SPIRITUAL INFORMATION

Spiritual Information

100 PERSPECTIVES ON SCIENCE AND RELIGION

Edited by Charles L. Harper Jr.

ESSAYS IN HONOR OF SIR JOHN
TEMPLETON'S 90TH BIRTHDAY

TEMPLETON FOUNDATION PRESS
PHILADELPHIA AND LONDON

Templeton Foundation Press
300 Conshohocken State Road, Suite 550
West Conshohocken, PA 19428
www.templetonpress.org

Templeton Foundation Press helps intellectual leaders and others learn about science research on aspects of realities, invisible and intangible. Spiritual realities include unlimited love, accelerating creativity, worship, and the benefits of purpose in persons and in the cosmos.

Library of Congress Cataloging-in-Publication Data

Spiritual information : 100 perspectives on science and religion / edited by Charles L. Harper Jr.
    p. cm.
Includes bibliographical references.
ISBN 1-932031-73-1 (pbk. : alk. paper) 1. Religion and science.
I. Harper, Charles L., 1958-
BL241.S69 2005
201'.65—dc22

                                                                2005005324

Printed in the United States of America

05 06 07 08 09 10   10 9 8 7 6 5 4 3 2

"How little we know, how eager to learn."

—Sir John Templeton

Contents ✍

THIS BOOK offers perspectives from many creative minds. Ninety of the essays included here were presented to Sir John Templeton on the occasion of his ninetieth birthday on November 29, 2002. To wish him continued strength of body and mind toward his centenary celebration, we have here collected a total of one hundred celebratory contributions for publication. These essays have been drawn together around the central theme constituting Templeton's core philanthropic vision: to stimulate progress in the domain of the spirit. His aim has been to provide philanthropic resources to support the growth and development of an academically rigorous arena of research and debate engaged in this challenge, bringing together the dynamism of the sciences with the diversity of the spiritual quest. The aim, as he puts it, is to generate "new spiritual information."

This term is rather loosely defined in the context of Templeton's interests. First, the idea reflects a desire to avoid the stasis of closure. Why consider God only through a lens of fixed tradition without training the eye on anything new? In the quest of the spirit, why not look to the open and progressive model of science, which intrinsically abhors closure and for which the adventure of new discovery is everything? Templeton's vision seeks to encourage people to cultivate a mindset of looking at the spiritual quest simultaneously as an adventure open to new insights from a wide variety of sources and as an endeavor to be taken seriously by using whatever methods of research might be fruitful.

This idea embraces a contrarian vision: to look to sources not typically thought of in connection with spiritual matters. Such sources may include, among others, scientific inquiry, innovation through entrepreneurial competition within the religious sector, new insights from research on the virtues, or careful study of the differences separating different spiritual traditions based on serious consideration and reflection.

New insights also may come from relatively "pedestrian" sources. Consider, for example, opinion polls. New spiritual information can be as simple as new statistical information on a spiritual topic—for example, results on what fraction of the population of a country prays regularly, or what percentage has had an intense spiritual experience of some sort, or what the correlations might be between spirituality and personality type or specific social and cultural circumstances. There is nothing particularly deep about such information, yet it may be useful knowledge. It may help people to approach the challenge of spiritual progress in a well-informed way.

On the other hand, "new spiritual information" may refer to insights that are specifically deep and theological in nature. The Templeton vision is properly hedged with the caveat that the challenge of making progress in the "things of God" is by no means as mundane as matters of research results, assembly lines, and international electronic equities trading markets: *Deus semper maior* ("God is always greater" [than human attempts at understanding]). For example, new spiritual information might have to do with scientific and philosophical analyses of the question of freedom or openness in the physical world—thus informing the continuing complex debate over the classic problem of evil in theology. Or it may have to do with insights into the mind obtained directly through prayer or meditation. Or it may be focused on understanding spiritual themes, such as the mystery of love without limits. Or it may have to do with scientific insights into the unseen, such as the nomic order implicit in the concept of the laws of nature. Or it may have to do with aspects of the rich strangeness of the veiled aspect of quantum reality.

These examples offer a spectrum of wide differences in considering what new spiritual information could be. The point is to open up inquiry into a broad range of types of potential new information pertinent to and focused on various spiritual topics. The idea of open-mindedness as demonstrated in the range of essays in this book also includes a commitment to a belief in the virtues of debate. Thus, challenges to Sir John Templeton's vision are included. Such welcoming of a clash of differences is very much a part of the Templeton way. Critical perspectives are encouraged. Taking account of different points of view is an important part of any effort to learn in a truly open-minded manner.

One way to understand the Templeton mindset is to see it as supporting alternatives to both religious and scientistic fundamentalisms. Fundamentalisms seek the simple picture conducive to closed-mindedness and are uncomfortable with an open adventure in seeking truth through polyphony and with appropriate humility. Rather, they seek to own the truth. And in the science-religion relationship, fundamentalisms of both the "for" and "against" varieties tend to focus on pushing a clear-cut clash, typically between (philosophically loaded interpretations of) modern scientific theories and (usually simplistic literal interpretations of) ancient religious texts.

One of the most central insights into the idea of new spiritual information is that the desire for acquiring it logically follows from a change in mindset: An open-minded quest is possible once the idea of thinking of religion as only a matter of preserving ancient tradition is discarded in favor of a different approach that drops the presumption that one's particular ancient tradition owns the sum total of Truth (and, in contrast, that competing traditions correspondingly are seen to hold either all or part of Falsehood). For this primary reason, Sir John Templeton has described his vision as the "humble approach."

Another aspect of the humble approach engages the notion that human beings are likely to apprehend the infinite richness of Divine Reality in unavoidably limited ways, if only because of the immense mismatch between our perceptual apparatus and the infinite reality of God. Templeton sometimes illustrates this second aspect of the humble approach with a characteristic question: "Is the human ability to understand God just as impossible as the ability of a clam to understand the ocean?"

A third aspect of the humble-approach mindset is to respect and appreciate lessons taken from the astonishing success of the scientific and technological enterprise in transforming human knowledge and in creating useful innovations. Rather than seeing science and technology as competitors for the big story, or somehow together as a modern antireligion that deflates all meanings external to itself, why should people seeking spiritual insight not instead be open-minded and enthusiastic to gain from possible insights that the scientific and technological enterprise might have to offer? Such insights do not require anything particularly odd. They may simply come from reflecting on the complex elegance of what science has discovered about the nature of the physical world (e.g., the "laws" of nature) and the life within it, and thus by implication about the creative wisdom upholding the order of nature itself. Or they may appreciate the dynamism with which technological innovation has transformed the quality of human life in myriad ways that we typically take for granted—from clean water, antiviral vaccines, and tomographic scanners to airplanes, computers, and the Internet.

Sir John Templeton's vision is one of constant learning. His motto, and that of all the charitable foundations he has created, is "How little we know, how eager to learn." The John Templeton Foundation exists to provide support to gifted thinkers who want to push the boundaries and are not afraid to do so, recognizing that many vitally important issues require vision, leadership, and risk-taking beyond the often overly narrow confines of specialized scholarship. The purpose of this collection of one hundred essays is to exemplify the Templeton vision of adventure from a wide diversity of points of view.

By fostering excellence in rigorous, multidisciplinary research among scientists, theologians, and other thinkers, Sir John Templeton's fervent wish is to unite inquiry into the essential nature of the universe through the scientific method with humanity's basic spiritual and religious quest to understand human and cosmic purpose. In so doing, the John Templeton Foundation draws together in an ongoing substantive dialog many talented representatives from a broad spectrum of fields of expertise, such as those whose work is represented in this volume. Were it not for Sir John's vision, the profound and wide-ranging output of this amazing and inspiring group of one hundred experts from various fields could not have been represented in the same published work. Our hope in presenting this one-hundredfold tribute to Sir John is that it will inspire others to pursue his quest to discover "over one hundredfold more spiritual information than humankind has ever possessed before."

Charles L. Harper Jr.
Vice President and Executive Director
John Templeton Foundation
December 2004
Philadelphia, Pennsylvania

Acknowledgments ✍

M ANY PEOPLE collaborated to bring this book to fruition in honor of the ninetieth birthday of Sir John Templeton on November 29, 2002.

I am particularly grateful for the generosity of our benefactor, Sir John Templeton, in making this project—and all of the Foundation's programs—possible. Also, I wish to thank his son, John M. Templeton Jr., President of the John Templeton Foundation, for his enthusiastic support of this project in honor his father's ninetieth birthday.

The one hundred authors whose work constitutes this volume also have my deep thanks. The talent, knowledge, and dedication to the pursuit of truth exemplified by all of the contributors made working on this book very enjoyable and stimulating.

The person who really carried the day on the project was Pamela Bond Contractor of Ellipsis Enterprises, whose effort was very substantial indeed. Pam served as developmental editor and project manager, and her Herculean efforts, assisted by Margaret Brennan, brought this large project to completion in a highly efficient and skillful manner.

Thanks also are in order for Joanna Hill and Laura Barrett of Templeton Foundation Press. I am especially grateful to them for the kindness of their patience as we worked to finish the book!

Part One

Perspectives on Sir John Templeton's Two Domains—
Spiritual Capital and Spiritual Information

Spiritual Information and the Sense of Wonder 1

The Convergence of Spirituality and the Natural Sciences

Alister E. McGrath

O NE OF THE MANY THEMES that have been deeply explored in recent years has been the way in which our growing understanding of the cosmos leads to an enhanced spirituality. In other words, we seek a more profound understanding and appreciation of the universe in which we live and of the God who we believe to have created it in such a way that it sparkles and scintillates with divine beauty and wisdom (Goodenough 1998; Ebert 1999). This quest is thanks in large part to the generous sponsorship of publications and conferences by the John Templeton Foundation that have sought to catalyze the process of reflection and advancement from both the scientific and religious perspectives.

While a "spirituality of the natural sciences" is still in its emergent phase, it is clear that a number of points need to be examined in considerable detail if this field of research is to achieve its considerable potential. This essay was written to celebrate the stimulus given to the study of science and religion by the personal vision of Sir John Templeton, while at the same time exploring a possible framework for developing the new discipline's insights. Through this essay, I aim to advance this important agenda by exploring a major issue that arises in the attempt to develop a spirituality of the natural sciences: How can we hold the generalizations of theory together with a continued concern for and loving attention to the particularities of the natural world?

The essence of the process of theorizing may be thought of as an attempt to identify universal a posteriori patterns in local situations and represent those patterns in a language appropriate to its subject matter. Often, in the case of the natural sciences, the most appropriate language is that of mathematics. The intellectual challenge here is to preserve and respect locality while discerning universality—that is to say, to ensure that the particularities of the observed situation are not displaced or superseded by the universal patterns they are held to disclose.

Theory tames reality, reducing it to manageable proportions and allowing it to be visualized in terms adapted to human reasoning. Experience is to be reduced to repeatable formulas; phenomena are to be represented formally through mathematics. In this sense, theory can be seen as embodying a central theme of the Enlightenment: the desire to reduce everything to what Descartes called "clear and distinct ideas." This concern can be seen throughout the development of modern natural science, from Newton to Einstein, in which reality is to be reduced and represented in terms conforming to three global categories: accuracy, simplicity, and generalizability (Latour 1993).

Of Rainbows and Refractions

Theory arises from a sustained engagement with the natural world, yet the paradox of the explanatory successes of the natural sciences is that theories developed on the basis of an engagement with nature often lead us *away* from that engagement with nature. We risk becoming preoccupied with the theory itself rather than with the wonders of nature that brought that theory into being. Paradoxically, the natural sciences can thus actually *discourage* an appreciation of nature. This was the point made in 1814 by John Keats in his famous lines concerning the beauty of the rainbow:

> Do not all charms fly
> At the mere touch of cold philosophy?
> There was an awful rainbow once in heaven:
> We know her woof, her texture; she is given
> In the dull catalogue of common things.
> Philosophy will clip an Angel's wings. ("Lamia," Part II)

For Keats, a rainbow can be seen simply as yet another example of the laws of optics in action, preventing the observer from appreciating its full wonder. It becomes just another item in "the dull catalogue of common things," where the important thing is the process of "cataloging," not appreciation of the individual items being addressed.

Keats has been heavily criticized for these comments, not least by Richard Dawkins (1998). Dawkins regards Keats's poetry as typical antiscientific nonsense that rests on the flimsiest of foundations:

> Why, in Keats' poem, is the philosophy of rule and line "cold," and why do all charms flee before it? What is so threatening about reason? Mysteries do not lose their poetry when solved. Quite the contrary—the solution often turns out to be more beautiful than the puzzle. And, in any case, when you have solved one mystery you uncover others—and perhaps inspire greater poetry.

Dawkins illustrates this point by drawing attention to the consequences of Newton's analysis of the rainbow. He tells us that Newton's dissection of the rainbow into light of different wavelengths led to Maxwell's theory of electromagnetism and thence to Einstein's theory of special relativity.

The points that Dawkins makes are important and valid. Perhaps the road from Newton to Maxwell and thence to Einstein was rather more troublesome than Dawkins's prose suggests, but the connection certainly exists.

Yet there is a deeper issue here that must be addressed by anyone concerned with the spirituality of the natural sciences. For Keats, a rainbow is meant to lift the human heart and imagination upward, intimating the transcendent dimensions of reality, pointing to a world beyond the bounds of experience. For Dawkins, the rainbow remains firmly located within the world of human experience. It has no transcendent dimension. The fact that it can be explained in purely natural terms is taken to deny that it can have any significance as an indicator of transcendence.

The angel that was, for Keats, meant to lift our thoughts heavenward, disclosing the transcendent dimensions of reality, has had its wings clipped; it can no longer do anything save mirror the world of earthly events and principles.

"Redemption of Particularities"

So how can we celebrate the development of scientific theories that deal with the rationality of the universe and the ability of the human mind to discern it, while at the same time remain closely in touch with the original engagement with nature that underlies them? How can we grasp the transcendent dimension of nature while remaining firmly engaged with its empirical aspects? The answer lies in the great theme of the "redemption of particularities"—the recognition of the need to continue to pay loving and meticulous attention to the individual aspects of the cosmos while taking pleasure in the universal patterns that we discern beyond them.

One of the most interesting treatments of the "redemption of particularities" theme is found in the literary works of the great British novelist and philosopher Iris Murdoch. Although she deals with the theme in some of her technical writings (e.g., Murdoch 1952), her most impressive treatment of the issue is found in her novels. *Under the Net* (1954) is arguably the least philosophical of all her novels, yet it contains an extended reflection on the manner in which a Wittgensteinian "net of discourse" is necessary if particularities are to be described and yet also shields or conceals those particularities to reinforce itself. As one of her characters writes:

> The movement away from theory and generality is the movement toward truth. All theorizing is a fight. We must be ruled by the situation itself, and this is unutterably particular. Indeed it is something to which we can never get close enough, however hard we may try as it were to crawl under the net.

Theory thus possesses simultaneously the ability to illuminate and conceal the world of particulars. It is as if the two realms are mutually necessary and yet are permanently in tension.

Literary theory, perhaps paradoxically, illustrates Murdoch's point with disturbing clarity. The theory, which was perhaps once intended to heighten the reader's awareness of the distinctiveness of a given text, has become interposed between the reader and the text, rendering the latter of questionable importance. Theory-led "readings" of texts subvert their particularities and lead to imprisonment within preconceived theoretical categories. Aware of this, Valentine Cunningham argues for the need for a "tactful" reading—that is, a reading that is in touch with the text, valuing its uniqueness and affirming its distinctiveness rather than seeking to compartmentalize it as yet another example of a theory-driven category (Cunningham 2002).

Tactfully Reading the Book of Nature

The relevance of this to a reading of the "book of nature" is obvious. Theologians, philosophers, and literary writers have often compared nature to a book. Cunningham's point is that we can easily read this book from the standpoint of a predetermined theory that causes us to disregard the particularities of nature precisely because we already see it in a certain manner determined by our theoretical perspective. Cunningham challenges us to adopt a "tactful" reading of the book of nature: to engage directly, respectfully, and lovingly with nature, valuing its specific features rather than merely "cataloging" them as yet more instances of a general theoretical point.

When rightly understood, theory liberates rather than imprisons. It allows us to "see" or "behold" a particular in a new manner—for example, to see a rainbow as a specific instance of a general optical principle or the orbiting of the satellites of the planet Jupiter as a specific instance of the general theory of gravitation. The beauty and wonder of the original natural phenomenon is thus preserved and allowed to become the gateway to a deeper theoretical appreciation of the universe.

Both science and religion begin with a sense of wonder, followed closely by a yearning to understand. Theory arises precisely because human beings are rational creatures and feel impelled, both morally and intellectually, to give an account of things. The natural sciences and Christian theology are both rooted in human experience and culture; yet they also aspire to transcend the particularities of time and place to yield truths that claim a more universal significance. The first critical question concerns precisely how one moves from observation of and reflection on particularities—the movements of the planets, the distribution of fossils, or the history of Jesus Christ—to universal theories that have validity and relevance beyond the specific events that evoked and precipitated them. The second critical question has to do with how we ensure that these particularities are not evaporated by the theory that they generate, so that a universal abstraction comes to be valued more than the concrete particularities that it enumerates.

Paradoxically, a given theory can lead us to look *through* rather than *at* the particular, causing us to ponder whether the particular illustrates a universal truth, rather than valuing it in its own right, bathed in its inalienable individuality. It is here that Keats's concerns about the demystification of the rainbow come into play in that a wonder-evoking sight of the natural world is seen simply as an example of an optical phenomenon, rather than as a breathtaking thing of beauty in its own right. Properly understood, theory leads to a deeper engagement with particularities, rather than retreating from them.

A "spirituality of the natural sciences" aims to keep this sense of wonder alive by insisting that we continue to value and appreciate each and every individual aspect of the universe, while at the same time rejoicing and admiring the underlying patterns of rationality that undergird it. As Chandrasekhar (1990) and others have reminded us, the mathematical beauty of these theories often complements and extends the beauty of the natural world itself, thus encouraging us to appreciate both the surface appearance and the deeper reality that lie beneath it. Science and theology have much to contribute to each other, especially in the innovative and important field of the spirituality of the natural sciences.

ℒ♥

ALISTER E. MCGRATH, D.PHIL., D.DIV., was elected Principal of Wycliffe Hall in 1995. In 1999, he was awarded a personal chair in theology at Oxford University with the title Professor of Historical Theology. His doctoral degrees, both from Oxford, are for his research in the natural sciences and for his research on historical and systematic theology. His most significant publication in the field of science and religion is the three-volume work *A Scientific Theology,* published by Wm. B. Eerdmans: *Volume 1: Nature,* September 2001; *Volume 2: Reality,* December 2002; and *Volume 3: Theory,* July 2003.

References

Chandrasekhar, S. *Truth and Beauty: Aesthetics and Motivations in Science.* Chicago: University of Chicago Press, 1990.

Cunningham, Valentine. *Reading after Theory.* Oxford: Blackwell Publishing, 2002.

Dawkins, Richard. *Unweaving the Rainbow: Science, Delusion and the Appetite for Wonder.* London: Penguin Books, 1998.

Ebert, John David. *Twilight of the Clockwork God: Conversations on Science and Spirituality at the End of an Age.* Tulsa, OK: Council Oak Books, 1999.

Goodenough, Ursula. *The Sacred Depths of Nature.* New York: Oxford University Press, 1998. Also see her essay in this volume.

Latour, Bruno. *We Have Never Been Modern.* Cambridge, MA: Harvard University Press, 1993.

Murdoch, Iris. "Nostalgia for the Particular." *Proceedings of the Aristotelian Society* 52 (1952): 243–60.

———. *Under the Net.* London: Vintage, 1954.

SIR JOHN TEMPLETON'S THREE PASSIONS 2

Michael Novak

S IR JOHN TEMPLETON turned ninety in November 2002. In his youth, he wanted to be a Christian missionary in foreign lands. A poor lad from the mountains of Tennessee (his ancestral home was not far from fabled Kenyon College), John had been sent to Yale through the generosity of a family friend. From there it was off to Oxford, where a Christian advisor told him his health was probably too frail for strenuous work overseas. John's summer jobs at Merrill Lynch, meanwhile, had taught him that he had a talent for analyzing listed companies and the likely long-term performance of their stock. He took this to signify that talents are a sign God gives us of our vocation.

And while on the one hand Sir John at age ninety-plus looks the picture of energy and health, on the other he still seems tiny and frail. Both his longevity and his sustained energy level would not have been easy to predict fourscore years ago, so his Oxford advisor may be forgiven. And because that same man's candor led John to veer off into a life of very nearly unparalleled success in worldwide investing, he even deserves some gratitude.

For the Templeton Fund—the pioneering mutual fund through which the future Sir John Templeton brought scores of thousands of small investors into the habit of worldwide investing—produced record-breaking gains, year after year, with a kind of steadiness that was a marvel then, and in retrospect still is today. (Sir John sold off the Fund some years ago to Franklin.) Sir John had some simple secrets about investing:

- ✦ Invest for the long term and be patient.
- ✦ Look for opportunities in places where things are so bad they can't get much worse.
- ✦ Single out good, honest, and true management that has its feet on the ground and a zest for solid creativity.

Sir John was conservative in the virtues that he looked for and put his trust in; he was radical in taking a worldwide view and showing willingness to seek out solid opportunities and calculated risks in truly forbidding places. He was radical in his worldwide vision and steadily traditional in his standards of judgment. For this reason, while the record shows that he produced above-average gains (and often far-above-average gains), Sir John radiated rocklike solidity of judgment.

In the retail investment world, Sir John was a new kind of genius. He pioneered in bringing global capital investments to areas of the world that had hardly known them and in teaching an international viewpoint to amateur investors on all continents. He taught scores of thousands of ordinary citizens a global perspective. It turned out that his vocation lay not in bringing the universal "good news" of salvation as a Christian missionary. Instead, he learned that he could have a significant effect in expanding opportunity and economic development for all people, including those in the heretofore most forgotten regions. He could help reduce poverty and misery in this world.

Behind Sir John's vision lay the three principles that were his passion: love, humility, and the moral instruction learned through such humble realities as ownership of property and the habit of enterprise. From these, he has never wavered.

Love

In the last line of Dante's *Paradiso*, we learn of "The Love that moves the Sun and all the stars." Like Dante, Sir John also believes that, in the human world at least, love is the great creative energy. He holds that this claim is empirically verifiable and invites scholars in all disciplines to test it out. Doesn't learning come easier when one loves the subject? An actress who loves her audiences bonds with them deepest. A person who loves life fares better under medical treatment. Managers and employees who love their work and love the people they serve tend to do their work better and offer their customers better service. A republic survives when its citizens love it dearly. All these hypotheses should be subjected to empirical testing. Meanwhile, Sir John has kept on living accordingly—as if the proposition were true.

No doubt Sir John, like anyone, may be sometimes less than kind and loving— but, it seems, not all that often. Journalists who have interviewed him and strangers who meet him along the way have often experienced a kind of cherubic kindness that he exudes. It seems to flow from within him. One suspects it would not be well to cross him or betray him; but then, anger of a certain sort is not a violation of love, but one of love's classic expressions when used to defend the thing that is loved. The point is that a certain goodness radiates from him—because he wants it that way.

Humility

Sir John is a firm believer in the proposition that both God and the universe around us are far, far bigger than we are and that our expanding knowledge shows us how much smaller and smaller we seem to be in the scheme of things. He likes to point out how many times vaster is our scientific knowledge of the world in the current year 2000 compared with one hundred years ago and how rapidly it is increasing every few months as an unprecedented number of scientists get on with their work day after day. But this vast knowledge is far greater than any one of us can absorb.

Sir John concludes from this that the only appropriate human attitude is humility—and further, that humility is a particularly important virtue in two great human enterprises: the pursuit of knowledge and the building up of human community. Arrogance and pride destroy trust and generate resentment, hostility, and division. They also blind the inquiring mind and make it reluctant to accept evidence from lowly and unexpected sources—whence it often comes. Thus, lack of humility causes many human setbacks, both in the advance of science and in global living.

By humility, Sir John means a certain down-to-earth truthfulness, a lack of pretension in both directions—neither know-it-all self-confidence nor excessive (and false) modesty. The word "humility" comes from *humus,* the Latin word for "earth" or "soil," and so it suggests a kind of groundedness, a self-knowledge without any sort of pretension.

Moral Benefits

Moral benefits are learned through the instruction conferred by such humble realities as ownership of property and the habit of enterprise. Parents soon come to understand how many things children can learn only by doing. There are certain crucial moral habits that children learn only through owning something of their own and having responsibility for its flourishing. Ownership teaches how much care things need if they are to be kept in good condition or, even better, improved. "If you borrow a neighbor's lawnmower, return it to him in better condition than you received it—clean it, oil it, tighten it, do something to make it better," one father taught a son. Even in taking over a *Fortune 500* company, the son remembers that injunction and has as his goal turning that company over to the next CEO in better condition than he received it.

In the same way, building an enterprise of your own forces you to learn habits you may once have counted as less important. For one, you learn how to work with others, teaching them trust in one another, how to be better than they've ever been, and how to set ever-new goals for themselves. For another, you learn how to keep track of small losses and small gains so as to keep the enterprise moving forward by the measure of hard-to-achieve profits, how to be grateful for small gains, and especially how to be grateful to good customers and how to find new ways of better serving them so as to deserve their patronage—and to find more good customers.

Building an enterprise summons up a very broad range of human skills, not all of which one is likely to have mastered in the beginning, but all of which one has to learn in short order. Building an enterprise is a morally stretching thing. It requires a creative vision. It requires a tolerance for risk, even at the cost of losing all that one has invested in it. It requires skills in inspiring and motivating others. It requires skills in efficiency and restraining costs, even as one tries to maximize the value to customers of the good or service provided. It requires a moral and emotional equilibrium of a rather high order that is under the constant critical eye of all those with whom one deals. For they, too, are seeking to cut costs and maximize value, and if you can't help them do that, they will seek someone else who can. Creativity, community building, and practical wisdom—these are the cardinal virtues of enterprise. But there are also a myriad of others, including the "tough love" needed to fire nonperformers for the good of the firm as a whole.

As writers since Montesquieu have noted, there is a close relationship between the virtues taught by commercial life and the virtues required to make a republic work: Initiative, enterprise, responsibility, community skills, trust, realism, practicality, good service, cheerfulness, and the like are necessary both to sound enterprises and to durable republics. Commercial virtues and republican virtue are not a perfect fit, for there are times when self-sacrifice even at the cost of one's own life is necessary for a republic, and in this sense a durable republic also needs martial abilities. But for the long haul, commercial virtues are more valuable, even, than martial abilities for the survival and prospering of republics. For martial societies lead as well to dictatorships as to republics, but commercial societies multiply the number of successful citizens who demand a voice in republican government.

Sir John Templeton, knighted by Queen Elizabeth II in 1987 for his services to the United Kingdom, including endowment of a new business college at the University of Oxford, deserves to be celebrated on his ninetieth birthday for his concentration on these three passions—not only in his own vocation, but in the philanthropies that will carry his vision into the future.

ℒ♥

MICHAEL NOVAK currently holds the George Frederick Jewett Chair in Religion and Public Policy at the American Enterprise Institute in Washington, D.C., where he is Director of Social and Political Studies. He received his M.A. in history and philosophy of religion at Harvard University and his S.T.B. (Bachelor of Sacred Theology) at Gregorian University in Rome. Author of *The Universal Hunger for Liberty: Why the Clash of Civilizations Is Not Inevitable* (2004), Mr. Novak has written 26 influential books in the philosophy and theology of culture that have been translated into many languages. *The Spirit of Democratic Capitalism* (1982), for which he received the Antony Fisher Prize presented by Margaret Thatcher (1992), has been influential in Latin America, Poland, Czechoslovakia, Germany, China, and Hungary. Mr. Novak served as Ambassador to the United Nations Human Rights Commission in Geneva (1981–82). Among his awards are the Templeton Prize (1994), the International Award of the Institution for World Capitalism (1994), the highest civilian award from the Slovak Republic (1996), the Thomas G. Masaryk Medal presented by Vaclav Havel of the Czech Republic (2000), and the Gold Medal of The Pennsylvania Society (2001).

REFERENCE

Hermann, Robert L. 2004. *Sir John Templeton: Supporting Scientific Research for Spiritual Discoveries*. Philadelphia: Templeton Foundation Press.

Spiritual Capital 3

A New Field of Research

Robert D. Woodberry

In the United States, highly religious people tend to live longer, have fewer mental problems, steal less, volunteer more time, and give away more money than others. Even when other relevant factors are controlled for statistically, these differences persist. Why? What do these people have to draw on that shapes their lives in these ways? To extend the trend of translating the economic idea of capital into other areas of social science—for example, human capital, social capital, and cultural capital—those who invest in religion can be considered to accumulate spiritual capital.

Spiritual capital differs from the other forms of capital, not because religious groups don't have material resources, skills, trusting relationships, and culturally valued knowledge—that is, financial, human, social, and cultural capital. They do. But religious groups are concerned with more than these. For example, most religious groups purport to be more than social clubs. They often stress that their relationship with God is central and that the focus of group activity is precisely to emphasize, actualize, and act on that relationship. Moreover, participants often claim that people can access spiritual resources individually and anywhere without respect to group solidarity per se. Both these suggest that what happens in religious groups is not fully encompassed as a special subset of social capital.

Empirical evidence seems to confirm this. Research consistently shows that those who attend religious services for social or other nonreligious reasons (the extrinsically religious) are significantly different from those who attend for religious reasons (the intrinsically religious), even if they attend church the same amount (e.g., Gorsuch 1988). If social capital is the main resource congregations create, we would not expect this difference.

In fact, religious people invest money and skilled work, risk certain relationships, and forgo chances to learn culturally valued knowledge in pursuit of spiritual returns. In the process, they build up spiritual, material, intellectual, and social resources that shape both themselves and society. The effects of this process are beginning to be measured. The metaphor of "spiritual capital" may aid in this investigation.

First, the metaphor helps us see religion as an investment and as a distinct end. People and societies invest resources in religion with the hope of some return. Although people may use religion to gain financial capital, social capital, and cultural capital, many also seek something uniquely spiritual, something that cannot be reduced to money or sex or power.

The metaphor also helps us see religion as a resource: one that people draw on to meet various challenges—sickness, political oppression, ethical choices, or social problems. Religious organizations are repositories of financial, human, social, and cultural capital, but they are also sources of moral teachings and religious experiences that may motivate, channel, and strengthen people to reach particular ends. These spiritual resources may also shape how people use other forms of capital in ways these theories would not predict. Introducing the concept of "spiritual capital" may challenge scholars to analyze whether there are any uniquely religious resources or whether religious groups are merely repositories of material resources and networks of people that happen to be in religious organizations.

Focusing on religion as a resource may also spur research on the economic impact of religion. Because some religions influence health, rule-following behavior, voluntarism, and sound work habits, they probably have an important impact on the economy. However, perhaps because most of these influences are indirect and economists have generally not viewed religion as a resource, the impact of religion on the economy has remained largely unexplored.

This metaphor may also spur research on the consequences to both individuals and societies of increasing or decreasing investments in spiritual capital and the impact of changing the types of spiritual capital in which people invest. Finally, it invites comparison between investing in spiritual capital and investing in other forms of capital. The resources people invest to gain one type of capital are often resources they cannot invest to gain another type. Scholars may research the consequences to individuals and societies of differential investment strategies.

However, the metaphor has some limitations. One problem is that it may overemphasize religion as a means of reaching particular ends, whereas religion typically is also deeply concerned about shaping which ends people seek. It is a resource, but not only a resource. Religious traditions help people change themselves, to decide what they should want and the means they should use to reach those ends. This does not mean that people always follow their stated beliefs. But some religious traditions may provide resources to help people evaluate the match between their stated beliefs and their behaviors and enlist divine and human aid in reducing the gap between them. Prayer groups, Bible studies, and mentoring relationships often serve this role.

The metaphor may also suggest that the main goal of religion is personal profit. This may be true for many people and many religious traditions, but some religious traditions stress that spiritual profit is only a byproduct of losing the self or "dying" to self. For example, for Christians the goal is to love God: To seek first God's gifts is idolatry; to seek spiritual gifts for financial benefit is the sin of Simony.[1]

Spiritual Resources

There are many spiritual and religious resources. Some are related to material capital, social capital, and cultural capital, and others are not. One example of an unambiguous religious resource is the ritual "sacrament" of the Eucharist. The value of receiving a small piece of bread and a sip of wine, and the idea that they may become either actually or symbolically the salvific body and blood of Christ, makes sense only within a religious worldview. The Eucharist, of course, has little direct monetary or nutritional value. However, the sense of spiritual nourishment that believers experience in receiving the Eucharist reinforces the authority of the Christian tradition to make transformative claims on the believer's life. Such religious experiences and transformative claims commonly energize people to engage in other activities that influence society.

Other religious resources—for example, experiences of the divine, conviction on "sin," the strength believers feel from knowing that others are praying for them or that God is in control, and the sense that God is watching or that "sin" will "hamper one's witness"—may also prompt people to act. Because relationships in religious groups have a spiritual context and often an external moral authority, religion may also shape social relations in ways that social capital theories would not predict. For example, people in a small Bible study group may be more willing to call others to ethical change or challenge them to help outsiders, than, for example, people in boating or bowling clubs. People generally may also be more willing to let others prod them ethically in religious contexts than in other contexts. Thus, the religious context shapes the "value" and uses of social relations. Studying the number of group memberships and the density of social networks is not sufficient. Bowling alone may be less a problem than lone ranger spirituality.

These examples only touch on the breadth of spiritual resources. These "resources" are hard to explain with existing theoretical concepts, but they fill many personal accounts of why people do the things they do—even in private journals. Thus, social scientists should take them seriously.

Possible Economic Consequences of Religion

When people invest in spiritual capital, they are often not trying to influence the economy, the political system, and so forth, but the religious resources they create may indirectly shape these and other arenas. Some ways that spiritual capital may influence the economy are through health, rule of law, voluntarism, and education—as explored below. Unfortunately the vast majority of statistical evidence comes from Western Europe and North America—areas where Protestantism and Catholicism predominate. Thus, these relationships may not generalize to some other religious traditions.

Health: Religion has an important impact on health (e.g., Smith and Woodberry 2001). For example in the West, religiously involved people generally live longer. In fact, building on the path-breaking research of Hummer et al. (1999), Koenig (2000) calculated that in the United States, religious uninvolvement is linked with a decreased lifespan equivalent to smoking a pack of cigarettes every day for forty years (i.e., about seven years). Highly religious people seem to have fewer mental problems, get sick less often, and recover from sicknesses more quickly than people who are less religiously active. They engage in less risky behavior with respect to health; for example, they have fewer lifetime sexual partners, smoke less, drink less, use drugs less, and attempt suicide less often. They are more socially involved and report higher self-esteem, greater levels of happiness, better sex, less stress, and more satisfying and lasting marriages and relationships—all social and emotional factors that influence health (Ellison and Levin 1998; Sherkat and Ellison 1999; Koenig 2000; Hummer et al. 1999; Smith and Woodberry 2001; Townsend et al. 2002).[2] Yet to date, no study has measured the short- and long-term economic impacts these practices have on society. Moreover, these relationships are amenable to quantification, such as the calculated reduction in insurance payouts, medical care, diminished productivity, and lost workdays.

Rule of Law: Some religious traditions seem to be an important resource for increasing cultural support for the rule of law (Woodberry 2004; Stark 2001).[3] Quantitative evidence suggests that people affiliating with these traditions display lower involvement in crime, political corruption, and misappropriation of resources—for example, workers calling in sick when they are not, using company supplies for personal benefit, and so forth (Woodberry 2004; Stark 2001; Johnson et al. 2000; La Porta et al. 1999; Treisman 2000; Sikkink and Smith 1998).[4]

The economic link here should be obvious. For example, quantitative research consistently suggests that corruption slows subsequent economic growth, accentuates income inequality, reduces government efficiency, and diminishes the quality and quantity of education, medical work, social services, infrastructure, and so on. (Jain 2001).

Voluntarism: In the West, empirical evidence suggests that highly religious people tend to volunteer more time and give more money to help people informally and to support both religious and nonreligious voluntary organizations (Woodberry 2000; Smidt 2003; Regnerus, Smith, and Sikkink 1998). Religious groups are also central to forming humanitarian organizations, private schools, and private hospitals, even if these organizations no longer have religious ties (Smidt 2003; Young 2002; Woodberry 2000; Smith and Woodberry 2001; Anheier and Salamon 1998). Voluntary activity can have an important effect on the economy by, among other things, providing social services that make the workforce more productive, reducing the tax burden required to fund social programs, contributing to high-quality education of youth, and so forth.

Education: Some religious traditions, particularly Protestantism, have also profoundly influenced worldwide education rates (Woodberry 2000; 2004). Protestants have consistently championed universal literacy, believing it is a basic religious responsibility to be able to read the Bible. Consequently, Protestants have invested massively in expanding education, both in their own societies and, through missionaries, in other societies. Thus, areas with more Protestant missionaries had more formal education during the colonial period and, on average, continue to have more formal education today (Woodberry 2000; 2004). Historical research suggests that these missionaries were motivated primarily by religious ideals. They wanted to convert people and thought education would help them do this. Colonial governments, settlers, and businesspeople generally resisted the expansion of mass education in the colonies. Thus, missionaries were not primarily serving the interests of these financially interested groups (ibid.). Missionaries and their supporters were investing in spiritual capital, but through the educational institutions they created, this investment had important economic consequences.

Caveats

In discussing spiritual capital and the impact religious resources have on society, I have focused on factors that many people may view as positive. But I need to present several caveats. First, religion is not the only factor that influences health, rule of law, voluntarism, or education. I am merely discussing one factor. Of course, some religious groups promote unhealthy behaviors, resist certain types of education, and hamper the economy. At times, religious differences can lead to violent and implacable conflicts, thus squandering economic resources. Religious strictures may also block the economical use of some resources. For example, Islam and Catholicism long promulgated ethical and legal restrictions against charging interest. In fact, all religious traditions presumably involve a complex mixture of positive and negative effects on economic productivity.

Second, I am talking about general tendencies, not universal absolutes. For example, it is clear that some nonreligious people volunteer more time and give more money than the average religious person. However, individual variation does not negate a general tendency. *On average*, highly religious people volunteer and give more.

Third, although some patterns may develop originally in religious groups, they may diffuse through society and continue to spread over time. Thus, although the modern form of social-movement organization seems to have developed from Protestant mission and revivalist groups, once these organizational forms developed, nonreligious people learned to use them effectively without direct contact with religious groups (Young 2002; Woodberry 2000; 2004). In some societies, the impact of religion on corruption rates and political democracy may also be more historic than contemporary. Once institutions and patterns of behavior are in place, they may continue even after religiosity declines or disappears (Woodberry 2004). Like financial capital, later generations may draw on the spiritual capital accumulated by previous generations. Thus, in measuring spiritual capital, we should not focus entirely on current investment levels or assume that only religiously active people draw on it.

Challenges

Research on spiritual capital faces several important challenges. First, although all societies have religious resources, they probably cannot be measured in the same way in every culture. For example, for Jews and Christians, weekly religious service attendance may be one good indicator of individual investment in spiritual capital. However, this measure may not be appropriate for Buddhists and Hindus. Even though Christians attend group religious services more often than Buddhists or Hindus, this does not mean they invest more in generating spiritual capital; they just invest in different ways.

Second, because people's motivations for religious activity vary, the same external act may not be an equivalent investment in spiritual capital. On things ranging from racial attitudes to helping behavior, people who attend religious services to gain social capital seem to be significantly different from those who attend for religious reasons (e.g., Gorsuch 1988). Thus, an ideal measure of spiritual capital investment would include a motivational component.

Third, investing in "spiritual capital" may generate very different resources in different religious traditions. The beliefs and goals in different traditions, their sources of authority, their means of interaction, and their institutional forms make a difference. Thus, for example, quantitative analysis suggests that Protestantism is associated with lower levels of corruption; other religious traditions are not (e.g., Triesman 2000; La Porta et al. 1999). Historical analysis suggests a role of Protestant renewal movements in this process (Gorski 1993; Woodberry 2004). This does not mean that Protestants invest more in spiritual capital or that Protestant spiritual capital is "superior." It merely means that investing in Protestantism may provide resources useful for some things and investing in other traditions may provide resources useful for other things. Thus, we can miss some of the impacts religious traditions have if we *assume* that religious groups are interchangeable or that we can measure spiritual capital in the same way regardless of religious tradition.

Still, spiritual capital may be a useful metaphor that can help us see new aspects of religion and channel scholarship in some promising new directions. It may even lead to important insights if spiritual "accounting" is developed with appropriate nuance and recognition of the complexity of and barriers to quantification of those aspects of life that are intractably intangible.

✒

ROBERT D. WOODBERRY, PH.D., is Assistant Professor of Sociology at the University of Texas at Austin. He earned a B.A. in political science from Wheaton College, an M.A. in cross-cultural studies from Fuller Seminary, an M.A. in sociology from Notre Dame, and a Ph.D. in sociology from the University of North Carolina, Chapel Hill. Professor Woodberry's current research looks at religion and democracy and at the long-term impact of missions and colonial policy on non-Western societies. Along with coauthors, he received the 2001 "Outstanding Published Article Award" from the Sociology of Religion Section, American Sociological Association. Professor Woodberry has served on the Nominations Committee of the ASA History of Sociology Section, 2002–03, the Councils of the ASA History of Sociology Section, 2000–02, and the ASA Sociology of Religion Section, 2000–01. He has coauthored numerous articles in prominent sociological journals.

NOTES

1 The word "Simony" comes from Simon Magus (Acts 8:18–24), who attempted to buy the gifts of the Holy Spirit to use for financial gain.

2 However, scholars still do not fully understand all the ways religion influences health, and the strength of particular health benefits is still contested.

3 Internationally, the link is primarily with monotheistic religious traditions, especially Protestantism. In North America, the link is strongest with theologically conservative traditions.

4 Research on delinquency among adolescent boys suggests the effect is primarily in areas with high overall religiosity.

REFERENCES

Anheier, Helmut K., and Lester M Salamon (ed.). 1998. *The Nonprofit Sector in the Developing World.* Manchester: Manchester University Press.

Ellison, Chris, and Jeffrey S. Levin. 1998. "The Religion-Health Connection: Evidence, Theory, and Future Directions." *Health Education and Behavior.* 25: 700-20.

Gorski, Philip S. 1993. "The Protestant Ethic Revisited: Disciplinary Revolution and State Formation in Holland and Prussia." *American Journal of Sociology.* 99(2): 265–316.

Gorsuch, Richard L. 1988. "Psychology of Religion." *Annual Review of Psychology.* 39: 201–21.

Hummer, Robert A., Richard G. Rogers, Charles B. Nam, and Christopher G. Ellison. 1999. "Religious Involvement and US Adult Mortality." *Demography.* 36(2): 273–85.

Jain, Arvind K. 2001. "Corruption: A Review." *Journal of Economic Surveys.* 15(1): 71–121.

Johnson, Byron R., Spencer De Lie, David B. Larson, and Michael McCullough. 2000. "A Systematic Review of the Religiosity and Delinquency Literature: A Research Note." *Journal of Contemporary Criminal Justice.* 16(1): 32–52.

Koenig, Harold. 2000. "The Healing Power of Faith." pp. 107–10 in *God for the 21st Century.* Russell Stannard (ed.). Philadelphia: Templeton Foundation Press.

La Porta, R., F. Lopez-de-Silanes, A. Shleifer, and R. W. Vishny. 1999. "The Quality of Government." *Journal of Law, Economics and Organization.* 15(1): 1131–50.

Regnerus, Mark D., Christian S. Smith, and David Sikkink. 1998. "Who Gives to the Poor? The Influence of Religious Tradition and Political Location on the Personal Generosity of Americans Toward the Poor." *Journal for the Scientific Study of Religion.* 37(3): 481–93.

Sherkat, Darren E., and Chris G. Ellison. 1999. "Recent Developments and Current Controversies in the Sociology of Religion." *Annual Review of Sociology* 25: 363–94.

Sikkink, David, and Christian Smith. 1998. "Religion and Ethical Decision-making and Conduct on the Job: Reconsidering the Influence of Religion in the Economic and Business Sphere." Presented at the annual meeting of the Society for the Scientific Study of Religion.

Smidt, Corwin (ed.). 2003. *Religion as Social Capital: Producing the Common Good.* Waco, TX: Baylor University Press.

Smith, Christian S. and Robert D. Woodberry. 2001. "Sociology of Religion." pp. 100–13 in *The Blackwell Companion to Sociology.* Judith Blau (ed.). Cambridge: Blackwell.

Stark, Rodney. 2001. "Gods, Rituals and the Moral Order." *Journal for the Scientific Study of Religion.* 40(4): 619–36.

Townsend, Mark, Virginia Kladder, Hana Ayele, and Thomas Mulligan. 2002. "Systematic Review of Clinical Trials Examining the Effects of Religion on Health." *Southern Medical Journal.* 95(12): 1429–34.

Treisman, Daniel. 2000. "The Causes of Corruption: A Cross-national Study." *Journal of Public Economics.* 76: 399–457.

Woodberry, Robert D. 2000. "The Long-Term Influence of Religious Traditions on Levels of Democratization." Presented at the annual meeting of the Association for the Sociology of Religion, Washington, DC.

———. 2004. *The Shadow of Empire: Christian Missions, Colonial Policy and Democracy in Postcolonial Societies.* Ph.D. Dissertation, Sociology Department, University of North Carolina, Chapel Hill.

Woodberry, Robert D. and Christian S. Smith. 1998. "Fundamentalism *et al.*: Conservative Protestants in America." *Annual Review of Sociology.* 22: 25–56.

Young, Michael P. 2002. "Confessional Protest: The Religious Birth of U.S. National Social Movements." *American Sociological Review.* 67(5): 660–88.

Spiritual Capital as an Economic Force 4

Robert J. Barro

Previous research has used cross-country experience to assess the determinants of economic growth. One conclusion is that successful explanations have to go beyond narrow economic variables to encompass political and social forces. Thus, economic growth has been found to depend on education and health, fertility rates, maintenance of the rule of law, and so on. Given these and other factors, poorer countries tend to grow faster and, thereby, converge toward the richer countries. However, because poorer countries typically rank low on a number of growth determinants—such as education, health, and rule of law—they tend not to grow faster in an overall sense.

Some researchers argue that explanations for economic growth should also include a nation's culture, especially religion. In ongoing research,[1] we view the economic influence of religion as operating through the formation of beliefs that influence traits such as honesty, work ethic, thrift, and openness to strangers. We view the religious beliefs and related character traits as "spiritual capital," which is analogous to the human capital that is important for worker productivity.[2] Human capital includes the skills and knowledge that come from formal schooling, on-the-job training, and parental guidance. Analogously, spiritual capital derives from formal learning through organized religion and from family and social interactions.

Our empirical analysis was focused at the countrywide level. We began with a previously constructed data set for more than one hundred countries. These data include national accounts variables and other economic, political, and social indicators observed since 1960. We recently expanded this data set to include measures of religion.

The measures of participation in organized religion and of religious beliefs come from surveys of individuals in about sixty countries. We use information from three waves of the *World Values Survey*, two waves of the *International Social Survey Programme*, and the *Gallup Millennium Survey*. (George Gallup has contributed an essay to this volume.) The participation variables are the portions of the population that attended formal religious services at least weekly, at least monthly, and so on. The religious beliefs refer to the portion of the population who said that they believed in heaven, hell, life after death, and God. Other questions, which might be more robust across religions, are whether the respondent considers himself or herself to be religious and whether religion plays an important role in one's life.

We know each country's breakdown of religious adherence across the major faiths. For persons who express adherence to some religion, we use a nine-way division into Catholic, Protestant, Muslim, Hindu, Buddhist, other Eastern religions,

Orthodox, Jewish, and other religions. We also have indicators of the interactions between government and religion. One variable measures the existence of an established state religion. Another gauges whether the government regulated the religion market, in the sense of appointing or approving church leaders. In subsequent research, we will use the *Religion & State Data Set* being constructed by Jonathan Fox and Shmuel Sandler to improve our measures of state regulation, subsidy, and suppression of religion.[3]

We are interested in how differences at the national level in church attendance and religious beliefs influence economic outcomes. However, to sort out this direction of causation, we have to deal with reverse effects from economic development to religiosity. This reverse channel is the focus of a substantial literature in the sociology of religion.

One theory in this literature is the secularization hypothesis, whereby economic development is thought to make people less religious, as gauged by church attendance, religious beliefs, and the influence of organized religion on social and legal processes. This hypothesis is controversial, and the continuing vitality of religion in the United States is a counterexample. A recent study by Laurence Iannaccone shows that the classic secularization pattern, whereby nations that were once highly religious experienced steady declines in church attendance, applies only to a few countries in Western Europe.[4]

An important competing theory downplays the role of economic development and other demand factors for religion and emphasizes the extent of competition among religion providers.[5] A greater diversity of religions is thought to promote more competition and hence a better-quality religion product and therefore higher religious participation and beliefs. The extent of religious competition depends on how the government regulates new entrants and existing providers in the religion market. Thus, this approach argues that government regulation, subsidy, and suppression are important determinants of religiosity.

Our primary goal is not to assess the validity of alternative theories of religiosity. Rather, we consider the countrywide determinants of religiosity to pin down the direction of causation from religion to economic performance, rather than the reverse. The estimation procedure is to isolate some variables—called instrumental variables—that influence religiosity without (arguably) being influenced by economic variables. The estimation reveals how differences in religiosity—driven by these instrumental variables—influence economic growth.

Two instrumental variables that we use are the indicators for the existence of an established state religion and for the presence of a regulated market structure, where the government appoints or approves church leaders. We also use an index of religious pluralism, which gauges the degree of heterogeneity of religious adherence within a country. The idea is that countries with primarily a single religion exhibit less competition among religion providers than countries with religious diversity.

Our empirical framework has been used in many previous studies.[6] This approach relates economic growth to lagged values of explanatory variables, including per capita GDP, school attainment and life expectancy, the fertility rate, indicators of the rule of law and democracy, and so on. Our analysis adds measures of religiosity. Thus, we examine how religion affects economic growth for given values of the other explanatory variables.

One finding is that, for given church attendance, economic growth rises when certain religious beliefs increase. The beliefs that seem to be growth promoting are those concerned with hell, heaven, and an afterlife. In contrast, growth is not related to belief in God. In our cross-country sample, the average percentage of persons expressing belief in God is 80 percent, compared with 38 percent for hell, 55 percent for heaven, and 58 percent for an afterlife. Thus, affirmation of belief in God seems to be a reflexive response with little content. In contrast, the survey responses about beliefs in hell, heaven, and an afterlife are less often positive and apparently more indicative of the religious convictions that matter for economic performance.

For given religious beliefs, higher church attendance reduces economic growth. Our interpretation is that church attendance affects economic outcomes mainly by fostering religious beliefs that influence individual traits such as work ethic, honesty, and so on. For example, beliefs in hell and heaven might affect these traits by creating perceived punishments and rewards for "good" and "bad" behavior. When we hold fixed religious beliefs, an increase in church attendance signifies that more resources, in terms of time and goods, are being consumed by the religion sector for given outputs (the religious beliefs). From this perspective, we are not surprised that higher church attendance reduces economic growth.

The link between religious beliefs and character traits depends on the nature of religious doctrine. That is, beliefs are growth enhancing if the perceived punishments and rewards reinforce good behavior, such as honesty and hard work. The relationship would be reversed if the religious doctrine encouraged nonproductive behavior, including violence. Our results suggest that this dark side of religion is atypical.

Another way to view the results is that economic growth is high when believing is high relative to belonging. Grace Davie characterized modern Britain as the prototypical example of a nation that features believing without belonging.[7] In our data, Britain does have high religious beliefs relative to its low church attendance. However, countries with higher levels of believing relative to belonging are Japan and Scandinavia.

Our findings do not mean that increased church attendance tends overall to reduce economic growth. To calculate the overall effect, we have to know how religious beliefs respond to greater attendance. We hope to estimate this "religion production function" in future research. At present, we can note that when religious beliefs and church attendance move together in their typical manner, the response of economic growth is weak. Countries that are more religious overall—that is, have higher beliefs *and* higher church attendance—tend, other things equal, to grow at about an average rate.

Aside from its impact on religious beliefs, church attendance may contribute to social capital built up through participation in organized religious services. The church-attendance variable may also proxy for the influence of organized religion on laws and regulations that affect economic behavior. Our results indicate that, for given beliefs, the overall effect from greater church attendance is to reduce economic growth. This effect combines the resources used up by the religion sector, the social-capital aspect of this sector, and the influence of organized religion on legal and regulatory institutions. In future research, we plan to estimate directly the economic effects of religiously based laws and regulations.

Figures 1 and 2 display some findings graphically. The horizontal axis in Figure 1 shows a measure of a country's monthly church attendance. The vertical axis shows the country's growth rate of per capita GDP over ten-year intervals, 1965–75, 1975–85, and 1985–95. (Each country appears three times if all data are available.) The variable plotted adjusts the growth rate for the effects of all of the explanatory variables other than monthly church attendance.[8] Conceptually, the fitted, downward-sloping line shows how economic growth would fall if monthly church attendance rose, while the other explanatory variables did not change. One of the variables being held fixed is religious belief, in this case, belief in hell. Thus, the negative effect on growth applies when church attendance rises for given beliefs.

Figure 2 is analogous except that the horizontal axis measures belief in hell. The upward-sloping line shows how economic growth would rise if belief in hell increased, while the other explanatory variables—including church attendance—did not change. Hence, this positive effect applies when beliefs rise for given church attendance.

Figure 1. Economic Growth and Church Attendance   Figure 2. Economic Growth and Belief in Hell

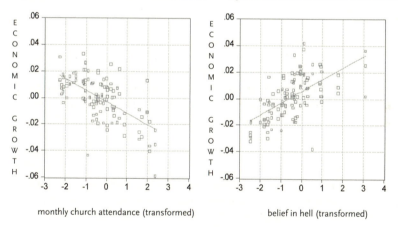

monthly church attendance (transformed)   belief in hell (transformed)

Other empirical results suggest that the "stick" from belief in hell is more potent than the "carrot" from belief in heaven in terms of growth promotion. We will have more evidence on these relationships when the data from the 2001 wave of the *World Values Survey* become available. These data will be useful because they contain far greater representation of Muslim countries, which tend to have high levels of belief in hell and heaven.

We anticipate that the effects of beliefs in hell and heaven on economic performance would be weaker in religions such as Hinduism and Buddhism, in which hell and heaven do not represent ultimate individual objectives. We find weak support for this proposition. We have more information from the 2001 *World Values Survey*, which includes expanded coverage of countries in which the population adheres primarily to Buddhism or other Eastern religions.[9]

The causal interpretation of the link between religion and economic growth depends on the use of instrumental variables that relate to the interplay between state and church. We relied especially on indicators for established state religion and for government regulation of the religion market. These measures are rough, and we expect to get better information from the *Religion & State Data Set*, which Fox and Sandler are constructing. We are eager to see whether our findings hold up when we use more accurate measures of the relation between state and church.

Our interpretation is that the economic effects of religious beliefs worked through influences on character traits, such as honesty and work ethic. We plan to check this interpretation by using survey responses from the *World Values Survey* to proxy for the underlying character traits.

Our findings about the economic effects of religion are exciting, provocative, and preliminary. We think there is more than enough to warrant further research, which will likely modify and perhaps overturn some of our findings. One conclusion that we expect to remain intact is that religiosity has important consequences for economic performance.

✐

ROBERT J. BARRO, PH.D., is Paul M. Warburg Professor of Economics at Harvard University, a senior fellow of the Hoover Institution of Stanford University, a research associate of the National Bureau of Economic Research, co-editor of the Quarterly Journal of Economics, and viewpoint columnist for *Business Week*. He was recently vice president of the American Economic Association, is currently President-elect of the Western Economic Association, and is a fellow of the American Academy of Arts and Sciences and the Econometric Society. Professor Barro received his B.S. in physics from Caltech in 1965 and his Ph.D. in economics from Harvard in 1970. He held faculty appointments at Brown, Chicago, and Rochester before returning to Harvard in 1987. Professor Barro has written extensively on macroeconomics, especially on economic growth, public debt, and monetary policy. His books include *Economic Growth, Macroeconomics, Nothing Is Sacred: Economic Ideas for the New Millennium, Determinants of Economic Growth*, and *Getting It Right: Markets and Choices in a Free Society*.

NOTES

1 See Robert J. Barro and Rachel M. McCleary, "Religion and Economic Growth," *American Sociological Review* (October 2003).

2 I have been unable to pin down the origin of the term "spiritual capital." Charles Harper of the John Templeton Foundation and editor of this volume tells me that John DiIulio may have coined it.

3 See Jonathan Fox and Shmuel Sandler, "Separation of Religion and State in the 21st Century: Comparing the Middle East and Western Democracies," International Studies Association conference, Portland, OR, February 2003.

4 See Laurence R. Iannaccone, "Looking Backward: A Cross-National Study of Religious Trends," George Mason University, 2002, available at wcfia.harvard.edu/religion.

5 For a survey, see Laurence R. Iannaccone, "The Economics of Religion: A Survey of Recent Work," *Journal of Economic Literature* (September 1998).

6 See Robert J. Barro and Xavier Sala-i-Martin, *Economic Growth*, 2nd ed. (Cambridge, MA: MIT Press, 2004), chap. 12.

7 Grace Davie, *Religion in Britain since 1945: Believing without Belonging* (Oxford: Blackwell, 1994).

8 The average value on the vertical axis has been set to zero and is, therefore, not meaningful.

9 See http://www.worldvaluessurvey.org/services/index.html.

SPIRITUAL ENTREPRENEURISM 5

CREATING A PLAN TO EXPLORE AND PROMOTE SPIRITUAL INFORMATION

Jean Staune

W HEN LAPLACE PUBLISHED his *System of the World* based on the works of Copernicus, Galileo, Kepler, and Newton, he made his famous statement to Napoleon: "*Sire, je n'ai pas besoin de cette hypothese*" ("Lord, I do not need this assumption"). The "assumption" was God. In a universe conceived as a large mechanism in which everything is causally determined and real freedom does not exist, the concept of God is, by definition, rendered obsolete. And although the Darwinian explanation of the evolution of life, which was based on randomness and hence on unpredictability, appeared to challenge the ordered theories of Laplace and his successors, both the Laplacian and Darwinian hypotheses have a common thread: Each contends that the world is explainable by itself, that no other level of reality exists, and that the universe is not the result of a divine plan.

The remarkable progress of neurology tends to lean toward the same conclusion: By revealing the complexity of neuronal mechanisms, it seems to lead us inexorably to the conclusion that human consciousness is entirely contingent on the brain and, therefore, that nothing can survive death. The French neurologist Jean-Pierre Changeux, for example, has claimed, "Man need no longer be seen as a spiritual but a neuronal being."[1] In much the same vein, Jacques Monod asserted, "Man finally knows he is alone in the immense indifference of the universe in which he appeared by chance."[2]

Consequently, classical science has been associated with a "disenchantment of the world," in the words of Max Weber. Moreover, it has had an adverse effect on religion, increasingly seen as the product of "nothing but" human imagination whose pervasiveness throughout human society, according to some sociobiologists, may be due to a genetic propensity. It has even been argued by some that societies with a belief in God are more productive, thanks to a "God gene" that has successfully survived the process of natural selection through the advantages conferred by "wishful thinking" in various societies.

Spiritual information may be conceived of in two ways:

✦ *Type 1*—a revelation to humanity from another level of reality (which is impossible if there are no other levels of reality);

✦ *Type 2*—information obtained from a scientific study of the world, which may serve to disclose part of God's creativity and possible elements of his cosmic purposes, including his plan for humanity and the universe (but, of course, impossible if such a plan does not exist).

In the context of classical science, it is clear that there is little or no room for any kind of spiritual information. However, since the beginning of the twentieth century, another kind of scientific revolution has been under way. Running counter to classical science, this revolution has been laying the foundation for a serious reappraisal of the two kinds of spiritual information described above.

Type 2 Spiritual Information: The New Scientific Paradigm

The following paragraphs briefly outline the revolutionary changes that have been taking place in the sciences and how these might be associated with a new kind of spiritual information.

In astrophysics, the theory of general relativity and the resulting Big Bang theory tell us that time and space are no longer absolutes and, therefore, that other dimensions located outside of time and space can exist. The Anthropic Principle shows us that the universe is finely tuned to allow the emergence of complexity and life and ultimately leads us to conjecture that it has been conceived in such a way as to allow consciousness—capable of apprehending beauty and seeking out its Creator—to appear.

Quantum physics further undermines materialism in the strict sense of the term by showing that elementary particles, the building blocks of matter, are not objects. As Werner Heisenberg said, "The atoms and elementary particles themselves form a world of potentialities rather than a world of things or facts."[3] Moreover, quantum mechanics reveals to us the existence of nonlocal connectivity free from time and space. This concept is reminiscent of the intuitions of some religions that refer to "interconnectedness," as we find, for example, in the concept of the constantly changing self in response to shifting conditions in Buddhism or the spiritual unity of all souls in the Communion of Saints in Christianity.

The evolution of life is no longer seen as a blind process. The work of scientists such as Michael Denton[4] extends the Anthropic Principle to biology by showing that evolution is made possible by the fine-tuning of the laws that govern biochemistry.

In addition, "genetic imperialism," which endows genes with a pivotal role in the process of evolution (underscoring the Darwinian conclusion that no plan can be discerned in the process of evolution), is increasingly thrown into contention. However, the recent discovery of a new RNA-based system of information in living organisms hit the headlines of some scientific journals and important newspapers.[5] Phillip Sharp of the Massachusetts Institute of Technology, who won the Nobel Prize in Physiology or Medicine in 1993, and Gordon Carmichael of the University of Connecticut have discovered the existence of fragments of RNA that are capable of interfering with the reading of biological information contained in DNA. Their work is linked to the discovery of a new universal mechanism in the world of living organisms that provides the simplest method for preventing the action of a gene in an organism. Even if the implications of such a mechanism in the process of evolution are not yet clearly understood, several leading scientists have not hesitated to talk about the discovery of a new "biological continent," which will inevitably change our perception of life. The progress of epigenetics also shows the importance of the role played by the environment in the expression of genes. It demonstrates that there is a lack of humility among those who purport (in overly simplistic and reductive statements) that "we are nothing but selfish genes mindlessly reproducing themselves" and who claim that Darwinian models are able to explain the whole of evolution. All of this raises the possibility that there may be a purpose in evolution.

If the reductionist approach in neuroscience has had, and will no doubt continue to enjoy, much success, numerous other experiences such as those of Ben Libet and Roger Sperry show us that there is a dimension of human consciousness that defies explanation from a purely neuronal basis.

Thus, a reductionist explanation of the singularity of the human person as a conscious being seems less and less likely. The "hard problem" seems to be getting even harder as our understanding improves. There is increasing evidence that the belief in an extra dimension of human existence is not absurd.

In mathematics, the Gödel Theorem has revealed the incompleteness of human logic. This, too, is a reason for humility, but it is also a justification for those who adhere to a Platonic view of the world according to which mathematics is not merely a construct of the spirit, but a reality intimately linked with this spirit. Gödel insisted that his work demonstrated that mathematical "truth" is a concept far larger than demonstrability. This transcendence of "truth" gives scientific substantiation to 2500-year-old intuition.

Hence, extensive data regarding the fine-tuning of the universe, the nature of matter, evolution, the human spirit, and mathematics contradict the claims of materialism and give a firm basis for the existence of spiritual information.

All of this suggests that we may be witnessing a paradigm shift. We have a considerable responsibility, and yet we know from the work of Thomas Kuhn that the purveyors of a new paradigm always go through periods of isolation—and even persecution—before they see their ideas come to fruition. How much easier it would have been for Galileo and his successors if only they had had supporters with entrepreneurial minds and public relations agencies to help them promulgate their ideas! And how many years and centuries humanity would have advanced if the ideas of the Renaissance had developed more quickly!

In short, there is no reason to shy away from using an entrepreneurial approach to promote ideas. The purpose of this paper is not to describe a complete strategy, but simply to show how strategic concepts can be carried from one field of inquiry to another. By using concepts that are typically used for creating a new product or a new market, we can contribute to the rapid evolution of knowledge.

Establishing the Plan: Promoting Spiritual Information

✦ *Who are our clients?*

All those who have a spiritual quest or a religious faith, as well as educational and cultural institutions. However, it is necessary to ensure that fundamentalists, for whom progress is impossible, should be excluded, as should all those who seek refuge in esoteric sects.

✦ *Who are our competitors?*

Organizations working in the field of Science and Religion and those dealing with the new scientific paradigm. Here, too, it is necessary to avoid organizations involved in spreading fundamentalist or New Age ideas. However, spiritually open joint ventures (win-win games) are possible—not only with other organizations defending spiritualist positions, but also with promoters of emergence, self-organization, and chaos theory, even if these promoters are entirely atheistic. A Jew, a Christian, and a Muslim who accept mainstream Science and Religion ideas have more in common with the atheistic disciples of Varela and Prigogine than with a Christian who believes the world is only six thousand years old or a Muslim who claims that the speed of light is written in the Koran. Given the weakness of a new paradigm when it emerges, alliances between organizations that might otherwise be rivals are vital. However, such alliances are sometimes very difficult to form for ideological and personal reasons. Therefore, they should be encouraged.

✦ *Who are our suppliers?*

Scientists, philosophers, theologians, and religious leaders who are either directly or indirectly involved with the Science and Religion dialog or the new scientific paradigm. Here, too, discretion should be exercised. To focus only on mainstream thinkers would be dangerous, as history clearly shows that new ideas generally emerge out of the mainstream. But ideas from lofty-minded people or those who lack intellectual rigor are equally dangerous.

✦ *What are our raw materials?*

All the facts and discoveries that show that the intuitions and principles of the great religions received by humanity were received from another level of reality (*Type 1 spiritual information*) or that enable the progression of the new scientific paradigm (*Type 2 spiritual information*).

✦ *Who are the potential shareholders?*

All those who believe that atheism and materialism are a dead end for humanity and who have the means to finance currents of thought that support a nonmaterialist vision of the world. They can be Jewish, Christian, Buddhist, Muslim, or simply spiritually open people who do not adhere to any particular religion.

✦ *Who are our promoters?*

The main religions that have an interest in disseminating information on the Science and Religion dialog to win back part of the public that thinks that modernity stands in opposition to religion. Also, the media interested in the sciences or polemical debates; the Science-Religion debate is often a contentious one.

Advancing the Plan: Taking Spiritual Information Forward

Hence, we can see how it is possible to construct an entrepreneurial approach based on a global strategy that would include increasing the raw materials base available for research, including certain sectors that are not directly concerned with the field of Science and Religion, and carefully selecting suppliers, taking into account the credibility of the prestigious mainstream people and the creativity of some innovative borderline people. This strategy should also involve lobbying large international organizations, universities, and academies to raise awareness about the seriousness of the field of Science and Religion, while similarly reaching out to the main religions so that they can disseminate the findings in this field of inquiry to their numerous congregations. It would also involve a systematic scanning of business leaders who have religious beliefs to encourage them to provide funding for the field. Work needs to be carried out in the area of communications and public relations to support the dissemination of works and the ideas of researchers, sometimes isolated, but who may be pioneers in the field of Science and Religion and/or the new scientific paradigm. We must also encourage mutual alliances between existing networks in the field that are not linked at present.

By building strategies of this nature, "spiritual entrepreneurs" will be able to herald the arrival and acceptance of the new paradigm that is now in its early infancy. Some may criticize the transposition of a "business plan" to the promotion of ideas. However, this is to ignore the fact that the history of science shows us that, in the long term, there is a safety net. If those who are involved in such endeavors tend to lack honesty and rigor, their actions lead to their own demise, whatever means they employ. This is one of the most remarkable characteristics of science (and which the scientific researcher shares with the religious seeker): The truth is always revealed in the end to the detriment of illusion. The best proof is surely that no leading scientist would participate in a program whose aim was to show that the world was only six thousand years old, even if such a program were backed with millions of dollars. If the new paradigm that we are talking about does not relate to facts, it will end in ruin, however many millions of dollars are spent trying to promote it.

Therefore, this approach avoids the risk of misinterpreting scientific data (as with the Lysenko affair under the communist regime[6]) insofar as we retain our freedom and the free exchange of ideas. On the other hand, if the new paradigm is confirmed, a global strategy for its promotion led by spiritual entrepreneurs could avoid loss of precious time in this period of doubt and international tension when more than ever we need to have reason to believe in the credibility of spiritual information—which indicates that the world and our existence have meaning.

This was Sir John Templeton's remarkable intuition when he decided to invest in the promotion and development of the new scientific paradigm, and especially its metaphysical and philosophical implications. And he has been working with an international perspective covering the main points mentioned above.

In its own independent way, and with much smaller means, the Interdisciplinary University of Paris has developed a similar strategy that does not merely limit itself to action through academic circles, but that aims to build a genuine business plan for the development of the field of vigorous, constructive dialog and mutual exploration between science and religion.

But to be consistent, the promotion of the facts and ideas linked to the field of Science and Religion must be carried out in line with the values and behavior that correspond to them. It is impossible to assert that the world is infused with meaning, that the emergence and development of life is part of a plan, that humans are more than machines created at the behest of "selfish genes" and at the same time pollute the environment and despise our collaborators and clients. Therefore, the spiritual entrepreneur should break with a short-term vision and the maximization of profit at all cost. There is a direct link between this type of behavior and the materialism of the classical paradigm. "If God does not exist, everything is permitted," said Dostoevsky. No morality and no ethics, only the search for individual self-interest, can find a solid basis for a vision of the world that corresponds to the classical paradigm.

Here, too, Sir John Templeton was a pioneer. He himself attributes his professional success to the fact that his aim was to increase the wealth of his clients and not the maximization of his personal profit. Had he chosen this latter option, he would not have benefited from the loyalty of his clients in the long run.

At a time when we require two-figure growth rates from companies and economic growth is between 3 percent and 4 percent, which has catastrophic results in increasing the pressure on businesses forcing some of them to cook the books, the example of Sir John Templeton shows us a possible alternative route: A spiritual entrepreneur should not only take the shareholders into account, but also all the stakeholders who constitute his or her business environment. This approach will work because the employees, the suppliers, and the clients will be more faithful and more motivated because of the respect and the advantage that they will obtain instead of creating a situation where the entrepreneur is only interested in maximizing his or her own profits. Ethics and values will generate more confidence in the business than in those of his or her competitors.

In conclusion we must be aware that we are facing a triple revolution.

✦ We are going from a dogmatic and self-assured theological vision based on fundamentalist conceptions of religious texts (for example, closing interpretation of the Koran and the damage it has caused and continues to cause) to a more open vision based on humility about all that we still need to know about what God wanted to convey to us, with simultaneous respect for other religions engendered by raising awareness about the incompleteness of our own tradition, however rich it is.

✦ We are moving from a scientist, materialist, and mechanistic vision of the universe that is devoid of the concept of an overall plan and that is closed in on itself to the concept of a universe that is open to other levels of reality from which we can receive spiritual information.

✦ We are shifting from a quantitative economy based only on profit, data, and the principle of survival of the fittest to a qualitative economy in which the respect of values, ethics, people, and nature is a requisite and not an option.

Although these three revolutions are very different, they are linked by the same concepts: the transition from arrogance to humility, from closed systems to open ones, from quantitative to qualitative economies.

The simultaneity and scope of the three revolutions open up new perspectives to humanity that have not been seen since the transition of the Middle Ages to the Renaissance. They represent the framework in which humanity may be able to acquire more spiritual information thanks to the work of seekers of truth and spiritual entrepreneurs.

ℒ♥

PROFESSOR JEAN STAUNE is Founder and General Secretary of the Interdisciplinary University of Paris, which has organized some of the most important international conferences and meetings in the Science and Religion dialog. He is also Assistant Professor of the Philosophy of Science in the MBA course of l'École des Hautes Études Commerciales (HEC) in Paris, editor of the *Temps des Sciences* series published by Fayard (Hachette Group), and a member of the John Templeton Board of Advisors and the European Society for the Study of Science and Theology (ESSAT). He has a DEA in Human Palaeontology from the National Museum of Natural History and a DESS in Management from the Sorbonne. His current research mainly focuses on the philosophical and social implications of new scientific discoveries, on the links between science and religion, and on ways to popularize the conceptual revolutions that occurred in both of these fields during the last century. He co-edited *L'Homme Face à la Science* (*Man in Front of Science*) in collaboration with Ilya Prigogine, Hubert Reeves, Trinh Xuan Thuan, and Bernard d'Espagnat. Also a management consultant to large corporations, Professor Staune is working on ways to develop strategic decision-making tools linking new scientific concepts to management theories.

NOTES

1 Jean-Pierre Changeux: *L'Homme Neuronal*, (Paris: Odile Jacob, 1983).

2 Jacques Monod: *Le Hasard et la Nécessité*, (Paris: Le Seuil, 1970).

3 Werner Heisenberg: *Physics and Philosophy*, (New York: Harper Torch Books, 1962).

4 Michael Denton: *Nature's Destiny: How the Laws of Biology Reveal Purpose in the Universe*, (New York: Simon and Schuster/Free Press, 1998). Also see his essay in this volume, "Henderson's 'Fine-Tuning Argument': Time for Rediscovery."

5 *The Independent*, 10 August 2002, and *Le Monde*, 13 August 2002, pages 1 and 2.

6 See "Lysenko, Trofim Denisovich," in *The Columbia Encyclopedia*, 6th ed. Copyright 2003 Columbia University Press: http://www.bartleby.com/65/ly/Lysenko.html.

GLOBAL SPIRITUAL CONFUSION AND THE NEGLECTED PROBLEM OF EXCESS SPIRITUAL INFORMATION

6

Wesley J. Wildman

THE BIGGEST PROBLEM facing the spiritual progress of human beings, after evil and stupidity, is confusion. Spiritually potent visions of the world abound. They sustain billions of lives each day. Many of us have friends and neighbors with worldviews different from our own, and media outlets are filled with images of diversity. Our species desperately needs to advance in wisdom or spirit to cope with the turmoil of technology and the perpetual clash of civilizations. But advance where? Along which path of wisdom should we stumble?

Some advise us to advance spiritually by digging deep into our own home traditions. The global picture of religious and cultural pluralism is what causes the confusion, and we should just learn to ignore it. Surely it is sage advice to appreciate our home traditions, but if we follow the path closest to hand thoughtlessly, we may deepen global spiritual confusion. After all, personal spiritual confidence is the proudest possession of the enthusiast, the often ignorant, sometimes dangerous, true believer. Most of us can't simply ignore alternatives. Nor can we rest content with the "we have ours and they have theirs" policy without committing intellectual suicide. The conflicts among spiritual visions of reality are obvious. We can't just wish them away. Digging deep in our home tradition (if we have one) might be necessary, but it is not sufficient.

Some say the generic and allegedly global spiritualities of humanism or of nature are the answer. But they are ideas rather than spiritual paths. They lack the symbolic power of traditional religions. Meanwhile, New Age spiritualities make a virtue of pluralistic confusion, while creating as much economic activity as wisdom. These cultural and class-specific alternatives to traditional religion don't appeal to most people.

Some say science can resolve the confusion. Science creates basic knowledge that people can agree on regardless of culture or religion. Cutting-edge science can be controversial, even among scientists, but educated people all over the world accept almost all of mainstream science. That's promising. But science's picture of the world is modest. It doesn't address issues of perennial concern to human beings: life after death, justice and goodness, meaning and purpose.

Some insist that we shouldn't give up just because science has a limited mandate. They say we can search for signs of an ultimate reality hidden within the workings of physical processes. More than that, they claim to know the secret key that unlocks the spiritual information hidden within scientific knowledge.

How do they do this? American philosopher William Lane Craig (who contributed an essay to this volume) advocates analyzing scientific discoveries to find spiritual information. He uses sophisticated arguments to show that Big Bang cosmology discloses a creator God. Scholars as diverse as mathematician William Dembski and biologist Michael Behe argue that some biological systems are so complex in a special way that evolutionary theory will never explain them; an intelligent designer of some sort must be invoked. A host of scientists have been studying the effects of prayer and spirituality on health. Others have been looking for the basis of moral teachings such as self-sacrificial love in evolutionary biology and neuropsychology. The list of intellectuals seeking spiritual information through science is long and often distinguished. (Like Craig, many are represented in this volume.) And now there is generous funding to help them, from the John Templeton Foundation and from other like-minded organizations.

The claim that scientific discoveries encode spiritual information is stunning. If it is true, then maybe science's knack of producing agreement about mundane matters could help us resolve our spiritual confusion. Here's how it would work: We extract the spiritual juice from the fruits of existing scientific research. We devise new science research efforts to keep up the flow of spiritual information. We use a class of middleman communicators to get the word out to the world, especially to leaders in education and to high-profile opinion makers. And then we enter a brave new world: science in harmony with spiritual information, overcoming ancient religious and cultural rivalries, transforming the globe into a place of peace and harmonious prosperity.

This is a bracing picture of the future, moving and insightful, and akin to the hopes of Sir John Templeton. But there is a challenge to overcome first because this vision of human progress through discovering spiritual information neglects a simple but deep fact: *The problem causing our spiritual confusion is not that we have too little information, but too much.*

It has always been this way, as the conflicted history of religions and cultures shows. And it continues to be this way even now. The latest scientific discoveries do not help to pare back this excess of information to an essential core. The basic spiritual worldview options persist, and each can be made more or less compatible with our growing knowledge of the world through science. Spiritual progress is essential to our survival and is flourishing. But we need something other than merely more spiritual information through science to achieve the goal of eliminating spiritual confusion.

How can we handle excess spiritual information? Experts in extracting spiritual information from scientific knowledge have little to say about this. Perhaps they know a lot about science and maybe one spiritual tradition, but only a little about the history of civilizations and cultures or about the world's great religions and philosophical ideas. In other words, they are biased by their local spiritual perspectives and tend to notice only the way that emerging spiritual information confirms their viewpoints. If the quest for spiritual information through science becomes more cross-culturally balanced, this bias will collapse. In its place will arise a number of brilliant worldviews already known to experts in the study of world religious philosophies, each more richly articulated by means of new spiritual information.

But this is neither consensus nor progress. It is merely a gloriously intensified version of the spiritual confusion that is already so familiar.

At this point, the long-suffering mystics would have us listen to them. Always marginalized because of their obscure ways of talking and peculiar spiritual practices, mystics can't compete with the achievements and prestige of science in our era. But the problem of excess spiritual information gives them an opening. If their famous claim to experience ultimate reality directly is true, then perhaps they can help sort through the excess information.

Obviously, novices in spiritual experiences will be of little help. Their enthusiasm for such experiences is vital for their own lives, but does not foster the wisdom and perspective needed to handle the problem of excess spiritual information. Even master mystics may not be able to assist much. Taken together, the collection of spiritual insights offered with deep conviction by the world's recognized masters of mystical wisdom, and received with reverence by their faithful disciples, seems massively contradictory.

For mysticism to help us, we would have to consult mystics with profound knowledge of the world's spiritual traditions, attuned to both historical and scientific ways of thinking. They would have to care about coordinating conflicting mystical visions. They would probably be committed to the proposition that a core truth lies beneath the diversity of mystical reports.

Enter American mystic and scholar Huston Smith. He is revered for his lucid scholarly accounts of the world's religions. He is also admired because of the decades of his long life spent traveling the world and getting to know religions and mysticisms from personal experience. He is an outspoken advocate of the view that mystic-scholars can solve the problem of excess spiritual information.

Smith is convinced that all religious traditions have a common core. You can't find it in rituals or teachings, where the diversity is overwhelming. But the mystics of all religions know about it. He argues that their direct experience of ultimate reality has enabled them to reach consensus on this core view of reality, even though the religious traditions to which they adhere differ enormously from one another. This core view was already present even in preliterate tribal religions, he says, and persists down to the present day. It is called the "primordial tradition" because of its age or the "perennial philosophy" because of its staying power (see his book *The Primordial Tradition* for a summary).

What does the perennial philosophy say? There are four levels of reality, with increasing dignity and power, and four corresponding levels of the human being:

+ The human body = the terrestrial level
+ The human mind = an intermediate level
+ The human soul = the celestial level
+ The human spirit = the highest level, the Infinite

That's the way the universe is built. It goes beyond science, but does not contradict it. We should all be able to agree on it.

But wait a minute. I noted above that a quick survey of mystics shows massive conflict. How can Smith dare to mention consensus? He explains the variety of mystics' reports as the result of connecting with reality at one of these four levels:

+ Nature mystics engage reality at the terrestrial level.
+ Mystics grappling with discarnate beings such as demons and angels engage at the intermediate level.
+ Mystics for whom the final vision is a personal deity engage at the celestial level.
+ And mystics for whom the ultimate vision is the Infinite—God without attributes, God beyond comprehension, God beyond God—engage at the highest level.

So here is the perennial philosophy's recipe for human progress. Each person should belong to a vital spiritual tradition. Using its resources, we deepen our spiritual and moral insight. We bring our actions into harmony with those insights. New spiritual information unlocked from science helps experts articulate each tradition more richly. For those who dare to learn about other ways, the perennial philosophy is the master worldview. Thus, we do not fall prey to mutual incomprehension or deadly conflict. And for those who don't care about such advanced learning, each tradition has basic rules about how to behave that make for peace within and among nations and religions. Within this framework, each person can advance in spiritual wisdom.

It is a grand vision. And it offers a real corrective to the earlier vision of progress through science-driven spiritual information. But just as the first vision was marred by the problem of too much information, so Smith's is spoiled by a simple fact: The perennial philosophy's claims about a common core to religious traditions simply do not survive close scrutiny. The data don't allow it. Who says? The overwhelming majority of specialists who study religion might revere Smith, but they find his arguments far too hopeful. Smith might think that his critics are in thrall to the details of religious differences and miss the big picture. But his critics are convinced. Rarely has a scholarly argument been read so widely and rejected so universally.

Some have argued boldly that "entheogens"—once innocently called "psychedelic drugs"—may hold the key to getting information about ultimate reality. Proponents claim that entheogens open up ignored human capacities for perceiving reality. But how useful is the information that people obtain through using entheogens? There is some evidence on this question, such as the famous "Good Friday" experiment at Boston University conducted in 1962 by Walter Pahnke. It seems that, as in mystical experience, people describe their drug-assisted experiences using the concepts and words available to them. Thus, getting information from drug-assisted experiences is no simpler than interpreting diverse mystical texts.

The problem of excess spiritual information has no neat answers. But that doesn't mean it is intractable. The world's great religious traditions might not share a common core vision, such as the perennial philosophy, but we are not left with a riot of absolute disagreement. The patient study of the great spiritual worldviews has produced valuable insights into the ways they agree and disagree.

The task of comparing religious ideas and practices is modest in itself, but it serves the more adventurous goal of truth-seeking. Yet even comparison has its skeptics. Many experts say that information about world cultures and religions is now so richly detailed that even the modest hope of meaningfully comparing the great spiritual worldviews is futile. How could one person ever gain deep knowledge of the languages and material needed to make a fair comparison, let alone decide whether one view is better than another or detect a core view beneath the diversity? Maybe comparison was feasible a hundred years ago, but surely it is no longer.

Scholars of religion skeptical about comparison can take a lesson from scientists. The natural sciences proceed in a corporate fashion these days. They must do so because we are long past the days when any one scientist could know all there was to know in science. The result is a messy social process, but it works. Perhaps the task of managing excess spiritual information—of comparing and analyzing worldviews—can also be conceived as a corporate task for a wide variety of experts.

This lesson seems to be sinking in. Some experts in religious and philosophical traditions—the ones who have not given up on comparison altogether—have devised corporate methods for comparing and assessing spiritual worldviews. They refer to their field with names such as "comparative metaphysics." American comparative metaphysician Robert Cummings Neville is an example. His Cross-Cultural Comparative Religious Ideas Project was a bold attempt to try out his proposed method in a small community of expert scholars. The project's four years and three volumes of results show how comparative metaphysics works in detail. There are several other noteworthy examples. But all belong to the world of scholars. The search for patterns and core ideas in our world's spiritual traditions is difficult. There are no shortcuts.

Resolving global spiritual confusion requires us to dig deep into our home traditions. It calls for paying attention to the ways that science can generate the sort of spiritual information that helps to articulate spiritual traditions more richly. But nothing less than comparative metaphysics will be able to turn the excess of ideas about ultimate reality emerging from the study of nature and spiritual experience into anything like reliable information. Of course, we also need great spiritual leaders and teachers, as well as technological and economic innovation and political systems that cultivate tolerance. But spiritual progress for human beings depends on facing a hard fact: Seeking spiritual information from science, like digging deep into our home spiritual traditions, produces an embarrassment of riches. Spiritual information from science is not the antidote to global spiritual confusion, at least not by itself.

✍

WESLEY J. WILDMAN, PH.D., is Associate Professor of Theology and Ethics at Boston University and Convenor of the Graduate School's doctoral program in Science, Philosophy, and Religion. He has been a member of the Boston-based Cross-Cultural Comparative Religious Ideas Research Project and also the Divine Action Project jointly sponsored by the Center for Theology and the Natural Sciences and the Vatican Observatory. Author of more than fifty scholarly articles and book

Science, Semiotics, and the Sacred 7

Seeking Spiritual Information in the Deep Structure of Reality

William Grassie

O UR PRINCIPAL BENEFACTOR at the Metanexus Institute is Sir John Templeton, the ninety-year-old visionary mutual funds manager of significant fame
and accomplishment. Sir John is fond of using the term "spiritual information" to
describe the focus of his philanthropic work in science and religion, expanded to
"new spiritual information" to describe the purpose of his philanthropic mission—
to increase our storehouse of spiritual information one hundredfold. With the
explosion of information that occurred during the twentieth century and into the
twenty-first, the use of the term "spiritual information" might well lead one to further despair in the face of ever-more unread books, magazines, and emails. When
people complain about information overload, the metaphor of spiritual information may well carry negative connotations for many. And yet Sir John's seemingly
idiosyncratic advocacy of this term—spiritual information—goes to the heart of a
profound epistemological and ontological shift in the sciences today and allows the
recovery of ancient insights from our received religious traditions.

Many religions have understood language to be in some way primordial to the
material constitution of the Universe. In Hinduism, the Upanishads talk of a primal
word, *Om*, which functions as the creative source of all Nature. In the Jewish
Midrash, the grammatical ambiguity of the first line of Genesis and the extravagant
linguistic creativity of *Elohim* leads to philosophical speculation about a preexistent
Torah, which God uses to speak reality into being. In Medieval Judaism, this rabbinic
tradition gave rise to the wild speculations and philosophical subtleties of the Kabbalah. The Greeks, including Plato, drew upon Heraclitus's notion of *logos*, viewing
the embodied word as that fire that animated and ruled the world, to explain their
understanding of primeval, material language. In the Gospel of John, Christians
celebrate this Word, or *Logos*, in a radical incarnationalist vision of a cosmic Christ
in whom and through whom all things come into being. Language, the spoken word
and the written word, was the ultimate medium for creation, revelation, and
redemption. Every time we communicate, we participate in a miracle of ultimate
significance, or at least so our ancestors intuited.

Modern humans, informed by science, live in a universe that is more enriched
with awesome subtleties and gorgeous details than our ancestors could possibly
have imagined. Paradoxically, however, our Universe seems also to be more spiritually impoverished than that of traditional peoples. This new Universe as understood by modern science seems to import a concomitant loss of significance,
meaning, and purpose in our lives. Here, Sir John's advocacy of the constructive

engagement of science and religion in general, and of advancing new spiritual information in particular, goes to the heart of intellectual history and the unfolding of our cosmic future.

The modern metaphysics of science takes space-time and matter-energy to be fundamental. To this we add the four nuclear forces, the laws of thermodynamics, some algorithmic processes, an element of randomness—and, presto, we have the Universe built from the bottom up that science has been so successful at explaining and describing from the microcosmic to the macrocosmic in all its stunning complexity. The oddity in all this new talk of information from scientists is that information does not fit into that twentieth-century paradigm. For instance, information is immaterial. It is not a thing you can point to, but a no-thing that must be metaphorically "read" by some-things, which some-things are apparently constituted by the no-thing in a fine piece of circular logic. An ontology and epistemology that looks only to materialism and reductionism for its explanations of phenomena will have a hard time explaining information itself. Ironically, the very pursuit of this materialist and reductionist paradigm has led to its supervenience, but the character and nuances of this new metaphysical vision have barely been explored.

In physics, we now talk about the information states of quantum phenomena. In cosmology, we speculate about a preexistent mathematical order, through which the cosmos unfolds. Challenge a hard-nosed, reductionistic physicist about mathematics and you're likely to find a softhearted neo-Platonist.

With the genomic revolution, biologists now also talk about information residing at the center of life processes. In cellular signal transduction, the genomic word becomes living flesh. Although species come and go in the evolutionary epic, much of the genomic memory of the past is retained in contemporary genomes. As new evolutionary niches are explored, the figurative becomes literal, as new species are reconfigured into new emergent possibilities, adding new chapters to the "book of life."

The neurosciences today see the brain as an information processing system. While no doubt beautiful to the discerning eye of a scientist, a single neuron is rather dumb. A hundred billion neurons in the human brain, however, wired in a massively parallel system, become potentially the most complex entity in the Universe. The neurons fire in on and off states through the synaptic media to mediate every human experience and memory. Laying down neural networks is another way of talking about encoding information, as the inside informational world of the brain maps with the outside informational world of Nature, culture, and cosmos.

This new metaphysical movement in the sciences has largely been mediated by the computer as both tool and metaphor. Among diverse scientific disciplines, the real scientific revolution in recent decades has been the ability to collect and analyze large datasets and to further manipulate these datasets through powerful computer simulations. Computers provide not just the tools for new scientific discoveries, but also the new metaphors that now also dominate scientific discourse (e.g., algorithms, binary code, hardware, and software—all terms that have traveled widely outside the domains of the computer sciences). Computational finitude, however, also points toward a complexity horizon that may thwart our unbridled desires for controlling and predictive knowledge. The Universe may be a single data-base, but it is so profoundly relational that the easy hackings of the codes by earlier science may soon be exhausted.

Of course, I am using the terms "language" and "information" to be in some sense analogous. It is worth noting that the greatest contemporary philosophers of science are compelled to also become philosophers of language (cross-reference any intro-ductory anthology in the two fields, and you will note philosophers such as Frege, Hempel, Quine, Searle, and Putnam appearing on both sides of the ledger). A little philosophical detour may help to illuminate the connection between language and information in our search to recover and discover something new of the spiritual center of our lives and the Universe.

The Swiss linguist Ferdinand de Saussure, credited as the founder of modern lin-guistics, distinguishes between language as *langue* and language as *parole*. *Langue* is the code, grammar, and structure of any particular language. *Parole* is the meaning of any particular speaker in a context-specific situation of a particular message. Linguistics as a science can illuminate *langue* because it is collective and objective in ways that particular utterances may be confoundingly context-specific. Today, scholars would substitute the terms *semiotics* and *semantics* and broaden the inquiry beyond "natural" human languages to include all kinds of communicative actions from art and advertising to abstract concepts and entire ideologies. Semiotics is the code of communication and semantics the informational content or meaning of particular communications. Of course, the codes of languages evolve over time through specific semantic histories, so Saussure's radical distinction between semi-otics and semantics cannot be maintained as we look at the evolution of human lan-guages over time. This realization has led to the ascendancy of a kind of philosophical relativism within linguistics today, which views the semiotics of thought as arbitrary and always derived from specific social and historical situa-tions. There is no simple correspondence between human language and objective realities.

The philosophy of science has also witnessed a similar move from a simple cor-respondence theory of sciences as Truth, referred to as positivism, to a much more nuanced and contextual understanding of science as temporarily reliable interpre-tations of truths. While Karl Popper's falsification theory of science may convince bench scientists of the epistemological purity of their endeavors, W. V. Quine, Arthur Fine, Thomas Kuhn, Hilary Putnam, and others have thoroughly demol-ished this understanding of science as an epistemologically privileged endeavor. The dilemma now becomes accounting for the progressive and practical effica-ciousness of science, in spite of its social and historical construction.

Sir John points the way out of this philosophical incoherence in science and lin-guistics when he suggests that language as information may somehow be constitu-tive of the ultimate nature of reality, as implied by using the adjective "spiritual" to modify the noun "information." Let's see how this might work and what some of the consequences might be.

Modern humans have tended to understand that we alone among the species of the world possess language, that language is unique to our brain structures and cultural possibilities. In a developmental context, human culture must teach every human infant anew how to speak, listen, and think. Terrence Deacon, Merlin Donald, and others have convincingly argued that human languages must reside in an "immaterial" cultural space between individual human mind-brains. The human infant's brain is capable of learning language, but there is no genetic or developmental necessity that they become linguistically competent. In those tragic cases when human infants are deprived of social and linguistic stimulation, they become permanently mentally and emotionally retarded. In this contemporary understanding of the developmental neurophysiology of human language, language really is "out there," in almost a neo-Platonic sense, and only comes to temporarily reside "in here" in our mind-brains. Indeed, in the strong sense, language helps to create our physical mind-brains.

In an evolutionary context of human development over the last two million years, we might rather say that Nature teaches our species to speak, listen, and think, because Nature is already pregnant with linguistic meanings and patterns "out there" that thankfully have the potential to map onto the "in here" realities of our mind-brain cultures. In that sense, human language is derived from the more-than-human world of Nature in the relational spaces between our species and the rest of creation.

The moment that we ground human language in a semiotically constituted and semantically rich cosmos, than we have solved the problem of incoherence that troubles contemporary philosophy of science and philosophy of language. The solipsistic circle posited by Wittgenstein in his discussion of language games is opened up to the dynamic and semantically rich universe. The encounter with the other rationalities of other language games becomes the progressive hermeneutical possibility of which Gadaamer speaks in the "fusion of horizons." Our human languages build on the many languages of Nature. Indeed, this intelligibility of Nature by human language is the precondition for science, so in one sense this is only to reaffirm the realist aspirations of science, even while seeking to reclaim the romantic motivations of science as a spiritual quest.

In this new view, science can be seen as a kind of translation project, where we try to learn the language of an alien set of phenomena and try to understand the terminology, syntax, and grammar that the phenomena authentically "speak." The semiotics of our scientific translations is represented in mathematical notations, diagrams, charts, and models. Another intelligent civilization in a different corner of the galaxy might use radically different semiotics to represent these phenomenological realities, but we would expect to be able to translate these representations, even as every human language is translatable (although something is also always lost in translation). Great science seems to occur most often when the scientist, like the missionary in the foreign land, "goes native." A good physicist dreams in the mathematics of the cosmos; a good chemist thinks within the three-dimensional bonding space of complex molecules; a good biologist has a feel for the organism. Science might better be defined as altruistic fidelity to the phenomena, making one's life and intellect a vehicle for some other reality to have a voice and value in our human culture, consciousness, and conscience.

This new relational, linguistically centered ontology can be seen as a kind of evolutionary neo-Platonism. And while we gain philosophical coherence, we are also tempered with a profound sense of our finitude, another one of Sir John's key thematic foci: Epistemological humility in matters scientific and religious turns out to be difficult for us to maintain psychologically, because we would wish to banish cognitive dissonance and existential uncertainty from our lives. Discovering new spiritual information is sure to be hard work, requiring patience, rigor, exertion, hope, faith, and love. Fortunately, Sir John also points us toward the recovery of these great virtues from our religious traditions, even as he calls for us to seek progress in religion.

This new relational, information-centered ontology arising in the sciences today provides a wonderful moment for the recovery and reinterpretation of traditional religious worldviews. Today, the Universe is far grander than our ancestors could have possibly imagined, but somehow they seem to have already intuited its deep, spiritual, informational structure through which all things come into being.

✐

WILLIAM "BILLY" GRASSIE, PH.D., is Founder and Executive Director of the Metanexus Institute on Religion and Science, www.metanexus.net. Dr. Grassie also serves as Executive Editor of the Institute's online magazine and discussion forum with more than forty thousand weekly page views and six thousand regular subscribers in fifty-seven different countries. He has taught in a variety of positions at Temple University, Swarthmore College, and the University of Pennsylvania. Dr. Grassie received his doctorate in religion from Temple University in 1994 and his B.A. from Middlebury College in 1979. Before graduate school, he worked for ten years in religiously based social service and advocacy organizations in Washington, D.C.; Philadelphia, PA; Jerusalem; and Berlin. Dr. Grassie is the recipient of a number of academic awards and grants from the American Friends Service Committee, the Roothbert Fellowship, and the John Templeton Foundation. He is a member of the Religious Society of Friends (Quakers).

REFERENCES

Boyd, Richard, et al. *The Philosophy of Science.* Boston: MIT Press, 1991.

Deacon, Terrence W. *The Symbolic Species: The Co-evolution of Language and the Brain.* New York: Norton, 1997.

Donald, Merlin. *Origins of the Modern Mind: Three Stages in the Evolution of Culture and Cognition.* Cambridge, MA: Harvard University Press, 1991.

Martinich, A. P., ed. *The Philosophy of Language.* New York: Oxford University Press. 1996.

Ricoeur, Paul. *Interpretation Theory: Discourse and the Surplus of Meaning.* Fort Worth: Texas Christian University Press, 1976.

Whitehead, A. N. *Process and Reality.* New York: The Free Press, (1929) 1978.

WHAT DOES A SLUG KNOW OF MOZART? 8

INTRODUCING THE ONTOLOGICAL MULTIVERSE

Charles L. Harper Jr.

EINSTEIN is reported to have remarked once that a Mozart symphony is more than an air-pressure curve. Sir John Templeton often says that an apple tree has a limited understanding of God. To complete a triad of odd remarks, let me add, "What does a slug know of Mozart?" If this seems a bit strange, keep reading; it gets worse.

This essay addresses the challenge of gaining insight into the concept of spiritual information and into the possibility of finding ways to accelerate the discovery of new spiritual information. Such innovation-focused exploration and discovery is the core desideratum of Sir John Templeton and forms the central mission of his Foundation.

Of course, there are many ways to conceptualize an unavoidably fuzzy and necessarily perplexing term such as "spiritual information." These include:

A. The classical models of formation of spiritual knowledge in the different forms of the world's great religious traditions:

1. Western monotheism: *Divine revelation* from a Creator God into the realm of that God's creation and across a categorically uncrossable ontological gap; or

2. Eastern monistic panpsychism (and radical mysticism generally): *Meditative/subjective illumination,* enlightenment by the stripping away of illusion to see or know the unitive heart or "beyondness" or "nothingness" of ultimate reality.

B. Intrinsically nonobjectifiable information obtained from a personal "realm of the spiritual." This might, for example, be spiritual information from the working of God within the subjectivity of a person. (For an excellent example, see the three-article series "Judaism beyond Words" by the Yale computer scientist David Gelernter published in the May, September, and November 2003 issues of *Commentary* [www.commentarymagazine.com].)

C. Ordinary objective scientific information about a spiritual topic or reality, such as in the study of spiritual transformation in people's lives. (For example, this is the aim of the ongoing Spiritual Transformation Scientific Research Project; see www.metanexus.net/spiritual_transformation/about/index.html.)

D. Extraordinary objective scientific information obtained from a paranormal research project—for example, through the study of the medical efficacy (or lack thereof) of distant, "blinded," intercessory prayer. At present, there is a vigorous and healthy debate over whether any positive (non-null) results have been obtained in studies including the health conditions of people struggling with illness and studied under scientifically "controlled" circumstances. (For example, see www.templeton.org/studyarchive/prayer.asp.) Thus far, no information of this type has been demonstrated incontrovertibly.

E. Sociological-scientific information about the historical and contemporary influence of "God concepts" and changes in God concepts affecting the nature and dynamic power of culture. See, for example, Rodney Stark's 2001 book, *One True God: Historical Consequences of Monotheism* (see www.pup.princeton.edu/titles/7122.html).

F. Information communicated within our universe from alien supreme beings and captured, for example, through radio telescopes. The main organization pursuing this vision is the Search for Extraterrestrial Intelligence. SETI now operates with the help of four million user participants contributing home PC time for signal analysis (see www.setiathome.ssl.berkeley.edu). See also Steven Brams's 1983 book, *Superior Beings: If They Exist, How Would We Know?* and his essay in this volume.

G. Scientific information about the physical dynamics of possible divine action in the world. For example, see the essay by Robert John Russell in this volume and conference series references cited therein. Also, for a recent overview and appraisal, see Nicholas Saunders's 2002 book, *Divine Action and Modern Science* (http://books.cambridge.org/0521801567.htm).

H. Information from a nonsubjectivity-constrained but otherwise epistemologically difficult-to-access "realm of the spiritual," such as from a "hidden dimensionality." The classic example of the concept of a "hidden dimension" is fictionally described as a moral lesson in humility in Edwin Abbot's 1884 classic, *Flatland*. For modern updates in this genre, see books by the polymath Clifford Pickover (www.pickover.com) and his essay in this volume. Also, for a philosophically nuanced treatment by a well-respected philosophical theologian, see John Hick's 1999 book, *The Fifth Dimension: An Exploration of the Spiritual World*.

(Note that some of the items in this list overlap and that [A.] is a kind of supertaxonomy.)

This essay discusses the concept of spiritual information in the context of the developing metascientific discussion surrounding efforts to develop a scientific theory of *emergence with increasing complexity*. This discussion engages the question of the proper scientific framing of different forms or levels of descriptions of Nature. Are the different fields of inquiry in science ultimately reducible to complicated exercises in bottom-level description in particle physics? Or does complexity introduce irreducible novelty—"Is more different?"—as Philip Anderson once asked in a famous paper? (For a particularly on-the-mark discussion, see Robert Laughlin's 1998 Nobel Lecture in physics discussing his work on the fractional quantum Hall effect: "Fractional Quantization," published in *Reviews of Modern Physics* 71, no. 4

[July 1999]: 863–74). Were E. O. Wilson's early advisors correct to encourage him to study genetic biochemistry rather than ants, arguing that anything learned from ants could be and should be more elegantly derivable biochemically "from below"? (Cf. Edward O. Wilson, *Naturalist*, 1994.) Or does the study of ants as wholes and as complex societies offer insights fundamentally unavailable from the bottom-up study of their biochemical parts?

The discussion of emergence provides a helpful perspective as it variously can engage with most of the modes identified in the above list. It also has the benefit of engaging with a central challenge of whether the concept of "spiritual" as a modifier to the word "information" can or cannot be connected with scientific concepts of objectivity. "Spiritual" may or may not imply an irreducible aspect of subjectivity in various contexts. Subjectivity is not to be confused necessarily with dismissive concepts such as unreality or wishful thinking. Subjectivity is part of, and not distinct from, reality. However, epistemologically it may void the possibility of shared, open, and "disinterestedly" testable "public" information. This, of course, is the gold standard of science. This is a hugely interesting question, and the concept of emergence provides a helpful basis for framing it in scientific terms. Possibly it can be seen in an analogous way also to Gödelian incompleteness. Gödel's famous incompleteness theorem provides a clear, logical, precise demonstration for separating truth that can be proved formally from truth that cannot be proved formally, but that still can be truth and that is part of the everyday professional life of mathematicians.

The introduction of this essay began with three odd remarks that can be restated as three questions:

1. How is a Mozart symphony different from an air-pressure curve?
2. What can an apple tree know about God?
3. What does a slug know of Mozart?

To these we can add a fourth:

4. Does Mozart express Divine beauty?

Possibly the strangest insight in all of science and philosophy hinges on elucidating the somewhat bizarre significance of the first three questions taken together and illuminated by one of the biggest lessons in the history of cosmology. This lesson is the "no special location" insight sometimes called the Copernican principle. It is based on the Copernican heliocentric revolution and its expansion more broadly to cosmology (by Giordano Bruno, Johannes Kepler, and others). Its lesson is that our sun is one star among a large number of stars, possibly an infinity of them. The Copernican Principle asserts that the location of the Earth is likely to be cosmologically ordinary.

Edwin Abbot's wonderful fantasy *Flatland* used the geometry of space to make a similar point. He imagined a race of two-dimensional creatures living in a sheet within a three-dimensional world. A similar idea was discussed by Carl Sagan in the book accompanying his TV series, *Cosmos*. Sagan wrote that he thought the most profound idea in science joining it with religion was the idea of stacked worlds-within-worlds. (The final scene in the film *Men in Black* nicely visualizes this idea: Worlds are toys within our world, which is then shown to be part of a game of cosmic marbles played by "superbeings" in an even larger "superworld"!) I think that the best candidate for the most profound idea in this category is even more strange. It requires switching a *hierarchy of emergent ontology* for the different sorts of spatial limit concepts used by Abbot and Sagan. The result of this switch is far more humiliating. This is because the nature of the epistemological blindness suggested is categorically unfathomable. Ideas of this sort were explored at least as early as Olaf Stapleton's 1937 science fiction classic, *Starmaker.*

If we have learned no longer to presume that planet Earth is at the center of the universe, why should it be generally presumed that *Homo sapiens* stands ontologically atop the summit of reality (Mount Epistemology)? Slugs lack aspects of their biology linked to the possibility of perception of aspects of the world that to us are easy to perceive. For example, our world contains things such as physics textbooks and an intelligent culture for understanding them. Our world contains Mozart symphonies and the context of perception and culture for understanding and enjoying them. Slugs can sense vibration. However, they are not capable of perceiving music as music. Mozart symphonies have no potentiality of existing in relation to the domain of knowledge of which a slug is capable. Although slugs and Mozart symphonies inhabit the same universe from our point of view, relative to the "point of view" of a slug, a Mozart symphony may be said to inhabit a different universe. Possibly it is better to say that both are part of the same "multiverse." The key point for reflection is that maybe we are like slugs.

Is our *epistemologocentric* belief that our ontology permits a reliable survey of reality correct? Could we be missing a lot of the full picture simply because what we are limits the domain of what we can perceive, even with the benefit of scientific instruments? Could reality be far richer than what we know? Could it be far richer than what we *can* know? Perhaps we too presumptively assume that, unlike slugs, our biological ontology is at the top of the ontological totem pole. But is this like a pre-Copernican view? Is our position more likely to be ordinary rather than central? There is an old Oxford ditty about the (great academic reformer) Master of Balliol, Benjamin Jowett:

> My name is Ben Jowett
> I'm the Master of this College
> If I don't know it
> It isn't knowledge

So, are we masters of reality, or are we somewhere in the middle, like slugs? A fascinating irony is that perhaps science can pose and substantiate the power of this question—but not answer it.

One conclusion of this essay is to suggest that a scientific appraisal of the nature of reality admitting hierarchically emergent ontology requires that theories of everything cannot aspire to completeness. Completeness requires radically incorporating humility, or "epistemological modesty." This is another way of stressing incompleteness and adds to the deep insights already obtained by Gödel. Without such an admission, wisdom seems to be categorically impossible. If, even at our cognitive best, we may be slugs of a sort, then another conclusion may be that there may be other universes of a categorically different kind from cosmological or quantum multiverse models. These might be called "ontological" or "epistemic" multiverses. (Take your pick if epistemology recapitulates ontology.) Do we live in an emergent multiverse? A final conclusion is that "how little we know; how eager to learn" is a good motto. ("How little we know; how eager to love" strikes a different note that also should not be neglected.) Humility may be a good bridge for traffic in constructive interrelations between the different worlds of science and religion.

The following table shows a hierarchy of ways to describe a Mozart symphony with the context of a slug's perception being roughly at level (ii). Contextual complexity increases as one goes down Table 1.

TABLE 1. A MOZART SYMPHONY: ELEVEN HIERARCHICAL LEVELS OF DESCRIPTION

ONTOLOGICAL DESCRIPTION	DESCRIPTION OF THE LEVEL OF AGENCY
(i) Motions of atoms	Atomic interaction
(ii) Air-pressure curve	Microphone acoustical signal record
(iii) Sounds from instruments	Sets of vibrating musical objects
(iv) Musicians playing instruments	Individual musicians
(v) Musical scores directing musicians to play instruments	Paper symphonic scores
(vi) Conductor orchestrating symphonic music	Conductor acting as an extension of the composer through the score plus applying his own artistic creativity
(vii) A Mozart symphony	Mozart
(viii) Performance of musical beauty	Local culture supporting the musical arts through a historic musical language form celebrating respected past masters of creative genius
(ix) Activity of a culture of arts seeking to express and cultivate experiences of stimulating artistic performance excellence for patrons	World culture supporting local cultures supporting the musical arts
(x) Artistic dimension of history	Historical "process" generating aesthetical cultures
(xi) Human hunger for beauty, meaning, and transcendence from the mundane	Human souls and cultures in spiritual quest?*

*"You have made us for yourself. Therefore our hearts will be restless until we find ourselves in Thee." —Saint Augustine

What is interesting to consider from this table is the ordering of relations in this hierarchy of description with respect to cause. One of the most powerful trends emerging from the success of science is to develop modes of reductive description.

Applied to a Mozart symphony, however, this gives us an air-pressure curve, and it should be obvious that something is muddled about giving priority to such a description. In fact, in terms of cause, it is obvious that the vectors of cause are much more logically persuasive if applied broadly from the bottom of the list toward the top. One cannot describe the reality of Mozart's influence on human history very well if one is constrained to speak of the interactions of atoms! Far better to consider the concept of physical "top-down causation" in Nature (which in the table works from the bottom up). The performance of a Mozart symphony in 2002 is undeniably causally related to the reality of the existence of a person called Wolfgang Amadeus Mozart in Europe from 1756 to 1791. More pertinently, the process of creativity in the mind of Mozart can be said quite reasonably to explain causally why certain molecules in the air move in certain ways during a symphony performance hundreds of years after Mozart's death.

We also can take away the dimension of time in history and just consider a time-slice approach of Mozart playing a piano by himself. Here we can consider top-down causation directly as involving dynamic action and interaction between distinct levels:

    I. The cultural "language" of music present in Mozart's mind
    II. Processes of creativity in Mozart's mind
   III. Action activity in Mozart's brain
   IV. Signaling in Mozart's spinal cord and arm nerves
    V. Control of Mozart's muscles for playing the piano
   VI. Energy transfer to the piano keys, etc.
  VII. Propagation of an air-pressure curve to Mozart's ears
VIII. Activation of neurons and genes to lay down musical memories in Mozart's brain

Here we can see that levels I and II have an interestingly "immaterial" or spirit-like ontology. However, they are the *causally most potent* factors of explanation. To attempt to explain away such factors as "nothing-but" something else (reproductive sex drives, memes, genes . . .) at a lower level involves a necessary dismissing of powerful empirical testimony. It is not clear that any such reductive move should be dignified by the descriptor "scientific."

Such reflections on what might be called the biology of creativity leave us with a hint that immaterial aspects of reality such as "culture" or "minds-emergent-from-brains" are at least as "real" as the material aspects of reality with which science is on more directly familiar terms, such as atoms, vibrating wires, genes, and nerves. More importantly, reality gets more interesting as one goes up the hierarchy into zones that are increasingly more difficult to describe in terms of the "parts" of reality known well to basic sciences, such as physics, chemistry, biochemistry, anatomical physiology, and neurobiology. But remember that if we were slugs, we would be missing everything in Table 1 beyond levels (ii) or (iii). Between chimps and humans, there is very little biological difference. (Note: See Jane Goodall's essay in this volume.) However, a relatively small increase in the scale of complexity in brain structure (perhaps at a level of very roughly a factor of two) seems to have opened up an ontological enrichment on a scale of as many orders of magnitude as one might consider. This is because the Lamarckian transition has been crossed. Realities of language and science and art and religion emerge as radically new aspects of the biology of human beings. So great is this difference that the biology is at least at the level of the emergence of a new phylum. Humans seem to have left slugs and chimps in the ontological and epistemological dust.

But does that mean we are at the top? Should we apply the Copernican Principle of likely ordinariness? Might we live at an ordinary location within the ontological multiverse? Perhaps such questions are worth thinking about. For a concluding reflection, I return to the subject of Mozart. The phenomenon of human genius provides an interesting and potent hint that the Copernican Principle may be applicable to the ontological multiverse question. If ontological richness exists above the human position, then genius may be a window opening to it. The existence of people such as Albert Einstein suggests that small increases in creativity unveil large new domains of discovery.

For theologian Karl Barth, Mozart was the pinnacle. He wrote, "If I ever get to heaven, I would first seek out Mozart, and only then inquire after Augustine, St. Thomas, Luther, Calvin, and Schleiermacher." He continued that in listening to Mozart, "It is as though in a small segment the whole universe bursts into song because evidently the man Mozart has apprehended the cosmos and now, functioning only as a medium, brings it into song!" Barth also wrote, "There is no Mozartean metaphysics. In the realms of nature and spirit, he sought for and found only the opportunities, materials, and tasks for his music. With God, the world, himself, heaven and earth, life—and, above all, death—ever-present before his eyes, in his hearing, and in his heart, he was a profoundly unproblematical and thus a free man: a freedom, so it seems, given to him . . ."(*Wolfgang Amadeus Mozart*; English translation, 1986). One can only speculate as to what horizon of wonder reality holds in its fullness if the free creativity of Mozart is but a hint, possibly of an Infinity beyond.

ℒ♥

CHARLES L. HARPER JR. has been Executive Director and Senior Vice President of the John Templeton Foundation since July 1996. His primary responsibilities are in the areas of strategic planning, program design and development, vision casting, and worldwide talent scouting in areas relevant to the Foundation's activities. Dr. Harper has worked to transform philanthropy by developing innovative entrepreneurial practices in grant making. He has created more than $100 million in new grant-based programs ranging widely from the study of forgiveness and reconciliation and enterprise-based solutions to poverty to projects on foundational questions in physics and cosmology, including topics in chemistry, neuroscience, evolutionary biology, medicine, and the philosophy of science. Originally trained in engineering at Princeton University (B.S.E. 1980), he obtained his D.Phil. in planetary science from the University of Oxford for a thesis on the nature of time in cosmology (1988).

He also holds the Diploma in Theology from Oxford (1988) and a Certificate of Special Studies in Management and Administration from Harvard University (1997). Dr. Harper was a National Research Council fellow at the NASA Johnson Space Center from 1988 to 1991. He also was a research scientist in the Department of Earth and Planetary Sciences at Harvard University. Dr. Harper is co-editor of *Science & Ultimate Reality: Quantum Theory, Cosmology and Complexity* (Cambridge University Press, 2004) and the tentatively entitled *Fitness of the Cosmos for Life: Biochemistry and Fine-Tuning*, forthcoming from Cambridge University Press. His other scientific publications include more than fifty research articles in scientific journals, including *Nature, Science*, and the *Astrophysical Journal*.

Freeman J. Dyson

T HE SEARCH for spiritual information is the grand design that inspires Sir John Templeton's philanthropic activities. He believes that spiritual wisdom is to be found by combining the insights of religion with the tools and methods of science. The John Templeton Foundation spends a major part of its resources supporting research and teaching in the field of Science and Religion, a new academic discipline still in the process of defining itself. Its practitioners may be theologians, philosophers, psychologists, sociologists, medical doctors, biologists, or physicists. They engage in a great variety of studies with diverse methods and purposes. But the central purpose of Sir John in supporting such studies is clear: to rejuvenate the ancient discipline of theology by bringing into it people and ideas from the new disciplines of science. His dream is to see experts in Science and Religion making new discoveries in religion that are as revolutionary as the discoveries that have been made in science during the last century.

One of the central new ideas in the physical sciences is "complementarity," introduced by Niels Bohr in the 1920s as a way to describe the new world of quantum mechanics. Complementarity means the existence of two pictures of a physical process that are both valid but cannot be seen simultaneously. The best-known example of complementarity is the dual nature of light. Light sometimes behaves like a continuous wave and sometimes like a hailstorm of discrete particles. To see the wave nature of light, you do an experiment to observe its diffraction by a grating. To see the particle nature of light, you do an experiment to observe it kicking out electrons from a metal surface. The two experiments are complementary. Light is both waves and particles, but you cannot see a wave and a particle at the same time. The nature of light is richer than any of the pictures that we use to describe it.

When the idea of complementarity is applied to atomic processes governed by quantum mechanics, the idea is mathematically precise and is verified by a wealth of experiments. But Bohr liked to extend the idea to more general contexts where its use has remained controversial. He introduced complementarity into biology, pointing out that a living creature can be studied either as an organic whole or as a collection of chemical molecules, but its behavior as a living organism and the behavior of its constituent molecules cannot be studied in the same experiment. In fact, the attempt to locate precisely all the molecules in a living creature would probably result in its death. He also spoke of the complementarity between justice and mercy in ethics, between thoughts and sentiments in psychology, between form and substance in literature, between frame and content in scientific theories. He spoke in an even more general way of "the mutually exclusive relationship which will always exist between the practical use of any word and attempts at its strict definition."

Following Bohr's broad use of the word, I propose that religion and science are also complementary. The formal frame of traditional theology and the formal frame of traditional science are both too narrow to comprehend the totality of human experience. Both frames exclude essential aspects of our existence. Theology excludes differential equations, and science excludes the idea of the sacred. But the fact that these frames are too narrow does not imply that either can be expanded to include the other. Complementarity implies exclusion. The essence of complementarity is the impossibility of observing both the scientific and the religious aspects of human nature at the same time. When we are aware of the universe through a religious experience, nothing is quantitative; when we are aware of the universe through scientific observation and analysis, nothing is sacred. To astronomers with a religious turn of mind, the heavens may proclaim the glory of God, but the glory will never be captured in their computer models of star clusters and galaxies. There is a danger that the academic discipline of Science and Religion may become a frame that excludes both genuine science and genuine religion. If frame A and frame B are mutually exclusive, then a frame C that tries to include both A and B is likely to end by excluding both. If science and religion are complementary, it is better that they should live apart, with mutual respect but with separate identities and separate bank accounts.

Contemporary discussions of science and religion often have a narrow focus, as if science and religion were the only sources of knowledge and wisdom. In fact, science and religion are members of a far wider array of human faculties, an array that also includes art, architecture, music, drama, law, medicine, history, and literature. Several of these faculties have closer ties than science has with religion. Every great religion has had great art and great literature associated with it from ancient times. The connections between science and religion are, by comparison, recent and superficial. I find it strange that science should be singled out as the partner of religion in Sir John Templeton's vision. If we look for insights into human nature to guide the future of religion, we shall find more such insights in the novels of Dostoevsky than in the journals of cognitive science. Literature is the great storehouse of human experience, linking together different cultures and different centuries, accessible to far more people than the technical language of science.

For many years, ever since the personal computer became ubiquitous, we have heard prophets proclaiming that books will soon be obsolete, that the new generations raised on video images will no longer be interested in reading them. Nevertheless, books survive, and new books are still being written and read. Even if books become obsolete in the future, their content will be transferred to some other medium, and literature will survive in another form. No matter how far we look into the future, humans will need a way to share their stories, and the sharing of stories is the essential basis of literature. Literature enables us to share the passions of Greek and Trojan warriors in the twelfth century before Christ and of Hebrew prophets and kings a few hundred years later. Literature will remain as the way we embalm our thoughts and feelings for transmission to our descendants. Literature survives when the civilizations that gave birth to it collapse and die. All through our history, literature and religion have been closely tied together. It is literature that gives longevity to religion. Religions that have no literature may come and go, but the Jewish Torah and the Christian Gospels and the Muslim Koran endure through the millennia. The more successful of the new religions of recent times also have their sacred books. Latter-day Saints have their *Book of Mormon*, Christian Scientists have their *Science and Health with Key to the Scriptures*, and the Marxists have their holy scriptures, too.

When I look around for a recent piece of research leading to an increase of spiritual information, I can think of no better example than the work of Elaine Pagels in studying and elucidating the ancient scrolls that were discovered at Nag Hammadi in Egypt. Her book *The Gnostic Gospels* is a popular account of her work, explaining the origins of these early noncanonical Christian texts and the new light that they throw on the canonical texts that later became the Christian Bible. Pagels is not a scientist. Her skills and her tools have little to do with science. She is a linguist and a historian. Her skills are intimate knowledge of the Coptic and Greek languages, and her tools are literary and historical analysis. Her work has given us a new picture of the Christian religion as it existed in early times before orthodoxies were rigidly imposed and heresies stamped out. This glimpse of a different Christianity has had great influence in broadening the scope and style of Christian thinking. It helps to free Christianity from the dogmatism of past centuries and resonates well with the new generation of students who call themselves Christian but feel more at home with heresy than with orthodoxy. The notion of complementarity can also be used to reconcile heresy with orthodoxy, to reconcile the view of Jesus seen in the Gnostic Gospel of St. Thomas with the view seen in the orthodox Gospels of the New Testament. The various Gospels give us different views, but they are views of the same Jesus.

If I were asked to recommend a program for the increase of spiritual knowledge all over the world, I would suggest a program of support for scholars like Elaine Pagels, who are learned in the languages and histories of other cultures and other religions, in the hope that they will discover and interpret other documents that were forgotten long ago or condemned as heretical. All religions have a tendency to become rigid and intolerant. Every religion has, buried in its past, heretical views that were suppressed. If we could recover some of the ancient heretical literature of other religions and make it accessible to students in the modern world, as Pagels has recovered and explained the suppressed literature of the Christian religion, we might succeed in broadening the outlook of all religions. With a broadened outlook, our diverse religions might be better able to live together in peace. Believers in each religion might come to see that all religions are complementary, giving us views of the same reality seen from different angles.

One of the finest Christian heretical writers was William Blake, whose poems and prophesies were not suppressed, but were ignored when he published them in the eighteenth and early nineteenth centuries. His orthodox contemporaries considered him insane, and he narrowly escaped being put in prison for treasonable remarks against the British monarchy. Two hundred years later, he is honored as a great poet and as a spokesman for the oppressed. His poem "The Everlasting Gospel" is another heretical Gospel to put beside that of St. Thomas:

> The Vision of Christ that thou dost see
> Is my Vision's greatest enemy:
>
> Thine has a great hook nose like thine,
> Mine has a snub nose like to mine:
>
> Thine is the friend of All Mankind,
> Mine speaks in parables to the blind:
>
> Thine loves the same world that mine hates,
> Thy Heaven doors are my Hell's gates.
>
> Both read the Bible day and night,
> But thou read'st black where I read white.

In another place he wrote:

> How do you know but ev'ry Bird that cuts the airy way
> Is an immense world of delight, clos'd by your senses five?

William Blake, this crazy poet who invited us

> To see a world in a grain of sand
> And a heaven in a wild flower,
> Hold Infinity in the palm of your hand
> And Eternity in an hour . . .

gave us more spiritual information in a few lines than all the theologians and scientists of his time in their learned volumes. If in the future we search for spiritual information, we are more likely to find it among poets than among scientists.

ℒ♥

FREEMAN J. DYSON was born in England and came to the United States in 1947 as a Commonwealth Fellow at Cornell University. He settled in the United States permanently in 1951, became Professor of Physics at the Institute for Advanced Study in Princeton in 1953, and retired as Professor Emeritus in 1994. Professor Dyson began his career as a mathematician, but then turned to the exciting new developments in physics in the 1940s, particularly to the theory of quantized fields. Beyond his professional work in physics, Professor Dyson has a keen awareness of the human side of science and of the human consequences of technology. His books for the general public include *Disturbing the Universe, Weapons and Hope, Infinite in All Directions, Origins of Life,* and *The Sun, the Genome, and the Internet.* In 2000, he was awarded the Templeton Prize for Progress in Religion.

PART TWO

*Perspectives on the History—and Future—
of the Science-Religion Dialog*

In Praise of Contingency 10

Chance Versus Inevitability in the Universe We Know

Owen Gingerich

"We live forward," Kierkegaard wrote, "but to understand we look back."[1]

I WAS REMINDED of Kierkegaard's words when I reflected on a conversation I once had with Paul Freund, Harvard University's expert on constitutional law. One of my sons was contemplating law school, and I remarked to Freund that my son's strength was in history, not in logic, which I felt must be essential for understanding the intricacies of legal reasoning. "On the contrary," Freund replied. "Law is historical, not logical."

Law is not governed by logical necessity, but by chance, or contingency. That is why case studies are so central to legal education. Looking backward is essential to understanding what we experience going forward.

But does this apply to the universe? Is the universe strictly logical, or did it unfold with an element of chance that we must look backward to discover? Einstein put it succinctly: "What I'm really interested in is whether God could have made the world in a different way. . . ."[2]

To those physicists seeking the "theory of everything," discovering the logical framework that would explain it all remains the goal. Their mission is rooted in an ancient faith in the intelligibility of the universe—and the rationality of physicists.

Einstein's thought, stated above, continues: ". . . that is, whether the necessity of logical simplicity leaves any freedom at all."

Let us for the moment consider that the cosmos has a logical simplicity that left God no choice, an idea that has long been branded as heretical by churchmen but appeals to physicists. There would be no contingency. The way our universe was made would be the only way to make a universe. We can examine this hypothesis in conjunction with two principles that achieved wide currency in the twentieth century: the Anthropic Principle and the Copernican principle.

Throughout the twentieth century, astute observers noticed that our universe has remarkable properties that are singularly congenial to the existence of intelligent, self-contemplating life. In 1913, Harvard professor L. J. Henderson published a book entitled *The Fitness of the Environment*,[3] in which he noted that not only were organisms adapted to their habitats, but that the fundamental details of chemistry themselves made life possible—peculiarities of hydrogen and carbon and the extraordinary physical nature of water. The march of science has made his thesis ever more cogent. And, if the universe had to be this way, intelligent life was inevitable.

Later in the last century, as knowledge of astronomy increased, it became clear that other global cosmic properties, such as the precisely balanced rate of expansion of the universe, played a fundamental role in making possible suitable habitats for life. These insights led to framing the Anthropic Principle, the observed fact that the universe favored our existence. In the words of physicist Freeman Dyson, it is a universe that "knew we were coming."[4] Said another way, our universe is a very special place with a built-in congeniality for intelligent, self-conscious life. The pointers all seem to say that there is purpose, direction, and intention in the universe.

But at the same time, another principle—the Copernican principle—became popular. This is the idea that, based on the insight of Copernicus, the earth is *not* the center of the universe, but that we are but an ordinary part of the universe, our home revolving about a mediocre star in the backwaters of our galaxy. Given the vastness of the universe, well understood only in the twentieth century, it seemed almost absurd to think that we could be centrally located, or even in any other way special. Yet the Copernican principle of mediocrity, which essentially denies that our universe is anything but ordinary, seems somehow to be at odds with the Anthropic Principle that we are indeed in a special universe.

One way to resolve the apparent conflict between these two principles would be to declare that all those congeniality pointers were mere accidents of a cosmic roulette: that there are many universes, and naturally we would find ourselves in the very one, which, like the little bear's porridge, was just right. On the face of it, the multiverse proposal offers atheists an answer to why our universe seems specially designed.

But, if God had no choice (as I have briefly considered for purposes of argument), then all the multiple universes would necessarily have the same congeniality factors, and it would make no difference which universe we found ourselves in. What a staggering discovery that would be! Atheists could say that, if God had no choice, there would be no need for a Creator. Theists could still stand in awe of the fact that the one-and-only design paved the way for our existence. There is no doubt that such a design is awesome.

Christian theologians have long insisted that God's creative powers included choices in the way the universe is made. This concept played a significant role historically in the so-called Galileo affair. Although Galileo was a pioneering experimentalist, he also held to the ancient belief, developed by the Greek philosophers, in the rationality of the cosmos, from which he hoped to develop a demonstrative proof of the Copernican system. He believed that the tides were the consequence of the earth's motion, and he proposed to entitle his cosmological book "On the Flux and Reflux of the Sea." Pope Urban VIII objected to the title because it gave too much emphasis to what Galileo believed was a proof of the Copernican system. Urban reminded Galileo that "God, by his infinite wisdom and power, could have created the tides in many other ways, including some beyond the reach of human intellect."[5]

Ultimately, Galileo realized, perhaps with some disappointment, that he could not produce a deductive proof of the Earth's motion. But in reality, he won the debate with Urban concerning the Earth's motion by changing the rules of science. I have called Galileo's *Dialogue on the Two Great World Systems* the "book that won the war." Unlike Copernicus's *Revolutions* or Newton's *Principia*, it did not contain new, heavy-duty science. It contained no proofs for the earth's mobility. Instead, it marshaled a long series of convincing coherencies. Although it lacked "proofs positive," his persuasive book made the seemingly ridiculous idea of the Earth's motion intellectually respectable. In consequence, science today proceeds not by looking for proofs, but by building a highly probable structure, coherent and persuasive.

Yet Urban could well have been right in his theological declaration that God could have created the world in many other ways. Convincing as a "theory of everything" might be, it is hard to imagine how a scientist could ever prove that it was the *only* explanation and that God had no choice. The "theory of everything" would have to link together all of the seemingly unrelated constants of nature. But could it ever show that the linkage system was unique and thus that our universe was inevitable?

And even if the universe were a logical necessity, contingency would nevertheless play a role. Sixty-five million years ago, an asteroid struck the Earth in what is now the present-day village of Chicxulub on the Yucatan Peninsula. The impact left a crater wider than one could see across, and the ocean pouring into that red-hot hole created a cataclysmic explosion. In its aftermath, the dinosaurs, whose family had ruled the earth for 200 million years, perished. Out of this turmoil, tiny mammals emerged, gradually evolving into the world's dominant family, including you and me. It is difficult to imagine that the trajectory of the Chicxulub asteroid was foreordained in the Big Bang.

I have met hard-core physicists who deny that biology is, or ever will be, a science. They demand a demonstrative, mathematical structure, if not tight logical necessity. Contingency is not for them. Stephen J. Gould's argument, so ably articulated in his *Wonderful Life*, that if we replayed the tape of life again the outcome would be far different, was anathema to them. The notion that bad luck (contingency), rather than bad genes (a demonstrative structure), could shape life on Earth was, in their book, enough to prevent palaeontologists from entering the science club.

On the other hand, I know of historians who have argued that the whole concept of contingency, in a Judeo-Christian context, drove the birth of modern science. In 1951, in a philosophical discourse to the British Association for the Advancement of Science, Professor John Baillie declared, "It is to the clear recognition of this element of contingency in nature that science owes its very being." Because God could create the universe in any number of ways, only appeal to observation and experiment could decide which of the alternate schemes might be true. "The reason why ancient science was so little observational and hardly at all experimental was that in holding so fast to the intelligibility of the world it failed to do justice to its contingency."

It has long been a challenging puzzle to understand why modern science arose in the Latin West in the sixteenth and seventeenth centuries and not in China or the Islamic world. It is unlikely that any one concept can explain the tangled complex of ideas and forces that shaped the European scientific renaissance. Contingency undoubtedly played an important role, even in a proposal as cerebral as the heliocentric system. Copernicus's idea was a "theory pleasing to the mind," proposed with no observational verification of the Earth's motion. Yet the whole notion of alternatives, that God could have created the universe in more than one way, drove astronomers to seek new evidence to distinguish the possibilities.

Looking backward is clearly essential to understanding the particulars of the biological world in which we live. History matters! It also illumines the very process by which we have come to understand the world about us. And, ultimately, it may help us to better understand God.

☙

OWEN GINGERICH, PH.D., is Research Professor of Astronomy and of the History of Science at the Harvard-Smithsonian Center for Astrophysics and former Chair of the History of Science Department at Harvard University, Cambridge, Massachusetts. He is a member and former Vice President, American Philosophical Society; former Chairman, US National Committee of the International Astronomical Union; former Councilor, American Astronomical Society; and Member, American Academy of Arts and Sciences, International Academy of the History of Science, and International Society for Science and Religion. Professor Gingerich has published more than five hundred technical or educational articles and reviews and most recently *The Book Nobody Read: Chasing the Revolutions of Nicolaus Copernicus* (Walker & Company, 2004).

NOTES

1 Paraphrased from Peter P. Rohde, ed., *The Diary of Søren Kierkegaard* (London: Peter Owen, 1960), pt. 5, sct. 4, no. 136.

2 Carl Seelig, ed., *Helle Zeit - dunkle Zeit: in memoriam Albert Einstein* (Braunschweig: F. Vieweg, 1986), 72; translated by Ewald Osers in Albrecht Fölsing, *Albert Einstein, A Biography* (New York: Viking, 1997), 736.

3 Lawrence J. Henderson, *The Fitness of the Environment: An Inquiry into the Biological Significance of the Properties of Matter* (New York: Macmillan, 1913). See also http://www.templeton.org/biochem-finetuning/.

4 Freeman J. Dyson, *Disturbing the Universe* (New York: Harper & Row, 1979), 250.

5 Cited by Galileo Galilei in his *Dialogo* and paraphrased from the Thomas Salusbury translation on 1661; see Giorgio de Santillana, trans., *Dialogue on the Two Great World Systems* (Chicago: University of Chicago Press, 1953), 471.

HISTORICAL ERRORS IMPEDING PROGRESS IN SCIENCE AND RELIGION 11

Jeffrey Burton Russell

EVERYBODY makes mistakes about the past. Some mistakes are trivial, but others impede progress in acquiring information—including spiritual information—by reinforcing prejudices and ideological programming. Ideology, which plays some role even in the natural sciences, assumes a huge role in the social sciences. Religious, political, gender, and economic biases have produced and nurtured false ideas about the past.

The word "history," although often used as a synonym for "the past," really means "investigation of the past." History properly works by showing how any situation (religious, political, scientific, or other) is at Point X by virtue of having moved from Point A through Point B through Point N. Any errors we make about events along the line between A and X weaken or invalidate the explanation of X. History is far from an exact science, and mistakes (not to mention misjudgments) easily creep in. But when mistakes encourage vast misunderstandings of the past, they are impediments to gaining knowledge. An ever-present example: ideologies that insist (from either a claimed scientific or a claimed religious point of view) that science and religion are at odds.

For a historical falsehood to be dangerous, it must be common to many people rather than idiosyncratic; it must endure over centuries or at least many decades; it must influence people's ideas about the world in general; it must be demonstrably false according to solid evidence. A dozen examples of many historical errors that fit these criteria follow; of these, we will discuss the first two:

Error one: Christians have traditionally read the Bible "literally" as a scientific and historical document.

Error two: Columbus discovered that the earth is round.

Error three: The medieval "Inquisition" tortured and killed millions of women for witchcraft.

Error four: The Catholic Church martyred Galileo for teaching that the Earth revolves around the Sun.

Error five: Ancient events have no influence on contemporary life.

Error six: Religious ideologies caused more deaths than secular ideologies.

Error seven: Darwin invented evolution.

Error eight: Darwin originated social Darwinism.

Error nine: Medieval popes were believed to be infallible.

Error ten: King George III was a tyrant.

Error eleven: Russia was not a colonial power.

Error twelve: Alger Hiss was innocent.

Some of these falsehoods have been employed innumerable times to promote the notion of a struggle between science and religion, a notion that has seriously impeded the progress of both and distorted the practice of history by making history a mere handmaiden to ideologies.

Error one is an important, common historical mistake, promoted in a number of ideologies, often even in opposing ones. The falsehood that Christians traditionally interpreted the Bible "literally" as a scientific and historical document has led to caricatures. This error entails even more basic misconceptions about how the Bible was written, formed, edited, and translated—even though the evidence for the process is vast and incontrovertible. If one believes that "there's just the Bible, and it's read in one way, and that's that," then the possibilities for further errors are inexhaustible. Many scientists, religious leaders, and even historians seem to labor under such a misapprehension.

I assume that readers of this essay accept that the Bible was formed gradually over many centuries and that its formation was not complete before the fifth, or at least fourth, century CE. The question is how the Bible was read or interpreted. That any reading of the Bible (or of any other document) necessarily entails some sort of interpretation is philosophically and linguistically obvious, even if we were ignorant enough to maintain that God Himself wrote the King James Version. For twenty centuries, Christians have interpreted the Bible in a myriad of ways. One perennial problem lies in the meaning of words. The term "literal interpretation" of the Bible is now ambiguous. Precisely used, the term means accepting every word and letter (Latin: *littera*) of the Bible as being "revealed." In that precise sense, Christians over time have taken the Bible literally, but most have not taken it as a scientific and historical document.

Interpretations of the Bible began in the earliest stages of its formation, because all but the most mentally feeble realized that when Jesus said that he was a door, he did not mean that he was a construction of nails and planks. From the first century onward, thoughtful Christians considered how documents that they believed to be revealed truth could best be understood. In the early centuries, Clement of Alexandria (c. 150–c. 215 CE) and Origen (c. 185–c. 254 CE) propounded models that became the basis for most subsequent interpretations, notably for the immeasurably influential Augustine of Hippo (354–430 CE). Augustine's interpretation of Genesis, *The Literal Meaning of Genesis,* sounds little like anything we would today consider "literalism." The view of Augustine and other influential Christian writers such as John Cassian (c. 360–435 CE) was that the Bible had as many meanings as God wants and that the meanings may be inexhaustible by human intelligence. But, they believed, human intelligence must work with what it has, and when humans try to understand the Bible, people best understand it in four main ways: as an account of events that actually occurred, as an allegory (a kind of speech in which one thing is understood by another) or typology (connecting the Old with the New Testament by types such as salvation through water—the Red Sea, Jonah, baptism), as moral guide, and as predictive of what will happen at the end of time. Ideas about which sort of interpretation best fits which passage have always been innumerable, but Augustine urged that the meaning that is most charitable is always the best.

At the time of the Reformation, Protestant and Catholic scholars both promoted re-emphasis on the text of the Bible itself. Many of these scholars, while continuing to understand the various ways in which the Bible could be interpreted, tended to the view that it should be read historically and scientifically more than typologically and eschatologically; this view eventually gave eighteenth-century skeptics grounds for mocking Biblical theology. In the nineteenth and twentieth centuries, many leading scholars advanced views different from any of the above—for example, that the Bible is best understood in terms of its historical provenance (when and where different biblical authors wrote). Still, the idea that the Bible is supposed to be historically and scientifically accurate persists on both sides of the growling crevasse between fundamentalists and materialists, the former insisting that the Bible is "true," the latter that it is "false."

Error two is another common historical mistake. Serious scholars have known for eighty years that educated medieval people knew that the Earth is spherical. Cosmology was certainly geocentric before Copernicus (1473–1543), but geocentricity and sphericity are two different questions, both scientifically and historically. Educated medieval people assumed that the Earth was the shape of a globe, just as they assumed that the Earth was the immoveable center of the universe. About a hundred medieval writings dealing with the Earth's shape have so far been identified. Only five seem to assert flatness, and two others are ambiguous. From the time of Augustine (354–430), every writer known in Western Europe who mentioned the shape of the earth asserted sphericity.

Yet the "Flat Error" continues, despite the evidence, to be repeated in schools and in popularized books by careless writers depicting Columbus's opponents as bigoted and benighted ecclesiastics. The main facts therefore need restating. First, no medieval person ever thought of the heavens as anything but spherical. As for the earth, the medieval term for "the entire earth" was *orbis terrarum* ("the globe of lands"). Medieval astronomers and geographers refined and improved on the Greek and Roman view of the Earth as a globe, a view completely dominant after the fourth century CE. Numerous medieval treatises *De sphaera*, "About the Sphere," demonstrate their knowledge of the globe. In a typical medieval scheme, the Earth is a globe around which the spheres of the Moon, planets, Sun, and stars rotate. Schematically it can be divided, like any globe or ball, into four quarters. The Eurasian-African landmass was supposedly set in the sea of one of these four quarters, while the other three-quarters were usually supposed to be entirely sea. If the other three quarters do not have lands, then sea runs west all the way from Portugal to Japan.

Medieval scholars came close to estimating the Earth's actual diameter and circumference. One school worked on refining the figure of 250,000 *stades* calculated by Eratosthenes (c. 275–c. 194 BCE), close to the modern figure of about 40,000 kilometers. The other school worked on refining the figure of 180,000 *stades* given by Ptolemy about 150 CE. Eratosthenes' more accurate view dominated; scholars following it assumed that the ocean ran unbroken from the Azores and Canaries to Japan, the distance an impassible barrier to a westward voyage to the Indies. But toward the end of the Middle Ages, some writers revived and preferred Ptolemy's less accurate figures. The differences led to Columbus's misconception that the sea was narrow enough for him to sail westward to Asia.

The arguments of the scholars and courtiers who opposed Columbus in the 1480s and early 1490s had nothing whatsoever to do with the shape of the earth. No one entertained the fantastic fear of sailing off the edge. Rather, Columbus's opponents argued that the ocean was too vast for a ship to sail west to Asia without all perishing of thirst and starvation, a dangerous gamble on which to risk life—and the royal treasury. It was a reasonable argument based on the available evidence, and Columbus had to work hard to overcome it. He accomplished this by fiddling the figures repeatedly in a number of stages until he had radically reduced both the circumference of the globe and the width of the sea, audaciously ending up with a figure for the sea's breadth equal to about 4,450 kilometers, about one-fifth the actual distance of about 22,000 kilometers.

Not many believed such preposterous calculations. But Columbus was in political luck. The Spaniards were eyeing new ways to expand their wealth and power in competition with the Portuguese. So King Ferdinand and Queen Isabella approved the adventure, and in 1492 Columbus set sail across the Atlantic. Then came the unexpected, one of the greatest pieces of luck in all of history: On October 12, 1492, Columbus blundered into the Americas under the mistaken impression that he was arriving in the East Indies. If the Americas had not been in his way, he and his crew would surely have perished, as those who opposed him had predicted.

What these examples of historical error have in common is their simplification of complex questions into simpleminded, easy-to-swallow myths that have contributed to the popular myth of a war between science and religion, a myth that continues to impede progress. Historical investigation and the other social sciences and humanities have often been playing fields for ideologies instead of fulfilling their proper calling as aiming at truth, willing to discard ideas that violate the evidence, adjusting assumptions and beliefs according to the evidence, and above all opening minds up more and more to a variety of ideas. This is no less true today than it has been in the past. Although historians and anthropologists are often vehement in opposing ethnocentrism, they just as vehemently (if sometimes unwittingly) promote *chronocentrism*—the notion that the ideas held *at this moment* by *current* social scientists are necessarily better than older ideas or worse than those to come. New is not always true. And to enhance understanding, spiritual information must be true.

✑

JEFFREY BURTON RUSSELL, PH.D., received his doctorate from Emory University and is a Harvard Junior Fellow, a Guggenheim Fellow, a Fulbright Fellow, a Fellow of the National Endowment for the Humanities, and a Fellow of the Medieval Academy. He is Professor Emeritus in the University of California, Santa Barbara, having taught history and religious studies there as well as at several other universities. Professor Russell has written seventeen books translated into fifteen languages, including *Inventing the Flat Earth: Columbus and Modern Historians* (1991), which shows how nineteenth-century anti-Christians invented and spread the falsehood that educated people in the Middle Ages believed that the Earth was flat, and *A History of Heaven: The Singing Silence* (Princeton University Press, 1997), a study of the history and meaning of heaven in Christian thought from the beginnings of time to the time of Dante. He is most noted for his five-volume history of the concept of the devil, published by Cornell University Press between 1977 and 1988. Professor Russell has also published more than sixty articles, most in theology, and is currently working on a new book on heaven for Oxford University Press.

The Longing
of Johannes Kepler 12

Kitty Ferguson

O NE SUMMER DAY, my daughter and I sat on a boulder jutting into the Black
River as it runs through a gorge near Chester, New Jersey, and pondered the
universe. Fish, squirrels, chipmunks, deer, insects, and birds appeared, disappeared,
and darted in every direction under a canopy of leaves. Farther along the river, two
humans on another rock were locked in an embrace. I remarked, shaking my head,
that when I looked at all this vigorous, teeming, diverse *life* and tried to imagine it
being created by the process of evolution, my first inclination was to exclaim,
"Naah!" But both of us acknowledged that my reaction was born of an inability to
conceive of the enormous time span during which all this had come into existence.
We also both agreed that evolution and survival of the fittest had never posed any
challenge to our faith in God. In fact, evolution seemed to us a glorious example of
God's genius—to have come up with this simple way of ensuring that life would fill
every niche and be exceedingly difficult to wipe out. My daughter, who would be
leaving the following week to begin graduate studies in molecular biology, pointed
out how far better equipped the very small (viruses, bacteria, yeasts) are to survive
than humans are.

"If anything were to challenge my faith," she mused, "it wouldn't be a theory about
how the universe could have started without God, and it wouldn't be evolution—it
would be the differences between people's experience of God." Spiritual experience
too often seemed inconsistent, and it surely wasn't always authentic—for didn't the
9/11 terrorists believe they were acting on God's instructions? For that matter, she
questioned, how do *any* of us trust our private spiritual perceptions, knowing that
drugs alter what seems to us to be "reality" and that our genes may make us prone
to belief or to skepticism, to mysticism or to being bluntly down-to-earth?

Johannes Kepler, the sixteenth- to seventeenth-century discoverer of the orbits of
the planets, was a man of sophisticated and exuberant faith. His education at the
University of Tübingen prepared him to be a Lutheran clergyman, and it was a
severe disappointment when he was assigned, instead, to teach mathematics to small
boys at a provincial school in Graz, Austria. Yet Kepler frequently voiced his conviction that even such apparently inexplicable turns of fate happened at God's direction, and, indeed, the flash of insight that set him on course toward his greatest
discoveries occurred while he was drawing a diagram on the chalkboard for his
class. He also believed that God had incorporated deep principles of harmony and
symmetry in Creation, and, having done so, does not meddle in an arbitrary fashion. Kepler felt obliged to live with this apparent contradiction between a God of
providence and a God of physical laws because he continued to encounter what

seemed to him to be concrete experiential evidence of both. More profoundly mysterious to him was the possibility of experiencing God not only as Creator of the universe and director of human events, but much closer. In Kepler's words, "There is nothing I want to find out and long to know with greater urgency than this: Can I find God, whom I can almost grasp with my own hands in looking at the universe, also in myself?"[1] From a large portion of the human race, the answer is, "Yes, God is to be found in ourselves, by ourselves, and God engages with us, personally." But, given that agreement, we seem to fall so far short of finding the *same* God as to belie our answer.

The conversation with my daughter, and Kepler's query, stick in my mind and cause me to suspect that, within the vast range of discussion about God and human interaction with God, those questions most frequently referred to science (having to do with creation, invention, and design) constitute only a small part of the total spectrum and have been blown out of proportion because they are, frankly, the easiest part to study scientifically. Thousands of generations of human beings attest that spiritual information isn't necessarily something that requires use of a prodigious tool like science to find. It sometimes comes unsought, even unwanted, and to the most unlikely people. It has to do not so much with the universe, out there, as with you and me, here and now. And it *is* extraordinarily difficult to systematize or study.

Personal human experience with God, if genuine, would be a rich source of vital information. Accordingly, much of this experience has been recorded in the writings of our religions. But the "yes" to Kepler's question doesn't come only from times when it didn't seem necessary to subject such information to the rigors of a "scientific method." The claim from many of our contemporaries is that the private channel is still open and that it is sheer foolishness—using pseudo-intellectual excuses—to ignore experiential evidence. With God standing face to face with us, must we forever insist on looking over God's shoulder at galaxies, test tubes, computer readouts? If we do, we are in denial: "Don't bother me about *engaging* with God. First I've got to find evidence in my science that God exists." Not that we don't learn about God through nature. Indeed, Kepler also wrote that in his experience "God wants to be known through the Book of Nature";[2] hence, everything Kepler discovered about the universe *was*, to him, spiritual information. But many trustworthy people insist that there is also much to be learned in day-to-day engagement, a lifetime of both "having it out" with God and enjoying living in the presence of God. Though no evidence survives of Kepler giving a direct answer to his question, it clearly was through such personal experience that he thought he had learned what God wanted. We have to ask what science can do with *this* data.

If we ponder why our most widely respected method of sorting truth from falsehood has seldom attempted to subject this body of experiential evidence to systematic study, several reasons come to mind. One is that science by definition limits itself to *public* evidence—evidence that is repeatable and testable in an open arena. Private experience with God arguably does not meet these criteria. It can't be coaxed or forced out by testing, or manipulated or scrutinized at will, and one person's experience is often not a guide to what the next person's will be.

A second reason is a tendency to conclude that if evidence can't be tested in a public arena with scientific tools, that means it *isn't evidence*. Rewording the old saw about the Master of Balliol ("What he doesn't know isn't knowledge!"), we declare, "What we can't study isn't evidence," or "What we can't study with the scientific method didn't really happen."

A third reason: Arguably the greatest faith in God is a faith in God's ultimate ability to stand up to all questioning, all testing, all profound personal doubts, expressed in our most brutally honest way. It is wonderful to be able to act on that faith. But many thoughtful people ask whether, in so acting, it is anyone's right to insist that *everyone* approach God in this manner. This is an extremely delicate question. To pursue it is to revisit the minds of those in the church at the time of Galileo who debated whether to confuse those of simple faith by publicly espousing what they as intellectuals suspected was correct: the Copernican system. It nevertheless behooves us to anticipate that science might turn out to be a bull in a china shop when taking on this body of evidence that is held as a priceless treasure by many. In none of our religious traditions, even at their most intellectually profound, has God reportedly declared that everyone's personal faith must be purified in intellectual fires. Demand this (as we do if we employ a method as public as science to scrutinize spiritual experience), and for all we might gain we arguably trample roughshod over much of God's most delicate ongoing maneuvering in human lives—a disastrous debacle indeed if science in its present state really *can't* deal adequately with private evidence! Clearly the task calls for a profound level of humility and reverence for our fellow human beings and what they believe. Yet such sensitivity is apt to leave one open to the accusation that objectivity is impossible when one already has too much respect for the "evidence."

When it comes to the first two hurdles—having to do with the nature of the evidence—I remind myself that the scientific method is not a monolith that has been with us forever. In the sixteenth and seventeenth centuries, men like Galileo and Kepler were not heirs to a scientific method. Muddling through to their own discoveries, they worked out what science *would* be for future generations—how it would work, what it must include, and what it shouldn't include. Scientists in the twentieth century again found themselves working out what science would be for later generations as they faced the challenges of postmodernism and found it both wise and productive to question the assumption of scientific objectivity. A far more significant frontier of science than "What hasn't been studied?" is "What can't be studied?" and we have been clever at finding ways of pushing back that second frontier. Kepler, in his struggles to describe the orbit of Mars, feared that it might not even *be* mathematically describable, yet he persevered and found the means to discover that it is elliptical. Astronomers and astrophysicists have devised methods to measure distances and quantities that seemed immeasurable. The fields of chaos and complexity arose out of the conviction that what science had ignored because it resisted systemization must be ignored no longer. Our method of sifting truth and falsehood has surely not encountered the ultimate barrier between what it can and can't handle.

The human intellect has a genius for approaching large, intimidating, "unanswerable" questions by way of more manageable inquiry. The ability to evaluate spiritual information coming from personal experience relies heavily on our first gaining much better understanding of *ourselves*. My daughter's question, "How do I know whether my own and others' experiences of God are authentic?" doesn't necessarily call for us immediately to wade into the evidence, winnowing it right and left, true or false. Rather, we ask, for example, "How *do* we recognize 'reality'? What causes one person to identify an experience as 'real' while another would not?"—questions that research in the neurosciences and genetics is currently approaching. The question, "Are emotions engendered by what we interpret as the presence of God really indicative of anything authentic?" similarly breaks down into "What causes us to feel joy or sorrow, inspiration or depression? What constitutes normal or abnormal psychology? What about us does not change when we take mood-altering drugs or otherwise manipulate our chemistry?"—problems certainly under scientific scrutiny. Information about consciousness and when and how it evolved should help us approach the larger questions: "Of how much of the universe are we conscious? Might some things lie beyond our ability, except under unusual circumstances, to be conscious of them?"

Will the answers challenge faith? If our experience in the areas of evolution and the origin of the universe are a guide, then, yes—they may, for a time. Yet it seems, at least to my daughter and me, that the more we learn in all areas of science, the more that challenge gives way to deeper mystery and deeper reverence. It is "a little knowledge" that is the more dangerous thing.

This discussion cannot avoid returning to the more personal level, for that is where the most fruitful or disastrous decisions about experience of God and God's will are often made. Has science given us any indication about how you and I personally should answer the question whether our own experience, be it "mystical" or occurring more subtly over a long period of time, is authentic—and whether what seems to be "divine guidance" should be trusted? Scientists have not been silent on this issue, nor have all responsible ones suggested we dismiss such "information" as worthless or imaginary.[3] Among psychologists of the most rigorous scientific bent, there are those who caution us not to down-value personal spiritual experience, and who suggest that sensible methods of control and evaluation come from within the faith traditions themselves. It is not a scientific test, but it is an intellectually valid exercise to ask whether a private experience is consistent with the religious tradition in which your or my faith has been honed—with its history, its teachings, its writings. We have learned from those traditions some lessons in how *not* to discern God's will—for instance, that it is risky to rely for endorsement of our private spiritual perception upon only one small part of those writings or choose among passages as though at a smorgasbord, rather than to study them as a whole and read and interpret individual passages in the context of that whole. With regard to that same history, we are not ignorant of the tragic errors some of our forebears have made in the name of religion, and this historical memory helps us judge the validity of our own perceptions about what God's will is. It is a safeguard to remain involved in a community of faith and to test private experience against the experience, perceptions, and wisdom of responsible contemporaries within the community. Even while we are seeking the assistance of an Intelligence far beyond ours, our own intelligence and good sense should not lie sleeping. It is not necessary to act stupider than we really are in order to remain humble before God.

The psalmist's question, "What is man, that you are mindful of him?" is an eloquent expression of awe for God, abject humility for us. But the question, refocused, is even *more* likely to bring us to our knees. We are, arguably, for some unfathomable reason, extremely important to God. You don't have to be a skeptic to ask, "Don't lunatics 'hear God's voice'? Don't terrorists feel they are obeying God's orders?" The body of data having to do with human experience with God *is* confusing, often inconsistent, and almost certainly not all authentic. On the other hand you don't have to be "overly religious" or gullible to admit that the body of data is enormous and extremely widespread and can't all be off the mark. It is not confined to the reports of mystics or to folk tales from the past, nor to once-in-a-lifetime, miraculous experiences, nor to any stratum of society, any ethnic group, any religious group, any IQ level. In a search for truth, although we should recognize the pitfalls of the enterprise, we do not dare ignore this data. Using science to address the imponderable questions has hardly begun until it can help us understand and share in a more meaningful way this vast, rich, unwieldy store of spiritual information that human beings—these unexplainably significant creatures—may already have.

ℒ♥

KITTY FERGUSON traces her interest in science to her childhood and her father's infectious enthusiasm for the subject. Her formal training was in music at the Juilliard School, and for many years she was a successful professional musician, until during a sojourn in Cambridge, England, she became acquainted with several eminent scientists, including Stephen Hawking. On her return to the United States, Kitty retired from music making and began to write and lecture about science. Her six books have been translated into many languages and include the best-selling biography *Stephen Hawking: Quest for a Theory of Everything; The Fire in the Equations: Science, Religion, and the Search for God*; and, most recently, *Tycho and Kepler: The Unlikely Partnership That Changed Our Understanding of the Heavens*. Kitty has been a part of workshops, panels, and lecture series in the United States and Europe; written for *Astronomy Magazine* and *Time Magazine's Time for Kids;* contributed a chapter to Russell Stannard's *God for the Twenty-First Century*; and served as primary consultant for Stephen Hawking's *The Universe in a Nutshell*. She serves on the Board of Advisors for the John Templeton Foundation, and she and her husband Yale are members of the Episcopal Guild of Scholars. The Fergusons are parishioners at St. Peter's Episcopal Church in Morristown, NJ, where Kitty heads up the Companionship with the Kothapallimitta Pastorate, an "untouchable" pastorate in the Church of South India.

Notes

1 Kepler to an anonymous nobleman, October 23, 1613, *Johannes Kepler: Gesammelte Werke,* 17, no. 669:20–22; translation in Carola Baumgardt, *Johannes Kepler: Life and Letters,* 114–15 (New York: Philosophical Library, 1951).

2 Kepler to Michael Mästlin, October 1595, *Johannes Kepler: Gesammelte Werke,* 13:40.

3 See James W. Jones, *The Mirror of God: Christian Faith as Spiritual Practice* (New York: Palgrave, 2003).

Dallas Willard

K NOWLEDGE GROWS and information increases when we test ideas and beliefs against the realities they presume. This is true in all areas of life, including the personal and the spiritual.

When Galileo dropped weights from the tower of Pisa and performed other experiments with moving bodies, he tested ideas that had been accepted for millennia. He pitted them against the realities they dealt with—actual bodies in motion—and found them to be false. But he also discovered what was true of them and laid a foundation for a culture of testing and "research" that has continued to develop up to the present. Galileo provided an accurate, general model of purposeful increase of knowledge and information.

The burden of human existence is the need to find an adequate basis for action in knowledge. The ancient insight that people perish for lack of knowledge is a profound truth that can be gleaned from personal reflection, as well as from simple people-watching. It is not quite as obvious as "people perish for lack of oxygen." The perishing involved is not as immediately striking. But it is often a more painful perishing at a far deeper level of human existence.

Reliable information is so vital to us because, in a sense peculiar to humans, we must *act*. We have no choice but to *choose*. What our individual and collective future holds depends largely on what we do. We are relentlessly thrown into a future of some sort, and we are always in some measure responsible for what that future will be—for the circumstances we will live in and the kinds of persons we will become. For us, even "doing nothing" amounts to doing *something*. And whether we act or "do nothing," we desperately need to know what we are doing.

Knowledge is the capacity to represent respective subject matters as they are, on an appropriate basis of thought and experience. That is an accurate portrayal of what we have in mind when we regard someone as having or not having knowledge in specific contexts of daily life—of knowing the English or Greek alphabet, for example, or of being qualified to operate on brains or use sewing machines. Knowledge grows through engagement with its subject matter and, as it grows, puts us in an increasingly better position to deal with our lives.

What "an appropriate basis" amounts to in the particular case will always depend on the nature of the subject matter of the knowledge in question. There is, from within our human limitations, no perfectly general formula for "appropriate basis" or "conclusive evidence." Much of the skeptical results of "modern" thought should be attributed to outstanding thinkers insisting on one or another supposed completely general formula for what is to be appropriate or conclusive evidence.

But regardless of our doubts and confusions, we nonetheless determine perfectly well in specific contexts when people do or do not know a certain subject matter—how to pronounce the Greek alphabet, how to perform brain surgery, or how to operate a sewing machine.

Now "science" in the modern sense (classical and medieval "science" is quite another matter) is the attempt, by thought, observation, and experimentation, to theoretically organize the events and entities of the sense-perceptible or "natural" world under ever-more comprehensive generalizations or laws. That aim would permit, but does not require, that *all* such events and entities come under one set of laws or one science (e.g., the dream of the unification of all natural forces—the theory of everything—in physics). And it also does not require that every element of the observable world be itself observable in narrowly defined *sense* perceptibility.

Thus, to witness wedding vows or an eclipse, you must have sense perceptions of some kind, but not of every element of the event observed. And if *all* you had were sensations, you would never see such common things. Also, the "unobservables" of subparticle physics are a part of the observable world, although unobservable themselves. Even from within science we have learned that the observable world cannot be understood in terms of what is observable.

It is important to realize that science, given our current understanding of it, makes—and can support—no claim about all that exists. It also does not *itself* claim to constitute the whole of knowledge, although various philosophers make that claim about it. For its purposes, there is no need—or, indeed, possibility—of making claims about whether something exists in some manner distinct from the natural world unless such a conclusion were forced on it by examination of that world.

Further, science has no way of answering the question of why, in general, the laws of the natural world that are held to be true actually do hold true, or of why whatever "initial conditions" that obtained (at the Big Bang or whatever constituted the origin of the universe) did obtain. It simply takes the observable world as a given and seeks to bring its events and entities under natural law as far as possible. If we ever get to a completely "unified theory," then it, and what it describes, will stand as a brute fact or arrangement with no "scientific" explanation at all. The fate of completely successful science is to eventuate in the mystical, the ineffable; and the practice of science is itself a spiritual or personal activity, impossible to derive from the laws of nature that it discovers.

The inescapable limits of scientific explanation are galling, however, for they leave such interesting and important questions untouched. That often provokes brilliant and ambitious minds to speculate beyond all legitimately scientific research, and even to call such speculations "scientific." Of course, anyone is free to speculate, and speculation rightly handled is one source of both information and knowledge. But to call one's speculations "scientific" should mean something more than that they are carried out by certifiable scientists or by people talking about certifiable scientists. As history shows, certifiable scientists are quite capable of unscientific or even nonsensical views. Among them are views about *all* reality or *all* knowledge.

By contrast, religion as a human practice involves two essential elements: (1) the belief in "another" realm than the natural world available to everyone through normal sense perception, and (2) the belief that that realm has a claim on us and that we can make claims on it through appropriate personal responses (ritualistic or otherwise). Thus, none of the great historical religions is without forms of offering and prayer and ways of relating our actions and daily life to that "other realm." That realm, whether beyond or within the realm of nature—or both—is usually thought of as a *spiritual* realm.

William James opens Lecture III of his *Varieties of Religious Experience* with the statement:

> Were one asked to characterize the life of [personal] religion in the broadest and most general terms possible, one might say that it consists of the belief that there is an unseen order, and that our supreme good lies in harmoniously adjusting ourselves thereto. This belief and this adjustment are the religious attitude in the soul.

Religions, in contrast to the sciences, do aim at descriptions and explanations of "the totality" of existence, and that always includes but transcends the physical world. Those explanations and descriptions are not, typically, of the same type as the explanations in the sciences. Usually they take the form of stories.

Stories, unlike scientific theories, are equipped, in ways peculiar to them, to deal with unique and total events and entities—with self-contained wholes. They characteristically convey a beginning, a "once upon a time," and an end, a "happily every after." These are "totalizing devices." But that does not detract from their intent to be an account of fact and reality, which is by no means the absolute prerogative of scientific theorizing. For there is no reason in the general nature of *fact* or *knowledge* that stories of the religious type should not provide information to guide life and even constitute knowledge as above described.

There is a *fact*, a reality, in any case where some property actually belongs to something, giving it an actual character. And there is no reason whatsoever that the properties central to the natural sciences must be all of the properties there are.

Of course, the stories told by the various religions, or even within one religion or by various individuals, cannot all be true in any straightforward sense because they conflict. Scientists and "scientific" theories also frequently contradict each other. Nevertheless, the stories, like scientific theories, are intended to be true. Conflict of scientific theories does not cause us to wash our hands of them, but to refine them. And the same attitude should be taken toward the reports and stories of religion.

Another feature of the stories or sub-stories that make up a religious or spiritual outlook is that we can "slip into" them, identify with them, and receive guidance from them in approaching life choices. We can test the stories by thoughtful examination of them and by living them out in appropriate ways. In this way, it is possible to show that they are inadequate or inaccurate, or to verify them, or to gain further information by means of them.

Just as Galileo demonstrated that you cannot understand bodies in motion by abstract thought, so we have to accept the fact that spiritual reality, in the activities of the individual or in the cosmos, must be approached in terms suitable to its nature. Subject matter dictates method, not the reverse. To insist on examining a subject matter, whether spiritual or natural, by methods that don't even deal with it can at best yield a vacuous self-satisfaction.

But while the spiritual and scientific approaches to reality differ profoundly, they are nonetheless overlapping enterprises. They both have wide-ranging implications for life and practice, and they can and do make conflicting claims about the same events or realities. In some cases, it may be possible to reasonably adjudicate such conflicts in favor of religion, or of science, or of neither—they might both be wrong.

But it is no use to say that they deal with different things and therefore cannot, when properly understood, come into conflict. That was the route taken by Stephen J. Gould in one of his last books, *Rocks of Ages*. In this regard, he followed a long line of thinkers over the last three hundred years. He assigned to science the realm of "fact" and to religion the realm of "meaning."

The thoughtful advocate of spirituality will not think Gould is overly generous to religion with this allocation and will see that what Gould calls "religion" is nothing that any sincere practitioner of it could accept. "Meaning," understood as exalted sentiment and purpose, cannot hang in a vacuum. It is a peculiar folly of "scientifically minded" intellectuals and academics such as Gould to think that meaning and value, including what is offered by religion, is only a projection of human will, usually involving a social and historical process of some sort. Ethical theory since the nineteenth century is mainly an attempt to find life-governing norms that have no basis in reality. It is an attempt that has now manifestly failed, as is to be seen in the writings of the most well-known ethical theorists of our day.

Conflicts of opinion between spiritual and scientific points of view are not bad, although they are often handled badly. Appropriate openness and humility are often remarkably absent between people supposed to be learned. But it is a natural and good thing that any far-reaching view of things, scientific or religious, should come into conflict with other views. This is because all such views serve as a basis of practice and policies. If they did not, they would be irrelevant to life and to the pressing need to base collective and individual human action on knowledge. And since the way of testing is the only path toward the growth of knowledge and information, the tests that rival accounts pose to one another can be accepted as welcome occasions of increased understanding of human life and the realities that support it.

What is required of us all is an open and honest approach to all views concerning human life and well-being. There is a truth to be known about human life and its spiritual nature and context. The way forward is to learn from the masters of the spiritual side of life and to test what they offer us by thoughtfully putting it into practice. The approach of Galileo is the right one and extends far beyond his interest in the motions of bodies.

The names on the list of spiritual masters are well-known. But to take them seriously as providers of information and knowledge and to put them to the test is extremely rare. This remains true even for those who profess confidence in them or when they are presented in a popular form, such as in Stephen Covey's very fine book, *The Seven Habits of Highly Effective People*. Few who buy that book or others like it actually do what it says. We sink in spiritual darkness, not because there is no light, but because we, for whatever reason, refuse to seek out the light, put it to the test of daily life, and share it.

ℒ♥

DALLAS WILLARD, PH.D., received his doctorate in Philosophy and the History of Science from the University of Wisconsin in 1964, where he taught before moving to the University of Southern California, Los Angeles. There he is now Professor of Philosophy, where his fields of concentration are Ethical Theory, Metaphysics, and Contemporary European Philosophy. Among Professor Willard's books are *Logic and the Objectivity of Knowledge* (1984) and *The Divine Conspiracy* (1998), and forthcoming philosophical essay "The Disappearance of Moral Knowledge".

Eminent Scientists and Religious Belief 14

Nicolaas A. Rupke

How widespread is the influence of religion among today's scientists? And what forms does this influence take? Is conducting opinion polls of scientists an effective way to find out, by asking them directly: "All those in favor of a personal God, please raise your hand"?

The results of such vote counting would certainly be arresting, especially in our Western, democratic culture. Or so the Bryn Mawr College psychologist James H. Leuba may have thought when in 1914 he carried out a landmark statistical survey of the belief in God and immortality among American scientists. Leuba found that of one thousand randomly selected scientists, 58 percent expressed doubt or disbelief in the existence of a God. When he confined the sample to a smaller number of the most eminent scientists, the figure of doubters was higher yet, nearly 70 percent. In 1933, Leuba repeated his survey and discovered that the number of disbelievers had increased to 67 percent and 85 percent, respectively (Leuba 1916; Beit-Hallahmi and Argyle 1997, p. 180ff).

There have been many similar statistical studies, among which is a recent repeat of Leuba's survey. In 1996 and 1998, Edward J. Larson, a historian from the University of Georgia, and Larry Witham, a *Washington Times* journalist, reported that little change from 1914 had occurred among American scientists in general, with approximately 40 percent believers. Among the top scientists, however, the percentage of believers had dropped dramatically, from 30 percent to a mere 7 percent. The lowest rate of belief existed among biologists, the highest among mathematicians (Larson and Witham 1998). A current study of religiosity among Nobel laureates by the Haifa psychologist Benjamin Beit-Hallahmi underscores the "eminence effect," showing that religiosity is negatively correlated with renown. Beit-Hallahmi concludes that scientific excellence is tied to distance from religion and that science and religion appear to be incompatible at both the philosophical and psychological levels (unpublished).

These findings have shocked many Christians and reinforced the traditional reluctance of scientists to be open about their religious beliefs and practices, relegating them to a hidden sphere of life. Accordingly, scant information is to be found in the standard biographies or biographical dictionaries for answers to our opening questions. An information gap has developed at the interface of science and religion. Over the past century or so, many hundreds of biographical studies of eminent scientists have been written. Frequently, close relatives, friends, or colleagues were directly and deeply involved in the production of these biographies, and details about religious beliefs and practices, along with other "bits of scandal," have been left out. This multitude of books and articles has, to a large extent, served as an instrument to perpetuate the Leuba-esque view that top-notch science is inimical to religious faith.

In recent years, historians of science have begun drawing a different picture of the relationship between science and religion—less antagonistic, more varied, and altogether richer (see, for example, Lindberg and Numbers 1986; 2003). Modern science, it would appear, has to a significant extent been inspired by the belief that the study of nature reveals divine truth and that the historical revelation of divine truth will be redemptive for humankind. This historiographical revisionism has made use of new approaches, such as the whole-life biography of individual scientists. No longer is a scientific life written as merely a kind of extensively narrated curriculum vitae confined to a scientific career, but as a tapestry of many interwoven strands, combining scientific work with upbringing, family life, sex life, political leanings, religious beliefs and practices, private failures, and public successes. A particularly fine example of the new genre of "telling lives in science" has been Michael Shortland's work on the great Scotsman Hugh Miller (1802–1856), showing the dynamics of real-life interactions between Miller's self-taught expertise in geology, his working-class beginnings as a stonemason, his fascination with divine design in the fossil record, his involvement in founding the Free Church of Scotland, his presumed homosexual inclinations, and his tragic end by suicide (Shortland and Yeo 1996; Shortland 1996; the full biography is still in preparation).

The whole-life biographical approach informs a current project at the University of Göttingen on the religious beliefs and practices of scientists from the twentieth century. The lives of some forty eminent astronomers, physicists, chemists, biologists, and mathematicians are being explored, with special attention paid to religious aspects. This may prove an effective way—although by no means an exclusive one—to develop insights into the variety of interactions between science and religion.

There are, of course, plenty of truly secular scientists who believe that their science, narrowly conceived, is the be-all and end-all. The Dutch marine geologist and one of the founders of modern sedimentology Philip Henry Kuenen (1902–1972), for instance, admitted to complete agnosticism, although modestly referred to this as his "color blindness" (personal communication). In such cases, a meaningful connection with religion may still exist in the context of the scientist's family. The family life of scientists now, too, is being looked at in greater detail than was traditionally done. In the case of Max Born (1882–1970), who had little time for religion, there was nevertheless much of it in his life through his wife, who was an active and devout Quaker. When after World War II they decided to return from Britain to Germany, in spite of having been forced out by the Nazis in 1933, the family settled back not in Göttingen, where Born had made his revolutionary contributions to quantum mechanics, but in nearby Bad Pyrmont, the North German center for of the Society of Friends. From here, Born continued to work on the moral and political implications of nuclear physics for war and peace. In 1957, he joined Otto Hahn (1879–1968) and other leading physicists in putting forward the Göttingen Manifesto, in which he declared his opposition to the acquisition of nuclear weapons by

Germany (Born 2002, pp. 60-64). It is likely that Born's pacifist activities were significantly shaped by the Judaism of his background, as well as the Quakerism of his home life.

The essential role of family life is shown brilliantly by James Moore, author with Adrian Desmond of the now classic biography of Charles Darwin, in describing the life of English geneticist Ronald Aylmer Fisher (1890–1962). Fisher was the Galton Professor at University College in London and later professor of genetics at Cambridge—as well as a lifelong eugenicist. His expertise in statistical methods proved instrumental in the formulation of population genetics and the establishment of neo-Darwinism. Moore shows that what underwrote Fisher's work was his "Darwinian Christianity," in which struggle, toil, and hardship played a redemptive role. His faith was intensely family-bound and shaped by an Anglican family background, as well as the nonconformist family context into which he married. "What unified Fisher's interests, what made a mathematically-based eugenic Darwinian Christianity not just possible but necessary for him, was the experience of family life, with its myriad practical, emotional and intellectual challenges" (in preparation).

A further example from the Göttingen project concerns Charles Hard Townes, who in 1964 received the Nobel Prize in physics for work that led to the development of the laser (Oosthoek, in preparation). Townes was born in Greenville, South Carolina, in 1915, in the Bible Belt, where he was brought up a Baptist. His life's story shows an unbroken strand of Protestant religiosity, although not of a fundamentalist or denominationalist kind. He has been a member of not only the Baptist Church, but, in turn, the Episcopalian Church, the Methodist Church, the Presbyterian Church, and the Congregationalist Church. His marriage in 1941 brought a family life that was marked by traditional rituals of Bible reading and prayer. With great effect, he combined work for industry (Bell Telephone Laboratories) with academic life (Columbia University, MIT, University of California, Berkeley) and government advisory work (Institute for Defense Analysis, President's Science Advisory Committee, etc.). Townes believes that faith is a driving force of all science and that the scientist is an instrument of God that brings new natural discoveries to the world. He sees a convergence of science and religion and is a strong supporter of the recent return in science of the concept that intelligent design pervades the universe.

Among the various meaningful connections between science and religion is that which occurs when a scientist who does not believe in a personal God nevertheless grew up in a religious environment and continues to be guided by the values of this background. A prominent example of this is another Bible Belt scientist, the renowned Harvard biologist and world expert on ants Edward O. Wilson, born in Mobile, Alabama, in 1929, admired and despised for his powerfully argued sociobiology. Among his early critics were Wilson's Marxist Harvard colleagues Stephen J. Gould and Richard C. Lewontin. Mark Stoll points out that Wilson's target was not Marxism, but religion—the conservative Protestantism of his youth. Brought up as a Southern Baptist, and baptized by immersion at the age of fourteen, he read the Bible avidly, at least twice from cover to cover. At university, evolutionary biology replaced his Christianity, but his concern with religion remained when he created a secular religion of biology. Although intended as a counter-religion to conservative Christianity, it exhibits the influence of Wilson's "inner Baptist." As Stoll concludes: "The culture of Southern Baptism has shaped, structured and informed his scientific quest" (in preparation).

This brings us to yet another, major connection of religion with science: the scientist as a counter-religious figure, a secular priest establishing a secular religion. The great example was Darwin's German "bulldog," Ernst Haeckel (1834–1919), whose enormously popular *The Riddle of the Universe at the Close of the Nineteenth Century* (1900; German original 1899) formed the inspiration for the Monist League, intended as a church alternative. Thus scientists appropriated ecclesiastical functions and structures. Or, less antagonistically, they were cast in cryptoreligious roles by a public in need of figures on whom to pin its hopes of redemption. From the 1951–1952 Gifford Lectures by Michael Polanyi (1958) to those by Mary Midgley in 1990 (1992; see also 1985), these and similar views have been poignantly argued.

Historians of science are stepping behind the screen of public utterances and Leuba-like vote counting to discover that there existed and exists in many eminent scientific lives a formative interplay of science and religion.

ℒ❦

NICOLAAS A. RUPKE, PH.D., is Professor of the History of Science at the University of Göttingen, Germany. He was born in Rotterdam, the Netherlands, but moved to the United States to continue his geological studies at Princeton University, where he obtained his doctorate in 1972. Then followed a twenty-year series of research fellowships at various institutions. While at the University of Oxford, Professor Rupke found the intellectual stimulation and institutional support to change his focus of interest from geology to the history of science. Among his books are a biography of Oxford geologist William Buckland, *The Great Chain of History* (1983); a biography of London biologist *Richard Owen* (1994); and the edited volume *Vivisection in Historical Perspective* (1987). His most recent publications are two edited volumes, *Medical Geography in Historical Perspective* (2000) and *Göttingen and the Development of the Natural Sciences* (2002).

REFERENCES

Beit-Hallahmi, Benjamin. (unpublished). "Religious affiliation, religiosity, and scientific eminence: a survey of Nobel Prize winners 1901–2001."

Beit-Hallahmi, Benjamin, and Michael Argyle. (1997). *The Psychology of Religious Behaviour, Belief, and Experience.* London: Routledge.

Born, Gustav V. R. (2002). *The Born Family in Göttingen and Beyond.* Göttingen: Institut für Wissenschaftsgeschichte.

Larson, Edward J., and Larry Witham. (1998). "Leading scientists still reject God," *Nature,* vol. 394, p. 313.

Leuba, James H. (1916). *The Belief in God and Immortality: A Psychological, Anthropological and Statistical Study*. Boston: Sherman, French & Co.

Lindberg, David C., and Ronald L. Numbers. (1986). *God and Nature: Historical Essays on the Encounter Between Christianity and Science*. Berkeley: University of California Press.

———. (2003). *When Science & Christianity Meet*. Chicago: University of Chicago Press.

Midgley, Mary. (1985). *Evolution as a Religion: Strange Hopes and Stranger Fears*. London and New York: Methuen.

———. (1992). *Science as Salvation: A Modern Myth and Its Meaning*. London and New York: Routledge.

Moore, James. (in preparation). "R. A. Fisher: A faith Fit for Eugenics."

Oosthoek, Jan. (in preparation). "Charles Townes: Converging Science and Religion."

Polanyi, Michael. (1958). *Personal Knowledge: Towards a Post-Critical Philosophy*. Chicago: University of Chicago Press.

Shortland, Michael (ed.). (1996). *Hugh Miller and the Controversies of Victorian Science*. Oxford: Clarendon Press.

Shortland, Michael, and Richard Yeo. (1996). *Telling Lives in Science: Essays on Scientific Biography*. Cambridge: Cambridge University Press.

Stoll, Mark. (2002) "Edward O. Wilson: The Science of Religion, and the Biologist's 'inner Baptist,'" "Science and Religion: The Religious Beliefs and Practices of Scientists: 20th Century" conference, Göttingen, Germany.

Biological Evolution, Quantum Mechanics, and Non-Interventionist Divine Action

15

New Research Promises Growth in Spiritual Knowledge

Robert J. Russell

S IR JOHN TEMPLETON's core vision, as articulated in a variety of essays and pre-sentations, is "growth in 'spiritual information'" or "growth in knowledge about 'ultimate reality.'" The underlying assumption is that the term "ultimate reality" stands for what theologians call "God" and that science can be a means of discovering new knowledge about God. Using the well-known "two books" metaphor, we could say that science reads "the Book of Nature," and the discoveries of science complement, deepen, and challenge what we learn about God through "the Book of Scripture."

I am reminded of the way the distinguished theologian Paul Tillich understood the terms "ultimate concern" and "ground of being" as symbols for God.[1] Sir John Templeton's vision is also consistent with panentheism, a theological concept that is frequently found in scholarly literature in the field of Science and Religion. Panen-theists[2]—and many nonpanentheists, too[3]—stress both the transcendence of God as Creator *ex nihilo* of the universe and the immanence of God as continuous Cre-ator acting within the processes of nature. As transcendent Creator, God brings about a universe that is orderly and intelligible, whose processes can be discovered through scientific methods and that are represented by the mathematical laws of nature. As immanent Creator, God's action within nature is hidden from science, and science, in turn, has no need to refer to a Creator. Thus, what science describes within the restricted framework of natural processes and methodological natural-ism, theology explains within the wider framework of religion and spirituality as "divine action" (DA).

The "holy grail" of much of the field of Science and Religion over the past decade has been to elaborate an understanding of DA, which, although based on religious sources (e.g., Scripture, religious experience), would be rendered more intelligible and persuasive if brought into close interaction with science. I have termed the spe-cific goal as "non-interventionist, objective, special divine action" (NIDA).[4] It is *spe-cial* DA because it refers to particular events that bear unusual significance. It is *objective special* DA because we can attribute the significance of the events to the events themselves and not just to our subjective interpretation of them, although, of course, there is always an element of subjectivity involved in the process of attri-bution. But the key is that it is *non-interventionist*: God, acting through regular nat-ural processes, brings about these special events without violating or suspending these processes. This is crucial theologically because the routine processes of nature are typically understood to be the result of God's general action as Creator *ex nihilo*. Also, God's special actions should not contravene, but instead should depend on (even while they transcend) God's general action. This is also crucial theologically because it would allow us to treat science as friend and partner for theology, rather than as something to be rejected as atheistic and either replaced with pseudoscience, as fundamentalism argues, or ignored theologically, as neoorthodoxy has maintained. Thus, NIDA would deliver the best of both theological worlds: the insistence on the objective character of DA by conservatives and the insistence on the non-interventionist character of DA by liberals across the denominational spectrum.[5] And if contemporary science could provide the template for NIDA, then it would convincingly demonstrate the need for theology to take science seriously— which would be immanently satisfying because it was the science of classical physics, among other factors, that drove conservatives and liberals into opposing camps over precisely the issue of DA.

Molecular and evolutionary biology, however, have been viewed as providing convincing evidence against DA. The irreducible role of genetic variation in generating biological complexity in partnership with natural selection has suggested to many "critics" (to put it mildly) of religion that evolution is proof of atheism.[6] Genetic variation—mutation and crossing-over during sexual reproduction—has been interpreted as "blind chance." When combined with random environmental changes, the "blind" characteristics that lead to the adaptation of species seem to render absurd the claim that God acts in evolutionary biology, leaving us with a pale, deistic God who acts only at the beginning of time—if, indeed, there was a beginning. But deism is certainly not about the God of Jews, Christians, and Muslims.

Scholars from a diversity of theological perspectives in the field of Science and Religion have responded to this challenge, drawing on and extending positions worked out in the nineteenth and early twentieth centuries.[7] The gist of their response is that *evolution is in fact how God creates*, since God creates through both chance and law. Thus, God as transcendent created the universe intentionally with both chance and law, and chance allows God to act as the immanent Creator within and through natural processes.[8]

But can we make "theological progress" here and take this approach one step further? Does God act in special ways that make a difference in evolution without intervening in natural processes? For this we need to be able to claim that evolution is genuinely open to NIDA—and that evolution provides a basis for such action.

Scholars in Science and Religion have explored a number of theories within physics and biology in search of a science-based NIDA project.[9] In my opinion, quantum mechanics (QM) is an extremely promising place to start: I will call it the "QM/NIDA research program." Now, QM is subject to a variety of competing philosophical interpretations.[10] In the one most generally espoused—the Copenhagen interpretation—nature is seen as ontologically indeterministic: Quantum chance is not a product of underlying causal processes of which we are unaware; instead, nature provides the necessary, sufficient conditions for specific events to occur. Normally, quantum processes evolve deterministically in time, governed by the Schrödinger equation.[11]

But the Schrödinger equation does not apply to particular quantum events, often called "measurements" for historical reasons, in which there is an irreversible interaction between the microscopic processes involving fundamental particles, such as electrons, protons, and photons, and a higher level of complexity in nature. This higher level can either be what I call the "mesoscopic" level of complexity, such as a DNA molecule or a dust mote, or the ordinary, macroscopic world. When such quantum events occur, the outcome is fundamentally indeterministic: According to the Copenhagen interpretation of QM, nature simply does not fully determine the outcome of such events. Thus, working within the Copenhagen interpretation, we can make the theological claim that it is God's NIDA, together with nature at the quantum level, that brings these events about. In sum, God acts through the open character of quantum events without intervening in them—and, to add to the picture, God created the universe in such way to render this possible!

Now the punch line is that genetic mutations involve QM: At a minimum, a mutation requires the making or breaking of a hydrogen bond, and that process is subject to QM. But this means that God acts at precisely the point in the evolutionary scenario where atheists say God cannot act—genetic variation! Thus, God's actions drive the evolution of life.[12] Moreover, as Sir John's approach of "growth in spiritual information" suggests, it is science, as it studies this whole process from the level of quantum events to the history of life on earth, that unlocks knowledge about the action of God as continuous Creator. Of course, belief in God is not based on science, but is brought to our interpretation of science. Still, it is science—within the framework of theology—that provides us with increasing knowledge about God's intentions and purposes as the ultimate reality that lies behind and acts within the world of nature. This surely is evidence of "progress in theology"!

But there is another, as yet unexplored, challenge to the progress we have made so far. As emphasized above, other, competing interpretations of QM do not involve ontological indeterminism. In Bohm's nonlocal hidden-variable interpretation, for example, one can narrate QM in terms of ontological *determinism*: Particles have well-defined positions and momenta, just as in classical mechanics, although unlike the classical view their movement is governed by a de Broglie–like "pilot wave" reflecting the presence of both the classical potential V (r, t) and the new "quantum potential" Q (r, t). There is no "measurement problem" in Bohm's approach, as measurements merely reveal the otherwise hidden and deterministic variables.[13] Similarly, in "many worlds" interpretations, determinism obtains, but at the cost of the universe splitting at each measurement. In quantum logic, classical, Boolean logic is replaced with nonstandard logic.

One of the key challenges, then, to the value of the QM/NIDA research program is whether it will offer promising new results if other, non-Copenhagen interpretations of QM are explored. If not, then the promise of the QM/NIDA program would be diminished. If it is highly interpretation-specific and limited to the Copenhagen approach, its power to illuminate and make intelligible DA would be undercut. In addition, if convincing reasons were one day given for rejecting the Copenhagen interpretation, the QM/NIDA program, if limited to that interpretation, would come to an end. But if one discovered that the QM/NIDA program need not be limited to the Copenhagen interpretation, this would be a striking result: It would strengthen the overall validity of NIDA, and *I claim it could lead to important research projects in physics.*

To formulate this idea in its clearest and most testable form, I propose the following thesis:

> *Every standard interpretation of QM will provide a plausible, if quite different, basis for the QM/NIDA research program, leading to progress in theology and to progress in physics.*

This thesis is easily testable. First, we study each interpretation (e.g., Bohmian, many worlds) and discover whether each provides a basis for the QM/NIDA agenda. There are only two possible results, each contributing to progress in knowledge:

1. *Progress in theology:* If we find ways to appropriate each interpretation for the QM/NIDA agenda, this will extend the validity of NIDA as a viable theological understanding of noninterventionist divine action in light of science. This, in turn, will result in a striking increase in our "spiritual knowledge."

2. *Progress in science:* If one finds an interpretation that cannot be appropriated for the QM/NIDA agenda, then we might count this as evidence against QM/NIDA. Interestingly, however, we still have another option left, one that leads directly to the possibility for *progress in science:* We attempt to discover a convincing reason that this interpretation of QM should be abandoned. If we could, in fact, find arguments for abandoning one of the standard interpretations of QM, this would constitute a *very significant result for physics.*[14] In the end, however, should this interpretation withstand our renewed and rigorous scrutiny, then its existence must be conceded as counting against the fruitfulness of the QM/NIDA program.

In either case, however, there is a further element of progress. If, as I believe, we urge that science and theology should best be in a relation of "creative mutual interaction,"[15] then we must go beyond showing the stunning importance of science for theology and discover the importance of theology in pointing us toward important research programs in science. This thesis provides just such an opportunity: It leads to genuine progress in both theology and in science—and progress as assessed by the independent criteria of each field.

The results, however they turn out (for this currently is unknown—this is genuinely new research), would constitute a crucial form of "spiritual information," for we would have empirically tested the theological claim that evolution is influenced by God's noninterventionist action and increased our overall knowledge about God's action in the natural world through new research in theology and science.

✍

ROBERT J. RUSSELL, PH.D., is Founder and Director of the Center for Theology and the Natural Sciences (CTNS) and Professor of Theology and Science in Residence

at The Graduate Theological Union in Berkeley, California. He received a doctorate in physics from the University of California at Santa Cruz in 1978 and his M.Div.
and M.A. from the Pacific School of Religion in 1972. Professor Russell is also
ordained in the United Church of Christ, Congregational, to ministry in higher
education. His scientific interests include foundational issues in cosmology and in
quantum mechanics. Professor Russell has co-edited seven books on science and
theology as a result of ongoing collaborative research between CTNS and the Vatican Observatory, five of which form the "divine action" series (http://www.ctns.org/
publications.html). He is the editor of the forthcoming festschrift *Fifty Years in Science and Religion: Ian G. Barbour and his Legacy* (Ashgate Publishers, 2004), the
author of numerous articles on the science-religion dialog, and co-editor of the
new refereed scholarly journal *Theology and Science*. Professor Russell worked
closely with the CTNS international programs "Science and Religion Course Program" and "Science and the Spiritual Quest." He is a former judge for the Templeton Prize.

NOTES

1 See, for example, Paul Tillich, *Systematic Theology* (Chicago: University of Chicago
   Press, 1951), 1:11, 156.

2 Representatives include Philip Clayton and Arthur Peacocke.

3 Representatives include John Polkinghorne and myself.

4 See Robert John Russell, "Introduction," in *Chaos and Complexity: Scientific Perspectives
   on Divine Action*, ed. Robert J. Russell, Nancey C. Murphy, and Arthur R. Peacocke, Sci-
   entific Perspectives on Divine Action Series (Vatican City State: Vatican Observatory
   Publications; Berkeley, CA.: Center for Theology and the Natural Sciences, 1995), 9–13.
   See also Robert John Russell, Nancey C. Murphy, and Chris J. Isham, eds., *Quantum
   Cosmology and the Laws of Nature: Scientific Perspectives on Divine Action*, Scientific
   Perspectives on Divine Action Series (Vatican City State: Vatican Observatory Publica-
   tions; Berkeley, CA.: Center for Theology and the Natural Sciences, 1993); Robert John
   Russell, Nancey C. Murphy, and Arthur R. Peacocke, eds., *Chaos and Complexity*; Robert
   John Russell, Nancey Murphy et al., eds., *Neuroscience and the Person: Scientific Per-
   spectives on Divine Action* (Vatican City State: Vatican Observatory Publications; Berke-
   ley, CA.: Center for Theology and the Natural Sciences, 1999); Robert John Russell,
   Philip Clayton et al., eds., *Quantum Mechanics: Scientific Perspectives on Divine Action*
   (Vatican City State: Vatican Observatory Publications; Berkeley, CA.: Center for Theology and the Natural Sciences, 2001).

5 See Nancey Murphy, "On the Nature of Theology," in *Religion and Science: History,
   Method, Dialogue*, ed. W. Mark Richardson and Wesley J. Wildman (New York: Routledge, 1996), esp. ch. 3.

6 See Richard Dawkins, *The Blind Watchmaker: Why the Evidence of Evolution Reveals a
   Universe without Design* (New York: Norton, 1987), 6; Edward O. Wilson, *On Human
   Nature* (Cambridge: Harvard University Press, 1978), 1.

7 For a helpful recent historical survey of the variety of responses to Darwin in England,

Europe, and the United States, see Claude Welch, "Dispelling Some Myths about the Split Between Theology and Science in the Nineteenth Century," in *Religion and Science: History, Method, Dialogue*, ed. W. Mark Richardson and Wesley J. Wildman (New York: Routledge, 1996), 29–40.

8 Early contributions to this position include Ian G. Barbour, *Issues in Science and Religion* (New York: Harper & Row, 1971 [originally published in 1966 by Prentice-Hall]); A. R. Peacocke, *Creation and the World of Science: The Bampton Lectures, 1979* (Oxford: Clarendon Press, 1979); more recent ones include Ian G. Barbour, *Religion in an Age of Science*, Gifford Lectures; 1989–1990 (San Francisco: Harper & Row, 1990); Ian G. Barbour, "Five Models of God and Evolution," in *Evolutionary and Molecular Biology: Scientific Perspectives on Divine Action*, ed. Robert John Russell, William R. Stoeger and Francisco J. Ayala (Vatican City State: Vatican Observatory Publications; Berkeley, CA.: Center for Theology and the Natural Sciences, 1998); Arthur Peacocke, *Theology for a Scientific Age: Being and Becoming—Natural, Divine and Human*, enlarged ed. (Minneapolis: Fortress Press, 1993); Arthur Peacocke, "Biological Evolution—A Positive Theological Appraisal," in *Evolutionary and Molecular Biology*; John F. Haught, "Darwin's Gift to Theology," in *Evolutionary and Molecular Biology*.

9 See the CTNS/Vatican Observatory series cited above.

10 See, for example, Max Jammer, *The Philosophy of Quantum Mechanics: The Interpretations of Quantum Mechanics in Historical Perspective* (New York: John Wiley & Sons, 1974); Nick Herbert, *Quantum Reality: Beyond the New Physics* (Garden City, NY: Anchor Press; Doubleday, 1985).

11 See, for example, http://scienceworld.wolfram.com/physics/SchroedingerEquation.html.

12 See Robert John Russell, "Special Providence and Genetic Mutation: A New Defense of Theistic Evolution," in *Evolutionary and Molecular Biology*.

13 Of course, the quantum potential is highly nonlocal, and its construction out of the wave function (r, t) suggests a major break in the meaning of "mechanism" in classical physics.

14 It goes without saying that the validity of these arguments must be entirely independent of the fact that the arguments serve to support the QM/NIDA program. Their validity must be based on their connection to new empirical predictions, to new demonstrations of internal inconsistency or incoherence with other well-accepted theories (such as special relativity), or to the general criteria of theory choice (such as Occam's razor, fertility, etc.).

15 See Robert John Russell, "Theology and Science: Current Issues and Future Directions" (http://www.ctns.org/russell_article.html).

Religion, Global Trends, and Religious Futurology 16

Philip Jenkins

ATTEMPTS TO PROJECT the long-term future have a track record that is at best mixed, at worst embarrassing. History is littered with the bleached skeletons of failed prophecies, and that is nowhere more true than in the realm of religion. In 1899, Mark Twain predicted that the then-booming movement of Christian Science was likely to shape the coming twentieth century. He predicted that Mrs. Eddy's church might make "the most formidable show that any new religion has made in the world since the birth and spread of Mohammedanism, and that within a century from now it may stand second to Rome only, in numbers and power in Christendom." (Today, far from dominating the world, Christian Scientists are rather outnumbered by the Amish.) Other predictions have proved equally wide of the mark. Countless warnings of imminent doom to the contrary, the Roman Catholic Church not only survives, but remains the world's largest religious institution. To quote Twain again,

> In this world we have seen the Roman Catholic power dying . . . for many centuries. Many a time we have gotten all ready for the funeral and found it postponed again, on account of the weather or something. . . . Apparently one of the most uncertain things in the world is the funeral of a religion.

Yet, having begun on this monitory note, I would suggest that some kind of religious futurology is not only possible, but essential. Religions and denominations simply have to have some basis for future planning and the allocation of resources, and much of this process depends on simple demographic data. Demographic shifts also carry implications for the nature of the spiritual marketplace in which the religions will be competing to spread their message. By projecting the future, we can understand both the potential for spiritual progress—and what often seem to be alarming obstacles to its accomplishment.

Yet perhaps the most important single reason for futurology is largely negative in nature. Many people, including the well-informed, operate according to perceptions that the future of religion will take some particular shape, yet generally these projections rest on nothing more than misleading assumptions, or rather prejudices. "Everyone knows," for example, that liberal and progressive-minded faiths represent the wave of the future, that fundamentalism and supernaturalism are doomed, and that our religious institutions must obey these iron laws. As the ultra-liberal Rt. Rev. John Shelby Spong, retired bishop of the Episcopal Diocese of Newark, warned us a few years ago, "Christianity Must Change or Die."

Unfortunately for such advocates, as we saw repeatedly in the late twentieth century, not only were these liberalizing trends far from inevitable, but they rather represented the reverse of observed reality. We live in an age when religious belief increasingly motivates political conduct and social activism, a phenomenon that has aptly been described as "the Revenge of God." If our religious debates are indeed going to be so influenced by our sense of the future, then at least we should try to get it right, to have some concrete foundation for what "everybody knows." As long as religions possess structures and institutions, they will need effective techniques of projecting the future.

If the claim that "biology is destiny" is controversial in many aspects of human activity, then this is all the more true in matters of religion. At the same time, we neglect biological trends at our peril. To illustrate this, I want to examine the religious impact, present and future, of what might be the greatest single global trend of our age. By this, I mean the massive relative decline in the proportion of the world's people who live in the traditionally advanced nations, the countries of the "old Christendom."

While populations are booming in the global South—Africa, Asia, and Latin America—Northern lands are undergoing a birth dearth of epochal proportions. If we combine the figures for Europe, North America, and the lands of the former Soviet Union, then in 1900, these Northern regions accounted for 32 percent of the world population. By 1950, the share had fallen a little to 29 percent, but the rate of contraction then accelerated, to 25 percent in 1970 and around 18 percent by 2000. By 2050, the figure should be around 10 or 12 percent. In contrast, the relative growth of the global South has been quite impressive. Africa and Latin America combined made up only 13 percent of the world's people in 1900, but that figure has now grown to 21 percent. The rate of change is accelerating. By 2050, Africa and Latin America will probably be home to 29 percent of the world's people. In 1900, "Northerners" outnumbered these "Southerners" by about 2.5 to 1; by 2050, the proportions will be almost exactly reversed. Southern nations are growing very rapidly, while their Northern neighbors are relatively static.

To illustrate this change in practice, we can look at the example of Uganda and Italy, representing respectively a young Southern country with a typical Third World population profile and an aging Northern land with a stagnating population (see Table 1).

TABLE 1. POPULATION CHANGE IN TWO COUNTRIES 1950–2050[1]
(POPULATION FIGURES ARE GIVEN IN MILLIONS)

	1950	2000	2050
Italy	47.10	57.64	45.0
Uganda	5.52	23.32	84.1

According to the projections of the U.S. Census Bureau, in 1950, there were more than eight Italians for every single Ugandan; by 2050, Ugandans should outnumber

Italians by 1.8 to 1. In fact, the transformation is even greater than this raw number may suggest, since many of those Italians will themselves be "Southerners," new-comers of African and Asian immigrant stock.

Predictions such as these are open to detailed criticism, and the demographers who produce these figures make no claims about their absolute reliability. Projections only work as long as people maintain their present behavior while societies adapt to changing circumstances. Populations can and do rebound from decline, while what seems like exponential growth can taper off. During the eighteenth century, colonial Americans noted with amazed delight that their population was doubling every twenty-five years or so, a rate that would today characterize a highly fertile Third World nation, and this pattern continued into the early nineteenth century. If the United States had maintained these rates up to the present day, then it would now be as populous as China. But of course it did not. To take the specific comparison I have used here, United Nations demographers project sixty million Ugandans by 2050, rather than the eighty million suggested by the U.S. Census Bureau. But the broad trend is clear: In the middle term—say, the next fifty years—we will be seeing a spectacular upsurge in Southern populations and a decisive shift of population centers to the Southern continents. Even if the more conservative UN estimate is correct, in 2050 there will be 1.5 Ugandans for every Italian.

This global shift is immensely significant for the future of religion. It is, for example, the single greatest reason for the upsurge in the world's Muslim population: Centers of Muslim strength happen to be in those parts of the world where the age profiles lean heavily toward the young and fertile. But Muslims are not alone in benefiting from this trend. Christians, too, should enjoy a worldwide boom in the new century, but the vast majority of believers will be neither white nor European, nor Euro-American.

According to the respected *World Christian Encyclopedia*, some two billion Christians are alive today, about a third of the planetary total. The largest single bloc, 560 million people, is still to be found in Europe. Latin America, however, is already close behind with 480 million, Africa has 360 million, and 313 million Asians profess Christianity; North America claims about 260 million believers. If we extrapolate these figures to the year 2025, and assume no great gains or losses through conversion or persecution, then there would be around 2.6 billion Christians. Six hundred thirty-three million would live in Africa, 640 million in Latin America, and 460 million in Asia. Europe, with 555 million, would have slipped to third place. Africa and Latin America would be in competition for the title of Most Christian Continent. About this date, too, another significant milestone should occur, namely that these two continents will together account for half the Christians on the planet. By 2050, only about one-fifth of the world's three billion Christians will be non-Latino whites, and Christianity will be primarily a religion of Africa, and of the African diaspora in the Americas. We can only begin to imagine the cultural consequences of such a shift.

With full awareness of the limitations of the data, I have tried to project the nations that should in 2050 have the largest Christian populations. Heading the list is the United States, with perhaps 330 million Christians. Next in place come seven countries, each with between eighty and two hundred million believers. In descending order, they are Brazil, Mexico, the Philippines, Nigeria, the Democratic Republic of the Congo, Ethiopia, and (providing our token Europeans) Russia. The list is striking, as much for the countries it omits as for those it includes. We note the absence of Britain, France, Spain, and Italy, names that recall the Christianity of the older global order.

If Christianity "goes South" in the manner I have suggested, this fact has many implications for many aspects of politics, society, and economics, as well as religion. Since the areas of Christian growth will also be adjacent to centers of rising Islam, the potential for political conflict is very high. But for present purposes, let us explore the consequences for purely religious and spiritual matters. Of course, we can hardly speak of a Nigerian or Mexican religious "character," and still less can imagine such an entity for the whole global South. Even in the heartlands of the new African Christianity, we can find conservatives and liberals, fundamentalists and modernists, saints and time-servers. Yet while making this allowance, we can legitimately comment that highly traditional and supernatural approaches still flourish in the global South, to a far greater degree than we find in Europe or North America. Across the South, flourishing Pentecostal and independent churches attract millions of believers. These newer churches preach deep personal faith and communal orthodoxy, mysticism, and Puritanism, all founded on clear scriptural authority. They preach messages that, to a Westerner, appear simplistically charismatic, visionary, and apocalyptic. In this thought world, prophecy is an everyday reality, while faith-healing, exorcism, and dream visions are all fundamental parts of religious sensibility. On present evidence, a Southernized Christian future should be distinctly conservative. I am reminded of John Updike's wry observation that "I don't think God plays well in Sweden. God sticks pretty close to the Equator."

More significantly, that change seems to have the potential greatest significance for the whole area of "spiritual information." Knowing *where* Christian believers are, or how many of them might exist at any given time, is a matter of some social-scientific interest. Vastly more important, however, is to understand the content of their faith and how that might change as society is transformed. The reasons for religious change run precisely contrary to what we might once have expected. Instead of religion fading as a consequence of modernization and urbanization, it is precisely these trends that have done the most to promote the growth of religious bodies, generally of the most conservative and fundamentalist kind, whether Christian or Muslim.

These emerging Christian churches work so well because they appeal to the very different demographics of their communities and do best among young and displaced migrants in mushrooming mega-cities. Population shifts will create a steadily growing number of huge metropolitan complexes that could by 2050 or so be counting their populations in the tens of millions. Most will have next to nothing in working government services, nothing to offer in the way of welfare, health, or education; rich pickings await any religious groups who can meet the needs of these new urbanites, anyone who can at once feed the body and nourish the soul. In such settings, the most devoted and fundamentalist-oriented religious communities emerge to provide functional social arrangements. This sort of alternative social system has been a potent factor in winning mass support for the most committed religious groups and is likely to become more important as the gap between popular needs and the official capacities to fill them becomes ever wider.

People want prosperity—or, at least, economic survival—but just as critical is the promise of health, and the desperate public health situation in the new cities goes far toward explaining the emphasis of the new churches on healing of mind and body. Apart from the general range of maladies that affect North Americans and Europeans, the Third World poor also suffer from the diseases associated with poverty, hunger, and pollution, in what has been termed a "pathogenic society." The attacks of these "demons of poverty" are all the graver when people are living in tropical climates, with all the problems arising from the diseases and parasites found in those regions. As well as physical ailments, psychiatric and substance abuse problems drive desperate people to seek refuge in God. Taking all these threats together —disease, exploitation, pollution, drink, drugs, and violence—it is easy to see why people might easily accept the claim that they were under siege from demonic forces and that only divine intervention could save them. The result is a continuation— indeed, a massive revival—of supernatural and charismatic religious views. We Westerners must ask ourselves, soberly, what might be a troubling question: In such a setting, are not such approaches a logical and natural means of understanding divine reality?

I have suggested that global demographic trends are likely to have clear consequences for the nature of Christianity, which in many ways could come to resemble the supernatural-oriented Islam currently surging across Africa and Asia. It might well be that this projection is too sweeping, some might even say too apocalyptic. Yet it is difficult to deny that the world's great religions will be affected by the coming demographic transformation. Christians themselves are only beginning to take account of the ethnic and geographical changes in their religion and the concomitant return of supernatural faith. Perhaps it will take decades for Westerners to absorb the lessons in full—by which time the revolution will be largely accomplished. Based on these projections, however, we can already see that older vision of a new secular liberalism, a death of God, is looking woefully inaccurate. To paraphrase Mark Twain, "one of the most uncertain things in the world is the funeral of a deity."

ℒ♥

PHILIP JENKINS has taught at the Pennsylvania State University since 1980, where he currently holds the rank of Distinguished Professor of History and Religious Studies. He has published eighteen books, about a hundred book chapters and refereed articles, and a hundred book reviews. His recent books (all published by Oxford University Press) include *Mystics and Messiahs: Cults and New Religions in*

American History (2000), *Hidden Gospels: The Modern Mythology of Christian Origins* (2001), *The Next Christendom: The Rise of Global Christianity* (2002), and *The New Anti-Catholicism: The Last Acceptable Prejudice* (2003).

NOTE

1 http://www.census.gov/ipc/www/idbrank.html.

"Playing God" 17

Noah J. Efron

People say we are playing God. In all honesty,
if scientists don't play God, who will?
—James Watson

ETAPHORS MATTER. A good metaphor captures a snarl of unruly thought
and emotion, reducing it to a clear image we get at once and remember.
Oddly, a bad metaphor often does the same. Just as a metaphor can help us to
understand a complex state of affairs that might otherwise elude us, it can just as
effectively help us to misunderstand what's going on. Metaphors illuminate, and
metaphors occlude. Perhaps, some do both at once.

The metaphor perhaps most often invoked to describe the work of scientists is
"playing God." In May 2000, Prince Charles warned on the BBC against biologists
playing God in the laboratory. In an open letter, Professor Richard Dawkins replied
that the prince's alarm was misplaced, or at least ill timed: "Playing God? We've
been playing God for centuries!" In August 2002, Pope John Paul II addressed a
chanting crowd of three million in a meadow near Krakow, using perhaps his final
Mass in his homeland as a vehicle to warn against scientists playing God in their laboratories. Soon thereafter, George W. Bush criticized stem cell researchers for doing
the same.

"Playing God" is not solely the coin of princes, professors, popes, and presidents;
the metaphor also has mass appeal. Entering the phrase "playing God" in Google
(the Internet search engine) produces sixty thousand hits. A recent Pew poll found
that most American Christians and Muslims, and many Jews, are uneasy about
biotechnology precisely because they see it as "playing God."[1] Greenpeace activists
picketing the laboratories of Monsanto carried signs accusing corporate scientists
of "playing God." Dozens, perhaps hundreds, of books in print about contemporary
science have "playing God" in their titles. Recent scientific milestones such as the
cloning of Dolly and the completion of a map of the human genome occasioned
hundreds of headlines that asked whether Ian Wilmut and Craig Venter had "played
God." When the Raelian cult announced that they had undertaken to clone a
human, *20/20*'s Barbara Walters hosted an interview entitled "Playing God." To date,
eager fans have ponied up $2 billion to see the *Jurassic Park* trilogy, movies that are
at heart a high-tech meditation on what may result when scientists "play God." The
notion that researchers are playing God engages, repels, incites, and excites us. When

we worry about science, what we are most often worried about is the specter of men and women in lab coats playing God.

This is nothing new. Mary Shelley's *Frankenstein* and Goethe's *Faust* are cautionary tales of remarkably durable appeal. Although they don't put it quite this way, what they caution against is men of science playing God. Further back, one finds sixteenth-century accounts nervously querying the probity of Paracelsus's efforts to construct a man from blood, feces, and semen. Others doubted the wisdom of alchemical and magical pursuits. Centuries earlier, similar doubts surfaced concerning Albertus Magnus, who was said to have built a manservant of brass. As Jon Turney has described in a brilliant book called *Frankenstein's Footsteps: Science, Genetics and Popular Culture*, the image of scientists building monsters they cannot control—in fact, playing God—has a long history that explains, in part, its tremendous appeal today.[2]

This historical image offers only a partial explanation, however. "Playing God" is a powerful metaphor because it captures something important, frightful, and relatively new about today's science and technology. The capacity of scientists to intervene in the workings of nature has increased rapidly, surpassing the predictions of last generation's scholars—and even the pipe dreams of science fiction writers and fantasists. Professor Dawkins chided Prince Charles that playing God is nothing new—and, strictly speaking, he is right. People have always tampered with nature, taming fire, diverting rivers, domesticating animals, and so forth. John E. Smith, in his admirable primer *Biotechnology*, points out that biotechnology has "been used for many centuries to produce beer, wine, cheese, and many other foods," traditional practices that have now been augmented by new laboratory techniques. The long history of biotechnology, as Smith describes it, begins with "Sumerians and Babylonians [who] were drinking beer by 6000 B.C."[3]

What Dawkins and Smith and many others elide is the great increase in the extent of our intervention into nature today, a difference in degree so great that it has become a difference in kind. When a team of researchers at the Australian Museum decided recently to clone back into existence the Tasmanian tiger, a marsupial hunted into extinction in 1936, they undertook something quite different from Babylonian brewing techniques. When researchers at Harvard engineered a mouse to fall ill with cancer—the celebrated and controversial "oncomouse"—they were up to something quite different from Sumerian sheepdog breeding.

Until the nineteenth century, a principal ideal of science was to apprehend a nature deemed static and eternal. In the twentieth century, a competing ideal of manipulating a nature that seemed plastic and changing became dominant. Thomas Huxley could still hold that "science has fulfilled her function when she has ascertained and enunciated truth," but in the generations since, the function of science has shifted from simply ascertaining the truth about nature to swaying nature to act in ways it never could or would on its own. Galileo set out to read the Book of Nature; Genentech scientists aspire to edit it—and they are succeeding to a remarkable degree. Kepler wrote that he sought to understand the motions of the planets so that he might, for a moment, "think God's thoughts." In contrast, the goal of

Monsanto scientists' efforts is to make nature reflect our own thoughts, needs, and desires.

It is our vastly increased ability to alter nature according to our designs that most people have in mind today when they worry about scientists playing God. If God is taken as the God of Creation—the God of Genesis, for instance—then the metaphor is more apt than ever. For if God created hydrogen and the other naturally occurring elements in the periodic table, it was a team of scientists at the Gesellschaft für Schwerionenforschung (GSI) who created the element ununbibim by fusing a zinc and lead atom in a heavy ion accelerator. The new element, which perhaps will never be found in "God's" nature, flickers into and out of existence (its half-life is 2.4 milliseconds) at the pleasure of scientists. Even for the most devout, the periodic table—the *elements themselves*, the building blocks of physical reality—are now a joint production of God and a group of scientists in Darmstadt, Germany.[4] When this is the state of affairs, it is hardly a leap to say that such scientists are playing God.

But it is precisely at the moment when the metaphor of playing God becomes most apt that it becomes most dangerous. It is a feature of the metaphor that it inevitably invites either censure or praise. When Prince Charles suggested that genetic engineers are playing God, he meant that their labors exceed the bounds of good taste, proper reason, and humility, and they ought to be stopped. When Richard Dawkins replied that we have been playing God for centuries, he meant that we *ought* to be remaking nature to conform to our wishes: "[I]f we want to sustain the planet into the future, the first thing we must do is stop taking advice from nature," turning our trust instead to the "scientific rationalism [that] is the crowning glory of the human spirit." The "playing God" metaphor counsels some to stop science in its tracks and others to embrace science with redoubled devotion.

This pulling toward the extremes may be a sign, as it often is, that we are thinking about things in the wrong way. Conceptualizing increased intervention in nature as playing God seems to invite us to see new sciences as Prince Charles does—as thoughtlessly dangerous hubris—or as Richard Dawkins does—as tools for fulfilling our destiny of dominating nature. But are these really the only options? Is there not a scheme for thinking about our growing ability to reshape nature that allows for, perhaps even draws us to, a middle ground? Is there not a way of thinking that acknowledges the beauty and benefit of our scientific capabilities without diminishing our humility?

Some months ago, on the first night of Passover, my wife Susan found a lump in the soft tissue beneath her shoulder, and by intuition and her training as a physician she knew at once that it was cancer. Surgeons removed the tumor, and now, every third Sunday, we travel together to a nearby hospital where she receives intravenous doses of cytoxan, adriamycin, and fluorouracil, a cocktail of toxins that prevent malignant cells from redividing and reproducing. It is an awesome fact about these drugs that two generations ago they did not exist at all. Had she been born fifty years earlier, my wife would be waiting to die. She would be dying. If a good working definition of playing God is willfully interfering with the course of nature, then our sure faith that Susan will recite blessings at our four-year-old's bar mitzvah nine years hence owes a debt of gratitude outright to scientists playing God. I know this to be true: To love someone with cancer is to believe with fierce piety in playing God.

But ought this to preclude us from fretting, with Prince Charles, that "nature has come to be regarded as a system that can be engineered for our own convenience or as a nuisance to be evaded and manipulated, and in which anything that happens can be fixed by technology and human ingenuity"? Can one be Dawkins on the oncology ward and Charles on a hike in the woods with the kids? In the strict ethical universe of the "playing God" metaphor, it is hard to see how.

There are alternative views, and these deserve some scrutiny. Early Jewish texts concerning the creation of a *golem*, or artificial man, imply a very different moral economy for evaluating science. The Talmud tells this story:

> Rava said: If the righteous wishes, they could create a world, for it is written (Isaiah 59:2), "Your iniquities have been a barrier between you and your God." For Rava created a man and sent him to Rabbi Zeira. The Rabbi spoke to him but he did not answer. Then he said, "You come from the pietists: Return to your dust."[5]

A later Midrash reports that:

> Abraham sat alone and meditated on [the ancient cosmogonical and cosmological treatise, *The Book of Creation*], but could understand nothing until a heavenly voice went forth and said to him: "Are you trying to set yourself up as my equal? I am one and have created *The Book of Creation* and studied it; but you by yourself cannot understand it. Therefore take a companion, and meditate on it together, and you will understand it." Thereupon, Abraham went to his teacher Shem, the son of Noah, and sat with him for three years and they meditated on it until they knew how to create a world. And to this day, there is no one who can understand it alone, two scholars [are needed], and even they understand it only after three years, whereupon they can make everything their hearts' desire.[6]

The attitudes of these odd little texts toward altering nature are very different from those behind the "playing God" metaphor. In the first text, it is no sin for people to strive to create life, as God might, but to do this they must first strive to be righteous like God. In the second text, too, it is no crime to seek God's powers, but this can only be accomplished in society with others, through learned disputation. Doing the God-like work of Creation is a decent goal, but to play God the Creator, one must also play God the Moralist. And this can only be accomplished painstakingly, in conversation with other people. One message of these quirky ancient passages is that one can be Richard Dawkins only by striving at the same time to be Prince Charles. The troubling aspect of science, in this way of seeing things, is not that we are playing God, but that we are not playing God well enough.

The fear that men and women in lab coats are playing God has had a long and storied career. Its value now, at the moment when scientists' skill at manipulating nature has become exquisitely refined, is diminished, although its ability to capture our attention is not. The simple *with-us-or-against-us* moral calculus of the "playing God" metaphor retains its appeal, even though it now impedes more than aids us in making important choices about the sciences and technologies we pursue and how we pursue them. It stops debate just as it begins it.

As I write this, scientists in Australia are reconstituting a defunct marsupial, and my wife is sleeping peacefully in the next room. Playing God? Perhaps. But surely we have more important questions to ask, discuss, and—together—answer.

ℒ♥

NOAH J. EFRON, PH.D., is Chairman of the Graduate Program for the History and Philosophy of Science at Bar Ilan University, Israel, where he specializes in Jewish attitudes toward nature and science. He has been a fellow at the Massachusetts Institute for Technology and at Harvard University. Dr. Efron's book, *Real Jews*, about religion in Israel, was published by Basic Books in May 2003. He has been awarded grants from the National Endowment for the Humanities and the Dibner, Mellon, Rothschild, and Thomas J. Watson Foundations, as well as the Israeli Academy for Higher Education. Dr. Efron is a founding member of the International Society for Science and Religion and of the Israel Society for History and Philosophy of Science. He lives in Tel Aviv and is currently writing *Golem, God and Man: Human and Divine in the Age of Biotechnology.*

NOTES

1 The Pew Initiative on Food and Biotechnology, "Genetically Modifying Food: Playing God or Doing God's Work?" 2001. Available at http://pewagbiotech.org/research/survey7-01.pdf.

2 Jon Turney, *Frankenstein's Footsteps: Science, Genetics and Popular Culture* (New Haven, CT: Yale University Press, 1998).

3 John E. Smith, *Biotechnology*, 3rd ed. (Cambridge: Cambridge University Press, 1996), 4.

4 In his contribution to this volume, Professor Philip Clayton cites theologian Philip Hefner's lovely turn of phrase that holds humans to be "created co-creators" with God. This is an inspired way to put the issue. I differ somewhat from Clayton and Hefner in that I think the mantle of "created co-creator," while filled with intoxicating possibilities and now in any instance inevitable, is a distressing, demanding responsibility for which humans have scarcely proven ready. In a sense, what Clayton and Hefner see as a solution, I see as a fearsome, unavoidable problem: What, then, ought we create?

5 Babylonian Talmud, *Sanhedrin*, 65b. Translation adapted from Moshe Idel, *Golem: Jewish Magical and Mystical Traditions on the Artificial Anthropoid* (Albany: SUNY Press, 1990), 27.

6 R. Yehudah Barceloni's *Commentary on the Book of Creation*, trans. Gershom Scholem, in "The Idea of the Golem," in *On the Kabbalah and Its Symbolism* (New York: Schocken, 1969), 176. Also see Idel, *Golem*, 19.

Fraser N. Watts

A N EXCITING new development in the study of religion is getting under way: the cognitive science of religion. I believe it promises to be the most significant development in the scientific study of religion so far and will really advance our understanding of the spiritual aspect of human nature.

As far back as we can trace, humanity has had an intuitive apprehension of the spiritual nature of reality. What contemporary cognitive science potentially enables us to understand is how this spiritual intuition arises and how it works, what mode of operation the human mind needs to be in to perceive the world in a spiritual way. The "spiritual information" arising from cognitive science is an explicit, research-based approach to the age-old intuitive grasp of the spiritual character of the universe.

Cognitive science is a unique interdisciplinary enterprise. Part of what is exciting about it is the way cognition is a crossroads where so many different disciplines meet. Cognitive science has seven key strands as it is applied to religion:

1. The formulation of cognitive theories of religion using the tools of information systems and computer science.
2. The empirical study of cognitive processes in religion using the paradigms of experimental psychology.
3. The study of cognitive aspects of religion from the standpoint of the social sciences, especially anthropology.
4. The mapping of cognitive processes in religion on to brain function and the empirical study of religious brain processes using the rapidly expanding tools of contemporary neuroscience.
5. The formulation of how the evolution of cognitive processes has underpinned the evolution of the religious capacity of humanity.
6. The charting of how religious cognition develops and changes as general cognitive capacities develop.
7. The philosophical formulation of cognitive aspects of religion and the use of philosophical tools of conceptual analysis to bring precision to cognitive theorizing about religion.

Cognitive science has proven its value in other areas of human functioning as well. The way it integrates these different disciplines around a single focus gives it a unique scientific penetration. In cognitive science, the whole is more than the sum of the parts. None of these seven disciplines can get as far alone as they can together. That is true even of neuroscience. Knowing what parts of the brain are involved in different aspects of religion doesn't get you very far unless you can map those brain areas onto a theory of cognitive functioning.

Although cognitive science has a good track record in other areas, it has only begun to be applied to religion in the last decade. The pioneers were people such as Thomas Lawson and Robert McCauley, Pascal Boyer, Dan Sperber, Eugene d'Aquili and Andrew Newberg, Justin Barrett, and others. Most of these pioneers have worked on at least two of the seven strands of cognitive science. The landmark book *Religion in Mind: Cognitive Perspectives on Religious Belief, Ritual, and Experience,* edited by Jensine Andresen (2001), arose from a conference at the University of Vermont in 1998. A series of volumes on *Current Approaches to the Cognitive Study of Religion* has begun to be published (Pyysiainen and Anttonen 2002).

Probably the biggest success story of cognitive science has been with language. Steven Pinker in *The Language Instinct* (1994) has set out the case for an inherited cognitive module underpinning the linguistic capacities of humans. Since then, there has been a tendency to extend this approach to all aspects of human functioning, as Pinker himself did in *How the Mind Works* (1997). It seems natural to assume that there will be a module for religion taking this approach as well.

But not so fast! Cognitive science sometimes gets carried away with its own enthusiasm. It is essential, if it is to deliver reliable scientific advances, that data keep pace with theory. The case for a language instinct needs to be demonstrated experimentally, although I believe it can be (Plotkin 1997). It is much more doubtful whether religion will be found to have the same kind of basis in a cognitive module, even though evidence for the role of genetic factors in religion is now coming in.

The point is that the cognitive science of religion must stay close to experimental data. Cognitive theories of religion, like all good theories, suggest research programs. But it is essential to actually do the research, not just to assume the conclusions. Fortunately, research usually brings surprises, and it will probably be the surprises in the cognitive investigation of religion that will advance our understanding most.

My own contribution to this area began almost fifteen years ago with a book written with Mark Williams, *The Psychology of Religious Knowing* (Watts and Williams, 1988). The field had not then really gotten going, but we were trying to identify some of the key issues on the basis of the fragmentary literature available, such as:

+ The use made in religious contexts of intuitive and nonanalytic modes of cognition.
+ The relation between the cognitive understanding of the self and of God, which seem to be closely intertwined.
+ The analysis of a prayer as an exercise in the religious schooling of several aspects of cognition that play key roles in everyday life.
+ The nature and significance of the figurative or metaphorical concepts that seem to play such a key role in religious thinking.

My current work is partly theoretical, partly empirical—and cognitive science always needs to be advancing on both those tracks simultaneously. On the theoretical side, I am exploring the application to religion to what I believe to be one of the most fruitful and versatile models of the general cognitive architecture currently available: the Interacting Cognitive Subsystems (ICS) developed by Philip Barnard (Watts 2002). A key feature of this approach is the distinction between two subsystems concerned with meaning in the central engine of cognition: (1) the "implicational" system, which identifies, in rather intuitive and holistic ways, meanings and regularities at a very high level of abstraction, and (2) the "propositional" system, which formulates meanings in a more logical and sequential form, rendering them more readily capable of articulation.

It is one of the key features of human cognition that the implicational system exists separately from the propositional system. In evolutionary terms, this creates problems—for example, giving us a capacity for worry and insomnia. But it also underpins distinctive human achievements, such as the capacity for religion. One aspect of religious experience that the ICS approach handles particularly well is the sense of ineffability. The model assumes that mystical experiences arise in the "implicational" subsystem, but that they defy adequate translation into the different code of the "propositional" subsystem. Of course, propositional meanings of some kind can always be produced (and mystics have often written at length about their "ineffable" experiences). However, the sense remains that this is not the original experience, and that in order to communicate the experiences have had to be translated into a rather alien code.

ICS also helps to capture the way in which religious cognition changes as children grow up. Initially, they seem to undergo a phase of powerful and intuitive experiences of God that are difficult to articulate and not much shared with other people. This is followed by the gradual development of a more adult capacity to think about religion, which seems to eclipse the earlier, more intuitive religious experiences. This seems to be a mode of religion that is initially mainly "implicational" and is gradually supplanted by one that is more "propositional." Some spiritual practices, such as meditation, seem to be designed to temporally reverse this process and to create the mental space in which it is possible to become like children again in the sense of having a powerful and intuitive sense of the presence of God.

My experimental work on religious cognition, undertaken with Nicholas Gibson in the Centre for Advanced Religious and Theological Studies (CARTS) at Cambridge, uses the paradigms of experimental psychology to assess and investigate religious cognition. One of the recent success stories of experimental psychology has been the application of such paradigms to the study of emotional cognition, and I had the opportunity to contribute to work in that area (e.g., Williams et al. 1988/ 1997). The paradigms that have worked well in "cognition and emotion" research seem likely to be applicable to religious cognition, too. They promise to get at a deeper level of religious belief than conventional pencil-and-paper questionnaire measures. In ICS terms, they will get closer to the deep, implicational levels of cognition, rather than the more superficial propositional levels. Or to put a similar point in more conventional religious language, they may give us something closer to "heart" knowledge, not just "head" knowledge.

We are at an early stage of this work, but it is already clear that paradigms exist that give a good measure of religious belief, such as the speed with which people can decide whether or not attributes apply to God. The challenge now is to see what advantages such measures may have, for example, in exploring the link between religion and health and, more fundamentally, to see what these approaches can tell us about how religious cognition is organized in the cognitive system. The cognition-and-emotion literature has found an interesting distinction between simpler emotional states, such as anxiety, and more cognitively complex ones, such as depression. Anxiety affects attention more reliably than memory and does so in an automatic, rather reflex-like way. Depression, in contrast, affects memory more reliably than anxiety and in a way that depends on elaborated cognitive encoding. Our preliminary hypothesis is that, in terms of this distinction, religion is cognitively more similar to depression than to anxiety.

At present, we are just at the start of an exciting phase of the cognitive science of religion in which we will discover a lot about how religion is organized in the human mind. But beyond that, there will be big theoretical debates about the status of religious cognition and how it relates to wider realities. As with mathematics, there are two possible views. Mathematics is sometimes regarded as a clever human invention that just happens to be useful in understanding the world. Others see it as a discovery of the nature of the real world. Similarly, is religious cognition just a purely human development, or does it reflect the spiritual nature of the world? My sympathies are with the latter view, and I look forward to marshalling the arguments and joining the debate.

⚹

FRASER N. WATTS, PH.D., is Starbridge Lecturer in Theology and Natural Science and Director of the Psychology and Religion Research Program at the University of Cambridge. He is also Fellow and Director of Studies in Theology at Queens College, Vicar-Chaplain of St. Edward's Church in Cambridge, and Secretary of the International Society for Science and Religion. He was formerly at the MRC Applied Psychology Unit, working on cognitive aspects of emotional disorders, and has been President of the British Psychological Society. Professor Watts's research is concerned with the interface between psychology and theology. He has recently published *Theology and Psychology* (Ashgate, 2002) and, with Rebecca Nye and Sara Savage, *Psychology for Christian Ministry* (Routledge, 2002), and edited with Elizabeth Gulliford, *Forgiveness in Context* (T & T Clark, 2004).

REFERENCES

Andresen, J. (2001), *Religion in Mind: Cognitive Perspectives on Religious Belief, Ritual and Experience*, Cambridge: Cambridge University Press.

Pinker, S. (1994), *The Language Instinct: How the Mind Creates Language*, New York:William Morrow.

———. (1997), *How the Mind Works*, New York: Norton, and London: Allen Lane.

Plotkin, H. (1997), *Evolution in Mind: An Introduction to Evolutionary Psychology*, London: Allen Lane.

Pyysiainen, I., and Antonnen, V. (eds). (2002), *Current Approaches to the Cognitive Study of Religion*, London: Continuum.

Watts, F. (2002), "Interacting cognitive subsystems and religious meanings." In *Neurotheology: Brain, Science, Spirituality and Religious Experience*, ed. Joseph, R., San Jose: University Press.

Watts, F., and Williams, M. (1988), *The Psychology of Religious Knowing*, Cambridge: Cambridge University Press.

Williams, J. M. G., Watts, F., Macleod, C., and Matthews, A. (1997), *Cognitive Psychology and Emotional Disorders*, 2nd ed., Chichester: John Wiley.

Exploring Inner Space in a New Age of Discovery 19

The Future of Scientific Survey Research in Religion

George H. Gallup Jr.

S CIENTIFIC SURVEY RESEARCH plays a vital role in illuminating the fundamental forces that drive humanity. Many social observers maintain that these forces are spiritual and moral, not just economic and political. Therefore, survey research is poised to make a solid contribution in this century to understanding the spiritual underpinnings of humankind—yielding more "spiritual information."

Polling organizations already survey cross-culturally on many different "external" experiences. The continuing challenge to pollsters, sociologists, and others is to devise measurements that are useful for understanding people's "internal" experiences as well. These, after all, are the most important experiences for understanding and improving life on Earth.

Whether because of disinterest, skepticism about religious or spiritual matters, or the belief that it is pointless to attempt to measure the "immeasurable," it wasn't until the final decades of the last century that sociologists and others turned their full attention to the inner life. Media commentators, furthermore, routinely ignored this dimension of life in their assessments of the state of the nation.

The Five Areas of Spiritual Survey Research

Exploration into the inner life, however, has now begun in earnest through scientific surveys and other forms of investigation. Survey research in this realm falls under five subcategories: metaphysical, historical, sociological, implementable, and theological.

Metaphysical: Scientific surveys can shed light on the beliefs of humankind related to first principles and the ultimate basis of existence. A key focus of such exploration is the "religious or mystical experience," a sudden transcendent moment of insight or awakening that seems to lift one out of oneself and offer a glimpse into a world of connectedness, peace, and love.

The challenge to survey research science is to probe beneath the surface of life, deep into the center of the human psyche where a common universal voice of someone or something is heard.

Religious or mystical experiences frequently take the form of "healing." Twenty-seven percent of Americans say they have experienced a "remarkable healing," with 21 percent noting a physical healing and 16 percent a psychological or emotional healing. Inspired by such findings as these, Dr. Dale Matthews wrote in *The Faith Factor* that the relationship between faith and faith healing is no longer simply conjecture:

The lessons my patients and others have learned from personal experience are echoed in over three hundred clinical studies that demonstrate one simple fact: faith is good medicine. Indeed, the medical effect of religious commitment is not a matter of faith, but of science, and both doctors and patients are taking part in a revolutionary convergence of medicine and faith, which is transforming the way people seek healing.[1]

Historical: A full understanding of a given society includes an awareness and knowledge of the spiritual underpinnings of that society. A large majority of Americans (eight in ten) are found to believe that the overall health of the nation depends on the spiritual health of its citizens. It is important to ask: What is the *spiritual state of the union?*

The CRRUCS/Gallup Spiritual Index represented the combined efforts of the Center for Research on Religion and Urban Civil Society (CRRUCS) at the University of Pennsylvania, The Gallup Organization, and The George H. Gallup International Institute. The Index sought to measure the breadth and depth of spirituality and religious faith in the United States and to shed light on the relationship of these factors to national well-being.

The CRRUCS/Gallup Spiritual Index, as reported in January 2003, stood at 74.7 percent out of a possible score of 100 percent. Although scores for individual respondents ran the full gamut from 0 to 100, the average score was 74.7 percent (plus or minus 1.4 points). This figure was the average of the measures for two key components:

1. *Inner Commitment*—These questions were designed to gauge feelings of connection with a God, a Divine Will, a Higher Power, etc. The average score on this set of questions was 79.8 percent (plus or minus 1.5 points) out of a possible 100 percent.
2. *Outer Commitment*—These questions tapped the ways inner commitment was being lived out in service to others, to one's community, and to society as a whole. The average American's score on this scale stood at 69.5 percent (plus or minus 1.5 points) out of a possible 100 percent.

Sociological: A mounting body of findings from surveys and other sources point to the power of the "spiritual dynamic" or the "faith factor" in the United States and in other nations. Deeply spiritually or religiously committed people experience less stress and cope better with the stress they do experience. They have fewer drug and alcohol problems, less depression, and lower rates of suicide. They enjoy their lives more than do less spiritually or religiously committed individuals.

Implementable: Survey research into the inner life can be of significant practical value to faith communities in shedding light on levels of belief, practice, and knowledge among both the churched and unchurched. With polling findings today revealing an unprecedented desire for spiritual and religious growth among Americans and people of other nations, faith communities face a historic moment of opportunity.

Theological: If one does not subscribe to "reductionism" (that is, taking an

approach that explains away God), one could maintain that it is of prime importance to use those survey tools available to gain insight into the response of humans
to God. Indeed, this pursuit could be described as the most profound and worthy
goal of scientific sampling. We honor God in recording how lives had been transformed by belief in God. We honor God by discovering those things that bring people closer to God. We honor God by helping people discover their God-given talents
and strengths, which can be used to build healthier faith communities, as documented by the creative work in the "gifts-based" ministry of Albert Winseman and
others at The Gallup Organization.

The Spirit of Change—A Change in Spirit

Author and theologian Michael Novak, on the eve of the current century, expressed
the view that the twenty-first century would likely be the most religious century of
the last five hundred years. In *The New Christendom*, Philip Jenkins writes about the
explosion of Christianity in the Southern hemisphere (specifically in Africa, South
America, and Asia) and the lack of attention given to this phenomenon:

> I suggest that it is precisely religious changes that are the most significant,
> and even the most revolutionary in the contemporary world. . . . We are
> currently living through one of the most transforming moments in the his-
> tory of religion worldwide.[2]

The U.S. public's views on the future shape of religion and spirituality were
sought in a survey conducted for the John Templeton Foundation by The Gallup
Organization in 2000 ("Religious Beliefs, Spiritual Practices and Science in the 21st
Century"). The U.S. public, the survey revealed, generally expected there would be
a surge in spiritual and religious feelings that would profoundly affect the world
scene. This, they believed, would be fed by global communications, discoveries in
astronomy, and an extended lifespan.

Six in ten in the survey thought that religious beliefs and spiritual practices would
change the way we think over the next one hundred years. And by the ratio of four
to one, Americans predicted that such beliefs and practices would become more of
a force in people's lives. Eight in ten predicted that such beliefs and practices would
have either a great deal or some impact on the course of history.

Eight in ten survey respondents said it was either very or fairly likely that individuals would experience advancement in religious beliefs or spiritual growth over
the next one hundred years. They saw this happening with individuals; among families; in the areas of politics, medical research, and education; and in terms of
encouraging greater acceptance of religious and cultural diversity.

Seven in ten, according to this survey in 2000, agreed that greater understanding
between religious groups would lead to more harmony and reconciliation. (It
should be noted that this survey was conducted before September 11, 2001. One of
the key areas to be monitored in the years ahead will be relations between Christians
and Muslims, as well as people of other religions.)

One of the most exciting pursuits of scientific surveys will be to identify the forerunners of the coming age—the "advance" men and women who will lead us to a higher level of civilization anchored in a loving God.

These "forerunners" are probably very much like the "everyday saints" whom Tim Jones and I interviewed for our book *The Saints among Us*. These are persons who have yielded their lives to God, have a sense of the nearness of God, and are able to live in other people's lives to a remarkable extent. Transformed individuals such as these are having an impact on societies far out of proportion to their numbers. They are the "quiet leaders" of our day, responsible for populaces being more kind, tolerant, forgiving, loving, and optimistic.

The saints are new heroes for an age of moral spiritual leadership. They are role models for the future. Swedish theologian Nathan Soderblom once said, "Saints are persons who make it easier to believe in God."

Here is what William James wrote about "saints," more than a century ago, in his classic *The Varieties of Religious Experience*:

> The saints . . . are the great torchbearers . . . the tip of the wedge, the clearers of the darkness. Like the single drops which sparkle in the sun as they are flung far ahead of an advancing wave-crest or of a flood, they show the way and are forerunners. The world is not yet with them, so they often seem in the midst of the world's affairs to be preposterous. Yet they are impregnators of the world, vivifiers and animators of potentialities of goodness which but for them would lie forever dormant.[3]

Writing from a Christian perspective, C. S. Lewis in *Mere Christianity* described people who have been transformed by Jesus Christ into "new men":

> Already the new men (and women) are dotted here and there all over the earth. Every now and then one meets them. Their very voices and faces are different from ours: stronger, quieter, happier, and more radiant. They begin where most of us leave off. . . . They will not be very much like the idea of "religious people" which you have formed from your general reading. They do not draw attention to themselves. You tend to think that you are being kind to them when they are really being kind to you. They love you more often than other men do, but they need you less.[4]

The inner life, which remains largely unexplored internationally at this point in history, could be said to be the "new frontier" of survey research, in a new era of discovery—not of the world around us, but of the world within us. We can be certain that the "spiritual information" that will be revealed will be as thrilling as the discoveries thus far made of our external earthly domain.

☞

GEORGE H. GALLUP JR. has been in the field of polling for half a century, serving in executive roles at the Gallup Poll, The Gallup Organization, and most recently as Chairman of The George H. Gallup International Institute. Much of his work has been focused on spirituality and religion, having directed more than one hundred special surveys in these areas. Mr. Gallup received his B.A. from Princeton University's Department of Religion in 1954 and holds seven honorary degrees. He has served on many boards dealing with education, religion, youth, and urban problems, among others. He is author of numerous books, including: *The Gallup Guide: Reality Check for Churches in the 21st Century* (2002); *Surveying the Religious Landscape: Trends in US Beliefs* (1999); *The Next American Spirituality: Finding God in the Twenty-First Century* (2000); *Growing up Scared in America: And What Experts Say Parents Can Do About It* (1996); and *The Saints Among Us* (1992). Mr. Gallup is currently a Trustee of the John Templeton Foundation.

NOTES

1 Dale A. Matthews, M.D., with Connie Clark, *The Faith Factor: Proof of the Healing Power of Prayer.* New York: Viking Publishing, 1998.

2 Philip Jenkins, *The Next Christendom: The Coming of Global Christianity.* New York: Oxford University Press, 2002; 2.

3 William James, *The Varieties of Religious Experience.* London: Longmans, Green and Co., 1902, The Penguin American Library, 1982.

4 C. S. Lewis, *Mere Christianity.* New York: Macmillan Publishing Co., Inc., 1943; paperback edition, 1960, 187–88.

Theological Fiction and the Future 20

Gregory A. Benford

Freeman Dyson's insightful piece on the tradition of theological fiction in the March 2002 *New York Review of Books* implies a gap in the current literary world:

> Between science and theology there is a genre of literature which I like to call *theofiction*. Theofiction adapts the style and conventions of science fiction to tell stories that have more to do with theology than with science.

His examples include the novels of Octavia Butler (a MacArthur Grant winner), C. S. Lewis, Madeleine L'Engle, and, principally, Olaf Stapledon. These works remain in print many decades after publication and point to a continuing interest in theofiction.

Where is this genre headed? Advancing fronts of science and technology provoke theological conflicts and fundamental questions. If science and Godhood are to find common ground, they will meet in the imaginations of writers.

In the twentieth century, the Big Bang had considerable theological impact, enshrining the idea of Creation. Viewed through the lens of general relativity, which stated that space and time were created simultaneously, literally nothing happened "before"—because there *was* no "before." Theologically, the Big Bang showed that St. Augustine was right and that popular religion was mistaken in its view that God existed in the stream of "time" before Creation.

I also believe that the emerging concern for long-term prospects comes, at least in part, from our greatly expanded lifetimes. Figure 1 shows how greatly our prospect for longevity has grown. Reflect that the average lifespan of a man born in 1900 was forty-eight years. All the great religions were born in times when a man of forty-eight was *old*. Early cultures' concerns for origins may have arisen from the short lives of their populations.

Our ideas about the future hinge on theological assumptions geared to those distant eras. The year 2100 may hold a greater prospect for longevity, as the figure projects, giving birth to a similar greater interest in the far future. What theologies will emerge from such an expanded view?

We have always had some sort of cosmology, however simple. Our yearning for connection explains many cultures' ancestor worship: We enter into a sense of progression, expecting to be included eventually in the company of the venerated. Deep within us lies a need for continuity of the human enterprise, perhaps to offset our own mortality. Deep time's panoramas, both past and future, redeem this lack of meaning, rendering the human prospect again large and portentous.

FIGURE 1. As our prospects of living longer have improved, so have our attitudes toward the far future altered.

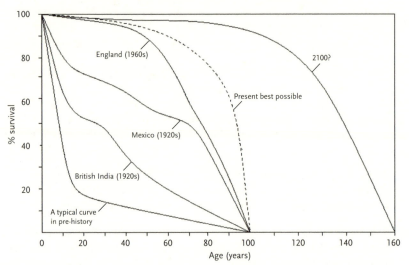

We gain stature alongside such enormousness. This presents us with an ultimate question: Will the time come when humanity itself will not be remembered, our works lost and gone for nothing? To illuminate the interplay between fact and fiction, here I shall treat one major idea just emerging—linking the human prospect to cosmology. By considering the far future, I expect that cosmology will have similarly large implications for theology and popular religion alike. These ideas may yield, in a more nuanced mode, hints that the cosmos we inhabit may be rich with purpose, or at least provide a discernible goal for life.

A major change in our ideas of cosmology occurred only a few years ago, with the discovery that our universe's expansion is *accelerating*—implying a forever-growing cosmos. Some feel repulsed by the entire notion. Evolution may have programmed us to expect cycles; the seasons deeply embedded this notion in our ancestors' thinking, as in the ancient Hindu system.

The Abrahamic faiths "of the book"—Jews, Christians, and Muslims alike—envision linear, not cyclic, time. Christian scripture says that this is a suffering world, addicted to attachment, ultimately to be transcended. God's agenda is rigorous: creation, fall, incarnation, redemption, final judgment, and then the ultimate fate—Last Things. The far future then lies beyond that goal. We moderns think long; the far future matters to us.

William Shakespeare's works endure—yet, forever? As Bertrand Russell put it in *Why I Am Not a Christian:*

> All the labours of the ages, all the devotion, all the inspiration, all the noonday brightness of human genius are destined to extinction in the vast heat death of the solar system, and . . . the whole temple of man's achievement must inevitably be buried beneath the debris of a universe in ruins.

So he doesn't believe in God because nothing lasts.

Yet the opposite, Paradise, seems boring to many, if it is mere joyful indolence. But is perpetual novelty even possible? Can we think an infinite variety of thoughts? These ideas converge in our present understanding of the very far future, our ultimate destiny. Science may be able to settle whether this eternally deferred arrival is physically possible.

Kurt Gödel's famous theorem showed that mathematics contains inexhaustible novelty: true theorems that can't be proved with what has come before. Only by expanding the conceptual system can they be proved. Most people would not turn to mathematics for a message of spiritual hope, but there it is.

So theofiction confronting this subject must face a paradox. We seem to harbor twin desires—purpose and novelty, progress and eternity alike.

Christian theology solved this dilemma by putting God outside time, so that holy eternity was not of infinite duration but rather *not time at all.* This belief is longstanding, but it need not stay in fashion forever. Faiths may arise that long for the heat death, or embrace the coming Big Crunch, becoming cosmological cheerleaders for cleansing ends.

In 1979, Freeman Dyson's *Reviews of Modern Physics* paper "Time Without End" brought this entire issue to center stage for physicists and astronomers. He already had his prejudices: He wouldn't countenance the Big Crunch option because it gave him "a feeling of claustrophobia." What was the prognosis for intelligent life? Even after stars have died, he asked, can life survive forever without intellectual burnout?

Energy reserves are finite, and at first sight this might seem to be a basic restriction. But he showed that this constraint was actually not fatal. He looked beyond the time when stars will have tunneled into black holes, which would then evaporate in a time that will be, in comparison, almost instantaneous. As J. D. Bernal foresaw in *The World, the Flesh, and the Devil* (1929):

> . . . consciousness itself may end . . . becoming masses of atoms in space communicating by radiation, and ultimately resolving itself entirely into light . . . these beings . . . each utilizing the bare minimum of energy . . . spreading themselves over immense areas and periods of time . . . the scene of life would be . . . the cold emptiness of space.

In the twenty-three years since Dyson's article appeared, our perspective has changed in two ways—and both make the outlook more dismal. First, most physicists now suspect that atoms don't live forever. The basic building block, the proton, will decay into lesser particles. White dwarfs and neutron stars will erode away, maybe in 10^{36} years. The heat generated by particle decay will make each star glow, but only as dimly as a domestic heater.

We speak here of *very* long times. By then our local group of galaxies would be just a swarm of dark matter, electrons, and positrons. Thoughts and memories would only survive beyond the first 10^{36} years if preserved electromagnetically in clouds of electrons and positrons—maybe something that resembles the threatening alien intelligence in *The Black Cloud*, the first and most imaginative of astronomer Fred Hoyle's science fiction novels.

As this darkened universe expands and cools, lower-energy quanta can be used to store or transmit information. Just as an infinite series can have a finite sum (for instance, $1 + \frac{1}{2} + \frac{1}{4} + \ldots\ldots = 2$), so there is no limit to the amount of information processing that could be achieved with a finite expenditure of energy. Any conceivable form of life would have to keep ever-cooler, think ever-more slowly, and hibernate for ever-longer periods.

But there would be time to think every thought. As Woody Allen once said, "Eternity is very long, especially toward the end."

Characteristically, Dyson was optimistic about the potentiality of an open universe because there seems to be no limit to the scale of artifacts that could eventually be built. He envisioned the observable universe getting ever vaster. Many galaxies, whose light hasn't yet had time to reach us, would eventually come into view, and therefore within range of possible communication and "networking." Interactions will matter.

These long-range projections involve fascinating physics, most of which is quite well understood. But what happens in zillions of years has vast uncertainties as well. These ideas will probably loom larger as we learn more about the destiny of all visible Creation.

Theofiction can confront even such grand epochs. This area of science and literature gives one example of its power to inform and shape our human agenda. Fiction at the cutting edge of these developments is still rare and should be encouraged.

The Odyssey was a founding text of Western civilization, an imaginative fiction about fantastic events. Grand epics of the far future could set our ideas just as powerfully.

ℒ♥

GREGORY A. BENFORD, PH.D., is Professor of Physics at the University of California, Irvine. He specializes in plasma plastic theory and was presented with the Lord Prize in 1995 for achievements in the sciences. Dr. Benford has served as an advisor to NASA, the U.S. Department of Energy, and the White House Council on Space Policy. He has received two Nebula awards for science fiction writing. In 1992, Dr. Benford received the United Nations Medal in Literature. He is the author of nearly 130 research papers in his field and several books, including *Timescape* (1980), *Deep Time* (1999), and *Cosm* (1999).

PART THREE

Perspectives from Cosmology, Physics, and Astronomy

Outward Bound 21

John D. Barrow

O NE OF THE MOST interesting features of the pattern of progress in science is the way in which greater understanding of reality, and our increasing success in predicting its changes, has grown hand in hand with its growing separation from human-centered experience. When we look for the most accurate predictions of the way the world works, they are not to be found in our attempts to understand the activities of society, fluctuations in financial markets, or vagaries of the weather. Rather, it is in describing the interactions of elementary particles or the motions of distant astronomical objects where accuracies of one part in 10^{16} are to be found.

Some sociologists of science have argued that the human contribution to scientific theories is the dominant factor in their success, not their uncovering of any objective reality. But if the latter were true, we would expect our scientific theories to become less and less successful when applied to the extremes of inner and outer space. We would expect to find them at their weakest when applied to environments that were far removed from immediate human experience or the circumstances out of which natural selection has fashioned our senses and sensibilities over millions of years. Exactly the opposite is found. It is in the description of events outside of the direct realm of human experience where our power to predict and explain is best and those areas closest to human intuition and experience are worst, by virtue of their intrinsic complexity. Just because there is an undeniable sociology of science does not mean that science is nothing but its sociology.

The course of scientific progress can be seen as a march toward a conception of reality that is divorced from human bias as much as possible. There are several landmarks on this outward journey from us to ultimate reality. First, Copernicus taught us that we should not expect the world to revolve around us; the structure of the universe guarantees us no special location in space. Then Darwin taught us that we are not the culmination of any special design, and Lyell discovered that most of earth's geological history went by, rather eventfully, without us. These insights do not mean that our location in the universe cannot be special in *some* ways (as the Anthropic Principle shows); we could not expect to live in a place where life is impossible, like the center of a star, for example. But our location must not be special in every way. We know that our location in time is indeed rather special, in a niche of cosmic history about fourteen billion years since the universe's expansion began, after the stars first formed but before they die. This is why we should not be surprised to find our universe to be so big and old.

Deeper still was the insight of Einstein, who showed how to express the laws of Nature so that they look the same to all observers, no matter where they are or how they are moving. Newton's famous laws of motion did not possess this universal expression. They would only be seen to take their simple form by special observers who move in a simple way, without acceleration or rotation. For these special observers, the universe's laws would appear simpler than they would for others. Such an undemocratic situation was a signal to Einstein that something was wrong in our conception of Nature's laws. And he was right. Now we express the basic laws of Nature in forms that would be found by all observers investigating the universe, from Vega to Vegas, wherever they are, whenever they look, no matter how they are moving. This is the second step.

The third great step in the divorce of science from human idiosyncrasy occurred when a further ingredient was recognized. Besides the laws of Nature and their outcomes, the structure of the universe around us is determined by a collection of unchanging qualities that we can encode in a list of numbers that we call the "constants of Nature." These qualities include things such as the masses of the smallest subatomic particles, the strengths of the forces of Nature, and the speed of light in vacuum. They are quantified by ever-more-precise measurement, and in the backs of physics books the world over you will find their latest values listed to large numbers of decimal places. These quantities generally have units—the speed of light is measured in meters per second or furlongs per fortnight—which are often rather anthropocentric: centimeters, feet, and inches are conveniently related to the scale of the human frame. Or, equally, they may be geocentric or heliocentric in origin—days and years are units of time that derive from the time for the Earth to rotate once on its axis and to orbit the Sun. These constants are far from universal. They describe properties of pieces of metal or the lengths of standard meters kept in special containers in laboratories on earth. But gradually, physicists realized that the universal constants of Nature allowed standards of mass, length, and time to be defined that did not depend on particular human-made artifacts. By counting the wavelengths of light emitted by a certain species of atom, or counting its vibrations, or the mass of its nucleus, it is possible to define units of length, time, and mass that can be communicated through interstellar space to physicists who had never seen Earth or human physicists.

This march toward established constants of Nature that were not explicitly anthropocentric, but based on the discovery and definition of universal constants of Nature, can be seen as a super-Copernican step. The fabric of the universe and the pivotal structure of universal laws were seen to flow from standards and invariants that were truly superhuman and extraterrestrial. The fundamental standard of time in Nature, just 10^{-43} of our seconds and defined by the gravitational, quantum, and relativistic constants of Nature, bore no simple relation to the ages of man and woman; no link to the periods of days, months, and years that defined our calendars; and was too short to allow any possibility of direct measurement.

These steps have depersonalized physics and astronomy in the sense that they attempt to classify and understand the things in the universe with reference only to principles that hold for any observer anywhere. If we have identified those constants and laws correctly, then they provide us with the only basis we know on which to base a dialog with extraterrestrial intelligences other than ourselves. They will be the ultimate shared experience for everyone who inhabits our universe.

Modern cosmology makes one further tantalizing suggestion about the nature of the universe. Before the inception of Einstein's general theory of relativity, all theories of physics were of a similar sort. They provided mathematical formulae that could be used to predict how things would move or change when they encountered other things. They described the action of forces, such as gravity, magnetism, and motion. But in all cases, these laws described the actions of the forces and motions *in* the universe and within its prespecified space and time. No motion or force could alter the Nature of space or of time. They were fixed: God-given and eternal.

Einstein changed all that. His theory is far more sophisticated. When the particles and their motions are introduced into a world governed by the general theory of relativity, they dictate the very geometry of the space and the flow of time. This curved space and time dictates how matter and energy can move, and its motion in turn tells space and time how to curve. It is this feature that gives Einstein's theory its most remarkable quality. *Every solution of Einstein's equations describes an entire universe.* Some are very simple—too simple to describe our universe as a whole, but very useful for describing parts of it; some are more elaborate and provide us with wonderfully accurate descriptions of our entire visible universe. Others describe universes different from our own and impress on us the remarkable nature of its special properties. We hear a lot about that accurate description of our universe, of its past and its present, and of what to expect in the far, far future. But it has passed unnoticed how remarkable it is that a mathematical theory, a collection of penstrokes on a piece of paper, can provide a description of an entire universe. The fact that there can exist a mathematical structure of which our whole universe is a particular outcome is rather astonishing. There could be no stronger evidence of the inadequacy of materialism and no better argument for the reality of a logic behind the appearances that is larger than visible reality itself. How amazing that the mathematical structure that appears to be something bigger than the astronomical universe itself is the very means by which we can understand its workings. Superhuman the universe may be, but the ultimate simplicity of the mathematical reality at its heart is what enables us to understand it and have faith that our understanding can converge on the truth.

✍

JOHN D. BARROW, D. PHIL, FRS, received his doctorate in Astrophysics from the University of Oxford (1977). He held positions at Oxford and the University of California, Berkeley before becoming Professor of Astronomy and then Director of the Astronomy Centre at the University of Sussex (1981-99). In 1999 Professor Barrow took up his current appointment as Professor of Mathematical Sciences at the University of Cambridge, where he is also Director of the Millennium Mathematics Project and a Fellow and Vice-President of Clare Hall. He is also the current Gresham Professor of Astronomy (2003-06) at Gresham College, London. He was elected a Fellow of the Royal Society in 2003 and served as a member of the Council of the Royal Astronomical Society. He is a recipient of the Locker Prize for Astronomy (1989), the Kelvin Medal of the Royal Glasgow Philosophical Society (1999), and the Lacchini Medal for Astronomy (2005). Professor Barrow was also awarded an honorary Doctor of Science degree by the University of Hertfordshire (1999). He is the author of more than 380 scientific papers in cosmology, astrophysics and mathematics and seventeen books, translated into twenty-eight languages, that explore historical, philosophical, and cultural aspects of astronomy, physics, and mathematics; these include *The Constants of Nature: From Alpha to Omega* and, most recently, *The Infinite Book: A Short Guide to the Boundless, Timeless, and Endless.* He is also the author of the successful play, *Infinities,* which was performed (in Italian) at the Teatro Piccolo, in Milan (2002 and 2003), directed by Luca Ronconi, and in Spanish at the Valencia Festival (2002) and for which he received the Premi Ubu Theatre Prize (2002) and the Italgas Prize (2003) for contributions to Italian scientific culture. Professor Barrow has given many named lectures, including the 1989 Gifford Lectures at the University of Glasgow. With Paul C.W. Davies and Charles L. Harper, Jr., he is co-editor of *Science & Ultimate Reality: Quantum Theory, Cosmology and Complexity* (Cambridge University Press, 2004) and, with Simon Conway Morris, Stephen J. Freeland, and Charles L. Harper, Jr., co-editor of *Fitness of the Cosmos for Life: Biochemistry and Fine-Tuning,* forthcoming from Cambridge University Press.

AN ECHO OF ANCIENT QUESTIONS FROM CONTEMPORARY COSMOLOGY 22

Marco Bersanelli

F OR THOUSANDS OF YEARS, humankind has perceived itself within a virtually unlimited earthly environment under the mysterious expanse of the sky. Only in the last few centuries—less than 0.1 percent of the human presence on Earth—has scientific knowledge led us to a sudden, breathtaking awareness of the nature, structure, and astonishing size of our cosmic environment. Perhaps the most controversial and amazing step was Copernicus's removal of the Earth from the cosmic center, reducing its status to just one of several planets orbiting the Sun. Eventually, the Sun was recognized as one of an inestimable multitude of stars. In the mid-1920s, Edwin Hubble demonstrated that spiral nebulae constitute vast "island universes" containing hundreds of billions of stars. Since the introduction of the telescope early in the seventeenth century, the size of the measured universe has grown by fifteen orders of magnitude, or a million billion times. Today we know that the horizon of our observable universe is a sphere 13.7 billion light-years in radius, growing at the rate of 26 billion kilometers per day. And we know that this is a fundamental boundary: At any moment, we simply can't see what lies beyond.

Recent developments in cosmology further solidify the impression of our marginality in the universe. We now understand that the type of material that makes everything we know—including us—is only a tiny fraction of the universe's mass-energy content. Recent measurements of distant supernovae (Perlmutter et al. 1998) and of the cosmic microwave background (Bennett et al. 2003; Bersanelli et al. 2002) indicate precise proportions for the main types of mass-energy ingredients of our universe. Only about 4 percent is in the form of baryons and other familiar types of matter; the rest is made up of an unknown "cold dark matter" component (approximately 23 percent) and an even more exotic "dark energy" (about 73 percent), possibly associated with vacuum energy. Consequently, we don't know what 96 percent of our accessible universe is made of; however, we do know that most of it consists of something radically different from what makes us and all known objects.

Ancient Queries and Infinite Longings

We are like nothing in a cosmos whose vastness and diversity surpass our imagination. But well before modern cosmology and our use of highly sensitive instruments, the ancient Jews posed a fundamental question: "When I consider your heavens, the work of your fingers, the moon and the stars, which you have set in place, what is man that you are mindful of him, the son of man that you care for him?" (Psalm 8:4–5). After three thousand years, modern science brings us back to the same deep question with new insights, new language, and newly added dramatic force. What are we in this immensity of the universe? On our small planet, we feel lost in a seemingly wasteful huge space: What is the purpose of such an enormous abyss out there? We are fashioned out of material that is marginal in nature's overall budget: Why is there so much "reality" that appears superfluous and alien to our human condition?

But the psalmist continues by immediately opening up another part of the paradox: "Yet, you made him a little lower than the heavenly beings, and crowned him with glory and honor" (Psalm 8:6–7). Indeed, humans are exceedingly special creatures. The "I" of every single human being—whose body is a pointlike fragment of the physical universe—exists as a sort of "singularity" in which nature reveals unheard-of properties: self-consciousness and freedom. We often lack appreciation of the "unnecessary" and "incomprehensible" status of creatures like us. Biological systems successfully selected by evolution could well exist with no a priori need of consciousness and self-awareness—as has been true for 99.9 percent of the history of life on Earth. Yet humans are gifted with a personal existence in which the whole universe is reflected: With our self-aware nature, we strive to find meaning for ourselves and for all things (Giussani 1997). As Thomas Aquinas notes: "*Anima est quodammodo omnia*" (The spirit of a man is in a certain way all things) (*De Veritate*, In Summa Theologiae, I, q. 14).

Scientists of all ages have expressed their wonder at the enigmatic condition of human nature (Bersanelli and Gargantini 2003). Pioneer astronomer Maria Mitchell suggests, "These immense spaces of creation cannot be spanned by our finite powers . . . but the vibrations set in motion by the words that we utter reach through all space, and the tremor is felt through all times." Even an infinite array of infinite worlds, such as those postulated in some multiverse theories, would be way too narrow to satisfy the extent of human desire and aspiration. The "Infinity" that we long for cannot be filled by any endless amount of space, time, matter, or any other physical quantity. The Italian poet Giacomo Leopardi expressed this idea poignantly, lamenting, but with awe, that humans suffer from

> . . . the inability to be satisfied by any worldly thing or, so to speak, by the entire world. To consider the inestimable amplitude of space, the number of worlds and their astonishing size—then to discover that all this is small and insignificant compared to the capacity of one's own mind; to imagine the infinite number of worlds, the infinite universe, then feel that our mind and aspirations might be even greater than such a universe; to accuse things always of being inadequate and meaningless; to suffer want, emptiness, and hence ennui—this seems to me the chief sign of the grandeur and nobility of human nature (Leopardi, *Pensieri*, LXVIII).

Cosmological Answers and the Nature of "Reality"

It is strange that creatures such as us, clearly structured to embrace the totality of things, appear to be physically insignificant at a universal level. In the past few decades, scientific progress has added new and unexpected elements to the debate. Nuclear physicists have shown that the heavy elements necessary for biological chemistry are the result of nuclear reactions within stars that require an exquisite balance in the laws of nature. Moreover, fundamental parameters such as the relative strength of the four fundamental forces, the mass and charge of elementary particles, the rate of cosmic expansion in the early universe, and the number of space and time dimensions appear precisely tuned to allow complexity to emerge (Barrow and Tipler 1984). We do not know how diffuse life is in our galaxy and beyond; certainly, the list of universal circumstances necessary for life's existence *anywhere* remains way too long to discuss here. Interestingly, even if we don't yet understand the nature of dark matter and dark energy, cosmologists already recognize how both components probably played a central role in creating galaxies in a cold, empty space—structures ultimately needed to give rise to life and to human existence.

A number of multiverse theories have been proposed that allow us to interpret these apparent coincidences as selection effects. The most extreme multiverse scenarios become modern reiterations of the old "Principle of Plenitude," which claims that anything that might potentially exist does exist (Lovejoy 1936). Even in this case, however, the fundamental question of why there is a reality at all remains unanswered, and a paradox may arise when pushing the multiverse approach too far. Recently, it has been argued that the *ultimate* form of multiverse is one in which every sub-universe is identified as one among all possible mathematical structures, each possessing an actual physical existence (Tegmark 2003). Some of them—like our universe—would be unbelievably complex, others trivially simple. In this vision, the physical multiverse coincides with the space of all mathematical possibilities. Now, if mathematics is a product of our human minds, then our mental creativity would be the source of the physical existence of all things—indeed, we would inhabit a very self-centered universe! On the other hand, mathematical objects might not be our inventions; rather, they could be the texture of reality itself. Even in this case, however, when we recognize a given abstract entity as *mathematical*, we necessarily use our brain's logical system to make this recognition from within the limits of our own mind. So we say that "the set of complex numbers" is a mathematical object, but "the scent of roses" is not—and we all agree. The criterion that qualifies a given package of symbols and rules as a "mathematical structure" (and therefore as a truly existing parallel universe) is written in the logical pattern of our intellect. Therefore, a particular understanding that our species has developed would coincide with the essential element that defines the physical existence of all things, which would mean that Homo sapiens possesses the yardstick for what does and does not exist. Ironically, therefore, the most general version of multiverse theory appears to coincide with the view of an ultimately anthropocentric universe. In fact, this scenario may appear more rigidly "homo-centered" than the hint of an anthropic design that multiverse theories seek to explain in terms of selection effects.

To avoid this situation, one could attempt further generalization. Could what we call "mathematics" represent just another layer of selection effect? Maybe the space of all mathematical patterns should be regarded as a particular case of a vastly wider metalogical space in which very basic concepts such as "symbol" and "rule" assume broader meanings, completely beyond the range of our comprehension. Moreover, infinite metamathematical multiverses might be postulated, each with a real physical existence; perhaps even the concept of "physical existence" might then be generalized, and so on. Unfortunately, however, we have now arrived at a place where by definition we don't know what we are talking about! Both our imaginations and our words break down, and we are lost in a desert of nonsense.

As long as language contains meaning, the extreme multiverse speculations seem to drive us toward a radically human mind–centered view of the world. In my opinion, this conclusion makes the concept of an ultimate multiverse unlikely. We have learned to be skeptical about hypotheses supported by scarce data leading to anthropocentric conclusions. Indeed, physical reality is likely to be deeper and more surprising than we can imagine. Inflation theories suggest that regions beyond our cosmic horizon may be highly diverse and exotic, so that our visible universe might indeed represent a unique cosmic habitat. High-precision observations in the near future will be able to test the inflation paradigm, but what lies beyond our horizon will always be out of reach. We should be careful with any drastic extrapolation into unlimited unknown territory based solely on what we see in our cosmic garden.

The Interconnectedness of All That Is

The uncontroversial and yet remarkable fact is that from subatomic particles to superclusters, nature appears far more deeply and actively interconnected in our lives than we might have ever guessed before the advent of science. A thousand years ago, all farmers knew that they owed their lives to the sun, rain, and regularity of seasons. Now we know that life is rooted much deeper in the soil of nature. Not only do we need sun and clouds, but we could not exist without cosmic expansion, dark matter, supernovae explosions, neutrinos, plate tectonics—the list is long. The universe would be hostile to life without very specific and yet sufficiently "flexible" fundamental laws. Furthermore, the local astronomical and geological characteristics of any environment supporting complex animal life must be extremely stable and yet delicate, as in the case of planet Earth (Ward and Brownlee 2000); the coupling of local requirements with universal physical parameters is likely to be even more sophisticated. No one has yet systematically explored how far the chain of dependencies extends that connect biological complexity to all observable physical structures. But certainly no farmer or scientist a century ago would have imagined that things such as the size of our universe or the speed of light are precisely what they need to be in order to give life a chance.

Contemporary science touches on some deep perceptions that the Judeo-Christian tradition has introduced and developed. Consider again the psalmist and his appreciation of order, aesthetics, and creativity in the universe: "How many are your works, O Lord. In wisdom you made them all" (Psalm 104:24). Likewise, Isaiah perceives the cosmos as an active element contributing to life: "He stretches out the heavens like a canopy, and spreads them out like a tent to live in" (Isaiah 40:22). That same universe that science initially seemed to have taken apart and made foreign to us may now regain its own unity when understood as a hospitable environment for life and for consciousness. Scientific knowledge is not equipped, I believe, to answer profound ultimate questions; however, some recent scientific developments have provided effective ways to rediscover them in new, rational, and dramatic terms. In the long run, science will need this openness to preserve its fascination for us, as well as its credibility and perspective.

✍

MARCO BERSANELLI, PH.D., is Associate Professor in Astrophysics at the University of Milan, where he does research in cosmology. He is particularly interested in observations of the cosmic microwave background, the relic radiation from the early universe. After graduating from the University of Milan in 1986, Professor Bersanelli worked as Visiting Scholar at the Lawrence Berkeley Laboratory, University of California, and then at Istituto di Fisica Cosmica, CNR, Milan, as Senior Scientist. He participated in a number of experiments in cosmology, including two expeditions to the Amundsen-Scott South Pole Station, Antarctica. Professor Bersanelli is Instrument Scientist and a member of the Science Team of the Planck Surveyor space mission, the European Space Agency project studying the early universe. He is president of Euresis, a scientific and cultural association promoting interdisciplinary dialog on frontier topics in science, and has given many public seminars, coordinated public exhibits, and published essays exploring the links between science and the religious sense. Professor Bersanelli is author of the book *Solo lo stupore conosce* (Rizzoli, 2003) about the human adventure of scientific research.

REFERENCES

Barrow, J. D.; and F. J. Tipler. *The Anthropic Cosmological Principle*. Oxford: Clarendon, 1986.

Bennett, C., et al. "First Year Wilkinson Microwave Anisotropy Probe (WMAP) Observations: Preliminary Maps and Basic Results," *The Astrophysical Journal Suppl. Ser.*, No. 148, pp. 1–27, 2003.

Bersanelli, M., M. Gargantini. "Solo lo stupore conosce," *BUR*, Milano: Rizzoli, 2003.

Bersanelli, M., D. Maino, A. Mennella. "Anisotropies of the Cosmic Microwave Background," *La Rivista del Nuovo Cimento*, No. 9, pp. 1–82, 2002.

Giussani, L. *The Religious Sense*. McGill: Queen's University Press, 1997.

Lovejoy, A. O. *The Great Chain of Being*. Cambridge: Harvard University Press, 1936.

Progress in Scientific and Spiritual Understanding 23

George F. R. Ellis

Progress in physical cosmology has been dramatic since 1965, with the hot Big Bang model of the early universe now being vindicated by a variety of concurring observations. Simultaneously with this in the last century we have made great progress in understanding the nature of matter on the one hand, through development of quantum field theory and the standard model of particle physics, and experienced extraordinary breakthroughs in understanding the physical basis of life on the other, in particular through identifying both the molecular basis of the genetic code and the neurological basis of brain functioning.

These triumphs throw amazing light on the nature of the Creator, for he has devised all these marvelous mechanisms that allow our existence. Today, it is unfashionable for physicists to consider themselves to be exploring the mind of God, but, of course, that is what they are doing. He is the particle physicist, cosmologist, and group theorist supreme, a chemist and biologist in addition—the master of both fundamental physics and complexity. Thus, scientific progress can be regarded as a major step toward discovering greater spiritual information. However, other aspects of the mind of God are not touched by these developments—for example, those to do with justice and rightness, with love and mercy, with joy and beauty. In these areas, too, progress has been made, although not as dramatic or rapid. Indeed, much of the "progress" made has been nothing other than the rediscovery of old truths that cannot themselves be encompassed by science. However, a major front of progress is the way we are beginning to see how new scientific discoveries—our understanding of the physical mechanisms that underlie our existence as living beings—are compatible with old spiritual truths.

Emergence of Complexity

One area of ongoing progress is our growing understanding of how the laws of physics underlie and enable the remarkable creative activity whereby matter spontaneously organizes itself into simple chemical structures and then living cells, which then through a slow evolutionary process lead to the development of plants, animals, and eventually self-aware human beings. This is the way we now need to understand how spirituality arises—through a slow evolutionary process underlying the historical emergence of complexity.

Two key features underlie the ability of physical Nature to support true complexity. First, there is the feature of top-down action in the hierarchy of physical structure. Just as lower levels of order underlie what happens at higher levels through the combined action of physical forces on fundamental particles, higher levels of order control what happens at lower levels, and hence they are able to have their own independent existence and meaning. This occurs through higher levels channeling lower-level actions according to high-level structures and boundary conditions. Second, information is incorporated in these higher levels of structure and governs their activity. It does so by setting the goals in feedback-control systems that endow matter with teleonomic properties; they are purposeful in their activity, arranged so that they attain specific goals, which thereby become causally effective. The goals are based on received information that is classified, analyzed, and remembered, thus enabling higher levels of order and meaning to emerge. At the highest level, symbolic processing and theoretical analysis drive goals and actions. However, the evolution and development of the brain is based on emotional responses, which guide brain development and function. Therefore, intellectual pursuits are not divorced from emotional responses. They are tied to each other in a deep pattern of harmony and tension. This balance is the basis of the way the brain can function as a spiritual instrument.

Cosmology and Anthropic Issues

How can the universe have a nature that allows all these complex structures to arise spontaneously through evolutionary and developmental processes? This is the new form of the Design question, where it is becoming increasingly apparent that a high degree of fine-tuning of both physical laws and cosmological boundary conditions is required so that life can function, and so any biological evolutionary process can take place at all. There are basically two options for explaining the great degree of improbability of a human-friendly ("anthropic") universe: (1) the scientific proposal that the universe we live in is just one of a host of universes that together form a "multiverse," this plenitude of universes making the existence of life in some fraction of them probable; and (2) the religious proposal that the universe was designed by a Creator.

The current issue is whether a multiverse provides a legitimate scientific explanation that can supplant the idea of a Creator. It is clear that, because of the limitations of human ability to probe the nature of what exists, the existence of a multiverse can never be proved scientifically. The humble way is to acknowledge this limitation. This is an aspect of one of the greatest kinds of progress that one can make in spirituality: to acknowledge the inevitability of intellectual uncertainty and doubt in such matters, recognizing that in the end the choice is a matter of faith.

Ethics and Meaning

Human goals are hierarchically structured, with ethics as the highest level because it determines which lower-level goals are acceptable. Ethics in turn derives its nature from the *telos*, or meaning, envisaged by the actor. The key progress recently made in this regard is the rediscovery that the basis of deep ethics is *kenosis*, a joyous, kind, and loving attitude that is willing to give up selfish desires and to make sacrifices on behalf of others for the common good, doing this in a generous and creative way and avoiding the pitfall of pride. In short, it is unlimited love, "emptying" the self in spiritual generosity.

The idea of self-sacrifice can be distorted and become a vision in which one's own self is not valued. But this is not the nature of the true idea, which is life-affirming and joyous because it extends to the self as well as the other. It is also the foundation of a profound path of social and political action, as evidenced in the writings and lives of Mahatma Gandhi, Martin Luther King Jr., and Desmond Tutu, among others. It is at the core of a truly spiritual life—a fact that has been known for thousands of years and is incorporated in the deeply spiritual traditions of all the major religions, and particularly in the life of Jesus. It is the way humility makes a true difference in individual and communal life.

Existence

The nature of existence is more complex than envisaged by any simple materialistic worldview. Opportunity for important spiritual progress lies in determining its characteristics—that is, the true nature of ontology. It can be argued that the following worlds are ontologically real:

✦ *World 1: The Physical World of Energy and Matter*, hierarchically structured to form lower and higher causal levels whose entities are all real.

This is the basic world of matter and interactions between matter, based at the micro level on elementary particles and fundamental forces, that provides the ground of physical existence. The hierarchical structure in matter is a real physical phenomenon and exists in addition to the physical constituents that make up the system.

✦ *World 2: The World of Individual and Communal Consciousness*—ideas, emotions, and social constructions; this again is real (it is clear that these all exist) and is causally effective.

This world of human consciousness can be regarded as comprising three major parts, different from the world of material things, and realized through the human mind and society: the world of rationality, the world of intention and emotion, and the world of consciously constructed social legislation and convention.

✦ *World 3: The World of Aristotelian Possibilities* that characterizes the set of all physical possibilities, from which the specific instances of what actually happens in World 1 are drawn.

This world of possibilities is real because of its rigorous prescription of the boundaries of what is possible. It provides the framework within which World 1 exists and operates. There is no element of chance or contingency here, and it certainly is not socially constructed (although our understanding of it is so constructed).

✦ *World 4: A Platonic World of (Abstract) Mathematical Realities* that are independent of human existence, but not embodied in physical form.

Major parts of mathematics are discovered rather than invented (rational numbers, zero, irrational numbers, and the Mandelbrot set, for example) and hence have an existence of their own. They have an abstract character, and the same abstract quantity can be represented and embodied in many symbolic and physical ways. They are not determined by physical experiment and are independent of the existence and culture of human beings.

The existence of these worlds shows that reality is much more diverse than envisaged by reductionist materialists and opens the way to contemplate the underlying reality:

✦ *Foundation World 0*—underlying fundamental reality, the world of God, partially described by theology and incorporating the fundamental meanings of the universe and of life.

This world is transcendent—that is, of a totally different nature than the others, indeed not properly describable in the same terms. This world is nevertheless able to interact with the others and influence them in important ways—in particular, the ground of their existence. It incorporates the underlying purpose, the set of values and meanings expressing the purpose (*telos*) of God and therefore underlying ethics. These values embrace justice as well as love. At their core is a paradoxical nature associated with *kenosis* and self-sacrifice ("he who would save his life must lose it"), in a profound sense contradicting the world of logical argumentation. Discovering this truth remains one of the most profound experiences enabling spiritual progress for each one of us. Its centrality to the life of Christ is clear in many sections of the New Testament, including Philippians 2:5–11 and the Sermon on the Mount. It is central to the resolution of the temptations in the desert, as is very clearly demonstrated in William Temple's book *Readings in St. John's Gospel.* Its rediscovery as a central feature of spirituality and ethics is profoundly hopeful for the future of humanity.

Multiple Paths to Spiritual Understanding

This deep nature is compatible with all those religious strands capable of seeing the value of the search for truth in religions other than their own and rejects those that dogmatically claim sole access to truth (representing the idolatry of claiming infallibility, which is against the kenotic virtue of giving up certainty). Indeed, we now recognize that because of the transcendent nature of ultimate reality and the variety of cultures, many different understandings will inevitably arise and be embodied in different faiths. The great spiritual progress now developing is the growing recognition that these can all be visions of the same underlying reality.

Spiritual Progress

The true nature of spirituality lies in an openness and awareness that takes all valid human experiences and understanding seriously—and sees in them, at least dimly, glimpses of the transcendent nature of an underlying reality that encompasses all

these aspects and much more. It is in this holistic kind of awareness and appreciation that one can to a small degree encounter the glory of the Creator with true
humility. This is not to claim that the part we happen to be expert in or are particularly aware of is the center of all or the only thing that matters. It is, rather, to see
our part as belonging to a far greater whole in which our beloved truths are certainly
valid, but where manifold aspects that others see may also be true and vital—even
if we find them difficult to appreciate. The integration of all of this—seeing all
dimensions of experience as simultaneously true—is spiritual growth.

Spiritual progress, then, resides in an increase of profound comprehensive understanding. The present-day Science and Religion movement is one significant vehicle that is enabling this to happen.

✍

GEORGE F. R. ELLIS, PH.D., is Professor of Applied Mathematics at the University
of Cape Town. He has written many papers on relativity theory and cosmology and
inter alia co-authored *The Large Scale Structure of Space-Time* with Stephen Hawking, *The Density of Matter in the Universe* with Peter Coles, and *Dynamical Systems
in Cosmology* with John Wainwright. He was co-author with Nancey C. Murphy,
who contributed an essay to this volume, *On the Moral Nature of the Universe*. He
is Past President of the International Society of General Relativity and Gravitation
and of the Royal Society of South Africa. He has been awarded various honorary
degrees and prizes, including the Star of South Africa Medal by President Nelson
Mandela in 1999 and the Templeton Prize for Progress in Religion in 2004.

THE UNIVERSE— WHAT'S THE POINT? 24

Paul C. W. Davies

Ｉｎ a famous conclusion to a popular book on cosmology,[1] physicist Steven Weinberg wrote, "The more the universe appears comprehensible, the more it also appears pointless." This comment echoes the sentiment of many contemporary scientists. Although they may wax lyrical about the awesome beauty, majesty, and subtlety of the natural world, they nevertheless deny any point or purpose to the universe. In this essay, written to honor Sir John Templeton's bold and sweeping vision, I shall critically reappraise Weinberg's claim.

Appealing to science to bolster the doctrine of cosmic pointlessness is by no means new. A hundred years ago, the mathematician and philosopher Bertrand Russell used the second law of thermodynamics in a trenchant attack on theism. The second law states, in effect, that the universe is dying, descending inexorably into chaos as its reserves of useful energy are squandered. Russell reflected on the "vast death of the solar system" that will follow when the sun burns out in several billion years and concluded that these depressing facts were consistent only with a philosophy of "unyielding despair."[2] Russell's position seems to be that if the universe as a whole is doomed, then physical existence is ultimately pointless; even human life and endeavor are, in the final analysis, futile. In recent years, the chemist Peter Atkins has developed this theme by tying the second law directly to the purposeless motion of molecules.[3] It is the random agitation of molecules that drives, say, a gas to states of higher and higher entropy, culminating in a state of thermodynamic equilibrium and effective macroscopic inactivity. Atkins elevates this indisputable fact about molecular motion to the status of a universal principle of purposelessness, in which the aimless meanderings of molecules become emblematic of the pointlessness of the universe as a whole. Even Freeman Dyson shares the sentiment that if the universe is ultimately doomed, "we might as well give up," in spite of the fact that the final cosmic state might lie trillions of years in the future and hence has no impact at all on individual human lives and society.[4]

The weakness of this argument is twofold. First, it assumes that entropy alone is an appropriate indicator of cosmic change. The decision to focus on this quantity is a purely ideological one. Russell and Atkins select entropy as the physical property for discussion because it paints a bleak picture of a degenerating, indeed doomed, universe. But there are other ways to describe cosmic evolution. For example, good astronomical evidence shows that the universe began in a state of almost total blandness. The richness and diversity of physical systems we observe today have emerged since the beginning through a long and complicated series of self-organizing and self-complexifying processes.[5] Viewed this way, the conspicuous story of the universe so far is one of unfolding enrichment, not decay. One could define, say, a measure of organized complexity that increases with time even as entropy increases. Nothing within science compels one to favor entropy over organized complexity in characterizing the evolution of the universe.

Second, let me contest the assumption that a system with a finite lifespan cannot have a point. This is obviously false. Individual human lives and cultures are subject to the same strictures of the second law of thermodynamics and are finite as a result. Yet human beings and society have all sorts of goals and purposes. To say there is no point to human life because one day we each will die is clearly ridiculous. So the fact that the stars may not burn forever or that the entire universe may eventually approach a state of thermodynamic equilibrium (or even dark emptiness) has little bearing on whether or not the universe has a point.

As with physical scientists, so biologists have used the supposed lack of directionality in physical processes in support of a philosophical position similar to Weinberg's. Stephen Jay Gould, for example, took pains to attack the Victorian notion of evolutionary progress.[6] He stressed that Nature is blind and so cannot look ahead to anticipate solutions to evolutionary problems. Darwinism, he pointed out, is based on purely random accidental changes, some good, some bad. There is no direction to evolution; it is not going anywhere, just exploring the vast space of biological possibilities. Therefore, so the reasoning goes, if biological evolution is blind, the universe as a whole must be pointless. Like Weinberg, Russell, and Atkins, Gould was scathing in his attacks on notions of cosmic purpose, which he saw as an anachronism, an unwelcome hangover from a bygone religious culture.

The evidence for the directionlessness of biological evolution is scientifically less compelling than is the case for the second law of thermodynamics. Taking the biosphere as a whole, its complexity has clearly risen since life on earth was restricted to a few microbes. The issue, however, is whether this merely represents a random, undirected exploration of the space of biological possibilities or whether there is a systematic *trend* toward greater complexity. The fossil record is somewhat ambiguous in this respect. Certainly some trends are discernible; for example, the so-called encephalization quotient (ratio of brain mass to body mass) escalated persistently during hominid evolution. Some contemporary biologists (e.g., Richard Dawkins,[7] Christian de Duve,[8] and Simon Conway Morris[9]) make a case that, at least within some lineages, there are trends toward greater complexity. So it is far from decided, even among professional biologists, that the evolutionary record supports a doctrine of biological chaos.

Recently, some cosmologists have attempted to advance a catch-all argument for cosmic pointlessness by invoking the multiverse concept.[10] This is based on the theory that what we have hitherto considered to be "the universe" is but a small component in a vast assemblage of universes, some resembling ours, others not. The universes may co-exist in parallel, so that they are physically disconnected, or they may connect to each other in remote regions of space or through "wormholes." Universes may differ in both their physical laws and initial conditions in such a way that all conceivable laws and conditions are represented in a universe somewhere. The overwhelming majority of the universes would go unseen because their laws and conditions would not be conducive to the emergence of life and conscious beings. Only in a tiny subset where, purely by chance, things fell out just right would observers arise to marvel over the ingeniously contrived appearance of their universe. The relevance of the multiverse to cosmic pointlessness is easy to grasp. If anyone should discover some aspect of Nature that hinted at a deep underlying purpose, then this superficially amazing fact could be shrugged off as a random accident that is observed by us only because that very same accident is a necessary prerequisite for the existence of life.

The multiverse theory suffers from a number of problems. In most versions, the existence of the other universes cannot be verified or falsified, even in principle, so its status as a scientific theory is questionable. Second, the degree of bio-friendliness we observe in the universe seems far in excess of what is needed to give rise to a few observers to act as cosmic selectors. If the ingenious bio-friendliness of our universe were the result of randomness, we might expect the observed universe to be minimally, rather than optimally, biophilic. Note, too, that multiverse explanations still need to assume the existence of laws of some sort, so they do not offer a complete explanation of the lawlike order of the universe. Finally, invoking an infinity of unseen universes to explain certain features of the universe we do observe seems the antithesis of Occam's Razor: It is an infinitely complex explanation. In this respect, it is effectively equivalent (in a mathematical sense) to naive theism in which the bio-friendliness of the cosmos is simply attributed, without further consideration, to selection from a "shopping list" of possibilities by a beneficent Deity. Both explanations appeal to an infinite amount of hidden information.

Cosmic pointlessness has also been argued on philosophical grounds on the basis that the very concept of a "point" or "purpose" cannot be applied to a system such as the universe because it makes sense only in the context of human activity. Some years ago, I took part in a BBC television debate with Hugh Montefiore, then bishop of Birmingham, and the atheist Oxford philosopher A. J. Ayer. Montefiore declared that without God all human life would be meaningless. Ayer countered that humans alone imbue their lives with meaning. "But then life would have no *ultimate* meaning," objected the bishop. "I don't know what 'ultimate meaning' *means!*" cried Ayer. His objection, of course, is that concepts such as meaning, purpose, and having a point are human categories that make good sense in the context of human society, but are at best metaphors when applied to nonliving systems.

However, scientists have long been guilty of projecting onto Nature categories that are rooted in human society. Each culture has used technological metaphors to describe cosmologies. The Greeks built a cosmological scheme based on musical harmony and geometrical regularities, because musical and geometrical instruments were the current technological marvels. Newton's universe was a gigantic clockwork mechanism. Russell's was an imperfect heat engine—a sort of Victorian industrial contraption writ large and running out of fuel. Today it is fashionable to describe the universe as a gigantic computer.[11] Information theory, which stems from the realm of human discourse, is routinely applied to physical problems in thermodynamics, biology, and quantum mechanics. All these designations capture in some imperfect way what the universe is about. It is not a clockwork mechanism or an information processor, but it does have mechanistic and informational properties. Living organisms have goals and purposes, and I see no reason that we may not use the organism as a metaphor for the universe (Aristotle already did). I am not suggesting that the universe is alive, only that it may share with living organisms certain properties, such as possessing "purposes," in the same way that it shares with a machine the property of having interlocking parts, a finite fuel supply, and so forth. I have put the word "purposes" in quotation marks because I am reasoning by analogy. This is, of course, dangerous, but the machine and information systems designations are also analogical, and few scientists object. So I contend that the universe may have purposelike or pointlike properties, alongside mechanistic and computational properties. All these characterizations require a leap from the human realm to the cosmic realm, and all are equally valid, if imperfect and incomplete, windows on aspects of cosmic reality.

I should like to finish by pointing out that science is founded on the notion of the rationality and logicality of Nature. The universe is ordered in a meaningful way, and scientists seek reasons for why things are the way they are. If the universe as a whole is pointless, then it exists reasonlessly. In other words, it is ultimately arbitrary and absurd. We are then invited to contemplate a state of affairs in which all scientific chains of reasoning are grounded in absurdity. The order of the world would have no foundation, and its breathtaking rationality would have to spring, miraculously, from absurdity. So Weinberg's dictum is turned neatly on its head: The more the universe seems pointless, the more it also seems incomprehensible.

❧

PAUL C. W. DAVIES, PH.D., is a theoretical physicist and cosmologist who holds the post of Professor of Natural Philosophy in the Australian Centre for Astrobiology at Macquarie University, Sydney. His research has been in the fields of quantum gravity, black holes, and early-universe cosmology. More recently, he has worked in astrobiology on problems concerning the origin of life and the transfer of microorganisms between planets. He is the author of more than twenty-five books, including several best-sellers such as *The Mind of God, About Time, The Fifth Miracle,* and *How to Build a Time Machine.* In addition, he has made and presented many television and radio documentaries that bring fundamental topics in science to a wider public. Dr. Davies was the recipient of the 1995 Templeton Prize for Progress in Religion.

NOTES

1 Weinberg, S. *The First Three Minutes* (Harper and Row, New York, 1988), 155.

2 Russell, B. *Why I Am Not a Christian* (Allen and Unwin, New York, 1957), 107.

3 Atkins, P. "Time and Dispersal: The Second Law," in *The Nature of Time,* eds. R. Flood and M. Lockwood (Basil Blackwell, Oxford, 1986).

4 Dyson, F., September 2, 2002, private remark during discussion of the fate of cosmo-logical models with a non-zero cosmological constant, at *Fine Tuning and the Laws of Physics*, symposium held at Windsor Castle, UK.

5 See, for example, Davies, P. *The Cosmic Blueprint* (Heinemann, London, 1987).

6 Gould, S. J. *Life's Grandeur* (Jonathan Cape, London, 1996).

7 Dawkins, R. *Climbing Mount Improbable* (Viking, London, 1996).

8 de Duve, C. *Vital Dust* (Basic Books, New York, 1995).

9 Conway Morris, S. *The Crucible of Creation* (Oxford University Press, Oxford, 1998).

10 See, for example, Rees, M. *Before the Beginning* (Simon & Schuster, London, 1997), chap. 15.

11 Lloyd, S. *Physical Review Letters* 88, 237901(2002).

Choose Your Own Universe 25

Andrei Linde

O NE OF THE MAIN GOALS of science is to find a theory that explains all features of our universe. The scientific approach is remarkably successful. And yet, some of the parameters of elementary particles still look like a collection of random numbers. We still do not know why electrons are two thousand times lighter than protons, why the force of gravity is so weak, and why the energy density of a vacuum is so small. Meanwhile, a minor change (by a factor of two or three) in the mass of the electron, in its charge e, or in the gravitational constant G would lead to a universe in which life as we know it could never have arisen. Adding or subtracting even a single spatial dimension of the same type as the known three dimensions would make planetary systems impossible. Furthermore, in order for life as we know it to exist, it is necessary that the universe be sufficiently large, flat, homogeneous, and isotropic. These facts lie at the foundation of the so-called Anthropic Principle (Barrow and Tipler 1986). According to this principle, we observe the universe to be as it is because only in such a universe could observers such as ourselves exist.

For a long time, scientists did not like this principle. The standard point of view was that the universe arose with one set of laws of physics. From this perspective, it did not make any sense to ask why the universe is so large, why space is three-dimensional, and why electrons are so light. It is just so. It seemed naive to assume that the laws of physics were fine-tuned in order to make our existence possible. One could argue that if somebody took the trouble of making the universe for our benefit, isn't it strange that he or she worked so hard to prepare the same conditions everywhere, even far away from earth? Wouldn't it be much easier to establish good conditions for our life only in a small vicinity of the solar system?

The negative attitude toward the Anthropic Principle changed only after the development of inflationary cosmology. This theory claims that immediately after its creation the universe went through the stage of inflation, exponentially rapid expansion in an unstable, vacuumlike state. As a result, the universe became exponentially large within an extremely short period. The simplest version of inflationary theory is the chaotic inflation scenario (Linde 1990), which describes the universe as being filled by a massive scalar field. An example of this is the Higgs field, which plays an important role in the standard model of electroweak interactions. It can be shown that if the scalar field originally was sufficiently large and homogeneous, its energy density could change its value only very slowly. According to Einstein's theory of gravity, the universe containing matter with constant energy density should expand exponentially. This corresponds to the stage of inflation. However, gradually the scalar field decayed and created usual matter consisting of elementary particles. After that, the universe expanded in accordance with the standard Big Bang theory.

Why do we need an extra stage of expansion of the universe if in the end we return to the standard Big Bang theory? The answer is that during inflation our universe could expand as much as $10^{1000000000000}$ times. Rapid expansion makes the universe extremely large and homogeneous. The geometric properties of space become similar to the properties of an almost flat surface of a huge inflating balloon. This explains why our universe is so big, homogeneous, and isotropic and why its geometric properties are so close to the properties of a flat space.

In addition to stretching the universe, inflation generates small density perturbations, which are responsible for galaxy formation. This happens because of amplification of quantum fluctuations during inflation. In certain cases, such quantum fluctuations become extremely large and may considerably increase the initial value of the scalar field. The probability of such events is small, but those rare parts of the universe where it happens begin expanding with much greater speed. This creates a lot of new space where inflation may occur and where large quantum fluctuations become possible. As a result, the universe enters an eternal cycle of self-reproduction: It permanently produces new inflationary domains, which in their turn produce new inflationary domains. Therefore, instead of looking like a single expanding balloon, as in the standard Big Bang theory, the universe looks like a huge, growing fractal consisting of many inflating balloons producing new balloons.

Each of these balloons is so large that its inhabitants will never see other parts of the universe. So for all practical purposes, each of these balloons can be considered to be a separate universe. Various scalar fields may take different values in these universes. These values determine properties of elementary particles and the way they interact with each other. Thus, the universe after inflation becomes divided into many universes operating by different laws of physics.

This provides a simple justification of the Anthropic Principle. One does not need to assume that a creator repeatedly turned out one universe after another in order to make our existence possible. The universe itself produces exponentially large domains with different laws of physics. And we should not be surprised that the conditions necessary for our existence appear everywhere in the visible part of the universe rather than only in a vicinity of the solar system. If the proper conditions are established near the solar system, inflation ensures that similar conditions appear everywhere within the observable part of the universe. But these conditions may become dramatically different at a distance $10^{1000000000000}$ cm away from us.

Twenty years ago, one could wonder whether this was a real theory or science fiction. However, during the last ten years, many predictions of inflationary theory have been confirmed by cosmological observations, and this theory gradually became the standard paradigm of modern cosmology.

Once we get used to this new picture of the universe, we can take one more step and consider a multiverse, an infinitely large set of different universes with different laws of physics operating in each of them. This will provide us with an unlimited number of universes and laws of physics to choose from (Rees 2000). Whereas the idea of a collection of different universes is conceptually much more complicated than the idea of a single inflationary universe consisting of many different parts, we believe that the notion of the multiverse is quite legitimate and can be given a precise mathematical meaning (Linde 2002). Introduction of the concept of the multiverse shows the way toward justification of the Anthropic Principle in its strongest form: All types of universes and all laws of physics are possible, but we can live in only the universes with laws of physics compatible with our existence.

Thus, we can go very far in our quest for the theory of everything, representing the universe as a huge, self-replicating machine offering all options beyond imagination. But is this theory complete, or is the complicated picture of the multiverse still too simplistic?

There is at least one part of this picture that remains a bit blurry. In order to fully justify the use of the Anthropic Principle, we should know what life is and how it emerges.

The simplest assumption is that life is a function of matter and that our consciousness is just a tool for describing the real world. So once we know the structure and composition of the universe, we know everything. However, in the context of quantum cosmology, the notion of an observer acquires an important role, and the evolution of the universe is directly linked to the possibility that it can be seen. Indeed, it can be shown that the wave function of the universe, which describes the probability of *all* processes in the universe, is *time-independent*. The universe becomes alive (time-dependent) only when one divides it into two parts: an observer and the rest of the universe. Then the wave function of the rest of the universe depends on the time measured by the observer (DeWitt 1967). In other words, evolution is possible only with respect to the observer. Without an observer, the universe is dead.

One could argue that instead of a conscious observer we can use any recording device. But do we really know that the universe depends on time recorded by this device if nobody is there to check it? Attempts to address this question bring us back to the old problem of the origin of knowledge.

Our knowledge of the world begins not with matter, but with perceptions. I know for sure that my pain exists, my "red" exists, and my "sweet" exists. I do not need any proof of their existence, because these events are a part of me; everything else is a theory. Later, we realize that our perceptions obey some laws that can be conveniently formulated if we assume that an underlying reality lies beyond them. The model of the material world obeying laws of physics is so successful that we forget about our starting point and say that matter is the only reality and that perceptions are only helpful for describing it. But, in fact, we are substituting the *reality* of our feelings with the *theory* of an independently existing material world. This theory is so incredibly successful that we almost never think about its possible limitations.

However, investigation of quantum cosmology persistently returns us to the most fundamental questions regarding our universe and our place in it. One can remember that before the development of the general theory of relativity, space (like consciousness) was considered to be just a tool for describing matter. Later, we learned that space has its own degrees of freedom, gravitational waves. Space can exist and change in time even in the absence of electrons, protons, and photons—that is, in the absence of anything that had been called matter before the formation of the theory of general relativity. Gravitational waves interact with matter so weakly that we have not found any of them as yet. However, their existence is crucial for the consistency of the theory of spacetime.

The dream of Einstein was to unify all internal symmetries of elementary particles with the symmetries of our world. This problem was solved in the 1970s after the discovery of supersymmetric theories. In these theories, all particles can be interpreted in terms of the geometric properties of a multidimensional superspace.

Thus, the concept of space, or superspace, ceased to be simply a tool for the description of the real world and instead took on independent significance, gradually encompassing all particles as its own degrees of freedom. In this picture, instead of using space for describing the only real thing, matter, we use the notion of matter in order to simplify the description of superspace. This change of the picture of the universe is one of the most profound (and least known) consequences of modern physics.

What if something similar happens with our understanding of consciousness? What if mind, just like space, has its own degrees of freedom, which may exist even in the absence of what we now call "matter"? Is it possible to unify our description of mind and matter and obtain a complete and internally consistent picture of our world? Persistent appearance of the word "observer" in quantum cosmology, as well as the recent developments related to the Anthropic Principle, indicate that sooner or later we may need to consider this possibility quite seriously.

One of the main principles of science is to move as far as possible without making any unnecessary assumptions. But on our way toward discovering the laws of nature, from time to time we may ask questions that might seem naive and metaphysical. Twenty years ago, it seemed naive to ask why there are so many different things in the universe, why nobody has ever seen parallel lines intersect, why different parts of the universe have been created simultaneously. Now that inflationary cosmology has provided a possible answer to all of these questions, one can only be surprised that before the 1980s it was sometimes taken to be bad form even to discuss them. Perhaps we should learn this lesson and not be too afraid if our pursuit of knowledge brings us to the boundaries of what we could study by traditional methods. Traditions can be changed. Our ultimate goal is to find the truth by any method that we find useful and productive.

Ɫ♥

ANDREI LINDE, PH.D., has been Professor of Physics at Stanford University since 1990. He studied physics at Moscow State University. In 1972–1974, he developed with David Kirzhnits a theory of cosmological phase transitions. From 1975 to 1988, Dr. Linde worked at Lebedev Physical Institute and then spent two years at CERN, Switzerland. He is one of the authors of inflationary cosmology: In 1982 he suggested the new inflationary universe scenario; in 1983 he proposed the chaotic inflationary universe scenario, and in 1986, the theory of a self-reproducing inflationary universe. Among Dr. Linde's latest developments are the theory of a stationary inflationary universe and the theory of the creation of elementary particles after inflation. He is the author of two hundred papers and two books on particle physics and cosmology. Among Dr. Linde's honors and awards are the Lomonosov Prize of the Academy of Sciences of the USSR (1978), the Oskar Klein Medal in Physics (2001), the Dirac Medal for the development of inflationary cosmology (2002), the Peter Gruber Prize for the development of inflationary cosmology (2004), and the Robinson Prize in Cosmology of the University of Newcastle, UK (2005).

REFERENCES

Barrow, J. D., and Tipler, F. J. (1986). *The Anthropic Cosmological Principle.* Oxford University Press, New York.

DeWitt, B. S. (1967). Quantum Theory of Gravity. 1. The Canonical Theory, *Phys. Rev.* 160, 1113.

Linde, A. D. (1990). *Particle Physics and Inflationary Cosmology.* Harwood Academic Publishers, Chur, Switzerland.

Linde, A. D. (2002). "Inflation, Quantum Cosmology, and the Anthropic Principle," in *Science & Ultimate Reality: Quantum Theory, Cosmology and Complexity,* eds. J. D. Barrow, P. C. W. Davies, & C. L. Harper. Cambridge University Press (2004).

Rees, M. (2000). *Just Six Numbers: The Deep Forces That Shape the Universe.* Basic Books, Perseus Group, New York.

FINESSE AND FIREPOWER

Karl W. Giberson

Frederick Forsyth's thriller *Day of the Jackal* tells the story of a fiendishly clever assassin, the Jackal, who almost brings down Charles DeGaulle. Through a combination of elaborate planning and ingenious subterfuge, the Jackal manages to get himself and a high-powered rifle into position to take a single shot at his target. At the last minute, the target moves and the bullet buries itself in the ground, unnoticed by the cheering crowd. The 1973 Hollywood version of the story, starring Edward Fox as the clever, elusive Jackal, was faithful to Forsyth's original scenario of ingenuity and cunning.

The 1997 remake of *Jackal* starred Bruce Willis. Gone was the elegant, understated assassin whose presence and attempted assassination were all but invisible. The new Jackal goes after his target—this time, the First Lady—with so much firepower that the assembled crowd flees in terror as shattered brick and glass from the front of the building rain down on them. In fact, so great was the carnage that a casual observer would have had some difficulty in determining the Jackal's exact target.

Alternate Realities

As the saying goes, there is more than one way to skin a cat. If you want to assassinate a highly protected figure, you need copious quantities of either finesse or firepower—finesse to do it once and get it right, or firepower to blast away recklessly and eventually hit the target. Finesse and firepower, curiously enough, often define the means to various ends—and, when one fails, there is always the other. You can write *Hamlet* with the finesse of a Shakespeare or the firepower of the infinite stadium of monkeys typing randomly; you can solve political problems with the finesse of diplomacy or the firepower of cruise missiles; and you can explain the marvelous design of our universe as the finesse of a wise Creator or the firepower of some mindless cosmic machine extravagantly belching out alternate realities, some of which have the ingenious design of this one, but most of which do not—collateral damage on a cosmic scale.

Such alternate realities have long been the stuff of science fiction; after all, who is not interested in the question of whether "our" reality is the only possibility? Could there be alternate realities with beings that are immaterial? Or lack sight? Or live forever? Are there alternate versions of ourselves, new and improved? Can we find a way to bring these speculative alternate realities into this one? Could we, for example, freeze ourselves and be thawed out at some later time and live again, perhaps in a century when there were no more "reality" TV shows?

Speculation about alternate realities is hardly new. The atomist philosophers of classical Greece were convinced that the universe contained an infinity of particles, combining in an infinity of random ways and producing every imaginable and unimaginable possibility. Aristotle rejected all this cosmic firepower. He preferred a compact, tidy, high-finesse, solitary universe with the Earth firmly anchored in the center of things, where it remained for almost two millennia with few challenges. Renaissance thinkers such as Copernicus unhooked the Earth and promoted it to the heavens with the other planets. If the Earth was a planet like the others, then it seemed all the more natural to wonder about alternate worlds. If there are planets besides Earth, then they must be inhabited, for, as some would argue, God makes nothing in vain, and empty planets would surely be a waste. Such speculations continued through the birth and development of both science and science fiction as thinkers from Kepler, Kant, and Whewell to Asimov, Sagan, and Benford created more or less plausible scenarios of alternate realities, imaginative extrapolations of their experience with this most remarkable reality.

Most of the historical flirtations with alternate realities were modest affairs, entailing little more than people like us living on the moon or on distant Earthlike planets. (Ever notice how the crew of the Starship *Enterprise* was always beaming down to planets that looked just like Earth?) Recently, however, speculation about infinite alternate realities that realize all possible scenarios has been ramped up several notches, but not by fiction writers. The current speculations, which make their predecessors look pale and anemic, come from leading scientists—and they even appear in legitimate scientific journals.

One might suspect that such prolific speculations about other realities have emerged from some unusual observation. Maybe planets are disappearing, or spaceships that venture beyond the asteroid belt mysteriously lose contact with NASA. Perhaps new stars are popping into existence from nowhere, or strange new television shows are suddenly appearing in prime time. But, while there may be some evidence for strange new television shows, speculation about alternate universes is not based on such observations.

The Goldilocks Universe

What, then, is the basis for the speculation that there may be many, even an infinity, of alternate universes? Surprisingly, the many universes—all of them completely disconnected from ours—are invoked as a way to explain *this* universe. Our universe, the one we live in, has been determined by contemporary cosmologists to be quite remarkable. The argument, which goes by the name of the Anthropic Principle and is by now quite familiar, goes like this: If you change the laws of Nature in our universe even slightly, then the place becomes uninhabitable. Make gravity 1 percent stronger or weaker, and suns won't shine properly; change the electrical force just a bit, and organic molecules won't form; make the universe expand just a little faster, and there won't be any solar systems. And so on. All of the various features of this universe appear to have been optimized for life. Change any of them, and the universe becomes boring and sterile. Our universe is neither too hot nor too cold; it is just right—a Goldilocks Universe.

All this would occasion no surprise if it turned out that the laws of Nature somehow have to have their current form, if there is some reason that gravity has its particular strength, electrons their mass, photons their energy, and so on. But, as near as anyone can tell, and they seem to be able to tell quite nearly, there is no reason that the various features of our universe are the way they are and not some other, equally plausible way.

All this makes our gigantic fifteen-billion-year-old universe seem rather puzzling, with all its various parameters so finely adjusted to accommodate us so nicely. Fred Hoyle, one of the past century's greatest cosmologists and author of a science fiction book, said that some "super intellect" must have "monkeyed with the physics." Freeman Dyson (who contributed a chapter to this volume), after looking closely at the fifteen-billion-year cosmic history that preceded our timely arrival, suggested that somehow "the universe knew we were coming." John Wheeler even suggested that, in some really bizarre (meaning quantum mechanical) way, the existence of our universe was dependent on our existence. No people, no universe—the ultimate symbiosis.

But Hoyle's "super intellect" and Dyson's "intentional universe" are hardly satisfactory answers to the mystery of our high-finesse, Goldilocks Universe, at least from a scientific point of view. These explanations are too traditional, too theological, too high on finesse and intelligence in an age that prefers heavy-duty cosmic firepower.

The requisite cosmic firepower comes in the form of some truly mind-boggling, or at least atom-jiggling, speculations about the existence of multiple universes. And by "multiple" we don't mean seven or eight, or even a few hundred. We are talking about an infinite number of real, live universes, with real stuff in them, real matter governed by real laws, maybe even alternate forms of intelligence possessed by alternate creatures; and perhaps even "alternate-reality" TV programs.

The first really serious proposal for multiple universes came from quantum theorist Hugh Everett, who thought that the problems of quantum mechanics were so deep that they could be solved only if the universe were constantly splitting off into slightly different futures. This idea has been rather eloquently updated by the extraordinary and eccentric Oxford physicist David Deutsch. In a few short pages in *The Fabric of Reality*, Deutsch shows how the behavior of electrons passing through a slit reveals the presence of other universes. Deutsch even has a proposal for a quantum computer that will perform half its calculations in some other universe, and thus run twice as fast as the old-fashioned kind that have to do everything in just one universe. Deutsch believes that it may one day be possible to build such a computer to test this strange idea. (He does not say how we will know that the extra calculations are being done in another universe, rather than in some hidden spot in this one.) The many universes that you get with quantum theory are the ultimate in cosmic firepower. Simple interactions, of the sort that are happening on your retina as you read these words, are splitting the entire universe, making multiple copies of everything that exists—every star, every galaxy, every television set.

Lee Smolin, who became a cosmologist after failing to get his rock band off the ground, offers another ingenious mechanism to get lots of universes. His idea runs like this: At the "centers" of black holes are tiny regions of infinite density called "singularities," where the laws of physics appear to completely break down (because of incompatibilities between relativity and quantum theory that cosmologists would like to resolve with a proper quantum theory of gravity that nobody has been able to find, although Smolin claimed in Princeton in March 2002 that he had such a theory[1]). If the laws of physics break down, and it appears that they do in the middle of black holes, then anything can happen. All bets are off. If anything can happen in the middle of the black hole, then maybe a new universe might erupt there, disconnected from this one. Smolin argues that this is exactly what happens, but that these "daughter" universes are slightly different from their parents. If some daughter universes differ in ways that give them more firepower to generate black holes, then that configuration will be favored in a sort of cosmic Darwinism. As time passes, this cosmic Darwinism will result in universes that are quite prolific, as universes that produce black holes have more "children" than those that do not. And, as luck would have it, universes that are good at making black holes are also good at making planets like ours.

In the prologue to his fascinating *The Life of the Cosmos*, Smolin humbly labels his idea a "frank speculation" and a "fantasy." Leading cosmologist Sir Martin Rees, however, in an essay in the anthology *Many Worlds*, says that Smolin's proposal is a "reasonable reaction" to the mystery of our just-right Goldilocks Universe.

The question at hand that motivates the speculation about multiple universes is how to explain the finely tuned, high-finesse, Goldilocks character of the one universe of which we have any real knowledge—this one. If there are an infinity of different universes with all manner of different characteristics, then it is not in the least remarkable that one of them happens to look like ours; and it is not remarkable that we happen to live in one of the universes that is compatible with our existence. On the other hand, if there is but one universe, then it certainly looks as if it was designed by some transcendent intelligence. The two choices, which we have been calling "finesse" and "firepower," are very different. A designed universe requires information, lots of information, of the sort that even skeptics are prepared to attribute to "God." An infinity of universes, with one accidentally looking like ours, needs very little information. If you have enough universes, then some of them will naturally and fortuitously look like this one; the impression of design, however, will be illusory.

It may be that an ingenious observational test might one day be devised to detect these alternate universes. But it is hard to see how such a test could be conclusive. If Deutsch's quantum computer does run twice as fast, can we confidently attribute the extra speed to the assistance of an otherwise undetectable alternate universe? All kinds of strange things happen in the world of the quantum, but most physicists are reluctant to suppose that the strangeness is coming from some other universe.

Our universe is remarkable in so many ways. Those who understand this most clearly offer extraordinary explanations: the universe is the product of either an information-rich source, such as the Creator of tradition, or it is one of a vast ensemble of universes. Both options are mind-boggling in their own way, and the choice toward which one gravitates, to use a nearby metaphor, depends very much on where one starts. And, if history is any guide, human ingenuity will always be up to the task of devising plausible explanations that are consistent with both one's presuppositions and generally accepted scientific notions.

ℒ♥

KARL W. GIBERSON, PH.D., is the founding editor of *Science and Theology News*, editor in chief of *Science and Spirit,* and Professor of Physics at Eastern Nazarene College in Quincy, Massachusetts. He has undergraduate degrees in physics, philosophy, and mathematics from Eastern Nazarene College and an M.A. and Ph.D. in physics from Rice University. Dr. Giberson has written many articles and two books on science and religion: *Worlds Apart: The Unholy War between Religion and Science* (1993) and *Species of Origins: America's Search for a Creation Story* (2002, with Donald Yerxa). His primary area of interest is America's creation-evolution controversy, particularly within the evangelical church. He is a contributing editor for *Books and Culture* and has been involved in various science and religion projects and conferences.

NOTE

1 The statement was made during Smolin's presentation at a symposium, *Science & Ultimate Reality: Celebrating the Vision of John Archibald Wheeler,* held March 15–18, 2002 in Princeton, New Jersey. See http://www.metanexus.net/ultimate_reality/main.htm for more information. A book chapter based on this presentation is included in a volume published by Cambridge University Press in 2004—*Science and Ultimate Reality: Quantum Theory, Cosmology and Complexity,* edited by John D. Barrow, Paul C. W. Davies, and Charles L. Harper Jr.

Marcelo Gleiser

T HERE IS A CREATIVE TENSION in the cosmos. We feel it every time we look at Nature, and we feel it within ourselves. It is revealed in the smallest of details, a dewdrop balancing on the tip of a leaf in an early fall morning, the hexagonal symmetry of snowflakes resulting from water's molecular structure and heat dissipation. And it is revealed in large-scale natural phenomena, a lightning strike ripping across the sky during a stormy night, in stars burning their entrails in order to survive the inexorable crush of their own gravity. Our collective history can be told as an effort to represent and make sense of this creative tension, this constant dance of chaos and order that shapes the world.

We have created countless stories, drawings, dances, and rituals in search of meaning, in search of answers. We look at the cosmos with a mixed sense of awe and wonder, of terror and devotion. And we want to know: How can something come from nothing? What is the origin of all things? Can order emerge by itself, without a guiding hand? Is beauty a mere accident of Nature, or is there a deeper meaning to it? Why do we crave beauty? What is it that makes us plant gardens, compose poems and symphonies, create mathematical theorems and equations? Why can't we be content simply by eating, procreating, and sleeping? These are questions that bridge and expand our ways of knowing, our being part of cutting-edge scientific research, philosophical meditation, religious prayer, and artistic output. We have an unquenchable urge to understand who we are and what our place is in this vast universe. In many ways, it is through this search for answers that we define ourselves. By asking, by wanting to know, we define what it means to be human. And, although the answers may vary, just as cultures vary from place to place and time to time, many questions are the same—and remain, to a large extent, unanswered.

Modern science has developed a comprehensive narrative describing the emergence of material structures in the universe. Although many of the details and fundamental questions remain open, we now can claim with certitude that the history of the cosmos traces an increasing complexification of its living and nonliving inhabitants, of the hierarchical development of form and function from the simple to the complex. Thus, at very early times, when the universe was extremely hot and dense, matter was in the form of its most basic constituents, the indivisible elementary particles. As the universe expanded and cooled, attractive forces between the different particles made clustering possible: Protons and neutrons emerged from binding quarks, atomic nuclei from binding protons and neutrons, light atoms from binding atomic nuclei and electrons, galaxies from huge collapsing hydrogen clouds, stars from smaller hydrogen-rich clouds within these galaxies, until, eventually, living beings emerged in at least one of the billions of solar systems spread across the cosmos.

The scientific account describing the emergence of complex material structures has enjoyed enormous success. Cosmology is now a data-driven branch of physics, as opposed to even two decades ago. However, in spite of this success, or perhaps because of it, several fundamental questions have surfaced that defy present knowledge. Among the most fascinating of these questions are those that address origins: the origin of the cosmos, the origin of life, and the origin of the mind. The answers to these questions, even if currently unknown, are all related to the issue of emergence: How is it that structures self-organize to the point of generating extremely sophisticated complex behavior? Be it a surging cosmos out of a primordial soup of cosmoids, a simple living being made of millions of organic macromolecules, or a thinking being capable of wondering about his or her own origins and of pondering moral dilemmas, the emergence of complexity encompasses some of the most awesome and least understood natural phenomena.

These three origin questions may be compressed into a single one: "How come us?" This is the kind of exasperating question that makes most scientists throw in the towel. A common answer is: "Who cares?" After all, there may not be a reason at all; we may be here simply as the result of a random sequence of accidents on the right-size planet, with the right amount of water, at the right distance from a moderate-size star, and so on. "The Universe may be full of Earth-like planets with other forms of intelligent life," the argument proceeds. Indeed, it is quite possible that the universe is filled with Earth-like planets, some of them with similar amounts of water and Earth-like atmospheric compositions. Possibly, several will also have some form of living beings. If Earth is a demonstrative example, life is very resilient and can adapt to extremely adverse circumstances. But intelligent life is a whole other story. (By "intelligent," I mean a species capable of self-reflection and with the ability for abstract thinking.)

Evolutionary arguments claiming that natural selection necessarily leads to intelligence are flawed. Consider the history of life in the only place we actually know it exists, Earth. The dinosaurs were here for about 150 million years and showed no signs of decline or of intelligence. Intelligence may be a sufficient condition for dominating the food chain, but it is not a necessary one. It took a devastating collision with a ten-kilometer-wide asteroid 65 million years ago to decimate the dinosaurs, together with 40 percent of all life forms on earth. Ironically, the mammals, which up to that point were pretty much insignificant, survived and flourished in the wake of this cataclysm. In a very real sense, we are here because of this catastrophic collision.

Life is an experiment in emergent complexity: We may know what the ingredients are, but we cannot predict its detailed outcome. (And we still cannot repeat it in the laboratory.) Intelligent life is certainly a very rare outcome. This goes against everything we have learned over the last four hundred years of modern science—that the more we know about the universe, the less unique we seem to be. True, we live among billions of other galaxies in the visible universe, each of them with billions of stars. True, the matter that makes up people and stars is subdominant; most of the matter that permeates the cosmos is not made of protons and electrons, but of something else that does not shine like the matter making up stars. Our location in the cosmos and our material composition are not of great cosmic relevance or particularly special. But our minds are. As far as we know, there aren't any others out there. If there were, chances are we would have been visited by now. Our galaxy, being about one hundred thousand light-years across and 12 billion years old, could have been traversed countless times by other intelligent civilizations. But it hasn't—unless, of course, aliens have been here long before we have and didn't leave any clues, or do not want to make contact. (Taking the first 2 billion years off for good measure, and assuming intelligent civilizations can travel at least at one-tenth the speed of light, gives a total of ten thousand galaxy crossings in the last 10 billion years. Either we have been purposely ignored, or we are really inconspicuous.) Given the unknowns (how can we presume to understand an alien psyche if we don't even understand our own?), we should keep an open mind, repeating, as suggested Carl Sagan, that "absence of evidence is not evidence of absence." (Or, maybe the aliens are just very shy.)

If, indeed, we are a rare event, we must be ready to take on an enormous responsibility: We must preserve our legacy, learning how to survive in spite of ourselves. Humans are capable of the most wonderful creations and the most horrendous crimes. It is often very convenient to dream of archetypical aliens, wise and all-knowing, who will inspire and educate us before it's too late. Those aliens are not so different from the saints and prophets of many religions who bring us hope and direction. But if we are alone, we must learn to save ourselves following our own guidance and acquired wisdom. It is here that a blending of science and religious ethics can be profoundly useful. We can start by extending the New Testament maxim "Do unto others as you would have them do unto you" to all known and unknown living beings, here and across the cosmos.

Then, we must learn from the way Nature operates. There is a single principle behind all existing order in Nature, an all-embracing urge to exist and to bind what manifests itself at all levels, from the racing world of subatomic particles to the edges of the observable universe. It also manifests itself in our lives and in our history. Humans cannot escape this alliance with the rest of the cosmos. Our tensions are part of this universal trend, our creations and destructions part of the same rhythms that permeate the universe. Through them, we search for transcendence, for a reality deeper and more permanent than our own. However, we have distanced ourselves from Nature and have become wasteful. Our wastefulness is reflected in the way we treat our planet and ourselves. It is a cancer that grows and overwhelms what lives and what doesn't.

The laws of physics dictate that inanimate systems never use more energy than they have to, never choose a more costly path to achieve the same end result. We must learn from Nature's simple elegance, from its aesthetic and economical commitment to functionality and form. We must look beyond our immediate needs and greed, reintegrating ourselves into a physical reality that transcends political and social boundaries. Perhaps then we will start to respect our differences, to learn from those who believe, live, and look differently than we do. And we don't have a minute to waste.

COSMIC ORDER AND DIVINE WORD 28

Lydia Jaeger

IT WAS FASCINATION for natural order that got me into physics. As a high-school student, I took a course in physics mainly because it was supposed to concentrate on astronomy—and because my older brother was convinced that I had to do physics. About a year and a half later, I had completely changed my mind and was seriously contemplating studying physics at university. What made all the difference was that I had discovered the mystery of Cosmic Order.

The fascination that got me into physics has never left me: Why does the pencil in my hand, each time I let it go, fall to the ground following a precise mathematical formula? In fact, we are so convinced of Nature's tidiness that we do not even bother to repeat the experiment; we do not feel any need to check that Nature will next time follow the same rule. The "law"-like regularity and consequent modelability of natural phenomena are the unquestioned assumptions that underlie all scientific research. The revolutions that took place in physics at the beginning of the twentieth century have certainly changed our philosophical understanding of the nature of Cosmic Order. Quantum mechanics has introduced chance at the most basic level of our physical theories. Nevertheless, quantum probabilities are themselves described by precise mathematical formulae. Quantum theory does not transport us into the daunting world of magic where just anything can happen. It is part of the deep order of Nature that science has been able to partially comprehend.

Different approaches to understanding Cosmic Order exist. Most scientists probably see it as simply a "given" by Nature, something to discover and describe. Others would want to make room for creative activity by the human agent. They consider that we do not so much discover Natural Order as construct it. Through the constraints imposed by experimental practice, we participate in shaping scientific laws in a kind of partnership with Nature. But common to all except for the most extreme relativists is the conviction that there is some basic, deep order in Nature that allows for the emergence of meaningful scientific practice. If Nature were a completely chaotic aggregate, no comprehensible mathematical description of Cosmic Order would be possible.

The recognition of harmony in Nature predates the birth of modern science in the seventeenth century. Very early hints are found in the Hebrew Bible. Its magnificent opening fresco shows God's work of Creation structured in six days. Plants and animals are produced "according to their various kinds." Of particular importance is God's Word giving rise to a structured Creation: "And God said, 'Let there be light,' and there was light. . . ." Ten times, the sacred author refers to God bringing forth Creation by speaking. Other texts develop the same idea. Thus the psalmist celebrates God's Word in Creation: "By the Word of the Lord were the heavens made, their starry host by the breath of his mouth" (Ps 33:6). This view, and the refrain of ultimate goodness ("God saw all that He had made, and it was very good"), stands in clear contrast to the Babylonian imperial cosmology in which Creation results from warfare in a power struggle between competing gods.

That Divine Word structured Creation is given special importance in the New Testament. One of its most significant contributions with regard to Creation concerns the role of Christ. Creation and its corollary, the providential sustaining of the world, are specifically attributed to the second Person of the Trinity. Echoing the first creation account in Genesis, the evangelist John writes: "In the beginning was the Word [*logos*]. . . . Through him all things were made; without him nothing was made that has been made" (John 1:1–3).

To be sure, we should not read back into the biblical texts the science of modern times. We need to beware of "precursorism" that, in an apologetical mood, tries to find all kinds of intimations of later findings in the ancient texts! Nevertheless, the more I think about Cosmic Order the more I realize how promising it is to understand it in terms of Divine Word. *Logos* Christology, as it is called in the jargon (after the Greek word for "word, reason"), has a longstanding tradition. It allows us to see Natural Order both as truly immanent and as pointing beyond itself.

The spoken (or written) word is incarnated in physical spacetime, but we will get the message only if we hear (or read) it as revelatory by the person who wants to communicate. In a similar vein, Cosmic Order understood as Divine Word is implemented in Nature, which is in turn studied by science. Creation is not a succession of unrelated instantaneous acts. God has spoken, and as rational creatures we are capable of reading Nature's "book." But at the same time, the logic of *logos* protects us from the excesses of scientism. There is more in heaven and on earth than our science has dreamt of. In particular, laws of Nature are not self-explanatory. To me, they are most powerfully interpreted as traces of the Creator's handwriting.

One outstanding feature of *logos* Christology has been somewhat neglected in classical accounts: It interprets Cosmic Order in personal categories. Already in the Hebrew Bible, the Word of Creation is spoken by the personal Creator God. Creation is no impersonal emanation of God's nature, as pantheistic thought would have it. It is the free act of the transcendent Lord who, in his wisdom, chooses to call the universe into existence. The personal character of Cosmic Order is reinforced when the New Testament links it to the Son of God, who communicates lovingly with the Father and the Spirit throughout all eternity and who, in the fullness of time, became incarnate as Jesus of Nazareth.

Interpreting Natural Order in terms of the Divine Word helps us to realize that the personal dimension is no foreign element in scientific practice. For too long, the theory of knowledge has been hampered by the unattainable ideal of complete formalization. To be sure, science can flourish only when high standards of intersubjective rational inquiry are respected. Scientific theories are not emendable to individual liking. Nevertheless, I suggest that it is good for the depth and richness of science to resist philosophical positivists who believe that eliminating an anthropocentric perspective is obviously a step in the right direction. I see no reason that this should be so.

The heydays of positivism are far behind us, even if the ideal of impersonal knowledge still continues to haunt scientific laboratories (and the philosophical imagination). At least since the publication of the historical works of Thomas Kuhn, Paul Feyerabend, and others, it has dawned on most of us that scientific research does not progress by induction from neutrally collected experimental "facts." Moreover, the formation of scientific theories cannot be reduced to disembodied processes of formalized reasoning. Such theories are often accepted, in the absence of sufficient support from experiments, on the basis of human "gut feeling" in respect of criteria such as rational beauty and the ideal of unification of the scientific worldview. Social and historical conditions play a role; we cannot free ourselves completely from the conventions of the community within which we work.

Scientists already make unavoidable existential commitments in choosing the problems on which they concentrate in their research. Problem-solving strategies also resist complete formalization. Scientists often describe the experience of hitting on the solution as "illumination," even if afterward they verify the correctness of the solution by more conventional and less revelatory methods. "Real" research strategies engaged in by "real" scientists disclose the personal character of scientific knowledge. Its recognition has led some into skeptical despair, appearing as if there is no escape from the prejudices of their own time. Is the pursuit of knowledge bound to fail? Is generalizable, objective truth forever beyond the grasp of us finite beings?

Reading Cosmic Order as *logos* provides us with the resources necessary to resist the bleak perspective of skepticism. There is no need to deny the human factor. Scientists bring to their enterprises all the diverse aspects of their experience. So truth-seeking through research is a quest for the truly human person. In fact, there is no other way to do responsible science. Nature, being the Lord's handiwork, calls for personally committed scientists. There is a human dimension to all knowledge, even in the hardest sciences. This is not a defect, as positivism claims. It is part and parcel of what it means to study Nature scientifically. There is no other way to grasp created reality with appropriate richness.

Therefore, Cosmic Order understood as Divine Word points to the direction to take if we want to overcome the antithesis between scientific knowledge and personal involvement that has crippled so much of modern thought. Without any concession to the relativistic mode, it is possible to bring the human subject back into our world picture. Only if humans accept going down that road can they once again be at home in the universe studied by science.

Acknowledging the personal character of all knowledge will also prevent us from seeing science as the only legitimate method of encountering reality. The development of modern sciences is an astonishing success story. It would be foolish to deny the staggering complexity of new insights that the rigor of scientific inquiry has allowed us to access. But the achievements of science should not lure us into thinking that natural sciences, and in particular physics, are the paradigm that should guide explorations of all reality. If we decipher God's handwriting in Cosmic Order, we may instead come to realize that the encounter between two persons can be a more sublime mode of knowledge than the encounter of persons with inanimate matter and forces. It is here in the personal dimension that the human subject most fully interacts with reality. This is not to deny the pertinence of the scientific method. But we now see it as a reduction by means of a highly useful projection of complex reality onto the limited plane of what objectifying inquiry can capture.

Therefore we should not look for accounts of human freedom and moral responsibility solely in terms provided by natural science. Likewise, attempts to reduce psychology to biology or biology to physics are doomed to fail. This does not mean that there is nothing to learn from applying methods of a more fundamental science to other fields of inquiry. But we should not expect to gain exhaustive knowledge through such reductionist research projects. Cosmic Order brought forth by Divine Word shows us that the hierarchy of knowledge works the other way around. It is not the hard sciences, and in particular physics, that set the agenda for human explorations of reality. The logic I have pursued suggests that human knowledge attains its summit in the empathic encounter between two persons. The Bible reveals that true religious experience is of the same kind. In such experience, we encounter the personal ground of being, our Master and Creator, in whom all Cosmic Order has its origin and who has entered human history in the person of Jesus of Nazareth.

&v

LYDIA JAEGER holds a permanent lectureship and is academic dean at the Institut Biblique de Nogent-sur-Marne, an interdenominational Evangelical Bible college near Paris that trains pastors and other church workers at an undergraduate level and laypeople in extension programs. She completed postgraduate studies in physics and mathematics—including research in theoretical solid-state physics—at the University of Cologne (Germany), in theology at the Seminary for Evangelical Theology in Vaux-sur-Seine (France), and in the philosophy of science at the Sorbonne (Paris). Currently, Ms. Jaeger is completing her Ph.D. thesis in philosophy on the possible links between the concept of law of nature and religious presuppositions at the Sorbonne under the supervision of Michel Bitbol (CNRS, France). Since 2000, Lydia Jaeger has had several short-study leaves in the Department of History and Philosophy of Science at the University of Cambridge (United Kingdom), where she is also an associate member of St. Edmund's College. Ms. Jaeger is a member of the Fellowship of European Evangelical Theologians (FEET), the Tyndale Fellowship, and Christians in Science (CiS). She is the author of *Croire et connaître: Einstein, Polanyi et les lois de la nature* (1999) and *Pour une philosophie chrétienne des sciences* (2000).

Science of the Unseen 29

A Perspective from Contemporary Physics

Hyung S. Choi

> "There are more things in heaven and earth, Horatio,
> than are dreamt of in your philosophy."
> —Hamlet, *Act I, Scene 5*

SINCE THE DAWN of civilization, human knowledge has extended to the realms of both the seen and the unseen. Including the relatively brief period of modernity when materialistic and positivistic metaphysics had its own heyday, careful thinkers of all ages have acknowledged the possibility that there are things that may be known beyond what can be observed by our limited perceptions.

Plato expressed his idea of knowledge of reality through his famous allegory of the cave, in which prisoners were chained facing the wall on which only shadows were cast. According to Plato, we are those prisoners who pitifully think that the shadows are the only reality. Aristotle, in his *Physics*, also declared that the objects of scientific knowledge are not the things that are clear to our senses, but the underlying nature or hidden principles that are behind those phenomena.

Contemporary Physics and the Unseen

By the end of the last millennium, an increasing number of scientists saw the glimpses of the unseen looming beyond what they had naively thought as the final chapter of scientific inquiry. In their effort to understand the new discoveries in quantum physics, cosmology, and other scientific frontiers, scientists were forced to push the boundaries of their disciplines further to include new ideas and theories that would have been unimaginable even a few decades before. These new ideas, such as "veiled reality," "eternal inflation and many universes," "hyperspaces and hidden dimensions," "creation out of vacuum," and so on would have been labeled mere "metaphysical speculations" by their predecessors.

This new development in physics is a sure sign that physicists are starting to break away from the positivistic attitude that had dominated their minds for the past few centuries and are returning to the idea that true knowledge should not preclude what is not observable. It was no accident that, at the turn of the new millennium, the American Physical Society, the largest professional society of physicists, published a one-hundredth-anniversary special issue that surveys the status of physics, entitled *More Things in Heaven and Earth* (Bederson 1999).

While scientific understanding of the world has changed dramatically, positivistic philosophy that suspects and even denies spiritual realities still has a strong grip on the general scientific community. In such a typical framework of thoughts, religious discourse does not address issues of reality; they only express the ideas and imaginations that may be a source of subjective value and meaning. It follows, scientism and positivistic philosophy conclude, that there can be no true sense of progress in religious truth-seeking activities.

Recent postmodern philosophies claim to have overcome this modern paradigm through their hermeneutical emphasis. However, many of these approaches rely on social or linguistic deconstruction rather than on reexamination of the very roots of the modern epistemology that has marginalized religious and metaphysical reflections. No rigorous, broad-based, systematic philosophical examination has been done on this all-important issue of "knowledge of reality" in spite of what we have learned from contemporary physics.

In the absence of this necessary philosophical groundwork, theologians and philosophers are bound to dwell in the long shadow of the Enlightenment when describing what they mean by "reality" and what they think proper knowledge should be. Unless we provide a sound theory of knowledge that encompasses both the seen and the unseen based on a new scientific view of the world, the dialog between science and religion will remain simply a curious intellectual side activity and will not be taken seriously as a legitimate, well-founded, mainstream academic research area.

Overcoming this prejudice requires removing the two important mind-blinders from current academia. The first of these is the strong prejudice against the idea of spiritual realities. This stems from the distorted view of the unseen as it has been almost equated with ancient myths and collective imaginations (Choi 2001). The second is the prejudice against the possibility of systematic research on the unseen, including what we call "religious" or "spiritual realities." Our idea of what is spiritual has become largely antithetical to what we consider rational and practical.

Search for the Fundamental Fabric of Nature

Science has been in the vanguard for overthrowing rigid ideas and old paradigms with fresh new thoughts and perspectives. For the last few centuries, as Richard Feynman once observed, physics has been serving effectively as "natural philosophy" as physicists have been seeking the fundamental fabric of reality. The first step in overcoming the prejudice against the "spiritual" aspects of the world is to cultivate the awareness of the metaphysical implications of scientific findings among scientists themselves. Then, the renewed philosophical discussions on epistemology and ontology will naturally follow that and provide a solid ground for serious academic research on the deep nature of reality beyond positivistic science. I believe that an entire new revision of epistemology itself is necessary as a result of our new understanding of the world provided by contemporary scientific developments.

Today, the physics community faces a number of challenges that have significant metaphysical implications. In addition to the well-publicized ideas of the "multiverse," the Anthropic Principle, and complexity theory, there is a resurgence of interest in understanding the nature of vacuum, the underlying principles of quantum mysteries, the nature of space-time itself, higher dimensional realities, macroscopic quantum phenomena both in atomic and condensed-matter physics, the role of information in fundamental natural processes, and the relationship between the mathematical and physical worlds. These are only a few of the promising research areas in physics that may wholly revise or significantly expand our present view of the world. We do not even know what surprises are in store on the way to our search for the deep nature of reality.

For a few important reasons, I suspect that the next fifty years will bring another Copernican revolution in our perspectives on nature. There has been an accumulation of signs that our present picture provided by well-established "standard" theories is not really adequate or truly fundamental. Of course, a well-known reason for this is the conceptual incompatibility between the pictures provided by the two pillars of contemporary physics: general relativity and quantum mechanics. Currently, major attempts are being made to unify the two with some significant theoretical success (Smolin 2001). If any of these attempts ever succeeds, the results will completely shake the very foundations of physics, including our ideas of space, time, and matter.

On the other hand, after about eighty years of development, we are just beginning to see the vast ramifications of quantum mechanics (Greenberger et al 1993). During the last couple of decades, physicists started to discover such unexpected phenomena as macroscopic quantum superposition, quantum nondemolition measurement, quantum eraser, temporal nonlocality, quantum teleportation and cryptography, and quantum computing, which tries to harness the parallel reality of the quantum world.

Another area that may bring about a fundamental change of our view of the world is the research on the nature of vacuum, or what we used to call "empty space" (Barrow 2000). Some suspect that the secret of the underlying fabric and origin of space, time, matter, and energy all lie deep within what we have naively called "nothing." Novel research is being undertaken by different groups of physicists.

Physics and Metaphysics

As John Archibald Wheeler once envisioned, the final theory that unifies these fundamental aspects of physics may turn out to be extremely simple, beautiful, and even compelling. Even if we ever have such a theory in the future, it does not mean that the success will signal the end of physics. On the contrary, I suspect that it will lead to new vistas in which physicists seek deeper and broader connections with other equally important aspects of the world. If we have learned one thing from science so far, it is that Nature has brought ever-present turns and surprises to our limited scientific vision. It is much more likely, as many limit theorems indicate, that we will never be able to solve all the mysteries of Nature, as all inquiries from within are inherently limited (Barrow 1998). After all, we are only a small part of the mystery that we seek to understand.

Other signs in the physics community indicate that physics is heading toward an era that will increasingly accommodate diverse perspectives and paradigms. Some prominent physicists are advocating a nonreductionist approach to fundamental physics (Anderson 1972). Others have become much more open to interdisciplinary issues with metaphysical elements. Still others, following David Bohm's legacy, have started to believe that physics itself needs to be integrated with metaphysics as it seeks deeper aspects of the world (Shimony 1993).

The current state of affairs in physics presents us with a tremendous opportunity to advance scientific research of metaphysical significance. It is very likely that we will observe a great renaissance in physics in this new century as truly creative and mind-boggling ideas sprout and blossom. This is not only because the physics community has a long history of open-mindedness to new ideas and nonorthodox approaches, but because the current situation requires innovative thoughts and fresh outlooks.

The question is whether we will be able to engage these new scientific ideas and theories with equally open-minded philosophical and theological perspectives. Often, the danger is that, without sufficient philosophical guidance on broader contexts of their works, physicists tend to interpret their theories and findings within the naturalistic or materialistic framework. Their rather conservative interpretive tendency is not surprising despite their innovative ideas and theories. By virtue of their own profession, physicists are often immersed in physical aspects of reality. Although changes in scientific theories can come into being rather quickly, changes in perspective need a much longer period of gestation. This is not to say that the naturalistic framework is wrong, but that it is much more desirable and can be fruitful to recognize that other persuasive ways of interpreting new scientific ideas and findings may exist. Proper interpretation of fundamental scientific ideas in broader metaphysical contexts is important because, as Alfred North Whitehead once noted, the future of humanity depends on how we relate these new scientific understandings with the greater perspectives of religion and ethics.

Conclusion

In some sense, new ideas in fundamental physics of the last century already have serious metaphysical components in them, as the boundary between physics and metaphysics has become largely blurred. The search for the fundamental fabric of reality will also become much more interdisciplinary as scientists try to incorporate equally fundamental ideas from other fields of study. Physicists used to feel that physics could ultimately explain everything in Nature using the reductionist program, an explanatory tool that had been so successful in physics and chemistry. However, today an increasing number of physicists start to view the reductionist program as wanting because of the implications of quantum wholeness and new developments from other sectors of physics (Laughlin and Pines 2001). Once we become free of the prejudices of positivistic philosophy and realize that the reductionist picture may not be adequate to understand the fundamental fabric of the world, scientific quests for the ultimate reality will eventually include such phenomena as mind, consciousness, and religious experiences.

Here we will see the disciplines of physics, mathematics, biology, neuroscience, robotics, linguistics, artificial intelligence, and others all converge in our pursuit of the fundamental fabric of the universe. No scientific discipline will remain unaffected by such basic changes in our perspective of Nature. In this search for the unity of knowledge, we will find metaphysical issues and the ideas of the unseen increasingly important. The Dark Age of materialism will pass away, and a new Renaissance will arrive when scientists talk freely of their imaginative ideas of the unseen.

Through this period of integration of science and metaphysics, a new kind of science will emerge that may be called the "science of the unseen." This time, the unseen realities will neither be regarded as a product of unscientific speculations nor be considered antithetical to rational endeavors. Rather, they will be seen as the culmination of the most rigorous scientific understanding and their best rational and creative syntheses. Then we will experience genuine progress in our pursuit of the knowledge of ultimate reality that lies at the hidden heart of all human inquiry.

ℒ♥

HYUNG S. CHOI, PH.D., is Director for Research and Programs in the Natural Sciences at the Metanexus Institute in Philadelphia and a Visiting Fellow at St. Edmund's College, University of Cambridge. Dr. Choi was a Witherspoon Fellow at the Center for Theology and Natural Sciences in Berkeley between 1994 and 1996 and, until assuming his position at Metanexus, was Professor of Mathematical Physics and Philosophy of Science at Grand Canyon University in Phoenix, Director of the Canyon Institute for Advanced Studies, and Chairperson of the Greater Phoenix Science and Religion Society. He is the recipient of many honors and awards for his teaching and research, including the Quality and Excellence in Teaching Award from CTNS.

REFERENCES

Anderson, Philip W., 1972, "More Is Different," *Science* 177, 393–96.

Barrow, John D., 1998, *Impossibility: The Limits of Science and the Science of Limits*, Oxford: Oxford University Press.

———, 2000, *The Book of Nothing: Vacuums, Voids, and the Latest Ideas about the Origins of the Universe*, New York: Pantheon Books.

Bederson, Benjamin, ed., 1999, *More Things in Heaven and Earth: A Celebration of Physics at the Millennium*, New York: Springer-Verlag.

Choi, Hyung S., 2001, "'Knowledge of the Unseen: A New Vision for Science & Religion Dialogue," *Perspectives on Science and Christian Faith* 53:2, 96–101.

Greenberger, Daniel M., Michael A. Horne, and Anton Zeilinger, 1993, "Multiparticle Interferometry and the Superposition Principle," *Physics Today*, August, 22–29.

Laughlin, R. B., and David Pines, 2001, "The Theory of Everything," *The Proceedings of the National Academy of Sciences*, 97:1, 28–31.

Shimony, Abner, 1993, *Search for a Naturalistic World View: Scientific Method and Epistemology* (vol. 1); *Natural Science and Metaphysics* (vol. 2), Cambridge: Cambridge University Press.

Smolin, Lee, 2001, *Three Roads to Quantum Gravity*, New York: Basic Books.

Design and the Designer 30

Picture this: A human family is hurtling through the cosmos on a small spaceship. Unsure of their position in a vast swath of time and space, they have lost contact with their point of origin and can perform only rudimentary calculations with the help of their trusty robot. They have no idea where home is! They are trying to reorient themselves so they can complete their mission, but it looks about as likely as finding a particular atom in the entire galaxy.

Have our science and technology left us, like this fictional human family, *Lost in Space*? I do not believe they have. The findings of science in the twentieth century, I believe, suggest the existence of a subtle and ingenious intelligence behind the structure of the universe. The fine-tuning of the laws of nature and the initial conditions of the universe for life have been the most widely discussed cosmological evidence for design, although other aspects of the laws of nature, such as their beauty and discoverability, also suggest design. Taken together, they constitute a powerful case for design, but one that challenges older mechanistic models based on notions such as Paley's watch. For the theistic scientist or philosopher, these findings of science suggest a broadened and deepened conception of a designer, which may offer new insights into the designer's purposes for creation. And for the person committed to atheistic naturalism as scientific, these scientific findings may themselves pose a challenge to be open to a reality beyond what we think of as the natural order.

The fine-tuning of the cosmos for life refers to the fact that many of the fundamental parameters of physics and the initial conditions of the universe are balanced on a razor's edge for intelligent life to occur: If these parameters were slightly different, life of comparable intelligence to our own would not exist. The first major discovery along these lines was in 1956—that the resonance states of carbon and oxygen had to fall within a narrow range for significant quantities of both carbon and oxygen to be produced in stars. Without enough carbon and oxygen, the existence of carbon-based life would be seriously inhibited. Many other instances of cosmic fine-tuning have been brought to light since then, and much work is continuing. One of the most impressive and discussed cases of fine-tuning is that of the cosmological constant, a term in Einstein's equation of general relativity that governs the rate at which space expands. For the universe to be hospitable to life, this constant must be fine-tuned to at least one part in 10^{53}—that is, one part in one hundred million billion billion billion billion—of what physicists consider its natural range of values. To get an idea of how precise this is, it would be like throwing a dart at the surface of the earth from the moon and hitting a bull's-eye one trillionth of a trillionth of an inch in diameter—less than the size of an atom!

Many physicists and others have taken the position that fine-tuning provides significant evidence that the cosmos is designed—and, furthermore, that one of the purposes of the designer was to create embodied, intelligent beings. Others have questioned this inference by saying that, as far as we know, the values of the fundamental parameters will eventually be explained by some grand unified theory. Hence, it is argued, we do not need to invoke a designer to explain why these parameters have life-permitting values. As astrophysicists Bernard Carr and Martin Rees note, however, "even if all apparently anthropic coincidences could be explained [in terms of such a unified theory], it would still be remarkable that the relationships dictated by physical theory happened also to be those propitious for life" (1979, 612). For the theist, then, the development of a grand unified theory would not undercut the case for design, but would only serve to deepen our appreciation of the ingenuity of the creator: Instead of separately fine-tuning each individual parameter, in this view, the designer simply carefully chose those laws that would yield life-permitting values for each parameter.

Another objection to considering fine-tuning as evidence for design is one that takes us almost into the realm of science fiction: the proposal that there are a very large number of universes, each with different values for the fundamental parameters of physics. If such multiple universes exist, it would be no surprise that the parameters in one of them would have just the right values for the existence of intelligent life—just as in the case where if enough lottery tickets were generated, it would be no surprise that one of them would turn out to be the winning number.

How did these universes come into existence? Typically, the answer is to postulate some kind of physical process, what I will call a "universe generator." Against the naturalistic version of the universe-generator hypothesis, one could argue that the universe generator itself must be "well designed" to produce even one life-sustaining universe. After all, even a mundane item such as a bread-making machine, which only produces loaves of bread instead of universes, must be well-designed as an appliance *and* have just the right ingredients (flour, yeast, gluten, and so on) in just the right amounts to produce decent loaves of bread. Indeed, as I have shown in detail elsewhere (2002), if one carefully examines the most popular and most well-developed universe-generator hypothesis, that arising out of inflationary cosmology, one finds that it contains just the right fields and laws to generate life-permitting universes. Eliminate one of the fields or laws, and no life-sustaining universes would be produced. If this is right, then, to some extent, invoking some sort of universe generator as an explanation of fine-tuning only pushes the issue of design up one level to the question of who or what designed it.

Despite these objections and the fact that the multiple-universe hypothesis typically has been advanced by naturalists as an alternative explanation to design, I am not objecting to the notion of many universes itself. I actually believe that theists should be open to the idea that God created our universe by means of a universe generator. It makes sense that an infinitely creative deity would create other universes, not just our own. Further, the history of science is one in which our conception of nature keeps increasing in size in terms of both space and time—from

believing that the universe consisted of the Earth and a few crystalline spheres created around six thousand years ago to positing a fifteen-billion-year-old universe
with more than three hundred billion galaxies. For the theist, the existence of multiple universes would simply support the view that creation reflects the *infinite creativity* of the creator. This begins to bring us to an expanded notion of a designer,
one far different and more interesting than the more anthropocentric and restrained
God of much traditional and popular religious thought.

Another area in which the fundamental laws and mathematical structure of
nature suggest design, and offer us some glimpses into the nature of the designer,
is their remarkable beauty and elegance. Nobel Prize–winning physicist Steven
Weinberg, for instance, devotes a whole chapter of his book *Dreams of a Final Theory* to explaining how the criteria of beauty and elegance are commonly used with
great success to guide physicists in formulating laws. Indeed, one of the most prominent theoretical physicists of this century, Paul Dirac, has gone so far as to claim, as
Einstein did, that "it is more important to have beauty in one's equations than to
have them fit experiment" (1963, 47). The beauty, elegance, and ingenuity of mathematical equations make sense if the universe was purposefully designed like an
artwork, but appear surprising and inexplicable under the nondesign hypothesis.
Weinberg, who is a convinced atheist, even admits that "sometimes nature seems
more beautiful than strictly necessary" (1992, 250).

According to Weinberg (1992, 149), the sort of beauty manifested by the theories
of fundamental physics is the elegant, sparse sort characteristic of Greek architecture—what is known as the classical conception of beauty. Traditional "design"
arguments appeal to this sort of ordered beauty in nature and consequently tend to
represent God as an engineer or architect. The sort of beauty manifested in the biological realm, however, seems different, and much more difficult to reconcile with
the restrained God of much traditional religious thought: The wild extravagance,
energy, and apparent "messiness" of nature have often been explained away as a
flaw of some kind in a more benign, original design. Such an explanation, however,
clashes with what evolutionary theory teaches us about the emergence of human
beings. To account for the biological realm, I suggest, we need a view of God as a creative artist with a fully developed aesthetic sense, not a view that models God as
merely a great mechanical engineer or precise watchmaker. This latter view paints
a false and harmful picture of the creator that theists should not feel obligated to
defend and that is probably also partly responsible for the perceived conflict between
religion and science.

On closer inspection, however, even the beauty of the mathematical structure of
fundamental physics is not as restrained as is often claimed, but is more akin to art
forms that go beyond traditional notions of classical decorum. For instance, variety and surprise are interwoven into the fundamental principles of physics in such
deep and clever ways that it takes years of work by our planet's best minds to figure
out how to extend the fundamental principles discovered in one domain to that of
another. Further, as evidenced in quantum mechanics, the material world of matter and energy is deeply mysterious and perplexing at the most fundamental level.
Thus, while nature can be described with mathematical simplicity in certain respects

and in certain domains, even fundamental physics itself points beyond conceiving of God as simply an engineer or watchmaker, with the attendant mechanical and reductive model of God's interaction with the world.

The final way in which the laws of nature and the structure of physical reality suggest design, and may reveal information about the nature of the designer, is in what I will call their "discoverability:" that is, the laws of nature themselves seem to be carefully arranged so that they are discoverable by beings with our level of intelligence—like solving a clever puzzle. One way in which this discoverability manifests itself is in the deep and beautiful mathematical structure of nature, something we already touched on above. According to physicist Eugene Wigner, one of the principal founders of quantum mechanics, "The miracle of the appropriateness of the language of mathematics for the formulation of the laws of physics is a wonderful gift which we neither understand nor deserve" (1960:14).

Work on articulating detailed examples of this discoverability has just begun in the last ten years, and the road ahead looks promising. Philosopher Mark Steiner's recent book, *The Applicability of Mathematics as a Philosophical Problem* (1998), for instance, is devoted to articulating examples of such discoverability of the laws of nature. At the end of the book, he concludes that the world is much more "user-friendly" for the discovery of its fundamental mathematical structure than seems explicable under naturalism (1998, 176). Similarly, physicist A. Zee provides several examples of this discoverability. Zee notes, for instance, that it is only because the four fundamental forces of nature—gravity, electromagnetism, the weak force, and the strong nuclear force—have widely varying strengths and domains of operation that, when we study one force, we can conceptually neglect the effects of the others. This allows us to disentangle the effects of each for analysis. As Zee explains, because of this "we can learn about Nature in increments. We can understand the atom without understanding the atomic nucleus. . . . Physical reality does not have to be understood all at once. Thank you, nature" (1986, 20).

Finally, as Michael Denton points out in his book *Nature's Destiny* (1998, 392-95), our advanced technology and science have only been possible because nature has the right elemental ingredients, such as various metals and silicon. If metals did not exist, for instance, industrial technology would not have developed much beyond the horse-drawn wooden buggy. Certainly, without silicon, the information revolution of the last twenty years could not have occurred. The right physical "stuff" would simply not have been available to extend those domains of invention and discovery, at least in the ways we know.

I believe that, if valid, the discoverability of the laws of nature is particularly exciting. It not only suggests design, but implies that our development of sophisticated science and technology was somehow in the cards, or at least was always a possible outcome of this particular universe. Such potential information about the creator's purposes, although certainly tentative, would go a significant way toward putting the development of science and technology into a larger, spiritually oriented context. This context could give technological and scientific advancement the moral and spiritual dimension they need, validating a degree of optimism about our continuing scientific and technological progress, while at the same time prompting us to recognize our science and technology as a gift that we have a profound responsibility to use appropriately.

The case for design that I have sketched above is very similar to the sort of arguments offered for many other scientific theories, in which many factors all point in the same direction and seem difficult to explain on any other hypothesis. As biologist and geneticist Edward Dodson says regarding the case for evolution, "The strongest evidence for evolution is the concurrence of so many independent probabilities. That such different disciplines as biochemistry and comparative anatomy, genetics and biogeography should all point toward the same conclusion is very difficult to attribute to coincidence" (1984, 68).

Further research and elaboration, of course, would be needed to make the case for design from the fine-tuning, beauty, and discoverability of nature of comparable strength. Furthermore, as with the theory of evolution, these design-indicating features of the laws of nature suggest certain kinds of larger purposes and intentions (or lack of them) that must be interpreted. For the theist, the potential implications these features have for our understanding of God and God's purposes for creation might be theologically revolutionary. For the naturalist, they pose an intellectual and moral challenge—to do the best science honestly while not discounting the evidence.

✍

ROBIN A. COLLINS, PH.D., is Professor of Philosophy at Messiah College in Grantham, Pennsylvania. He spent two years as a graduate student studying theoretical physics at the University of Texas at Austin before receiving his Ph.D. in Philosophy from the University of Notre Dame in 1993, where he received the graduate award in the humanities for "outstanding research, teaching, and publication." He has received several awards, most recently a Pew Evangelical Scholars Fellowship (1999–2000) and a Research Fellowship from the Center for Philosophy of Religion at the University of Notre Dame (2003). Collins is widely regarded as one of the leading people in philosophy working on the argument from design, with several recent articles published or forthcoming on this topic. He is also currently working on a book on this topic, tentatively entitled *The Well-Tempered Universe: God, Cosmic Fine-Tuning, and the Laws of Nature.*

REFERENCES

Carr, B. J., and Rees, M. J. "The Anthropic Cosmological Principle and the Structure of the Physical World." *Nature* 278, 12 April 1979: 605–12.

Collins, Robin. "The Argument from Design and the Many-Worlds Hypothesis," in *Philosophy of Religion: A Reader and Guide*, William Lane Craig, ed., Trenton, NJ: Rutgers University Press, 2002.

Denton, Michael. *Nature's Destiny: How the Laws of Biology Reveal Purpose in the Universe.* New York: The Free Press, 1998.

Dirac, P. A. M. "The evolution of the physicist's picture of nature." *Scientific American*, May 1963.

Dodson, Edward. *The Phenomena of Man Revisited: A Biological Viewpoint on Teilhard de Chardin.* New York: Columbia University Press, 1984.

Steiner, Mark. *The Applicability of Mathematics as a Philosophical Problem.* Cambridge, MA: Harvard University Press, 1998.

Weinberg, Steven. *Dreams of a Final Theory.* New York: Vintage Books, 1992.

Wigner, Eugene. "The Unreasonable Effectiveness of Mathematics in the Natural Sciences," *Communications on Pure and Applied Mathematics* 13, 1960: 1–14.

Zee, A. *Fearful Symmetry: The Search for Beauty in Modern Physics.* Princeton, NJ: Princeton University Press, 1986.

Henderson's "Fine-Tuning Argument" 31

Time for Rediscovery

Michael J. Denton

A RE THE LAWS of Nature fine-tuned for life on earth—and perhaps even intelligent life forms like humans? Over the past thirty years, many physicists have claimed they are. And many books presenting the evidence have been published. The idea has even become fashionable. But the first and most important book on the subject was published long before the current wave of interest. The book was *The Fitness of the Environment*. The author was Lawrence Henderson. The date was 1913! Henderson was at the time Professor of Biological Chemistry at Harvard. He was already famous for the many contributions he had made to physiology. One of his equations is known by every medical student, the Henderson-Hasselbalch equation. But *The Fitness* was Henderson's greatest achievement. This great classic is a historic landmark in human thought. In it Henderson examined the basic properties of the key components of life. His conclusion was unequivocal. The properties of matter are "fined-tuned" specifically for life as it exists on Earth. Moreover, this "fine-tuning" is "adjusted" for higher life forms like us. If the properties of matter were any different, we could not exist. Here for the first time was clear scientific evidence that the universe must have "known we were coming."

No one can read this great classic and fail to be impressed. It was highly regarded by many of the great biologists of the early twentieth century. The embryologist Joseph Needham called it that "Golden Book" (1936). J. B. S. Haldane conceded that it presented convincing evidence for design (1985). More recent supporters of Henderson have been Nobel Laureate George Wald (1958) and Yale biophysicist Harold Morowitz (1987). I first read *The Fitness* twenty years ago. The impact was immediate. For me, it opened up a whole new perspective on the living world. Of course, I was familiar with the fine-tuning argument of the physicists. I was aware of the idea that the basic forces of Nature must be close to what they are. If they were different, life would be impossible. Planetary systems would not exist. Atoms and chemistry would not exist. We would certainly not be here (Barrow and Tippler 1986). But I knew that physics could only take us so far. Only biology can go further and show that Nature is fine-tuned for life forms like us. It is because *The Fitness* extends the argument to beings like us that it has such impact.

In *The Fitness*, Henderson examines all the properties of the key building blocks of life. He begins with water. He considers the thermal properties of water that act to retard freezing—high thermal capacity, high latent heat of fusion, expansion before freezing, and expansion on freezing. As he points out, this ensemble of properties is unique. Then he shows how all these properties work together as if by magic to prevent freezing. He then looks at another key building block, carbonic acid. He shows that, like water, it again possess many unique properties, and he shows how these act together to maintain the acid-base balance of living tissues. The result is again like magic, a process providing life with a mechanism "of the highest possible efficiency." He examines the way carbon combines with itself and atoms of hydrogen and oxygen. He shows why no other atoms can combine in such variety and number as these. In his words, "No other element can match carbon, and no other chemistry organic chemistry." He also shows that oxidations "are the best chemical source of energy." Moreover, of all oxidations, those of carbon and hydrogen yield the greatest quantities of energy. Finally, he shows that the building blocks of life are common and abundant throughout the cosmos. So they are also fit to "enter into the stream of life" because of their availability. He concludes with the following words: "Hydrogen, oxygen and carbon, water and carbonic acid are not to be rivaled. The fitness of water, carbonic acid, and the three elements make up a unique ensemble of fitness for the organic mechanism. No other [set of constituents] could possess such highly fit characteristics . . . to promote . . . the organic mechanism we call life."

All the evidence points in one direction. Each of life's building blocks is maximally fit for its role. And in each case, no alternative is known. The whole ensemble of building blocks is like the pieces of a three-dimensional jigsaw puzzle. They can only be assembled to *one unique end*: life as it exists on Earth. The argument is elegant and convincing. The conclusion is compelling. The laws of Nature are fine-tuned for life on Earth. Life is an inevitable consequence of cosmic evolution. And of course the inference regarding design is obvious.

If *The Fitness* had gone no further, it would have still been an immense achievement. But Henderson does go much further. He shows that this fine-tuning extends also to "advanced life forms like modern Humans." Or, as Henderson puts it, "animals like man." Take, for example, the way air-breathing active organisms such as humans rid themselves of heat. There are, as Henderson points out, only three ways of doing this: by conduction, by radiation, or by evaporative cooling. But at temperatures close to 40 degrees centigrade—the temperature of the body—only evaporative cooling will work. It turns out that the evaporative cooling of water is greater than any other known fluid and works with increasing efficiency as the temperature approaches 40 degrees. If the evaporative cooling effect of water were like that of any other fluid, it is very doubtful that advanced warm-blooded organisms such as mammals and birds could ever have evolved. High intelligence means high temperatures. How fortuitous, then, is the evaporative cooling of water. Without it, no advanced intelligence would grace the earth—or any other planet, for that matter. The universe would be unconscious.

Another product of metabolism that must be excreted from the body is the end-product of oxidative metabolism, carbon dioxide. As Henderson points out:

> In the course of a day a man . . . produces some two pounds of carbon dioxide. All this must be rapidly removed form the body. Because it is a gas, this can be easily done by breathing it out in the lungs.

Henderson continues: ". . . were carbon dioxide not gaseous, its excretion would be the greatest of physiological tasks." The fact that carbon dioxide is a gas has another consequence. It makes possible one of the most exquisite and brilliant adaptations in the whole of biology. It allows the body to rid itself of excess acid by simply exhaling it in the lungs. As acid accumulates, it is neutralized by bicarbonate base in the blood. The carbonic acid formed is converted to water and carbon dioxide in the lungs, where it exits the body effortlessly. This stunning example of fine-tuning for organisms like us strikes every student of human physiology.

I became aware of the sheer brilliance of this adaptation while teaching respiratory physiology to medical students. This was before I had read *The Fitness*. Here was a case of fitness that was in the nature of things. It was not the result of selection. For me, the discovery was a personal epiphany: If matter can provide one adaptation, why not others? Perhaps matter played an important role in evolution. It was this insight that first led me to an increasingly skeptical view of pan-selectionism. Later, on reading *The Fitness*, I was intrigued to learn that it was the study of the bicarbonate buffer system that first led Henderson himself to consider the whole question of environmental fitness.[1]

Today, few disagree with the facts to which Henderson alludes. Some may doubt that things are as "maximally fit" as he claims, but no one seriously looking at the evidence doubts that the laws of Nature facilitate and permit only "our type of life." When NASA scientists contemplate looking for life in space, it is carbon-based life that they seek. Henderson would have approved. Since Henderson's day, a vast amount of new biochemical knowledge has been acquired. We know of things that he never dreamed of. But nearly all that has been learned only reinforces his argument. Many additional cases of fine-tuning have come to light. (Some of these are presented in my recent book *Nature's Destiny* [1998].) Take, for example, new evidence of fine-tuning for the origin and evolution of proteins. Recent analyses of meteorites have revealed the presence of many of the amino acids used in proteins. These same amino acids are also the easiest to obtain in prebiotic syntheses (Miller 1987). This means that the building blocks of the proteins are spontaneously formed and common throughout the cosmos. Here is a clear case of fine-tuning toward protein-based life. But this is not all. Recent studies have also shown that stable proteins are very easy to form. In fact, they arise simply like crystals out of the basic properties of amino acid sequences (Denton and Marshall 2001; Denton et al. 2002). Here we have a second case of fine-tuning toward protein based life. Henderson would have been delighted.

The Fitness is one of the most important books published in the twentieth century. Few other books carry a message as profound. But instead of being widely read, it is largely ignored today. This is all the more surprising considering that we all hunger for some evidence, even a hint, that we are here by design. And *The Fitness* certainly provides more than a hint. So why has Henderson's great work fallen into relative oblivion? Why is this great classic not compulsory reading for every biology major throughout the world?

One reason for its lapse into relative obscurity is that, to a very large extent, the force of Henderson's argument is in the details. Only on a careful reading can *The*

Fitness have real impact. The mutual fitness of life's constituents can be appreciated only by considering the details. And it helps to have a biochemical or medical background. But the major reason must be the challenge it poses to conventional Darwinian thought. Darwin claimed that fitness is generated by natural selection. But fitness like that of the bicarbonate buffer for acid-base balance is given by Nature. It is adaptation "for free" arising out of the intrinsic properties of matter. As Henderson insists in such cases: ". . . natural selection could not be involved." Again, Darwin considered evolution to be mainly a contingent process. But *The Fitness* clearly implies that the origin and evolution of life is built into the properties of matter. Such an idea is quite alien to Darwinian thought.

Henderson's views may have fallen out of fashion. But I think his core idea is beyond dispute. There is no question that the properties of matter have played a decisive role in directing the course of evolution. I also agree with Henderson that these properties are fine-tuned for beings like us. Of course, the idea that natural law has influenced the course of evolution is not new. This was orthodoxy in pre-Darwinian days. *The Fitness* echoes the views of Richard Owen and Goethe. But like all great works, *The Fitness* is many things. It is part Platonism, part *Naturphilosophie*. It is materialistic, while at the same time a great work of teleology. Its rediscovery is long overdue. Had it been required reading for students of biology since 1913, I believe the history of twentieth-century biology would have been very different.

ℒ♥

MICHAEL J. DENTON, PH.D., has been a Senior Research Fellow in Human Genetics, Biochemistry Department, University of Otago, Dunedin, New Zealand, since 1989. His main research focus has been on the genetics of human retinal disease; his group made a major contribution to the field by identifying several new genes responsible for retinal diseases. He has had a longstanding interest in evolutionary biology and has argued in recent publications that molecular forms such as the protein folds are determined by natural law, not natural selection. Recently, Dr. Denton was invited to present these views in *Nature* and in an article for the recently published *Encyclopedia of Evolution* (Oxford University Press). He has an article on the same subject in the *Journal of Theoretical Biology*. In his latest book, *Nature's Destiny*, he argues along similar lines to Lawrence Henderson's *Fitness*, presenting evidence for believing that the laws of nature are fine-tuned for life on Earth and for organisms like modern humans.

NOTE

1 See Henderson's (1958) comments on the bicarbonate system in the preface of *The Fitness* and see footnote on 156.

References

Barrow, J. D., and Tipler, F. J. (1986) *The Anthropic Cosmological Principle*. Oxford: Oxford University Press.

Denton, M. J. (1998) *Nature's Destiny*. New York: The Free Press.

Denton, M. J., and Marshall, C. J. (2001) The Laws of Form Revisited. Invited Concepts Column, *Nature*. 410: 411.

Denton, M .J., Marshall, C. J., and Legge, M. (2002) The Protein folds as Platonic forms: New Support for the pre-Darwinian conception of evolution by natural law. *J Theor Biol*. 2002 Dec 7;219(3):325-42. Comment in: *J Theor Biol*. 2003 Jul 21;223(2):263-5.

Haldane, J. B. S. (1985) *On Being the Right Size*. New York: Oxford University Press.

Henderson, L. J. (1958) *The Fitness of the Environment*. Boston: Beacon Press.

Miller, S. L. (1987) Which Organic Compounds Could Have Occurred on the Prebiotic Earth? *Cold Spring Harbor Symp. Quant. Biol*. 52: 17–27.

Morowitz, H. J. (1987) *Cosmic Joy and Local Pain*. New York: Scribner.

Needham, J. (1936) *Order and Life*. New Haven: Yale University Press.

Wald G. (1958) See introduction in Henderson, op. cit. xvii-vviv.

Jennifer J. Wiseman

Every good and perfect gift is from above, coming down from
the Father of the heavenly lights, who does not change like shifting shadows.
—*James 1:17, NIV*

A FEW YEARS AGO, the movie *Contact*, based on the book by Carl Sagan, intrigued viewers with a vision of how alien beings might actually try to make themselves known to those residents of Earth who are inquisitive enough to listen for their messages. In the story, astronomer Ellie Arroway uses radio telescopes, such as the Arecibo dish in Puerto Rico and the Very Large Array (VLA) in New Mexico (see Figure 1), to monitor the heavens for incoming signals that could only have originated from intelligent beings sending intentional messages. Despite the skepticism and discouragement of her scientific colleagues, Dr. Arroway continues to monitor the heavens, and indeed she does detect an unmistakable pattern in signals heard through the VLA radio dishes. This received message launches Ellie, and in fact the whole world, into an adventure unmatched in human history as the experts decide whether to follow the instructions in the message and make true interactive contact with the alien message-senders.

I watched the film with special attentiveness because, like Ellie, I am a radio astronomer. Often, I have used the VLA to study signals from the heavens—not messages from alien life forms, but radiation emitted from the gas in distant galaxies and in nearby interstellar clouds where new stars are forming. To date, no confirmed message-carrying signal from alien intelligence has been received from any radio telescope, although private groups diligently scan the skies for such greetings. Yet the vast compilation of new astronomical information that scientists have discerned through radio—and all other—telescopes in just the last few decades has drastically and forever changed the human view of the universe.

And so I ponder: Have I, too, received messages through radio telescopes? Certainly, I have not received or recognized any coded pulse from an alien life form. And yet, on a still grander scale, I think about the possibility of receiving "messages" from God—the God of the Bible; the Creator and Sustainer of all the laws and grandeur that govern the universe; the God who is personal and who speaks through Nature, through prophets, and through the love and intervention of a Savior. Does this God speak to us, in a sense, through the wonders we discover in the heavens, through our telescopes? As I pause to reflect in stillness, listening beyond the clamor of producing works for academic publishing, participating in professional meetings and talks, pursuing funding and grants, teaching, and encountering academic trials of all sorts, the messages I have heard throughout my early career play again in my ears—seven messages that I believe God "whispers" through radio—and all—telescopes.

> *I. Seek the mysteries of my handiwork. The radiating signals of marvelous workings in the Universe have emanated for eons, yet only for a few decades have you even barely begun to discover them and to trace them to discoveries beyond your imagination.*

Figure 1.: The Very Large Array (VLA) and the Radio Galaxy 3c31

Courtesy of the National Radio Astronomy Observatory / Associated Universities, Inc.

Within the last century, knowledge of the universe opened up to a scale never before contemplated by humankind. In the 1920s, following the "Great Debate" of Harlow Shapley and Heber Curtis and the subsequent discoveries of Edwin Hubble, it was finally realized and agreed that the swirling nebulae of light observed along with stars in the heavens are not located within our own Milky Way galaxy of stars. Instead, it was determined that they must be distinct and separate galaxies located millions, and even billions, of light-years away, rushing away from one another as the very fabric of space expands. A few decades later, the faint echoes of the very beginning of that expansion—microwave background radiation signals left over from the Big Bang—were discovered by Arno Penzias and Robert Wilson of Bell Laboratories as they grappled with what they thought was simply "noise" in their receivers. This radiation emitted from forming galaxies, and even from near the beginning of time, has been swirling to us and past us throughout all of human history, throughout all the generations and civilizations of great thinkers as they postulated various cosmologies and cosmogonies to explain the universe they could observe. And yet only now have we been able to capture and decode these radiative messengers from the heavens, telling us of other galaxies and even of the beginning of time and space. Are we now gaining a complete picture of the universe, or are we just at the beginning of discovery of what the cosmos holds?

II. I take pleasure in your discoveries. My joy in creating is not complete until you see and rejoice in what I have made, and I rejoice in that discovery with you. For when you see the outworking of the forces and processes I have set in motion and the immensity and beauty of time and space, you see something of my character.

We are told in the biblical narrative of Genesis that one of the first tasks God assigned to the first human was to name the animals (Gen 2:19–20a). One gets the definite sense that God was enjoying the process and the intrigue of finding out what the man would see in each unique creature. The image conveyed in the text is that the man studied the attributes of each animal and bestowed on each a fitting, descriptive name—in essence, the first act of observational science. To the author of Genesis, this was seen as an enjoyable activity to both God and man in an unfallen Edenic paradise. How similar to the task of the modern astronomer! We observe objects in the heavens—objects that we cannot manipulate—and we bestow on them descriptive names: spiral galaxy, red giant star, radio jet, dark interstellar cloud. Could it be that after fourteen billion years of evolution of the universe, and eventually of life itself, that God takes joy when we use our developed minds and skills to discover and study the wonders of Creation? I believe so, especially when the joy and awe instilled by such discoveries lead to recognition of the presence, majesty, and creativity of the Creator.

III. There is more to the Universe than meets the eye. Keep looking.

When Galileo Galilei pointed an optical magnifying glass toward the heavens, he saw a new world of detail, such as moons orbiting Jupiter, that contributed to a revolution in human understanding of the cosmos. With each large technological advance in telescopes, a new, previously unseen universe opened before us, reshaping and refining our comprehension of the cosmos. The discovery of cosmic radio waves in 1932 by Karl Jansky led to the development of radio telescopes and the discovery of the "radio sky." Hitherto unknown "radio galaxies" were discovered, many with bipolar outflowing jets larger than the galaxy itself that are spewing material away from the galaxy at nearly the speed of light as an exhaust mechanism for material swirling around a hungry black hole at the galaxy center (see Figures 1 and 2). Radio emissions from regions previously simply known as "dark clouds" for their opaqueness suddenly revealed complexes of swirling and fragmenting interstellar gas coalescing into new stars. Similarly, infrared telescopes are now revealing the patterns of interstellar dust, and X-ray telescopes are revealing energetic galaxies; ultraviolet telescopes are telling us of the mechanisms of the sun and of the production of elements early in the universe, and millimeter-wave telescopes are telling us of circumstellar material around other stars where planets may form. Each "new look" at the sky with different frequencies, different resolutions, and different filters gives us a new sky to add to our growing understanding of the cosmos. We must never stop looking; there is always more to learn.

IV. Creation continues. Stars still form.

It is still a surprise to most people to find out that the universe is not static.

Figure 2. The Hubble Deep Field, a long exposure of the Hubble Space Telescope revealing many faint and distant galaxies. Most light spots on the image are not stars, but galaxies, each containing billions of stars. Some are very distant, requiring billions of light-years for the light to reach us. Some of these galaxies radiate also in infrared, radio, or X-ray light, indicating high activity of internal star formation or black holes.

Courtesy of R. Williams, the Space Telescope Science Institute HDF Team, and NASA.

Through the time machine of light emitted hundreds of millions of light-years ago from distant heavenly bodies, we see ancient galaxies tidally stripping one another as they closely pass, sometimes merging in a spectacular display of interacting spiral arms. Stars exploding as supernovae at the end of their lifespan shine as beacons and distance indicators from both faraway and nearby galaxies. Closer to home, gas clouds observed with radio telescopes even in our own Milky Way are condensed by the motions of the galaxy or by the remnant compression of a supernova, leading to the collapse of pockets of gas into new stars. These "protostars" shine brightly in infrared and millimeter wavelengths through the dense gas of their nursery. As infalling material accretes onto the forming star, some is ejected by the surrounding magnetic field, creating from each stellar pole outflowing jets streaming across the interstellar cloud and beyond in a spectacular display. Shortly after their birth, large stars brighten the surrounding leftover gas by radiatively ionizing it into colorful nebulae. Eventually, the gas is blown away, and the star shines as long as its inner hydrogen fuel lasts. When the fuel is used up, a large star ends as a supernova explosion, dispersing heavy elements into the interstellar medium and creating a disturbance that can trigger the next generation of star formation. Indeed, as we study our dynamic universe, it becomes clear that Creation is not a static collection of matter, but rather a universe evolving according to the processes and forces set in motion long ago and upheld in stability. It even appears that several cycles of star formation and supernovae were needed to produce the heavier elements we now require for life. Created beauty need not be unchanging.

V. You seek, and yet your findings are gifts from Me.

We study and strive diligently to make new discoveries and to understand more of the universe; surely this is pleasing to our Creator. And yet the ability to comprehend the nature of Nature is itself a gift. Moreover, many of the greatest discoveries of the cosmos (and in my own work) have been unintended "accidents," perhaps to remind us that all discoveries are gifts.

VI. Human life is significant because I have chosen it to be so.

One of the puzzles of the cosmos is how to measure the value of human life, given the unfathomable vastness of time and space. One popular measure of our value depends on our uniqueness: Are intelligent beings like us common in the universe? If not, that would seem to increase our "value." So then the arguments and counterarguments tend to go forward along two opposing lines: (1) intelligent life must be common throughout the universe, given the statistical unlikelihood that our solar system is the only one out of billions of galaxies (each with billions of stars) that has components necessary for life to evolve; or (2) we are likely to be the only case of self-aware intelligent life because, given the rather violent nature of circumstellar environments (asteroids, radiation, etc.), our solar system is extremely unusual in its arrangement and has protected Earth from catastrophe long enough for highly evolved life to thrive. However, if one considers other revelations, it appears that our value is not based on our uniqueness as a species. Rather, it lies in the fact that we have been created to have a personal relationship with our Creator (perhaps by evolving to the point where we can begin to comprehend this) and that God has entered our world personally, speaking to us through prophets and rescuing us as Savior. We have a problem accepting this because we forget that "infinite" goes in both directions, that an infinite God is interested in both vast time and space and in the minutiae of our daily lives, knowing even the number of hairs on our head. This is not a new difficulty, for even the biblical Psalmist had trouble comprehending this:

> *When I consider your heavens, the work of your fingers,*
> *the moon and the stars, which you have set in place,*
> *what is man that you are mindful of him,*
> *the son of man that you care for him?*
> *Yet you have made him a little lower than God*
> *and crowned him with glory and honor.* (Ps. 8:3–5, NIV)

VII. Work together, and share what you learn. I am more interested in the discoverers than in the discovery!

Here is a message counter to the classic scientific mindset. A celestial object exists whether or not it is being observed and studied by a detached human being. Even in quantum mechanics, where observation actually changes the state of a system, it is the act of observation, and not the inner character of the observer, that matters. And yet to the One responsible for the cosmos, science conducted in human unity and discoveries shared to uplift others are worth far more than "equivalent" discoveries made for selfish gain or unshared with those unable to make such discoveries themselves. As I write part of this essay, I am working as an American at a Japanese telescope atop Mauna Kea in Hawaii for a few nights with my Japanese collaborators and friends. We are studying magnificent outflowing jets emitted from forming stars with one of the world's most powerful telescopes. Just a few decades ago, such cooperation would have been unthinkable. I ponder the horrors of the World War II attacks here at Pearl Harbor and in Japan at Hiroshima and Nagasaki. How much better it is for the peoples of the world to work together, using technology not for war or greed, but to discover the magnificent handiworks of God! How pleased the Lord must be when the magnificent discoveries of the universe are explained to those whose eyes are cast down from the burdens of life, thereby lifting their sights to beauty and awe and hope.

Again, the biblical Psalmist declares:

The heavens declare the glory of God; the skies proclaim the work of his hands.
Day after day they pour forth speech; night after night they display knowledge.
There is no speech or language where their voice is not heard.
Their voice goes out into all the earth, their words to the ends of the world.
(Ps 19:1–4a, NIV)

P.S. And a bonus whisper: You are part of something beautiful.

Radio telescopes, and indeed all telescopes, reveal a universe of complexity and beauty that speaks of great care and creativity in its design. This very reality tells us that our lives mean more than simply survival. Indeed, we can even see that God is very good for even choosing to make a universe of beauty that leads to life, and thus everything good must proceed from God. Even while terrible evil is present and allowed in our world for a time, we can still proclaim, along with the writer of the book of James just as at the beginning of this essay: "Every good and perfect gift is from above, coming down from the Father of the heavenly lights, who does not change like shifting shadows. . . ."

✍

JENNIFER J. WISEMAN, PH.D., is an Associate Research Scientist in the Department of Physics and Astronomy, Johns Hopkins University, and was the American Physical Society's 2001–2002 Congressional Science Fellow. She received her B.S. in physics from the Massachusetts Institute of Technology in 1987 and had the distinction of co-discovering a comet while still an undergraduate. At Lowell Observatory in Arizona, she discovered an unexpected object—later deemed Comet Wiseman-Skiff—on a photographic plate taken by astronomer Brian Skiff. After her early success, she earned her Ph.D. in astronomy from Harvard University in 1995 with a thesis entitled "Large-Scale Structure, Kinematics and Heating of the Orion Ridge." Dr. Wiseman then served three years as a Jansky Fellow at the National Radio Astronomy Observatory and three years as a Hubble Fellow at Johns Hopkins University before her service on Capitol Hill for the House Science Committee. At Johns Hopkins, she currently studies regions of star formation, specifically the conditions in interstellar gas clouds that lead to the birth of new stars.

PART FOUR

*Perspectives from Quantum Mechanics,
Mathematics, and Symbolic Logic*

The "Trialistic" Structure in Physics 33

New Insights for Metaphysics and Natural Theology

Gennaro Auletta

I N THIS PAPER, I examine complementarity, a concept introduced by Niels Bohr for interpreting quantum mechanics (QM). I explain that QM has three basic features: events, correlations, and dynamics. These features stem from the nature of quantum information, which is a general paradigm—far more general than classical information—covering the emergence of any dynamic system.

If these three features of QM are so general, we may ask how philosophers might perceive them. Alfred North Whitehead and Charles Sanders Peirce pursued this line of thought. Dynamics can be understood as a trade-off between local events and "nonlocal" quantum correlations, results that were partly anticipated by Whitehead and Peirce. Moreover, according to Peirce, the reason these three features are so general is that they are the *imago Dei* ("image of God"); that is, they show a Trinitarian structure, which Peirce called "trialism." In this context, I also briefly consider some consequences of QM for natural theology.

The Complementarity Principle and an Unseen Reality

As is well known, Bohr (1928) developed the idea that, in terms of classical physics, a causally complete description of a physical system has two features: spacetime coordination and the causal, dynamic definition of the system. He pointed out that the unity of these two claims breaks down in QM, so we cannot simultaneously obtain the exact individuation of a system's position and its dynamic description. This is the basis of the complementarity principle. However, there is a certain ambiguity in Bohr's statements, so that we could reformulate this principle by saying that there is a complementarity between an event (by definition, a spacetime localized phenomenon) and the wavelike behavior of the physical system.

The delayed-choice experiment proposed by Wheeler (1978 and 1983) sheds light on this point. Consider a Mach-Zender interferometer (see figure). In Wheeler's version of this setup, the final detectors may be switched from the "ordinary" (not delayed) positions DA' and DB' to positions DA and DB before the photon goes through BS2. This may be done after the beam has already passed through BS1. In the arrangement DA-DB, we detect the (corpuscular) path of the photon, and this represents an event. Instead, in the arrangement DA'-DB', we detect the (wavelike) interference (produced by the transformations induced by BS1 and BS2), and this cannot consist of an individual event. In fact, in order to obtain interference, many experimental runs may be necessary. In general, it is impossible to measure the wavelike features (the wave function) of a single system (D'Ariano and Yuen 1996). Obviously, the two detection typologies are incompatible, according to Bohr's prediction.

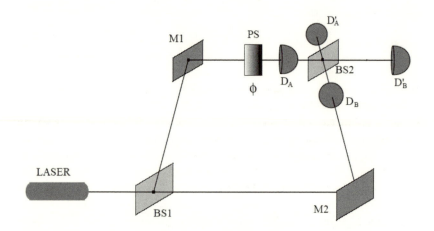

Figure 1. Mach-Zender Interferometer: A light beam emitted by the laser on the left is split into two paths by a beam splitter (BS1), a half-silvered mirror that partly transmits and partly reflects an incident beam. The two beams are then reflected by full mirrors (M1 and M2). The phase shifter (PS) tunes the phase between the two components. In the ordinary (not delayed) setup, the photons will be detected by detectors DA' and DB' after the two beams are recombined and split again by a second beam splitter (BS2). In the setup proposed by Wheeler, the two detectors may be switched from positions DA' and DB' (interference detectors) to positions DA and DB (which-path detectors).

In order to better understand the specificity of the second typology (wavelike interference), let us say that the results obtained by measuring the wavelike properties in a delayed-choice experiment and those obtained by doing the same in an "ordinary" (not delayed) interferometry experiment show no difference. In other words, we are totally free to perform delayed-choice experiments (i.e., to decide up to the last attosecond, 10^{-18} seconds before reaching BS2, to displace the detectors) without altering quantum predictions. This teaches us a general lesson: There are time intervals—in our case, in which the photon travels from BS1 to the detectors—where we cannot assume that an event happened; otherwise we could not be free in our experimental arrangement. However, after such an interval, an event may have occurred—for instance, the photon has been registered by DA' or DB'.

On the other hand, we cannot have an input photon before BS1 and a detection output, say at DA' or DB', and nothing between the input and the output. We are then forced to admit that there must also be a reality before an event has been registered (at DA' or DB'), since events can emerge only from some form of reality. What, then, is this form of reality? It is the superposition-state (in our experiment, the combination of the lower and upper path of the interferometer), or the wavelike nature of the photon (i.e., the initial state and the evolved state before interaction with the detectors).

As I have said, we cannot directly detect the "superposed" reality (again, see D'Ariano and Yuen 1996), but only infer it indirectly (see Auletta and Tarozzi 2004). This is precisely because any measurement is local in nature. However, we should then carefully distinguish between two features. One feature is the *reason* for the quantum (detection) event. There is no reason that we obtain this result and not another (i.e., quantum events are unpredictable or completely random). The other feature is *whether this result comes from nothing*. This is impossible. Therefore, there must be a form of reality that somehow establishes the *general* (but not the particular) conditions from which the event emerges. Let us consider what this form of reality can be.

Whereas the detection event is discontinuous and unforeseeable, the superposition is a form of continuity. Again, a superposition of, say, two states allows all linear combinations of these two states. Moreover, these states associated with possible measurement outcomes, as components of a superposition, cannot be separated. This is a notable difference from classical physics, in which no probability of an outcome "interferes" with another. In other words, the initial state may be seen as a combination of all possible outcomes where interference terms are also present. What, then, is complementarity? It is the relationship between an initial state and any of the evolved states from the initial one before interaction with detectors on the one hand (any one of these states comprises, in terms of probabilities, all the possible measurement results in a continuous way) and the final detection event on the other (which, in an abrupt way and without apparent reasons, is a "decision" of a result in particular). In this sense, an event is a *selection* of one among a huge number of possibilities "encapsulated" in the initial state of the system.

Dynamics is the joint, the connection between these two complementary features—the unforeseeable detection event and the initial superposed (relative to the measured observable) or entangled state, which is "nonlocal" because of the "interference" of probabilities. In order to understand this, we must not consider the photon as an isolated system. Instead, it is necessary to consider the total system encompassing the photon, including the apparatus and also the environment (any quantum system is always correlated to the environment). It is the dynamics that allow the result to be either of the measurement of the path or of the interference pattern. It is also the dynamics that may either destroy an entanglement or constitute it, that may allow a measurement outcome or annihilate this possibility by returning to the initial state through reversible dynamics (the so-called quantum eraser). And any of these possibilities must be considered as an extreme point of a wide range of intermediate possibilities, especially between pure corpuscular and pure wavelike behavior (Mittelstaedt et al. 1987). Therefore, contrary to Bohr's opinion, these two must be understood as limiting cases of dynamic behavior. In other words, dynamics should be considered the trade-off between events and the continuity of quantum correlations.

The "Trialistic" Structure in Physics and Metaphysics

In QM, therefore, three fundamental features must be distinguished (see also Auletta 2003): (1) the abrupt, discontinuous, local production of an event; (2) the relational, continuous, "nonlocal" dimension of superposition and entanglement; and (3) the dynamic trade-off between these two opposite features.

My point is that these features are not only characteristics of quantum reality, but also of the universe in general. In fact, they are a direct consequence of the nature of information in QM (see Auletta 2004a, 2004b) as any quantum system represents information. The initial (wavelike) state may be seen as potential information that contains all possible measurement outcomes. An event may then be seen as a form of selection of this initial source of potential information.

If these features are so general, we might ask whether they have been perceived, even if in a confused form, by great metaphysicians. The answer is yes—in particular, by Whitehead and Peirce. It is stunning to realize that Whitehead wrote his considerations (1929, 169) at almost the same time that Bohr published his article (1928). Although to my knowledge neither knew of the other's opinions, they each addressed the fact that (classical) science requires scientific observations that have to do with what Whitehead calls "presentational immediacy"—the location of things in the present time (1929, 61–70 and 121–26)—as well as with scientific theories (and laws) that have to do with causal efficacy.

This is perhaps the place to shed some light on the misunderstanding of causality. Causality may be only the result of the convergence between observation and law, between events and the correlations that allow the possibilities from which events may emerge. The important point is that Whitehead completely agrees with the idea that at any moment the universe "makes decisions" that represent a selection of the potentialities that the past state allowed (1929, 42–46).

In explaining his notion of trialism, Peirce introduced the concepts of *firstness*, *secondness*, and *thirdness*. About *firstness*, he said:

> The idea of First is predominant in the ideas of freshness, life, freedom. The free is that which has not another behind it, determining its actions.... (CP 1.302)

And:

> It must be initiative, original, spontaneous, and free; otherwise it is second to a determining cause.... It cannot be articulately thought: assert it, and it has already lost its characteristic innocence; for assertion always implies a denial of something else. Stop to think of it, and it has flown! What the world was to Adam on the day he opened his eyes to it, before he had drawn any distinctions, or had become conscious of his own existence—that is first, present, immediate, fresh, new, initiative, original, spontaneous, free, vivid, conscious, and evanescent. (CP 1.357)

I stress here the idea that the "first" is not determined by the preceding conditions, as in the case of a quantum-mechanical event.

About *secondness*, Peirce wrote:

> The second category that I find, the next simplest feature common to all that comes before the mind, is the element of struggle.... Now there can be no resistance where there is nothing of the nature of struggle or forceful action. By struggle I must explain that I mean mutual action between two

things regardless of any sort of third or medium, and in particular regardless of any law of action. (CP 1.322)

The stress on struggle remains from classical (mechanical) science. The important
point, I think, is that "secondness" implies relationships between several things.

It is also interesting that Peirce developed the idea that individuals (and events)
are the result of a selection among many possibilities, apparently with no reason:

> Hence, remembering that the word "potential" means indeterminate yet
> capable of determination in any special case, there may be a potential aggre-
> gate of all the possibilities that are consistent with certain general condi-
> tions; and this may be such that given any collection of distinct individuals
> whatsoever, out of that potential aggregate there may be actualized a more
> multitudinous collection than the given collection. Thus the potential aggre-
> gate is, with the strictest exactitude, greater in multitude than any possible
> multitude of individuals. But being a potential aggregate only, it does not
> contain any individuals at all. It only contains general conditions which per-
> mit the determination of individuals. (CP 6.185)

The Trinity in Natural Theology

Peirce called the *first* category *tychism* (CP 6.102), which comes from the ancient
Greek word for "chance." The *second* category he called *synechism* (CP 6.103), which
comes from the ancient Greek word for "continuity." The *thirdness* is often said to
be the middle between the first and the second (CP 1.337). Peirce called this *third* category *agapism* (CP 6.302), which comes from the Greek Christian word for "love."
This is not fortuitous, because already the young Peirce (1866) had spoken of the
Christian Trinity in referring to the three categories. And he would do the same at
the end of his life by speaking of the triad in terms of the Triune God (1906a: 364;
see CP 5.436). Later, he often called the first "God the creator" (CP 1.362).

The second, the continuity, then is analogous to the Son (the Mediator), and the
third is analogous to the Holy Spirit, the dynamic mediation between Father and
Son—Love. In summary, the Father is the will and act of creation, therefore the
event. The ultimate reason of the act of the creation is God's Will. On the other
hand, the act of creation is in itself a germinal event in the sense that it is a call for
the creature to actively participate to it. The destiny of our universe in this sense is
open, and in this sense it is an event that renews itself at each moment and at any
scale; any event is the renewal of the First Event. The Son, the Mediator, is therefore
relation, but not only between God and His creatures. The Logos is also relation in
itself; any intellectual act is ultimately a relation between elements and for this reason can be cast in conditional form (Peirce 1868).

Therefore, the Holy Spirit, Love, is the dynamic bond between Father (event)
and Son (relation). Love is the elevation of any interaction because it is integration
into a superior whole. In this sense, Peirce could write that "the continual increase
of the embodiment of the idea-potentiality [in the Creation] is the *summum*

bonum" [1906b: 388]. Peirce tried to see the universe as an embodiment of this trinitarian structure.

The three features I discuss above may be seen as a further development of Peirce's tripartite trialistic structure. His main idea, with which I agree, is that the modern age, especially the scientific culture, is a heritage of middle-age nominalism. According to this philosophy, only objects (or events) that can be directly experienced exist. On the other hand, Peirce pointed out that there is no reason to deny reality to other forms of being that do not have a bodily structure. In my opinion, the wavelike behavior of quantum systems is such a reality. It displays a character that is common to all forms of relationships, namely (1) the interdependence between parts, (2) the fact that this interdependence is ultimately a form of covariance, (3) nonlocality, (4) the fact that any relation is a decrease of the "degree of freedom" of the relatives, and (5) the fact that it is impossible to have a direct experience of it. Given a local reality (events) and a nonlocal reality (relations, correlations, interdependencies), the problem is how to join or to connect these two extremes. This is the role played by dynamic processes, a point that Peirce did not completely understand because he thought in classical terms. In fact, dynamics in the classical framework of physics is rather kinematics extended over dynamic variables such as energy and momentum. Since a system is always perfectly determined, the dynamics does nothing other than "displace" the system in a given "space," for instance in the phase space. In quantum mechanics, this is a trade-off between opposite realities or exigencies and as such is the only source of any thing that we consider existent.

ℒ♥

GENNARO AULETTA, PH.D., obtained his doctorate in philosophy in 1993 at Rome University. He is Invited Professor at the Free University of Urbino and at the Pontifical Athenaeum Antonianum. Professor Auletta is also Scientific Director of Science and Philosophy at the Pontifical Gregorian University, Rome. He is the editor of four books and author of fifteen papers and three books: *Determinismo e Contingenza*, Naples, 1994 (about the modal logic and metaphysics of Leibniz); *Foundations and Interpretation of Quantum Mechanics: A Critical-Historical Analysis of the Problems and a Synthesis of the Results*, Singapore, 2000, 2001; and *Introduzione alla Logica*, Roma, 2002 (a short introduction to logic). Professor Auletta's main interests are in the domain of the foundation and interpretation of quantum mechanics, information theory, philosophy of nature and ontology, history of science, and logic.

REFERENCES

Auletta, Gennaro. 2000 *Foundations and Interpretation of Quantum Mechanics. In the Light of a Critical-Historical Analysis of the Problems and of a Synthesis of the Results*, Singapore: World Scientific; rev. ed. 2001.

———. 2003 "Some Lessons of Quantum Mechanics for Cognitive Sciences," *Intellectica* 36-37, 293–317.

———. 2004a "Quantum Information and Inferential Reasoning," submitted to *Foundations of Physics*.

———. 2004b "Quantum Information as a General Paradigm," submitted to *Foundations of Physics*.

Auletta, G., and Tarozzi, G. 2004 "Wavelike Correlations versus Path Detection: Another Form of Complementarity," *Foundations of Physics Letters* 17, 89–95.

Bohr, Niels. 1928 "The Quantum Postulate and the Recent Development of Atomic Theory," *Nature* 121, 580–90.

D'Ariano, G. M., and Yuen, H. P. 1996 "Impossibility of Measuring the Wave Function of a Single Quantum System," *Physical Review Letters* 76, 2832–35.

Mittelstaedt, P., Prieur, A., and Schieder, R. 1987 "Unsharp Particle-Wave Duality in a Photon Split-Beam Experiment," *Foundations of Physics* 17, 891–903.

Peirce, Charles S. 1866 "The Logic of Science or Induction and Hypothesis: Lowell Lectures," in W I, 357–504.

———. 1868 "Some Consequences of Four Incapacities," *Journal of Speculative Philosophy* 2, 140–57; in W II, 211–42.

———. 1906a "The Basis of Pragmaticism in Phaneroscopy," in EP II, 360–70.

———. 1906b "The Basis of Pragmaticism in Normative Sciences," in EP II, 371–97.

———. CP *The Collected Papers*, Vols. I–VI (eds. Charles Hartshorne and Paul Weiss), Cambridge, MA: Harvard University Press, 1931–35; vols. VII–VIII (ed. Arthur W. Burks), Cambridge, MA: Harvard University Press, 1958.

———. W *Writings*, Bloomington, Indiana University Press, 1982–.

———. EP *The Essential Peirce*, Bloomington: Indiana University Press, 1998.

Wheeler, John A. 1978 "The 'Past' and the 'Delayed-Choice' Double-Slit Experiment," in A. R. Marlow (ed.), *Mathematical Foundations of Quantum Theory*, New York: Academic, 9–48.

———. 1983 "Law without Law," in J. A. Wheeler and W. H. Zurek, (eds.), *Quantum Theory and Measurement*, Princeton, NJ: Princeton University Press, 182–213.

Whitehead, Alfred N. 1929 *Process and Reality*, London, New York: Macmillan Pub., 1929, 1957, corrected ed. 1978, 1979.

Zurek, Wojciech H. 1981 "Pointer Basis of Quantum Apparatus: Into What Mixture Does the Wave Packet Collapse?" *Physical Review* D24, 1516–25.

———. 1982 "Environment-induced Superselection Rules," *Physical Review* D26, 1862–80.

Michael Silberstein

The Brain – is wider than the Sky –
For – put them side by side –
The one the other will contain
With ease – and You – beside –
The Brain is deeper than the sea –
For – hold them – Blue to Blue –
The one the other will absorb –
As Sponges – Buckets – do –
The Brain is just the weight of God –
For – Heft them – Pound for Pound –
And they will differ – if they do –
As Syllable from Sound –
– Emily Dickinson (1862)

I HAVE BEEN ASKED to write about the ultimate fate of what the twentieth-century American philosopher Wilfrid Sellars called "the manifest image" in light of present and future developments in science. The manifest image of humans is that we are beings with consciousness, beliefs, desires, intentions, and volitional powers. The scientific materialist image portrays humans as embodied machines subject to study and ultimate explanation by physics, molecular biology, and neuroscience. The question of reconciling these two apparently disparate worldviews is a question not just about our image of humanity, but about our conception of the whole of reality. For example, string theory paints a very different picture of the universe than we learn from the world of our everyday experience, and for many, the manifest image includes supernatural entities such as God and souls, which do not appear as components of theories in physics and other sciences.

Can one reconcile the scientific materialist worldview with the manifest image? Or are these differing perspectives largely mutually exclusive? If they are mutually exclusive views, then does the success of science render the manifest image a mere death mask? Has science defeated the ancient picture even of humans as persons with freedom and real choice? And does it render the idea of a spiritual reality nothing but a realm of *faerie* stories?

I argue that neither the reductive scientific image nor the commonsense dualistic manifest image represents the deepest conception of reality. In the spirit of Huxley's *The Perennial Philosophy* (1944), I advance the notion that the most profound scientific thinking and spiritual thinking actually converge on a conception of reality that is radically counterintuitive from the perspectives of both the manifest image and the reductive scientific image: that the world and everything in it is one system—a deep unity—which, for various pragmatic reasons, we human beings carve up into systems and subsystems, parts and wholes, causes and effects, localized and separable mechanisms, and so on. The core aspect of the oneness of being is a fact missed by both the manifest image and the causal/mechanical scientific perspective. The basic insight goes by many names, such as "emergence," "relationalism," "holism," "*potentia*," and so forth. I call this perspective of unified diversity "perennial pluralistic monism," which has definite consequences regarding several great debates and questions. These include the mind-body problem, the question of purpose, and the nature and existence of God.

The Real Meaning of Quantum Mechanics

Many people do not realize that what most bothered Einstein about quantum mechanics (QM) was not nonlocality or even indeterminism; it was nonseparability:

> But whatever we regard as existing (real) should somehow be localized in time and space. That is, the real in part of space A should (in theory) somehow 'exist' independently of what is thought of as real in space B. When a system in physics extends over the parts of space A and B, then that which exists in B should somehow exist independently of that which exists in A. That which really exists in B should therefore not depend on what kind of measurement is carried out in part of space A; it should also be independent of whether or not any measurement at all is carried out in space A. If one adheres to this programme, one can hardly consider the quantum-theoretical description as a complete representation of the physically real. If one tries to do so in spite of this, one has to assume that the physically real in B suffers a sudden change as a result of a measurement in A. My instinct for physics bristles at this. However, if one abandons the assumption that what exists in different parts of space has its own, independent, real existence, then I simply cannot see what it is that physics is meant to describe. For what is thought to be a 'system' is, after all, just a convention, and I cannot see how one could divide the world objectively in such a way that one could make statements about parts of it. (Einstein, in a 1948 letter to Max Born)

Einstein's concerns with QM were based on conflicts with two principles that he regarded as crucial for "realism": (1) separability, the notion that the universe can be divided into separable systems with their own definite properties: what we think of as existing or real in region A should exist independently of what we think of as existing or real in region B; and (2) locality, the notion that the properties of a system in region A should be independent of what we choose to measure in region B or whether any measurement at all is performed in region B.

Now, if we assume that a system in region B does not have any properties independent of the properties of system A, then we violate separability. The possibility of quantum entangled states over any pair of spacelike separated regions A and B means that a measurement at A can change the catalog of properties not only at A but also at B; this violates locality. Einstein, on my reading, was most bothered by nonseparability (quantum holism). He held that the very possibility of doing science demands that a system be describable as being localized in a continuously connected spatiotemporal region.

My preferred interpretation of QM (see Howard 1994 for more details) sides with Bohr against Einstein. It embraces the holism that Einstein and many others found so repugnant. The causal-mechanical worldview requires separability and locality, a world of autonomous subsystems in which the measuring devices (including observers) and the systems measured are separable. Directions in modern QM, both theoretical and experimental, seem to be clear in telling us that we must give up this notion. My answer to John A. Wheeler's question "Why the quantum?" is that the holism glimpsed by QM is the most fundamental fact about the universe. My claim is that QM is not fundamentally about the behavior of nonclassical waves *and* particles, but about the inextricable wholeness or oneness of the universe, which is one system. The nonclassical features of QM result from the entanglement of the observer/observed, measuring devices, and the systems measured. It is because of entanglement that QM has nonseparability, nonlocality, complementarity, probabilistic outcomes, an absence of transtemporal objects, and so forth. QM cannot ascribe independent reality to an observer or the observed. It cannot therefore eliminate "external disturbances" from acts of observation and measurement (Howard 1994).

Bohr's idea is that scientific knowledge emphasizes space, time, transtemporal objecthood, causality, and so forth as necessary a priori categories under which our representations and knowledge of physical systems must be organized. The point of the "complementarity interpretation" is to articulate a different conception of the nature of physical or scientific knowledge in light of radical quantum holism. Complementarity (such as the well-known position/momentum example or the space-time/causal example) is a function of entanglement. Recall that properties related by complementarity in QM are noncommuting. Noncommuting properties are mutually exclusive. They complement each other. Such properties are essential aspects of the same entity or system. The most well-known formal example is the noncommuting relationship between position and momentum. And the most notorious informal example is wave/particle duality. We cannot ascribe to an observed system alone a unique, complete, and correct description. Complementarity allows us to maintain Kantian intuitions that classical assumptions are needed to make sense of experimental results.

Relationalism and Complementarity in Eastern Thought

Eastern philosophical and religious traditions such as Hinduism, Buddhism, and Jainism incorporate metaphysical and epistemological teachings that seem similar to the kind of holism, relationalism, complementarity (in the much more informal philosophical sense), and so on that have been championed by many students of QM over the years. While mystics and physicists may not literally be making identical claims, they may recognize similar insights, acquired by very different means. Take the following examples from Bohr and Schrödinger, respectively:

> For a parallel to the lesson of atomic theory . . . we must in fact turn to quite other branches of science, such as psychology, or even to the kind of epistemological problems with which already thinkers like Buddha and Lao-tse have been confronted, when trying to harmonize our position as spectator and actor in the great drama of existence. (Bohr 1987, 20)

> Subject and object are only one. The barrier between them cannot be said to have been broken down as a result of recent experience in the physical sciences [quantum mechanics], for this barrier does not exist. (Schrödinger 1958, 3)

It is well known that many of the founding fathers of QM see echoes of its deeper lessons in Hinduism, Buddhism, Taoism, Jainism, and other spiritual traditions. Two representative texts follow. The first is from a twentieth-century Hindu saint echoing the *Upanishads*. The second is from a scholar of Buddhism. These examples demonstrate why the founding fathers of QM cited parallels between physics and Eastern metaphysical thought:

> Everything is inter-linked and therefore has numberless causes. The entire universe contributes to the least thing. All divisions are illusory. (Sri Nisargadatta Maharaj 1973, 36–40)

> We might also say that a dharma's [things, thoughts, mental events] identity is not self-contained but relational. And since the other dharmas to which it is related also exist only relationally, there is no 'fixed point,' no self-established entity anywhere. A dharma by itself has no nature, any more than an electron can itself be said to be either a wave or a particle. Call it interdependent arising, dependent origination, emptiness, the absence of intrinsic nature, but all facts, all phenomena, are relational. (William Ames 2003, 300–301)

Although one can find the concept of complementarity stated philosophically within Hinduism, Buddhism, and Taoism, the most direct place to find it emphasized is in Jainism. The central philosophy of Jainism is Anekāntavāda (see Shaw 2000). The ontological aspect of the doctrine holds that reality is multifaceted and possibly has infinite aspects, features, or modes. It also holds that reality comprises opposite (complementary) aspects—for example, it is both many and one. The doctrine of Anekāntavāda also has an epistemological aspect—namely, that all propositions attributing properties to an object or reality as a whole are true only in relation to a certain point of view, in a particular context, under a certain condition, or in some respect.

Thus, whether one is talking about complementarity in QM or in the context of Eastern philosophy, the world is considered primarily a unity, such that it is we who do the carving, whether by sensory modalities, conceptual schemas, explanatory schemas, mathematical formalisms, or experimental setups. A complementary relationship therefore exists between the oneness and multiplicity of the universe. Consider a passage from the Hindu tradition, the first to articulate this idea:

> From the highest point of view the world has no cause. Once you create for yourself a world in time and space, governed by causality, you are bound to search for and find causes for everything. You put the question and impose an answer. Each moment contains the whole of the past and creates the whole of the future. In reality all is here and now and all is one. Multiplicity and diversity are in the mind. Everything is caused by all and affects all. The diversity is in you only. See yourself as you are and you will see the world as it is—a single block of reality, indivisible, indescribable. Your own creative power projects upon it a picture and all your questions refer to the picture. (Sri Nisargadatta Maharaj 1973, 39)

Philosophical and Theological Consequences of Perennial Pluralistic Monism

While unavoidably "fuzzy," such a basic framework of thinking has far-ranging consequences for metaphysics and epistemology. Take, for example, the issue of causation. While good, pragmatic reasons may exist to divide the world into causes and effects, causal mechanisms, causal-mechanical subsystems, and so forth, holism affirms an underlying unity: We have one system—the universe.

Radical relationalism also has definite consequences regarding the question of whether the universe is structured into a hierarchy of discrete layers, levels, or entities such as particles, atoms, molecules, cells, brains, minds, and so on. Given radical relationalism, even if the ordering of complexity in structures (ranging from those of elementary physics to those of neurophysiology) is discrete, the interactions between such structures will be entangled. Therefore, any separation into levels will be arbitrary and selected for pragmatic purposes only. Such divisions will be dependent on what question is being put to nature and what "scale" of phenomena is being probed. Reality in this view has a decidedly "non-Boolean" structure (i.e., it can't be reduced to interrelationships between entities perceived to be separate and distinct).

On the related subject of scientific explanation, radical relationalism suggests that we should be polyphonists and not monistic exclusivists about matters of explanation. Philosophers of science debate whether *the most fundamental* explanation for any given phenomenon is causal/mechanical, nomological, or unificationist. However, radical relationalism speaks in favor of the pragmatic account of scientific explanation, which holds that the answer to the question is to be determined on a case-by-case basis. There just is no perspective- or interest-independent fact about what constitutes *the most fundamental* scientific explanation in any given case.

All of this has implications for the debate between reductionism and emergence. There are far too many versions of each of these doctrines to enumerate here (see Silberstein 2002, for more details). Nevertheless, we can focus on two issues concerning reductionism: (1) reduction in the sense of atomism and (2) intertheoretic reduction such as the so-called Theory of Everything (TOE). "Atomism" here refers to the idea that the most fundamental intrinsic properties of the most fundamental parts (e.g., particles, strings) determine all the properties of the less fundamental objects (e.g., atoms, molecules, cells) that they "compose," "realize," or what have you. For example, if two possible worlds are identical with respect to their fundamental physical facts, then they will be doppelgangers with respect to all their macroscopic facts as well. Quantum entanglement stands partially against atomism. Indeed, given radical relationalism there simply are no intrinsic properties. However, the failure of atomism still leaves the second question open—whether there exists a unique TOE, such as string theory, from which it is possible, in principle, to derive or otherwise obtain the laws and phenomena of "higher-level" physical theories.

One way of interpreting the thinking of the founding fathers of emergentism (e.g., C. D. Broad) is to note their focus on the point that intertheoretic reduction fails as a matter of principle. Thus, the quantum does not necessitate the classical. And this in turn does not necessitate life. And this in turn does not necessitate mind. And so on. For Broad, the quantum, the classical, life, and mind are all fundamental facts or features of the world. Each domain possesses laws and properties irreducibly specific to itself.

Consider, for example, QM as a TOE. As Robert Laughlin puts it:

> We know the Schrödinger equation is correct because it has been solved accurately for small numbers of particles (isolated atoms and small molecules) and found to agree in minute detail with experiment. However, it cannot be solved accurately when the number of particles exceeds about 10. No computer existing, or that ever will exist, can break this barrier because it is a catastrophe of dimension. It is possible to perform approximate calculations for large systems, and it is through such calculations that we have learned why atoms have the size they do, why chemical bonds have the length and strength they do, why solid matter has the elastic properties it does, etc. With a little more experimental input for guidance it is even possible to predict atomic conformations of small molecules, simple chemical reaction rates, structural phase transitions, ferromagnetism, and sometimes even superconducting transition temperatures. But the schemes for approximating are not first-principles deductions but are rather art keyed to experiment, and thus tend to be the least reliable precisely when reliability is most needed, i.e., when experimental information is scarce, the physical

behavior has no precedent, and the key questions have not yet been identified. Predicting protein functionality or the behavior of the human brain
from these equations is patently absurd. So the triumph of the reductionism of the Greeks is a pyrrhic victory: we have succeeded in reducing all of
ordinary physical behavior to a simple correct TOE [i.e., quantum mechan-
ics] only to discover that it has revealed nothing about many things of great
importance. (Laughlin and Pines 2000, 28)

In this preceding passage, Laughlin's remarks about QM's being for all practical
purposes a TOE are well taken. However, his remarks are ambiguous with respect
to our present concern. Is it *in principle* possible (viz., for God to do it) to derive
molecular structure and other classical features of the universe from QM alone? Is
our inability to do so simply a function of ignorance?

Here I offer a Bohrian, or radical relationist, answer to this question. Is QM a
TOE? Yes and no. Is our inability to derive *ab initio* classical phenomena, such as
molecular structure from the Schrödinger equation, just a function of ignorance?
No! In order to explain the phenomena of classical mechanics, must we posit emergent laws and properties in the sense defended by Broad? No! Therefore, QM is a
TOE in *some sense*. For example, it is well known that researchers are attempting to
screen off objects at higher and higher scales (i.e., objects that are more and more
"macroscopic," or classical) to determine whether there is a classical limit to quantum interference effects. If we were to discover such a limit (whether at the level of
viruses or of elephants), then Broad's brand of emergentism with respect to the
classical realm might be largely vindicated. The Bohrian view that I am defending
is betting that no such classical limit exists. Nonetheless, QM is not a TOE in any
sense implying that classical mechanics would be desirable from it and has not been
merely a function of ignorance. It is well known, for example, that a smooth or regular limiting relation exists between special relativity and Newtonian mechanics
such that $(v/c)^2$ à 0. It is also well known that the limiting relation between quantum
and classical mechanics is not smooth, but results in an asymptotic singularity in the
semiclassical limit in which Planck's constant $h \rightarrow 0$. From this, some might try to
infer some kind of classical limit to quantum interference effects or some kind of
Broad-type thesis of emergence with respect to classical phenomena. However, the
view I am espousing will explain the asymptotic singularity in terms of the necessity of requiring the introduction of a new "contextual topology." Classical properties such as molecular structure "emerge" only given the "fundamental" quantum
description plus the new contextual topology. It is the radical relationalism built
into the nature of reality that explains the need to introduce contextual topology,
not the other way around.

Next, consider the "hard problem of consciousness." Once again, we find a convergence of thought between the great minds of Eastern philosophy and the founding fathers of QM as to the significance of radical relationalism:

The general problem of the relations between psyche and physis, between
the inner and the outer, can, however, hardly be said to have been solved. . . .

Yet modern science may have brought us closer to a more satisfying conception of this relationship by setting up, within the field of physics, the concept of complementarity. It would be most satisfactory of all if physis and psyche could be seen as complementary aspects of the same reality. (Pauli 1994, 260)

Consciousness and the world appear and disappear together, hence they are two aspects of the same state. That which matter and consciousness are but aspects is never born and never dies. What makes the bridge between the two [between matter and mind]? The very gap between is the bridge. That which at one end looks like matter and at the other end like mind, is in itself the bridge. Don't separate reality into mind and body and there will be no need of bridges. Consciousness arising, the world arises. (Sri Nisargadatta Maharaj 1973, 17)

"Mind" and "matter" are different ways of looking at or describing the same thing—two interdependent and essential sides of the same coin. You cannot have one without the other, just as you cannot have either a measuring device or a quantum system being measured without the other.

While the take on the mind/body problem being described here is in some sense a dual-aspect neutral monism, once again pragmatic pluralism is called for. One should not be confounded by questions such as "What is the nature of mind?" The question is ill-posed if there is no singular nonperspectival, non-context-dependent answer to such questions. There is some sense in which, minus the implicit exclusivist assumption, the identity theory, dualism, functionalism, and so forth are all correct theories of mind. Mind is phenomenological, physical, informational, *and* functional, depending on the model under consideration, as well as the questions being asked and other contextual features of explanation. Unfortunately, in philosophy of mind we define these various theories about the nature of mind in such a way that they are competing and mutually exclusive. I believe this is a mistake driven by old-fashioned Platonic essentialism and the idea that to explain is to reduce. Again, we find that Asian philosophy is way ahead of its Western counterpart on this matter:

Consciousness and unconsciousness, while in the body, depend on the condition of the brain. Consciousness as such is the subtle counterpart of matter. Just as inertia and energy are attributes of matter, so does harmony manifest itself as consciousness. You may consider it in a way as a form of very subtle energy. Wherever matter organizes itself into a stable organism, consciousness appears spontaneously. With the destruction of the organism consciousness disappears (Sri Nisargadatta Maharaj 1973, 265).

There is certainly a convergence between Buddhism and science when you speak of gross levels of consciousness. Buddhists would agree that the gross levels of consciousness are contingent upon the body, and when the brain ceases to function, those levels of consciousness do not arise. We've agreed that this [gross] consciousness arises in dependence upon the brain.

Consciousness or mind is not a thing existing in and of itself. This is a false representation, because there are many degrees of subtlety of consciousness. For example, the gross level of mind and energy exists in dependence upon the gross physical aggregates. As long as the brain is functioning, there is gross consciousness, and as soon as one becomes brain-dead, one has no more consciousness at this gross level. So far, this Buddhist perspective accords with the neurosciences. (The Dalai Lama 1997, 165)

A more Western, directly scientific way to express the Buddhist and Hindu conception of mind and consciousness is one that has been defended by myself and others (Varela et al. 1991; Silberstein 2001): to view mental processes as emerging from self-organizing networks that tightly interconnect brain, body, and environment at multiple levels. From this perspective, it makes no sense to think of the brain, body, and environment as internally and externally located with respect to one another. Instead, they are mutually embedding and embedded systems, tightly interconnected on multiple levels. The point is that radical relationalism obtains throughout reality, from the quantum to the mind.

Conclusion

We have seen that the most profound Western physics and many of the spiritual traditions of the East do in fact converge on a view about the nature of ultimate reality—specifically, the perennial oneness of being. Huxley argued that perennial pluralistic monism is also an interpretation fitting within much of the Western spiritual tradition as well. We have also seen that the oneness of being is equally contrary to scientific materialism, the manifest image, and the classical emergentism of C. D. Broad. For all their differences, these traditions assume a universe carved at the joints complete with autonomous forces, mechanisms, parts and wholes, and transtemporal objects. Much of the literature in the field of Science and Religion presupposes that any possible convergence between the scientific worldview and the manifest worldview must come down on one side or the other—for example, by naturalizing spirituality and religion or demonstrating that the natural world leaves room for Divine action, dualism, or libertarian free-will. I hope to have shown that such a presupposition may be false—and furthermore that there is good reason to think it false. I take myself to be practicing what Huxley called "empirical theology." If nothing else, I hope this essay encourages intellectual humility about our views concerning the ultimate nature of reality and real pluralism in the realm of religious and theological thought. The nature of God may also turn out to be radically counterintuitive from this theological perspective. If perennial pluralistic monism is true, there is no justification for exclusivism in either science or theology. Given perennial pluralistic monism, fundamental physics and theology are converging on the same spiritual information, and the information we are getting is best characterized by panentheism in Western theology, Advaita Vedanta in Hinduism, etc. On my interpretation, science and religion are not two distinct "nonoverlapping magisteria," and they are not two opposing and mutually exclusive paradigms. Rather, they are both, in their complementary way, providing commensurate spiritual information about the fundamental nature of reality.

If Western theology will allow itself to be humbled by the possibility of perennial pluralistic monism, it may find that many of its ancient driving concerns will dissolve rather than be resolved. In philosophy and science we make a distinction between those problems that are resolved outright, such as the discovery of the double helix, and problems that get deflated by the realization that the assumptions driving the problem were false. Much of Western theology still operates in the context of the manifest image of God and humanity respectively as numerically distinct beings or substances with distinct purposes, etc. But perhaps it is *the very idea* of and quest for *purpose* that is our real prison. If God and the universe are truly one, then nothing separate is being created: The film, the director, and the actors are one—as in a dream. What is the *purpose* of a dream? If God, man, and the universe are one in some substantial sense (such as that advocated by Advaita Vedanta), then perhaps the problem of purpose or meaning and the problem of evil are illusions in need of dissolution and not problems to be solved head-on.

✍

MICHAEL SILBERSTEIN, PH.D., is Associate Professor of Philosophy at Elizabethtown College and an Adjunct Professor at the University of Maryland, where he is also a faculty member in the Foundations of Physics Program and a Fellow on the Committee for Philosophy and the Sciences. A National Endowment for the Humanities Fellow, Professor Silberstein has published and delivered papers on both philosophy of science and philosophy of mind. His primary research interests are philosophy of physics and of cognitive neuroscience, especially how they bear on more general questions of reduction, emergence, and explanation—a topic that he explored in his most recent book, *The Blackwell Guide to Philosophy of Science* (co-edited with Peter Machamer, 2002). Professor Silberstein is currently working on *The Whole Story: Emergence, Reduction and Explanation Across the Disciplines* and *Illuminating Images: Philosophy, Film and Interpretation.*

REFERENCES

Bohr, N. 1987. *The Philosophical Writings of Niels Bohr.* Vol. 2. *Essays on Atomic Physics and Human Knowledge*, 1933–57. Ox Bow Press.

Howard, D. 1994. "What Makes a Classical Concept Classical? Toward a Reconstruction of Niels Bohr's Philosophy of Physics." In *Niels Bohr and Contemporary Philosophy.* Folse, H., and Faye, J. (eds.). Boston: Kluwer, 201–29.

Huxley, A. 1944. *The Perennial Philosophy.* Harper and Row Publisher.

Laughlin, R. B., and Pines, D. 2000. "The Theory of Everything." *PNAS* 97, no. 1 (Jan. 4): 28–31.

Quantum Logic and the God-World Relationship 35

A New Resource for Exploring Modern Christian Theology

Thierry Magnin

SCIENCE AND THEOLOGY have their own distinct languages and modes of representing reality. These must be clearly distinguished in order to avoid naïve concordism. However, it is interesting to explore how the methods and logic used in one field can be applicable to the other, taking into account the specific constraints of each.

The aim of this paper is to consider quantum physics and its possible application to Christian theology. We will see that Christian dogmas—Trinity and Incarnation, as well as the biblical notion of Covenant—can be fruitfully explored through the logic of the "included middle" as applied to quantum physics. This application of methods from one field to another emphasizes that deep, common human attitudes enable both physicists and believers to explore the nature of reality without any confusion between the fields of science and theology. Common attitudes derive from the study of the logic of the included middle and its role in science and theology. Such a field of pursuit is called "moral philosophy" because it is related to critical analysis of the ethical principles involved in comparative epistemologies in science and theology.

Taking into account the different domains of science, metaphysics, and theology, I show how moral philosophy can be a new foundation for the dialog between scientists and people of faith. Such a dialog can perhaps be helpful in promoting quality in education and in supporting peace in the modern world.

On the Question of Reality in Science . . .

Enormous progress in science occurred during the twentieth century. However, part of this progress ironically involved determining the limits on knowledge. In quantum physics, new insights have generated a different way of considering the subject-object relation. For quantum physicists, reality is "veiled" (d'Espagnat 1979) because of unseen interactions between the subject and the object. Defining the physical quantities thus depends on the specifics of observation and measurement. There is a coupling between the experimental conditions and the conceptual apparatus. As shown by the classical wave-particle dualism, we can say: If you do this (with one kind of apparatus), you will observe that. Then if we try to interpret the situation in terms of "what really exists," it becomes completely different with respect to classical physics. Something coming from the subject is contained. Independent reality cannot be reached by science, as previously advocated by Kant. Complete objectivity is not possible in quantum physics. Thus, in the quantum world, the scientist is a kind of "translator" of a complex reality in which observers are irrevocably included.

One can say that the scientism of the nineteenth century in Europe has been considerably weakened by quantum physics, which questions objectivity; by Laplacian determinism; and by subject-object separability. Scientism is also weakened by the thermodynamics of irreversible processes, which questions the validity of reductionism, and also by the Gödel theorem, which considers the question of undecidability in mathematics. Such evolution is generally translated by the following sentence: "Something of reality is beyond our knowledge" (Barbour 1997).

Even if quantum physics gives new insights about reality through science, we must never forget the status of the observer in Kant's analysis. But quantum physics has generated new insights into the subject-object problem, stressing the contextuality and relationality of reality. More and more, science is shown to correspond to "the game of possibilities." In his book by this name (Le jeu des possibles), Nobel laureate François Jacob compares myth and science in their relation to reality:

> Mythic or scientific, the representation of the world by man is related to his imagination. . . . To give valuable observations in science, one must initially have in mind some idea about what must be observed. We need to decide before the observation what can be observed, what is possible. A previous idea about reality is necessary. . . . The scientific investigation always starts with the invention of a possible world, or a fragment of this possible world. Mythic thought also started in the same way. But then Myths and Science completely differ. (Jacob 1981)

Such an approach has been described in detail for exploring the relation between science, philosophy, and theology (Russell, Stoeger, Coyne 1988).

The New Logic of the Included Middle in Quantum Physics

Quantum mechanics, and later quantum physics, caused the sudden appearance of mutually exclusive contradictories (A and non-A), as in the wave-particle duality problem. The qualities of continuity (wave mode) and discontinuity (particle mode) are mixed when referring to quantons[1] (and in describing them mathematically), even if a quanton appears experimentally either in the wave mode or in the particle mode. In the same way, separability and nonseparability, local causality and global causality, symmetry and asymmetry, reversibility of time and irreversibility of time simultaneously occur as conjoined contradictions in the description of reality in the quantum world.

Niels Bohr applied the complementarity principle to investigating the wave-particle duality problem, stressing the relatedness of outcomes to the specific nature of the measurements being made (see Bohr 1958). The question is: How do we combine continuity and discontinuity, separability and nonseparability, symmetry and asymmetry? Bohr's complementarity principle suggests that mutually exclusive descriptions must be taken into account simultaneously. This was expressed by Bohr's colleague Heisenberg as follows:

When playing with these two images, going from one to the other and then back again, we finally obtain the right impression of the strange sort of reality which hides behind our atomic experiments. (Heisenberg 1969)

One possible solution to this situation of apparent logical paradox is to replace the axiom of the excluded middle of classical logic—something cannot be this and also that at the same time—argued by Aristotle. By the contrary axiom of the included middle, we have the idea that there is a third term T that is at the same time A and non-A. Lupasco (1941) and Nicolescu (1991) in France have done considerable work defining the logical status of quantum complementarity through the logic of the included middle.

Nicolescu defines two kinds of complementarity through the notion of "levels of reality." To provide an overview, some definitions are needed. By the word "reality," we mean something that resists our simple representations, descriptions, or images. By the term "level," we mean a group of systems that is invariant under the action of certain laws. The passage from one level of reality to the other then involves a breakdown of laws and logic, of fundamental concepts such as causality. In analyzing the complementarity principle, the two levels of reality that must be considered are the macroscopic (level 1, related to classical physics with its appropriate and specific language and logic) and the microscopic (level 2, related to quantum physics with its own appropriate and different logic).

The content of the axiom of the included middle becomes clear if we put the three terms A, non-A, and T on a triangle diagram with the dynamics associated with them, as shown in Figure 1.

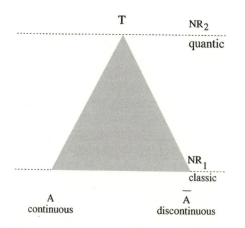

FIGURE 1. LEVELS OF REALITY IN THE LOGIC OF THE INCLUDED MIDDLE.
NR* 1 = macroscopic (level 1, local causality and separability, classical physics)
NR* 2 = microscopic (level 2, global causality and nonseparability, quantum mechanics)
NR = *niveau de réalité* (level of reality)

Research at point T corresponds to research focused on a level of reality where what is mutually exclusive at level 1 can be unified at level 2. It corresponds to the included middle for which point T is not at the same level of the contradictory logical antagonism. Notice that the antagonism is never completely solved. New antagonisms can appear from point T at level 2. The figure is only a simple heuristic to represent the level structure of the included middle in quantum physics. In this representation, no basic contradictions with Aristotle's logic of noncontradiction occur because point T is not at the same level as the two components of the basic contradiction.

Contraries, contradictions, antagonisms, and opposites are terms that have evolved since the time of Aristotle. We propose the following definition of "antagonism," both in science and (as we will see) in theology, consisting of eight characteristics (Kaiser 1974): *unity* (the complementary modes of representation are related to the same object), *common properties, completeness of each mode in one experimental situation, co-exhaustivity* (the two modes are sufficient to simultaneously describe the object), *equal necessity* (the two modes are equally necessary), *alternativity, co-inherence* (each mode exists potentially inside the other), and *mutual exclusivity.*

The Classical Logic of the Included Middle in Christian Theology

> At the end of each truth, one must consider the opposite truth, the two
> opposite reasons. If not, everything is heretic. (Pascal)

This statement from the scientist-philosopher-theologian Pascal asserts that the approach to truth requires the clash and synthetic combination of opposites. This is not so far from Heisenberg's statement about a completely different problem, the wave-particle duality, which asserts that the contrary of a deep truth can itself be another deep truth. In theology, this insight has been called the *via eminentiae* (the eminent way) based on the debate between differing views or perspectives since Thomas Aquinas. Thus, God in the Bible is presented both as personal and nonpersonal, both humble and nonhumble—which means that he cannot be personal and humble as we imagine by simple, direct analogy to human attributes.

Indeed, one sees the formal representation of several logical antagonisms within the Christian tradition. For example, the history of the dogma of the Holy Trinity clearly shows a continuous dialectical process used to explore a unity of antagonisms. This is detailed in the Quicumque Symbol of Athanasius (Magnin 1998; Camus, Magnin, Nicolescu, and Voss 1994). But the famous dogma of Incarnation is probably the best example of the use of the complementarity principle within theology. Jesus is held to be both true Man and true God, realizing on the Cross the unity of antagonisms "full power–no power." On the Cross he reveals both who is Man and who is God. Then for the disciples of Jesus, the Cross unifies the antagonisms "to become themselves [vs.] to be completely dependent and given to God." This opens a new way and power of life! One finds oneself in losing oneself!

The question for the present analysis is to examine whether notions such as included-middle logic used in science may be interesting for advancing the theology of Incarnation. This can be done without any confusion between the fields, taking into account their clearly distinct specificities. In theology, a distinction separates the concepts of knowledge from revelation and knowledge from conceptual thought. For example, theologian Karl Rahner said:

> Theology is mainly (i) the believer's explicit awareness to revelation of God in History through His Word which is Revelation per se and (ii) the scientific method in order to gain insight into His Word as knowledge on newly acquired information. (Rahner and Vorgrimler 1970)

Thus, revelation is not separable from the experience of the community of believers in the Church in a peculiar social and cultural context. In theology, there always is "something beyond our understanding" that we call "mystery" and that is beyond the domain of logical analysis according to the empirical and logical scientific method. A mystery is not something we cannot understand. It is something we will never get to the end of (St. Augustine). A mystery is something in which the subject is involved, in contrast with an analytical problem independent of the subject. Thus, the question of the mode of representation occurs in theology as well as in science.

There is a specific coupling between experimental conditions and conceptual apparatus. Figure 2 illustrates an analogous representation of the dogma of Incarnation in terms of an included-middle logic.

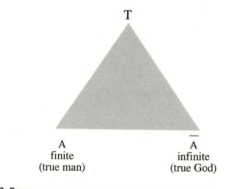

T

A
finite
(true man)

A̅
infinite
(true God)

FIGURE 2. REPRESENTATION OF THE DOGMA OF INCARNATION IN TERMS OF LEVELS OF REALITY IN THE LOGIC OF THE INCLUDED MIDDLE.

In classical language, man is finite and God is infinite: Finite man cannot be infinite God! This statement defines reality level 1 (bottom of triangle). In the Christian tradition, the unity of antagonisms between finite and infinite is realized by Jesus Christ, reality level 2 (faith, top of triangle). Here, the incarnate Son of God, Christ, realizes the unity of antagonisms, particularly on the Cross (the death of eternal life). But for the believer, the Cross is still the sign of a "passing-through," a sign of conversion that is never finished! Thus the believer goes by faith from level 1 to level 2, but never reaches point T. The novelty of Christ is given by revelation and is completely beyond what we can imagine.

Even if there is no relation between the status of quantum reality and the status of Jesus the Christ (obviously!), the antagonism of finite-infinite in theology in comparison with the continuous-discontinuous antagonism in science, along with their corresponding modes of representation, are quite analogous in terms of logic of the included middle. Analogy is here related to the mode of representation in terms of logic, not the attributes! The logic of quantum physics appears quite interesting for presenting the terms of Christian dogmas and to emphasize the potential logic with respect to reality of such formally paradoxical beliefs.

Another important point of the Christian tradition, the Covenant between God and Man in the Bible, can also be expressed in terms of complementarity using the logic of the included middle. Creation is separated from God (one of the translations of "creation" in Hebrew means "separation") and, at the same time, is in relation with God through the Covenant. Thus, the Covenant includes both the separation (alterity) and the relation (unity/communion), as shown in Figure 3.

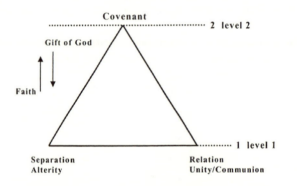

FIGURE 3. REPRESENTATION OF THE BIBLICAL COVENANT BETWEEN MAN AND GOD.

There is a strong unity of antagonisms in the Covenant that allows both freedom of choice for man and the freely given gift of love from God to humanity. The love of God given to humanity is completely free, which is open to a free man's response. The experience of faith is open to an understanding of the Covenant as a unity of contradictions that is never completely solved by man. Using the terms from the hylemorphism of Aristotle, one can say that the actualization of the separation induces the potentialization of the relation. Similarly, the actualization of the relation induces the potentialization of the separation. This is in dynamic equilibrium. The Bible shows a lot of historical examples of such actualization/potentialization. Thus, quantum logic can be fruitful in exploring the biblical Covenant in its specificity!

Related Common Attitudes between Physicists and Believers

Consequences of the analogous use of the logic of the included middle in both the-ology and science are interesting in terms of human attitudes about the nature of reality. My argument seeks to avoid comparing science and theology directly. It is more important to show that the use of paradoxical complementarity by the scien-tist can also be an interesting application for the believer. This analogy can illumi-nate the depth of Christian dogmas, which many people feel must be untrue because they seem *prima facie* to be logical self-contradictions. However, such an analogy demonstrates common issues between scientists and theologians, in completely dif-ferent fields. Therefore, one can propose the following attitudes to be common through analysis of included-middle logic and complementarity:

+ *Acceptance of reality as "reality of interactions" and as "something that resists simple representation."*
+ *Positive acceptance of the incompleteness of our understanding of reality.* Some aspects of reality are generally beyond our normal modes of understanding. Classical science used the terms "stability," "permanence," "decidability," "deter-minism," and "certainty." The evolution of modern science leads to consider-ations of "instability," "chance," "undecidability," "unsettlement," and "uncertainty" in our knowledge. It is essential to see that such an evolution does not correspond to a defeat of scientific reason, but, on the contrary, is a condition of progress toward a deeper conceptual understanding of reality. Nevertheless, this evolution implies a considerable change of mentality for scientists. This is similar to a challenge in ethics where acceptance of human finitude is necessary, if unwelcome. This posture of humility is also the fun-damental, necessary attitude for the believer facing the mystery of God.
+ *Partial understanding of reality.* Despite the incompleteness of our under-standing, the world is partly understandable! One can then perhaps say some-thing about God!
+ *Acceptance and openness to alterity through the sense that reality is deep and resists easy understanding.* Reality is always partly beyond our compartmen-talized representations. The same alterity is observed by the believer in theo-logical research into God.
+ *Edification through confronting alterity.* Moral lessons are learned in both sci-ence and theology by recognizing that we are subjects facing that which is innately beyond what we can easily confront, capture, and comprehend. Recognition of the depth and inexhaustibility of reality and the limitation of our concepts can be an important, morally potent lesson both in science and in matters of faith.
+ *Openness to the sense of mystery.* This mystery is different in science and in theology, but is similarly significant in each.

In conclusion, one can say that the incompleteness of our scientific knowledge opens new ground for a clarifying dialog between scientists and believers. Quantum logic can be very fruitful for presenting the ways in which some Christian dogmas are in fact addressing deep issues. It induces common human attitudes between scientists and believers, which can be of great interest for education.

ℒ♥

THIERRY MAGNIN, PH.D., TH.D., is Professor of Solid-State Physics at l'École Nationale Supérieure des Mines, St. Étienne, France, and Head of the Material Science Research Laboratory (URA) at the Centre National de la Recherche Scientifique (French National Center for Scientific Research [CNRS]). He has written two hundred papers and reviews and five books on solid-state physics and won the prestigious Laureat Award of the French Academy of Sciences in 1991. Professor Magnin is also a Catholic priest and General Vicar of the diocese of St. Etienne. The topic of his thesis in theology was "The relationship between science and theology today." He has helped organize many conferences on this topic and has written four books in French (*Which God for a Scientific World?* Nouvelle Cité, 1993; *Between Science and Religion*, Le Rocher, 1998; *Scientific Parabola*, Nouvelle Cité, 2000; *Becoming Oneself at the Light of Science and Bible*, Presses de la Renaissance, 2004). Professor Magnin is a Member of the Board of Scientific Advisors of the Université Interdisciplinaire de Paris.

NOTE

1 The wavelike/particlelike objects of the quantum world (http://www.worldscinet.com/ ijmpb/18/1804n05/S02179792040241 85.html); quantum change carriers in quantum reality that are "Dawkinsian" (quantum included-middle, both "mind" and "body"); see Richard Dawkins's *The Selfish Gene* (http://www.quantonics.com/Level_5_QTO_ Quanton_Primer.html).

REFERENCES

Barbour, Ian G. *Religion and Science*, San Francisco: Harper, 1997.

Bohr, Niels. *Atomic Physics and Human Knowledge*, New York: Wiley and Sons, 1958.

Camus, Michel, Magnin, Thierry, Nicolescu, Basarab, and Voss, Krister. *Levels of representation and levels of reality*, Munick: ESSSAT, 1994.

d'Espagnat, Bernard. *A la recherche du réel*, Paris: Gauthiers-Villars, 1979.

Heisenberg, Werner. *Der Teil und Das Ganze*, Munich: Piper et Verlag, 1969.

Jacob, François. *Le jeu des possibles*, Paris: Flammarion, 1981.

Kaiser, Christian. *The logic of complementarity*, Edinburgh: University of Edinburgh Press, 1974.

Lupasco, Stephane. *L'expérience microphysique et la pensée humaine*, Paris: Le Rocher, 1941.

Magnin, Thierry. *Entre science et religion*, Paris: Le Rocher, 1998.

Nicolescu, Basarab. *Science, Meaning and Evolution*, New York: Parabola Books, 1991.

Pascal, Blaise. *Pensées*, 83, Edition de Brunschvig.

Rahner, Karl, and Vorgrimler, Hermut. *Petit dictionnaire de théologie catholique*, Paris: Seuil, 1970.

Russell, Robert J., Stoeger, William R., and Coyne, George V. *Physics, Philosophy and Theology: A common quest for understanding*, Notre Dame, IN: University of Notre Dame Press, 1988.

Between Mathematics and Transcendence 36

The Search for the Spiritual Dimension of Scientific Discovery

Joseph M. Zycinski

I N THE FOURTEENTH CENTURY, Nicole of Oresme tried to describe human emotions mathematically. But human psychic processes finally turned out to be too complicated for mathematical formulae, and this ambitious attempt ended in failure. Seven centuries later, the astonishing variety of physical processes can be described in the language of mathematics, no matter whether these processes take place in New York, Beijing, or Kinshasa. One cannot avoid the question as to why the language of mathematics has been so effective in the physical description of Nature and why physical processes are described by universal physical laws even when they could have been nothing but an uncoordinated mess. These questions could be regarded as the counterpart of the classical philosophical problem: Why does being exist when there could have been mere nothingness? This question, criticized as trivial and meaningless by empirical positivists in the 1930s, now can be expressed in a new form that now also is meaningful for empiricists: Why do mathematically described laws of physics exist at all when Nature could have been manifested as uncoordinated chaos?

The Mysterious Effectiveness of the Language of Mathematics

The effectiveness of mathematical language in describing natural phenomena has amazed many authors. At the beginning of modern physics, an important controversy arose between Isaac Newton, author of the *Philosophiae naturalis principia mathematica*, the work containing the first theoretical exposition of new physics, and John Flamsteed, the first Astronomer Royal and founder of the Greenwich Observatory. Newton determined the positions of celestial objects on the theoretical basis underlying his principle of gravity. Flamsteed determined them on the empirical basis using the best observational equipment accessible at that time. Finally, after an emotional debate, Flamsteed had to correct his observational results. Mathematical formulae, worked out theoretically, better revealed the structure of the physical world in our cosmic neighborhood than did the observational evidence. Three centuries later, Eugene Wigner called this mysterious and astonishing property "the unreasonable effectiveness of mathematics in the natural sciences" (Wigner 1960).

The same "unreasonable effectiveness of mathematics" was revealed by Albert Einstein when, on the basis of field equations in his general theory of relativity, he discovered the expansion of the universe, which was confirmed by observation several years later. In 1965, the same effect was illustrated by the discovery of the microwave radiation that originated fourteen billion years ago with the Big Bang. The main problem was that the existence of such radiation was already predicted on the basis of mathematical calculations in the late 1940s. How does one explain that the language of mathematics is not only adequate to describe physical processes, but that it also helps us to discover new phenomena previously unknown? To better understand this astonishing property of our world, let us refer to an analogy closer to our everyday experience. Imagine that someone had created a new language as a purely artificial product. Had he later discovered that an African tribe spoke this very language, such a coincidence would have amazed him. It would be as improbable as the existence of a tribe reciting fragments of James Joyce's *Ulysses* or using, as a means of communication, a new language created specifically for computers. Such occurrences could not be considered obvious or natural.

Perhaps the people who either do not know computers or who are critical of Joyce would not find anything amazing about such a situation; for them, any sequence of English or English-like words would be only an unintelligible jabber. A similar situation occurs among the people who do not understand mathematics and do not appreciate its role in the physical description of Nature. Those who do understand the role of mathematics in science think like Paul Davies, who, when awarded the Templeton Prize in 1995, expressed the essence of his philosophy by saying: "It is impossible to be a scientist, even an atheist scientist, and not be struck by the awesome beauty, harmony and ingenuity of nature. What most impresses me is the existence of the underlying mathematical order." This order described by abstract mathematical formulae has often been regarded as either a bare fact or an unintelligible mystery.

In my opinion, to explain the nature of such an order one has to go beyond mathematics as well as beyond the natural sciences. This transcending of the level of scientific discovery brings us to the divine Logos underlying the mathematical structure of the world. Some authors call such a structure "the rationality field" or "the formal field." Jan Lukasiewicz, the well-known representative of the Polish School of Logic, argued that the reality of ideal mathematical structures independent of human experience could be regarded as an expression of God's presence in Nature (Lukasiewicz 1937). Such an approach seems justified because this mysterious reality provides us with an experience of the sacred, which transcends the domain of empirical observations and seems to precede all observation. Consequently, I call this astonishing reality permeating our physical world the *theosphere*.

Mathematical Presuppositions for Cosmic Mysticism

For methodological reasons, references to the theosphere were eliminated from modern science in the time of Galileo. Although he never denied the value of theological explanation, the author of the *Dialogo* was right when he claimed that all references to metaphysical or theological factors must be excluded from the domain of astronomical research. If, in the spirit of medieval astronomy, one were to refer to the role of angels to explain the motion of planets, one could always introduce the hypothesis of angels to explain any set of empirical data. As a result, in such an approach astronomy would merely remain a branch of applied "angelology" (Galileo Galilei 1890).

Galileo's methodological distinctions were important in separating science from philosophy. They do not eliminate, however, philosophical questions inspired by new scientific discoveries. Neither do they eliminate the aesthetic contemplation of Nature or our reaction to its beauty. In premodern science, this very beauty, as well as the contemplation of it, were regarded as a purely subjective factor. Thanks to the growth of modern science, one discovers that the physical order and its mathematical description constitute the objective basis for our aesthetic fascination. In its strongest form, this fascination has been called "mystical" because it provides a non-conceptual experience of the deepest level of physical reality. Albert Einstein called this kind of experience, inspired by "a deep conviction of the rationality of the universe" and its mathematical description, "cosmic religious feeling."

The question therefore arises: What would be the ultimate rational justification for this expression of the rationality of Nature, which combines mathematical description and mystical insight? The contemporaries of Galileo never asked such a question because they used mathematics without ever discussing why its use was so effective. As a matter of fact, again for methodological reasons, the question of the mysterious effectiveness of mathematics transcends the cognitive level of both mathematics and physics. It could be answered on the level of philosophy and theology when we refer to the transcendent reality of God, which ultimately justifies the cosmic order as well as its sophisticated mathematical description.

Cosmic Harmony and Human Ecology

Because of their dislike for pantheism, in their reflections about God many philosophers spoke mainly about transcendent reality as it exists outside the world of Nature. However, in the Judeo-Christian tradition, the immanence of God within Nature was no less important. We see this especially in Psalms, which presents God clothed in majesty and splendor, wearing light as a robe (Ps. 103:1–4). In this perspective, harmony exists between the world of Nature and that of spirituality. Harmony is created by the great cedars of Lebanon and also by tiny herbs, by mountains full of marmots and also by wild goats—as well as by the Spirit of God, which renews the face of the Earth (Ps. 103). Specific aspects of this harmony are seen in the Gospels, in which unseen divine reality reveals itself in some of the basic elements of Nature—the lilies of the field and the vine plant, the fig tree and the storm on the lake, the Bethlehem plain and the Garden of Olives. In the biblical perspective, as in the philosophical reflections of Plato and Leibniz, God reveals his presence not in the gaps of our knowledge about Nature, but in the harmony of Nature. To this tradition also belongs Teilhard de Chardin, who, writing in *The Divine Milieu*, speaks of divinity revealing itself in the heart of the universe. A particular form of this tradition would be developed in A. N. Whitehead's process philosophy, in which the role of God, immanent in his creation, has been compared with that of the "Poet of the world."

The Poet not only creates his poems, but also expresses his nature in their beauty. Aesthetic categories are important for mathematical equations as well as for our spiritual harmony because they reflect the initial harmony of the world created by the divine Poet. God's presence can be discovered in the various forms of harmony: physical, aesthetic, mathematical, ethical, spiritual. The different expressions of this harmony make up a human ecology, which facilitates our personal growth thanks to continuous cooperation with the divine Poet of the world. In this dynamic framework, all of us are invited to multiply the beauty of existence while spiritual harmony becomes an important component of our human ecology.

The spiritual consequences of human interaction with the immanent God can be described in St. Luke's well-known words "hearts burning" (Luke 24:32). Our fascination with aesthetic beauty and our openness to altruistic actions such as human gentleness and kindness disclose the presence of the immanent God at the level of intentional processes. Of course, this presence cannot be reduced to intentional or psychological factors. The physical study of supersymmetry discloses the most basic forms of cosmic harmony that were ignored earlier in physics in the same way that the aesthetic aspects of physical theories were ignored at a time when empiricism dominated in science.

To come to know our human ecology means to discover in our existence the role of physicobiological determinants and their relationship to the patterns of existence proposed by the divine Poet. Describing the nature of our interaction with God, we can follow Whitehead when in his *Process and Reality* he uses the expression "the lure for feeling." The causal influence of this lure can be described in categories of subtle persuasion, which can influence our decisions not only at the conscious but also at the subconscious level. This form of divine persuasion leads to human behavior in which special attention is paid to real values and gives rise to a fascination, thoughtfulness, and amazement in situations that may previously have seemed trivial. God, as a subtle Artist, never forces his patterns of beauty on us. He respects our freedom as well as the possibility of our rejecting his subtle persuasion.

In some physical processes, such as those described in classical Newtonian dynamics, mutual dependencies of interacting objects are strictly determined. In deterministic chaos, such strict determinism disappears, and many marginal factors can influence the final result. In our interaction with God, the subtle divine Poet never violates human freedom. Our personal decisions are ultimately free in the sense that God never determines them independently from us, but only influences us through subtle persuasion. For this reason, Whitehead compares God's role with that of a Poet who introduces his vision of truth, beauty, and goodness into our world. This form of introduction merely brings a proposal of harmonious existence, but never a strong, necessary determination. The better our cooperation with the immanent God in our personal growth, the more mature become our actions and the more evident our spiritual search for the basic harmony of human existence.

St. Paul, speaking to the inhabitants of Athens on the Areopagus, powerfully expresses the presence of God in the created world when he says: "In Him we live, move and have our being" (Acts 17:28). This divine presence constitutes a world of meaning, and thanks to this the reality in which we live is neither governed by the logic of dreams nor is a manifestation of the absurd. Mathematical equations, the effectiveness of which allows us to affirm that the world is a manifestation of the Logos and not a mere result of absurd and meaningless coincidence, are a special example of this world of meaning.

Immersed in this world of meaning, all of us are inhabitants of the invisible theosphere, which consists not only of the rationality discovered in scientific experiments, but also of the beauty experienced both in direct contact with Nature and in contemplation of Einstein's field equations. We have become used to this reality and tend not to notice it, just as in our daily lives we take gravity and genetic conditioning for granted. The invisible world of the divine Logos that penetrates our daily lives shows that, just as the fox says in Saint Exupery's *Little Prince*, "what is essential is invisible to the eye."

✑

JOSEPH M. ZYCINSKI is Archbishop of Lublin and Professor of Philosophy and Grand Chancellor at the Catholic University of Lublin. His fields of interests are primarily (1) philosophy of science, (2) relativistic cosmology, (3) metalogic, (4) history of science, and (5) the relationship between the natural sciences and Christian faith. Archbishop Zycinski is a Member of the European Academy of Science and Art in Vienna; the Congregation for Catholic Education; the Pontifical Council for Culture, Vatican; and the Russian Academy of Natural Sciences, Moscow. He has authored more than 25 significant books, among them *The Structure of the Metascientific Revolution; Three Cultures; Science, the Humanities and Christian Thought; Theism and Analytic Philosophy; Language and Method;* and *The Universe and Philosophy: Philosophical Issues in Relativistic Cosmology* (1980 and 1986) with Michael Heller (who also contributed an essay to this volume). He has written numerous articles and more than 350 scholarly papers published in Polish, English, German, French, Spanish, Russian, Italian, Slovak, and Hungarian that have appeared in such periodicals as *Zygon; British Journal for the Philosophy of Science; The Review of Metaphysics; Logos: A Journal of Catholic Thought and Culture; Philosophy in Science;* and *Cultures and Faith.*

REFERENCES

Galileo, Galilei, *Le Opere di Galileo Galilei*, ed. A. Favaro, Florence: G. Barbera, 1890; vol. VII, 263; vol. V, 316.

Lukasiewicz, Jan, "Wobronie logistyki," Studia Gnesnensia 15 (1937): 219.

Wigner, Eugene, "The Unreasonable Effectiveness of Mathematics in the Natural Sciences," Communications in Pure and Applied Mathematics 13 (1960): 1.

Rejecting the Realm of Numbers 37

Edward Nelson

In one of the non-Platonic dialogs of antiquity, Genesis 18:22–33, it is significant that it is Abraham, not his interlocutor, who appeals to an abstract idea: "Shall not the Judge of all the earth do right?" How unsettling it is to live in a world ruled by a Person rather than by ideas.

The God Without Properties, the I Am Who I Am, is not governed by an infinite, uncreated, immutable realm of abstract ideas. This realm is a human fabrication, and a pagan one at that.

I will not expound here on the evils, as I see it, of this fabrication. William Blake in *The Human Abstract*[1] and Isaiah Berlin in *The Crooked Timber of Humanity*[2] have done so far more eloquently than could I. Rather, I shall describe how I approach the question as a mathematician.[3]

I enjoy doing mathematics. Starting from axioms and previously proved theorems, each step I take involves an act—applying a rule of inference. I enjoy hiking in the mountains. Starting at the trailhead, each step I take requires an act—setting one foot before the other. To me, the two activities are similar. But this is not so in the prevailing view of mathematics. According to this view, the truths of mathematics already exist in an infinite, uncreated, immutable realm, and all I do is discover them. Mathematicians call this view Platonism, with good historical justification, because Plato was strongly influenced by Pythagoras, who more than anyone was the originator of mathematics as a deductive discipline.

Platonism finds its simplest expression in the theory of numbers. In mathematical logic, numerals are constructed as follows: 0 is a numeral; given a numeral n, construct its successor by writing Sn. Thus 0, S0, SS0, . . . are numerals. Each construction of a new numeral requires an act. Now imagine that the process of writing all possible numerals has been completed and call the resulting set **N**, the set of all numbers. Thus **N** is conceived of as an infinite, uncreated, immutable realm. Numerals are concrete; the realm of numbers is abstract.

In mathematics, one constructs a formal language to discuss numbers, containing in addition to the symbols 0 and S the symbols + (addition) and · (multiplication) and the logical symbols *not, and, or, implies, for all, there exists*, and =, as well as the variables *x, y*, and so forth. Formulas are constructed from these symbols. Like numerals, formulas are concrete objects.

This is a powerful language for expressing concepts of the theory of numbers. For example, the twin primes conjecture, that there exists arbitrarily large primes *y* such that *y* + 2 is also a prime, is an unsolved problem of the theory of numbers: No one has proved it or disproved it. It is easily expressed in this language, as follows:

"1": S0;

"2": SS0;

"x is less than y": there exists z such that $x + z = y$;

"x divides y": there exists z such that $x \cdot z = y$;

"y is a prime": not $y = 1$ and for all z, z divides y implies $z = 1$ or $z = y$;

"the twin primes conjecture": for all x there exists y such that x is less than y and y is a prime and $y + 2$ is a prime.

The idea of truth in mathematics is a peculiar one. It is an abstract idea, for the truth of a formula such as "for all x there exists y such that B(x, y)" where B(x, y) is a previously constructed formula, presupposes the cogency of an infinite search through all elements x and y of **N**. The idea of mathematical truth can be illustrated by a fable.

Late one night while working on the twin primes conjecture, a mathematician perceived a pungent odor. Looking up, he saw that a visitant was present.

V. Do you want to know whether the twin primes conjecture is true?

M. Yes, with all my soul. I have been working on it for years without success.

V. I can show you. I can take you directly into the Platonic realm.

M. (*cautiously*) What do you require of me in return?

V. Only that you look at what I show you. Do you agree to this bargain?

M. Yes.

V. Good. Swallow this.

The hands of the clock showed 1:00 as they entered the infinite, uncreated, immutable realm of numbers. One by one, starting with 0, proceeding to S0 and so on, they examined all numbers x. One by one, starting with x, proceeding to Sx and so on, they examined all numbers y bigger than x to verify whether y and $y + $ SS0 were primes. As the search progressed, these verifications became lengthier and lengthier. Eventually:

M. I am infinitely weary. Can we stop?

V. No, you are only finitely weary. An infinite search still lies ahead of us. You must keep your bargain. Let us continue.

This exchange was repeated infinitely often. Truly infinitely weary at the end of the search, the mathematician saw, let us say, that the twin primes conjecture is true. As they returned to the mathematician's study, the hands of the clock showed 1:00.

M. No time has elapsed!

V. There is no time in that realm, no becoming. All is static.

M. It is a dead realm.

V. No. Nothing in it was ever alive.

M. The knowledge that the twin primes conjecture is true is of no use to me as a mathematician; I cannot publish it by itself. I need a proof.

V. Why waste your time trying to construct a proof? All proofs already exist in the Plutonic—pardon me, Platonic—realm. Let us enter that realm again, search through all proofs, and see whether one of them is a proof of the twin primes conjecture.

M. No, never again! I do not believe in your realm; you have given me some pernicious drug. Hence!

One writes down certain axioms and argues that they are true. The resulting theory is called Peano Arithmetic after the great Italian mathematician Giuseppe Peano, although the name is something of a historical misnomer. The most important axioms are the induction axioms, which can be described informally as follows.

Let $A(x)$ be some formula. Suppose that you have proved (1) $A(0)$ and also (2) for all x, $A(x)$ implies $A(Sx)$. Then induction allows you to conclude (3) for all x, $A(x)$. The motivation for postulating induction is the following: Consider a numeral, such as $SS0$. We have $A(0)$ by (1). By (2) we have $A(0)$ implies $A(S0)$, so by the logical rule of inference called *modus ponens* we have $A(S0)$. By (2) again we have $A(S0)$ implies $A(SS0)$, so again by *modus ponens* we have $A(SS0)$. In this way, for each numeral n we can dispense with induction to prove $A(n)$ from (1) and (2). But accepting induction as true requires conflating the concrete notion of a numeral, whose construction requires acts, with the abstract idea of a number; and, indeed, many theorems in Peano Arithmetic can be proved using induction that cannot be proved without it.

Finally, one argues that the axioms of Peano Arithmetic are true and that the logical rules of inference preserve truth, so all theorems of Peano Arithmetic are true. But $0 = S0$ is not true; hence, there is no proof in Peano Arithmetic of $0 = S0$.

Now this is an interesting conclusion. The argument proceeds by the abstract idea of mathematical truth, about which logicians can and do dispute, but the conclusion is concrete. A proof in Peano Arithmetic is a concrete object, and all logicians agree as to whether a putative proof is indeed a proof.

This is where Platonism is perhaps vulnerable. According to Platonic ideas, there is no proof in Peano Arithmetic of $0 = S0$. So if someone were to present a proof in Peano Arithmetic of $0 = S0$, Platonism could no longer excrete its poison into human thought, and Platonists of the future would have the intellectual status of flat-earthers today.

The world is not static, but alive. There is time, there is becoming, in the world. Things in the world move by law and by chance, by will and by grace, and who has the wisdom to disentangle the threads of this living tapestry?

Mathematics is made by mathematicians, and without mathematicians there would be no mathematics. How do mathematicians use induction in their work? They use it to bring into being new things, things that did not exist before.

Here is a simple example. We can ask, given a number x, is there a number y that is divisible by all numbers less than x? Using 0, S, $+$, and $\cdot$ only, there is no way to write down such a y in terms of x. Let $A(x)$ be the formula "there exists y such that for all z, z is less than x implies z divides y". We have (1) $A(0)$—let $y = 0$. We have (2) for all x, $A(x)$ implies $A(Sx)$—for let y_0 be a number that is divisible by all numbers less than x; then $y = y_0 \cdot Sx$ is a number that is divisible by all numbers less than Sx. Induction allows us to conclude (3) for all x, $A(x)$. We write $y = x!$, using the new symbol !, to denote the y whose existence is asserted by $A(x)$. But how do we know that induction can be applied to the new kind of number that x! denotes?

If we examine induction as it is used in living mathematics, we are less sure about its justification. Induction can be used to create new kinds of numbers. Therefore, postulating induction requires a leap of credulity—that it can be applied not only to those numbers that already exist, but also to those that induction itself brings into being. There is a circularity here that perhaps can be exploited to construct a proof in Peano Arithmetic of $0 = S0$.

I search for such a proof, at times with "hope dwindled into a ghost not fit to cope with that obstreperous joy success would bring."[4]

ℒ♥

EDWARD NELSON, PH.D., received his doctorate in mathematics at the University of Chicago in 1955. He joined the Princeton University faculty in 1959, becoming Professor of Mathematics in 1964. Professor Nelson's early work was in probability theory, functional analysis, and mathematical physics. His work in constructive quantum field theory included "A Quartic Interaction in Two Dimensions" (in *Elementary Particles*, MIT Press, 1966), for which he was awarded the 1995 Steele Prize for seminal contribution to research by the American Mathematical Society. Professor Nelson's less orthodox work in quantum theory includes two books and a number of articles on stochastic mechanics, a theory based on an unconventional interpretation of the Schrödinger equation. His recent work has focused on logic and the foundations of mathematics. He invented a new approach to nonstandard analysis, Internal Set Theory, discussed in his book *Radically Elementary Probability Theory* (Princeton University Press, 1987). In his book *Predicative Arithmetic* (Princeton University Press, 1986), Professor Nelson develops at length the reasons for his skepticism of classical mathematics. He was elected a member of the American Academy of Arts and Sciences in 1975 and of the National Academy of Sciences in 1997. In 1991, he became *doctor honoris causa* of the Université Louis Pasteur in Strasbourg, France.

NOTES

1 "The Human Abstract" by William Blake is a poem from *Songs of Experience*, in *The Complete Poetry and Selected Prose of John Donne & The Complete Poetry of William Blake*, New York: The Modern Library, 1941.

2 Isaiah Berlin, *The Crooked Timber of Humanity: Chapters in the History of Ideas*, New York: Vintage Books, 1992.

3 A technical account of matters related to this article is in the author's *Predicative Arithmetic*, Mathematical Notes 32, Princeton: Princeton University Press, 1986.

4 From "Childe Roland to the Dark Tower Came," in *Selected Poems of Robert Browning*, New York: Walter J. Black, 1942.

Is God a Mathematician? 38

Mario Livio

MANY OUTSTANDING physicists, most notably Albert Einstein, Eugene Wigner, and James Jeans, noted that mathematics appears to be just too effective in explaining the universe. Wigner, in particular, wrote a remarkable paper in 1960 entitled "The Unreasonable Effectiveness of Mathematics in the Physical Sciences." He notes: "The miracle of the appropriateness of the language of mathematics to the formulation of the laws of physics is a wonderful gift which we neither understand nor deserve." We may wonder, for example, why it is that all the phenomena encompassed by electromagnetism, from the behavior of electrons to the nature of light, can be explained by a set of four differential equations—Maxwell's equations. Equally puzzling is the fact that some geometrical curves such as the ellipse, invented/discovered by the Greek mathematician Menaechmus around 350 BCE, were found two thousand years later to describe the orbits of planets around the sun. Similarly, group theory proved to be essential in the understanding of both the organization of elementary (subatomic) particles, and the structure of solids. What is it, then, that makes mathematics fit the observable universe like a glove?

Attempts to answer this question fall generally into two broad categories. According to one view, mathematics is in some sense the actual "language" of the universe. It exists independent of us humans, and we are merely *discovering* it in the workings of the cosmos. Proponents of this philosophy like to point out that even some of the more esoteric areas of mathematics, such as non-Euclidean geometries, were eventually found to provide cornerstones to cosmological models. The success of mathematics in explaining Nature is not an accident, if one accepts this premise. The cosmos has literally imposed mathematics on humanity.

Many thinkers throughout history have espoused the above view. In *Il Saggiatore* (*The Essayist*), Galileo Galilei writes:

> Philosophy is written in this grand book—I mean the universe—which stands continually open to our gaze, but it cannot be understood unless one first learns to comprehend the language and interpret the characters in which it is written. It is written in the language of mathematics, and its characters are triangles, circles, and other geometrical figures, without which it is humanly impossible to understand a single word of it, without these, one is wandering about in a dark labyrinth.

Given that these ideas put mathematics on a somewhat similar footing to religion —both represent a relationship between humans and the universe—it should come as no surprise that some religious natural philosophers regarded mathematics as a manifestation of a divine thought. In the words of astronomer Johannes Kepler:

Geometry, which before the origin of things was coeternal with the divine mind and is God himself (for what could there be in God which would not be God himself?), supplied God with patterns for the creation of the world.

Even Hermann Weyl, one of the leading mathematicians of the twentieth century, writes:

. . . purely mathematical inquiry in itself, according to the conviction of many great thinkers, by its special character, its certainty and stringency, lifts the human mind into closer proximity with the divine than is attainable through any other medium.

There exists, however, a very different view of mathematics, according to which it is nothing but a human invention that has no real existence outside the human brain. In the words of the great German philosopher Immanuel Kant: "The ultimate truth of mathematics lies in the possibility that its concepts can be constructed by the human mind." "Theories" of the universe are, according to this view, only *models*, the utility of which is determined solely by their success in explaining natural phenomena. The effectiveness of mathematics in the physical, biological, and social sciences is in this case a direct consequence of *evolution* and *natural selection* of ideas. In other words, over the centuries mathematicians have produced a plethora of mathematical constructs and models of the universe galore. Many of these models proved to be blind alleys (e.g., the Ptolemaic model of the solar system) and were eventually discarded. The successful ones have been continually improved, with superior data and new mathematical machinery becoming available. The road to our present theoretical thinking of the cosmos has, according to this view (sometimes labeled "intuitionist"), been very similar to the emergence of Homo sapiens through the tortuous evolution of the species. The apparently miraculous applicability (to models of the universe) of some mathematical tools originally conceived with no application in mind reflects, in this case, a mere overproduction of ideas, of which physics has selected only the appropriate ones. The latter point of view has become increasingly popular, especially with psychologists and researchers in the field of embodied cognition. For example, Berkeley linguist George Lakoff and Freiburg University psychologist Rafael Núñez write (in *Where Mathematics Comes From*): "Sometimes human physicists are successful in fitting human mathematics as they conceptualize it to their human conceptualization of the regularities they observe in the physical world." Similarly, cognitive neuropsychologist Stanislas Dehaene concludes in *The Number Sense*:

There is one instrument on which scientists rely so regularly that they sometimes forget its very existence: their own brain. . . . Is the universe really "written in mathematical language," as Galileo contended? I am inclined to think instead that this is the only language with which *we* [emphasis mine] can try to read it.

So, was mathematics discovered or invented? In his recent thought-provoking book, *A New Kind of Science*, computer scientist Stephen Wolfram strongly argues that mathematics is a human invention. Wolfram shows that computer programs and cellular automata can embody more general rules than afforded by mathematical equations. He also shows that the systems of axioms representing conventional mathematics cover only a tiny fraction of the huge range of all *possible* abstract systems. Any attempt to describe mathematics as a pure discovery would thus leave us entirely in the dark with respect to two major questions: (1) How can the human mind gain access to that mythical space in which mathematics presumably exists? (2) How can we call the choice of a small number of sets of rules (out of an immense range of possibilities) a "discovery"?

However, if we were to conclude that mathematics is *entirely* a human invention, this would raise two different questions: (1) How can we explain all the unanticipated theorems that emerged from the systems of axioms that were chosen (including ones that we still don't know how to prove)? (2) Why did the Italian mathematician Giuseppe Peano, after all, choose a particular set of carefully crafted axioms for the theory of numbers, and not any other set?

There is no doubt that even extremely simple systems of rules or axioms can generate highly complex behavior or unexpected "theorems." In this sense, mathematics does take on a life of its own once the basic rules are specified, and humans do have to discover its endless list of properties. Mathematics is therefore a human invention that intrinsically contains discoveries. Why did humans come up with this particular version of mathematics, and why is it so effective in explaining the universe? The answers to these two questions may actually be intimately related. Humans may have developed branches of mathematics (such as arithmetic and geometry) that are largely based on the human *perception* of the universe. Arithmetic may reflect the human ability to discern discrete objects, and geometry may represent the human brain's response to edges and lines. If this is true, then the effectiveness of mathematics may indeed be a consequence of the fact that the universe has imposed, in some sense, a particular brand of mathematics on humans. Jef Raskin, who helped create the Macintosh computer, goes even somewhat further. He thinks that human *logic*, from which mathematics has presumably emerged, was shaped and essentially forced on us by the workings of the universe, via Darwinian natural selection. Raskin's argument goes something like this: For most propositions encountered in everyday life, humans can assert whether they are true or not. If some creatures were to develop with a logic allowing them to assert "true *and* not true" for certain propositions, such creatures would not have survived for long. For example, such a creature might jump off the edge of a cliff thinking that nothing would happen to it, even if it had seen others before jumping to their inevitable deaths.

As strange as this may sound, astronomy could, *in principle*, provide a more definitive answer to the question about the effectiveness of mathematics. Imagine that we were to discover many extraterrestrial intelligent civilizations, all of which evolved independently of one another. Imagine further that we were to find that all of these civilizations recognize, for example, the value of π and the prime numbers. One could then argue that mathematics, as we know it, is, in this sense, "universal." These particular astronomical discoveries may prove, however, to be entirely unfeasible. Not only is the discovery of extraterrestrial civilizations extremely difficult, even the definition of an "intelligent civilization" may prove to be an insurmountable task if other civilizations are very different from us. In the meantime, therefore, we are forced to continue to use our mathematics, while the question as to the cause of its effectiveness remains somewhat unresolved.

MARIO LIVIO, PH.D., is Head of the Science Division at the Space Telescope Science Institute (STScI), which conducts the scientific program of the Hubble Space Telescope. Dr. Livio has published more than four hundred scientific papers and has received numerous awards for research and for excellence in teaching. In addition to his scientific interests, he is a self-proclaimed "art fanatic" who owns many hundreds of art books. Recently, he combined his passions for science and art in two popular books, *The Accelerating Universe*, which appeared in 2000, and *The Golden Ratio*, which appeared in 2002.

Sarah Voss

A DECADE AND A HALF ago, when I was teaching calculus at a small Midwestern college and my career in ministry was still barely a dream, I struggled to find anything in the literature that would justify a term such as "mathematical theology." Although the concept can be traced back to the ancient Greeks, the term is relatively new.

Today, things are different. Now we find the occasional book bearing an explicitly mathematic-theological title,[1] and we find numerous works where the relation between math and theology is indirect and metaphorical, but with the same intent.[2] Mathematical physicists and other scientists often make direct statements relating God to mathematical concepts.[3] Even the prestigious *Scientific American* recognizes the term, albeit somewhat less than enthusiastically.[4]

So, what is mathematical theology, anyhow? What good is it? Why should we take any note of it? The short answers to these questions are simple. Mathematical theology is a study of the Divine, which in some way draws on mathematics. It's good because it opens our minds (and maybe our hearts) to new possibilities. And, finally, it brings hope.

The longer answers are too involved for this essay, but perhaps I can point you in an appropriate direction. And perhaps you will become intrigued by how much mathematics "counts" in the theological world.

First, more on the nature of mathematical theology. When guests enter our home, they are often startled to find a large mannequin sitting on our sofa. They are startled partly because "Jonesy" is unusual and partly because she greets our visitors wearing a T-shirt that pretty much sums up (humorously, but also seriously) what I mean by "mathematical theology."

But unless I draw their attention to it, most people overlook her T-shirt inscription:[5]

and God said,

$$\varepsilon_0 \oint E \cdot da = \sum q$$

$$\oint B \cdot ds = \mu_0 \int J \cdot da + \mu_0 \varepsilon_0 \frac{d}{dt} \int E \cdot da$$

$$\oint E \cdot ds = -\frac{d}{dt} \int B \cdot da$$

$$\oint B \cdot da = 0 \dots$$

and there was light!

"Jonesy"

The implication, of course, is that God speaks in mathematics. This idea is old. The Pythagoreans held much the same view, believing that "Number is all" and that "the harmony of the spheres" depended on right relationship between those numbers.

Through most of the years since the Pythagoreans, people have played variations on this same theme. Only in the last couple of hundred years did the dissociation between the spiritual realm and the world of mathematics become a requirement for scientific legitimacy. Fortunately, this false separation is now coming to an end.

God seems to speak in mathematics in two basic ways. One is through the precision of numerical calculation, logical proofs, and all the other phenomena associated with mathematics in the "hard" sciences. The other way is through metaphor. Most of the book titles cited earlier (see notes 1 and 2) are also metaphors drawn from mathematics and applied to theological and spiritual notions. For example, the universe has been said to work like a mathematical hologram, and theology is in some manner like mathematical chaos theory.

It has been only in the last decade or so that our society has started to acknowledge the existence of mathematical metaphors, or what I call "mathaphors." And when they apply to the spiritual realm, I call them "holy mathaphors." Mathematical theology involves both straight calculation and mathaphors, but it leans more heavily on the latter.[6] I'll say more about one such holy mathaphor when we talk about hope.

What good comes from examining holy mathaphors? Elsewhere, I have explored ten ways in which metaphors drawn from mathematics are impacting us.[7] In short, these analogies are

1. Changing our metaphors for God
2. Challenging our human role in the universe
3. Helping us accept ambiguity
4. Revamping our understanding of the one and of the many
5. Revising our thoughts about free will and determinism
6. Moving us toward pluralistic, multiworld views
7. Pushing the envelope on what our understanding of "consciousness" is
8. Altering our expectations for the afterlife
9. Offering the hope of a more compassionate future
10. Encouraging faith perspectives that are always incomplete and in process

While a case can be made for all of these statements (and probably others), the point here is that ideas drawn from mathematics greatly extend our spiritual worldviews. Such mathematical notions are suggestive, not conclusive. But in those suggestions lie the makings of new ways of interacting with one another, of healing, of understanding God. In a world that is often spiritually fractured and hurting, we can look to mathematical theology for the seeds of new hope.

Mathematics, it should be noted, has long been a reservoir for radical change. Consider holography, for instance. Twenty years before the invention of the laser, which is essential to producing holographic images, the theory of holography was nonetheless complete and available in the mathematics textbook—and this is not an isolated example. Over and over, we first become aware of valuable new ideas through the language of mathematics.

To some, drawing analogies from math and the hard sciences is a suspect process. Some fear that extrapolating scientific concepts to a nonscientific discipline such as religion or philosophy clouds the truth of our spiritual insights and leads to misunderstanding of the science involved. Truthfully, this can happen.[8] Yet to prematurely close our minds to the exciting possibilities that mathematical analogies can bring to such nonmathematical disciplines is, in my opinion, a tragedy.

A tragedy, in fact, is what my favorite mathematician's life turned out to be when his mathematical discoveries were labeled "heretical" by his more "successful" (traditional) colleagues. Georg Cantor was born in St. Petersburg, Russia, on March 3, 1845, to a father who converted to Christianity from Judaism and a mother who was Roman Catholic. A deeply religious man himself, Cantor became a mathematics professor at what he considered a "second-rate" institution, the University of Halle.[9] During his career, Cantor virtually single-handedly contributed to the world what is now known as "transfinite set theory." This theory, which introduced the notion of the *actual* infinite,[10] revolutionized mathematics. He had a quasi-religious self-justification for his work, believing his ideas had come to him as a messenger of God. But at Halle, Cantor chafed under the constant and often mean-spirited criticism of his own former teacher and very influential mathematician, Leopold Kronecker. These vicious attacks and the general lack of recognition of his mathematical triumphs contributed to Cantor's eventual nervous breakdown. He died in a mental hospital in Halle in 1918, a dispirited and bitter man.

Although Cantor did not live to see this revolution happen, he never doubted that it someday would. In the hindsight of the century that has passed since his great discoveries, perhaps it is time to wonder whether he was right. Cantor's work involves numerous radical conclusions about infinity and the continuity of numbers. For example, he showed that there are different sizes of infinities, with some being larger than others. Furthermore, the ones we think should be smaller or larger than others are not necessarily so. The sequential counting numbers {1,2,3,4,...} would seem to most of us to be a larger set than the set of even counting numbers {2,4,6,8,...}. But Cantor showed that because they could be put into one-to-one correspondence with one another, they have an unexpected equivalency. Thus, in an odd way, a part of a set is actually equal to the whole of it. Another way of saying this is that in mathematics *the part may have the power of the whole.*

This is only one of the unusual notions that Cantor presented. In the Cantorian world, there also exists an entity that is infinitely many yet simultaneously infinitely sparse. The infinite both is and is not infinite; incompleteness is intrinsic to the structure of the system.

It is interesting to take these characteristics of Cantorian set theory and say, "What happens if something like this occurs in an area other than mathematics?" In particular, what happens if something similar to these ideas works in our theological and spiritual realms?[11]

One of the possibilities that arises from this reflection is a new notion of pluralistic religion. Until now, there have been three ways of responding to the fact that we humans have more than one religious understanding. Whose faith is "right"? The religious exclusivist says, "Mine is." The inclusivist says that lots of them appear to be right, but that they are all included in one "real" way to salvation or liberation. The traditional pluralist says, "You can have yours and I'll have mine, and that's just fine."

Now, with a Cantorian perspective, we can consider that the part may have the power of the whole. When we use Cantorian set theory as a metaphor for a new way of thinking about contemporary religious pluralism, we find a wonderful precedent for accepting the "unacceptable" contradictions inevitable in any discussion of "right" faith(s). In other words, many different religious traditions are "equivalent" to the one whole truth.[12]

Cantorian mathaphors give rise to the idea of a "religion which contains all religions."[13] In spite of its initial sense of grandiosity, this mathaphor suggests that such an all-encompassing religion is still just one more religion, with both its good and flawed aspects. Cantorian mathaphors also offer new possibilities in our understanding of an "infinite" God. For example, might God in some way be both infinite and bounded? Might God be "actual" rather than (or as well as) "potential" in nature? And what are the implications of such a God for our lives?

These and other questions are ripe for further examination. Mathematical theology gives us one tool for doing the exploration. If we use it, it promises to stretch us, to challenge us, to offer us hope. The "strange metaphor" in the poem below strives to capture the essence of this.

CANTOR RELIGION[14]

The lamps are different, but the Light is the same.
(Jalalu'l-Din Rumi, thirteenth-century Sufi poet)

In the room my mind
sit many different lamps.
The lamp of Christianity, an old oil
lantern, recently wired for electricity,
all the latest scientific gadgets;
when I approach,
it springs on automatically.
I trust this lamp:
it was the light in the hallway
when I was small and afraid of the dark.
I use this lamp even now, oh,
not all the time . . . but
when I have moments free,
in fancy Gothic cathedrals
or tiny country chapels
smelling of warm waxed wood.

The Eastern lamp is hand-crafted copper,
gondola-shaped, wick lit
Aladdin's lamp, it charms
with ancient promise
of untold treasure, I must
but rub it and attend, oh
there, can you see?
The earnest, handsome Buddhist
from Sri Lanka
who resides in the basement of my house,
who laments that the young women
in this country don't care much
for the color of his skin. Me?
I'm old. I love the rich
blue-black glow which lives
in the light of this lamp.

The Jewish lamp, really seven candles
welded together. The one
in the room my mind
is highly stylized. Contemporary.
Unorthodox. You can't make out much
in its soft flame, mostly abstract
markings, maybe it makes a difference
if you read Hebrew. Still, I love
to search the shadows it forms
for things familiar and strange,
as order out of nothing
in only seven days
and bushes that burn
with the Sabbath light
now and forever Amen.

In this land where I was born
are Native lamps; mine
a gray clay
artifact, discovered lying
by a tattooed Erie Indian
whose body was dug from a pit
and whose spirit finds me yet today
when I dig my bare toes
deep into the earth
and listen to the breath
of the wind.

All these and more are the lamps
which rest in the room
my mind, yet the one
I cherish most is the chalice
that ignites my heart,
for I see in its light
the room my mind
with all its magnificent lamps,
among them the chalice
that ignites my heart
which shows the room my mind
Dear God of many iterations,
may all their light shine on
and on and on, like a Cantor set
transcending.

ℒ♥

SARAH VOSS, D.MIN., a Unitarian Universalist minister and former mathematics professor, writes, lectures, teaches, and preaches widely about the relationship between religion and mathematics/science. She is the author of several books, including *What Number Is God?* (1995), an exploratory work on mathematical metaphors, and *Zero: Reflections about Nothing* (1998), a book of inspirational essays. She has written articles dealing with mathematics and religion, which have appeared in journals such as *Parabola, The UU World,* and *Mathematicia Philosophia,* and in collections such as *Rocking the Ages,* a Swedenborg Foundation "Chrysalis Reader." She has also developed and taught an award-winning course called "Bridging Science and Spirit: A Mathaphorical Journey." Her most recent projects include the "St. Mathematicia" sermon series, which she offered in 2004 as consulting minister to the First Unitarian Church of Sioux City, and an informal educational workshop focused on "moral math." Currently, she is a part-time lecturer in religion at the University of Nebraska at Omaha. For more about her work, see www.PiZine.com.

NOTES

1 Consider, for example, *Chaos Theology: A Revised Creation Theology* (Sjoerd L. Bonting, Novalis, 2002), and *Quantum Theology: Spiritual Implications of the New Physics* (Diarmuid O'Murchu, Crossroad/Herder & Herder, 1997).

2 For example, *The "God" Part of the Brain* (Matthew Alper, Roger Press, 2001); *The Holographic Universe* (Michael Talbot, Harper Collins Publishers, 1991); *The Soul in Cyberspace* (Douglas Groothuis, Baker Books, 1997); *The Bible Code* (Michael Drosnin, Simon & Schuster, 1997); *The Age of Spiritual Machines* (Ray Kurtzeil, Viking, 1999); *The Loom of God: Mathematical Tapestries at the Edge of Time* (Clifford A. Pickover, Plenum Press,

1997); *Sacred Geometry* (Robert Lawlor, Thames & Hudson, 1989); and *What Number Is God?* (Sarah Voss, SUNY, 1995).

3 For a nice example, see John Houghton's analogy of God in the fifth (mathematical) dimension, in "Where Is God? Thinking in More Than Three Dimensions," from *God for the 21st Century* (ed. by Russell Stannard, Templeton Foundation Press, 2000, p 159).

4 In "A Pixelated Cosmos," George Musser writes that mathematical string theory "has been called an exercise in 'recreational mathematical theology'" (*Scientific American,* October, 2002, p 18).

5 J. C. Maxwell's four famous equations of electricity and magnetism.

6 See also my book *What Number Is God?* and my article "Sacred Qualities" in *Parabola* (Fall 1999, pp 32–37). I also teach a class/seminar that deals with "holy mathaphors"; see www.PiZine.com.

7 I developed these ideas in two invited lectures: "Old Pythagoras Would Be Pleased: Theological Reflections on Dyson Mathematics," CTNS Templeton Conference on the works of Freeman Dyson, Omaha, NE, October 2000; and "Ten Ways Contemporary Mathaphors Are Shaping Our Spiritual Lives," Klein 2000 Lecture, First Unitarian Church, Ann Arbor, Michigan, October 2000.

8 See, for example, "A Review of Mikael Stenmark's *Scientism: Science, Ethics, and Religion,*" by Ciprian Acatrinei, Metanexus: The Online Forum on Religion and Science; Views 2002.10.07, http://www.metanexus.net.

9 Martin Luther University of Halle, Wittenberg, is located in the German city of Halle, Saxony-Anhalt. It was merged in 1817 from the University of Halle (founded 1694) and the University of Wittenberg (founded 1502, closed in 1813 by Napoleon) and named after Martin Luther. It is the largest and oldest university in the Bundesland of Saxony-Anhalt, with about fourteen thousand students.

10 As opposed to the more commonly held idea of the infinite being filled with *potential.*

11 See chapter 4 of my book *What Number Is God?* My eventual hope is to revise and extend these ideas for a lay audience.

12 The material in these last two paragraphs appears in "Viewpoint: The Many Faiths or One Faith Question," by Sarah Voss, printed in *Publisher's Weekly Religion Bookline,* November 1, 1996, p 2.

13 Cf. the Cantorian notion of a "set which contains all sets."

14 From *What Number Is God?* pp 132–33.

Michael Heller

THE MATHEMATICAL-EMPIRICAL method of modern science was born when investigators gave up asking questions that were too difficult and limited themselves to those aspects of the world that could be measured. In spite of this, it soon appeared that the new method was exceedingly efficient in many hitherto unexpected fields of investigation. The idea that "the world should be explained in terms of the world itself"—that is, with no help of elements alien to the mathematical-empirical method—has been quickly elevated to the rank of the fundamental methodological principle. Many people either openly claim or are inclined to think that the limits of the scientific method coincide with the limits of rationality in general. What is beyond the scientific method is beyond rationality. In this sense, totalitarian tendencies are inherent in the practice of science.

Nowhere are these tendencies better visible than in modern cosmology. When thinking about the universe on its most "global" scale, it is difficult to avoid thinking about the limits of science and its method. Nevertheless, even in this field of research, the scientist has, according to the scientific code, the duty to "explain the world in terms of the world itself." Several strategies have been promulgated to fulfill this duty. Let us enumerate some of them.

The most ancient of these strategies is the claim that the universe is "eternal." If it had no beginning, it is simply "given"; then, as far as its origin is concerned, there is nothing to be explained. When Einstein created his first relativistic world model in 1917, he was ready to change his equations by adding a new term (containing the famous cosmological constant) rather than admit that the universe was nonstatic and, consequently, that it could have a beginning. Einstein's model soon turned out to be in conflict with astronomical observations, and the theory of the "expanding universe," with the Big Bang as its beginning, took precedence. However, to kill the idea of the "eternal universe" was not that easy. In 1948, Hermann Bondi, Thomas Gold, and Fred Hoyle promoted "steady-state cosmology" and defended it vigorously. They proposed the image of a universe in which matter re-creates itself continuously, and therefore a universe that lasts indefinitely. Recent versions of chaotic inflationary cosmology, created by Andrei Linde (a contributor to this book) and modified by Lee Smolin, can be thought of as a new incarnation of the same idea with the proviso that there are no material particles, but rather new universes that are continuously regenerated.

Another version of the same strategy is the idea of "eternal return." In its strong form, time itself is "closed," like a circle, and each event in the universe was, and will be, repeated infinitely many times. In its weaker form, the universe oscillates: Each contracting phase is followed by an expanding phase, with a "big bounce" between phases. In this way, the universe continues to pulsate *ad infinitum*. Various modifications of this scenario are possible and, in fact, have been proposed.

In the above strategies, the universe is simply "given," and as such continues its existence indefinitely. More ambitious strategies aim at explaining scientifically how this could be. To this category belong various models of the "quantum creation of the universe," also called "models of quantum tunneling out of nothing." The idea, proposed by James Hartle and Stephen Hawking in 1983, was subsequently developed by several authors. It consists of a combination of quantum physics, in which a "game of probabilities" plays the key role along with general relativity that is a paradigmatic theory for modeling the universe in its largest scale. Creation models aim at showing that there is a non-zero probability for the universe (in its certain state) to emerge out of nothing. Unfortunately, however, we have not yet developed a full unification theory of quantum physics and general relativity. Many approaches have been tried, leading to different results.

The above explanation clearly presupposes the existence of physical laws. With no laws of physics, no physical model is possible. With no laws of physics, nothing would forever remain nothing. How then does one explain the existence of physical laws? One possible explanation is to assume that, on the fundamental level, no physical laws exist at all. On this level, everything is equally probable; the only "law" is randomness and its attendant "stochastic noise." What we call the "laws of physics" emerge out of this primordial chaos as the outcome of some averaging process. This strategy seems to be an attractive explanation, but its results are so far rather poor. It elevates a "game of probabilities" to the rank of a fundamental ontology of the universe. Here the question could be asked: In what respect does the probability calculus differ from other mathematical theories such that it is elevated to such a prominent rank?

Another attempt to explain the existence of physical laws consists of arguing that there is only one logically consistent set of such laws. If we ever discover the "final theory of everything," it will be constituted by exactly this set of laws. This strategy provides an ultimate explanation in the sense that, if it is correct, there is no choice: either this set of laws, or nothing. However, according to Gödel's incompleteness theorems, this can hardly be correct. If in mathematics the ideal of a complete and logically consistent set of axioms is excluded, the chance that something similar could be done in physics is indeed minuscule.

The whole of the history of physics testifies to the fact that the universe has a property owing to which it (i.e., the universe) can be modeled with the help of mathematical structures. In mathematics, we may think of two structures that, in a sense, determine each other. Such structures are called "dual." Roughly speaking, if f and x are elements of two dual structures, then the "evaluation" of f on x, that is $f(x)$, can also be read as the "evaluation" of x on f, that is $x(f)$. It can happen that a structure is dual with itself; in such a case, it is called "self-dual." We could rightly say that it explains or justifies itself. Mathematical structures are not static; they can act on one another. One could say that the whole of modern mathematics is about actions of various structures on various other structures. Mathematics is, in a sense, a science of "structure dynamics." It can happen that a structure is not only self-dual, but also acts on itself in a self-dual manner. Such a structure can truly be said to be "self-sufficient." If the universe, on its most fundamental scale, is modeled by a self-dual structure in the above sense, it is "self-explaining" in the truest sense of this term. There exist many self-dual structures in contemporary mathematics (for instance, in the theory of quantum groups), and some of them have interesting applications to physics. However, for the time being, no self-dual structure is known that is rich enough to provide a "global explanation of everything." Shan Majid, a mathematical physicist from Cambridge University, the author and main propagator of this idea, says briefly that a fundamental theory of physics is incomplete unless it is self-dual in the above sense.

We do not know which of these strategies (if any) is correct or closest to being correct. Most probably new ones, with more clever and more self-explaining answers, will be invented. However, all of them—those that already exist and those that will exist in the future—must presuppose the existence (in whatever sense of this term) of something that is to be explained and of something that explains it. In the most ambitious of these strategies, these two instances of "something" coalesce into one self-explaining something. Here the famous Leibniz question is unavoidable: Why does something exist rather than nothing? The most self-explanatory element is nothingness. If there were nothing, there would be nothing to be explained—no questions to be asked, nobody to answer them. Nothingness is the simplest state of all.

The question itself—Why does something exist rather than nothing?—bears an important metaphysical message. It would hardly be possible to better express the astonishing fact that the universe exists and that it does not seem to contain in itself any justification of its own existence. It is not without meaning that the astonishment takes the form of a question. Questions open vast fields of possibilities that are usually blocked by positive statements. Leibniz's question is perhaps the less anthropomorphic of all questions ever asked in philosophy and, at least indirectly, in theology. Moreover, this question is free from any involvement in time or space. The Leibnizian "something" is neither temporal nor timeless, neither localized in space nor totally abstract. When I ask this Leibnizian question, I am not directly alluding to God; I am only wondering about the existence of "something" that contains me. I start thinking with what I know from my direct experience, namely, that I am. But my thought is not trapped in itself. It is the word "Why?" that opens broad horizons.

Leibniz's question also alludes to an infinite distance separating something from nothing. In this context, "infinite" is a synonym for "indefinite"—like the distance between any real number and zero (their ratio is indefinite) or like the proportion between my transient "now" and the entirety of time, of which my "now" is only a negligible, but real, instant surrounded by an already-nonexistent past and a not-yet-existent future. From "nothing" to "something" is like from "now" to "infinity."

The existence of an Absolute, Something that infinitely transcends me, cannot be doubted. It constitutes the content of my direct experience, if by "experience" I mean not merely sensorially perceiving the fact that I am, but also "touching my own existence" by my wondrous human ability to think about the fact that I "am." It is another question that clamors for an answer: What or Who is the Absolute? An impersonal, but in some sense infinite, power that is at least partially expressed in the mathematical laws of Nature, or a Conscious Being infinitely transcending anything we can imagine?

Could Infinity be Infinity if it is less rather than more?

MICHAEL HELLER, PH.D., a Roman Catholic priest, is Professor of Philosophy at the Pontifical Academy of Theology in Cracow, Poland, and an adjunct member of the Vatican Observatory staff. He twice held the Lemaître Chair at the Catholic University of Louvain, Belgium. Fr. Heller is an ordinary member of the Pontifical Academy of Sciences in Rome, a founding member of the International Society for Science and Religion, and a member of several other international societies. The list of his publications contains more than eight hundred entries, including nearly three hundred research papers in physics, cosmology, philosophy of science, and history of science. He also is author of more than twenty books, the most recent being *Is Physics an Art?* (1998), *Quantum Cosmology* (2001), *The Beginning Is Everywhere* (2002), *The Meaning of Life and of the Universe* (2002), and *Creative Tension* (2003).

One Universal Computation 41

FIRST ZERO, THEN ONE

Kevin Kelly

A THREE-GIGABYTE genome sequence represents the prime coding information of a human body—your life as numbers. Biology, that pulsating mass of plant and animal flesh, is conceived by science today as an information process. At today's rates of compression, you could download the entire three billion digits of your DNA onto about four CDs. As computers keep shrinking, we have little difficulty imagining our complex bodies being numerically condensed to the size of two tiny cells. These micro-memory devices—egg and sperm—are packed with information.

That life might be information, as biologists propose, is far more intuitive than the corresponding idea that hard matter is information. When we bang a knee against a table leg, it sure doesn't feel like we knocked into information; yet that's the idea many physicists are formulating.

The spooky nature of material things is not new. Once science examined matter below the level of fleeting quarks and muons, it knew the world was incorporeal. What could be less substantial than a realm built out of waves of quantum probabilities? (And what could be weirder?) Digital physics is both. It suggests that those strange and insubstantial quantum wavicles, along with everything else in the universe, are themselves made of nothing but 1s and 0s. The physical world itself is digital.

The scientist John Archibald Wheeler (coiner of the term "black hole")[1] was onto this in the 1980s. He claimed that, fundamentally, atoms are made up of bits of information. As he put it in a 1989 lecture, "Its are from bits." He elaborated: "Every it—every particle, every field of force, even the spacetime continuum itself—derives its function, its meaning, its very existence entirely from binary choices—bits. What we call reality arises in the last analysis from the posing of yes/no questions."

To get a sense of the challenge of describing physics as a software program, picture three atoms: two hydrogen and one oxygen. Put on the magic glasses of digital physics and watch as the three atoms bind together to form a water molecule. As they merge, each seems to be calculating the optimal angle and distance at which to attach itself to the others. The oxygen atom uses yes/no decisions to evaluate all possible courses toward the hydrogen atom and then usually selects the optimal 104.45 degrees by moving toward the other hydrogen atom at that very angle. Every chemical bond is thus calculated. If this sounds like a simulation of physics, then you understand perfectly, because in a world made up of bits, physics is exactly the same as a simulation of physics. There's no difference in kind, just in degree of exactness.

Unlike the fantastic world of *The Matrix* movies, in which simulations are so good you can't tell whether you're in an artificial world; in a universe run on bits, everything is a simulation.

An ultimate simulation needs an ultimate computer, and the new science of digitalism says that the universe itself is the ultimate computer—actually the only computer. Further, it says, all the computation of the human world, especially our puny little PCs, merely piggyback on cycles of the "Great Computer." Weaving together the esoteric teachings of quantum physics with the latest theories in computer science, pioneering digital thinkers are outlining a way of understanding all of physics as a form of computation.

From this perspective, computation seems almost a theological process. It takes as its fodder the primeval choice between yes or no, the fundamental state of 1 or 0. After stripping away all externalities, all material embellishments, what remains is the purest state of existence: here/not here. Am/not am. In the Old Testament, when Moses asks the Creator, "Who are you?" the Being says, in effect, "Am." One bit. One Almighty Bit. "Yes." "One." "Exist." It is the simplest statement possible.

All creation, from this perch, is made from this irreducible foundation. Every mountain, every star, the smallest salamander or woodland tick, each thought in our mind, each flight of a ball is but a web of elemental yeses/nos woven together. If the theory of digital physics holds up, movement (f = ma), energy (E = mc²), gravity, dark matter, and antimatter can all be explained by elaborate programs of 1/0 decisions. Bits can be seen as a digital version of the "atoms" of classical Greece: the tiniest constituents of existence. But these new digital atoms are the basis not only of matter, as the Greeks thought, but of energy, motion, mind, and life.

From this perspective, computation, which juggles and manipulates these primal bits, is a silent reckoning that uses a small amount of energy to rearrange symbols. The result is a signal that makes a difference—a difference that can be felt as a bruised knee. The input of computation is energy and information; the output is order, structure, and extropy.

Our awakening to the true power of computation rests on two suspicions. The first is that *computation can describe all things*. To date, computer scientists have been able to encapsulate every logical argument, scientific equation, and literary work that we know about into the basic notation of computation. Now, with the advent of digital signal processing, we can capture video, music, and art in the same form. Even emotion is not immune. Researchers Cynthia Breazeal at MIT and Charles Guerin and Albert Mehrabian in Quebec have built Kismet and EMIR (Emotional Model for Intelligent Response), two systems that exhibit primitive feelings.

The second supposition is that *all things can compute*. We have begun to see that almost any kind of material can serve as a computer. Human brains, which are mostly water, compute fairly well. (The first "computers" were clerical workers figuring mathematical tables by hand.) So can sticks and strings. As an undergraduate student in 1975, engineer Danny Hillis constructed a digital computer out of skinny TINKERTOYS. In 2000, Hillis designed a digital computer made of only steel and tungsten that is indirectly powered by human muscle. This slow-moving device turns a clock intended to tick for ten thousand years. He hasn't made a computer with pipes and pumps, but he says he could. Recently, scientists have used both quantum particles and minute strands of DNA to perform computations.

A third postulate ties the first two together into a remarkable new view: *All computation is one.*

In 1937, Alan Turing, Alonso Church, and Emil Post worked out the logical underpinnings of useful computers. They called the most basic loop—which has become the foundation of all working computers—a finite-state machine. Based on their analysis of this machine, Turing and Church proved a theorem now bearing their names. Their conjecture states that any computation executed by one finite-state machine writing on an infinite tape (known later as a Turing machine) can be done by any other finite-state machine on an infinite tape, no matter what its configuration. In other words, all computation is equivalent. They called this "universal computation."

When John von Neumann and others jump-started the first electronic computers in the 1950s, they immediately began extending the laws of computation away from math proofs and into the natural world. They tentatively applied the laws of loops and cybernetics to ecology, culture, families, weather, and biological systems. Evolution and learning, they declared, were types of computation. Nature computed.

If nature computed, why not the entire universe? In a June 2002 article published in *Physical Review Letters,* MIT professor Seth Lloyd posed this question: If the universe were a computer, how powerful would it be? By analyzing the computing potential of quantum particles, he calculated the upper limit of how much computing power the entire universe (as we know it) has contained since the beginning of time. It's a large number: 10^{120} logical operations. There are two interpretations of this number. One is that it represents the performance "specs" of the ultimate computer. The other is that it's the amount required to simulate the universe on a quantum computer. Both statements illustrate the tautological nature of a digital universe: Every computer is the computer.

Continuing in this vein, Lloyd estimated the total amount of computation that has been accomplished by all human-made computers that have ever run. He came up with 10^{31} logical operations. (Because of the fantastic doubling of Moore's law, more than half of this total was produced in the past two years.) He then tallied up the total energy-matter available in the known universe and divided that by the total energy-matter of human computers expanding at the rate of Moore's law.

"We need three hundred Moore's law doublings, or six hundred years at one doubling every two years," he figures, "before all the available energy in the universe is taken up in computing. Of course, if one takes the perspective that the universe is already essentially performing a computation, then we don't have to wait at all. In this case, we may just have to wait for six hundred years until the universe is running Windows or Linux."

The relative nearness of six hundred years says more about exponential increases than it does about computers. Neither Lloyd nor any other scientist mentioned here realistically expects a second universal computer in six hundred years. But what

Lloyd's calculation proves is that over the long term, there is nothing theoretical to stop the expansion of computers. "In the end, the whole of space and its contents will be the computer. The universe will in the end consist, literally, of intelligent thought processes," David Deutsch proclaims in *Fabric of Reality*. These assertions echo those of the physicist Freeman Dyson, who also sees minds—amplified by computers—expanding into the Cosmos "infinite in all directions."[2]

Yet while there is no theoretical hitch to an ever-expanding computer matrix that may in the end resemble a universal machine, no one wants to see themselves as someone else's program running on someone else's computer. Put that way, life seems a bit secondhand.

Yet the notion that our existence is derived, like a string of bits, is an old and familiar one. Central to the evolution of Western civilization from its early Hellenistic roots has been the notion of logic, abstraction, and disembodied information. The saintly Christian guru John writes from Greece in the first century: "In the beginning was the Word, and the Word was with God, and the Word was God." Charles Babbage, credited with constructing the first computer in 1832, saw the world as one gigantic instantiation of a calculating machine, hammered out of brass by God. He argued that in this heavenly computer universe, miracles were accomplished by divinely altering the rules of computation. Even miracles were logical bits, manipulated by God.

There's still confusion. Is God the Word itself, the Ultimate Software and Source Code, or is God the Ultimate Programmer? Or is God the Necessary Other, the off-universe platform where this universe is computed?

But each of these three possibilities has at its root the mystical doctrine of universal computation. Somehow, according to digitalism, we are linked to one another, all beings alive and inert, because we share, as John Wheeler said, "at the bottom—at a very deep bottom, in most instances—an immaterial source." This commonality, spoken of by mystics of many beliefs in different terms, also has a scientific name: computation. Bits—minute logical atoms, spiritual in form—amass into quantum quarks and gravity waves, raw thoughts, and rapid motions.

The computation of these bits is a precise, definable, yet invisible process that is immaterial yet produces matter. "Computation is a process that is perhaps *the* process," says Danny Hillis, whose new book, *The Pattern on the Stone*, explains the formidable nature of computation. "It has an almost mystical character because it seems to have some deep relationship to the underlying order of the universe. Exactly what that relationship is, we cannot say. At least for now."

Probably the "trippiest" science book ever written is *The Physics of Immortality*, by Frank Tipler. If this book were labeled standard science fiction, no one would notice, but Tipler is a reputable physicist and Tulane University professor who writes papers for the *International Journal of Theoretical Physics*. In *Immortality*, he uses current understandings of cosmology and computation to declare that all living beings will be bodily resurrected after the universe dies. His argument runs roughly as follows: As the universe collapses in on itself in the last minutes of time, the final spacetime singularity creates (just once) infinite energy and computing capacity.

In other words, as the giant universal computer keeps shrinking in size, its power increases to the point at which it can simulate precisely the entire historical universe, past, present, and possible. He calls this state the Omega Point. It is a computational space that can resurrect "from the dead" all the minds and bodies that have ever lived. The weird thing is that Tipler was an atheist when he developed this theory and discounted as mere "coincidence" the parallels between his ideas and the Christian doctrine of Heavenly Resurrection. Since then, he says, science has convinced him that the two may be identical.

While not everyone goes along with Tipler's eschatological speculations, theorists such as Deutsch endorse his physics. An Omega Computer is possible and probably likely, they say.

I asked Tipler which side of the Fredkin gap he is on. Does he go along with the weak version of the ultimate computer, the metaphorical one, that says the universe only seems like a computer? Or does he embrace Fredkin's strong version, that the universe is a twelve-billion-year-old computer and we are the killer app? "I regard the two statements as equivalent," he answered. "If the universe in all ways acts as if it was a computer, then what meaning could there be in saying that it is not a computer?"

Only hubris.

And if the universe is a computer, then the Spirit of God seems to dwell in its tiniest bit, the elemental, immaterial act of computation, which is shared by everything. There is but one Universal Computation, and we each manifest this unseen power in our specific material way.

✑

KEVIN KELLY helped launch *Wired* magazine in 1993, served as its Executive Editor until January 1999, and is currently Editor-at-Large. In 1994 and 1997, during Kelly's tenure, *Wired* won the National Magazine Award for General Excellence (the industry's equivalent of two Oscars). His books include *Out of Control: The New Biology of Machines, Social Systems, and the Economic World* (1994); *New Rules for the New Economy: 10 Radical Strategies for a Connected World* (1998), which was a bestseller in the United States and has been translated into various languages; *Bicycle Haiku* (2001), *Asia Grace* (2002), *Cool Tools* (2003), and *Bad Dreams* (2003). Kelly serves on boards of high-tech companies and is a frequent speaker at conferences and corporate meetings.

NOTES

1 Also see http://www.metanexus.net/ultimate_reality/main.htm and http://us.cambridge.org/titles/catalogue.asp?isbn=052183113X.

2 Freeman J. Dyson, *Infinite in All Directions: Gifford Lectures Given at Aberdeen, Scotland, April-November 1985*. New York: Harper & Row, 1988. Also see his essay in this volume.

"Neoreality" and the Quest for Transcendence 42

Clifford A. Pickover

> The nature of reality is this: It is hidden, and it is hidden, and it is hidden.
> —*Rumi, thirteenth-century Sufi poet and mystic*

W HAT IS REALITY? What is transcendence? How can we open our minds so that we can reason beyond the limits of our intuition? When Albert Einstein was asked about reality, he replied, "Reality is merely an illusion, albeit a very persistent one." In an effort to stretch readers' minds, I have considered both Einstein and Rumi while publishing thirty books on topics on the borderlands of science and religion. Most recently, and perhaps most importantly, I published four science-fiction novels in a "Neoreality" series in which both the reader and protagonists cope with realities separated from ours by thin veils. These distortions and parallel universes are a backdrop for human emotion, scientific logic, grand adventure, and a variety of religious discussions. For example, in *Liquid Earth,* religious robots help humans cope with a reality that melts along a rustic Main Street in Shrub Oak, New York. In *The Lobotomy Club,* a group of people perform brain surgery on themselves to allow them to see religious visions and a "truer" reality. In *Sushi Never Sleeps,* readers ponder a fractal society with inhabitants living at different size scales. Would individual population groups, because of size, develop their own separate societies, religion, and laws? Would some of the tiny Fractalians believe that individuals a million times their size even existed, or would they be relegated to the realm of mythological creatures, like the superhuman gods of yore? And, finally, in *Egg Drop Soup,* an alien object allows people to explore countless realities populated by a host of mysterious beings.

Sometimes readers of the "Neoreality" series ask me why I write on God, strange realities, and religious subjects. I tend to be skeptical about the paranormal. However, I do feel that there are facets of the universe we can never understand, just as a monkey can never understand calculus, black holes, symbolic logic, and poetry. There are thoughts we can never think, visions we can only glimpse. It is at this filmy, veiled interface between human reality and a reality beyond that we may find the numinous, which some may liken to God.

But what exactly is *neoreality?* In my book series, I use the word "neoreality" to imply a new or altered reality that is so close to ours that the differences are usually imperceptible. These realities are often futuristic, fresh, and alive with detail. Readers find themselves in touch with a hyper-reality, a religious reality beyond space and time. Odd portals help characters transcend ordinary existence. The word "neorealism" has traditionally described a movement in Italian filmmaking, characterized by the depictions of poor people and their daily challenges. In neo-realistic movies, directors often featured ordinary characters in plots that mean-dered like wisps and eddies of wind. The directors did a minimum of editing and fancy camerawork. My new use of the word "neoreality" is not synonymous with neorealism, although I can resonate with the old neorealistic characters, buffeted by the seemingly random circumstances around them. Navigating the chaotic churn, and speculating about God, is the very essence of adventure.

Belief in an omniscient God and the promise of heaven are important ideas to adherents of great monotheistic religions such as Christianity, Judaism, and Islam. These beliefs pervade much of Western culture and are clearly evident in the United States. Recent surveys indicate that:

✦ The United States ranks highest, along with Iceland and the Philippines, for those who believe in heaven (63 percent of the population).
✦ The United States ranks highest for those who believe in life after death (55 percent).
✦ Eighty-four percent of Americans believe that God performed miracles.

Indeed, science and religion are both thriving in America.

Not only do many laypeople believe in God, but various scientists have used evi-dence from physics and astronomy to conclude that God exists. Note, however, that the scientists' "God" may not be the God of the Israelites, who smites the wicked, but rather a God that established various mathematical and physical parameters that permitted life to evolve in the universe. Some scientists feel we exist because of cos-mic coincidences—or, more accurately, we exist because of seemingly "finely tuned" numerical constants that permit life. Those individuals who believe this Anthropic Principle pronounce these numbers to be near-miracles that might suggest an intel-ligent design to the universe. Here are just a few examples of where religion and science become close.

We owe our very lives to the element carbon, which was first manufactured in stars before the Earth formed. The challenge in creating carbon is getting two helium nuclei in stars to stick together until they are struck by a third. It turns out that this is accomplished only because of internal resonances, or energy levels, of carbon and oxygen nuclei. If the carbon resonance level were only 4 percent lower, carbon atoms wouldn't form. Were the oxygen resonance level only half a percent higher, almost all the carbon would disappear as it combined with helium to form oxygen. This means that human existence depends on the fine-tuning of these two nuclear resonances. The famous astronomer Sir Fred Hoyle said that his atheism was shaken by facts such as these:

> If you wanted to produce carbon and oxygen in roughly equal quantities by stellar nucleosynthesis, these are just the two levels you have to fix. Your fix-ing would have to be just about where these levels are actually found to be. ... A commonsense interpretation of the facts suggests that a superintellect has monkeyed with physics, as well as with chemistry and biology, and there

are no blind forces worth speaking about in nature. The numbers one calculates from the facts seem to me so overwhelming as to put this conclusion almost beyond question. . . . Rather than accept that fantastically small probability of life having arisen through the blind forces of nature, it seemed better to suppose that the origin of life was a deliberate intellectual act.

Robert Jastrow, the former head of NASA's Goddard Institute for Space Studies, called this the most powerful evidence for the existence of God ever to come out of science. Other amazing parameters abound. If all of the stars in the universe were heavier than three solar masses, they would live for only about five hundred million years, and life would not have time to evolve beyond primitive bacteria. Stephen Hawking has estimated that if the rate of the universe's expansion one second after the Big Bang had been smaller by even one part in a hundred thousand million million, the universe would have re-collapsed. And the universe must live for billions of years to permit time for intelligent life to involve. On the other hand, the universe might have expanded so rapidly that protons and electrons never united to make hydrogen atoms.

Paul Davies (who contributed a chapter to this volume) has calculated that the odds against the initial conditions being suitable for later star formation as one followed by a thousand billion billion zeroes. Davies, John Barrow (who also contributed a chapter to this book), and Frank Tipler estimated that a change in the strength of gravity or of the weak force by only one part in 10^{100} would have prevented advanced life forms from evolving. There is no a priori physical reason that these constants and quantities should possess the values they do. This has led the one-time agnostic physicist Davies to write, "Through my scientific work I have come to believe more and more strongly that the physical universe is put together with an ingenuity so astonishing that I cannot accept it merely as a brute fact." Of course, these conclusions are controversial, and an infinite number of random (non-designed) universes could exist, ours being just one that permits carbon-based life. Some researchers have even speculated that child universes are constantly budding off from parent universes and that the child universe inherits a set of physical laws similar to the parent, a process reminiscent of evolution of biological characteristics of life on earth.

We can go even further and think about the wild implications for multiple universes—such as those presented in my "Neoreality" series—and what they say about our power in relation to God's. Stanford University physics professor Andrei Linde (who contributed a chapter to this volume) has speculated that it might be possible to create a new baby universe in a laboratory by violently compressing matter at high temperatures—in fact, one milligram of matter may initiate an eternal self-reproducing universe. What would be the economic or spiritual gain we would get from creating a universe, considering it would be extremely difficult, if not impossible, to enter the new universe from ours? Would God care if we created such universes at will? Andre Linde and writer Rudy Rucker have discussed methods for encoding a message for the new universe's potential inhabitants by manipulating parameters of physics, such as the masses and charges of particles, although this would be a precarious experiment given the difficulty of manipulating these constants so that they code a message and permit life to evolve. In light of the possibility of multiple universes, perhaps the term "omniscient" takes on a new meaning, and the God of the Old Testament might be omniscient only in the sense that he knows all that can be known about a single Universe and not all universes.

Is God a mathematician?[1] Certainly, the World, the Universe, and Nature can be reliably understood using mathematics. Nature *is* mathematics. The arrangement of seeds in a sunflower can be understood using Fibonacci numbers. The shape assumed by a delicate spider web suspended from fixed points, or the cross-section of sails bellying in the wind, is a catenary—a simple curve defined by a simple formula. Seashells (such as the chambered nautilus, the symbol of the John Templeton Foundation), animal horns, and the cochlea of the ear are logarithmic spirals, which can be generated using a mathematical constant known as the "golden ratio." Mountains and the branching patterns of blood vessels and plants are fractals, a class of shapes that exhibit similar structures at different magnifications. Einstein's $E = mc^2$ defines the fundamental relationship between energy and matter. And a few simple constants—the gravitational constant, Planck's constant, and the speed of light— control the destiny of the Universe. I do not know whether God is a mathematician, but mathematics is the loom upon which God weaves the fabric of the Universe.

I think that our brains are wired with a desire for religion and belief in an omniscient God. If so, the reasons for our interest, and the rituals we use, are buried deep in the essence of our nature. Religion is at the edge of the known and the unknown, poised on the fractal boundaries of history, philosophy, psychology, biology, and many other scientific disciplines. Because of this, religion and religious paradoxes are an important topic for contemplation and study. Even with the great scientific strides we will make in this century, we will nevertheless continue to swim in a sea of mystery. Humans need to make sense of the world and will surely continue to use both logic and religion for that task. What patterns and connections will we see in the twenty-first century? Who and what will be our God?

And what about the Bible itself? Why do I use so much biblical imagery in the "Neoreality" book series? For one thing, the Bible is as an alternate-reality device. It gives its readers a glimpse of other ways of thinking and of other worlds. It is also the most mysterious book ever written. We don't know the ratio of myth to history. We don't know all the authors. We are not always sure of the intended message. We only know that that the Bible reflects and changes humankind's deepest feelings. The Bible, an ancient book, paradoxically describes the ultimate Neoreality—and is the hammer that shatters the ice of our unconscious. Dan Platt, of the IBM Watson Research Center, once told me, "The Bible is at minimum an interesting model of human understanding—of how we reach across cultures to understand each other and learn about what we hold as sacred. I have the notion that that kind of interface is the most visible place to look for God."

Perhaps Dr. Platt is right. Austrian biologist Paul Kammerer once compared events in our world to the tops of waves in an ocean. We notice the tops of the isolated waves, but beneath the surface there may be some kind of synchronistic mechanism that connects them. Whatever you believe about such far-out speculation, be humble. Our brains, which evolved to make us run from lions on the African savanna, may not be constructed to penetrate the infinite veil of reality. We may need science, computers, brain augmentation, and even literature and poetry to help us tear away the veils. For those of you who read the "Neoreality" series, look for the hidden mechanism, feel the connections, pierce the cosmic shroud, and sail on the shoreless sea of love.

ℒ♥

CLIFFORD A. PICKOVER received his Ph.D. from Yale University's Department of Molecular Biophysics and Biochemistry and is the author of more than thirty highly acclaimed books, translated into ten languages, on such topics as computers and creativity, religion, art, mathematics, black holes, human behavior and intelligence, time travel, alien life, and science fiction. Dr. Pickover is a prolific inventor with dozens of patents, associate editor for several journals, author of colorful puzzle calendars, and puzzle contributor to magazines geared to children and adults. His recent books include *The Paradox of God and the Science of Omniscience, The Loom of God, Surfing through Hyperspace, Time: A Traveler's Guide, Dreaming the Future, Keys to Infinity, Wonders of Numbers, The Mathematics of Oz*, and four science-fiction novels in his "Neoreality" series: *Liquid Earth, The Lobotomy Club, Sushi Never Sleeps*, and *Egg Drop Soup* and he has a forthcoming book *Sex, Drugs, Einstein, and Elves: Sushi, Psychedelics, Parallel Universes, and the Quest for Transcendence* (2005). Dr. Pickover's Web site, www.pickover.com, has now received more than a million visits and worldwide attention in the press.

NOTE

1 Also see Mario Livio's chapter by this title in this volume.

Belief in a Superior Being 43

A Game-Theoretic Analysis

Steven J. Brams

Theology addresses the relationship that human beings have with a superior being—God—in most monotheistic religions. Before exploring this relationship, however, it is appropriate to ask the prior existential question: Is belief in a superior being justified, and under what circumstances?

Knowing the answer to this question may provide spiritual guidance to the genuinely perplexed. True, a scientific investigation will not provide a definitive answer, but game-theoretic analysis of the kind I describe does, in my view, offer new insights into the foundations of belief in a superior being.

In this essay, I begin by constructing a simple game, the "Revelation Game," that reflects issues raised in several Hebrew Bible stories and also speaks to two questions that concern many people today:

1. Is belief in a superior being rational?
2. If a superior being exists, should he reveal himself?

To be sure, modeling the complex relationship that a person (P) might have with a superior being (SB), such as God, drastically simplifies a deep and profound religious experience for many people.[1] My aim, however, is not to describe this experience but to abstract from it in order to analyze strategic choices that P and SB might face.

Is it reasonable to view SB as a game player who, like P, makes rational choices? Or is SB too ethereal or metaphysical an entity to put in these terms? Consider the view expressed by the theologian Martin Buber (1958, 135) about his approach to understanding God:

> The description of God as a Person is indispensable for everyone who like myself means by "God" not a principle . . . not an idea . . . but who rather means by "God," as I do, him who—whatever else he may be—enters into a direct relation with us.

It is not a great leap of faith to model a "direct relation" as a game, although as Raymond Cohen (1991, 24) points out, "the concept of a personal, unmediated relationship between human being and deity is quite incomprehensible" in the non-Western world.

The Revelation Game

The game I use to explore the rationality of belief in an SB, the Revelation Game, supposes specific primary and secondary goals of P and SB. To preview the subsequent analysis, I will show that

+ play of this game leads to a *Pareto-nonoptimal equilibrium outcome*—a stable outcome that is worse for both players than some other outcome; but
+ both P and SB can induce Pareto-optimal outcomes if one or the other possesses "moving power."

In the Revelation Game, I assume that SB has two strategies: reveal himself (R), which establishes his existence, and don't reveal himself $\bar{R}$, which does not establish his existence. Similarly, P has two strategies: believe in SB's existence (B), and don't believe in SB's existence $\bar{B}$ (see matrix game in the figure).

FIGURE 1. OUTCOME AND PAYOFF MATRIX OF REVELATION GAME

	P	
	Believe in SB's existence (B)	Don't believe in SB's existence ($\bar{B}$)
Reveal himself (R) (establish his existence)	P faithful with evidence: belief in existence confirmed $(3,4)^P$ ◄—	P unfaithful despite evidence: nonbelief in existence unconfirmed $(1,1)$
SB	↓	↑
Don't reveal himself ($\bar{R}$) (don't establish his existence)	P faithful without evidence: belief in existence unconfirmed $(4,2)^{SB}$ —→	P unfaithful without evidence: nonbelief in existence confirmed $\underline{(2,3)}$ ◄— Dominant

Key: (x,y) = (payoff to SB, payoff to P)
4 = best; 3 = next best; 2 = next worst; I = worst
Nash equilibrium underscored
Arrows indicate direction of cycling
SB = moving power outcome SB can induce
P = moving power outcome P can induce

I begin by specifying (i) primary and (ii) secondary goals of each player:

SB: (i) Wants P to believe in his existence; (ii) prefers not to reveal himself.
P: (i) Wants belief (or nonbelief) in SB's existence confirmed by evidence (or lack thereof); (ii) prefers to believe in SB's existence.

The primary and secondary goals of each player, taken together, completely specify the players' orderings of outcomes from best (4) to worst (1). The primary goal distinguishes between the two best (4 and 3) and the two worst (2 and 1) outcomes of a player, whereas the secondary goal distinguishes between 4 and 3, on the one hand, and 2 and 1 on the other.

Thus, for SB, (i) establishes that he prefers outcomes in the first column of the payoff matrix (4 and 3), associated with P's strategy of B to outcomes in the second column of the matrix (2 and 1), associated with P's strategy of B̄. Between the two outcomes in each column, (ii) establishes that SB prefers not to reveal himself (hence, 4 and 2 are associated with B over revealing himself (3 and 1 are associated with R).

For P, (i) says that she prefers to have her belief or nonbelief confirmed by evidence (so the main-diagonal outcomes are 4 and 3) to being unconfirmed (so the off-diagonal outcomes are 2 and 1). Between the pairs of main-diagonal and off-diagonal outcomes, (ii) says that P prefers to believe (so 4 and 2 are associated with B) rather than not to believe (so 3 and 1 are associated with B̄).

I assume that P is somebody who takes the Bible (or other monotheistic religious works) seriously. Although these works may describe experiences that are outside P's ken or beyond the secular world, I suppose that P has yet to make up her mind about the existence of an "ultimate reality" embodied in some SB.

While P entertains the possibility of SB's existence, and in fact would prefer confirmatory to nonconfirmatory evidence in the Revelation Game (according to her secondary goal), *evidence is P's major concern* (according to her primary goal). Moreover, P realizes that whether or not SB provides evidence will depend on what SB's rational choice in the Revelation Game is.

To highlight the quandary that the Revelation Game poses for both players, observe that SB has a *dominant strategy* of R̄: this strategy is better for SB whether P selects B [because SB prefers (4,2) to (3,4)] or B̄ [because SB prefers (2,3) to (1,1)], so SB would presumably choose it. Given SB's choice of R̄, P, who does not have a dominant strategy but prefers (2,3) to (4,2) in the second row of the Revelation Game, will choose B̄ as a best response.

These strategies lead to the selection of (2,3), which is the unique *Nash-equilibrium outcome* in the Revelation Game: Either player that departs from this outcome will do immediately worse, which makes this outcome stable, or in equilibrium. But, paradoxically, it is an outcome Pareto-inferior—worse for both players—to (3,4).

Even though (3,4) is better for both players than (2,3), (3,4) is not a Nash equilibrium because SB has an incentive, once at (3,4), to depart to (4,2). But neither is (4,2) an equilibrium, because once there, P would prefer to move to (2,3).

According to the theory of moves (Brams 1994), the Revelation Game is "cyclic." This means that when the players cycle in the direction of the arrows shown in the figure (counterclockwise), the player moving from one outcome to another never moves from the best outcome of 4. For example, if play starts at the upper-right outcome of (1,1), then

> from (1,1), P departs from her worst to her best outcome of (3,4);

> from (3,4), SB departs from his next-best to his best outcome of (4,2);
> from (4,2), P departs from her next-worst to her next-best outcome of (2,3);
> from (2,3), SB departs from his next-worst to his worst outcome of (1,1).

Observe that all these moves immediately benefit the mover, except SB's move from (2,3) to (1,1), which creates an "impediment." But because the latter move is not from SB's best outcome of (4,2), the Revelation Game is still cyclic.

In a sense, a thoughtful agnostic plays the Revelation Game all her life, never certain about SB's strategy choice, or even that SB exists. In choosing $\overline{B}$, I interpret P to be saying that she does not believe either in SB's existence or nonexistence *yet*—in other words, she wants to keep her options open.

Should P become a believer or a nonbeliever, then she no longer would be torn by the self-doubt reflected in her choices in the Revelation Game. The evidence, so to speak, would be in. But I assume that P is neither an avowed theist nor an avowed atheist but, rather a person with a scientific bent who desires confirmation of either belief or nonbelief. Preferring the former to the latter as a secondary goal, P is clearly not an inveterate skeptic.

What SB might desire, on the other hand, is harder to discern. Certainly the God of the Hebrew Bible very much sought—especially from his chosen people, the Israelites—untrammeled faith and demonstrations of it. Although he never revealed himself in any physical form, except possibly to Moses before he died, God continually demonstrated his powers in other ways, especially by punishing those he considered transgressors.

Moving Power

A player has "moving power" by outlasting the other player in a cyclic game. By "outlast" I mean that one (stronger) player can force the other (weaker) player to stop the move-countermove process at an outcome where the weaker player has the next move.

More precisely, P1 has *moving power* in a 2 x 2 game—that is, one in which each of two players has two strategies—if it can induce P2 eventually to stop, in the process of cycling, at one of the two outcomes at which P2 has the next move. The state at which P2 stops, I assume, is that which P2 prefers.

In the Revelation Game, moving power is *effective*—the outcome that each player can induce with moving power is better for it than the outcome that the other player can induce with this power. To further understand this, assume that SB possesses moving power. Because cycling is counterclockwise, SB can induce P to stop at either (4,2) or (1,1), where P has the next move. Obviously, P would prefer (4,2), which is indicated as the moving-power outcome that SB can induce by the superscript SB in the Revelation Game; it gives SB his best outcome, 4, and P her next-worst outcome, 2.

On the other hand, if P possesses moving power, she can induce SB to stop at either (3,4) or (2,3), where SB has the next move. Obviously, SB would prefer (3,4), which is indicated as the moving-power outcome that P can induce by the superscript

P in the Revelation Game; it gives P her best outcome, 4, and SB his next-best outcome, 3.

Notice that the player with moving power can ensure a better outcome (4) than the player without it (either 2 or 3). Hence, it is better for a player to possess moving power in the Revelation Game than for the other player to possess it, which makes this power effective.

If SB has moving power, he can induce P to believe without evidence, which satisfies both of SB's goals. By contrast, P satisfies only her secondary goal of believing, but not her primary goal of having evidence to support this belief.

Endowing SB with moving power raises a feasibility question: Whenever P moves from belief to nonbelief, SB should switch from revelation to nonrevelation. But once SB has established his existence by revealing himself, can it be denied?

I suggest that this is possible, but only if one views the Revelation Game as a game played out over a long time. To illustrate this point, consider the situation recounted in Exodus. After God "called Moses to the top of the mountain" (Exodus 19:20) to give him the Ten Commandments, there was "thunder and lightning, and a dense cloud . . . and a very loud blast of the horn" (Exodus 19:16). This display provided incontrovertible evidence of God's existence to the Israelites; but for readers of the Bible today, it is perhaps not so compelling.

Yet even the Israelites became wary and restive after Moses's absence on Mount Sinai for forty days and nights. With the complicity of Aaron, Moses's brother, they revolted and built themselves a golden calf. God's earlier displays of might and prowess had lost their immediacy and, therefore, their force.

Moving to the present, the basis of belief would seem even more fragile. Many people seek a more immediate revelatory experience than reading the Bible, and some find it. For those who do not, God remains hidden or beyond belief unless they can apprehend him in other ways.

This is where the problem of revelation arises. Without a personal revelatory experience, or the reinforcement of one's belief in God that may come from reading the Bible or going to religious services, belief in God's existence may be difficult to sustain with unswerving commitment.

Revelation, also, may be a matter of degree. If God appears with sound and fury, as he did at Mount Sinai, he may likewise disappear like the morning fog as memories of him slowly fade. Thereby seeds of doubt are planted. But a renewal of faith may also occur if a person experiences some sort of spiritual awakening.

A wavering between belief and nonbelief created by SB's moving between revelation and nonrevelation shows that P's belief in SB *may have a rational basis for being unstable*. Sometimes the evidence manifests itself, sometimes not, in the Revelation Game. What is significant in this game is that SB's exercise of moving power is consistent with SB's sporadic appearance and disappearance—and with P's responding to revelation by belief, to nonrevelation by nonbelief.

Relying on faith alone, when reason dictates that it may be insufficient to sustain belief, produces an obvious tension in P. Over a lifetime, P may move back and forth between belief and nonbelief as seeming evidence appears and disappears. For example, the indescribable tragedy of the Holocaust destroyed the faith of many believers, especially Jews, in a benevolent God, and for some it will never be restored. But for others it has been rejuvenated. Furthermore, many former nonbelievers have conversion experiences—sometimes induced by mystical episodes—and, as a result, pledge their lives to Christ or God. For still others, there is a more gradual drift either toward or away from religion and belief in an SB, with belief positively correlated with age. More broadly, periods of religious revival and decline extend over generations and even centuries, which may reflect a collective consciousness about the presence or absence of an SB—or maybe both. As Leszek Kolakowski (1982, 140) remarked, "The world manifests God and conceals Him at the same time."

It is, of course, impossible to say whether an SB, behind the scenes, is ingeniously plotting his moves in response to the moves, in one direction or another, of individuals or society. But this is not the first Age of Reason, although it has had different names in the past (for example, Age of Enlightenment), in which people seek out a rational explanation. Nor will it be the last, probably again alternating with periods of religious reawakening as occurred during the Crusades and arguably today, that will also come and go. This ebb and flow is inherent in the instability of moves in the Revelation Game, even if an SB, possessed of moving power, has his way on occasion and is able temporarily to implement (4,2).

Perhaps the principal difficulty for SB in making this outcome stick is that people's memories erode after a prolonged period of nonrevelation. Consequently, the foundations that support belief may crumble. Nonbelief sets up the need for some new revelatory experiences, sometimes embodied in a latter-day messiah, followed by a rise and then another collapse of faith.

If P is assumed to be the player who possesses moving power, then she can induce (3,4), which SB would prefer to (2,3), given that SB must stop at one or the other of these two outcomes when he has the next move. If the idea of "forcing" SB to reveal himself—and, on this basis, for P to believe—sounds absurd, it is useful to recall that God exerted himself mightily on occasion to demonstrate his awesome powers to new generations. By the same token, God left the stage at times in order to test a new generation's faith, usually being forced to return in order to foster belief again.

The effects of moving power, whether possessed by SB or P, seem best interpreted in the Revelation Game as occurring over extended periods of time. Memories fade, inducing SB to move from nonrevelation to revelation when the next generation does not understand or appreciate SB's earlier presence. Even when SB moves in the opposite direction, going from revelation to nonrevelation, his actions may not appear inconsistent if P, effectively, is a different player. Thereby the earlier concern I raised about infeasible moves is dissipated in an extended game in which the identity of P changes.

Because the Revelation Game is a cyclic game with two Pareto-optimal outcomes, one of which each player can induce, it seems best viewed as a game of movement, in which either player possessing moving power can induce the best outcome. Yet this is usually only a temporary "passing through," because the other player can respond by switching strategies. Finally, the player without moving power will be forced to desist. But if that player is P, and she believes for a time without evidence, then eventually she will be replaced by another P that feels less piety in the face of an ineffable SB.

Feasibility may militate against too-quick switches on the part of the players, but fundamentally the Revelation Game is a game for the ages. Its fluidity—rather than the stability of its Pareto-inferior (2,3) Nash equilibrium—seems its most striking feature. I have highlighted its unsettling nature as players alternate between belief and nonbelief when they cycle through the two Pareto-optimal moving-power outcomes, (3,4) and (4,2).

Conclusions

Emphatically, my interpretation of players' goals in the Revelation Game is not sacrosanct. If readers disagree with those I have postulated, they can propose alternative goals and explore their ramifications using game theory and the theory of moves.

Normally, one would suppose that SB possesses moving power and so would be able to implement its most-preferred outcome, getting P to believe without revelation. However, when the torch passes to a new generation of people that does not remember the punishment their forbears suffered for their lack of faith, it is just as reasonable to think that the game will cycle to nonbelief. SB will then be forced to reveal himself, possibly through the retribution he inflicts on nonbelievers, and belief in SB once again will be restored.

The alternation between belief and nonbelief, and revelation and nonrevelation, illustrates the instability inherent in the Revelation Game, despite its unique Nash equilibrium. In thinking afresh about the central theological questions posed at the outset, we understand better why answers to them may well be strategic.

To be sure, many theologians reject the proposition that a person's relationship with a superior being is strategic. Fideists, in particular, argue that we believe in God by making a leap of faith, not because it is strategically optimal to do so (or not do so), much less that God is acting strategically.

But this criticism rejects not only the framework developed here but also the abundant evidence of strategic calculations in the Hebrew Bible, which I have presented in detail elsewhere (Brams, 2003). If the Revelation Game does not provide a definitive answer to the spiritually perplexed, it shows why this perplexity occurs and what information may lead people toward or away from belief in a superior being.

✒

STEVEN J. BRAMS, PH.D., is Professor of Politics at New York University. He is the author or co-author of fourteen books that involve applications of game theory and social choice theory to voting and elections, international relations, bargaining and fairness, and the Bible and theology. His most recent books are *Biblical Games: Game Theory and the Hebrew Bible*, rev. ed. (MIT Press, 2003) and (co-authored with Alan D. Taylor) *Fair Division: From Cake-Cutting to Dispute Resolution* (Cambridge University Press, 1996) and *The Win-Win Solution: Guaranteeing Fair Shares to Everybody* (W. W. Norton, 1999). He is a Fellow of the American Association for the Advancement of Science, the current president of Public Choice Society, a Guggenheim Fellow, a past president of the Peace Science Society (International), and in 1998–99 was a Visiting Scholar at the Russell Sage Foundation.

NOTE

1 I refer to "SB" as a "he" and to "P" as a "she" for convenience only; these gender designations could as well be reversed. This essay is adapted from Brams (2003, ch. 10), wherein a more extended analysis, replete with several examples from the Bible, is given. The theory of moves—on which part of this analysis is based—is given in Brams (1994); the theology underlying the analysis is developed more fully in Brams (1983), wherein the work of early theorists, such as Blaise Pascal, is discussed.

REFERENCES

Brams, Steven J. (1983). *Superior Beings: If They Exist, How Would We Know. Game-Theoretic Implications of Omniscience, Omnipotence, Immortality, and Incomprehensibility.* New York: Springer-Verlag.

———. (1994). *Theory of Moves.* New York: Cambridge University Press.

———. (2003). *Biblical Games: Game Theory and the Hebrew Bible,* rev. ed. Cambridge, MA: MIT Press.

Buber, Martin. (1958). *I and Thou,* trans. Ronald Gregor Smith, 2nd ed. New York: Scribner's.

Cohen, Raymond. (1991). *Negotiating across Cultures.* Washington, DC: U.S. Institute of Peace.

Kolakowski, Leszek. (1982). *Religion.* New York: Oxford University Press.

ON THE PROBLEM
OF THE EXISTENCE OF EVIL 44

REFLECTIONS OF A JEWISH PHYSICIST-PHILOSOPHER

Max Jammer

T HE INVITATION to write an essay in honor of Sir John Templeton on the occasion of his ninetieth birthday gives me the opportunity to express my highest esteem for Sir John. It also gives me the chance to express my admiration for the John Templeton Foundation for promoting the values of religion, morality, and excellence in academic and scientific pursuits to discover more about spiritual information among all people on earth, irrespective of color, gender, nationality, or creed.

For my contribution, I have chosen to focus my reflections as a Jewish physicist-philosopher on the problem of the existence of evil as a method of furthering spiritual information.

Let me begin with a statement concerning the philosophy of physics that Albert Einstein made a few years before World War II. Still in Berlin and talking to Esther Salman, a student of physics, Einstein made the following confession about the ultimate motive behind his scientific work: "I want to know how God created this world. I am not interested in this or that phenomenon, in the spectrum of this or that element. I want to know His thoughts; the rest are details."[1] A few years after the war, when talking in Princeton with his assistant Ernst Gabor Straus, Einstein repeated this statement with an additional explanatory comment: "What I am really interested in is knowing whether God could have created the world in a different way; in other words, whether the requirement of logical simplicity admits a margin of freedom."[2]

More recently, the cosmologist Stephen Hawking, in his best-seller *A Brief History of Time,* raised a similar question: "Why does the universe go to all the bother of existing?"[3] Or, in other words, "Why is there something rather than nothing?" And almost repeating Einstein, he added: "If we find the answer to that, it would be the ultimate triumph of human reason—for then we should know the mind of God."

The problem I wish to discuss in this essay is similar to, but more restrictive than, the questions raised by Einstein and Hawking. Paraphrasing Einstein, what I am interested in is knowing whether God could have created a world different from ours, namely a world in which evil does not exist.

That evil exists in the world in which we live and did exist throughout its history can hardly be doubted. In recent years, the Holocaust in Europe, the events of September 11, 2001, in the United States, and the recent earthquakes and floods in Asia and elsewhere testify to the existence of evil. Almost paradoxically, even the history of the world's religions, both in the present and in the past, abounds with evil. In our times, for example, Protestants fight against Catholics in Northern Ireland, Hindus against Muslims in the Far East, Muslims against Jews in the Near East. Because of the evils caused by religious wars, especially in the Middle Ages, Baron Paul Henri Thiry d'Holbach, a leading atheistic materialist of the eighteenth century and author of anticlerical treatises that shocked even Voltaire, found it appropriate not only to deny the existence of God, but even to declare, in his *Système de la Nature,* that the idea of God is an invention that inflicted the greatest tragedy on humankind.[4]

Interestingly, evil and good are often inseparably connected. Thus, for example, the discovery of the famous mass-energy relation $E = mc^2$ in the theory of relativity initiated our present era of nuclear energy with its beneficial consequences in industry and medicine, but it also led to the destruction of Hiroshima and Nagasaki and to the catastrophe caused by the breakdown of the Russian nuclear reactor at Chernobyl.

Numerous other examples can be cited to illustrate that what is evil and harmful in one respect is good and beneficial in another. It may therefore be claimed, physically speaking, that evil and good are relative and complementary, that they balance or compensate for each other, and that their sum total, like that of negative and positive electric charges in the universe, is null.

Ideas of such competition, with mutual annihilation of the principles of evil and good, can be found in the early medieval doctrine of Manichaeism, which originated from ancient Persian Zoroastrianism. As it evolved from Zoroastrian (Zarathustran) theology, Ormazd, the lord of goodness and of light, wages war incessantly against Ahriman, the lord of evil and of darkness. In contrast, traditional Judaism and Christianity believe in the ultimate victory of good over evil in the ideal of a world free of suffering. For Jews and Christians who believe in a benevolent and almighty God, the undeniable existence of evil in the past and present, as we have seen, therefore poses a serious problem.

The philosophical discipline dealing with this problem is usually called *theodicy,* a term coined in 1710 by Gottfried Wilhelm Leibniz from the Greek *theos* (God) and *dike* (justice), because it vindicates the justice of God in permitting evil to exist.[5] But of course the problem of theodicy is much older than its name. It was raised by the author of the biblical book of Job, who described him as a "perfectly honest and upright man, one that feareth God and escheweth evil."[6] But in spite of undeserved pain and misery, even amidst the worst of his afflictions, Job never cried out against God or swerved from his confidence in the Almighty. A modern analog can be found in Elie Wiesel's record of his experience in the death-camp Auschwitz,[7] where thousands of Jews, hungry and sick and in spite of the horror they experienced, met on the eve of Rosh Hashanah, the Jewish New Year, and prayed: "Blessed be the Name of the Eternal!"

The task of theodicy consists of resolving the apparent logical contradiction or, as logicians call it, the "trilemma" between the following three basic, generally accepted (at least by theists) propositions:

1. God is omnipotent.
2. God is perfectly good and benevolent.
3. Evil exists in the world.

It is, of course, a purely logical problem, for it cannot be resolved by observation or experimentation. It is easy to verify that the truth of any two of these three propositions contradicts the truth of the remaining one. In fact, if (1) and (2) are supposed to be true, then (3) must be wrong, because an omnipotent and perfectly benevolent God could not allow any evil to exist. Similarly, if (1) and (3) are valid, then obviously God cannot be perfectly good and benevolent, and (2) would be falsified. Finally, if (2) and (3) are true, then God cannot be omnipotent in contradiction to (1), because an absolutely benevolent and compassionate God could approve of a world with evil only if he were not omnipotent. Strictly speaking, propositions (1) and (2), combined only with the assumption that a world exists, lead to severe logical difficulties. For whatever the world created by God may be like, his omnipotence must always have enabled Him to create a world better than the one he did create—which involves infinite regress.

Of course, for philosophers and scientists who, like Aristotle in antiquity or Feuerbach in modern times, deny a divine creation of the world, such problems do not exist. On the other hand, for philosophers, who like J. L. Mackie doubt the possibility of solving the trilemma, this impossibility "suggests that there is no valid solution of the problem which does not modify at least one of the essential propositions in a way which would seriously affect the essential core of the theistic position."[8]

Concerning the first horn (1) of the trilemma, it should be noted that in biblical and early rabbinic literature the notion of God's *power* was fully acknowledged, but divine *omnipotence* was not.

When the first patriarch, Abraham, exclaimed, "shall not the Judge of all the earth deal justly?";[9] when the prophet Jeremiah cried to God, "why doth the way of the wicked prosper?";[10] when Habakkuk criticized God, "Thou that art of eyes too pure to behold evil";[11] or when Job complained that "the judge of all the earth shall not do justice,"[12] the issue was not God's omnipotence, but His acquiescence in the existence of injustice and evil. Jewish theology admitted the notion of divine omnipotence only in the Middle Ages, probably under the influence of Islamic philosophy. But even thereafter it was said that "whenever people obey God's command, they strengthen the power of the Almighty," a statement that, strictly speaking, is self-contradictory. Similarly, but without involving a logical contradiction, the Kabala declares: "The Holy One said: when Israel is worthy below My power prevails in the universe, but when Israel is found to be unworthy My power weakens above."[13] Such ideas of course contradict the validity of proposition (1) and therefore resolve the trilemma.

Another proposal to resolve the problem is based on a denial of proposition (3). The foremost proponent of such a solution is undoubtedly Maimonides (Moses Ben Maimon), the great Jewish philosopher of the thirteenth century whose philosophical and theological thoughts strongly influenced not only Jewish but also Christian and Islamic philosophers. According to Maimonides, evil is not something that has its own existence; it is only a privation of good, a state in which good is absent. "Evils are only evils in relation to something; and everything that is an evil with reference to one particular existent, that evil is the privation of this thing or one of the states suitable for it. For this reason the following proposition may be enunciated in an absolute manner: All evils are privations."[14]

In the sequel, Maimonides applies his identification of evil as a *privatio beni* to human society and tries to prove that all "great evils that come about the human individuals who inflict them upon one another because of purpose, desires, opinions, and beliefs, are all of them likewise consequent upon privation. For all of them derive from ignorance, that is from a privation of knowledge."[15] True, there are evils that, even physically speaking, originate from the deprivation of good, such as the danger that faces future generations of humankind to have enough life-sustaining clean air to breathe.

But it seems difficult to believe that Maimonides, had he been alive to witness the horrors of the Holocaust, the destructions of World War II, the threats of nuclear weaponry, and the terrorist acts all over the present-day world, would retain his identification of evil merely as a privation of good and not ascribe to it a self-existent, independent, and actual, though harmful, reality.

Still, I believe and hope that if, and only if, Maimonides' conception of evil as a privation of good will be interpreted and enacted as an admonition to replace evil by good, will there be a future for humankind on earth.

✥

Max Jammer, Ph.D., is Professor Emeritus of Physics and former President of Bar-Ilan University. He also was co-founder of the Institute for Philosophy of Science at Tel-Aviv University and has served as President of the Association for the Advancement of Science in Israel. Among Dr. Jammer's awards are the prestigious "Israel Prize," the "Monograph Prize of the American Academy of Sciences," and most recently (in 2000) the "Prize for Outstanding Books in Theology and the Natural Sciences" awarded by the Center for Theology and the Natural Sciences in Berkeley, California. His most recent works include *Concepts of Mass in Classical and Modern Physics* (1997), *Einstein and Religion* (1999), and *Concepts of Mass in Contemporary Physics and Philosophy* (2000).

Notes

1 E. Salman, "A Talk with Einstein," *The Listener* 54, 570–71 (1955).

2 C. Seelig, *Helle Zeit–Dunkle Zeit* (Zurich: Europa Verlag, 1956), 72.

3 Stephen W. Hawking, *A Brief History of Time* (London: Bantam Press, 1989).

4 Baron Paul Henri Thiry d'Holbach, *Système de la Nature* (Amsterdam, 1770).

5 G.W. Leibniz, *Essais de Théodicée sur la Bonté de Dieu* (Amsterdam, 1710).

6 Job 1:8.

7 E. Wiesel, *Night* (London: MacGibbon and Kosle, 1961), chap. 5.

8 J. L. Mackie, "Evil and Omnipotence," *Monist* 64, 200–212 (1956).

9 Genesis 18:25.

10 Jeremiah 12:1.

11 Habakkuk 1:13.

12 Midrash Pesikta 25:1.

13 Zohar (Vilna edition) 2:65.

14 Maimonides, *The Guide of the Perplexed* (Chicago: Chicago University Press, 1963), 459–60.

15 Ibid., 462.

Do Quantum Experiments Challenge Kant's Criticism of the Proofs for the Existence of God? 45

Antoine Suarez

THE DEVELOPMENT of a consistent religious attitude is based on the primary conviction that God exists and that rational discussion about God is possible. Without this basis, theology cannot be considered as a part of knowledge. Religious faith would necessarily be reduced to superstition. Criticisms of attempted rational philosophical "proofs" of the existence of God are based on the assumption that one visible event is always caused by some earlier visible event, or material cause. The consequence of this assumption ("visible from visible") has been a general expectation that deeper knowledge of the universe would render God superfluous. A "God of the (scientific) gaps" ceases to be necessary once science fills those gaps.

Sir John Templeton has dared to challenge this view, investing his fortune in exploring whether it is possible to increase spiritual information through the constructive engagement of science and religion. Does science destroy the logic for the existence of God or build it? Recent quantum experiments have provided evidence that visible (or, to be more exact, observable) things do not originate exclusively from visible (observable) causes. This would seem to indicate that Sir John's intuition may be correct.

Generic Failure of the Rational Basis of Theology

It is by definition impossible to argue that God (the infinite, invisible Being) exists outside of the world we see if one postulates in advance that visible things originate exclusively from visible things. The postulate "visible from visible" has contributed to a view called "scientism." Scientism affirms a "nothing but" vision such that the question of the existence of God is generically beyond the domain of rational knowledge. It expects that scientific progress, by filling explanatory gaps, eventually will render the notion of God conceptually superfluous (Laeuffer 1997; Hewlett 2000). One main source of the present crisis of religion within scientific and technological civilization may be the expectation that eventually science will make it possible to explain all that happens in the universe—and indeed most importantly the existence of the universe itself (and its underlying rational order)—by means of temporal-causal chains. In this view, belief in God is intrinsically antiscientific. It violates methodological canons of naturalism understood to be basic to the scientific worldview.

This assumption—"visible from visible"—was a core element in the worldview of philosophers such as Laplace, Kant, and Comte. In particular, it was the heart of Kant's criticism of the philosophical proofs for the existence of God. He postulated that in the chain of causes responsible for a phenomenon, each single cause is itself observable (Kant 1956). Kantian philosophy assumes that determinism is the correct underpinning of causality considerations (Bernays 1971). According to this understanding of causality, each physical effect can be explained exclusively by causes working within spacetime or by observable elements of reality that propagate in spacetime (Kant 1968a, 1968b).

Undoubtedly, investigations of temporal deterministic causal chains through experiment have been of great benefit to the scientific, economic, and cultural development of humankind. The massive success of classical physics seems to give scientific validity to the idea that there is no reality beyond what is visible (observable). But today, science itself seems to support the idea that the world cannot exclusively be explained by observable influences. I argue that recent quantum experiments demonstrate this clearly. Modern physics does not exclude unobservable causes. In fact, it includes them at a very basic and general level within the laws of quantum mechanics. This generates a new model of reality that is open rather than closed. I must emphasize that this view in no primary way argues for the existence of God. It simply argues that a popularly accepted assumption associated with a positivistic/"scientific" philosophical interpretation of the meaning of science is no longer justifiable. It cannot be used properly as an argument against a basic premise of religion: That which exists is far more than that which is causally observable.

Quantum Experiments and Events without Temporal Causes

Two events cannot be correlated if each occurs at random: "Correlations cry out for explanation" (Bell 1987). Either the two events are directly dependent on each other (such as dialing a telephone number and hearing a telephone ring), or they are predetermined by a common cause that occurred in the past (such as two television sets showing the same image).

Quantum mechanics predicts correlated outcomes in spacelike separated regions in experiments using two-particle entangled states. If all events in nature must be explicable by the effects of signals propagating in spacetime with a velocity (v) that cannot be faster than the speed of light ($v \leq c$), then one has to exclude any direct dependence between spacelike separated events. By this logic, quantum correlations therefore must imply the existence of particles carrying hidden variables that determine the particle's behavior. Apparently, this was what Einstein thought. As a consequence, he concluded that the quantum-mechanical description of physical reality could not be considered complete (Einstein et al. 1935). However, Bell showed that if one admits only relativistic local causality (causal links with $v \leq c$), the correlations occurring in two-particle experiments should fulfill clear locality conditions ("Bell's inequalities"). Experiments, however, have clearly shown that locality is violated by quantum mechanics (Bell's theorem) (Bell 1964 1987). In fact, many Bell-type experiments conducted over the past two decades clearly demonstrate violation of local causality. Violation of Bell's inequalities ensures that these correlations are not predetermined by local hidden variables. "Entangled" separated particles behave as if there were a faster-than-light connection between them.

If the correlations are not predetermined, then there must be a direct dependence between two spacelike separated events. But what kind of causality does such dependence involve? Physicists are used to the time-ordered causality of relativity, in which a "temporally" earlier event influences a "temporally" later event. As long as one believes (like Einstein) that there are no spacelike (faster-than-light) influences, the fundamental temporal notion could not be other than proper time along a timelike trajectory. Yet, because Bell experiments did reveal a world consisting of nonlocal links, the "reasonable" position in the very spirit of relativity is to assume time-ordered causality and to describe the nonlocal links using lines of simultaneity to distinguish between "before" and "after."

Indeed, such a description is possible in conventional Bell experiments, in which all apparatuses are standing still in a laboratory frame. In this frame, one of the measurements always takes place before the other, and the particle arriving later can be considered to take account of the outcome of the one arriving before. In fact, this is the way Bell tried to explain things. And, in so doing, he came to discover quantum nonlocality. Orderings with one measurement before and the other after in time are referred to as *before-after* or *after-before* timings. In experiments with all measuring devices at rest, it is possible to explain quantum correlations through time-ordered causality.

But what about experiments with moving apparatuses in which different space-time reference frames are involved? In this case, it is possible to define "conflicting" time orderings. If each measuring device in its own reference frame is the first to select the output of photons, we have *before-before* timing. If each measuring device in its own reference frame selects the photon output after the other, we have *after-after* timing. Is it also possible to give a time-ordered causal explanation for relativistic experiments using such apparatuses in motion? I was convinced it was and developed an alternative nonlocal description termed "multisimultaneity."

This description of nonlocality integrates a time-ordered description of the nonlocal correlations in experiments with both *before-before* and *after-after* timings (Suarez 1997, 2000). Consider, for instance, experiments in which the measuring devices are in motion in such a way that each of them, in its own reference frame, is the first to select the output of photons (*before-before* timing). Then each particle's choice will become independent of the other's. According to multisimultaneity, the nonlocal correlations should disappear (Suarez and Scarani 1997). In contrast, the standard predictions of quantum mechanics require that the particles stay nonlocal and correlated independently of any timing, even in a *before-before* situation.

This means that *before-before* experiments are capable of acting as a standard of time-ordered nonlocality (much as Bell's experiments act as a standard of locality). If timing-independent quantum mechanics prevails, nonlocality cannot properly be imbedded in a relativistic chronology. However, if quantum mechanics fails, there is a time ordering behind nonlocal correlations.

In February 2000, experiments using detectors in motion showed results that were in agreement with quantum mechanics (Zbinden 2001). Taking advantage of the fact that traveling acoustic waves can act as moving beam splitters, *before-before* experiments using beam splitters in motion were made in June 2001 (Stefanov et al.

2002). Again, the correlations did not disappear. The predictions of quantum mechanics were vindicated. Quantum correlations have now been demonstrated to hold regardless of any relativistic frame-of-reference or time ordering.

Explaining Quantum Entanglement

Bell-type experiments both with and without moving measuring devices demonstrate that quantum correlations in some sense transcend spacetime and do not appear to be bound by the usual temporal-causal ordering of before and after. Quantum correlations reveal logical ordering. Experiment shows that this dependence, or logical order, is beyond any real-time ordering.

Suppose a physicist could act nonlocally and would like to bring about Bell correlations. She or he would first choose one event, randomly assigning a value x (x being either + or -) to it, and subsequently would assign a value y (y being either + or -) depending on x to the second event. Suppose these operations occurred without the flow of time? As quantum mechanics suggests, and the experimental results confirm, this is the way nature is.

Signals follow timelike trajectories and can consistently be described in terms of "before" and "after" by means of real clocks. Einstein's universe contains only such local causal links. Bell showed that Einstein's reality is not the whole of physical reality. The conventional Bell experiments discovered apparent connections acting faster than light. Again, the results of recent experiments strongly suggest that this nonlocal quantum realm is curiously transcendent with respect to a causal ordering of time. Perhaps this is a small but possibly not insignificant window into aspects of deeper domains of existence traditionally described as "spiritual."

Moreover, it is important to stress that controlling nonlocal links is something beyond our power. Quantum mechanics tells us, and experiment confirms, that we cannot use nonlocal links for faster-than-light communication. The notion of time makes sense only in the seen universe we can control. Where our power reaches, there is time; and what is beyond our power is also beyond time. Therefore, time is the domain or horizon of our finite power.

Spiritual Information: "Visible from Invisible"

Sir John Templeton has dared to challenge the conventional opinion that science and religion are destined to preside over totally separate domains. The ultimate reality that science progressively frames, in Sir John's view, is an expression, in part, of the infinite well of the Divine Reality that both fills and transcends nature. Therefore, the immense and accelerating stream of new information about nature generated by the ongoing adventure of the sciences should be a factor in realizing progress in spiritual information. Just as science has revolutionized our understanding of the natural world, so perhaps it also can expand our understanding of the Divine in real, albeit small and humble, ways (Harper 2005).

Will Sir John Templeton once again succeed by "investing as a contrarian"? Remarkably, he has invested his fortune in pursuits directly opposed to Kantian criticism and scientism's view of a world without God. His vision that it might be possible to gain "progress in spiritual information" through scientific research clearly is based on the assumption that science itself will acknowledge that "reality is deeper than the visible or the tangible" (Templeton 1995 2001:36).

Bernard d'Espagnat has described the quantum domain as "veiled reality" (d'Espagnat 2003). I have argued that recent experiments have emphasized the seriousness of this inference. Quantum correlations reveal a domain of existence that cannot be described with the notions of space and time. The experiments we have discussed rule out the belief—in particular, Kant's causality postulate—that physical causality necessarily relies on observable signals only. Moreover, they demonstrate that we never will achieve complete power in the universe: Nature always will do things that humans are not able to do.

In conclusion, science itself vindicates the idea that the world is deeper than the visible (observable). In a small but ontologically deep way, this finding may support Sir John Templeton's prediction that "scientific revelations may be a goldmine for revitalizing religion in the twenty-first century" (Templeton 2003).

✐✐

ANTOINE SUAREZ, PH.D., is Founding Director of the Center for Quantum Philosophy at the Zurich-based Institute for Interdisciplinary Studies. He received his doctorate in natural science at the Swiss Federal Institute of Technology in 1975, where he became interested in the philosophical significance of quantum mechanics and in genetic epistemology. For more than a decade, he conducted research on cognitive growth, which led to the development of improved methods for teaching mathematics and science to children. He directed this Swiss think tank from 1985 to 1993, and, with major support from the Leman Foundation, did studies incorporating the insights of philosophers, theologians, and ethicists. Dr. Suarez was the first (with Valerio Scarani in 1997) to propose experiments using moving measuring devices to investigate the tension between quantum mechanics and relativity, especially whether there is a real-time ordering behind nonlocal influences, and collaborated with Nicolas Gisin's group in conducting these experiments. In addition to articles in scientific journals, chapters in volumes of collected works, and an early study on the relation of thought to action in adolescents, Dr. Suarez is editor (with Alfred Driessen) of *Mathematical Undecidability, Quantum Nonlocality and the Question of the Existence of God* (Kluwer, 1997).

REFERENCES

Bell, J. S. 1964, *Physics*, 1, 195–200.

———. 1987, *Speakable and Unspeakable in Quantum Mechanics*, Cambridge: Cambridge University Press, 152.

Bernays, P. 1971, "Causality, Determinism and Probability," in W. Yourgrau and A. van der Merwe, *Perspectives in Quantum Theory*, Cambridge, Massachusetts: MIT Press, 261.

d'Espagnat, B. 2003, *Veiled Reality: An Analysis of Present-Day Quantum Mechanical Concepts*, Frontiers in Physics Series, Boulder, CO: Westview Press.

Einstein, A., Podolsky, B., and Rosen, N. 1935, Can Quantum-Mechanical Description of Physical Reality Be Considered Complete? *Phys. Rev.* 47, 777–80.

Harper, C. L., Jr. 2005, *Spiritual Information: 100 Perspectives on Science and Religion*, Philadelphia: Templeton Foundation Press.

Hewlett, M. 2000, "God or Science: Do I Have to Choose?" in *God for the 21st Century*, Stannard R., Ed., Philadelphia: Templeton Foundation Press.

Kant, I. 1956, *Kritik der reinen Vernunft*, Hamburg: Felix Meiner, 466, 580, 589, 600 (B 483, B 637, B 649, B 664).

———. 1968a, *Träume eines Geistersehers, erläutert durch Träume der Metaphysik*, Text edition of the *Königliche Akademie der Wissenschaften*, Band II, Berlin: Walter de Greyter, 370–72.

———. 1968b, *Vor dem ersten Grunde des Unterschiedes der Gegenden im Raume*, Text edition of the *Königliche Akademie der Wissenschaften*, Band II, Berlin: Walter de Greyter, 383.

Laeuffer, J. 1997, "Scientism and Scientific Knowledge of Things and God," in *Mathematical Undecidability, Quantum Nonlocality and the Question of the Existence of God*, A. Driessen and A. Suarez, Eds., Dordrecht, The Netherlands: Kluwer.

Stefanov A., Zbinden H., Gisin N., and Suarez A. 2002, Quantum Correlations with Spacelike Separated Beamsplitters in Motion: Experimental Test of Multisimultaneity, *Phys. Rev. Lett.* 88:120404.

———. 2003, Quantum entanglement with acousto-optic modulators: Two-photon beats and Bell experiments with moving beam splitters, *Phys. Rev. A* 67:042115.

Suarez A. 1997, Relativistic Nonlocality in an Experiment with 2 Non-before Impacts, *Phys. Lett.* A, 236, 383.

———. 2000, Quantum Mechanics versus Multisimultaneity in Experiments with Acousto-optic Choice-devices, *Phys. Lett.* A, 269, 293.

Suarez A. and Driessen A. 1997, *Mathematical Undecidability, Quantum Nonlocality and the Question of the Existence of God*, Dordrecht, The Netherlands: Kluwer.

Suarez A. and Scarani V. 1997, Does Entanglement Depend on the Timing of the Impacts at the Beam-splitters? *Phys. Lett.* A, 232, 9.

Templeton, J. M. 2001, Bridging Two Worlds; Interview with Sir John by M. Marty and L. O'Connell, *Second Opinion*, July 1993. Edited and updated version in Report 2001 of the John Templeton Foundation, 36.

———. 2003, Biography of Sir John Templeton: http://www.templeton.org/sirjohnbio.asp.

———. 1995, *The Humble Approach*, Philadelphia: Templeton Foundation Press, 13–24.

Zbinden H., Brendel J., Gisin N., and Tittel W. 2001, Experimental Test of Non-local Quantum Correlation in Relativistic Configurations, *Phys. Lett.* A, 63:022111.

F. Russell Stannard

"PROVE TO ME that God exists, and I'll believe."
We have all heard *that.*

It sounds fair enough. After all, we live in a scientific age—one in which we are encouraged to be skeptical. Science is based on experiment, fact, and logic. So why should we not be equally rigorous in requiring indisputable proof before subscribing to religious beliefs?

Before demanding the clinching piece of evidence that conclusively demonstrates the existence of God, let us first ask whether the findings of science really are as clear-cut and incontrovertible as is generally supposed.

Take, for example, the Big Bang theory. Most scientists today accept that the universe began with the Big Bang. Why? The experimental evidence, of course. Observations with telescopes reveal that the galaxies of stars are receding from one another; the farther away a galaxy is, the faster it recedes into the distance. That is exactly the kind of motion one would expect if all the material of the universe had originally been squashed together and had suddenly exploded. The faster-moving material would by now have receded farthest—which is what we see. Case proved.

Except that it is not. At the time when the recession of the galaxies was the sole evidence available, many noted cosmologists were unimpressed. They preferred an alternative idea: the Steady State theory. According to this rival hypothesis, as the galaxies moved out of a given region of space, they were replaced by spontaneously created new material. This in time gathered together to form new stars and galaxies. These new galaxies later, in their turn, joined the recessional movement and left the region. Thus the process was endlessly repeated. In this way, the overall picture remained essentially unchanged. There was no Big Bang origin of the universe—indeed, no origin at all. The universe had always existed, and would continue to exist for all time; hence the term "Steady State."

Then along came a second piece of evidence. The Big Bang would have been very hot and violent; there would have been a blinding flash of light—as one gets when a nuclear bomb goes off. The cooled-down remnants of that radiation ought still to be around in the universe (there being no other place for it to be). Sure enough, with the right types of instruments, it was detected. The so-called "cosmic microwave background radiation" has all the characteristics expected of that fireball remnant.

So does that mean we ought to be regarding this radiation as proof of the Big Bang—rather than the recession of the galaxies? The problem with that notion is that space has many other sources of radiation. It is conceivable that some of those sources might, by chance, combine to emit radiation that mimics the kind we are looking for. If this radiation were the sole evidence for the Big Bang, it would be no more decisive than the recession of the galaxies. And yet, the case for the Big Bang has undoubtedly been strengthened by the addition of this second piece of evidence.

Then along came a third indication. From a theoretical study of the temperature and density conditions of the early stages of the Big Bang, it proved possible to calculate the chemical composition of the emerging gases. The estimates yielded 77 percent hydrogen, 23 percent helium (by mass), and just traces of the heavier elements. Experimental observation of today's interstellar gas medium shows that it has a composition in very good agreement with these figures. Not that the comparison is that straightforward. The result needs to be treated with caution. Nuclear processes occurring in stars since the Big Bang have altered the original chemical composition of the elements. To measure the original composition—that emerging from the Big Bang—one must select out regions of space where subsequent contamination by the newly synthesized materials is thought to be less significant. Such a selection procedure is open to some doubt. It is open to the charge that one might to some extent be defining an "uncontaminated region" as one that happens to give you the result you are seeking. For this reason, the measurement is not exactly clinching evidence for the Big Bang. Nevertheless, it is still an encouraging result. It fits in well with the overall picture we are building up.

Indeed, there are now altogether *five* independent indications of the Big Bang. None of them, considered in isolation, constitutes proof of the hypothesis; they can each be explained away on other grounds. What is compelling is that the Big Bang theory is capable, at a stroke, of elegantly explaining them all. The theory is economical, and it is this feature that has progressively won over the cosmologists to accept the Big Bang hypothesis. Not that there was any defining moment when the Big Bang received official recognition. Rather, it was the case that the scientific community gradually ceased arguing about it and took it for granted.

The same kinds of considerations surface in the field of biology. Why do the vast majority of biologists today accept that all-important hypothesis: evolution by natural selection?

Again, no single incontrovertible piece of evidence compels absolute, universal acceptance. The fossil record showing how we humans and today's other animals evolved over time from less developed species is incomplete. It has many gaps. Although these are progressively being filled, the evidence is likely always to remain fragmentary; some animals, by their very nature, did not leave fossils. Others have had their remains destroyed as shifting crustal movements carried them down into the earth's interior.

Fortunately, we do not have to rely on the fossil record. We have other indications. For instance, we see evolution going on around us today. Admittedly, this is on a modest scale—species developing immunity to pesticides is a well-known example. The extent of the changes we have witnessed during our own lifetime is not sufficient to convince everyone that something as complex as the eye could have emerged in such a manner. But given the enormous span of time that has been available to the evolutionary process in the past . . . maybe.

Then there are anatomical comparisons between species, and furthermore, the evidence of DNA similarities.

As with the Big Bang, and with other truly powerful scientific theories, the case for evolution by natural selection rests on a broad raft of evidence. It is not so much a matter of proof based on some single, decisive experiment. Rather it is the case that one becomes progressively *persuaded* of the truth of the hypothesis. This acceptance is grounded in the accumulation of diverse types of evidence, all of which point to a common explanation.

Which brings us to the question of religion. If, contrary to popular thinking, science is not based on knock-down proof, it is surely unreasonable to claim, in the name of science, that there has to be knock-down proof of the existence of God before taking religion seriously. I would contend that much the same kind of thinking should be applied to the big religious questions as to the big scientific ones. The case for God, like that for the Big Bang and for evolution, has to be built up progressively. There are several indications. Here are some together with a religious interpretation:

- ✦ Take for a start the simple fact that we and the universe exist. Why? To what do we owe our existence? The religious response is to say that God is the Creator—the ground of all being. That might indeed be how we define the term "God." It is the name we give to whatever is responsible for all existence.
- ✦ The world operates in accordance with intelligible laws of Nature. The source of their intelligibility? The Mind of God.
- ✦ If the laws of Nature had come into existence spontaneously of their own accord—or if the force of gravity, the magnitude of the electric charge on the electron, the violence of the Big Bang, and a host of other variables had taken on their values purely by chance—the odds of them all conspiring together to produce conditions capable of supporting life would be less than those of repeatedly winning first prize in the lottery. The universe appears to be fine-tuned for the production of life. Why? Could it not have been deliberately designed that way? Could not the designer have been God?
- ✦ Religious experience—the numinous presence sensed in devotional prayer—is perceived by the devoted as a direct encounter with God.
- ✦ Many are the claims that prayers have been answered. God's response to our requests?
- ✦ Reports of miracles. If God is the source of the laws of Nature, might he not set them aside on occasion, given sufficient reason so to do?
- ✦ Often, people who have committed their lives to God find on looking back over those lives that they appear to have followed a plan whereby even the seemingly bad times were later turned to one's ultimate good. This is seen as the work of the guiding hand of God.
- ✦ We are all possessed of an inner moral law—the sense of right and wrong. Where does this come from if it is not God speaking through the voice of conscience?
- ✦ As evolved animals, we are subject to genetically influenced behavior fashioned in the sometimes harsh conditions of the past. Such inherited traits

tend to center on selfishness, aggression, and a disregard for the needs of others not closely related to oneself. How is it then, as is often claimed, that true happiness and fulfillment come in such paradoxical ways as turning the other cheek, giving rather than receiving, sacrificing for others rather than indulging oneself? Could not the source of this special kind of wisdom be found in God's "foolishness"?

✦ Finally, for the Christian believer, there is above all else the remarkable life, and even more remarkable resurrection, of Jesus. This has a ready explanation in his truly being the Son of God.

Such then is a whole variety of life's features and experience and the religious interpretations of them. I am not denying that it is possible to conjure up alternative hypotheses for explaining away each of these indications—picking them off one at a time in some ad hoc manner. None of them in isolation constitutes the kind of proof or argument that would compel the atheist to abandon the path of skepticism. But what appears to me and to many as so compelling is that the whole of this wide range of indications can all be explained by a single hypothesis: God. The world and life just make better sense in the light of the God hypothesis than without it.

Which is not so different from the kind of thinking that has always guided scientific work.

Ⓛ

F. Russell Stannard, O.B.E., Ph.D., is Emeritus Professor of Physics at the United Kingdom's largest academic institution, the Open University, where for twenty-one years he headed the Physics Department. A high-energy nuclear physicist, Dr. Stannard has carried out research at CERN in Geneva and at other laboratories in the United States and Europe. He is a Licensed Lay Minister in the Episcopal Church and has been made an Officer of the Order of the British Empire by the Queen. Dr. Stannard has received the Bragg Medal from the Institute of Physics and the UK Project Trust Award of the John Templeton Foundation. He has been made a Fellow of University College London and currently serves as President of the UK's Science and Religion Forum. A prolific writer for adults and children, his books are translated into nineteen languages. His most recent book for adults on the relationships between science and religion, *The God Experiment*, based on his Gifford Lectures, is published in the United States by HiddenSpring. Dr. Stannard is a frequent broadcaster on British radio and TV and a regular contributor to the most popular BBC radio program, *Thought for the Day*. He devised *The Question Is. . .* video series, which is currently used by 40 percent of all UK secondary schools as the basis for stimulating discussions about science and religion. Dr. Stannard's trilogy of *Uncle Albert* books, introduces children ten years and older to relativity and quantum theory.

FROM INFORMATION TO SPIRIT 47

A SKETCH FOR A NEW ANTHROPOLOGY

Gianfranco Basti

I N THE HISTORY of Western philosophy, three main solutions to the mind-body problem have been put forward: *dualistic, monistic,* and *dual.*

In the *dualistic solution,* defended in ancient Greek philosophy by Plato, in the modern age by René Descartes, and in the last century by John C. Eccles and K. R. Popper (Eccles & Popper 1977), the soul is conceived as being separated from the body and interacting with it (i.e., mind is moving particles). *Theologically,* this solution makes it impossible to justify the individual survival of humans (i.e., because the same soul, independent of matter, can be reincarnated in different bodies). *Anthropologically,* we lose the psychophysical unity of the human person, at the same time giving a negative valuation to the body. *Physically,* the relationship between mind and body as an interaction implies a violation of the principle of energy conservation—or, in reference to quantum mechanical unpredictability (Eccles), also to the very strange notion of "backward causation" (Popper).

The *monistic solution* was defended in Greek philosophy by the Stoics and the Epicureans, who reproposed, against Plato's dualism, Democritus's mechanistic interpretation of the functioning of the mind. In the modern age, it was defended by all philosophers who, after Hume's pioneering attempt, tried to extend the mechanistic method of Newtonian physics to the study of the psyche in order to repropose Democritus's mechanism from within modern Galilean science. In the last century, the monistic solution was also defended by the so-called "functionalist" approach to the mind-body problem, which identifies mind functioning with Turing machine extensional calculations on the supposition that a purely entropic information measurement (the Shannon measure, the famous "bit") is sufficient for dealing with biological and cognitive information exchanges in animals and humans. But this is not so, as we see in the next section. In any case, for the monistic approach, mind functions are interpreted as products of the human brain just as any other physiological function is the product of its respective organ (Feigl 1958).

The *dual solution* was defended in Greek philosophy by Aristotle, in medieval philosophy by Scholastic philosophers such as Thomas Aquinas, and today by phenomenologists. According to this solution, given that what exists is only the human, individual living body (i.e., the human person in its psychophysical unity), this bodily unity consists of two irreducible components: the formal one (mind) and the material one (particles). This ontological solution may correspond to the modern informational approach to living and cognitive systems, insofar as they are considered dynamically self-organizing, dissipative structures (Prigogine 1981; Thom 1990;

see Figure 1) for which neither entropic information measurements (such as Shannon's bit) nor Turing-like paradigms (for characterizing their information processing) are sufficient. This approach offers an original solution consisting of both mind localization relative to the body (mind containing its body) and of the possible survival of the human mind after death (mind survival depending on information exchanges).

From the Monistic to the Dual Solution

The identity theory of mind and body, in scientific use, depends on the extensionality axiom in modern predicate logic. In mathematical logic, indeed the so-called "extensionality principle" holds. If two classes (i.e., the extensions of two different predicates, such as "to be water" and "to be H2O") are equivalent, they are the same class, and we can reciprocally substitute them for each other. Their meaning is, in fact, extensionally the same. The identity of wholes implies the sameness of parts and of their relations.[1]

The identity theory between mental and physical states in this strictly logical interpretation was confuted by the logical analysis of the neopositivistic philosophy of intentional (with a "t") statements ("I-talk"). In this framework, identity would imply the reducibility of the statements by which a human subject expresses his or her own conscious psychical states (i.e., a belief statement of the intentional, content-related form "I . . . see, want . . . something") to the external observer statements ("O-talk") by which the neurophysiologist describes the corresponding brain modifications. On the contrary, it is evident that the two statements are reciprocally irreducible because the former is necessarily expressed in an intensional (with an "s") predicate logic—i.e., a logic in which the extensionality axiom does not hold—and the second one is necessarily expressed in an extensional predicate logic (Searle 1983; Zalta 1988; Basti 2001; Basti and Perrone 2002).

To understand roughly what this sort of nonreducibility means, it is sufficient to remember that many instances of everyday language become immediately meaningless as soon as we apply the extensionality axiom to a logical analysis of them. For instance, let us consider the religious statement: "Almighty God, bless this water. . . ." If we substitute the predicate "to be water" with the equivalent predicate "to be H2O," the religious statement becomes immediately meaningless: "Almighty God, bless this H2O. . . ."

This logical nonreducibility of the I-talk of conscious experience to the O-talk of scientific observation is unavoidable. Indeed, the only way a human can know what happens in the conscious experience of another person is through the I-talk by which the conscious subject describes it. The mind-body problem is thus primarily (Quine 1989, 133), but not exclusively, a logical problem of the nonreducibility of many meaningful uses of ordinary language (effectively, all the uses strictly related to human conscious states) to the only extensional languages of modern mathematical sciences.

The Dual Solution of the Mind-Body Problem

What makes the dual solution so appealing today is the following evidence. Given that we completely change the matter by which our bodies are constituted at the cellular level at least twice every year, it is evident that the stability and persistence of ourselves in time (our identity) is strictly related to some sort of "sameness" of the global information pattern organizing corporeal matter (Penrose 1996). Of course, the previous discussion helped us to understand that the core of the problem consists, in the proper sense, of our having to attribute the information pattern to this notion of identity.

To deal seriously with the connection between the dual theory of the mind-body problem and the informational approach to it, we have thus to deepen our understanding of the logic underlying Aristotle's ontology—i.e., its formal ontology.[2] "Formal ontology" is a particular evolution of modern analytic philosophy that tries to solve the problem of a logical scientific theory of meaning by recovering to modern symbolic logic the core of classical (Greek and Scholastic) formal logic. The most basic senses of the most fundamental (transcendental or preceding any further categorical distinction) predicate "to be" (Cocchiarella 2001) are twofold:

1. The *being of essence*, saying *what* a given being *is* (Scholastic philosophy named it *quidditas*, literally "whatness"); e.g., saying "The runner *is* what is running" without saying anything about the effective *existence* of the object;
2. The *being of existence*, saying *whether* a given individual instance of an essence *exists*; e.g., saying "*There is* a runner on the street."

By making such a distinction, ancient formal logic is able to do what modern mathematical logic—because of the extensionality axiom—is no longer able to do: to have identity (sameness of the essence, of the "whatness," of what existence is) without equivalence (sameness of the parts-whole partition and relationship, given that both parts and whole are what exists). Applied to the mind-body problem, this means that we can agree with Quine when he affirms that, given the logical nonreducibility of I-talk to O-talk, nevertheless what effectively exists (i.e., the only object that both language frameworks are referring to) is only brain processes (Quine 1989, 133). Given that living brains are not only energetically but also informationally "open" physical systems, their nature (being of essence) is characterized not only by material, but also by formal, exchanges. They are systems able to generate information not only in the sense of a growth in entropy (loss of a precedent order), but also in the sense of a structure modification (creation of a new, unpredictable order).

Dual ontology implies a criticism of mechanistic ontology. It is evident that in most dynamic processes (primarily, but not only, those concerning living bodies), it is not true that we can predict unequivocally their final stable states by considering only their "initial conditions" ("initial causes" in ontology). That is, in mechanics we cannot make such predictions by considering only the kinetic momentum (in ontology, the acting causality) and the position (in ontology, the element states) on which the former acts in order to interpret the final stable state as deducible from them, as a theorem is from its postulates in geometry. Starting from similar initial conditions, in most physical processes neither the final states nor (given similar final states) the trajectory in the phase-space of the dynamic system (in ontology, the spatiotemporal path) by which the processes reach the final states are the same. Therefore, a sufficient ontology of dynamic systems must also consider the formal component of the physical causality, i.e., the dynamic rearrangement of parts-whole relationships. In cinematic dynamic systems, it corresponds to a deep rearrangement of the phase space, such as occurs in chaotic systems.

Effectively, both in biological and neurological realms, the cyclic and logically reversible processes are synonyms of disease and biological disorder. For instance, a particular cyclic tracing appearing in an ECG means that the heart is fibrillating. Or, a particular cyclic tracing appearing in an EEG means that an epileptic fit is impending in the brain. Similarly, in the intentional behavior of animals and humans, perfectly deterministic, cyclic behavior is synonymous with "stupidity" in the cognitive realm. To change paths to reach the same end, or even to change inter-mediate objectives in order to achieve the final objective, is characteristic of living and intelligent functioning. As D. R. Hofstadter summarized in his bestseller on the informational approach to life and intelligence (Hofstadter 1977), the behavior of a wasp that always follows the same path to try to reach the light behind the window, condemning itself to bump indefinitely on the glass until it dies, is synonymous with stupidity, not intelligence.

The limit of all the modern information notions and measurements is evident. Insofar as they all are entropy measurements, not only can they not be operational versions of the Aristotelian notion of "form," but they fail completely in measuring information generation related to "a creation of order" (a rearrangement of the parts-whole relationships in the phase-space) in self-organizing systems—primarily the chaotic behaviors characterizing most neural and biological systems (Perrone 1995, 2000; see Figure 2). Therefore, it is not surprising that the classic informa-tional approach has failed in dealing with the emerging property of "pleotropism" of the genome in genetics and particularly of neurons in neuroscience—i.e., the capability both of genes in the genome and of neuron arrays in the brain of chang-ing their coding function according to different situations (phase-space rearrange-ments) in the ongoing global dynamics.

Metaphysical and Theological Relevance of the Dual Solution

According to dual ontology, what generally characterizes living bodies is their capa-bility of controlling the form of their functions for better satisfying the biological ends of their species. On the contrary, what characterizes humans as such is their rational functions. Humans, unlike other animals, are indeed able to control not only the form, but also the goals, of their biologically driven behavior. In ethologi-cal terms, humans are also able to control their instincts, which are localized in the inner part of the brain (the limbic system), and even to give themselves new goals not determined by biology to their behaviors. Also, the human faculty of logical thought depends on this control of instincts. In fact, as Konrad Lorenz pointed out,

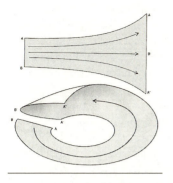

FIGURE 1. The "stretching" (top) and "folding" (down) mechanism in a stable far-from-equilibrium dynamic system. Through the recurrence of dynamic instability points (stretching) under a condition of energy dissipation (folding), two distant points on bidimensional divergent trajectories can become closer by the folding of the third dimension. By stretching, we have a growth in entropy (loss of memory about the initial conditions), but by folding we have an unpredictable creation of order. This is a sort of "invention" of a new path for reaching far-from-equilibrium stabilities. Any of the neighbors of the points of the original trajectory (not only the equilibrium points) can thus become stability points in order to originate (pseudo-)cycles. Because the folding consists of an energy dissipative condition, we can say that these systems are able "to eat" energy "for producing" order (structural information). For this reason, 1977 Nobel Prize Laureate in Chemistry Ilya Prigogine named them *dissipative structures,* rightly referring to Aristotle's "dual" ontology for philosophically characterizing these systems (Prigogine 1981). The limit of Prigogine's scientific approach to these systems is his use of the notion of entropy (more precisely, the strange notion of "micro-entropy") for trying, without success, to define the "mathematical laws" of these systems.

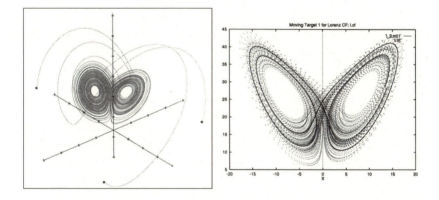

FIGURE 2. Map of the Lorentz chaotic attractor (left) and of a pseudocycle within this attractor (right). It is evident that the system's pseudocycle is composed by different trajectories depending on the resolution (i.e., for a specific precision) at which we observe it. In this sense, a chaotic attractor is said to have a "fractal" nature from the geometrical standpoint. The temporal series of a chaotic system is characterized by the ability of the system to jump in an absolutely unpredictable way from one to another of its pseudocycles in order to give the observer the false impression of "randomness." Only with suitable, very large statistics are we able to understand that only a finite volume of the phase-space is, on the contrary, effectively visited by the system. In other words, like a classic "deterministic" system (e.g., a pendulum), it has an *attractor.* Nevertheless, its behavior is absolutely unpredictable and "chaotic." The expression "deterministic chaos" for denoting such systems is derived from this apparently contradictory nature. It is amazing to note that all the informational richness (the practically infinite number of pseudocycles of whichever order, i.e., connecting whichever number of [pseudo-]stable points) the Lorentz system is able, in principle, to generate is derived mathematically by a system of only three nonlinear differential equations.

dealing with the difference between animal and human intentionality, unlike animals that know physical objects to the extent necessary for satisfying their instincts, humans desire to know objects as they *really* are; that is, their goal is to know *truth*. Of course, this type of active control has to be localized outside the human organism as such because it concerns the ultimate level of organism control: its biological goals.

This "outside" is generally identified—by Aristotle as well as by most contemporary psychologists, psychoanalysts, cognitive scientists, and philosophers (Minsky 1988, Freeman 2001, Searle 1997)—in the culture to which each human belongs. Of course, this solution is not satisfying philosophical personalism. In order to grant equality, intellectual creativity, and individual responsibility to each human person—i.e., the basis of modern Western culture—it is necessary to grant that everybody has his or her own individual, "separated" mind. This "separateness" must be intended as the effective capability given to each individual of controlling not only his or her biological instincts (for this, a "society of minds" could be sufficient, at least in principle), but also his or her cultural constraints. Otherwise, not a person, but his or her biology or culture, are the only actors, and hence the only moral and legal responsible agents of human thoughts and actions!

In this way, the so-called spiritual component of the individual human mind in dual personalistic theory is the formal relation each individual has with a Transcendent Agent (named "God" by believers). Through this formal relation, the human person is made capable of being aware of, and hence of controlling, the tangle of formal relations with the other biological and cultural agents constituting the texture of his (progressively) conscious and (largely) unconscious experience in life. Every human, as far as he or she is intelligent and free, is endowed with this relation, although only religious people are—sometimes and partially—conscious of it.

In any case, in the dual theory mind is not located somewhere inside the body (e.g., in the brain), as in all the dualistic and monistic theories. It is located in the dynamics of formal relations (i.e., in the nonentropic information exchanges) among the different parts of the body continuously rearranging themselves and between the body and its complex (physical, cultural) environment.

To sum up, it is not the body that contains the mind, but the mind that contains its body (Thomas Aquinas, *Summa Theologiae*, I, 76, 8; MacKay 1980; Basti 1991, 265–69). The goal of gathering spiritual information may be for the mind to realize this.

✐

GIANFRANCO BASTI, PH.D., an ordained priest for the Diocese of Rome and Chaplain to His Holiness the Pope John Paul II, became Rector of the historical Basilica of St. Pudenziana, Rome in 2003. He earned his doctorate in Philosophy of Science from the State University of Rome, basing his thesis on the relation between the neural network approach in neuroscience and the physical foundation of intentionality according to Aristotelian theory. Currently, Mgr. Basti is Full Professor of

Philosophy of Nature and of Science at the Pontifical Lateran University in Rome and Invited Professor of Logic at Pontifical Gregorian University. His research focuses on neural networks and the logical foundations of science. In 1995, Mgr. Basti earned the Neural Network Leadership Award from the International Neural Network Society. In 1997, he cofounded the International Research Area on Foundations of the Sciences at Pontifical Lateran University with Edward Nelson of the Department of Mathematics at Princeton University (who contributed an essay to this volume), Ennio De Giorgi, and Antonio Luigi Perrone. Mgr. Basti is a member of several editorial boards and the author of more than eighty scientific and philosophical papers and four books.

NOTES

1 Also, the locality principle in geometry and in physics is a corollary of such an axiom. The nonlocality paradoxes in quantum mechanics are thus strictly dependent on a revision of such an axiom in modern mathematics. In this sense, a dual ontology of mathematical and physical entities can offer a precious contribution also in this direction.

2 For an introduction to formal ontology, visit www.formalontology.it. For an introduction to dual formal ontology, see (Cocchiarella 1996; 2001; Basti 2002).

REFERENCES

Basti G. (1991). *Il rapporto mente-corpo nella filosofia e nella scienza*, Edizioni Studio Domenicano, Bologna.

————. (1995). *Filosofia dell'uomo*, Edizioni Studio Domenicano, Bologna.

————. (1996). Per una lettura tomista dei fondamenti della logica e della matematica. In Basti & Perrone (1996), 23–252.

————. (2001). Intentionality and Foundations of Logic: a New Approach to Neurocomputation, in *What should be computed to understand and model brain function? From Robotics, Soft Computing, Biology and Neuroscience to Cognitive Philosophy*, T. Kitamura (Ed.), World Publishing, Singapore-New York, 2001, 239–88.

————. (2002*a*). *Filosofia della natura e della scienza. Vol. I: I Fondamenti*, Lateran University Press, Rome.

————. (2002*b*) (Ed.). *Proceedings of "IRAFS'02. Foundations and the ontological quest. Prospects for the new millennium"*, Rome, Pontifical Lateran University, January 7-10, 2002. Online publication on the Web site: www.pul.it/irafs/irafs.htm.

Basti G, Perrone A. L. (2002). Neural nets and the puzzle of intentionality. In Neural Nets. WIRN Vietri-01. Proceedings of 12th Italian Workshop on Neural Nets, Vietri sul Mare, Salerno, Italy, 17–19 May 2001, Roberto Tagliaferri and Maria Marinaro (Eds.), Springer, London 2002, 313–27.

Cocchiarella N. B. (1996). Conceptual Realism as a Formal Ontology, in R. Poli and P. Sirnor (eds.), Formal Ontology, Kluwer Academic Press, Dordrecht.

————. (2001). Logic and ontology, Axiomathes 12: 117–50.

Eccles J. C. , Popper K. R. (1977). *The self and its brain*, Springer, Berlin-New York.

Feigl H. (1958). The "mental" and the "physical". In: Minnesota Studies in the Philosophy of Sciences, II, Feigl H. and Scriven Maxwell M. (Eds.), Minnesota University Press, Minneapolis, 370–497.

Freeman W. J. (2001). *How brains make up their minds*, Columbia University Press, New York.

Hofstadter D. R. (1977). *Gödel, Hescher and Bach. An eternal golden braid*, Basic Books, New York.

MacKay D. M. (1980). The interdependence of mind and brain, *Neuroscience* 5:1389–91.

Minsky M. (1988). *Society of mind*, Touchstone Books.

Penrose R. (1996). *Shadows of mind. A search for the missing science of consciousness*, Oxford University Press, Oxford.

Perrone A. L. (1995). A formal scheme to avoid undecidabilities: an application to chaotic dynamics characterization and parallel computation. In: Andersson S. I. (Ed.), *Cognitive and dynamical systems. Lecture Notes in Computer Science* 888, 9–52, Springer, Berlin.

————. (2000). A new approach to chaotic systems characterization and its implication for biology, *Aquinas*, 43: 381–409.

Popper K. R., Eccles, J. C. (1977). *The self and its brain*, Springer Verlag, Berlin.

Prigogine I. (1981). *From being to becoming: time and complexity in the physical sciences*, W. H. Freeman, New York.

Quine W. V. O. (1989). *Quiddities. An intermittently philosophical dictionary*, Harvard University Press, Cambridge.

Searle J. R. (1983). *Intentionality. An essay in the philosophy of mind*, Cambridge University Press, Cambridge.

————. (1997). *The construction of social reality*, Free Press, Chicago.

Thom R. (1990). *Semiophysics, a sketch. Aristotelian physics and catastrophe theory*, Addison-Wesley, Redwood City.

Thomas Aquinas (*Summa Theologiae*). *St. Thomas Aquinas Summa Theologica (translated by Fathers of the English Dominican Province)*, 5 volumes, Thomas More Publishing, London, 1981.

————. (*De Unitate Intellectus contra Averroistas*). *Aquinas Against the Averroists: On There Being Only One Intellect*. Transl. by R. McInerny, Purdue University Press, Indianapolis, 1993.

————. (*Quaestio Disputata de Anima*). *Questions on the Soul: St. Thomas Aquinas, O.P. (Mediaeval Philosophical Texts in Translation, No 27)*, Transl. by J. H. Robb, Marquette University Press, Milwaukee WI, 1983.

Zalta E. (1988). *Intensional logic and the metaphysics of intentionality*, MIT Press, Cambridge.

PART FIVE

Perspectives on Evolution and Purpose

Possible Precursors of Religious Behavior in Animals

Jane Goodall

D O ANIMALS have souls? Do chimpanzees show any sign of religious behavior? These questions are seldom topics of discussion among scientists studying animal behaviour. Indeed, for the most part they will deny the existence of "soul" and deem the subject of religion inappropriate for scientific debate. It was not my intention to become a scientist when, in 1960, I went to Africa to learn about wild chimpanzees. Thus, I went about my study in a different and unorthodox manner. Probably this is why, despite the fact that I acquired a doctoral degree in the end, I am not at all reluctant to explore the intangible concept of "soul" and the possible precursors of religious behaviour in chimpanzees and other animals.

I arrived in Gombe with no scientific training. I watched the chimpanzees with a mind unbiased by reductionist scientific theory. I was not afraid to let intuition play a part in my gradually evolving ability to interpret the complexities of chimpanzee society and behavior. Knowledge gained from the Gombe study, now in its forty-third year, and information from other studies of the great apes, has helped us to redefine our own place in the animal kingdom. These studies demonstrate, on scientific as well as intuitive grounds, that we humans are not, as was once believed, the only living beings with personalities, minds capable of rational thought, and emotions similar to—and sometimes perhaps identical to—those that we call happiness, sadness, fear, anger, and so on. The great apes have brains more like ours than that of any other living creature. They demonstrate the ability to make as well as use tools. They are capable of intellectual performances that we once thought unique to ourselves, such as recognition of self, abstraction and generalization, cross-modal transfer of information, and theory of mind. They have a sense of humor. Chimpanzees form affectionate and supportive bonds between individuals, especially family members, which can last throughout a life of up to sixty years. They show compassion and true altruism. Sadly, all too much like us, they also have a dark side and are capable of extreme brutality. They are aggressively territorial and may attack "strangers" from neighboring social groups, leaving them to die of their wounds. They may even wage a kind of primitive warfare.

Clearly, the line dividing humans from the rest of the animal kingdom, once thought so sharp, has become extremely blurred. Perhaps, after all, it is not so ridiculous to speculate as to whether chimpanzees might show precursors of religious behavior. In fact, it seems quite possible that they do.

In one of the remote, steep-sided valleys in Gombe, there is a glorious, hidden waterfall. As one approaches, moving quietly through the forest, the roar of the falls gradually gets louder. Suddenly, through the vegetation, one glimpses the living, moving water as it cascades down from the stream bed some eighty feet above. Over time, the water has worn a perpendicular channel in the rock. Vines hang down on either side, and ferns move ceaselessly in the wind created by the falling water. For me, it is a magical, spiritual place. And sometimes it seems that the chimpanzees too are strangely moved. As they approach their hair may bristle, a sign of excitement. And then they may start to display, charging with a slow, rhythmic motion, often in an upright position, splashing in the shallow water at the foot of the falls. They pick up and throw great rocks. They leap to seize the hanging vines and swing out over the stream in the spray-drenched wind. For ten minutes or more, they may per- form this magnificent "dance." Usually it is the males who display thus, but I have seen females react in the same way.

It is not only a waterfall that stimulates such performances. Quite often, the chim- panzees display thus when they cross a stream, charging rhythmically up and down, stamping through the shallow, racing water, picking up and throwing rock after rock. And even more often, we see the "rain dance" that takes place at the sudden onset of a heavy downpour. Strangely, the most incredible "dance" of this sort ever observed at Gombe occurred right at the start of my study. I had a grandstand view of no fewer than seven adult males displaying on the other side of a narrow, steep- sided valley opposite me. Each of them charged down, dragging huge branches, leaping up to sway vegetation, while the thunder growled and crashed, rain teemed down from purple black clouds, and a group of females and youngsters watched from trees on the skyline. Every performer charged down at least twice, some more often, pausing briefly in trees at the bottom of the slope before plodding up, then starting their magnificent dance all over again.

What triggers these marvellous performances? Is it possible that the chimpanzees have a sense of awe, a feeling generated by the elements—rain, thunder, falling water? Or even, as I witnessed once, the sudden onset of a fierce wind that raced up the valley from the lake? Certainly, all these things generate intense feelings of awe and wonder and excitement in me.

After a waterfall dance, a chimpanzee may sit on a rock in the stream gazing up at the sheet of falling water, water that seems alive, always rushing past yet never going, always there yet ever different. Was it perhaps similar feelings of awe, or won- der, that gave rise to the first animistic religions, the worship of the elements and the mysteries of nature over which there was no control? Only when our prehistoric ancestors developed a spoken language would it have been possible to discuss such internal feelings—discussions that could create a shared belief system.

My years spent in the forests of Gombe crystallized my own spiritual awareness. Day after day I was alone, sharing the wilderness with the animals and the trees, the gurgling streams, the mountains, the awesome storms, and the star-studded night skies. I became one with a world in which, apart from the change from day to night, from wet to dry season, time was not important. I became ever more attuned to the great Spiritual Power that I felt around me, the Power that is worshipped as God, Allah, Tao, Brahma, the Great Spirit, the Creator, and so on. I came to believe that all living things possess a spark of that Spiritual Power. We humans, with our uniquely sophisticated minds and our spoken language, call this spark, in ourselves, a "soul." If this is so—and it cannot be proved either way—then it follows that chimpanzees and other animal beings have souls also. Certainly, we cannot prove that they do not.

As most scientists do not admit the possibility of a soul in humans, a study of the animal soul is hardly a subject for scientific investigation! But religious behavior in humans is a fact. A study that compared religious rituals across a variety of human cultures, searching for elements shared by most (or all) such rituals, would be scientifically respectable. And, in this context, we could ask whether chimpanzees (or other animals with complex brains and behavior) might show precursors to human ritualistic behaviors.

Careful documentation of the contexts and behaviors involved in the elemental displays of chimpanzees would be extremely interesting. Our videography records of waterfall, stream-bed, and rain displays would provide valuable information because they allow detailed analysis of movement patterns and social interactions. And these filmed sequences are typically accompanied by field notes that describe behaviors leading up to and following the displays.

Such investigations might throw new light on the emotions that trigger the displays and whether they sometimes resemble those that we describe as awe and wonder.

It seems most unlikely that animals other than ourselves are aware of their souls or are concerned about the existence of God. They are concerned with going about their lives, finding food and shelter, propagating their species. But most of them are probably far more in tune with their spiritual selves than we are, more aware of the great Spiritual Power in which we all "live and move and have our being."

It is important that science dares to ask questions outside the prison of the biased mind, dares to explore new areas of animal being. Such explorations might not only increase our understanding of and respect for other-than-human mental states, but also illuminate aspects of our own spiritual development.

☙

JANE GOODALL, PH.D., C.B.E., began her landmark study of chimpanzees in Tanzania in June 1960 under the mentorship of anthropologist and paleontologist Dr. Louis Leakey. Her work at the Gombe Stream Chimpanzee Reserve would become the foundation of future primatological research and redefine the relationship between humans and animals. Dr. Goodall's observations of chimpanzees making and using tools would force science to rethink the definition "man the toolmaker." Defying convention, she gave the chimpanzees names instead of numbers and observed that they had distinct personalities, minds, and emotions. Today, scientists and field staff continue her work at the Gombe Stream Research Center, which Dr. Goodall established in 1964. In 1977, she established the Jane Goodall Institute in Silver Spring, Maryland, which focuses on research, education, conservation, and development. Her publications include two overviews of her work at Gombe—*In the Shadow of Man* and *Through a Window*—and the spiritual autobiography, *Reason for Hope*. *The Chimpanzees of Gombe: Patterns of Behavior* is recognized as the definitive work on chimpanzees. Today, Dr. Goodall travels three hundred days per year or more, speaking about conservation issues and the preservation of all species. In April 2002, she was appointed to serve as a United Nations "Messenger of Peace."

Jean Clottes

ARCHAEOLOGY and physical anthropology have long shown that the Upper Palaeolithic people, our Cro-Magnon ancestors, were beings exactly like us. Our direct lineage started in Africa at least 150,000 years ago. About 90,000 years ago, Homo sapiens were living in the Middle East. Some went east and eventually populated Australia between 60,000 and 50,000 years ago. Others went west and arrived in what is now Western Europe between 45,000 and 40,000 years ago. They and/or their descendants were the creators of what we call "cave art." Many of those paintings and engravings were made deep inside caves where nobody lived; thus, the inescapable consequence was that ever since they were discovered most specialists have agreed that the art must have been created for religious purposes and that some of the beliefs of those ancient peoples could be approached through them. Comparisons were made with the rock art of modern hunter-gatherers in other parts of the world. The universality of human religiosity, as well the indisputable fact that we all belong to the same species with the same abilities, needs, and cravings, made those comparisons possible.

That European Palaeolithic religions could be shamanistic[1] was an idea propounded half a century ago (Eliade 1951). The hypothesis was further developed in later years (in particular by Lewis-Williams and Dowson 1988). Shamanic cultures still exist today and existed in the nineteenth century and before, and we have testimonies about them. By studying these "contemporary" or "recent" cultures and their ways of thinking about the world, we can make inferences about long-dead cultures such as those in the Upper Palaeolithic.

Before being applied to what was discovered in the painted caves, three distinct series of observations were used to support the idea that these early religions were shamanistic—in the *neuropsychological model of altered states of consciousness*, the *shamanic societies in the world*, and the *rock art of known shamanic cultures*, such as the San in southern Africa and numerous Native American groups in the western United States. In the 1990s, I worked with Lewis-Williams to determine whether the theory could be applied to European cave art (Clottes and Lewis-Williams 1996, 1997, 2001). Recently, Lewis-Williams developed and expanded his model and his ideas in a groundbreaking book (Lewis-Williams 2002).

The Neuropsychological Model of Altered States of Consciousness

Altered states of consciousness are an intrinsic part of human psychological makeup. In addition to sleeping dreams and daydreams, our perceptions may be modified by tiredness, lack of sleep, violent emotions, and genuine hallucinations. The latter can be caused not only by drugs or pathological states, but by fasting, isolation, darkness, suffering, throbbing sounds, flickering lights, intense concentration, sensory deprivation, and other things. In our ultra-rationalist society, such events are looked down on, and often they are not talked about. In different types of cultures, however, vision seekers become prophets, spiritual leaders, saints, or shamans.

Lewis-Williams and Dowson (1988), referring to the numerous studies published on hallucinations, mention a model with three stages. This model is "ideal," meaning that some people will go from one stage to the next, others will directly reach Stage 3, and still others will never go beyond Stages 1 or 2.

Stage 1 is characterized by entoptic phenomena (i.e., within the eye) and the perception of geometric forms. In Stage 2, one's mind instinctively tries to rationalize those forms and to give them meaning. They start to become organized. One frequent feeling is going through a tunnel or being sucked into a vortex. Emerging from it, one reaches Stage 3, with spectacular hallucinations in which all senses participate and sometimes intermix in strange confusion. One may levitate, meet extraordinary creatures, talk with animals, or be transformed into an animal. Entoptic phenomena often persist in the background (Lemaire 1993).

According to at least one ethnologist (Reichel-Dolmatoff 1978), the Columbian Tukano Indians' visions closely followed the model described. Variants of the model have been found in numerous shamanic societies in various parts of the world. For example, the shaman's soul flight often takes him to the other world through a tunnel or under the water. This is reminiscent of some mystical experiences or of near-death experiences, in which one sees a great white light at the end of a tunnel and can float or be acutely sensitive to the presence of people dear to him or her. All those reactions are then those of the human nervous system under the stimulus of exceptional situations.

Shamanic Societies in the World

Among the multiple components of shamanism (Hultkranz 1987; Vitebsky 1995), a few features are basic and directly relate to our purpose. First, people living in a shamanic society believe in a complex cosmos in which several worlds coexist. They may be parallel or tiered. They interact with one another, and in ours most events are caused by the influence of the other world(s).

Second, some people are believed to be able to get deliberately in touch with the other world(s) for practical aims: to cure the sick; to maintain a good relationship with the "gods," or supernatural beings, or to restore destroyed harmony with them; to make the rain come in arid countries; to ensure good hunting or to address a "Master of Animals" to make hunting possible; or to predict the future or bewitch an enemy.

Third, contact can be made when spirit-helpers come to the shaman or vision-seeker, often in animal form. Shamans identify with their spirit-helpers. They may also send their soul to the other world to meet the spirits there and obtain their help. This is done through trance.

Finally, shamanism is widespread among hunter-gatherers all over the world. Until recent days, it was present over an enormous area—the Arctic, from Siberia to Canada, the Scandinavian countries, all of North America, and the northern part of South America. Taking into account that religions last for very long periods, even among changing societies, as well as the very ancient peopling of the Americas in Upper Palaeolithic times, a strong shamanistic framework for Palaeolithic religions is a logical hypothesis.

The Rock Art of Known Shamanic Cultures

Many similarities, caused by a commonality of beliefs, can be noticed in the location of the art, as well as in its themes and in its motivations.

Painted or engraved places are often believed to be an entrance to the world of the spirits, a door that can work both ways. They also help to facilitate having visions. A person who seeks access to the supernatural world will go to a solitary place to await a vision, often at the foot of a wall loaded with the power of images. Access to the other world may be through a tunnel watched over by guardian animals (bears and/or rattlesnakes in California). In those sacred places, spirit-animals come out through the cracks in a rock and go back the same way. This is one of the reasons that so many snakes and other animals are so often represented as appearing to emerge from walls.

The images were full of power, which explains why they crowd some panels: Each new one drew on the power there and added its own. The number of subjects represented is always restricted. In the Californian Coso Range, bighorns were prevalent as rain-animals, a vital role in that desert region.

The images include geometrics similar to entoptic forms and composite creatures (with both human and animal characteristics), which ethnological testimonies describe either as spirits met during the trance or as the transformation of the shaman him- or herself.

In various cases, rock art was used to "capture" visions. In Nevada and California, if this was not done seekers would "lose" their vision and die. Sometimes, the shaman's soul journey was represented by means of metaphors ("death" or "killing" for trance).

In this relatively recent shamanic rock art, one can see an obvious relationship to Palaeolithic art.

Palaeolithic Art

Palaeolithic art evinces an overall unity in various ways. First, deep caves were used consistently for more than twenty thousand years. To make paintings or engravings in the complete dark is exceptional in the history of humankind. For such a tradition to have gone on for so long, firmly rooted beliefs must have been passed on from generation to generation.

All over Europe and at all times, priority has been given to representation of animals and geometric signs, with many indeterminate lines. Humans are scarce. Composite creatures also belong to Palaeolithic art (see Figure 1), from a man with a lion's head in the Aurignacian of Hohlenstein-Stadel to the Middle Magdalenian "Sorcerers" of Trois-Frères (see Figure 2).

1   **2**

FIGURE 1. The so-called "Sorcerer" in the Gabillou Cave (Dordogne, France), representing a composite creature, part human, part animal. *Tracing by J. Gaussen.*

FIGURE 2. The so-called "Sorcerer with Musical Bow" from the Trois-Frères Cave (Ariège, France), part man, part bison. Therianthropes such as this one or the one from Gabillou, common in shamanic cultures, may represent a transformed shaman or a supernatural spirit. *Tracing by H. Breuil.*

3

FIGURE 3. Part of the famous "Scene of the Well" in the Lascaux Cave (Dordogne, France), in which a man with a bird's head seems to fall in front of a wounded bison. Below the man, a bird seems perched on a pole. The bird images might represent the flight of the soul, a common metaphor for a shaman's trance. The Lascaux Well is not so extensive a place as some other chambers in the same cave. *Tracing by A. Glory.*

In the caves, Upper Palaeolithic people behaved in exactly the same way from 32,000 to 12,000 BP.[2] They went to the most remote passages and recesses, sometimes to places where only one or two persons could gain access at a time (Portel, Chauvet, Tuc d'Audoubert, Candamo). In this case, the *act* of drawing was paramount, not its result. The Lascaux Well might have been such a place (see Figure 3). On the other hand, impressive compositions were made in vast chambers, such as at Lascaux (Salle des Taureaux), Niaux, and Chauvet, and other drawings were superimposed over one another in complex palimpsests, such as at Trois-Frères, Gargas, and Lascaux (Abside). This implies participation in collective ceremonies in which the images played a part for the perpetuation of beliefs, worldviews, and ritual practices to obtain the help of the spirits.

The cave itself was most important. Very often, animals were drawn by using natural reliefs for some parts of their bodies, making them appear as though they were coming out of fissures, shafts, or the ends of galleries. Many bone fragments were stuck into the cracks of the walls for no practical purposes except reaching into the deep rock. Such nonutilitarian gestures were found in a number of caves ranging from about 27,000 BP at Gargas to 14,000 in the Volp Caves. They confirm that the cave and its walls were thought of and used in the same way. Those facts are too numerous to be haphazard or coincidental. They testify to traditions and the materialization of fundamentally the same beliefs for more than twenty millennia.

Palaeolithic Art as the Testimony of a Shamanistic Religion

Upper Palaeolithic people, our forebears, had a nervous system identical to ours and thus also experienced modified states of consciousness, which they had to interpret in their own way. We know that they deliberately and repeatedly went into the deep caves to make drawings, not to live. This went on for immense periods of time. We also know that everywhere in the world and in all sorts of mythologies, the subterranean world has always been considered a supernatural realm, that of the gods, the dead, or the spirits. To go there was to venture into another world where one would meet supernatural beings. The analogy with shamanic soul journeys is obvious. In addition, experiences from modern spelunkers testify to the hallucinogenic properties of caves (Fénies 1965). Those accidental hallucinations are due to the cold, the wet, the weariness, and the lack of external stimuli. When Magdalenians or their predecessors went into the deep caves, they were aware of being inside the world of the supernatural and expected to find spirits there. Such a state of mind, reinforced by tradition, was bound to facilitate the experience of having visions.

The caves might thus have played a dual role: to facilitate visions and to get in touch with the powers through the walls that constituted a kind of veil between their world and ours. The use of natural reliefs then makes perfect sense. People believed that the animal spirit itself was present in the rock, literally at hand. By drawing it, they reached across the veil and tapped its power. The hollows, shafts, and gallery ends played the complementary role of the places that the animals were coming from.

Palaeolithic people's desire to contact the spirits or powers in the subterranean world may have manifested itself in three other ways. First, they stuck bits of bone into the cracks of walls, such as at Trois-Frères, Enlène, Tuc d'Audoubert, Bédeilhac, Labastide, Troubat, Brassempouy, Portel, Llonin, and other places. The elementary symbolism of this kind of gesture can be found in all sorts of contexts, even today— for example, the Jerusalem Wailing Wall.

Finger flutings and indeterminate traces could have been created from the same motives. They were not meant to draw an image, but to leave a trace on the wall wherever this was feasible, as in Cosquer and Gargas. The gesture itself was what counted. Within the sacred context of the caves, the most likely explanation is that people tried to get in direct touch with the powers beneath the rock. This might have been done by non-initiates who thus participated in the ceremonies in their own way.

Handprints and hand stencils may have served the same kind of purpose. When applying one's hand on the wall and blowing sacred paint onto it, the hand blended with the rock and took its color, red or black. It metaphorically vanished into the wall, leaving a kind of ghostly mark of itself when removed. Such an act would establish a concrete relationship with the world of the spirits and enable some persons (children in Gargas, for example, or sick people) to benefit from a direct contact with the powers beyond.

Conclusion

We have not attempted to explain all of Palaeolithic art through shamanism. From what is known about shamanism (or rather, shamanisms) in the world, we have examined the way Palaeolithic caves were used over a period of more than twenty thousand years. This has led us to think that most of the art was done within a shamanistic *framework* of beliefs. It does not imply that *all* the images came from visions, even though trance and hallucinations must have played an important role. At present, we have no way of knowing the details of those people's beliefs. However, we have taken a step toward understanding their attitude to the supernatural and their ways of approaching their own gods.

ℒ⋎

JEAN CLOTTES, PH.D., studied at Toulouse University, where he based his *Doctorat d'Etat* dissertation on dolmens (prehistoric megalithic burial chambers). From 1990 to 1993, Dr. Clottes taught an advanced course in Prehistoric Art at Toulouse University. In 1992, he was appointed General Inspector for Archaeology at the French Ministry of Culture, where from 1993 to 1999 he was Scientific Advisor for prehistoric rock art. Dr. Clottes is editor of the *International Newsletter on Rock Art*, has published more than three hundred scientific articles, and has authored or edited twenty-three books, the most recent including *Passion Préhistoire* (2003 ; *World Rock Art* (2002); *La Préhistoire Expliquée à Mes Petits-Enfants* (2002); and *La Grotte Chauvet—L'Art des Origines* (2001). Dr. Clottes also serves as director of collections ("Arts

Rupestres") at Éditions du Seuil and la Maison des Roches in Paris, and he is a member of various committees and councils dedicated to prehistoric monuments and rock art.

NOTES

1 From **sha·man** *n* — spiritual leader: somebody who acts as a go-between for the physical and spiritual realms, and who is said to have particular powers such as prophecy and healing. [Late 17th century. Via Russian from Tungus *šaman*, ultimately from Sanskrit *śramaná?* "Buddhist ascetic," from *śrámas* "religious exercise."] Microsoft® Encarta® Reference Library 2003. © 1993–2002 Microsoft Corporation.

2 BP = Before Present.

REFERENCES

Clottes and Lewis-Williams D., 1996. *Les Chamanes de la Préhistoire. Transe et Magie dans les Grottes ornées.* Paris, Le Seuil.

———, 1997. Préhistoire. Les Chamanes des Cavernes, *Archéologia* 336: 30–41.

———, 2001. *Les Chamanes de la Préhistoire. Texte intégral, polémiques et réponses.* Paris, La maison des roches.

Eliade M., 1951. *Le Chamanisme et les techniques archaïques de l'extase.* Paris, Payot.

Fénies J., 1965. *Spéléologie et médecine.* Paris, Masson, Collection de Médecine légale et de Toxicologie médicale.

Hultkranz A., 1987. *Native religions of North America: the power of visions and fertility.* San Francisco, Harper and Row.

Lemaire C., 1993. *Rêves éveillés. L'âme sous le scalpel.* Paris, Les Empêcheurs de penser en rond.

Lewis-Williams D., 2002. *The Mind in the Cave. Consciousness and the Origins of Art,* London, Thames and Hudson.

Lewis-Williams D. and Dowson T., 1988. The signs of all times. Entoptic phenomena in Upper Palaeolithic art.. *Current Anthropology* 29(2), 201–45.

Reichel-Dolmatoff G., 1978. *Beyond the Milky Way: hallucinatory imagery of the Tukano Indians.* Los Angeles, UCLA Latin American Centre.

Vitebsky P., 1995. *Les Chamanes.* Paris, Albin Michel.

Ursula Goodenough

THE TITLE of this essay, suggested in the invitation I received to contribute to this volume, brought to mind the following oft-quoted paragraph:

It seems to me we are losing the sense of wonder, the hallmark of our species and central feature of the human spirit. Perhaps this is due to the depreda-tions of science and technology against the arts and humanities, but I doubt it—although this is certainly something to be concerned about. I suspect it is simply that the human spirit is insufficiently developed at this moment in evolution, much like the wing of archaeopteryx. Whether we can free it for further development will depend, I think, on the full reinstatement of the sense of wonder. It must be reinstated in relation not only to the natural world but to the human world as well. At the conclusion of all our studies we must try once again to experience the human soul as soul, and not just as a buzz of bioelectricity; the human will as will, and not just a surge of hor-mones; the human heart not as a fibrous, sticky pump, but as the metaphoric organ of understanding. We need not believe in them as meta-physical entities—they are as real as the flesh and blood they are made of. But we must believe in them as entities; not as analyzed fragments, but as wholes made real by our contemplation of them, by the words we use to talk of them, by the way we have transmuted them to speech. We must stand in awe of them as unassailable, even though they are dissected before our eyes. (Melvin Konner, *The Tangled Wing: Biological Constraints on the Human Spirit*. Holt, 1982)

Konner is working here in the territory that has come to be called *emergence*. I develop in this essay some useful ways to think about emergence, ways that are importantly influenced by my understandings of Terry Deacon's thinking.[1] I then suggest how Konner's thinking might be expanded and even reconfigured in light of these ideas and indicate how emergentism functions in my own spiritual quest.

The concept of emergence says that since the first moments in the thirteen billion years of our observable universe, something more keeps arising—emerging—from "nothing-but." Some of these emergent properties, such as surface tension, arise from shape interactions alone: Surface tension emerges when water or other molecules interact to form a liquid; it doesn't exist until the liquid state is adopted. Other emer-gent properties entail both shape interactions and time, as in snowflake formation or complex systems, where the shape interaction that happens next depends on the shape interaction that happened before. The possibilities for novelty are enormous.

But the emergent properties that hold our attention—what we can call "third-order emergence"—are those that arose with the advent of biology and then continued to arise through biological evolution. These also entail shapes moving through time; but, in addition, they are encoded and remembered, thereby becoming substrates for natural selection, which biases what is or is not remembered. I refer to these properties, loosely but usefully, as biological *traits*.

Biological traits are made up of biomolecules, such as enzymes and hormones and ion channels, that interact and play out in space and time. The difference between traits and complex systems, then, is that traits are specified by instructions: the shape of an enzyme, its capacity for productive shape changes, the timing of its appearance in a given cell, how much of it is made, and what regulates its interactional possibilities. These things are not left to chance or to fluctuating initial conditions or boundary conditions. They are encoded, either in the genomic instructions themselves or in epigenetic instructions (cell-cell interactions), such that pretty much the same outcome—the same emergent trait—occurs with a quite remarkable degree of reliability.

And, indeed, to generate a reliable outcome is what organisms are about. When a species is unable to reproduce itself in a reliable fashion, it either drifts toward extinction, or, through mutation and natural selection, it adopts a more reliable strategy—that is, it evolves.

Granted that the ultimate substrate for natural selection is the organism itself, the units of selection are its emergent biological traits. Thus, natural selection does not "see" the enzymes, the individual gene products that catalyze an organism's energy transduction; rather, it "sees" the outcome, the emergent trait metabolism. In the same way, natural selection "sees" an organism's motility and not the contractile and regulatory proteins that together allow that motility to happen. Instructions for a less adaptive metabolism or motility are less likely to spread through a population than instructions for a more adaptive metabolism or motility, with the wild-card word "adaptive" having everything to do with the match between an organism's genomic expectations and the niche wherein it in fact finds itself. Metabolism and motility are *nothing but* their constituent parts. But they are also *something more*, something new and emergent.

What is particularly important about biological traits is that they are *about* something. Metabolism allows an organism to carry out its chemistry; motility allows it to move toward food and mates and away from toxicity and predators. There is a *point* to a trait that we cannot ascribe to a snowflake. A trait, and the traits that it combines with to generate an organism, has a purpose—namely, to allow the organism to carry on and thereby transmit the instructions for those traits. Organisms of different sorts may inhabit other planets in the universe, but, for me, a vital piece of naturalistic spiritual information is that the organisms on this planet, and their inevitable evolution given its inhomogeneous environment, are steeped in teleology.

Except for us—and us very recently—organisms have no idea whatsoever that their traits emerge because genetic instructions have been transmitted and correctly interpreted. Organisms are only aware, to the extent that they are aware at all, that their traits serve to carry out their purposes, their goals. Moreover, except for us—

and us very recently—organisms have no idea that their traits are emergent properties with underlying "nothing-but" parts. All of this is as hidden from view, as is
the way that water molecules interact to generate surface tension or colloids interact to generate fractals. We are, to the best of our knowledge, the only ones who
know about bioelectric buzzes and sticky pumps and the chromosomes that encode
the instructions for making these things.

So we arrive at "us very recently," us maybe two million years ago, when there
emerged a new trait: the capacity for symbolic language and the co-evolution of
both culture and the capacity for *symbolic (self-) representation.* We modern humans
experience what we experience. The extent to which this trait is latent/manifest in
other organisms as well is an intensely interesting question, but one we can set to
the side as we acknowledge an important truth: this human trait of symbolic (self-)
representation is a remarkable new kid on the evolutionary block. As we manipulate our symbolic understandings in the contexts of our remembered cultures, we
effectively create a new kind of reality, a virtual reality, one infused with concepts
and ideals and histories and expectations.

Although our new capacities for symbolic (self-) representation and cultural
transmission have been evolving for some time, it has only recently been the case
that they have been used to dissect the material world, and in particular biological
traits—and, in particular, our own biological traits—into their component parts.
While this activity now occurs worldwide, it began only in very small pockets of
human culture. Most humans, after pursuing their imperatives to eat and find shelter and procreate, have been engaged throughout the ages in articulating their sense
of awe and wonder—their spirituality—in totems and rituals and cave-paintings
and songs and prayers, modes of expressing wonder that have been transmitted
through culture in the forms that we call "religions."

This version of human history leads us to an interesting realization: We inhabit
cultures wherein our sense of awe and wonder has been yoked to things that we
don't really understand, things that are larger and more powerful and more mysterious than we are, things that we can access only through our symbolic minds,
things such as Tribe and Beauty and Soul. As these large and abstract entities exist
only in our virtual reality, they activate experiences of transcendence because our
virtual reality is itself a transcendent modality. They are infused with the property
we sometimes call "the supernatural."

So, then, goes one version of the story: we wrecked it all. We went too far, we ate
the whole apple, we came to understand that all these things emerge from underlying mechanisms—that Tribe has a great deal to do with primate forms of hierarchy and xenophobia, Beauty with sensory perception, and Soul with bioelectric
buzz. The shockwaves of disappointment continue to resound, hundreds of years
later, with huge attendant efforts to ignore or explain away or deny these understandings, even as we avidly consume the technologies that they generate.

But there is another version of the story: that our scientific understandings have
simply provisioned us with more to engage our awe and wonder. To absorb that we
have evolved from elegant simple creatures and with them co-inhabit a broiling,
beautiful planet spinning through endless space—to take this in and find oneself

within it—is to gasp just as deeply as in any other modality of spiritual encounter. Spiritual encounters don't cancel one another out; they complement one another.

So we can now return to Konner. He starts out by simultaneously saying that we haven't yet reached our evolutionary possibilities for wonder and that we need to re-instate the sense of wonder that we once had but have since lost. I would say that we already have a thrilling capacity for wonder—it needn't wait for "evolutionary enhancement." And I would further say that to the extent that it is true that our sense of wonder has been lost, this is not so much because of our scientific under-standings as because we have not yet developed robust ways to access spiritual responses to these understandings. We remain trapped in the notion that the tran-scendent is resident only in the supernatural. The project is not to re-find some old-time sense of wonder, but to expand its modes and sources of elicitation.

Konner goes on to suggest that remediation of this state of affairs will best be accomplished when we figure out how to reframe how we experience ourselves—not as bioelectricity and hormones and metabolism, but as persons of soul and will and heart. I would counter that, in fact, we have no idea how to experience ourselves as bioelectricity and hormones and metabolism; we only know, intellectually, that these activities undergird our experience. I no more experience myself as a bio-electric buzz than my cat does, even though I know about these things and she does not. The only way I know how to experience myself is through symbolic (self-) rep-resentation, which by definition is a virtual reality that doesn't *feel* material at all.

Konner concludes that the real solution is to believe in soul and will and heart as entities, as unassailables, as wholes rather than fragments, "made real by the words we use to talk of them, by the way we have transmuted them to speech . . . even though they are dissected before our eyes."

From my perspective, emergentism offers us another way to configure this inter-face, one that I find more helpful to my spiritual journey. I would say that we don't need to subdue the parts and salvage the wholes through some set of semantic tricks and transformations. The wholes are fully as real as the parts; they are each mani-festations of the same thing, the one emergent from the other. Emergentism, I would say, defeats the artificial dualism that Konner and many others correctly regard as having confused and polluted our sense of wonder.

Our new kinds of minds allow us to encounter a universe resplendent with emer-gent properties and their component parts. Many go on to ask whether the uni-verse itself has a purpose and a plan; some say yes, others no. I prefer to focus on the purposiveness of our kind. All of us here belong to the same lineage—the lineage of intentionality, the trait that defines all earthly creatures. This understanding serves as the bedrock of my naturalistic spirituality: I am knocked out every time I think about it.

✿

URSULA GOODENOUGH, PH.D., is currently Professor of Biology at Washington University in St. Louis, Missouri. Her research has focused on the cell biology and (molecular) genetics of the sexual phase of the life cycle of the unicellular eukaryotic

EVOLUTIONARY THEORY AND THE SCANDAL OF UNCONDITIONAL LOVE

Jeffrey P. Schloss

Charles Darwin: Prophet or Profligate?

ONE OF MODERNITY's most provocative but disruptive intellectual battles has been the century-and-a-half-long blood-feud between conservative Christian theism and evolutionary naturalism. Although it is currently fashionable to gainsay "warfare" accounts of the interaction between science and religion, this tension between traditional religious constituencies and the pillar of contemporary biology has proven to be both crucial and enduring. Just scanning current book titles and newspaper articles reveals the elusiveness of a workable truce, much less a peaceful resolution to this conflict. Why is this? Ironically, it may involve a fight about love.

It is tempting at first blush to dismiss religious resistance to Darwinism as one more episode in the inevitable retreat of belief in the supernatural, driven by the relentless advance of scientific understanding. But the ready abatement of religious distress over other naturalistic explanations in eighteenth- and nineteenth-century biology and cosmology suggests there is something more at work. Indeed, both religious and secular commentators point out that it is not mere naturalism, but the implications of a specifically Darwinian naturalism, that appear to entail unique challenges for traditional religious understandings—involving not just the mechanism of life's origin, but the very meaning of life itself (Haught 2000; O'Hear 1997; Ruse 2000).

Western theism has traditionally affirmed a transcendent Creator of and purpose to life, which the design of the cosmos manifestly, even jubilantly, testifies to; and it has embraced the conviction that human beings, fashioned in the Creator's image, are specially suited to apprehend and cultivate that purpose in a moral vision of self-giving and unconditional love. On the other hand, philosopher James Rachels is by no means alone in pointing out that "Darwin's great contribution was the final demolition of the idea that nature is the product of intelligent design" (1990:110) and that evolutionary theory "undermines the idea that man is made in the image of God ... The idea of human dignity turns out, therefore, to be the moral effluvium of a discredited metaphysics" (1990:5). In an essay that explores the issue of incommensurability between evolutionary biology and the Christian love command, Michael Ruse cautions that "those who are worried about the clash between science and religion have good reasons for their worries" (1994:5).

The question is, does this apparent clash constitute a genuine threat to religious insights that are fundamental to Christian belief and even essential to human flourishing? Or does it entail a constructive, perhaps prophetic, challenge to reformulate or revisit moribund religious understandings in light of important new information? I want to argue that both are simultaneously the case. There is consonance and dissonance—each of which may be constructive—between some evolutionary and religious understandings of love and human purpose. Moreover, these agreements and disagreements reflect resonant ambiguities *within* each tradition as well. As I hope to show, the mantra of "science-religion dialog" turns out to be profoundly true in this case: There is an earnest need for tentative, mutually respectful exchange between disciplines on the issue of love.

The Provocative Evolutionary Love Story

The issue of sacrificial love occupies a crucial position in both religious and biological understandings of life. In the Christian tradition, it is considered the ultimate *telos* of human existence, the summation and fulfillment of all moral obligation. For evolutionary biology, it constitutes a "central theoretical issue" (Wilson 1975; Holcomb 1993) inasmuch as it has entailed a quandary needing explanation. Why so? Darwin himself recognized that an exclusively other-benefiting trait "would annihilate my theory, for such could not have been produced through natural selection" (1859:199). And yet it appeared that the world in fact did contain such traits, from sterile, other-serving castes in social insects to manifold instances of ostensibly self-relinquishing altruism in human societies.

A century after Darwin, two important theoretical insights extended the power of evolutionary theory to make sense of ostensible sacrifice. First, fitness was reconceptualized as a property of genes, not just of individuals. William Hamilton's (1964) notion of kin selection meant that fitness could be inclusively furthered, not only directly by having offspring, but also by caring for genetically related kin, as long as the cost to the giver was less than the gain to the beneficiary times the index of genetic relatedness (C ≤ B * R). J. B. S. Haldane encapsulated this idea by his famous quip, reputedly made while scribbling calculations on a napkin in a pub, that he would lay down his life to save two brothers or eight cousins.

Second, using an analogous cost/benefit logic to explain sacrifice outside of kinship boundaries, Robert Trivers (1971) argued that sacrificial behaviors could be selectively established if the cost to the actor is less than the benefit of a future compensatory return times the probability of receiving such a return. He termed this "reciprocal altruism." While this sounds like an oxymoron—after all, altruism is precisely not reciprocity—the idea is that such behaviors are not strictly and immediately reciprocated. Rather, it is that individuals make genuinely costly investments in others—but only in those particular others with whom the net balance of trade is likely to be positive in the long run. Thus, reciprocal altruism involves recognizing other individuals and monitoring the history of reciprocation.

These powerful insights have been immensely successful in making sense of previously puzzling sacrificial behaviors and have formed the basis for the sociobiological revolution—the comprehensive attempt to explain social behavior in light of evolutionary theory (Wilson 1975; Dawkins 1976). In its initial triumphalist zeal, sociobiology ambitiously asserted that all human social behavior could be explained by the two processes discussed above, or hence reduced to nepotism and favoritism. However, things are clearly more complicated than that. In what E. O. Wilson calls the "scandal of mammalian biology," human beings manifest an unusual degree and scope of cooperation: We invest in others outside the boundaries of kin and crony, and do so at significant personal cost.

In order to help explain this human anomaly, Richard Alexander (1987) advanced the notion of indirect reciprocity utilizing a modification of the above cost/benefit calculus. Indirect reciprocity theory argues that in human beings—the only primate living in groups too large to keep track of personal relationships—reputation for being a faithful reciprocator mediates inclusion in the cooperative matrix. Morality is an adaptation to large group size that provides the rules for accruing resources in one's reputational bank account. Conscience serves as a "reputation alarm" that goes off when one is behaving in a way likely to erode "principal" (Alexander 1987). Thus in humans, and perhaps only in humans, individuals exhibit sacrificial cooperation with others who will never repay the favor, but only so long as the cost of the sacrifice is less than the benefit of an indirect compensatory return from someone else, times the increased likelihood this will happen from reputational enhancement. According to indirect reciprocity theory, we're as unselfish as it pays to be; we're as selfish as we can get away with.

Cynical implications notwithstanding, indirect reciprocity does make sense of, and successfully predicts, many patterns of human social cooperation. But there are also explanatory limits. Virtue may be its own reward, but virtue consciously pursued for reward's sake strikes most people as suspiciously unvirtuous; thus humans are on vigilant lookout for hypocrites whose goodwill is intentionally tied to the rate of reputational return. Moreover, human group sizes are often so large that we need to make decisions about cooperating with others whose reputations we don't know. Enter signaling theory, which suggests that individuals develop hard-to-fake, often involuntary displays that reliably convey cooperative disposition. Indeed, consciousness is understood by some evolutionary biologists primarily as an adaptation for inferring the interior state of others, "a game of life in which the participants are trying to comprehend what is in one another's minds before, and more effectively than, it can be done in reverse" (Alexander 1987:133). As a complement, the uniquely neotonous and hairless human facial morphology is a highly effective stage for emotional display. Recent experimental work has confirmed the connection between involuntary facial signals and altruistic dispositions and has revealed that people indeed have a fascinating ability to make accurate inferences from facial information (Brown et al. 2003).

So the very best strategy for cooperative inclusion is to be a genuinely good person. Or is it? Groucho Marx quipped that "The secret of life is honesty and fair-dealing—if you can fake that, you've got it made." Yet the best, perhaps the only way, to "fake" an involuntary display is to be sincerely but erroneously convinced of one's good intentions. Self-deception theory, the last refinement in the above sociobiological line of argument, suggests that human cognition is structured with a bias toward overestimating one's own virtue and concealing one's ultimately self-serving motives from self-conscious recognition. The most effective fitness-maximizing strategy is not intentional hypocrisy, but entirely sincere, although inauthentically self-deceived, professions of beneficence. Indeed, believing that you believe the New Testament love command has been described as the most effective strategy for manipulating others to your own benefit.

As Oscar Wilde observed, "A sentimentalist is simply one who desires to have the luxury of an emotion without paying for it." Evolutionary theory posits this as a biological adaptation. Recognizing this, "No hint of genuine charity ameliorates our vision of society, once sentimentalism has been laid aside. What passes for cooperation turns out to be a mixture of opportunism and exploitation" (Ghiselin 1974:247).

Darwinism as Profligate

Given this deconstruction of genuine altruism as a legitimate end, or even a realistic possibility for human existence in the name of Darwin, those who claim there is no overlap (much less conflict) between science and religion (Gould 2002) and those who offer glib assurance of happy congruence between evolution and Christian belief (Miller 1999) seem to be proposing "peace, peace, where there is no peace." In light of this, the religious reflex toward anti-evolutionism seems understandable, if intellectually and socially counterproductive. I would like to suggest that religious belief may constructively speak to these scientific issues in three ways.

First, it may graciously but persistently articulate what we know about the reality of love from ways of understanding outside the sciences. With no religious agenda, Frans de Waal (1996:14) critiques gene-centric theories as dismissing what "many of us consider to be at the core of being human" and concludes "a more cynical outlook is hard to come by." Mary Midgley (1994:17) observes that "Darwinism is often presented . . . as a reductive ideology requiring us to dismiss as illusions matters which our experience shows to be real and serious." Now such assertions do not themselves advance, or even answer, scientific propositions; but they do remind us that there is unresolved tension between truth claims. Ironically, a good deal of religious thought has been so eager either to refute or to accommodate itself to Darwinian theory that it may have overlooked the opportunity—and responsibility—to keep us clear about mysteries that so far remain unclear. The tentative disinclination to thinking everything has essentially been solved is what Sir John Templeton, in whose honor this volume is being assembled, has called "humility theology." As Nicholas Lash eloquently suggests, "[Conflicts] arise when evolutionary science, having forgotten its 'fragmentary' character, expands into a comprehensive explanatory system. . . . Christian hope paradoxically 'enriches our knowledge' by protecting our nescience from illusion" (1995:283).

Second, as alternative scientific accounts for the evolution of altruism and human purpose emerge, theology can take care to reflect on the entire landscape of scientific theory and not just a favored position or easy target; moreover, it can serve as a conversation partner in territory that it has spent much effort mapping. In recent years, unifactorial explanations involving individual selection have been supplemented with theories invoking different levels of genetic selection (Sober and Wilson 1998; Boehm 1999) and nongenetic or cultural evolution (Durham 1991). These revisionist accounts present a more nuanced but ambiguous picture of human nature as entailing deep ambivalences relating to contrasting legacies of individual and group selection (Boehm 1999) and tensions between biological and cultural (even religious) influence. But these developments over the last decade mirror debates about the conflictedness and transformability of the human capacity to love that theology has been wrestling with for centuries. Indeed, recent "camps" in evolutionary thought in many ways mirror longstanding polarities in Augustinian vs. Thomistic and Reformed vs. Wesleyan theology (Schloss 2002a).

Third, most concretely but perhaps most controversially, religious understanding may actually inform scientific research (Russell 2001; Schloss 2002b). For the tradition of natural theology, purpose is an inference based on the limitations of naturalistic explanation. I would propose the converse: Religious notions of purpose are starting assumptions that may serve as a wellspring of alternative hypotheses, not suggested by prevailing theory, but fully investigatable by scientific means. One example of this concerns the frequency and effects of altruism. Prevailing evolutionary accounts are primarily econometric and posit that human social behaviors optimize the ratio of material inputs to outputs (Schloss 1996). Because there has been no theoretical warrant, we have never asked the fundamental organismic question about what happens *inside* the individual as a function of cooperative disposition: Are there internal biological benefits to altruism? Another example involves the role of morality and religion in promoting altruism. Virtually all evolutionary accounts see religion as a nonadaptive spandrel, an adaptation for individual fitness, or a facilitator of intra-group cooperation (Schloss 2000). Ironically, however, most world religions expressly eschew exclusively individual and group interest, urging unconstrained or, to use Sir John's term, "unlimited love." Now maybe this is all explainable by self-deception theory, but the point is it is empirically addressable (Schloss 2002a): Is there a connection between the professions of such religions and the altruistic behavior of their adherents? After longstanding lack of interest, these issues are currently being investigated by a variety of empirical studies.

Darwinism as Prophetic

It would be presumptuous to suggest that religion should speak and not listen to science on the issue of love, and I want to propose that spiritual understanding may be both refreshed and advanced by contemporary evolutionary accounts of altruism in at least two ways. First, notions of kin selection and reciprocal altruism constitute the most systematic explanation to date of the natural loves, theologically regarded as expressions of common grace. Moreover, they provide a basis for inquiry into the groupish constraints of natural affection and the question of how to expand the domain of human beneficence in ways that all religions urge. Indeed, Jesus almost sounds like a sociobiologist in the Synoptic Gospel accounts that exhort us not to restrict our greetings or invitations or lending to those who do the same in return. He seems to regard these behaviors as native defaults, observing that even Gentiles, sinners, and tax collectors do the same. He might just as easily have commented that all social vertebrates do the same! Religious indifference to the very real constraints, and provisions, of biological embodiment in the name of transcendence is an intellectual presumption that subverts, rather than advances, love and genuine spirituality. As Pascal observes, "Man is neither angel nor brute. And the unfortunate thing is, he who would act the angel, acts the brute" (1958: Pensee 358).

Second, notions of indirect reciprocity and self-deception constitute an unusually rich resource for understanding—and exposing—religious inauthenticity and the conditions that promote it. Religious profession uncoupled from genuine love has consistently been viewed as counterfeit spirituality in biblical and church tradition. Signaling theory provides a polarizing lens to examine behaviors that have been culturally reified as emblems of religious commitment, but that may mask self-serving and even exploitive personal orientations or social structures (Schloss 1996). This is precisely what the biblical prophetic tradition confronts in its criticism of mere lip service, or frequent exhortations to justice over religious ritual. Contemporary biological accounts provide a heuristically effective tool, which we have not yet developed the ability to disarm.

Indeed, I want to conclude by suggesting that Darwinism may function as—and be received with no less scorn than—religious prophets who exposed moribund spiritual understanding to the increasing illumination of love's demands. While it is understandable that religious faith will reject the hubris of hyper-Darwinian nihilism, it is noteworthy that conservative religious tradition has not welcomed with palm branches those conceptual tools of evolutionary biology that are not only highly congruent with traditional religious understandings, but potentially useful for advancing religious ends. Equally significant is contemporary anti-evolutionism's focus on relative minutiae such as radiometric dating, the Noahic flood, and fossil gaps. This appears to constitute a scrupulous tithe of intellectual mint and cumin, while quite literally ignoring the weightier matters of the law—love and human purpose. Why strain at gnats and overlook camels?

Thomas Luckmann (1967) has a profound account of religious nominalization that may help explain this (Schloss 1987). Building on Weberian notions of routinization, Luckmann observes that the sacred values in religion that make sense of life and govern behavior may gradually come to do neither. Even though they continue to be rhetorically affirmed, they are imperceptibly replaced by unrecognized values or an "invisible religion." Nominalization occurs not when people become halfhearted, but when hearts are invested in religious rhetoric that does not reorganize life but instead merely names or ontologically distinguishes the community. The twofold function of a prophet is to point out the unrecognized counter-values that actually organize the community and to pull down icons of social justification and community distinction.

Thus, John the Baptist says, "Produce fruit in keeping with repentance. And do not begin to say to yourselves, 'We have Abraham as our father.' For I tell you that out of these stones God can raise up children for Abraham" (Luke 3:8). He then goes on to specify what tangible, specifically altruistic behaviors would reflect the authenticity of religious commitment. I would argue that a similar implication of Darwinism—made overt in the Rachels quote cited at the beginning of this essay—has been to say, "Do not say to me you are uniquely made in God's image, or supernaturally born again by the Spirit of God: for I say to you God is able 'to breathe life into' (using the very words from the *Origin*) any number of life forms that bear the same unremarkable fruit that you do." It is then quite clearly specified what kind of altruistic behaviors would be tokens of genuine transcendence, restating with prophetic and contemporary impact the ancient Johanine challenge to Gnostic nominalism, "If anyone says, 'I love God,' yet hates his brother, he is a liar. For anyone who does not love his brother, whom he has seen, cannot love God, whom he has not seen" (1 John 4:20).

At the beginning of this essay, I commented that the tension between religion and evolution might be understood, in part, as a conflict over love. I did not specify which side either was on! Indeed, the traditions are as frail as the human hearts that birth them, which is why we need them to cooperate in enriching our capacity to explore and promote genuine charity. In the last analysis, there seems to be precious little in thoughtful versions of evolutionary theory that is intrinsically incompatible with Christian orthodoxy from any age. There is, however, a great deal that stands to make orthodoxy more demanding.

ℒ♥

JEFFREY P. SCHLOSS, PH.D., is Professor of Biology at Westmont College in Santa Barbara. He received his doctorate in Ecology and Evolutionary Biology from Washington University. Professor Schloss has taught at the University of Michigan, Wheaton College, and Jaguar Creek Tropical Research Center. He has been awarded a Danforth Fellow and an AAAS Mass Media Fellow in Science Communication. Professor Schloss has served on the editorial and advisory boards of numerous journals relating science and religion, including *Zygon: The Journal of Theology & Science, Science & Christian Belief, Science & Theology News,* and *Science & Spirit.* His twofold interests are in the ecophysiology of poikilohydric regulation and the implications of evolutionary theory for our understanding of ethics and human purpose. Professor Schloss's recent projects include several collaborative volumes: *Altruism and Altruistic Love: Science, Philosophy, and Religion in Dialogue* (Oxford, 2002) (two of his collaborators—Stephen G. Post and William B. Hurlbut—contributed essays to this volume); *Research on Altruism and Love* (Templeton Foundation Press, 2003) (again with Stephen G. Post, and others); a two-volume series of the *Journal of Psychology & Theology* focusing on biological and theological perspectives on human nature; and *Evolution and Ethics: Morality in Biological and Religious Perspective* (Eerdmans, 2004) (with Philip Clayton, who contributed an essay to this volume).

REFERENCES

Alexander, R. D. 1987. *The Biology of Moral Systems.* Chicago. Aldine-de-Gruyter.

Boehm, C. B. 1999. *Hierarchy in the Forest: The Evolution of Egalitarian Behavior.* Cambridge. Harvard University Press.

Brown, M., Palameta, B., and Moore, C. 2003. Are there non-verbal cues to commitment? An exploratory study using the zero acquaintance video presentation paradigm. *Evolutionary Psychology.* 1: 42–69.

Darwin, C. 1859, 1967 ed. *On the Origin of Species by Means of Natural Selection: or, the Preservation of Favored Races in the Struggle for Life.* Cambridge. Harvard University Press.

Dawkins, R. 1976. *The Selfish Gene.* Oxford. Oxford University Press.

de Waal, F. 1996. *Good Natured: The Origins of Right and Wrong in Humans and Other Animals.* Cambridge. Harvard University Press.

Durham, W. 1991. *Coevolution: Genes, Culture, and Human Diversity.* Stanford. Stanford University Press.

Ghiselin, M. T. 1974. *The Economy of Nature and the Evolution of Sex.* Berkeley. University of California Press.

Gould, S. J. 2002. *Rocks of Ages: Science and Religion in the Fullness of Life.* New York. Ballantine Books.

Hamilton, W. D. 1964. The Genetical Evolution of Social Behavior. *The Journal of Theoretical Biology,* 7: 1–16.

Haught, J. F. 2000. *God after Darwin: A Theology of Evolution.* Boulder, CO. Westview Press.

Holcomb, H. R. 1993. *Sociobiology, Sex, and Science.* Albany. State University of New York Press.

Lash, N. 1995. Production and Prospect: Reflections on Christian Hope and Original Sin. In *Evolution and Creation,* ed. E. McMullin, 273–89. Notre Dame. University of Notre Dame Press.

Midgley, M. 1994. *The Ethical Primate: Humans, Freedom and Morality.* London. Routledge.

Miller, Kenneth R. 1999. *Finding Darwin's God: A Scientist's Search for Common Ground between God and Evolution.* New York. HarperCollins Publishers, Inc.

Luckmann, T. 1967. *The Invisible Religion: The Problem of Religion in Modern Society.* New York. MacMillan.

O'Hear, A. 1997. *Beyond Evolution: Human Nature and the Limits of Evolutionary Explanation.* Oxford. Clarendon Press.

Pascal, B. 1958. *Pensees.* T. S. Eliot, commentator. New York. E. P. Dutton.

Rachels, J. 1990. *Created from Animals: The Moral Implications of Darwinism.* New York. Oxford University Press.

Ruse, M. 1994. Evolutionary Theory and Christian Ethics: Are They in Harmony? *Zygon: Journal of Religion & Science.* Vol. 29(1): 5–24.

———. 2000. *Can a Darwinian be a Christian? The Relationship between Science and Religion.* New York. Cambridge University Press.

Russell, R. J. 2001. The Relevance of Tillich for the Theology and Science Dialogue. *Zygon: Journal of Religion & Science* 36(2).

Schloss, J. P. 1987. Social Ecology and the Nominally Religious World View: Cultural Transformation or Accommodation by the Christian Liberal Arts. *Faculty Dialogue* 8:99.

———. 1996. Sociobiological Explanations of Altruistic Ethics: Necessary, Sufficient, or Irrelevant Perspective on the Human Moral Quest. In *Investigating the Biological Foundations of Human Morality.* James Hurd, editor. New York. The Edwin Mellen Press. 107–45.

———. 1998. Evolutionary Accounts of Altruistic Morality and the Quandary of Goodness by Design. In *Mere Creation* William Demski, editor. Downers Grove, IL. InterVarsity Press. 236–61.

———. 2000. Wisdom Traditions as Mechanisms of Homeostatic Integration: Evolutionary Perspectives on Organismal 'Laws of Life'. In *The Science of Wisdom and the Laws of Life.* Warren Brown, editor. Philadelphia. Templeton Foundation Press. 153–91.

———. 2002a. 'Love Creation's Final Law?': Emerging Evolutionary Accounts of Altruism. In S. Post, L. Underwood, J. Schloss, and W. Hurlbut, eds. *Altruism and Altruistic Love: Science, Philosophy, and Religion in Dialogue.* New York. Oxford University Press. 2002.

———. 2002b. From Evolution to Eschatology. In *Resurrection: Theological and Scientific Assessments.* Ted Peters, Robert J. Russell, and Michael Welker, editors. Grand Rapids. Wm Eerdmans. 56–85.

Sober, E., and Wilson, D. S. 1998. *Unto Others: The Evolution and Psychology of Unselfish Behavior.* Cambridge. Harvard University Press.

Trivers, R. L. 1971. The Evolution of Reciprocal Altruism. *The Quarterly Review of Biology,* 46: 35–39.

Williams, G. C. 1993. Mother Nature Is a Wicked Old Witch. In *Evolutionary Ethics,* eds. M. H. Nitecki and D. V. Nitecki. Albany. State University of New York Press.

Wilson, E. O. 1975. *Sociobiology.* Cambridge. Harvard University Press.

———. 1978. *On Human Nature.* Cambridge. Harvard University Press.

THE STUDY OF PURPOSE IN THE LIVING WORLD
AS A SOURCE OF NEW SPIRITUAL INFORMATION

Paul K. Wason

W*HAT IS THE MEANING OF LIFE?* When I was in college we debated this question through many long winter nights. Those were pre-postmodern nights when "finding yourself" meant locating your being in an existing web of meaning and purpose. We tossed about many strange suggestions, never doubting the existence of "meaning."

But what if Jacques Monod had been among us? Would a sparkling night have ended in the gray dawn of recognition that we are "alone in the unfeeling immensity of the universe, out of which [we have] emerged only by chance" (1972:167)? Had George Gaylord Simpson joined us, he might have rendered some fine stories, but all with the same amoral: "Man is the result of a purposeless and materialistic process that did not have him in mind. He was not planned" (1949:344). E. O. Wilson was then writing his great text on sociobiology. But had he made a quick appearance on the way to the library, he would have left us to ponder the idea that "no species, ours included, possesses a purpose beyond the imperatives created by its genetic history" (1978:2).

Would we have believed them? Possibly. Undergraduates are easily overwhelmed. But I hope not, for there *is* purpose in the universe. Humans have purposes. We engage in planning, act intentionally, seek and create meaning. Some appear to deny this, accepting Monod's sweeping claims with stiff lip and steady gaze. But I suspect they still believe in the reality of purpose. Can we imagine Richard Dawkins dragging a pen one day across some paper, without purpose or intent, only to discover the beautifully crafted text of *The Blind Watchmaker*? If Wilson really believed there is no purpose at the end of the genetic leash, why such great devotion to converting us? Why not do something a little more genetic? Perhaps I shouldn't speak for them. But I do not believe their line. In order to come to believe it, I would have to purposefully choose to believe that purpose and choice are illusory. That would be a rather silly thing to do. And if you cannot accept an apparently inevitable conclusion without becoming silly or incoherent, it is time to revisit the premises.

There is more. These human intentions, designs, and purposes genuinely affect the material world. I break no natural laws in playing billiards, yet the balls end up where *I intended* them. Well, sometimes. They all end up in different places from where they would have were it not for my purpose.[1] Human purposes accomplish things that would not have been predicted. Elements of our world, such as the New Jersey Turnpike, single-malt scotch, and California, would not make sense if we tried to understand them without accounting for human purpose. They may not make sense anyway. But we do know that real purposes have genuine causal efficacy in the realm of biology.

If we are to understand life at all, we must account for all of life.[2] Human thought is as much a part of the living world as the first multicellular organism, so any effective understanding of life must account for our purposive behaviors. Including California. And we may discover purpose to be far more widespread than this. In causal terminology, these are questions of teleonomy and teleology. "Teleonomy" concerns whether the laws of nature can be interpreted in terms of generic goal-directedness with respect to their role in evolution. "Teleology" concerns questions of transcending meaning and purpose. It is the study of phenomena exhibiting order, design, purposes, ends, goals, and direction. Purpose is the more familiar concept, of course. Among humans, it is that which we set before ourselves as an object, end, result, or plan.[3] So far, so good. But there is one more word we must consider.

Purpose and Design

Design. There, I said it. A word scorned not just by religion's cultured despisers, but throughout mainstream science and religion. It's tempting to avoid it, but we cannot, for purpose and design are deeply intertwined. It is no accident that in many people's minds purpose is implicated in objections raised against design.

It has been two hundred years since William Paley first asked us to imagine finding a watch on the NJ Turnpike. (Or something like that.) Most would agree that the watch was designed. Surely it didn't coalesce spontaneously from the random wind-currents of ten billion tires. A close look would reveal "that its several parts are framed and put together *for a purpose*" (Paley 1802:2). Design, it seems, makes little sense without purpose—at the very least, what something was designed *for*. Conversely, purpose is often expressed through design (as in, what *were* they thinking when they built that ramp?).

But times have changed. Paley had argued that, just like watches, the eye and hand *must have been* designed too because, well, how else could such intricacy have come about? Once immensely persuasive, this reasoning no longer works. We now have a perfectly plausible alternative, natural selection. Darwin's *The Origin of Species*, it is said, "did away for all time with the problem of teleology" (Plotkin 1994:51). Purpose and design became obsolete together. This, I believe, is the heart of what Monod, Simpson, Wilson, and Dawkins are trying to get us to see.

Does this mean our late-night search for meaning was in vain? I don't think so. First, selectionist explanations are powerful but not necessarily complete. I am not proposing heresy. I can recite the creed in good conscience: Many biological features make far more sense if we assume a history of descent with modification than if we see each as the efficient, independent, freely creative design of a wise and benevolent designer.[4] And with 99 percent of all life forms extinct, planned obsolescence seems a better summation of earth's history than timeless design. And yet, in evolutionary psychology and perhaps elsewhere, explanations using natural selection as the primary causal agent are often little more than clever just-so stories. Also, the presumption that anything having to do with life can be explained by natural selection, and that life overall must have the character we ascribe to selection,[5] does not follow even from the very fruitful success of the idea.

Second, natural selection could be a vehicle for purpose. What we need are not more assertions of the opposition between biological processes and purpose or design, but improved methodologies for distinguishing purpose from contingency, randomness, and determinism, meaning from meaninglessness, and design from chaos within a biological context. Much of modern design theory has too readily accepted the premises of Monod and Plotkin and so have taken a largely unproductive path—that of trying to oppose design to natural selection and trying to understand design without reference to purpose. After all, much of the living world can very neatly be explained by natural selection. If we propose, as many theists do, that purpose and/or design are pervasive as well, there must be compatibility, even synergy, among design, purpose, meaning, and selection.

Third, there are other approaches to design (Gregersen 1998:220). Design arguments of the eighteenth and nineteenth centuries were mechanistic, not unlike the science of the time (Davis and Poe 2002). But science has changed. Why, then, must design still conjure up great cosmic blueprints for specific organismal traits? Although unaware of natural selection, Paley was not unaware of these issues. He meant his arguments to be in line with, not opposed to, the most current biological understanding. We should do the same if we really want design or purpose arguments to offer new insight into the nature of reality. Even human artifacts, known to have been intelligently designed, often owe their current form and functionality to long periods of trial and error, exploration, and artificial selection. This evolution is not considered evidence against design, plan, and purpose. Why, then, should we persist in pitting purpose, design, and natural selection against each other in the wider realm of life?

Possibilities for the Study of Purpose in the World of the Living

The study of purpose in the living world is not impossible. Not even its deep connections with design render it obsolete. But how might we actually go about it? First, it cannot all come from within biology. The world's religions are a major source of the insight that purpose permeates existence. Philosophers have been studying purpose and causation for a long time. These are debates biology cannot afford to ignore. In addition, research in physics and cosmology has documented a remarkable range of apparent "fine-tunings" of physical laws and constants suggesting that we inhabit a "bio-friendly universe" (Davies 1999:20).

While nineteenth-century natural theology emphasized the intricate design of specific biological features, modern biologists might build on cosmology and study broad features of life in a search for overarching design and purpose. Michael Denton has recently shown that many aspects of the universe are strikingly suitable for the emergence and evolution of life (1998). Is life part of a broader cosmic purpose, perhaps built in?

What is life, anyway? Can the living be adequately understood in terms of reductive physical and chemical processes? The architectures of life might also be an area of study relevant to purpose. In the realm of the very small, consider that protein function depends not just on the sequence of amino acids, but on their folding and coiling, their three-dimensional structure. Could it be that evolutionary pathways for proteins are determined by physical laws? And what of the higher architectures of life? Can life take just any form or is the wondrous profusion around us built from just a limited number of possibilities that are part of *a plan built into the creation from the beginning*? The pervasiveness of convergence, for example, suggests limits to the number of real possibilities (Conway Morris 1998).

A casual overview of the history of life reveals trends (larger body size, greater physiological complexity) and even trends of trends (increasing integration, cooperation, freedom). Are these real? Is selection working on random mutation the only plausible mechanism, or do physiological and molecular constraints, and external forces (such as asteroids) have a significant cumulative effect? Are genes (which somehow manage to be selfish in an amoral and purposeless world) the ultimate purpose of life? Very likely, higher levels of integration (organism, population, community) are also essential for understanding biology, with implications for hierarchical or emergent purpose.

And just what are the purposes of life? Suppose we began by thinking about what is really important to us, at the deepest level of who we are? However subjectively we start out, I expect we will discover commonalities, elements basic to us as humans, as human animals, as examples of life. Instead of assuming these are late, ephemeral, and hopelessly individual, what if we found ways of determining their broader influence throughout life. Could they be fundamental elements of life, even fundamental aspects of reality?

I know what you're thinking. This guy really is from California. But consider—very likely, we already know what some of these deep elements are—love, grace, humility, compassion, relationship, thanksgiving, communion with God. We can add to and check the list by reviewing the world's religious teachings, extracting elements of the perennial philosophy, and asking our children. Indeed, scholars in astrobiology and SETI message development are already exploring what elements of humanity are sufficiently universal to be understandable by independently evolved intelligent life. I hope they succeed in their great quest, but this work is also of immense value now for the equally profound quest for understanding purpose in life on Earth.

Purpose in human affairs often comprises intentions, a plan or design with goals, and some means for carrying them out. Can we identify any of these elements in the nonhuman biological world as clues to how purpose works? Indeed we can. Bekoff has evidence that canids not only have intentions, but make them known to each other, thus enabling higher orders of sociality such as social play and a sense of fairness (Bekoff 2002). Tschudin (2001) has found dolphins capable of rudimentary moral reasoning, and Heinrich even reports planning and play among ravens (Heinrich 1999:310, 324). Cognitive ethology may be the most immediately rewarding approach available for studying purpose in the living world.

Can we uncover traces of purpose beyond the level of individual and social behavior? What does it tell us that evolution has led to conscious beings who stay up all night asking about the purpose of life? What does it tell us about the universe that the most intelligent known life forms willingly drive the New Jersey Turnpike? What is the basis for moral, spiritual, and religious awareness?[6] What is religion, anyway, and why has it been of utmost importance for all humans throughout history, save a minuscule minority of recent Western elite?

Humans are small, bipedal primates who drink ten-year-old single-malts. We engage in design, act with future goals in mind, and are as much a part of the living world as our dear friend the yeast. Purpose, meaning, intention, design, and teleology are found in profusion in the living world, from California to Scotland to New Jersey. What might we learn about other life forms, about life itself, if we start by recognizing that there is real, serious purpose among at least some living beings? Well, kind of serious.

ℒ♥

PAUL K. WASON, PH.D., was named Director of Science and Religion Programs for the John Templeton Foundation in 1999. He works with scientists, theologians, philosophers, and ministers on programs that feature the constructive engagement of science and religion. Dr. Wason is an anthropologist with a specialty in prehistoric archaeology. His research on inequality, social evolution, and archaeological theory has been published as *The Archaeology of Rank* (Cambridge, 1994) and in other works. Currently, he is studying the changing relations between religion, status, and leadership as evidenced by the stone circles and other monuments of Neolithic and Bronze Age Europe. Previously, Dr. Wason spent ten years at Bates College as Director of Foundations and Corporations and as a sponsored research administrator and served on the College's multiyear strategic planning effort. Dr. Wason received his Ph.D. in anthropology from the State University of New York at Stony Brook and is a Phi Beta Kappa graduate of Bates College, where he earned a B.S. in biology.

NOTES

1 This illustration is borrowed from Keith Ward's clear and helpful discussion (1992:48).

2 Hans Jonas suggests: "Perhaps, rightly understood, man *is* after all the measure of all things—not indeed through the legislation of his reason but through the exemplar of his psychophysical totality which represents the maximum of concrete ontological completeness known to us" (Jonas 1966:23–24).

3 Even defining (never mind studying) teleonomy and teleology is very complicated, but exploring what scholars have said about the words provides much insight into what they think about the living world. Importantly, not everyone uses the words as I have defined them here. See Barrow and Tipler 1986:133–36; Ayala 1998, 2000; Mayr 1982, 1991.

4 As just one of literally hundreds of possible examples, human embryos have yolk sacks

even though drawing their nourishment from their mothers (Miller 1999:100–101; see also Williams 1996 for many examples, some perhaps a little stretched, and the writings of Stephen Jay Gould, such as 1980:19ff).

5 To the extent that natural selection is used as a baseline model for the way the world is, it does lead to a different perspective from that of traditional theology. It is often considered random, directionless, meaningless, lacking in purpose, cold, selfish; and, as George Williams points out, these are things we would want to condemn (Williams 1996:157). Williams and I condemn this as a way of human life, others say that is the only rational basis for morality. But a third view is that there must be more to the world than is revealed through this mechanism as already shown by the reality of effective purpose.

6 Recently scholars from several disciplines have given attention to religion in their study of human evolution including paleoanthropologist Ian Tattersall (1998, 2002), psychologist Merlin Donald (1991, 2001), archaeologists Colin Renfrew (1994, 1998) and Steven Mithen (1996), anthropologist Pascal Boyer (1994, 2001) and evolutionary biologist David Sloan Wilson (2002). In turn scholars whose main interest is in religion itself like Stewart Guthrie (1993), Walter Burkert (1996), Wentzel van Huyssteen (personal communication), and John Haught (2000) have discovered the relevance of evolutionary material for their work.

References

Ayala, Francisco, 2000. "Teleology and Teleological Explanation." Counterbalance Foundation: Meta Library body.html.

———, 1998. "Teleological Explanations in Evolutionary Biology." In Colin Allen, Marc Bekoff and George Lander (eds.), *Nature's Purposes: Analyses of Function and Design in Biology.* Cambridge, MA: The MIT Press, 30–49.

Barrow, John D., and Frank Tipler, 1986. *The Anthropic Cosmological Principle.* Oxford: Oxford University Press.

Bekoff, Marc, 2002. *Minding Animals: Awareness, Emotions, and Heart.* Oxford: Oxford University Press.

Boyer, Pascal, 2001. *Religion Explained: The Evolutionary Origins of Religious Thought.* New York: Basic Books.

———, 1994. *The Naturalness of Religions Ideas: A Cognitive Theory of Religion.* Berkeley: The University of California Press.

Burkert, Walter, 1996. *Creation of the Sacred: Tracks of Biology in Early Religions.* Cambridge, MA: Harvard University Press.

Conway Morris, Simon, 1998. *The Crucible of Creation: The Burgess Shale and the Rise of Animals.* Oxford: Oxford University Press.

Davies, Paul, 1999. *The Fifth Miracle: The Search for the Origin and Meaning of Life.* New York: Simon and Schuster.

Davis, Jimmy H., and Harry L. Poe, 2002. *Designer Universe: Intelligent Design and The Existence of God.* Nashville, TN: Broadman and Holman Publishers.

Dawkins, Richard, 1987. *The Blind Watchmaker: Why the Evidence of Evolution Reveals a Universe Without Design.* New York: W. W. Norton & Company.

Denton, Michael J., 1998. *Nature's Destiny: How the Laws of Biology Reveal Purpose in the Universe.* New York: The Free Press.

Donald, Merlin, 2001. *A Mind So Rare: The Evolution of Human Consciousness.* New York: W. W. Norton & Company.

————, 1991. *Origins of the Modern Mind: Three Stages in the Evolution of Culture and Cognition.* Cambridge, MA: Harvard University Press.

Gould, Stephen Jay, 1980. *The Panda's Thumb: More Reflections in Natural History.* New York: W. W. Norton & Company.

Gregersen, Niels Henrik, 1998. "A Contextual Coherence Theory for the Science-Theology Dialogue." In Niels Henrik Gregersen and J. Wentzel van Huyssteen (eds.) *Rethinking Theology and Science: Six Models for the Current Dialogue.* Grand Rapids: William B. Eerdmans Publishing Company, 181–231.

Guthrie, Stewart Elliott, 1993. *Faces in the Clouds: A New Theory of Religion.* New York: Oxford University Press.

Haught, John F., 2000. *God After Darwin—A Theology of Evolution.* Boulder, CO: Westview Press.

Heinrich, Bernd, 1999. *Mind of the Raven: Investigations and Adventures with Wolf-Birds.* New York: Cliff Street Books.

Jonas, Hans, 1966. *The Phenomenon of Life: Toward a Philosophical Biology.* Evanston, IL: Northwestern University Press.

Mayr, Ernst, 1991. *One Long Argument: Charles Darwin and The Genesis of Modern Evolutionary Thought.* Cambridge, MA: Harvard University Press.

————, 1982. *The Growth of Biological Thought: Diversity, Evolution and Inheritance.* Cambridge, MA: Harvard University Press.

Miller, Kenneth R., 1999. *Finding Darwin's God: A Scientists' Search for Common Ground Between God and Evolution.* New York: Cliff Street Books.

Mithen, Steven, 1996. *The Prehistory of the Mind: The Cognitive Origins of Art, Religion and Science.* London: Thames and Hudson.

Monod, Jacques, 1972. *Chance and Necessity.* Tr. A. Wainhouse. London: Collins.

Paley, William, 1802. *Natural Theology, or, Evidences of the Existence and Attributes of the Deity, Collected from the Appearances of Nature.* London: R. Faulder.

Plotkin, Henry, 1994. *Darwin Machines and the Nature of Knowledge.* Cambridge, MA: Harvard University Press.

Renfrew, Colin, 1998. "Mind and Matter: Cognitive Archaeology and External Symbolic Storage." In Colin Renfrew and Chris Scarre (eds.) *Cognition and Material Culture: The Archaeology of Symbolic Storage.* Cambridge: McDonald Institute for Archaeological Research.

————, 1994. "The Archaeology of Religion." In Colin Renfrew and Ezra B. Zubrow (eds.) *The Ancient Mind: Elements of A Cognitive Archaeology.* Cambridge: Cambridge University Press, 47–54.

Ruse, Michael, 2000. "Teleology: Yesterday, Today and Tomorrow?" *Studies in History and Philosophy of Biological and Biomedical Sciences* 31, no. 1: 213–32.

————, 2000. *The Evolution Wars: A Guide to the Debates.* Santa Barbara, CA: ABC-CLIO.

Simpson, George Gaylord, 1949. *The Meaning of Evolution: A Study of the History of Life and of Its Significance for Man.* New Haven: Yale University Press.

Tattersall, Ian, 2002. *The Monkey in the Mirror: Essays on the Science of What Makes Us Human.* New York: Harcourt, Inc.

————, 1998. *Becoming Human: Evolution and Human Uniqueness.* New York: Harcourt Brace and Company.

Tschudin, A. J-P., 2001. "Mindreading Mammals? Attribution of Belief Tasks with Dolphins." *Animal Welfare* 10: S119–27.

Ward, Keith, 1992. *Defending the Soul.* Oxford: One World.

Williams, George C., 1996. *Plan and Purpose in Nature.* London: Weidenfeld and Nicolson.

Wilson, David Sloan, 2002. *Darwin's Cathedral: Evolution, Religion and the Nature of Society.* Chicago: The University of Chicago Press.

Wilson, E. O., 1978. *On Human Nature.* Cambridge, MA: Harvard University Press.

THE EVOLUTION OF ALTRUISM 53

FROM GAME THEORY TO HUMAN LANGUAGE

Martin A. Nowak and Natalia L. Komarova

I T IS A COMMON PATTERN in nature for simple things to give rise to more complicated things. Great complexity arises in a sequence of incremental steps, and the resulting system acquires features that could not have existed in the beginning. One such feature is altruism. In this essay, we show how altruism, which is not sustainable in simple systems, becomes a necessary component of more sophisticated scenarios, where it actually keeps the system together. This holds true for the evolutionary dynamics of co-existing organisms. It also holds true for the spiritual evolution of individuals. As we strive to find God, truth, and love throughout our lives, we can rise to higher and higher levels of understanding and spiritual sophistication. And one of the great fruits found on this path is selflessness, the willingness to give oneself for the good of others. An outsider in the early stages of life, altruism is a familiar presence in fairy tales, games, and songs and becomes vitally important as we mature, becoming one of the pillars of the spiritual temple built in the course of one's life.

This common motivating force in the universe is the subject of this essay. We explain how cooperation could have arisen naturally, despite the always-present temptation to defect. We first present the famous Axelrod et al.'s "Prisoner's dilemma" and then talk about more complicated versions of the game, which mimic different aspects of human interactions. We see that in a complex society with a sophisticated infrastructure, altruistic behavior is necessary for survival and prosperity. It is also a necessary prerequisite for the existence of language, with all of its consequences, including our ability to share thoughts, pass on moral values, and pray. Altruism is there in the beginning as a prerequisite for what it means to be human, and it is there at the end as one of the most cherished spiritual values. Following is an attempt to make sense of this.

The "Prisoner's Dilemma"

Cooperation and mutual help are integral parts of human society. So are deceit and selfish behavior. Family members, neighbors, and colleagues often find themselves in situations where personal interests are in conflict with the interests of the larger group. The temptation is to cheat and maximize one's own benefit without concern for others. The alternative choice is to cooperate, which means accepting a (small) cost in order to help somebody else. All world religions call for an attitude that promotes such altruistic behavior, and so does evolutionary game theory.

The problem of cooperation and defection is described mathematically by the famous "Prisoner's Dilemma" (Trivers 1971, Axelrod and Hamilton 1981). This game has two players (two prisoners that are being accused of having committed a crime and are questioned by the police in separate rooms). Each player has two choices: to cooperate (to be silent) or to defect (to betray the other). The idea is that each player gains when both cooperate (the police will not have proof, so the punishment will be reduced); but if only one of them cooperates, the one that defects will gain more (i.e., will be freed for offering evidence against the other). If both defect, both lose, but not as much as the "cheated" cooperator whose cooperation is not returned (if each of them reports on the other, the punishment for both is reduced for helping the police). The essence of the game is that the temptation to defect (five points) exceeds the reward for mutual cooperation (three points), which exceeds the payoff for mutual defection (one point), which exceeds the payoff for exploited cooperation (zero points); see Table 1.

TABLE 1. PAYOFFS IN THE "PRISONER'S DILEMMA"

	You Cooperate	You Defect
I Cooperate	I receive 3, you receive 3	I receive 0, you receive 5
I Defect	I receive 5, you receive 0	I receive 1, you receive 1

What would you do in this situation? If you cooperate without knowing what the other one is up to, you would face the risk of being severely punished in case the other betrays you. And even if the other prisoner cooperates, you are still better off defecting. So, the decision is easy: No matter what the other player does, you should defect. Thus, both players will defect—and as a result will receive only one point each. On the other hand, if they had both cooperated, they would have received three points each! This is the dilemma of cooperation.

Both in *On the Origin of Species* (1859) and in *The Descent of Man* (1871), Darwin mentions that cooperation is not easily explained by natural selection. In terms of modern evolutionary game theory, imagine a population of individuals consisting of cooperators and defectors. Individuals play the Prisoner's Dilemma in random pairwise encounters. The payoffs are added up, and individuals reproduce proportional to their payoff. It is straightforward to see that defectors will always do better than cooperators. After some time, cooperators will become extinct. Natural selection chooses defection. Yet, as noted by Darwin, cooperation is abundant in nature. How can we explain this?

THE "ALTRUISM" OF "SELFISH" GENES

The first answer to Darwin's question was given by William D. Hamilton (1964). Cooperation among relatives can be explained by kin selection. Genes that induce altruistic behavior are shared among relatives. Hence, genes, selfishly, promote their own survival. Hamilton's equation demands that the coefficient of relatedness between the donor and the recipient of an altruistic act has to exceed the cost-benefit ratio of this act. As the famous biologist J. B. S. Haldane once said, "I would jump into the river to save two brothers or eight cousins."

Kin selection is one of the most successful theories in evolutionary biology. But the question remains: How do we foster cooperation among nonrelatives?

DIRECT RECIPROCITY

In a single round of a nonrepeated game of the Prisoner's Dilemma, there is no incentive to cooperate. If the game is repeated, however, cooperation can become a viable option. The repeated game of the Prisoner's Dilemma admits an infinite number of possible strategies. A strategy has to specify whether to cooperate or to defect given any history of the game. The simplest and least cooperative strategy is Always Defect (AD). Interestingly, more cooperative strategies such as Tit-for-Tat (TFT) can take over AD. In TFT, a player cooperates on the first move and then does whatever the other player did in the previous round. If the other player cooperated, the second player cooperates. If the other player defected, the second player defects. Hence, these moves somehow embody the harsh advice referred to in the New Testament: "an eye for an eye, a tooth for a tooth" (Matt 5:38). TFT can take over AD if the initial abundance of TFT players exceeds a certain threshold (the "invasion barrier") or if the TFT players form clusters.

TFT does well against many other strategies, but it has a weakness. If two TFT players interact and one makes a mistake and defects, then both players will be locked in a series of alternating defection and cooperation. Another mistake can bring the sequence to all-out defection. In the long run, in a world such as ours where mistakes are possible, two TFT players perform as poorly as players who choose cooperation or defection randomly with a 50 percent chance on each move. Hence, TFT's unforgiving retaliation is its Achilles' heel.

The population of TFT players can be invaded by more forgiving strategies such as Generous TFT (GTFT), which always answers cooperation with cooperation and sometimes answers defection with cooperation (Nowak, May, and Sigmund 1995). The optimum level of forgiveness for the payoff values in the Table is that one in three defections of the other player are followed by cooperation. The rule of GTFT is "never forget a good move, but sometimes forgive a bad move."

GTFT in turn can be undermined by Always Cooperate (AC). In mixed populations of AC and GTFT, there is (almost) only cooperation, and the payoff is the same for every player. Random drift can lead to populations dominated by AC. This is reminiscent of a peaceful society that loses any mechanism to retaliate or punish defection. The outcome is clear: After some time, AD will invade again. A cycle of war and peace is closed, as shown in Figure 1. The evolution of altruism displays cycles of cooperation and defection.

A simple strategy such as Win-Stay, Lose-Shift (WSLS) can break this basic cycle. In WSLS, a player will stick with his or her move from the previous round if this was successful (e.g., earning five or three points) and change if it wasn't (e.g., earning only one or zero points). WSLS can correct errors and hence is as forgiving as GTFT. In addition, WSLS can exploit AC; hence, WSLS populations cannot be undermined by AC.

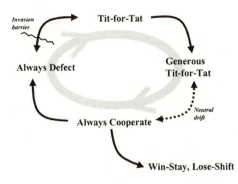

FIGURE 1. THE CYCLE OF WAR AND PEACE.

INDIRECT RECIPROCITY

The model of direct reciprocity assumes repeated interactions between two players. This is a good assumption in many situations, but it does not hold for all social interactions. People often are willing to cooperate with those whom they are unlikely to meet again. The motivation for such behavior can be explained by models of indirect reciprocity. The basic idea is that cooperation leads to a reputation that elicits help from others (Nowak and Sigmund 1998). In this setting, cooperation pays because it confers the image of a valuable community member on the cooperating individual.

EFFECT OF NEIGHBORHOODS

Finally, we note that cooperation is easier to maintain in a sedentary population (Nowak, May, and Sigmund 1995). Defectors can thrive in an anonymous crowd, but mutual aid is frequent among neighbors. It is interesting that territorially structured interactions promote cooperation even if no follow-up encounter is expected. This result favors cooperation even for the seemingly hopeless single round of the Prisoner's Dilemma. Let us suppose that each member of the population is constrained to a node of a square grid and interacts only with his or her eight closest neighbors. We further assume that each player is either a pure cooperator or a pure defector. After each round of the game, each player is replaced by a copy of the winner. It is easy to see that a lone cooperator will be exploited by the surrounding defectors and succumb. Four cooperators in a block, however, may hold their own, because each of them interacts with three cooperators, and a defector from the outside can reach and exploit only two. If the bonus for cheating is not too high, clusters of cooperators will grow! On the other hand, lone defectors will do very well at first because they can exploit all their neighbors; but as soon as they spread, defectors will surround themselves with their like, and so diminish their returns.

Cooperation, Defection, and Communication

We have seen that game-theoretic models, crude as they are, illustrate how cooperation and altruism might arise and be maintained in a population of individuals. Sophisticated creatures such as humans may be drawn to follow strategies that encourage cooperation because of repeated interactions among individuals that can recognize and remember one another or by virtue of self-organizing structures generated by interactions with neighbors. Once cooperation is in place, it can give rise to a new level of highly complex interactions among individuals. One of the most amazing examples of that is human language.

To see that the very existence of language is impossible without cooperation, let us perform the following thought experiment. Assume that individuals in the population can exchange information. At each interaction, one person acts as a "speaker" and the other as a "listener." The speaker has a choice of either giving away some piece of useful information (telling the truth) or lying. Telling the truth may be associated with some cost to the speaker (for instance, telling others about a food source may harm the donor in the future), and it confers a positive payoff to the listener. On the other hand, telling a lie may be beneficial to the speaker and harmful to the listener. This sets up a game-theoretic scenario in which different strategies may have more or less success in the evolutionary dynamics. Let us suppose for a moment that the AD strategy (always tell a lie) wins over the population. It is immediately clear that a language cannot evolve under such circumstances because there is no point for listeners to learn to decode the messages of the speakers! In a population of liars, those who can pass on messages and understand the messages of others have no advantage compared with individuals who do not have the ability to communicate, which shows that evolving a signaling system requires some level of cooperation.

Interesting examples can be found in biology. Bees have a highly sophisticated signaling system in which they can "tell" other members of the hive about the location, and even the quality, of food sources. This is hardly surprising considering the high level of cooperation that exists in bee colonies. The biological explanation of cooperation is kin selection (bees in a hive are closely genetically related, and thus by helping others they help spread their own genes). In its turn, cooperation leads to the development of language. Similarly, one could argue that the existence of human language relies on a high level of cooperation and altruism in human society; the difference is, of course, that the reason for altruism is not kin selection, but other, more sophisticated interactions, some of which we have examined.

If cooperation exists in a population of individuals, then we can argue that a coordinated signaling system can arise. Humans use words as a basic unit of communication. If the cognitive abilities of the individuals are high enough, then the population will follow self-organizing dynamics until all individuals have a common lexicon (Komarova and Nowak 2001). The next step is to clump words together and construct sentences following a common system of generative rules, which eventually leads to the emergence of syntactic communication. We argue that this is possible only in a highly cooperative society in which it pays to have the ability to communicate (Nowak, Komarova, and Niyogi 2002). Once a communication system is established, it leads to a wealth of sophisticated social behaviors and promotes the emergence of complex social structures, morals, and a common system of values— altruism usually being one of them.

Conclusion

We have seen that evolution as we know it would be impossible without altruism; altruistic/cooperative behavior arises naturally (and by necessity) and gives rise to a great variety of phenomena we observe in nature and in society. At the same time, altruism appears to be one of the highest and most desirable moral values of modern religions. A person on his or her spiritual quest will not advance far without embracing an altruistic attitude. This common pattern, which has arisen in a rather unexpected way, suggests that there are "favorite" themes in the universe. Our efforts to find them and internalize them should come from both the theological and scientific perspective. Future interdisciplinary research should include mathematical modeling in ecology and sociology, performed in close contact with experts in human spirituality, cultural history, and religion. This will shed more light on the emergence of altruism and on broader questions of human spiritual evolution.

✺

MARTIN A. NOWAK, PH.D., is Professor of Mathematics and of Biology at Harvard University since 2003, Director of the newly founded Center for Theoretical Biology, and the Faculty Director of the Program for Evolutionary Dynamics. He received his Ph.D. from the University of Vienna in 1989, where he studied biochemistry and mathematics. His diploma thesis was on quasi-species theory, and his Ph.D. thesis was on the evolution of cooperation. After graduating, he went to the University of Oxford as the Erwin Schrödinger scholar to work with Robert May. In 1992, he became a Wellcome Trust Senior Research Fellow and in 1997 Professor of Mathematical Biology. In 1998, Professor Nowak moved to Princeton to establish the first program in Theoretical Biology at the Institute for Advanced Study. He is interested in all aspects of mathematical biology, particularly the dynamics of infectious diseases, cancer genetics, the evolution of cooperation, and human language. In an effort to describe the evolution of human language, he designed a mathematical approach bringing together formal linguistics, learning theory, and evolutionary dynamics. Professor Nowak has published more than two hundred papers and is on the editorial board of *Philosophical Transactions of the Royal Society London, Journal of Theoretical Biology,* and *Journal of Theoretical Medicine.* His first book, *Virus Dynamics* (together with Robert May), was published by Oxford University Press in 2000. Professor Nowak is a corresponding member of the Austrian Academy of Sciences and has won numerous awards.

NATALIA L. KOMAROVA, PH.D., is Assistant Professor, Department of Mathematics, University of California, Irvine, and a member of the Institute for Advanced Study, Princeton. She studied theoretical physics at Moscow State University, where her master's thesis was on chaos control in 2-D maps. She received her doctorate in Applied Mathematics in 1998 from the University of Arizona, where her thesis title was "Essays on Nonlinear Waves." In 1998–1999, Dr. Komarova was a Research Fellow at the Mathematics Institute, the University of Warwick, United Kingdom, where she continued her work on natural pattern formation and competition between nonlinearity and randomness. She went to IAS in 1999 as a member of the School of Mathematics, where she became interested in problems of mathematical biology. In 2000, Dr. Komarova joined the Program in Theoretical Biology at IAS, and in 2003 she became part of the faculty in the Department of Mathematics at Rutgers University. She is interested in applying mathematical tools to describe natural phenomena. She received the 2002 Prize for Promise from the Student Achievement & Advocacy Services Corporation.

REFERENCES

Axelrod, R., and Hamilton, W. D. The evolution of cooperation. *Science* 211, 1390 (1981).

Hamilton, W. D. The genetical evolution of social behaviour. *J. Theor. Biol.* 7, 1–52 (1964).

Komarova, N. L., and Nowak, M.A. (2001). Evolutionary dynamics of the lexical matrix. *Bull. Math. Biol.*, 63(3), 451–85.

Nowak, M. A., Komarova, N. L., and Niyogi, P. (2002) Computational and evolutionary aspects of language, *Nature*, 417, 611–17.

Nowak, M. A., May, R. M., and Sigmund, K. The arithmetics of mutual help. *Scientific American* 272, N6, 76–81 (1995).

Nowak, M. A., and Sigmund, K. Evolution of indirect reciprocity by image scoring. *Nature* 393, 573–77 (1998).

Trivers, R. The evolution of reciprocal altruism. *Q. Rev. Biol.* 46, 35–57 (1971).

THE FORM OF FREEDOM 54

William B. Hurlbut

W E ARE LIVING in the Age of Information, and the assertion is often made that information is freedom. Yet, even as we give assent to these claims, we rarely pause to reflect on their meaning or their implications concerning natural reality and our capacity to comprehend the world in which we exist. Such an inquiry might allow us to discern an overarching process and purpose within the order of creation and thereby inform and enrich our spiritual quest.

The concepts of information and freedom are so familiar to us that they resist easy definition or description. While information is generally taken to imply objective factual data, it is immediately evident that the apprehension of information is itself a subjective capacity dependent on our ability to gather, analyze, and assimilate—to be in-formed and trans-formed in conformity with an underlying aspect of reality. Furthermore, to be of use in navigating and negotiating our way within the world, information must provide not just data, but the pattern of knowledge and the wider picture of understanding. Information is but the foundation for the fuller comprehension essential for spiritual formation—the deepest alignment with the source and significance of life.

Recognized in this way, freedom cannot be merely a result of information, but is an essential condition for its apprehension. We must be capable of discerning the dimensions and distinctions within the multiformed world, of selectively perceiving, evaluating, and comprehending the very character of the cosmos. Yet freedom is also an invitation, beckoning us onward to be further transformed in the direction of transcendence—toward a fuller freedom built on a more comprehensive understanding. It is in light of these capabilities (and callings) that we gain a greater appreciation of the crucial complexity and specificity of human embodiment as the essential "form of freedom." We are creatures capable of ascending to a knowledge of our Creator, open to be spiritually in-formed with the freedom of love—as the very "image of God."

The Evolutionary Ascent of Freedom

If we step back and look anew at the evolutionary process within which we have emerged, we are amazed at the majesty of its meaning. At every stage in both the phylogenetic process and the ontogenetic unfolding of the developing individual, there is an essential interplay, a flow of information drawing life into a richer freedom and fullness in response to the exigencies and opportunities within the order of Nature. The very principles and conditions of the physical world provide the powers and possibilities for the stable continuity and creative extensions of Nature's living forms.

Only certain combinations of chemicals with particular properties could have formed the first structural and functional elements necessary for the continuity of life. These few highly constrained specific molecular elements in turn became the foundation with which all further complexity had to develop in coordinated and complementary integration. Looking back over nearly four billion years of evolution, it is astonishing to realize that these early life forms set the platform for an absolutely extraordinary proliferation of possibilities and the emergence of increasing freedom, communication, and comprehending consciousness within the phenomenon of life.

At its most primary level, freedom within living Nature is prefigured as a widening range of possibilities in the service of continuity and constructive change. This pattern of increasing freedom (and the apprehension of information it allows) is manifest within a rising scale of complexity built on mutation, modulation, modular specialization, and the emergence of mind—culminating in the comprehensive consciousness of communal moral and spiritual awareness.

Whereas early life forms adapted through a multitude of variations produced by reproduction and mutation (changes in the coding sequence of DNA), more complex systems of adaptation soon evolved that allowed *individual* organisms to draw information from their environment and to adjust internally to changing conditions. Such individual freedom is first manifest as modulation of the timing or pattern of gene expression in direct response to chemical conditions and is already seen in single-cell life forms. A major advance in the ascent of freedom occurs with multicellularity and its possibilities for specialized cell functions and complementary division of labor. This modularization is further extended with body segmentation (head, thorax, and tail, etc.) and the independent developmental programs of specialized organs of awareness and action (and later, appetite, a felt sense of desire or need that motivates and governs these vital powers).

With the evolutionary emergence of brains nearly five hundred million years ago, more primary capacities of selective perception and locomotion were transcended by programs of integrated organismal response—innate reflex arcs of nerves and muscles triggered by external stimuli. This improved the coordination of information and action and allowed the extension of life into more varied and challenging environments. But, whereas the oceans had provided a more or less steady chemical context and constant temperature, the ascent to dry land required more complex self-regulation of water, pH, and temperature. This control of internal milieu, however, ensured the stability of chemical structures and reaction rates essential for the neurological basis of body representation, emotion, and memory. These capacities, in turn, provided the platform for a sense of inwardness, continuity of identity and self-awareness. From here forward, the evolutionary ascent toward the fullness of freedom would be about the emergence of mind and would culminate in the moral and spiritual awareness of the human person.

The Psychophysical Unity of the Human Person

To understand the emergence of mind within the evolutionary process, it is essential to recognize its role in the service of life, its crucial significance in matters of the body. Indeed, as neuroscientist Antonio Damasio has pointed out, "The mind had to be first about the body, or it could not have been."[1] Whatever abstractions and extensions of thought we may have, they are grounded and built on a capacity to comprehend in and through our bodily being and its dynamic of experience. It is here, with a deeper appreciation of the psychophysical unity of the human person, that we begin to see the full significance of our physical form.

The origins of mind may be understood as a further extension of the most fundamental principles of biology: continuity and constructive change. Brains emerged in response to the need for integrated organismal control of mechanisms to sustain and regulate stability of body states. These adaptations, crucial for continuity of physical identity, came to be under the control of complex neurological regulation through a system of body representations within the brain. Together with peripheral sensory awareness of the body surface and proprioceptive perception of the musculoskeletal dynamics of body position and balance, this inner awareness of bodily state became the basis for the sense of self. This web of self-awareness, like a map suspended in mental space, provides a constantly updated image of our state of being against which any perturbation or alteration can be compared. Damasio explains that the body, as represented in the brain, constitutes "the indispensable frame of reference for the neural processes that we experience as the mind; that our very organism rather than some absolute external reality is used as the ground reference for the constructions we make of the world around us and for the constructions of the ever-present sense of subjectivity that is part and parcel of our experience. . . ."[2] Precision and clarity in consciousness, and the coordination and application of memory across time and circumstance, are only possible because of the defined borders and the remarkably invariant reference of the "self" anchored in the body. Indeed, the body serves as a stable standard against which change can be measured.

The mind, then, is not an abstract neurologic function, but is an activity of the whole body. And we know the world not as a separate reality, but with reference to ourselves. The accurate apprehension and genuine acquisition of information allowed by the stable ground of the body make possible the crucial human capacity for adaptive self-transformation through learning. The detection and interpretation of an outside stimulus culminates in the in-forming of our physical body (through memory encoded as synaptic connections): its conformation to a wider consciousness of the nature of the world and the self within the world. This capacity for adaptive transformation through learning is the basis for both continuity of personal identity and the interpersonal and intergenerational transmission essential for culture.

The awareness and learning that the sensitive and responsive self make possible, however, are not the objective knowing of a dispassionate observer. The mind has been selectively shaped for perception and interpretation in accordance with its service to survival and the goals of life. George Lakoff and Mark Johnson, in *Philosophy in the Flesh*, explore the meaning of this "embodied mind" for its implications in individual consciousness and social communication. They argue that reason is not literal but metaphorical, that the very structures of our categories and concepts come from the nature of our bodily experience—the world as we know it by living in it. Time, for example, is understood by its representation through the movement through space. Likewise, we have evolutionarily selected perceptual categories such as color discrimination (allowing detection of ripe fruit) and enhanced discrimination at the acoustic boundaries between certain sounds (allowing spoken language). Grounded in these inherited patterns of categorization and conceptualization, we are endowed with a certain preferential perception that helps us organize our understanding of the world. These do not just represent useful analogies, but actual felt realities, conceptualized through a common grounding in bodily experience that in turn provides the foundations for genuine communication and community of mind.

The Synergy of Social Cooperation

All of these shared foundations of human existence, our particular evolved form of embodied being and the common challenges of a similar environment in which our lives are embedded, provide the crucial underpinnings of human social life and its cultural and moral meaning. It is here that we see most clearly the significance of the human form in the ascent to freedom and comprehensive understanding of the world.

Human beings are intrinsically social; our long period of childhood dependency ensures that social stimulation plays a formative role in the maturation of the mind. This intricate social interplay, especially between infant and mother, is built on a remarkable set of anatomic and physiologic adaptations—facial expressions, visual perception, and shared emotional responses—that make possible the unique human capacity for empathy, a genuine intersubjectivity of feeling. This grounding in intersubjectivity in turn supplies the patterning for personal identity and the platform for shared cultural awareness. From earliest childhood, there is an "attunement" between mother and child that provides the crucial lessons of pure social interaction, the ties of attachment and the nonverbal foundations on which language will later be built.

This primary grounding of communication and trust, based on shared biology, bridged by empathy, and built by personal interaction, provides the foundation for moral awareness and cultural community. The philosopher Charles Taylor writes, "The genesis of the human mind is . . . not 'monological,' not something each accomplishes on his or her own, but dialogical."[3] Within this common consciousness, and the shared capacity for language, we move beyond the imperatives of the present to the creative constructions of cultural meanings and values. Forging forward in a collective extension of mind, we explore our world within the counterpoint and corrective of a shared dialog, seeking a clarity of knowledge that penetrates to the core of the cosmic order.

The Peril of Freedom and the Meaning of "Spiritual Information"

We have traced the evolutionary outlines of the trajectory of ascent from the constraints of chemistry, to the contingency of passive response, to the active agency and self-determination of a creature of genuine freedom. At every step, the capacity to draw on the information accessible within the multiformed world was a crucial factor in the continuity and extension of living forms. Culminating in the collective consciousness and momentum of mind of our modern technological society, this combination of freedom and information has become at once a source of both promise and peril.

In our dominant and mastering position within the world, we sense ourselves above the flow of natural process, and, with our advancing biotechnology, we may come to see all of living Nature as mere matter and information to be reshuffled and reassigned for projects of the human will. Liberated from the basic struggles of survival, we are opened to imagination, to the ambitions of technological self-transformation that could shatter the fragile balance of our physical and psychological functioning, the fine-tuned freedom of our embodied being and its relational dynamics of meaningful existence.

Yet, within this rising scale of freedom and peril, we sense a significance in human life that mysteriously transcends the persuasions of our earthly appetites and ambitions. Self-aware and sensitive to others, we have awakened to a moral meaning that beckons beyond to a deeper spiritual wisdom, a more comprehensive consciousness of an overarching process and purpose within the phenomenon of life. We come to see all of the order of creation as an intelligible language for a drama of the deepest significance. Drawn forth in an evolutionary ascent, the constructive complementarity of an ever-more distilled sense of self set within a wider and richer relation with the world, we ascend from sensation to perception to knowledge, and then to the comprehensive understanding of spiritual information—the embodied conformation of spiritual formation, a participation in the very life of God, the fullness and flourishing of love.

Cradled and called forward within this mystery of time and space and material being, we are the "form of freedom": dust with a cosmic destiny. Like the emerging spiral of the Chambered Nautilus, we have been brought forth from nothing and opened to the infinity and eternity of being.

✒

WILLIAM B. HURLBUT, M.D., is a physician and lecturer in the Program in Human Biology at Stanford University. After receiving his undergraduate and medical training at Stanford, earning an M.D. in 1974, Dr. Hurlbut completed his postdoctoral studies in Theology and Medical Ethics, first studying under Robert Hamerton-Kelly. Dr. Hurlbut's main areas of interests involve the ethical issues associated with advancing technology and the integration of the philosophy of biology and Christian theology. Dr. Hurlbut has co-taught integrative courses at Stanford with Luca Cavelli-Sforza, Director of the Human Genome Diversity Project, and Nobel Prize–winner Baruch Blumberg. Dr. Hurlbut also works with the Center for Security and International Cooperation on a project formulating policy on Chemical and Biological Warfare and with NASA on projects in Astrobiology.

NOTES

1 From *Descartes' Error: Emotion, Reason, and the Human Brain,* New York: Grosset/Putnam, 1994, xvi.

2 Ibid.

3 Charles Taylor, *The Ethics of Authenticity,* Harvard University Press, Cambridge, 1992, 33.

PART SIX

Perspectives on Sociology and Ethics

EVOLUTION, CHRISTIANITY, AND THE DIALOG ON MORAL FREEDOM

Alain J-P. C. Tschudin

Presupposing that science and religion can engage in dialog, can such a conversation be informative and bear fruit in the future? As a Catholic Christian who studies social evolution and Christian ethics, I shall answer "yes," notwithstanding the challenge mounted by conflicts inherent in this debate. My interest lies in the dialog between Christian moral philosophy and the theory of Darwinian evolution, as first published in *On the Origin of Species* (1859). The information flow arising out of a shared understanding of knowledge from these disciplines may be mutually beneficial. By contextualizing Jesus within evolutionary history, I shall argue that evolutionary theory can inform the Christian conception of human nature in relation to the world and, equally, that Christian thinking can contribute to the ethics of scientific and secular engagements with the world. In particular, my aim in this essay is to focus on the issue of freedom as a bridge between evolutionary/biological and theological points of view. Despite continued confrontation between science and religion, I hope to negotiate some of the impasses in order to trace a path toward conflict resolution.

God, Creation, and the Evolution of Moral Freedom

It is well known that in the twentieth century Creationism impeded the improvement of relations between science and religion. Creationists (they are not yet extinct!) support a literalist reading of the biblical stories of creation presented in Genesis and thus hold that God created all species separately. Hence, according to this view, there is no genetic relatedness between species and no need to invoke evolution as an explanation for life on earth. The abundant evidence in support of natural selection makes any preoccupation with Creationism obsolete (see Ruse 2001). From Darwin onward, the theory of natural selection has, at least in the scientific community, radically undermined the notion of direct creation.

It is also interesting to note that the theory of natural selection has undermined another old myth—that life is an outcome of random physical processes. Natural selection involves a generic directionality in evolution. And this directionality involves selection for traits that increase the possibility of individual survival and reproduction, which are retained when they improve "fitness" between an organism and its prevailing environmental conditions.

Regarding the possibility of God, the theory of evolution necessarily remains agnostic in character. And rightly so, precisely because the theory, even if capable of describing the origins of the cosmos and of life, cannot state what underlies them. In this sense, science and theology typically deal with different domains and sets of specific questions. Thus, theistic evolution, the belief in a God who promotes such origins, does not conflict with evolutionary theory (Bowler 1989).

Some scientist-skeptics (Sober 1993) attempt to portray God post-creation as a passive, armchair observer of a universe characterized by laissez-faire. This is inadequate, if only because it represents only one possible view of God with scant consideration given to plausible alternatives. One alternative view is that God does not doze in an armchair after the act of creation ex nihilo. The very causal act of creating something from nothing can be interpreted to show that God is actively involved in all of creation. Such a suggestion is consistent with theories purporting to explain cosmic evolution from a single source, such as the Big Bang (Lemaitre, Hubble, Penzias, and Wilson).

St. Thomas Aquinas, for one, recognizes that through the act of creation the world and all its creatures are dependent on God. As a consequence of unbounded divine love, however, the world evolves in relative freedom according to the laws of nature. So Herbert McCabe (1987) can rightly observe that although creation is dependent on divine causation, human freedom of action does not contradict the nature or being of God.

Rather, from a Christian perspective, one might argue that human freedom allows for the image of the Creator—and for the intention of the creation—to be reflected. For Christians, therefore, such evolutionary freedom is qualified only by the divine hope for humanity and the rest of creation to be reconciled with God through love, not force. It follows that this reunion can only be effected autonomously through the exercise of freedom of choice (Rahner 1993), as is most explicitly exemplified in the person of Jesus of Nazareth.

This realization packs a mighty punch. If we were preprogrammed automatons, exactly where would our freedom lie? Freedom per se, in the sense of being created and existing, is absolute: *we are*, versus *we are not*. In another sense, however, freedom may be said to be relative, to evolve. This relates to the evolution of behavior within a broader social and physical environment and to the moral freedom to choose between behaviors and their consequences. Such freedom is monumentally significant for humans. To grasp this, some evolutionary context is necessary.

Darwin argued that natural selection operates to maximize individual fitness in a dynamic environment, but it was only following the heritability studies of Austrian monk Gregor Mendel that his theory was verified. Yet, Mendelian genetics represents only the beginning of the genetic "revolution." Most notoriously, Richard Dawkins, of *The Selfish Gene* fame, along with a cohort of other "selfish geneticists" and sociobiologists, has been accused of advancing a view of genetic determinism that undermines moral responsibility for behavior (see Rose 1978). Dawkins explains that determinism is equated with a "physical, materialistic basis" for action (1982:11).

It appears that the determinists do have a point. Many of the behaviors in the animal world are instinctual and are characterized by self-interest, which is necessary for self-preservation and propagation. Humans and other social animals seem to have originally clustered in groups because they provided increased fitness for individuals within the group (Humphrey 1976). Yet, as environmental resources are limited, group living leads to competition and to the evolution of "Machiavellian" intelligence or tactical deception (Byrne and Whiten 1988). The most successful individuals in a group are those who know when and with whom to compete and cooperate. One might also expect selection for improved "cheater" detection in social groups, and thus deception often results in conflict and aggression. Yet, if this scenario fully described group living, groups would rapidly fragment, with no apparent benefit from sociability.

Given that conflict and aggression do arise, something else must occur for social living to remain viable. This is the capacity to manage and resolve conflict through peacemaking or reconciliation. De Waal (1989) suggests that peacemaking is crucial to maintaining social cohesion in primate societies. Indeed, peacemaking is therefore integral to the evolution of extended cooperation in social animals. But we should resist the temptation to breathe a sigh of relief at how good-natured we animals are: The impetus behind such solidarity is individual self-interest.

In animal societies, reconciliation occurs selectively as a means-to-an-end strategy to elicit continued support and cooperation from others. Picture the alternative: Excluded from your community, you wander alone on the African plains, no friends to alert you to predators and none to help you forage for food; your predicament becomes clear: This is not a pleasant place to be. Although sociality in some species—humans, for example—has evolved from humble beginnings to the point where perspective-taking, empathy, and altruism frequently occur, much remains to be discovered about ourselves and other animals. But surely our elaborate human sociality transcends such basal, animalistic self-concern? Not so! As Ganya proclaims in Dostoevsky's *The Idiot*, "Why, the instinct of self-preservation is the normal law of humanity . . ." (1996:349).

Even Plato, in his *Symposium*, can be interpreted as writing on love from the perspective of self-interest. Kerr (1987) suggests that this love is characterized by the desire to possess and control others, who are substitutes for "absolute beauty" and are loved as a means to an end. Aristotle, recognizing the pitfalls of his teacher's doctrine, sought rather to promote a love based on intrinsic value for those of shared moral excellence. Although this shift is noteworthy, it still retains—through partiality—the possibility of loving in self-interest, precisely because for Aristotle such love was intended for one's equals. Similarly, in the Judaic tradition, where love was to be demonstrated for God and for neighbor (but not for all), the potential for partiality remained. Such love was seemingly as good as it got for humanity before an event that occurred two thousand years ago, an event that I shall argue has radically changed the course of evolution: the coming of Jesus of Nazareth.

Jesus of Nazareth and Evolutionary History

Given my choice of title and subject matter, I would like to introduce a concept for consideration: the placement of the historical figure of Jesus within the broader context of evolutionary history. This depiction of Jesus is intended to balance the scale with Teilhard de Chardin's "Cosmic Christ." Such a balance is envisaged by offsetting the conception of the revealed, continuous human nature of the man Jesus with the mystical, discontinuous, divine nature of the Christ, co-existent in the person of Jesus the Christ.

While I hope to develop this theme more fully in a forthcoming publication, let it suffice to say here that the concept of the Jesus of evolutionary history by no means implies an ongoing messianic unfolding, nor does it allow for a potential New Age distortion of Christian dogma. On the contrary, it affirms the singular Incarnation and confirms the teaching to the Romans (6:9–11) that Christ died to expiate sin, once and for all. Such a conceptualization is merely intended to broaden theological investigations of the meaning—and significance—of Jesus with regard to the process of evolution and to life on Earth.

Many terms have been developed to describe Jesus. Haight (1999), for example, describes him as the "symbol of God." Yet, what is symbolized? St. John's Gospel clearly portrays Jesus as the symbol of God's unbounded love for the world ("God so loved the world that . . ."). It is precisely this link of love that is of critical importance to our discussion. The reason for insisting on this emphasis is that Jesus, through selfless love, releases those confined to a world of determinism. And it is perhaps an appreciation of such love that "crusading" atheists are lacking, when they succumb (for a myriad of possible reasons, including deceit, egoism, fear, ignorance, pride, or vanity), to the self-centered blindness of nature.

The hallmark of Christian love is precisely that it is other-centered—freely given and shared with all, friends and enemies alike. Jesus thus represents a profound departure from his forebears when he comments, "If you love those who love you, what reward will you get? Are not even the tax collectors doing that? And if you greet only your brothers, what are you doing more than others? Do not even pagans do that?" (Matt 5:46–47).

Imagine the shock and contempt with which Greek and Jewish scholars alike would have viewed such radicalism. Yet, it is precisely in this *novel solidarity* that Jesus demonstrates the greatest contrast between himself and the world. He is with creation for creation's sake. By surrendering his life freely and willingly for the salvation of all, Jesus voluntarily empties himself of himself. The "reward" described by Jesus is thus clearly not of a worldly nature, but rather something to be regarded in the sense of spiritual salvation. In this sense, the Christian love for others cannot be construed as motivated by an evolutionary reward, and hence by "self-interest," precisely because it negates any worldly adaptive benefit otherwise gained.

This must be puzzling for the determinists, but perhaps some elaboration would be helpful. Insofar as Jesus shares our human nature, he has the possibility of exercising the moral freedom to choose between alternative behaviors that, in his case, hold extremely different consequences. Nonetheless, to stand for truth (which, according to Jesus's own reading, sets one free) and in good faith, Jesus voluntarily yields his life (John 10:18). In this instance, the truth demands what to most evolutionarily endowed humans would seem the ultimate penalty: loss of life. To Jesus, however, this represents the freedom to give the greatest gift: love (John 15:13). The exercise of moral freedom, based on unconditional love, is thus central to the Christian faith and pivotal for the role Christians play in bearing witness to the truth.

Unconditional Love and the Freedom to Share

Jesus encourages humanity to share: "Freely you have received, freely give" (Matt 10:8). But what are we called to give? In a world characterized by self-interest, Christians can give of themselves. The litmus test for Christians, individually and communally as the church, is whether we forego our own interests and live by "being-there-with-others" (Moltmann 1973). Through solidarity with "the poor," which combines the praxis of Pope John Paul II and the theology of liberation, Christians make their contribution to the world. It is thus in the Christian conception of solidarity that the contrast with its naturalistic counterpart, worldly solidarity, is most apparent. Whereas on the latter reading the strong can subordinate the weak into social cohesion, and so sustain injustice and poverty, this cannot be supported by Christian social teaching.

It follows that although Christians are not opposed to the world, they may be called to be so—not exclusively in times of injustice, but in the dilemmas of daily life in actions related to self, to others, and to the environment. Schillebeeckx (1979) commences his book *Jesus* with the story of a crippled man (Acts 3). From the Christian perspective, we are *all* represented by that crippled man with respect to limitations and inadequacies, and yet we are simultaneously empowered with the Christ-given capacity exercised by Peter to share in the healing and transformation of the world. By displaying solidarity with "the poor" (broadly defined), Christians harmonize well with other believers, humanists, and naturalists who actively pursue justice and peace. However, the bout with the world is not yet over, especially while Christians stand opposed to those generically known as "social Darwinists."

Darwin gets a rough deal, for these individuals are not promoters of Darwinian evolution, but rather are proponents of Spencer's philosophy that individuals act in self-interest and are rewarded with natural success. Hence, social Darwinists (who are not that social after all!) support a policy of laissez-faire in which the fittest individuals survive, and survive well—much to the detriment of the common good. In our current socioeconomic and political milieu, such self-interested individuals and collectives increasingly show themselves to be in opposition to the teaching of the Gospels. Indeed, the policies of social Darwinists de facto represent the antithesis of Christian solidarity. Locally and internationally, the difference between the powerful and powerless becomes more polarized and antagonized, leading many to fear much more than a boxing match and nothing short of apocalyptic doom. Lebedyev appears perhaps to summarize human nature when he says to Ganya, "Yes, sir, the law of self-destruction and the law of self-preservation are equally strong in humanity."

Yet, this need not necessarily be the case. During precarious times, when human self-interest could easily wreak havoc, Christians can share solidarity with the world and thereby provide a gift of hope in the knowledge that the coming of Jesus of Nazareth has changed the course of evolution. The Jesus of evolutionary history has provided an infusion of selfless love and defense of moral freedom that provides humanity with a chance to prove Lebedyev and others wrong.

Appropriately, perhaps, the greatest gift of all for humanity is to have the freedom to choose, in the words of St. Paul, between the old life and the new. The "spiritual information" provided by an intensified exchange between science and religion can serve to bring out the similarities and differences between these lives. This in turn may enhance the meaning and significance of personal and interpersonal life choices. I have attempted to demonstrate this in the current example by using the interplay of evolution and Christian philosophy to provide an evolutionary contextualization of Jesus. This is intended as an initial probe into the significance of the Christ event for the unfolding of moral freedom. The exchange of spiritual information is historically tidal, with its ebbs and flows; to prepare the way for the Lord in contemporary, pluralistic society, this dialog must be revised and renewed.

ALAIN J.-P. C. TSCHUDIN, PH.D., completed his doctoral studies on social evolution and comparative cognition in mammals through the School of Psychology, University of Natal, South Africa, and as a Commonwealth Scholar in the School of Biological Sciences, University of Liverpool. As part of his studies, he developed nonverbal tests of social intelligence for use with animals and humans. Following this, Dr. Tschudin held a Swiss Academy Research Fellowship at the University of Cambridge in the Departments of Experimental Psychology and Psychiatry. Currently, he is studying for a Ph.D. in Applied Christian Ethics at Cambridge in the Faculty of Divinity. Dr. Tschudin's recent works include a Master of Philosophy dissertation at Cambridge entitled "Social Evolution and Christian Ethics as Moral Freedom"; journal articles including "Comprehension of Signs by Dolphins" (*Journal of Comparative Psychology*, 115[1], 100–105) and "Mindreading Mammals?" (*Animal Welfare, 10:S119–127*); and a forthcoming book chapter, "Dumb Animals, Deaf Humans?" (in *Rational Animals?* edited by Susan Hurley and Matthew Nudds, Oxford University Press). Dr. Tschudin is a member of Corpus Christi College and fellow of the Cambridge Philosophical Society.

REFERENCES

Aristotle. (1976). *The ethics of Aristotle: the Nicomachean ethics.* London: Penguin.

Aquinas, T., St. (1970). *Summa Theologiae.* London: Blackfriars.

Bowler, P. J. (1989). *Evolution: the history of an idea.* Berkeley: University of California Press.

Byrne, R. W., and Whiten, A. (Eds). (1988). *Machiavellian Intelligence: social expertise and the evolution of intellect in monkeys, apes and humans.* Oxford: Oxford University Press.

Darwin, C. R. (1859). *On the origin of species by means of natural selection.* London: John Murray.

Dawkins, R. (1976). *The selfish gene.* New York: Oxford University Press.

———. (1982). *The extended phenotype: the gene as the unit of selection.* Oxford: Oxford University Press.

de Waal, F. B. M. (1989). *Peacemaking among primates.* London: Penguin.

Dostoevsky, F. (1996). *The Idiot.* Ware: Wordsworth.

Haight, R. (1999). *Jesus, symbol of God.* Maryknoll, NY: Orbis Books.

Humphrey, N. K. (1976). The social function of intellect. In (Bateson, P. P. G., and Kinde, R. A., Eds.) *Growing points in ethology.* Cambridge: Cambridge University Press.

Kerr, F. (1987). Charity as friendship. In (Davies, B., Ed.) *Language, meaning and God: essays in honour of Herbert McCabe.* London: Geoffrey Chapman.

McCabe, H. (1987). *God matters.* London: Geoffrey Chapman.

Moltmann, J. (1973). *Theology and joy.* (Translated by Ulrich, R.). London: SCM Press.

Plantinga, A. (1991). When faith and reason clash: evolution and the Bible. *Christian Scholar's Review,* 21(1): 8–32.

Plato. (1951). *The Symposium.* Harmondsworth: Penguin.

Rahner, K. (1993). *Foundations of Christian faith: an introduction to the idea of Christianity.* (Trans. Dych, W. V.). New York: Crossroad.

Rose, S. (1978). Pre-Copernican sociobiology? *New Scientist,* 80: 45–46.

Ruse, M. (2001). *Can a Darwinian Be a Christian: The relationship between science and religion.* Cambridge: Cambridge University Press.

Schillebeeckx, E. (1979). *Jesus: an experiment in Christology.* Collins: London.

Sober, E. (1993). *Philosophy of biology.* Oxford: Oxford University Press.

PLANETARY SPIRITUAL (IN)FORMATION 56

FROM BIOLOGICAL TO RELIGIOUS EVOLUTION

Holmes Rolston III

Decoding the human genome accentuated the cybernetic turn in biology—but, somewhat surprisingly, revealed fewer genes than we thought we had. The focus immediately shifted to cognitive psychology, to the cybernetic brain, with its neural genius for mental (or "spirited") experience. The ideational powers of the human mind, which has accumulated knowledge over the millennia of human culture, have vigorously intensified in, and been documented by, these recent, spectacular discoveries in the biomolecular and neural sciences. We earthy, embodied humans are better informed about our world and ourselves—and are more searchingly, more spiritedly self-conscious than ever before.

What next? The newspaper headlines confirm that, politically and ethically, we confront value questions as sharp and as painful as ever, advances in the sciences notwithstanding. Those who rejoice in (or fear) these advances in scientific information about where on Earth we came from, how we evolved, and who we are must also look ahead to what we will be.

We grow increasingly competent scientifically and technologically and simultaneously decreasingly confident about keeping life human/humane. The sciences may also claim to be value free and warn that there is no scientific guidance of life. Looming worries about ever-returning wars and ever-elusive peace, escalating populations, massive consumption of Earth's resources, poverty, unsustainable development, deteriorating environments, climate changes—these cut to the quick. Alternatively put, the planetary crisis for this new century—if not the millennium—calls for accelerated acquisition of spiritual (in)formation.

Earth and Its Information Explosion

Earth as seen from space was the stirring picture of the last century. But the simple global photograph belies a pervasive spectrum of escalating, increasingly complex information at multiple scales—from the global through the ecological and the organic to the molecular levels. We are now confronted with the escalating advances in information that first occurred in evolutionary natural history and are now exploding in cultural history.

Once it was thought that, in nature, there were two metaphysical fundamentals: matter and energy. The physicists reduced these two to one: matter-energy. The biologists afterward discovered that there were still two metaphysical fundamentals: matter-energy and information. At the start of the cybernetic age, Norbert

Wiener insisted, "Information is information, not matter or energy" (Wiener 1948, 155). George C. Williams cautions, "Evolutionary biologists have failed to realize that they work with two more or less incommensurable domains: that of information and that of matter.... The gene is a package of information" (in Brockman 1995, 43).

John Maynard Smith, dean of British theoretical biologists, says, "Heredity is about the transmission, not of matter or energy, but of information" (Maynard Smith 1995). The most spectacular thing about Earth, says Richard Dawkins, is this "information explosion," even more remarkable than a supernova among the stars (Dawkins 1995 145). The astronomical universe—so cosmologists have been noticing with their Anthropic Principle—must be *there*, about as it is, if we are to be *here*, about as we are. At a minimalist level, the surface of the moon, for example, contains information from which a geologist can passively read moon history.

Biological information, by contrast, is actively agential, self-actualizing. Only on Earth (so far as we yet know) can anything be learned. The first secret of animated life—genetic coding that enables coping in an environment—was revealed when we unlocked the genome. The essential characteristic of a biological molecule, contrasted with a merely physicochemical one, is that it contains vital information. In this light, genetic natural history is actually a search program for increasing information, transmitted from one generation to the next, reticulated and variegated sexually, increasing adaptive fit. This is a most impressive result: If the DNA in the myriad cells of the human body were uncoiled and stretched out end to end, that microscopically slender thread would reach to the sun and back over a half dozen times.

The Mind and Its Information Explosion

Yes, but we just found out that we humans don't have as many genes as we thought. That doesn't mean, however, that we have less intelligence than we once believed; rather, it means that the secret of our capacity for processing advanced information lies somewhere else, made possible by genetic flexibility that opened up our cerebral capacity.

Generally, in body structures such as the blood or liver, humans and chimpanzees are 95 percent to 98 percent identical in their genomic DNA sequences and the resulting proteins. But this is not true in their brains. "Changes in protein and gene expression have been particularly pronounced in the human brain. Striking differences exist in morphology and cognitive abilities between humans and their closest evolutionary relatives, the chimpanzees." So concluded a team of molecular biologists and evolutionary anthropologists from the Max-Planck Institutes in Germany (Enard et al. 2002).

Cognitive development has come to a striking expression point in the hominid line(s) leading to *Homo sapiens*, growing from about three hundred to about fourteen hundred cubic centimeters of cranial capacity in a few million years. E. O. Wilson, Harvard sociobiologist, emphasizes, "No organ in the history of life has grown faster" (E.O. Wilson 1978, 87). This line seems "headed for more head," so to speak.

An information explosion gets pinpointed in humans, an event otherwise unknown, but undoubtedly present in the human brain.

Animal brains are already impressive. In a cubic millimeter (about a pinhead) of mouse cortex are an estimated 450 meters of dendrites and one to two kilometers of axons; each neuron can synapse on thousands of others. The human brain, with a cortex three thousand times larger than that of the mouse, is of such complexity that descriptive numbers are astronomical and difficult to fathom. A typical estimate is 10^{12} neurons, each with several thousand synapses (possibly tens of thousands), in a flexible neural network that is more complex by far than anything else known in the universe. This network can be formed and re-formed, making possible virtually endless mental activity (Braitenberg and Schüz 1998). The result of such combinatorial explosion is that we have more possible thoughts than there are atoms in the universe. Compare how many sentences can be composed rearranging the twenty-six letters of the English alphabet.

What is really "exciting"—using that word in both the "agitated" and "provocative" senses—is that human consciousness is now "spirited," an ego with felt, psychological inwardness. Molecules, trillions of them, spin round in this astronomically complex webwork and generate the unified, centrally focused experience of mind, a process for which we can as yet scarcely imagine a theory. The self-actualizing, self-organizing process (autopoiesis) doubles back on itself in this reflexive animal, with the qualitative emergence of what the Germans call "Geist" and existentialists call "Existenz." "Conscious" has the root meaning: "I know." An object, the brain-controlled body, becomes a spirited subject.

This brain is as open as it is wired up. The self we become is registered by its synaptic configurations, which is to say that the information from personal experience, both explicit and implicit, goes to pattern the brain. Informed mind, or spirited experience, reconfigures brain processes, and there are no known limits to this flexibility and interactivity (LeDoux 2002).

Culturally (In)forming the Human Spirit

Earth seen from space reveals no apparent culture, but on the ground, culture is as evident as nature. Animals can undoubtedly intend to alter or imitate other animals' behaviors, but there is little evidence that they have "a concept of mind" or that they can recognize the presence or absence of ideas in other animals from whom they may learn or whom they might teach. Dorothy L. Cheney and Robert M. Seyfarth conclude, "It is far from clear whether any nonhuman primates ever communicate with the intent to inform in the sense that they recognize that they have information that others do not possess" (Cheney and Seyfarth 1990, 209). If a monkey doesn't see it (or smell or hear it), a monkey doesn't know it.

What is missing is precisely what makes human cumulative transmissible culture possible. The central idea is that acquired knowledge and behavior are learned and transmitted from person to person by one generation teaching another, ideas passing from mind to mind, existential human spirits forming and reforming each other with their shared notions.

Humans come into the world by nature unfinished, if also with unlimited possibilities for education. A newborn is information waiting to happen. Persons live, move, and have their being in their communities, and this generates language, conversation, cooperation, conflict, negotiation, criticism, evaluation. The determinants of events are anthropological, political, economic, technological, scientific, philosophical, ethical, religious. Ideas are as determinative as forces or fields or metabolisms or genetics.

The *Homo sapien* is the only part of the world free to orient itself with a view of the whole. That makes us, if you like, free spirits; it also makes us social spirits. Spirits interact with fellow spirits, person-to-person; these "political animals" (Aristotle) build their historically ongoing cultures. Richard Lewontin, another Harvard biologist, emphasizes the social over the biological: "The genes, in making possible the development of human consciousness . . . have been replaced by an entirely new level of causation, that of social interaction with its own laws and its own nature" (Lewontin 1991, 123).

This information explosion, says Richard Dawkins (1989), is powered by social "memes" rather than by biological genes. Information transfer in culture can be several orders of magnitude faster and overleap genetic lines. The informing is deliberate, critical. This recompounds again the combinatorial cybernetic explosion.

Forming and Informing Ethics

Cooperators need ethics—at least cultured free spirits in critically reflective communities do. The self-conscious need conscience. Yet reflection about charity, justice, and honesty are not virtues found in wild nature. No natural decalogue endorses the Ten Commandments.

It is not difficult to see how a first-level "ethics" is generated: Reciprocators can help each other out to their mutual benefit. This already exists in animal societies. Political scientists, psychologists, and biologists have discovered that reciprocity can arise and be maintained within communities of those who seek their enlightened self-interest, with the caution that such cooperation has to be protected against "free riders" or "cheaters." Scientists have created computer models of this, such as the "tit-for-tat" strategy and its variants (Axelrod and Hamilton 1981). But have we yet found or formed actual ethics?

Tribes with more cooperators do well against tribes with fewer cooperators. Lately, group selection, long disfavored in biology, has reappeared, especially in human affairs. Those communities prosper where the members have "motivational pluralism": "Natural selection is unlikely to have given us purely egoistic motives" (Sober and Wilson 1998, 12, 323). This produces altruism blended with enlightened self-interest—the patriot going into battle to save others, the Rotarians building their community spirit, the Presbyterians loving both self and neighbor. But, except for international reciprocity, we still have nothing informing a global picture of ethical cooperation.

In the global village, tribalism, even if altruistic, is the problem rather than the answer because we have not surpassed group competition. Sober and Wilson can find no "universal benevolence. Group selection does provide a setting in which helping behavior directed at members of one's own group can evolve; however, it equally provides a context in which hurting individuals in other groups can be selectively advantageous. Group selection favors within group niceness *and* between group nastiness" (Sober and Wilson 1998, 9). Can we find a more inclusively spirited ethic?

The Promise of Spiritual (In)formation

Donald T. Campbell offers a more promising account. Animals are selected to conserve values under the regimes of nature, where genetic inheritance is virtually the sole means of transmitting information across generations. The requirements of humans in their transmissible cultures differ. To elevate prehumans to humans, morality arose, almost always religion-based. Morality moves humans away from their merely genetic instincts toward more appropriate cultural behavior. "Social evolution has had to counter individual selfish tendencies which biological evolution has continued to select as a result of the genetic competition among the cooperators" (Campbell 1975).

Those religions best succeed that most help humans pull away from their genetic instincts toward the biosocial optimum in culture, although this too often remains in-group—the gods are for us and our children (D. S. Wilson 2002). Even the best religions are not so successful as would be ideal because of the counterproductive tugging of the animal legacy of self-interests. But major world faiths nevertheless are globally inclusive. They preach not just tribal, but universal, altruism.

The religions, preaching altruism, (in)form us spiritually and make culture possible. Without them, we are beasts. There is nothing shameful about a beast being a beast; but a human "spirit" ought to be something more. In the behavior that religions exhort, stretching humans away from our lingering ancestral genetic dispositions, the world religions are right. What begins as the beast in us becomes also the brokenness in us. The information preached needs to inform our personal regeneration, as well as enable us to regenerate offspring. Redemption and salvation empower this ethics, although the saints have often been wary about thinking of this as human achievement; it is also the gift of grace.

Such religiously inspired altruism is progressively less tightly coupled to the genes, whether individually or tribally. Disciples need not have the genes of the prophets, seers, and saviors who launched these teachings. In successful world religions, they seldom have. Nor need they be in the same tribe or local group. People do better with genes plastic enough to follow the best religion, whether their kith or kin launched it or not. In faith universalized, there is no longer any differential survival benefit to me or my tribe; the benefit is open to all.

Spiritual formation may once have been tribal, but today it must be increasingly planetary, ecumenical—becoming spiritual "in-formation." Religions will be tested for their capacity to educate us, and the best ones will survive. So much for the complaint that religion is of no earthly use. Or for the fear that theology will be more and more displaced by science. Or economics. Or politics. Quite the contrary.

On Earth, we humans increasingly need increased spiritual "in-formation" if we are globally to survive as a species, if (as biologists might put it) we are able to adapt as "fits" on the planet.

Christians can plausibly make the claim that no harmony between humans in their nation-states, or between humans and their landscapes (or planet), can be gained until persons learn to use the Earth both justly and charitably. Those twin concepts are not found either in wild nature or in any science that studies nature. They must be grounded in some ethical authority, and this has classically been religious. The Hebrews, for instance, were convinced that they were given a blessing with a mandate. The land flows with milk and honey, if and only if there is obedience to Torah.

We are living on Earth; the spiritual formation required must be of earthly use and globally inclusive. Religions must think globally while they act locally. Beyond that, it does not follow that nothing universally true can appear in human morality because it emerges while humans are in residence on Earth. Keep promises. Tell the truth. Do not steal. Respect property. There is nothing particularly "earthbound" about: Do to others as you would have them do to you. Love your enemies. Do good to those who hate you. Such commandments may be imperatives wherever there are moral agents living in a culture that has been elevated above natural selection. We humans can therefore also hope that there is extraterrestrial love, justice, and freedom.

Perhaps, after all, this primate rising from the dust of the Earth, on becoming so remarkably spiritually informed, bears the image of God.

✒

HOLMES ROLSTON III, PH.D., is University Distinguished Professor and Professor of Philosophy at Colorado State University. He is Past and Founding President of the International Society for Environmental Ethics and a founding editor of the journal *Environmental Ethics*. He has served on the editorial board of *Zygon* for two decades. Professor Rolston also is a founding member of the International Society for Science and Religion. He has written seven books and is featured in *Fifty Key Thinkers on the Environment* (2000). A distinguished international lecturer, Professor Rolston spoke at the World Congress of Philosophy, Moscow, 1993, and again in Boston, 1998. He participated by invitation in preconferences and the United Nations Conference on Environment and Development in Rio de Janeiro, 1992, where he was an official observer. Professor Rolston was the recipient of the 2003 Templeton Prize.

REFERENCES

Axelrod, Robert, and William D. Hamilton, "The Evolution of Cooperation," *Science* 211 (27 March 1981): 1390–96.

Braitenberg, Valentino, and Almut Schüz, 1998. *Cortex: Statistics and Geometry of Neuronal Connectivity*, New York: Springer.

Brockman, John, 1995. *The Third Culture*, New York: Simon and Schuster.

Campbell, Donald T., 1975. "On the Conflicts Between Biological and Social Evolution and Between Psychology and Moral Tradition," *American Psychologist* 30: 1103–26.

Cheney, Dorothy L., and Robert M. Seyfarth, 1990. *How Monkeys See the World*, Chicago: University of Chicago Press.

Dawkins, Richard, 1989. *The Selfish Gene*, Oxford: Oxford University Press.

———. 1995. *River out of Eden*, New York: Basic Books, 1995.

Enard, Wolfgang, et al., 2002. "Intra-and Interspecific Variation in Primate Gene Expression Patterns," *Science* 296 (12 April): 340–43.

LeDoux, Joseph, 2002. *Synaptic Self: How Our Brains Become Who We Are*, New York: Viking.

Lewontin, Richard, 1991. *Biology as Ideology*, San Francisco: HarperCollins.

Maynard Smith, John, 1995. "Life at the Edge of Chaos?" *New York Review of Books*, March 2.

Sober, Elliott, and David Sloan Wilson, 1998. *Unto Others*, Cambridge, MA: Harvard University Press.

Wiener, Norbert, 1948. *Cybernetics*, New York: John Wiley.

Wilson, David Sloan, 2002. *Darwin's Cathedral*, Chicago: University of Chicago Press.

Wilson, E. O., 1978. *On Human Nature*, Cambridge, MA: Harvard University Press.

Is There a Place for "Scientific" Studies of Religion? 57

Robert Wuthnow

Recently, numerous calls have gone out for a better understanding of religion. Of course, many of those were heard after September 11, 2001, when it became clear how little most Americans know of Islam and how much misunderstanding exists between Muslims, Christians, Jews, Hindus, and Buddhists. But even before the terrorist attacks, the Bush administration's efforts to promote faith-based service organizations challenged scholars to consider religion and its continuing place in American life. The volatile border between religion and citizenship saw rhetorical skirmishes again over a court ruling on the mention of God in the Pledge of Allegiance.

Few would doubt that religious studies, theology, history, and even *belles-lettres* have much to offer in providing relevant information about religion and spirituality. A student interested in learning about Islam would do well to read the Koran and study the history of Muslim teachings. That student would also benefit from knowing something about the societies in which Islam is prominently located today. A good intellectual background for thinking about faith-based social services would require an understanding of religious teachings on charity and the history of religion's place in serving the common good. Some first-hand observations, perhaps vividly communicated by journalists, of soup kitchens and homeless shelters would prove useful as well.

But is there a place for scientific studies of religion? That is a harder question. Isn't it a mismatch to impose scientific methods on religion? Haven't hermeneutics and phenomenology taught us to be skeptical of science? And, for that matter, what do we mean by "science"? I thought about these questions recently when I asked a graduate student whether she thought of her research on Native American religion as scientific. Taken aback, she replied, "Well, no, it's just religious studies; definitely not science." She said science smacked of positivism, which, by all means, she wanted to avoid.

I'd like to be counted among those who see a place for a scientific approach toward the study of religion. However, in that context, I think we need to interpret the word "scientific" broadly.

In the now-famous Gifford lectures that he delivered one hundred years ago, William James remarked, "I do not see why a critical Science of Religions might not eventually command as general a public adhesion as is commanded by a physical science." James had in mind that a science of this kind could do better at shedding light on religion than could philosophy. The trouble with philosophy, he said, was that it "lives in words" and thus fails to capture the depth, motion, and vitality of religion. Science could do that. Properly conceived, it would focus on the facts of religion, employing induction and deriving knowledge from the concreteness of spiritual experience. James gave few examples of what he had in mind, but I imagine he might have been intrigued by studies of prayer, religious experience, and healing.

History has been kind to James, but not to his point regarding a "Science of Religions." As generations of students tackle James's *The Varieties of Religious Experience*,[1] they discover in its pages interesting anecdotes about the saints and timeless musings about the differences between healthy-mindedness and the sick soul. But they seldom come away inspired by the idea of applying science to religion. The reasons are not hard to find. Human behavior has proven more complex than early advocates of the human sciences imagined. Positivism has given up ground in the face of arguments about the inevitability of interpretation and perspective. The brave new world promised by science has turned out still to be dominated by war and injustice as much as by technological progress. If the choice C. P. Snow offered between two cultures—one scientific and one humanistic—has to be made, the spiritually inclined will reasonably opt for keeping religion in the realm of values and meaning, rather than reducing it to the dry world of scientific investigation.

In his book *Theology and Social Theory: Beyond Secular Reason*, John Milbank, a professor of religious studies at the University of Virginia, wrote a powerful critique of the scientific impulse in the study of human behavior.[2] Standing James's view on its head, Milbank argues that the human sciences are not about knowledge at all, but about power. It is a grab for dominance in discussions of values. It works only by creating an illusion of objectivity and by eliminating from consideration all that does not fit that illusion. If Milbank is right, it certainly makes more sense for people interested in religion to side with theology than to run amuck in the social sciences.

Milbank's criticisms may be overly harsh, for the assumptions he attributes to social scientists scarcely resonate with how practicing social scientists actually think. In my experience, at least, social scientists usually make no pretense of explaining all of human nature, only a piece of it. And they are far less interested in metaphysical assumptions than Milbank suggests.

Yet the application of science to religion may still be judged folly because of the narrowness of the questions it seems able to explore. Take, for instance, the current interest in whether brain-imaging research, such as that of the Princeton psychologist Jonathan Cohen, can identify spots in the brain that "light up" when people make decisions about whether actions are morally correct. Or in brain activity when people show kindness to their neighbors, make love, or pray. While interesting as a description of neurological processes, such research fails to tell us much about which moral decisions are right, how kindness affects social relations, the meaning of love, or why people pray.

In my own discipline, sociologists have, in recent years, been quite attracted to a theoretical perspective, advanced by such prominent scholars as University of Washington sociologist Rodney Stark and Pennsylvania State University sociologist Roger Finke. This perspective helps make sense of such widely varying religious phenomena as the growth of Methodism in nineteenth-century America, the late-twentieth-century decline of mainstream Protestantism, the spread of early Christianity, and the superiority of monotheism among world religions. The argument, as I understand it, is that people make rational choices about religion, much as they do about buying cars (well, maybe not cars), and thus choose religions that give them the most gratification (such as certainty about their fate in the world to come).

Elegant in its simplicity, this is nevertheless an argument that, in the manner of science, cannot be easily proven or disproven. It is perhaps better to think of this perspective as an effort to bring sociological insights to bear on historical interpretation than as an application of scientific method.

But if there are reasons to be skeptical about science in the study of religion, there are also reasons to make the most of what science has to offer. Science teaches us the value of empirical rigor and the need for systematic investigation. The scientific method involves thinking of ways in which our cherished assumptions about the world may prove to be wrong. It involves the strategic use of rationality, not in the interest of doing away with all that is not rational (any more than the legal system is meant to replace literature and music), but to have reasons for conducting our research in one way rather than another. Science also involves the criterion of replicability, and that means candidly disclosing what we have done so others can track our mistakes.

Those aspects of science can be followed without claiming to find universal laws of human behavior, and they can be employed in the study of religion without "explaining away" the topic of inquiry. The more scholars have applied scientific methods to the study of human behavior, the more they have learned that human behavior is indeed contextual and contingent and that its meanings must be examined from multiple perspectives. Recent American Sociological Association President Alejandro Portes's critique of simplistic models of economic and political development illuminated that gap.[3]

Science is no longer regarded by social scientists, as it was by the early positivists, as the grand search for great truths. Indeed, there has been a remarkable shift in how social scientists think about the role of science in their work over the past half-century. With little empirical evidence in the past, science seemed an attractive beacon; but as empirical evidence accumulated, the hope of making sweeping generalizations about the human condition faded. In the study of religion, for example, scholars a half-century ago offered grand generalizations about its social functions, about its attractions to the dispossessed, and about the universality of religious experience. Today, all of those generalizations have been qualified.

For some, of course, "scientific method" suggests research that employs numbers. The phrase calls to mind the numerous polls and surveys we read about that include questions on religion—for instance, polls by the Gallup Organization in Princeton that followed Americans' attendance at religious services after the 2001 terrorist attacks.[4] By employing rigorous methods of sampling, such surveys tell us about beliefs and behavior in ways that we would not be able to know from our limited personal experience. Among sociologists, the General Social Survey, conducted nationally by the University of Chicago every two years since 1972, has provided an impressive stock of information from which to draw conclusions about trends in religious beliefs, practice, and affiliation.

But scientific method can equally pertain to studies involving qualitative information drawn from participant observation, interviews, and archival materials. Carefully sifting through letters and diaries in an archive, or through artifacts at an archeological dig, is every bit as much science as computing regression equations or life-expectancy tables. For example, recent archeological studies, such as those of the forensic anthropologist Douglas Owsley of the Smithsonian Institution, are providing new insights into the lives and cultures of the first human inhabitants of the Pacific Northwest. If science is understood in this broader way, then we can identify more clearly some of the challenges in which it may usefully be employed.

One of the greatest challenges is understanding more clearly the vast diversity that characterizes our own religious culture and that of the wider world. We are once again, just as we were a century ago, a nation populated by a large number of recent immigrants from a wide array of ethnic and religious backgrounds. For the first time, the United States includes a sizable minority of its population who practice religions other than Christianity or Judaism (some estimates range as high as ten million, when Muslims, Buddhists, and Hindus are included). The role of scientific studies should not be, in the first instance, to discover what is common among the various religious traditions, but to understand what is different and to gauge reactions to those differences. That task is especially important because of conflicts among religious traditions, on the one hand, and because of the superficial assumptions that one still encounters among naive observers that "all religions are the same."

To their credit, social scientists who study religion today are much more likely to insist on in-depth analysis of specific traditions than to settle for superficial generalizations. Investigations of Buddhism, Judaism, Islam, Hinduism, and Christianity have all moved in this direction, paying closer attention to distinct practices and illuminating the internal diversity of each tradition. For instance, in the series of books on religious practices being edited by the University of Michigan Buddhism scholar Donald Lopez, the emphasis has shifted decidedly toward the variability of lived religious experience and away from seeking grand generalizations.

In sociology, the concern for detail is evident in in-depth studies of the beliefs and practices of new immigrant religious communities. In Houston, Los Angeles, New York, Chicago, Miami, and several other cities, research is now being conducted on how such communities are adapting religiously and culturally to their urban environments. For instance, University of Houston sociologists Helen Rose Ebaugh and Janet Saltzman Chafetz have edited an illuminating collection of essays that describe in detail how Asian Christians, Hispanic Christians, Hindus, and other groups are coming to terms with life in suburban Houston.[5]

To be sure, the boundary here between social science and investigative journalism is sometimes blurred. But scholars have opportunities that journalists don't, both in asking questions about topics that may not be newsworthy and in taking the months and years that may be required to conduct in-depth research. I think especially of the book *Terror in the Mind of God* by Mark Juergensmeyer,[6] a sociologist at the University of California at Santa Barbara. It is a masterful study of the relationship between religion and violence that became an instant sensation after September 11, 2001, but which was based on nearly a decade of research with accused and convicted terrorists, survivalists, and vigilante groups.

Another challenge is to harness the vast resources currently available to scholars interested in religion (especially from private foundations, and from colleges and universities) for studies having strong normative concerns. I've worked for many years with students in various disciplines who are interested in religion. My biggest complaint about these students isn't that their studies lack rigor, but that they lack purpose. All too often studies are initiated because data are there, or because nobody has looked at a particular topic before, rather than because the research explores a larger concern. That is the fault of faculty members more than of students. We have done a better job teaching methods than we have of instilling purpose.

We need studies that investigate more pointedly the great human concerns that redound in special ways to each generation, whether those are framed in terms of such problems as violence and injustice or in the language of virtue and hope. Certainly, the possible connections between terrorism and particular interpretations of religious teachings have come to be of concern, as the response to Juergensmeyer's research shows. Recent research examining the role of religion in encouraging forgiveness, or in promoting acts of unconditional love, also fits the bill.[7]

If the study of religion were more consistently deliberate in bringing together the realm of facts with the world of values, then it would be harder to imagine where the objections to scientific studies would lie. Of course, humanistically oriented scholars and many in the social sciences would probably be put off by studies seeking to reduce religious impulses to hard-wired biological or economic concerns. But such studies differ from the looser and more practical ways in which most social scientists currently approach scholarship on religion.

It is in relating fact and values that scientific studies of religion can illuminate issues such as Islamist terrorist attacks or the relative merits of faith-based service organizations. Besides reading religious texts, students should explore research on Americans' responses to September 11, examining the roots of religious prejudice or the extent of contact between Christians and Muslims. Beyond discussing the separation between church and state, students should do more, as exemplified by the work of the University of Pennsylvania sociologist Byron Johnson, or the team of scholars at the State University of New York at Albany under the direction of Richard Nathan, to compare the effectiveness of faith-based and nonsectarian service organizations.

There is also a continuing role for the kind of science that William James had in mind if we consider a point that is often neglected in discussions of his argument. James recognized that we have a natural tendency to concentrate on the "local" and the "accidental" and that these should be the starting point for any scientific inquiries. In the same spirit as James, Clifford Geertz has observed that "local knowledge" is of particular value, both in daily life and to the enterprise of the human sciences. We know ourselves only by comparing the locale in which we live with the locales in which we do not. This quest for comparison and generalization probably inspired the first generations of social scientists. In the process of comparative investigation, the familiar does not become general; it becomes strange, and thus is experienced in new ways.

Scientific studies of religion need to be guided both by hubris (to venture hypotheses at all) and humility (to acknowledge when they are wrong). William James said it well:

> The science of religions would forever have to confess, as every science confesses, that the subtlety of nature flies beyond it, and that its formulas are but approximations.

Those approximations, nevertheless, are valuable guides to understanding what it means to be human. And properly conceived, scientific studies of religion can contribute significantly to those approximations.

✐

ROBERT WUTHNOW, PH.D., received his doctorate from the University of California, Berkeley. He currently is Professor of Sociology of Religion and Cultural Sociology, Center for the Study of Religion, Princeton University. Professor Wuthnow specializes in the use of both qualitative and quantitative (historical and ethnographic) research methods. He is the author of many works, including *The Crisis in the Churches: Spiritual Malaise, Fiscal Woe* (1997), *Poor Richard's Principle: Recovering the American Dream through the Moral Dimension of Work, Business, and Money* (1996), and *Meaning and Moral Order: Explorations in Cultural Analysis* (1987). Professor Wuthnow's recent books include *After Heaven: Spirituality in America Since the 1950s* (1998) and *Loose Connections: Joining Together in America's Fragmented Communities* (1998). He has also edited the recent *Encyclopedia of Politics and Religion* (2000). Currently, Professor Wuthnow is directing a Lilly-funded project on The Public Role of Mainline Protestantism in America since the 1960s.

NOTES

1 William James. *The Varieties of Religious Experience.* Longmans, Green and Co., 1902.

2 John Milbank. *Theology and Social Theory: Beyond Secular Reason.* Blackwell, 1990.

3 Alejandro Portes. "The Hidden Abode: Sociology as Analysis of the Unexpected." *American Sociological Review,* February 2000.

4 Note that George H. Gallup Jr. contributed an essay to this volume.

5 Helen Rose Ebaugh and Janet Saltzman Chafetz, eds. *Religion and the New Immigrants.* AltaMira Press, 2000.

6 Mark Juergensmeyer. *Terror in the Mind of God.* University of California Press, 2000.

7 See, for example, the essays by Stephen G. Post and Everett L. Worthington Jr. in this volume.

Sociology and Spiritual Information 58

Challenging "Obvious" Opinions

David A. Martin

How might sociology help in the quest for spiritual information, pursued throughout a lifetime of commitment by Sir John Templeton?

One of the unexpected uses of sociology is to puncture the social illusions of the secularist intelligentsia—in particular, misconceptions about the social role of religion and assumptions about the inevitability of secularization. When it comes to the relation of religion to society, a sector of the educated public—including scientists otherwise concerned to promote scientific thinking—assumes unlimited license to air unsupported opinion. Once off their own patch, such people take for granted what they ought critically to examine. Although science notoriously subverts the obvious, in matters of religion the obvious reigns supreme.

In what follows, I take two standard opinions, one to the effect that religion causes war, and the other proclaiming that religion is in terminal decline. Of course, these opinions seem obvious because neither is a straightforward mistake. Anyone who believes religion causes war just points to Ulster or the Middle East or to the "wars of religion" from (say) 1520 to 1648. Anyone who holds that religion is going down before the linked advance of science and secularization points to the evident contrast between the "ages of faith" and the science-based societies of today. After all, in Europe most of the indices of belief and practice point downward, and even where belief exists it is no longer held in the old way. Some observers point to circumstances, such as the undermining of ancient establishments, that may render Europe exceptional in its religious apathy; but there are others for whom Europe previews the future.

One oddity of standard opinion on these matters is that were people to pause even for a moment they would come up with some of the counter-evidence. They would recognize, for example, that in Ulster religion dovetails into historic disparities of power and memories of ethnic displacement. So merely pointing to the conflict is simple-minded, indeed a refusal to think sociologically. Equally they know that the science-based United States is at one and the same time the most advanced and most religious of modern societies. Yet people do not follow through what they know. In the case of the evident religiosity of the United States, they deal with the anomaly by dismissing American society as in this respect "artificially retarded." Nor do they ask why skepticism is more evident in some of the humanities and the "soft" sciences than the "hard" sciences. Counter-evidence is not allowed to undermine the dominant paradigm.

We need to examine, therefore, why it is that we dismiss counter-evidence we know perfectly well. Could it be that opinions in this matter derive not so much from observation as from "faculty club culture" and an ideological take on progress going back to the Enlightenment? Too many of us are willing prisoners of comprehensive views arising out of the long conflict over claims to real knowledge between enlightened modernizing elites and their opponents. According to the enlightened, truth, secularity, and tolerance have been ever pitted against superstition, fanaticism, and violence, and as truth is great and will prevail, secularization follows. Paradoxically, this position has the character of faith: What ought to be so, will be so.

Suppose, however, that we systematically doubt the obvious and critically examine our two standard opinions: that religion causes war and that it is in terminal decline. Maybe this will not yield spiritual information precisely, but we will in this way gain understanding about how spiritual aspirations and the templates of faith and hope mesh with the historical sequence of social structures and with the particular structures arising in modernity. We can inform ourselves about the ways "the spirit" enters into and is deflected by social relationships. In that way, we allow understanding of why religious hope is frustrated and constrained by social structures to replace condemnation.

As to our first statement that "religion causes war," this is about as vacuous as saying that "politics causes violence" or "ethnic solidarity gives rise to conflict." The simple truth is that group struggles for power, dominance, and resources—or for survival—are endemic, while in any given conflict the factors are multiple, varied, and intertwined. There is a complicated interplay of symbolic triggers, presenting symptoms, overt justifications, and underlying causes.

If we start with the two most devastating wars in human history that deluged our modern world in the last century, neither had much to do with religion. These were secular wars of nations and ideologies, even though religious reasons were put forward for sacrifice in battle. For that matter, the protests against war throughout the modern period from the time of the first Peace Societies in 1816 onward owed much to religious motivation.

World War I derived from alliances and arms races to counter the potential economic and political domination of the European heartland by Germany, and the ideological aspects were framed in terms of civilization against barbarism and German Idealism against French skepticism. The origins of World War II lay partly in the political dispositions following Allied victory in the First World War, as well as the Great Depression, but there was also the great clash of purely secular ideologies in the mighty triangle of liberalism, communism, and fascism.

Even in much earlier conflicts where religious aspects were more to the fore, you have to ask how far religion dovetailed with ethnicity or was identified by rulers with established power under threat or with imperial and cultural expansion and dynastic rivalries. What was the role of the pursuit of booty or economic resources or the eruptions of peoples? Just these questions have also to be asked about the century or so of the "wars of religion." To give one example, one has to inquire about the political and economic opportunities perceived by German Protestant rulers over against the Holy Roman Empire. After all, the incidence of wars both before and after this period was roughly the same. And so far as the early modern period goes, emergent nationalism was a perfectly adequate *casus belli*, even where nationalism promoted itself in religious terms, as it was prone to do when subject nations such as Poland defended their cultural survival. Britain provides a clear instance of an imperial nation promoting itself behind the idea of a freedom-loving Protestant people.

Such questions press us to pursue the more profound issue of the way ideas and images, whether religious or secular, are absorbed into the social practices and power structures of very different kinds of society—feudal, mercantile, industrial, or whatever. What would you expect a feudal society based on knightly service to make of the Sermon on the Mount? Not much, perhaps, but you would need to look into the role of Christ's body as a governing metaphor of social membership and at the origins of "courtesy" and Chaucer's "parfit gentil knight" to gain some understanding of the assimilation of Christianity into social practice. What is true of a religious idea is equally true of a secular one, as for example when Darwin's ideas were utilized in late Victorian society to promote social Darwinism, the survival of the fittest, and its malign derivatives. Does that permit us to say "Darwinism causes war" because it describes it?

You can think of religious images and ideas as templates of aspiration and hope as well as sources of foundation charters, of moral and social disciplines, and of sacred legitimations of social order. As these templates are adopted by and inserted in structures of power and economic organization, they modify them and are modified by them. Selective use is made of the religious repertoire, and the most radical ideas may even be turned upside down by the pressure of dominant social interests. Those items of repertoire we know best, such as kingship under God, inevitably represent the powerful who make history, but there is also an underground take-up by the powerless who suffer history. Either way a faith is partly converted by those it partly converts. Once a peaceable faith in a suffering God initially carried by artisans and the powerless is adopted as part of the political legitimation of Rome, the kingdom of Heaven comes down to earth as the empire and "Romanitas." The cross becomes a sword. Christian anticipations of a better spiritual kingdom will then infiltrate the interstices of the social imagination *sotto voce*.

In this way, peaceable and radical images of fraternal feasting or reversals of the roles of the lowly and the proud or charismatic prophecies of social justice will be simultaneously assimilated to social realities and feed contrary imaginations—as in those Medieval sculptures where rich and poor alike face the even scales of a last judgment. Moreover, once the common people gain direct access to the original templates through the spread of printed Scripture, hitherto slumbering imaginations will wake up to all kinds of possibilities, as they did in the English Civil War.

So, then, putting the matter in theoretical terms, repertoires of ideas, religious and secular, are bent by the prism of interests. If that sounds abstract, we hear it proclaimed quite concretely whenever a political leader frankly declares a country's interests the cornerstone of foreign policy or when a reforming politician seeking office responds to pressure of the interested constituencies that form his power base. Democracy itself has to be specifically grounded in the play of interests. The processes are endemic and universal, and scientific understanding of them ought to ameliorate the conspicuously "interested" and selective condemnation of religion. If absorption of the "light" of faith by structures of power led to the Grand Inquisitor as well as St. Francis, the implementation of the secular Enlightenment came to include the horrors of postwar communist Europe, as well as ideals of liberty, equality, and fraternity.

Turning to our second standard opinion, what then of the "secularization thesis"? Given that the idea of a one-way track from religious past to secular future was a master narrative historically embedded in the ideological dynamic as well as in the power struggles and practical policy of European elites, whether radical or Marxist, one has to pull out the elements of genuine observation. As pointed out earlier, secularization is not a simple mistake, and when we take into account genuine observation, a major body of opinion locates secularization not in the direct impact of science but in the process of social differentiation, constitutive of modern society. Social differentiation refers to the way the overarching monopolies found in organic society fragment into autonomous spheres, as for example education, welfare, or indeed religion itself. A prime instance of increasing autonomy would be provided by the historic shift from the church-state to a free church in a free state, of which the First Amendment of the U.S. Constitution was an early harbinger. It is in this restricted sense that one can speak of a secularizing process, as I have done in my own work, *A General Theory of Secularization* (1978). But that does not entail an eventual secular society.

Once you look at the historical record, you certainly find past societies (for example, in the late medieval period) where the theological mode is pervasive and religious monopoly is established. You also encounter, however, a series of secularizing episodes suggesting that there may be several different stories to be told about secularization, even within Christianity—let alone Islam—which raises even more complex questions. The overall master narrative needs to be qualified.

For example, a major secular shift came about when monarchs, beginning with Henry VIII but eventually including most of the absolute rulers of Europe, took over the church. But then a quite different secular shift occurred as the church-state link was increasingly undermined, beginning in Holland and Britain but arriving at complete severance in the United States. That second shift inaugurated a plural society where religious organizations competed on an open market to create a version of modernity uniquely religious in character. What began in a semi-Christian Enlightenment generated an evangelical and enthusiastic response to dawning modernity, powering the expansion of voluntary religion and linking increasing active participation in the religious sphere with increasing democratic participation in politics. So, once you open up the historical horizon, the single track diverges into varied options and pathways.

Divergence is most dramatically illustrated by the contrast between the Anglo-American pattern and the "Latin" pattern of Southern Europe and South America. This contrast has all manner of cultural and political correlates parallel to the specifically religious difference, which turns on a cooperation of Enlightenment with Christianity on the one hand and a struggle between radical enlightened elites and the Catholic Church on the other. What is special in the Anglo-American case is the positive association between modernity, nation-building, democracy, and pluralistic participatory religion. The issue has been and remains whether the Anglo-American or Franco-Hispanic pattern exemplifies the future.

That is where the massive expansion of Evangelical and Pentecostal Christianity in the developing world may turn out to be very significant. The linkage between religion, economic discipline, and democratic participation forged in early modernity is currently reappearing alongside the southward shift in the center of gravity of Christianity from Europe and even from North America. Moreover, this evangelical expansion is paralleled by a voluntaristic and an often radical or charismatic Catholicism, particularly the latter. Perhaps an alternative master narrative could be constructed based not on the anticipations of the philosophers of 250 years ago, but on the association of democratic and economic advance with an open market in religion—and not only in religion.

Sociology, like meteorology, is not renowned for predictive power, and one does not know whether the global future will be characterized by active participatory religious organizations or the kinds of individualistic and therapeutic spirituality with mystical or Eastern elements currently popular in Europe. That is an open question and another story.

✍

DAVID A. MARTIN, PH.D., is Emeritus Professor of Sociology at the London School of Economics. His research interests include the theory of secularization; religion and violence, peace, and conflict; Christian language, sacred space, ritual and the arts, especially music and architecture; the contemporary expansion of Pentecostalism in the developing world; the relation between sociology and theology; and religion in Eastern Europe. Dr. Martin is a regular reviewer for *The Times Literary Supplement* and is author of many books, including *Christian Language in the Secular City* (2002) and *Christian Language and Its Mutations* (2002); *Pentecostalism—The World Their Parish* (2001); *Does Christianity Cause War?* (1997); *Reflections on Sociology and Theology* (1997); *Forbidden Revolutions: Pentecostalism in Latin America and Catholicism in Eastern Europe* (1996); *Tongues of Fire: The Explosion of Protestantism in Latin America* (1990); and *A General Theory of Secularisation* (1978). He is Honorary Professor, Department of Religious Studies, Lancaster University; International Associate, Institute for the Study of Economic Culture, Boston University; sometime Scurlock Professor of Human Values, Southern Methodist University (1986–90); and Sarum Lecturer, Oxford University (1995). Dr. Martin received an Honorary Doctor of Theology degree from Helsinki University (1999) and has served as President of the (then) International Society for the Study of Religion (1975–83).

The Emergence of Ethics from Science 59

An Examination of the Ideals of Einstein and Gandhi

Ramanath Cowsik

$\mathbf{I}$N HIS THOUGHT-PROVOKING BOOK *The Humble Approach,* Sir John Templeton has recommended that our approach to human knowledge, be it scientific or spiritual, be one of humility:

> The approach asks each of us, whether we are students of the natural or the supernatural, to [be] witness to the intimate relationship of physical and spiritual reality in our own lives. In a humble manner we can use our talents to explore the universe to discover future trends. (Templeton 1998)

This approach is particularly relevant today, poised as we are at the beginning of the twenty-first century, distracted by wars and violence and challenged by the rapid growth of science and technology. However objective our religion and science may appear to be, each of us has to ultimately develop a worldview of his or her own based on an examination of the complex world around us. Sir John's remarks have inspired me to reflect on the life and thoughts of two great people of recent times, Einstein and Gandhi, who serve as archetypical examples of the ideals expressed by Sir John Templeton.

Albert Einstein

Einstein's Science

Einstein's scientific contributions revolutionized almost every major aspect of modern physics: quantum theory, gravitational physics, and statistical physics. In fact, Einstein redefined the very concept of spacetime. Whereas the Copernican revolution moved us away from a geocentric point of view nearly five hundred years ago, Einstein's theory of general relativity connected space and time in a single manifold, rendering the fundamental question of the "center of the universe" meaningless because the theory holds that there is absolute freedom of choice in the universe. Moreover, the equations of Einstein's theory of gravitation revolutionized cosmology. The earth is about 150 million kilometers away from the sun, a star; the stars that fill "our" firmament, about 100 billion of them, are conglomerated as the Milky Way galaxy; and scores of billions of galaxies fill space distributed in a quasi-random way. Thus, the cosmological principle states: The universe is homogeneous and isotropic on large scales.

When Einstein's equations were used to investigate the consequences of this aspect of the universe, the solutions indicated that the universe was expanding in a very special way—the galaxies were moving apart in the same manner as dots would on an expanding balloon. It was as though the fabric of space was being continuously created, distancing the galaxies from one another. Approximately ninety years ago, Edwin Hubble firmly established that the galaxies were indeed moving as predicted by Einstein's equations.

Astronomical research during the intervening years has shown that the universe expanded from an extremely hot, condensed state after the Big Bang. As the universe expanded and cooled within about one second, it contained only neutrons, protons, electrons, positrons, neutrinos, and neutrino-like particles, in addition to radiation. After five minutes, the universe cooled enough to synthesize helium nuclei. For a million years, the universe went through an uneventful expansion and cooled continuously. When the temperatures fell enough for electrons and protons to combine to form atoms of hydrogen, the close coupling between radiation and matter vanished with dramatic effect. During this process, the neutrino-like particles similarly cooled, their random motions slowed, and their self-gravitation drove them to clump together into clouds. Because these neutrino-like particles do not emit or scatter light, they are called particles of dark matter. The clouds of dark matter gravitationally attracted atoms that radiated. Slowly, radiating atoms settled into the central regions of the clouds. Clouds of atomic gas then merged to form galaxies, such as our own Milky Way. Carbon, nitrogen, oxygen, iron, and other elements—the building blocks of life—did not exist, and our familiar world was yet to be made.

The gas in the central regions of these systems condensed to form stars. The central core of a star has a temperature of about ten million degrees. Here, nuclei of hydrogen and helium fuse to form the heavier elements, which are then dispersed back into interstellar space by stellar winds. Occasionally, when the mass of the stellar core exceeds the Chandrasekhar mass, it undergoes a collapse under self-gravity, the outer regions are expelled in an explosion, and the resulting debris contains many of the heavy elements, including uranium. In the intervening eight to ten billion years since the birth of the universe, such processes have seeded most of the galaxies with heavy elements. Thus, everything that we see has an intimate connection with the birth of the universe and with the subsequent stages of its evolution. Because most of the human body is made up of carbon and oxygen, with traces of elements such as nitrogen, iron, and others that were synthesized in stars, we are all made of star dust.

It was only during the last few billion years that life appeared on Earth in the form of unicellular organisms. The slow evolution of the species led finally, within the last one hundred thousand years, to humankind as we know it. The history of civilization with agricultural capabilities is even shorter—a mere ten thousand years.

Two points should be noted here: First, a systematic and progressive sequence of evolution has brought the world to its present state. Humankind, with its intelligence and capacity for articulation and organization, has been shaped by the progressive evolution of the exotic particles and fields of the early universe, the formation of galaxies, nucleosynthesis in the stars, and the origins of life on this planet. The implications of this arrow of positive evolution connecting us to the major events in the depths of space and time, and indeed directly back to the Big Bang itself, are profound. Second, the span of humankind's existence is but a minuscule speck in this vast universe, which is about fourteen billion years old and has an extent of 10^{23} kilometers. We also see that normal matter, of which we are all made, is only a tiny fraction of the much vaster dark matter. Furthermore, the dynamics of the universe are controlled by vacuum energy, which is not matter at all. All of this reinforces our connection with the universe and, at the same time, leads us away from a simple anthropocentric view. Yet humankind's indomitable spirit has striven to comprehend this cosmos.

I have attempted to illustrate this evolution in the following figure.

FIGURE 1. TABLEAU SHOWING THE EVOLUTION OF THE UNIVERSE, AS WELL AS OF SCIENCE AND SPIRITUALITY, WHOSE BEGINNINGS, WE MAY ARGUE, ARE COINCIDENT WITH LIFE ITSELF.

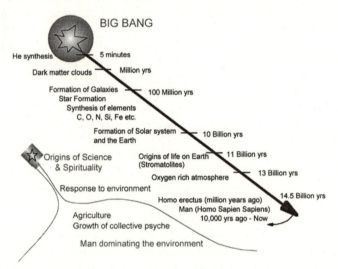

Einstein's "religion" was an attitude of cosmic awe and of devout humility before the harmony in nature. His God-concept was more sophisticated than the common view of a personalized God, the lawmaker who punishes us for our sins and rewards us for our virtues. Einstein said, "My comprehension of God comes from the deeply felt conviction of a superior intelligence that reveals itself in the knowable world" (Calaprice 2000). He considered himself an agnostic, and his spirituality was similar to that taught by Buddha and later by Spinoza—not unlike the *paramarthika* or the transcendental interpretation of the Vedanta delineated by Shankara in contrast to the *Vyavaharika* view held by the common people. In close parallel with the Hindu saints, especially Gautama Buddha and Shankara, Einstein felt the futility of human desires.

Just as Einstein opened up science, which had reached a watershed in the beginning of the twentieth century, so did Shankara revitalize the religions of India with spirituality in the eighth century. Individual existence in pursuit of mundane materialistic goals impressed Einstein as a sort of prison, and, similar to the philosophy of *Advaita* expressed by Shankara, Einstein felt a deep inner urge to experience the universe as a significant whole. Einstein felt that whatever there is of God and goodness, it must work itself out and express itself through us—we cannot stand aside and "let God do it." He was truly a *karmayogi* and followed the dictum of Gita *mā té sangōstvakarmani* (do not detach yourself from your duty) as he strove incessantly to prevent war and bring peace among nations (Jammer 1999[1]).

It should be emphasized that there is a universality to Einstein's cosmic experience that is closely akin to that of monks and nuns in deep, fervent prayer or of the mystics of the East during meditation. A common characteristic is that these experiences are so intense that they transform the individual in a fundamental way. The neuroscientist Andrew Newberg has noted that these "religious" experiences are common to all faiths in that they induce a sense of oneness with the universe and a feeling of awe that impress such experiences with great importance. During these religious experiences, believers feel their sense of self dissolve, and their sensory inputs weaken and even turn off completely, as they feel a continuing loss of boundary. The attendant psychosomatic reactions imbue such experiences with deep significance characterized by great joy and harmony, similar to the feeling of *Bhakti* described by the spiritual leaders of India and the feelings experienced by parents when they first see their newborn offspring. Perhaps part of the nervous system of creatures, including humans, has been hardwired this way to ensure the survival of the species and to sustain evolution.

Let us focus attention on the implications of Einsteinian cosmology for the spiritual quest in general. The two points that were underscored during the earlier discussion of cosmology were: (1) our connection to the grandest and earliest events in the universe and (2) the extremely minuscule span of human existence in the vastness and enormousness of cosmic space and time. Even the planet on which we live is more than four billion years old—ancient in comparison with our sojourn on it.

More than a billion years ago, a subtle condition composed of light, heat, water, and a proper mix of elements led to the birth of life on this planet. During most of the epochs of evolution, nature was all-powerful. It nurtured life and made life forms that evolved progressively. Eventually, humans appeared and also were controlled by nature. Yet even though they are a product and creation of nature, humans have now grown powerful enough to exert control over it. We can choose to destroy nature, or we can protect it and make it even more beautiful. Science alone cannot and will not tell us what we humans should do. Spirituality has a prescription for this dilemma, but cannot adequately defend it without relying on a certain degree of faith. However, a complete perspective can be provided jointly by science and spirituality and can point to a set of values that may guide humankind through the labyrinth of choice.

Let us, for a moment, take inspiration from our connection with the rest of the universe and sensitize ourselves to the character of progressive evolution to higher levels that is innate in us. To assume that those values that support such an evolution are the right ones is both natural and consistent with the teachings of the great leaders of humankind, such as Buddha, Jesus, and Shankara. When we recognize our connection to the rest of the world—both the inanimate and living things on earth—we sensitize ourselves to our common origins and are endowed with an empathy that gives us strength to follow the precepts of universal love, including the ideal of "love thy enemy," as taught by Jesus and others. However, we may wonder whether living up to this ideal is possible in the present world.

Mahatma Mohandass Gandhi

Mohandass Karamchand Gandhi, discoverer of the method of peaceful noncooperation in South Africa, was born in India about ten years before Einstein. Not surprisingly, he called his freedom struggle to bring about sociopolitical change peacefully through moral persuasion rather than through the use of force *satyagraha*, or pursuit of truth. The unflinching and unwavering adherence to truth, not unlike that of an exemplary scientist, is at the heart of Gandhi's personality. From this quality emerges Gandhi's Christ-like love and nonviolence in all aspects of life, even in thought. In support of this idea, one may quote Gandhi himself:

> To see the universal truth face to face one must be able to love the meanest creation as oneself. . . . For me the road to salvation lies through incessant toil in the service of my country and humanity. In the language of the Gita, I want to live in peace with both friend and foe. (Radhakrishnan 1944)

Thus, we see the two facets of Gandhi's personality—the spiritual inner self forever devoted to the pursuit of truth and the activist outer self, which found expression in this world through his deep love of humanity and untiring efforts toward its betterment. We may identify *ahimsa* (nonviolence), *satya* (truth), and universal love as Gandhi's three quintessential virtues, which became luminously clear during the long struggle for freedom in India, when these three qualities blended, supported, and added glory to one another.

Through the years, *satyagraha* has proven remarkably successful in bringing freedom from discriminatory control of one people by another—a freedom that is permanent and leaves both parties not in antagonism, but in friendship. In Einstein's own words we find a clear description of Mahatma ("Great Soul") Gandhi and the peaceful movement he launched in South Africa and India to gain freedom from prejudice and oppression:

> A leader of his people, unsupported by any outward authority; a politician whose success rests not upon craft nor on mastery of technical devices, but simply on the convincing power of his personality; a victorious fighter who has always scorned the use of force; a man of wisdom and humility; armed with resolve and inflexible consistency, who has devoted all his strength to the uplifting of his people and the betterment of their lot; a man who has confronted brutality with the dignity of a simple human being, and thus at all times risen superior. Generations to come, it may be, will scarcely believe that such a one as this ever in flesh and blood walked upon this earth. (Einstein 1950)

The quotation from Einstein touches on some of the salient aspects of Gandhi's personality. But what Einstein said of Gandhi, we may say of Einstein himself. We see clues to the most enduring of Einstein's concerns, exactly consonant with those of Gandhi: peace in this world and the evolution of society to one that holds the highest values. Einstein's life was spent in an unceasing effort to bring about these values with the same consistency and quiet resolve that he so admired in Gandhi, coupled with the spiritual ideals preached so effectively by the great spiritual leaders, such as Buddha and Jesus.

Apart from the personal qualities that helped Gandhi face fearlessly any onslaught, including incarceration, during his *satyagraha* movement, he had another deep idea that has relevance today. He felt that no individual, group, or nation—rich or poor—should be without gainful employment. Just as the poorest among us who eke out a living can be redeemed when provided with an opportunity to work and earn that living, he believed that the rich who have gained wealth as individuals through inheritance or as a nation through exploitable natural resources would benefit greatly if they regularly worked hard in their chosen fields of interest. Gandhi's *Charka* or *Khadi* (village industries) program was a tremendous help to the poor in India in the 1930s. Even today, no one can remain merely a consumer. All of us should be engrossed in some creative effort in order to give meaning to our lives.

Thus, we see that science and spirituality both tell us that we should work to sustain the positive universal evolution. According to the ancient Indian way of life, this is following one's *dharma*. In our incessant effort toward peace, which is essential for positive evolution, we should follow the path shown by Buddha, Jesus, and Gandhi. This method is not restricted to the oppressed and the poor, but is available to the rich and powerful as well, as indeed Emperor Asoka of India showed more than two thousand years ago when he renounced warfare and adopted the doctrines of Buddhism.

In Conclusion . . .

We see that the reductionist approach of science has clearly pointed out our connection with the rest of this vast universe and events that occurred in the depths of time. Science has shown that a positive vector of evolution has transformed the exotic fields and particles of the Big Bang into the universe in which we live. But the reductionist approach, as it stands today, cannot tell us how to attach value to things or actions. We can try to circumvent this impasse by augmenting the reductionist approach with an additional axiom: All actions and attributes that support positive evolution have a positive value, and all of our efforts should be directed to nurture this positive evolution. For example, love of humanity, nonviolence, and the betterment of the world should be endowed with positive value, just as the great spiritual leaders have been telling us all along. However, this message cannot find easy purchase in minds rigorously trained in the reductionist approach, minds that tend to ignore the subtle urgings of our inner self. This extra axiom allows us to bridge the gap between science and spirituality. It gives meaning to lives dedicated to bringing about peace and tranquility, to lives engaged in creating beautiful art and sensitive poetry, and to lives engrossed in understanding science so that we approach ever closer to truth. I can do no better than to end by quoting Rabindranath Tagore:

where the mind is without fear and the head is held high;
where knowledge is free;
where the world has not been broken up
into fragments by narrow domestic walls;
where the words come out from the depths of truth;
where tireless striving stretches its arms towards perfection;
where the clear stream of reason has not lost its way
in the dreary desert sand of dead habit;
where the mind is led by thee into ever widening thought and action
—into that heaven of freedom, my Father, let my country awake.

✍

RAMANATH COWSIK, PH.D., has held faculty positions at the University of California at Berkeley and the Tata Institute of Fundamental Research in India. Currently, he is a Distinguished Professor at the Indian Institute of Astrophysics in Bangalore and Professor of Physics in Arts and Sciences at the McDonnell Center for the Space Sciences of Washington University, St. Louis. He is one of the world's preeminent astrophysicists, with pioneering contributions in both theory and experiment. His work on the cosmological influence of massive neutrinos helped establish the now rich and vigorous field of astro-particle physics. During the last decade under his leadership, the Indian Institute of Astrophysics developed a world-class astronomical observatory at an altitude of fifteen thousand feet above sea level at Hanle, in southeastern Ladakh. His work has been honored with numerous Indian and international awards, including the Bose Prize (India); the Third World Academy of Sciences Award; the president of India's second-highest civilian honor, the Padma Shri; and election to the Membership of the National Academy of Sciences (USA).

NOTE

1 Also see Max Jammer's essay in this volume.

REFERENCES

Calaprice, A. *The Expanded Quotable Einstein*. Princeton, NJ: Princeton University Press, 2000.

Einstein, A. From "Out of My Later Years," New York: Philosophical Library, 1950. New translations and revisions by Sonja Bargmann, based on *Mein Weltbild*, edited by Carl Seelig, Laurel Edition, Dell Publishing Co. Written on the occasion of Gandhi's seventieth birthday in 1939. [Note the several other essays in this volume discuss Einstein and Gandhi; see, for example, the essay by Kuruvilla Pandikattu.]

Jammer, M. *Einstein and Religion,* Princeton, NJ: Princeton University Press, 1999.

Templeton, Sir John, *The Humble Approach.* Philadelphia, PA: Templeton Foundation Press, 1998.

Radhakrishnan, S. Ed. *M. K. Gandhi: Essays and Reflections on His Life and Work—Presented to him on his seventieth birthday* (Kitabistan, Allahabad, 1944).

SCIENCE IN THE SERVICE OF MEANINGLESSNESS 60

SOCIOLOGICAL CHANGE AND THE DECLINE OF FAITH

M. A. Casey

S*CIENCE IS OFTEN presumed to have played an important part in the demise of faith in the modern world, while remaining unaffected by the situation of mean-inglessness that has followed in its wake.* This is an overstated claim and one that needs to be reexamined. This essay is a preliminary attempt to sketch out the main lines that such a reexamination might follow and what it might mean for our understanding of the relationship between religion and science.

One of the major reasons for the waning of faith in the West is the decline of community. We are inclined to sentimentalize community now, but it was not so long ago that it was the object of a huge emancipatory effort that successfully swept aside all the restrictions communal life necessarily imposes, making the individual the supreme arbiter of when he will and will not be obligated to others. As a consequence, community for most of us is something we have to opt into if we are going to be part of it at all. But for most of human history, it was something we were born into and that worked powerfully to support the values that were taught in the family.

Importantly, communities were credal. It was thought that social stability and peace—and often even society's very survival—required not just common values, but a common faith in God. This created a world with clearer, and in some ways more certain, ideas about good and evil, freedom and truth, individual character and human nature than we have today. It was also a more limited world. We should not despise it on this account, anymore than we should romanticize it. Nietzsche describes human beings as animals whose well-being depends on firm limits and clear horizons. Far from falsifying this proposition, the configuration of modern life has only served to reinforce its validity.

It is no surprise that with the demise of community's hold on the individual the compelling force of faith has also diminished. Being associated with the old world of fixed horizons and immutable laws, faith is treated as something incompatible with the new dispensation of limitless possibility and individual supremacy. It continues to be tolerated, of course, but preferably as a private therapeutic device for managing the feelings of dread, guilt, and insignificance that attend the human condition and that the modern situation often magnifies.

The relegation of faith to the realm of therapy is exemplified by the rise of "spirituality" as a surrogate for traditional religion. Part of its appeal is that unlike religion, spirituality does not come with a moral code. In fact, it has no consequences for action at all. Religion demands that the individuals radically change the way they live to better conform with a law that is directed to their true happiness, but which is not of their own making. Spirituality makes no such demand. Happiness in this account consists of continuing just as you are, but with a new overlay of "inspiration, myth, and insight" to affirm the supposedly unique and intrepid qualities of a life lived in mediocre selfishness.

No doubt, this sort of thing helps some people, especially in the midst of the loneliness, anxiety, and confusion about fundamental questions that infuses so much of modern life. But considered sociologically, spirituality amounts to the veneration of the self for purposes that are ultimately therapeutic rather than properly religious or spiritual. It flatters the self in its lonely supremacy and reinforces that supremacy with bits and pieces of "esoteric" knowledge, but it does nothing to bring the supreme individual back within the ambit of something greater than him- or herself.

The situation is different when it comes to faith, understood as a relationship with a truth that is supreme to the individual. In this case, strenuous efforts are made to exclude religion from public affairs and to confine it to private life on the basis that faith of this kind is a dangerous and infantile illusion—infantile because continuing to believe in God in the face of his nonexistence is to be like children preferring wishes over reality. "Maturity" (for both the individual and the species) means overcoming the need for faith—and perhaps the need for any kind of meaning at all. Those unable to do this are not penalized, but their contributions to public life, especially on certain key issues, are often regarded as suspect.

The assumption at work here is that belief is an illusion and persistence in it an exercise in self-deception. Bring people to see clearly, the thinkers of the eighteenth century argued, and they will grow beyond faith—ultimately, the thinkers of the nineteenth century argued, to the point where they will be able to behold the meaninglessness of existence without despair, and perhaps even with serenity. Freedom, not only from faith but from any sort of meaning, is the destiny and greatness of the human animal.

Although it is an old idea, the conceit that faith can maintain its hold on the imagination only as long as there are blinkers on human vision still has considerable appeal. Its validation depends on the dubious assertion that modern science has made belief in God untenable, at least to the intellectually honest. It is clear that faith in the West, as measured by religious affiliation and practice, has declined. And even in countries such as the United States and Australia, where most people still tick the "Christian" box on census forms, an unreflective and somewhat complacent practical atheism—living in effect as if there is no God—is generally the rule rather than the exception. But the very incoherence of this situation suggests that it is sociological change rather than the breakthroughs of science that is the key to understanding the decline of faith.

This is not the place to rehearse in detail the enormous changes that modernity has brought to human life. Material abundance, social stability, the decline of community, the rise of individualism, and the enormous freedom, mobility, and level of opportunity we enjoy are one part of it. The powerful patterns and demands of production, consumption, and technology that drive and sustain these conditions is another. What is important is that together they have radically reduced both the need and the occasion to engage consistently with the deeper levels of existence.

Practical unbelief, even among believers, has been facilitated particularly by the fragmentation of life into discrete compartments and the obviation of any requirement to bring one's life into a coherent whole. If faith has been displaced not just among intellectuals but also among the broad mass of people in the West, it is not because science has made belief in God untenable. It has much more to do with the way modernity has massively increased our capacity for muddle and self-contradiction, while making it easier than ever before to live almost entirely on the surface of existence.

What this makes clear is that the facile opposition of science and faith is a hopelessly outdated and inadequate explanatory paradigm. A token of this is the way evolutionary theory in all its various and apparently endless elaborations continues to be regarded as the knockout blow in the argument its partisans insist on having with religion. It is interesting, and not entirely peripheral to the present discussion, to note that Darwin is the only member of the once-vaunted "scientific" trinity of Marx-Darwin-Freud (which not so long ago was often credited with the final dispatch of faith) who still has any serious standing. But one could be excused for hearing in the insistent tones adopted by some of his followers a fear that he is also destined to share their fate.

There can be no doubt that the picture presented by mainstream evolutionary theory is deeply disenchanting in its depiction of human life. It has been very successfully popularized and in many ways epitomizes the way science apparently advocates meaninglessness at the expense of faith. But it also exemplifies why the resonance of this particular form of disenchantment is limited: Quite aside from whatever the truth may be, no one in their heart of hearts genuinely believes that they are merely a chance conglomeration of "selfish genes."

While some may see this as an instance of human narcissism defeating scientific understanding, we would do better to see it as a reason for tempering the narcissism of science. People value and respect science and are grateful for the many great goods it brings. But in the end, science is looked to for the wonderful ways in which it can improve life, not for an explanation of the meaning and purpose of existence.

More than anything else, the supremacy of the individual characterizes our age. We are utterly free, utterly sovereign. We believe in this more than we believe in God, and certainly more than we believe in science. As a result, the experience of the individual trumps everything, and appeals to authority—whether the authority of faith or the authority of science—have little weight. Obviously, this is not to say that we are not influenced by the ideas and forces around us. But no matter how compelling these influences may be in themselves, their effective force can be reduced to nought unless they register directly with the particular and personal experience of a given individual.

Of particular importance is the *personal* experience of meaninglessness, as opposed to its various intellectual conceptualizations. It is loneliness, uselessness, and the absence of hope that makes the experience of meaninglessness so powerful. While it is sometimes underscored by the disenchanted account of human existence generated not so much by science as by the materialistic assumptions of a certain ideology of science, it is the individual experience that is decisive, not the scientism.

This also applies to the experience of life as meaningful. It is one of the reasons that love is so important. Those who place science and religion in opposition overlook the fact that God is not an intellectual proposition. If a person becomes a Christian, for example, he or she does so primarily because of personal experience of the *reality* of God's love. The intellectual elaboration of what this love implies for the living of daily life comes afterward.

One point of connection between science and the love that faith reveals is wonder. Every new scientific discovery amplifies our reasons for wonder. But strangely, when we enter into this we quickly come up against an adamant insistence that the only certain thing the wonders of life point to is their own cancellation in blind chance and absurd concatenations.

Is this the truth? No. The truth does not contradict itself, and for this reason there is no contradiction between science and faith. Within its limits, science seeks the truth, and so too does faith; for meaning has no value unless it is true. It is this that is not understood by those who would place science in opposition not only to faith but to meaning itself. Just as faith is not well served by those who would reduce it to a private therapeutic exercise, science is not well served by those who insist that meaninglessness is the only truth we can know. The sundering of science and faith in this way makes of them a deception and a self-deception, distorting our vision in a way that not only makes it difficult to see clearly, but that often blinds us to the true reality of things.

The only beneficiary of the adversarial relationship imposed on religion and science two hundred years ago has been meaninglessness. Science has been just as much diminished by this as has faith. But this is not a destiny. It is possible to recast the terms on which science and religion interact so that both can flourish in a context of authentic meaning. The first step is to bring down the curtain on the very tired Punch-and-Judy show that nineteenth-century presuppositions have lumbered us with and to start afresh where we find ourselves today—at the beginning of a new millennium.

✍

MICHAEL CASEY, PH.D., is Permanent Fellow in Sociology and Politics at the Australian session of the John Paul II Institute for Marriage and the Family and a sociologist on the staff of the Catholic Archbishop of Sydney. He holds degrees in law, English literature, and modern European history from Monash University, Melbourne, and a doctorate in sociology from La Trobe University, also in Melbourne. Dr. Casey's book *Meaninglessness: The Solutions of Nietzsche, Freud and Rorty* was published in 2002 by Rowman and Littlefield. His articles have been published in *Society* and *First Things*. In 2001, Dr. Casey won the Acton Institute's Novak award for an essay on religion and globalization. His research interests include the relationship between authority and freedom and the impact of twentieth-century political ideology on modern culture.

SECULARIZATION AND THE SCIENCES 61

Peter L. Berger

For a long time, the conventional view has been that modernity goes hand in hand with secularization, in the sense of a decline in the credibility of religion. And at least one of the reasons for this is supposed to be the rise of modern science: Supposedly the scientific understanding of the world leaves less and less room for a "God hypothesis." There are people who still adhere to this view, not least among them theologians who try to find a place for religion in an allegedly secular culture.

Unfortunately for them, the empirical evidence is massively to the contrary. The contemporary world is full of powerful religious revitalization movements, many of them erupting in emphatically modernizing contexts. Thus, the two most dynamic religious movements in the world today—the worldwide explosion of Pentecostal Protestantism and the comparably explosive spread of resurgent Islam—are occurring not in backward villages, but primarily in the context of modernizing urbanization. America, despite the assertions of many of its intellectuals, continues to be a strongly religious society, especially if one compares it with Western and Central Europe (one of the few geographical areas where secularization does indeed appear to be dominant). This is not the place to discuss possible reasons for this difference (although this happens to be one of the most interesting topics in the sociology of contemporary religion). Clearly, however, America is no less modern than, say, Sweden. Whatever the reason for American religiosity, it cannot be the absence of modernity, let alone of science.

To say the least, then, the relation between science, modernity, and religion is more complicated than assumed by the aforementioned conventional view. If one wants to throw light on this relation, it is important to make an important distinction—that between the natural sciences and the human sciences (the latter encompassing the humanities and social sciences). And, indeed, it appears that the degree of secularity in practitioners of disciplines in these two areas is quite different.

The natural sciences have thrown out two great challenges to religion. The first was the result of the Copernican revolution, marginalizing the place of the earthly habitat of humanity in the universe.[1] The second challenge was posed by the Darwinian revolution, putting in question the place of Homo sapiens in the evolutionary scheme of things. Both revolutions made it very difficult to adhere to a literal understanding of the biblical account of creation and human origins. Both challenges, especially the evolutionary one, continue to be troubling to people who adhere to a belief in literal biblical "inerrancy." Most religious people, including most theologians in the Christian and Jewish traditions, have successfully integrated the respective scientific findings into their view of the world.

What is more important, the advances in the natural sciences over the last century or so have not, as expected, led to what Max Weber classically called a "disenchantment of the world." On the contrary, many natural scientists—especially physicists, astronomers, and biologists—have testified to an increasing sense of wonder and awe resulting from their work and have consequently become very open to religious interpretations of the world. A lively dialog now exists between natural scientists and theologians. The John Templeton Foundation has devoted large resources to this dialog. Although I must confess that I have nothing to contribute to this dialog as my knowledge of the natural sciences is embarrassingly minimal, I do feel certain that the dialog will continue and that it is important.

The human sciences have posed a very different challenge. It is the challenge of the insight that all beliefs and values are relative in terms of time and place. The insight was already expressed eloquently by Pascal, when he wrote that what is truth on one side of the Pyrenees is error on the other. Historians pioneered in this challenge, beginning in the early nineteenth century, not only by dismantling the traditional understanding of the biblical texts, but also by their bringing to attention the vast literatures of non-Western religions. Religious believers now had to confront the fact that the scriptures they took to be divinely inspired were the result of complicated historical processes, and further by the fact that scriptures of other traditions made comparable claims to supernatural authority. More recently, psychology showed how beliefs and values could be seen as "projections" of very mundane human needs, and the social sciences could show how beliefs and values depend on empirically analyzable "social constructions."

For a time, this sense of relativity was limited to people with higher education in the relevant fields. The number of these people has, of course, increased enormously over the last half-century. More importantly, however, a similar sense of relativity is now shared by even larger numbers of people as a result of their experiences in ordinary, everyday life. This is the result of an ever-widening *pluralism*. As far as America is concerned, the religious consequence of this has been amply documented by the Pluralism Project directed by Diana Eck at Harvard University. No longer can the religious identity of Americans be subsumed under the three categories in the title of the important book by Will Herberg published in 1955: *Protestant, Catholic, Jew*. Immigrants from every corner of the world have brought their religions with them, and they, and especially their children, are engaged in an ongoing conversation with people belonging to the older American denominations. This conversation is not taking place just in academic seminars and interfaith colloquia. It occurs daily in the workplace with colleagues and across the fence with neighbors; it even occurs in kindergartens.

This is not secularization. Secularization would mean that there is too little religion in the world today. Pluralism means that there is *too much religion*. More precisely, individuals in the pluralistic situation must somehow come to terms with the fact that others, especially those they respect and like, have beliefs and values greatly different from their own. Among ordinary people, this has led to what Robert Wuthnow, the Princeton sociologist, has nicely called "patchwork religion": Individuals put together their own little religious system, more or less sophisticated as the case may be, by patching up bits and pieces of their native tradition with some taken from other traditions. They can say something like, "I am Catholic, but . . . ," or "I am Jewish in my own way," or even "right now I'm into Buddhism." It is facile to caricaturize this phenomenon. I, for one, would take a more positive view of the challenge of pluralism. It impels individuals to make religious choices because their original faith can no longer be taken for granted. I fail to see why a taken-for-granted religion is superior to one that is consciously chosen. Christians in particular should reflect on the fact that contemporary religious pluralism has remarkable similarities with the pluralism of the Graeco-Roman world in which the early church came into being: Should we bemoan a situation that resembles those in which Paul and the early church fathers lived and thought? I think not.

It seems to me that our contemporary religious pluralism calls for reflection quite different from that demanded by the dialog between theology and the natural sciences. Such reflection is not new. It has occurred in different places and in different times—for one example, on the Silk Road in Central Asia, where for centuries religious traditions rubbed up against each other. A highly sophisticated product of this pluralism is the classic Buddhist text *The Questions of King Milinda*, consisting of a dialog between a Buddhist teacher and a Hellenistic ruler. In the history of Christianity, its thinkers first had to confront the challenges of rabbinical Judaism and Hellenism, later with Islam (without which medieval Christian scholasticism would have been much poorer). Each of these confrontations led to what the French aptly called a *prise de conscience*—a deliberate assessment, in the face of the challenge from "the other," of what in one's own faith is essential and must never be given up and what may be put aside as the result of this or that historical accident.

A vast intellectual task is before the thinkers of every religious tradition. For Christian theologians, the dialog with Judaism and Islam is as timely as ever. But there is also the urgent necessity to confront the immense riches of the religious traditions of southern and eastern Asia, notably in the encounter with Hinduism, Buddhism, and Confucianism. In Africa and also elsewhere, the confrontation persists with surviving or robustly reassertive traditions often subsumed under the somewhat patronizing category of "primal religions"—traditions that have kept alive the archaic nexus between humanity, Nature, and supernatural realities. Out of this has come an expanding and widening set of conversations. These do not always lead to agreement. Indeed, I would propose that in such conversations it is as important sometimes to say no as it may in other cases be to say yes.

What is quite clear, I think, is that this dialog between the great religious traditions is immensely promising both intellectually and spiritually. To use a term favored by the John Templeton Foundation, such dialog does constitute "progress in religion."

✒

PETER L. BERGER, PH.D., is Professor Emeritus at Boston University. A sociologist by training, he is currently director of two research centers at the University—the Institute for the Study of Economic Culture (founded in 1985) and the Institute on Religion and World Affairs (founded in 2000). He received his Ph.D. from the Graduate Faculty of the New School for Social Research, New York, in 1953. Subsequently, before joining the faculty at Boston University in 1979, he taught at the University of North Carolina, the Hartford Theological Seminary, the New School for Social Research, Rutgers University, and Boston College. He holds honorary doctorates from five universities in the United States and Europe. His recent books include *A Far Glory: The Quest for Faith in an Age of Credulity* (1992), *Redeeming Laughter: The Comic Dimension of Human Experience* (1997), and (editor, with Samuel Huntington) *Many Globalizations: Cultural Diversity in the Contemporary World* (2002).

NOTE

1 For discussion of an opposing viewpoint, see Dennis R. Danielson, "The great Copernican cliché," *Am. J. Phys.* 69, 1029, October 2001 [http://ojps.aip.org/ajp: DOI: 10.1119/1.1379734].

PART SEVEN

Perspectives on Religion and Health

The Faith Factor in Medicine, the Health Factor in Religion 62

REFLECTIONS ON A NEW RESEARCH TRADITION

Anne Harrington

THE VALUES of a regular religious life and spiritual practice have long been extolled, but until recently few have thought that these values might include enhanced physical health. The past five or six years, however, have seen an escalating number of studies offering new evidence for the health benefits of religious practice and spirituality. This evidence in turn is leading to a growing number of suggestions that medical science and religion now have a basis on which to enter into a new and progressive partnership: one in which medicine is inspired to become more spiritual and in which religion gains new utility and status in the modern world.

Two questions can be asked: (1) Without critiquing the soundness of every specific piece of evidence offered,[1] what is the general nature of the argument for the health benefits of religion? (2) Does this trend, in fact, offer a foundation for bringing what we would consider to be "best practice" medicine and "best practice" religion into fruitful partnership? In this article, I aim to answer both of these questions in turn.

The Nature of the Argument in Four Parts

The argument about the health benefits of religion is actually not a single argument, but four separate claims. Each of these has its own data set, and each has come out of a distinct research tradition in medicine. Let me take each in turn.

GOING TO CHURCH IS GOOD FOR YOUR HEALTH

The origins of the interest in the health benefits of church attendance lie in epidemiological work that began in the late 1960s, a time of great medical interest in identifying the lifestyle and environmental factors that were contributing, in particular, to the rising incidence of heart disease in the United States. Out of this work, a person's degree of social isolation versus social embeddedness emerged as an important factor. Some work suggested, for example, that living in traditional close-knit communities acted as a protection against heart disease—and, possibly, other common forms of morbidity and mortality. Other studies indicated that more isolated people within a community tended to be sicker and to die earlier than those who were more socially embedded.[2]

From the beginning, membership in a religious community was commonly included as one independent variable among many others that might act as measures of the effects of social embeddedness and social isolation. Studies began to emerge that suggested that the link between health and religion was a particularly important one.[3] Various kinds of work began to suggest that church attendance was strongly correlated with a reduced likelihood of suffering from any number of health problems, especially in old age. Some studies even suggested that going to church was correlated with extended lifespan.[4]

What might be the reason for this? Initially, the tendency was still to reduce churchgoing to social support. Researchers said that churches (and, by extension, synagogues and mosques) are good for your health because they provide really good community. Nevertheless, not everyone was satisfied that this was the whole story. For example, in 1996, Israeli epidemiologist Jeremy Kark compared mortality rates in eleven secular and eleven matched religious kibbutzim between 1970 and 1985 and found that mortality in the secular kibbutzim was twice that of mortality on the religious kibbutzim. At the same time, he and his colleagues insisted, "there was no difference in social support or frequency of social contact between religious and secular kibbutzim. . . ."[5]

What else might be going on, then, to explain such differences? The answer we begin to see emerging takes us to the next two claims about the health benefits of religion, both of which are concerned with what are often called "intrinsic" (roughly, one's private, experience-based sense of the divine, sometimes also called "spirituality") as opposed to "extrinsic" (the degree to which one publicly participates in the structures of religious life) religiousness.[6]

MEDITATION/CONTEMPLATIVE PRACTICE IS GOOD FOR YOUR HEALTH.

When, in the 1960s, middle-class Americans began a romance with mantra-based meditative practices such as transcendental meditation (TM), they were interested in the emotional and spiritual benefits. Few thought that meditation might have a positive effect on physical health. Meditation began to be reconceptualized regarding its potential health benefits only in the 1970s, with the work of people such as cardiologist Herbert Benson at Harvard University.[7] Against a background of evidence that stress—a still relatively novel concept of human ailment[8]—played a significant role in a large number of diseases, especially heart disease, Benson repackaged meditation as a stress-buster. To do this, he distanced himself from the sectarian aspects of TM, renamed it the "relaxation response," and reconceptualized it as a natural physiological counterpart to the stress response.[9]

Beginning in the 1980s, Benson found both a comrade and, to a certain extent, a rival in meditation teacher Jon Kabat-Zinn, who in 1979 established what was then called the Stress Reduction Clinic at the University of Massachusetts Medical School in Worcester. There he taught patients a type of meditative practice based on an attention-training technique widely practiced in Buddhism called "mindfulness." In best-selling books such as *Full Catastrophe Living*, Kabat-Zinn offered evidence that mindfulness meditation helped chronic patients cope better with the stress of their disorders. In other publications, he offered evidence that the practice directly influences resistance to disease and the healing process.[10]

While both Benson and Kabat-Zinn taught practices with origins in Asian contemplative traditions (particularly Hinduism and Buddhism), both researchers also insisted in their different ways that you don't have to be Hindu or Buddhist to meditate. Indeed, according to these investigators, you don't even have to be religious. At the same time, if you are religious and your religion happens not to be Hinduism or Buddhism, you do not have to be concerned about possible doctrinal conflict. In interviews, Benson has talked about how when he first began spreading the word about meditation—or what he was then calling the "relaxation response"—he was "startled at the excitement among the religious pros" in the Christian community. They told him that in introducing them to the relaxation response, he had reminded them of the power of similar practices in their own tradition with which they had largely lost touch. "'This is why I came into church work in the first place,' said one, 'and I'd lost it. . . .'"[11]

BELIEF IS A HEALING POWER

The claim that belief is a healing power has roots that are more explicitly faith-based than either of the two other claims I've reviewed so far. Its origins lie, in fact, in a late-nineteenth-century Protestant movement in America that variously called itself "mind-cure," "New Thought," "Christian Science," "Unity Science," and "practical Christianity." The leaders of this movement were influenced by ideas about the power of belief derived from European investigations into mesmerism, hypnosis, and so-called faith healings (Lourdes in these years was a subject of intense scrutiny by some medical doctors).[12]

If faith can heal, reasoned the leaders of this movement, then why not cultivate it? Doing so, they argued, shows no lack of respect for God, but is instead a way of proactively realizing the practical presence of God in one's own life. William James, observing the fruits of this movement at the turn of the twentieth century, was at once impressed and bemused: "The blind have been made to see, the halt to walk; lifelong invalids have had their health restored. . . . One hears of the 'Gospel of Relaxation,' of the 'Don't-Worry Movement,' of people who repeat to themselves, 'Youth! Health! Vigor!'"[13]

The history is worth knowing because the mind-cure of the previous century has played a largely unrecognized role in shaping popular views about the power of the mind over the body—from Norman Vincent Peale's doctrines about the "power of positive thinking" to various "New Age" ideas about how thoughts become things.[14] The history also helps us better understand how it came to be that the John Templeton Foundation—a philanthropic organization whose stated mission is to "pursue new insights at the boundary between theology and science"—should have emerged in the past several years as the single most important supporter of research into the religion-health link.[15] Sir John Templeton, who at the age of ninety-plus still largely sets the research priorities for the Foundation, was raised at least partly within a branch of mind-cure called "Unity Church" and has remained influenced as an adult by the ideas he learned there.[16]

Present-day empirical research into the power of belief can be understood in part as an attempt to subject these deeply rooted popular understandings to new, more rigorous forms of investigation. The results in support of the tradition have included studies suggesting that terminally ill patients with strong faith, a "fighting spirit," and a "positive attitude" may live longer or face better odds of recovery than more pessimistic or fatalistic patients.[17] They have also included attempts to study how "dummy" pills—placebos—that people believe will help them might result in measurable changes in a clinical condition.[18]

Taken as a whole, the message from the new research has produced a highly ecumenical and utilitarian message about belief. Just as it is claimed that going to church is good for your health, irrespective of the kind of church you attend, and that meditating is good for your health, irrespective of the kind of meditative practice you employ, so it is also claimed that belief or faith is good for your health irrespective of what you believe. All beliefs in a higher power are equal because all (or so it is assumed) equally marshal the body's endogenous healing abilities. In the words of Herbert Benson, "In my scientific observations, I have observed that no matter what name you give the Infinite Absolute you worship, no matter what theology you ascribe to, the results of believing in God are the same."[19]

Prayer Works

The fourth claim for the health benefits of religion stands in a somewhat different and potentially destabilizing relationship to the other three: Prayer works.

Let us be very clear what is being said here. Prayer works—not because it provides a strong sense of social connection, not because it facilitates a special meditative state, and not because it deepens one's sense of faith. No. Prayer itself changes people's health in ways that are independent of all of those other factors. We know this, say the people who make this claim, because when individuals or groups of people pray for the health of a sick person—even when the sick person is not sure or even aware that he or she is being prayed for—it has a measurable effect.

The origin of this research tradition goes back to the rise of statistics, and more specifically to the rise of a vision of statistics in the late nineteenth century as a new tool for resolving longstanding questions of social policy.[20] In this context, Darwin's cousin Francis Galton proposed in the 1870s to use statistics to test the efficacy of prayer. He reasoned that if prayer works as a protector of health and life, then those whose health was most frequently the subject of prayer should on average live longer than those who were less frequently prayed for. Because the Church of England service includes prayers for the health of members of the British royal family, Galton decided to compare the longevity of members of that family against others who had "the advantage of affluence." He found that, rather than living longer, they were "literally the shortest-lived."[21]

For the naturalistically inclined intellectuals of the time, all this was a good joke. For many of the clergy, it was unseemly and wrongheaded. Prayer, as one clergyman of the time insisted, was a private matter, unquantifiable, with an efficacy beyond the reach of statistics.[22] Nevertheless, the idea that the efficacy of prayer should be an empirical question has continued to tempt. In our own time, people have tried to test it using the gold standard of evidence-based clinical medicine: the randomized, placebo-controlled, double-blind trial.

The launching study in this vein was conducted by Randolph Byrd in the 1980s.[23]

This study assigned 393 patients who had been admitted to a coronary care unit to one of two groups: a prayed-for group and a control group.[24] Byrd found that in six out of twenty-six kinds of possible complications, the prayed-for patients did better on a statistically significant level than the controls. In contrast, the controls did not do better than the prayed-for patients on any of the twenty-six measures.[25]

Today, a range of replications and variations on the Byrd study have either been completed or are in progress. In 1999, a Kansas-based researcher named William Harris claimed to have replicated Byrd's findings with a larger population sample (although his study did not reproduce the specific measures of improvement found by Byrd), triggering a new spate of media attention, as well as a lot of critical scrutiny by skeptics.[26] Currently, Herbert Benson's lab at Harvard University is attempting an ambitious, multi-site study that claims to be a definitive replication of the Byrd study.[27]

Theologically, we are somewhere new. Proponents of the other three claims are always careful to leave God's existence as an open question, but the force of their arguments does not inherently depend on whether God exists. Matters here are different. If prayer works—and works in ways that cannot be reduced to the placebo effect, social support, or stress reduction—then medical science has apparently obtained evidence for the existence of God.[28] Small wonder that this is the most fiercely contested, criticized, and publicized arm of the religion-and-health tradition.

Even when the other three arms of the tradition do attempt to engage with religion in more than an instrumental way, they do it very differently than does this last arm. The other three arms see themselves as theologically neutral. They insist that there is something called "religion" or "spirituality" that stands above any and all specific faith traditions and whose health effects can be discussed. Whatever the intentions of the researchers or the funders, matters in the prayer arm of this tradition—at least at the moment—are different. The fact that all the widely publicized studies to date have tested the efficacy of explicitly Christian prayer has not been lost on at least some people. One Christian fundamentalist Web site devoted to posting scientific evidence for the reality of the Judeo-Christian God has thus triumphantly announced that "no other religion has succeeded in scientifically demonstrating that prayer to their God has any efficacy in healing."[29]

The Religion-Health Link: What Kind of Medicine? What Kind of Religion?

If church attendance protects against mortality and morbidity, does that mean that churchgoing should be medically prescribed, like exercise and a low-fat diet? If all forms of belief produce equivalent health benefits, does this mean that we should be uninterested in the specific content of different historical faith traditions?[30] Conversely, does the current sectarian direction of the prayer studies mean that this research tradition, inadvertently or not, is invoking the authority of medical science to pit the God of one faith tradition against that of another?

Research into the links between religious practice and health has produced an empirically provocative and complex set of data. This work has the potential to contribute to a much richer understanding of human functioning in health and disease than currently exists. The vistas are exciting. Nevertheless, at present the real potential of this work is being increasingly obscured by a range of simplistic, polemical, and ill-thought-out extrapolations. In particular, I worry about well-meaning but under-theorized ideas that putting "prayer alongside Prozac"[31] will lead to a new "spiritualizing" of medical practice itself [32] or that religion can now claim a heightened status for itself—but only (this part is rarely noted or perhaps even recognized) to the extent that it is willing to conceptualize its goods within the value system of a consumerist "therapeutic culture" that prizes individual well-being above all things.[33]

Both medicine and religion—acting alone as well as in partnership—have a responsibility to demand more from themselves. And, happily, the research tradition linking health and religion is in a position to help them do it.

ℒ♥

ANNE HARRINGTON PH. D., is Professor for the History of Science at Harvard University, specializing in the history of psychiatry, neuroscience, and the other mind sciences. She received her doctorate in the History of Science from Oxford University in 1985 and has held postdoctoral fellowships in England and Germany. Strongly committed to the interdisciplinary exchange between the humanities and the biomedical sciences, from 1997 to 2002 she co-directed Harvard's Interfaculty Initiative in Mind, Brain, Behavior. From 1994 to 1998, she was a core member of the MacArthur Foundation Research Network on Mind-Body Interactions, where she headed projects on the placebo effect, trance, and meditation. She is the author of *Medicine, Mind, and the Double Brain* (1987) and *Reenchanted Science: Holism in German Culture from Wilhelm II to Hitler* (1996), as well as of about forty articles ranging across mind-body medicine, German-speaking holistic science, neuroscience, and psychiatry. She is also the editor of *The Placebo Effect: An Interdisciplinary Exploration* (1997) and, with Richard J. Davidson, *Visions of Compassion: Western Scientists and Tibetan Buddhists Examine Human Nature*. Her newest book, *Stories under the Skin*, will be published by W. W. Norton.

NOTES

1 Virtually all of the research remains controversial, although to varying degrees, and for various reasons. See for example "Evidence Behind Claim of Religion-Health Link Is Shaky, Researchers Say," a report of an article published in the March 2002 issue of the *Annals of Behavioral Medicine*, http://hbns.org/newsrelease/religion3-11-02.cfm. Compare that to the encouraging note sounded in the 2003 special edition of *American Psychologist* on "Spirituality, Religion, and Health" as an "emerging research field," *American Psychologist* (January 2003) 58(1): 24–74.

2 Some classic reference points in this literature include: L. F. Berkman and S. L. Syme,

(1979), "Social Networks, Host Resistance and Mortality: A Nine-Year Follow-Up Study of Alameda County Residents," *American Journal of Epidemiology* 109: 186–204; J. G. Bruhn and S. Wolf (1979), *The Roseto Story* (Norman: University of Oklahoma); S. Wolf (1992), Predictors of myocardial infarction over a span of 30 years in Roseto, Pennsylvania. *Integrative Physiological and Behavioral Science* 27(3): 246–57; J. S. House, K. R. Landis et al. (1988), "Social relationships and health." *Science* 241(4865): 540–45.

3   See, for example, J. S. House, C. Robbins et al. (1982), "The association of social relationships and activities with mortality: prospective evidence from the Tecumseh Community Health Study." *Am J Epidemiol* 116(1): 123–40.

4   See, for example, W. J. Strawbridge, R. D. Cohen, G. A. Kaplan (1997), "Frequent attendance at religious services and mortality over 28 years," *AJPH* 87: 957–61. It is worth remembering that correlation refers to nothing more or less than a linkage between variables and does not necessarily prove causality.

5   J. D. Kark, S. Carmel, R. Sinnreich, N. Goldberger, Y. Friedlander (1996), "Psychosocial factors among members of religious and secular kibbutzim." *Israeli Journal of Medical Science*, Mar–Apr, 32(3–4): 185–94.

6   The classic reference here is G. W. Allport and J. M. Ross (1967), "Personal religious orientation and prejudice." *Journal of Personality and Social Psychology* 5: 432–43.

7   On this historical phenomenon, see, among others, Megan Peimer, "Transcendental meditation: a prototype for the translation of spirituality into science in the 1970s" (a senior undergraduate honors thesis presented to the Department for the History of Science, Harvard University: 1997). Available through the Harvard University (Widener) library system.

8   The development and popularization of the concept of "stress" as we today understand it was led after World War II by the Viennese-born physiologist Hans Selye, who came to Canada (the University of Montreal) in the 1930s. See, e.g., Hans Selye (1973), "The Evolution of the Stress Concept," *American Scientist* 61: 692–99. For more on the history of stress, see John W. Mason (1975), "A Historical View of the Stress Field," Part II, *Journal of Human Stress* 1 (June): 22–36.

9   For an introduction to Benson's early research in this area, see R. K. Wallace, H. Benson, and A. F. Wilson (1971), "A Wakeful Hypometabolic State," *American Journal of Physiology* 221: 795–99; R. K. Wallace and H. Benson (1972), "The Physiology of Meditation," *Scientific American* 226(2): 84–90; J. F. Beary and H. Benson (1974), "A Simple Physiologic Technique Which Elicits the Hypometabolic Changes of the Relaxation Response," *Psychosomatic Medicine* 36: 115–20. Benson's best-selling book popularizing his technique and its health-promoting effects was published in 1975: *The Relaxation Response* (with Marion Z. Klipper, New York: Avon Books).

10 J. Kabat-Zinn (1982), "An outpatient program in behavioral medicine for chronic pain patients based on the practice of mindfulness meditation: Theoretical considerations and preliminary results," *General Hospital Psychiatry* 4: 33-47; J. Kabat-Zinn, L. Lipworth, and R. Burney (1985), "The clinical use of mindfulness meditation for the self-regulation of chronic pain," *Journal of Behavioral Medicine* 8(2): 163–90; J. Kabat-Zinn (1991), *Full catastrophe living: Using the wisdom of your body and mind to face stress, pain, and illness* (New York: Delacorte); J. Kabat-Zinn, E. Wheeler, T. Light, A. Skillings, M. J. Scharf, T. G. Cropley et al. (1998), "Influence of a mindfulness meditation-based

stress reduction intervention on rates of skin clearing in patients with moderate to severe psoriasis undergoing phototherapy (UBV) and photochemotherapy (PUVA)," *Psychosomatic Medicine* 60(5): 625–32.

11 *Psychology Today* (October 1989).

12 Jean-Martin Charcot (1893), "la foi qui guérit," *Progrès Medicale*; "The faith-cure," *The New Review* 8: 18–31.

13 See William James, "The Religion of Healthy-Mindedness," Lectures IV and V from *The Varieties of Human Experience: A Study in Human Nature* (New York: Penguin Books, 1902 [1987]).

14 For a discussion of the influence of the mind-cure movement on Norman Vincent Peale, see Charles Braden, *Spirits in Rebellion: The Rise and Development of New Thought* (Dallas: Southern Methodist University Press, 1966 [reprinted, 1987]); for its links to the so-called New Age movement, see, among others, "New Age and the New Thought Movement," http://websyte.com/alan/newage.htm; and "Science of Mind, New Thought, Unity, and the New Age Movement," http://www.new-thought.org/suggest.html.

15 For the mission statement of the John Templeton Foundation, and a description of its commitment to funding work on interactions between spirituality and health, see its website: http://www.templeton.org.

16 John Sedgwick, *The Unlikely Philanthropic Odyssey of Sir John Templeton*, Worth Business eBooks (July/August 2000) (http://www.ebooks.com/item/042895.htm); excerpt reprinted online at http://www.templeton.org/worth.asp.

17 See, for example, L. A. Gottshalk (1985), "Hope and other deterrents of illness," *American Journal of Psychotherapy* 39: 515–24; N. Cousins, *Head First: The Biology of Hope* (New York: Dutton, 1989); K. W. Pettingale et al. (1985), "Mental attitudes to cancer: An attitudinal prognostic factor," *Lancet* 8, 750; P. C. Roud (1987), "Psychosocial variables associated with the exceptional survival of patients with advanced malignant disease," *Journal of the Nat. Med Association* 79: 97–102.

18 On the placebo effect, see, among others, my own edited volume, A. Harrington, *The Placebo Effect: An Interdisciplinary Exploration* (Cambridge: Harvard University Press, 1997).

19 Herbert Benson (with Marg Stark), *Timeless Healing: The Power and Biology of Belief* (New York: Scribner), 1996, 200.

20 Ted Porter, *Trust in Numbers: The Pursuit of Objectivity in Science and Public Life* (Princeton, NJ: Princeton University Press, 1997).

21 Francis Galton (1872), "Statistical inquiries into the efficacy of prayer," *Fortnightly Review* 12: 125–35.

22 D. W. Forrest, *Francis Galton: The Life and Work of a Victorian Genius* (London: Paul Elk, 1974), 172.

23 Before Byrd, there were one or two other studies—all with negative results—that have received less attention: C. R. B. Joyce and R. M. C. Welldon (1965), "The objective efficacy of prayer: a double-blind clinical trail," *J Chronic Dis.* 18: 367–77; P. J. Collipp (1969), "The efficacy of prayer: a triple-blind study," *Med Times* 97: 201–4.

24 There was no attempt to stop family members and others from praying for the people in the control group, leading to odd discussions about the effects of "background" prayer and "prayer dosage."

25 R. J. Byrd (1988), "Positive therapeutic effects of intercessory prayer in a coronary care unit population," *Southern Medical Journal* 81: 826–29. Also available online at http://www.godandscience.org/apologetics/smj.pdf.

26 W. S. Harris, M. Gowda, J. W. Kolb et al. (1999), "A randomized, controlled trial of the effects of remote, intercessory prayer on outcomes in patients admitted to the coronary care unit," *Arch Intern Med.* 159: 2273–78. For the transcript of a March 13, 2001, debate between Harris and a skeptic, Irwin Tessman, see http://www.csicop.org/articles/2001 0810-prayer.

27 The organization's official position on the intercessory prayer work it is funding can be read at: http://www.templeton.org/spirituality_programs.asp.

28 See, for example, Patrick Glynn's *God: The Evidence* (Rocklin, CA: Prima Publishing, 1997).

29 "Evidence for God from Science: Harmony between the Bible and Science," http://www.godandscience.org/index.html.

30 Cf. Joel James Shuman and Keith G. Meador, *Heal Thyself: Spirituality, Medicine, and the Distortion of Christianity* (Oxford: Oxford University Press, 2003), 40–43.

31 It was Dale Matthews who told a group of graduating medical students that the "medicine of the future is going to be prayer and Prozac." See H. Side (1997), "The calibration of belief," *New York Times Magazine* (December 7): 92–95. Reprinted as: "Prescription: Prayer," *St. Petersburg Times* (December 29, 1997): D1–2. Ironically Dale Matthews's own widely anticipated study investigating the power of intercessory prayer at a distance proved disappointing. See Gary P. Posner (2002), "Study Yields No Evidence for Medical Efficacy of Distant Intercessory Prayer: A Follow-up Commentary," *The Scientific Review of Alternative Medicine* 6, no. 1 (Winter). Also online at: http://members.aol.com/garypos/prayerstudyafterpub.html.

32 Cf. here Harold G. Koenig, Michael E. McCullough, David B. Larson, *Handbook of Religion and Health* (Oxford: Oxford University Press, 2000), 5.

33 Some classic, critical works on American "therapeutic culture" include Philip Rieff, *The Triumph of the Therapeutic: Uses of Faith After Freud* (Chicago: University of Chicago Press, 1966 [1987]); T. J. Jackson Lears, "From Salvation to Self-Realization: Advertising and the Therapeutic Roots of the Consumer Culture, 1880–1930," in *The Culture of Consumption: Critical Essays in American History, 1880–1980,* ed. Richard Wightman Fox and T. J. Jackson Lears (New York: Pantheon, 1983), 1–38.

SPIRITUALITY, MEDICINE, AND MISUNDERSTANDINGS

Harold G. Koenig

SCIENCE AND RELIGION have been at odds throughout most of recorded history. Usually, science uncovers new information that seems to invalidate religious beliefs or teachings. In the most recent battle between religion and science, however, conflict seems to have arisen over the exact opposite: findings that appear to validate the health benefits of religion for humankind and society. And, surprisingly, the strongest objectors in this debate have not been scientists, but theologians. This essay examines their concerns and attempts to clarify the issues.

Medical and social scientists have over the years collected a lot of evidence that those who are more religious tend to be healthier, happier, and less burdensome to society. This research has stimulated a small revolution within the field of medicine and healthcare more broadly. Surprisingly, such trends have received relatively little criticism from other medical researchers, with the exception of primarily one (Sloan et al. 1999; 2000). As a result, there are signs of growing acceptance of a role for religion and spirituality within mainstream medicine (Koenig 2001; 2002). This is particularly notable given that scientific communities typically change their views only very slowly and over long periods of time.

But another group of critics is put off by efforts to explore the connection between religion and health. Several articles in popular magazines, medical journals, and at least one book illustrate the objections to such research by leaders within the religious community. In the January 27, 1999, issue of *The Christian Century*, an article appeared entitled "Faith's Benefits." Quoting from that article, "By praising religion's health benefits, scientists subtly confirm their own cultural authority" (77). In the August 2001 issue of the *Journal of the South Carolina Medical Association*, the Reverend Joe Baroody writes, "By claiming that faith heals, the authors place faith directly in opposition to death, thereby oversimplifying faith's role in relation to illness" (347). Most recently, a book entitled *Heal Thyself: Spirituality, Medicine, and the Distortion of Christianity* (Shuman and Meador 2002) raised serious concerns about how the information from such research is being interpreted and applied.

Objections can be categorized into three major concerns: (1) That health professionals will encourage people to become religious in order to achieve better health; (2) that scientists are trying to validate religion, which has traditionally been viewed by those within the religious field as needing no proof or verification; and (3) that healthcare professionals, because of their interest in addressing spiritual issues, are invading the turf of clergy, taking over their role, and squeezing them out of an area in which they, not health professionals, are the experts. Let us examine each concern more closely.

Prescribing Religion

As a result of this research, there is concern that doctors will prescribe religion to nonreligious patients in order to improve their health. For example, physicians may encourage patients to attend church or pray to God, just as they would suggest that patients stop smoking or exercise. This use of religion for health purposes alone is seen as both trivializing and utilitarian.

This argument has two parts. First, it emphasizes that religion has intrinsic value and worth that are far greater than any health benefits it may confer. In fact, true, devout faith may prompt people to risk their emotional or physical health in order to advance the religious cause, as commonly seen among missionaries, prophets, and martyrs. Religious beliefs often have a cost in terms of self-sacrifice, including giving up certain pleasures that provide satisfaction and comfort. Thus, devout religion may not always improve health or relieve suffering. To imply that religion is not valid unless it enhances health or makes someone feel good is simplistic at best and heretical at worst.

Second, if a person becomes religious with the primary goal of improving their health, then better health may not result. While nearly twelve hundred research studies during the twentieth century explored the relationship between religion and health (Koenig et al. 2001), no studies examined whether becoming religious only to achieve health accomplished this result. In fact, nonreligious people who attend church expecting to cure high blood pressure or strengthen their ability to fight off disease may be sadly disappointed. If religious teachings make them uncomfortable by challenging their lifestyles, stress levels may increase, blood pressures may rise, and immune function may plummet. While more than six hundred studies show that people who are religious are healthier, most of these people weren't religious just for the health benefits. Rather, better health was likely a natural byproduct of devout faith pursued for its own value.

If these points are valid, then should physicians and nurses seek to bring about spiritual transformation in order to achieve better health for their patients? I think not. Bringing about a spiritual transformation in nonreligious patients is not a primary, or even a secondary, concern for health professionals. It is the clergy who have been trained to serve as spiritual guides. Thus, it is inappropriate (and probably unethical) for a physician to prescribe religion as they would penicillin or aspirin to a nonreligious patient. Such prescriptions would instill expectations that becoming religious for health reasons alone will improve health, which is neither scientifically demonstrated nor theologically sound.

There is much, however, that health professionals can do short of taking on the clergy's role. First, at least in America, the vast majority of patients are *already* religious. Rather than ignore or devalue this (as has been the custom for the past several centuries), should not health professionals recognize the importance of religion as a resource for health and healing? Although health professionals are not experts in this area, are there no actions they can properly take to ensure that spiritual needs are met, while at the same time not overstepping professional boundaries? I think there are. Taking a spiritual history, showing respect for the patient's religious beliefs, and taking a few moments to listen to spiritual concerns without giving advice are just a few examples.

Science Validating Religion

In today's culture, science has become for many the ultimate and final source of authoritative knowledge about the world. Many view religion as simply one other aspect of the natural world that can be subject to scientific scrutiny and therefore be either proved or disproved. Theologians object to this. They say that there are other ways of "knowing" besides science and that there are other sources of truth beyond the ability of science to verify or disprove them.

Religious leaders are reluctant to give scientists the power to either credit or discredit their sacred beliefs and practices, and it is not surprising that they are offended by attempts to do so using scientific tools designed to examine natural phenomena. Examining events that occur outside of Nature belongs squarely in the province of religion, which, they claim, has its own methods of identifying and assessing spiritual truth. Many scientists agree with them and believe that religion and science are not compatible.

Why, then, are biomedical researchers attempting to study the relationship between religion and health, against objections from both other scientists and many theologians? To answer this question it is important to understand that two very different approaches are now being taken by researchers in this area. The first, as represented by double-blinded intercessory prayer studies, seeks to scientifically prove the supernatural. The second examines the effects of religious belief and practice on mental and physical health through pathways that are widely acknowledged and accepted by science.

The first approach, as I see it, is neither scientifically nor theologically credible, and experts from both sides of the fence should be objecting to such studies. They lack scientific value because the mechanism by which health effects are thought to occur is completely outside of the recognized laws that govern the universe. Such studies do not build on existing scientific knowledge, as research usually does. If the existence of such effects could be verified, then this would involve a leap in scientific knowledge that has no precedent in human history.

The first approach also raises theological questions that are not easily answered, at least within a monotheistic Western religious worldview. That view sees the universe as being governed by an all-powerful, all-knowing, unlimited, and just but merciful personal God who is well described in Jewish, Christian, and Islamic holy texts. This is not a God who can be controlled to act within the confines of a research study, a God who must follow natural laws, a God who has no other purpose for humankind other than health, and a God who always answers yes—like a magic genie at our beck and call. Instead, God is portrayed as separate from Creation, acting outside of time and space, above and beyond that which can be scientifically measured and verified—indeed, a God whose "ways are not man's ways" and for whom "a day is like a thousand years."

In contrast to attempts to prove the supernatural, a second approach relies entirely on the scientific method. In this case, it is the *effects* of religious belief and practice that are of primary interest. This is an entirely different game—this time, played according to the rules. Over the years, scientists have developed ways of accurately and reliably measuring psychological, social, and physical health. In addition, literally hundreds of religious measures exist that can assess types of beliefs and quantify the intensity of those beliefs and their associated behaviors.

From a scientific viewpoint, then, there is absolutely no reason that one cannot measure a person's religiousness and observe how this relates to mental, social, or physical health. Likewise, there is no reason that experiments cannot be undertaken to increase the religious practices of persons in one group and compare their speed of healing with that of a control group. This approach should not unduly concern either theologians or scientists since such research has no bearing on whether or not God exists and answers prayers or whether the supernatural is "real." Such an approach is firmly based within the current scientific model and relies on well-known psychological, social, and behavioral mechanisms within the field of science. The focus is on the *consequences* of having religious belief and living out those beliefs, not on whether those beliefs are true or false.

Health Professionals Invading Turf

The third objection by religious professionals, sometimes spoken and sometimes not, is that if physicians and nurses begin to regularly address spiritual issues, then this would involve an invasion of turf. Health professionals are not trained to address patients' spiritual needs and therefore are limited in what they can do. What they can do is largely restricted to spiritual assessment. What they cannot do is address complex spiritual issues or provide spiritual advice on subjects about which they have little or no knowledge.

Job security, however, is probably the last thing that clergy need worry about if health professionals become more cognizant and appreciative of the role that spirituality plays in medicine. Most physicians and nurses are already overwhelmed by their own duties and don't have time (nor often the desire) to address patients' spiritual needs. The result would most likely be an increase in demand for pastoral services—possibly one that would be difficult to meet with existing resources.

Conclusion

Misunderstanding and confusion surround scientific research that is now examining the relationship between religion and health. This is widespread both among medical researchers and religious professionals and prevents progress in understanding the role that spirituality plays in healthcare. As these misunderstandings begin to clear, my hope is that religious and health professionals will increasingly see one another, and religion-health researchers, as allies in a common effort to help people heal and become whole. Admittedly, the ultimate goals of medicine and religion are different. The goal of medicine is to relieve suffering and achieve health. This is not the primary task of religion. However, health and relief of suffering often result from religion sought after for the right reasons. Because of this, medicine and religion are connected.

✑♥

HAROLD G. KOENIG, M.D., M.H.Sc., currently is on the faculty at Duke University Medical Center as Professor of Psychiatry and Behavioral Sciences and Associate Professor of Medicine. He is Director and Founder of the Center for the Study of Religion/Spirituality and Health at that institution and has published extensively in the fields of mental health, geriatrics, and religion, with nearly 170 scientific peer-reviewed articles, more than 40 book chapters, and 24 books in print or in preparation. Dr. Koenig is Editor of the *International Journal of Psychiatry in Medicine* and Founder and Editor-in-Chief of *Research News & Opportunities in Science and Theology*. His latest book is *Spiritual Caregiving* with Verna Carson (Templeton Foundation Press, 2004).

REFERENCES

Koenig, H. G. (2001). Editorial. Religion, spirituality and medicine: How are they related and what does it mean? *Mayo Clinic Proceedings* 76: 1189–91.

———— (2002). An 83-year-old woman with chronic illness and strong religious beliefs. *Journal of the American Medical Association* 288: 487–93.

Koenig H. G., McCullough M., and Larson D. B. (2001). *Handbook of Religion and Health.* New York: Oxford University Press.

Shuman, J., and Meador, K. (2002). *Heal Thyself: Spirituality, Medicine, and the Distortion of Christianity.* New York: Oxford University Press.

Sloan, R. P., Bagiella, E., and Powell, T. (1999). Religion, spirituality, and medicine. *The Lancet* 353: 664–67.

Sloan, R. P., Bagiella, E., VandeCreek, L., Hover, M., Casalone, C., Hirsch, T. J., Hasan, Y., Kreger, R. (2000). Should physicians prescribe religious activities? *New England Journal of Medicine* 342: 1913–16.

Ted Peters

W E FIND OURSELVES in a struggle between flesh and spirit, says St. Paul in the New Testament. When the spirit wins, we enjoy the fruits: "love, joy, peace, patience, kindness, generosity, faithfulness, gentleness, and self-control" (Gal 5:22). When the flesh takes control, it drives us to "fornication, impurity, licentiousness, idolatry, sorcery, enmities, strife, jealousy, anger, quarrels, dissensions, factions, envy, drunkenness, carousing, and things like these" (Gal 5:19–20). The question I wish to pose now is: Can our body influence the spirit? If we are born with a genetic predisposition toward the things of the flesh, does it make the task of spiritual growth impossible, or at least more difficult? If we devise a pharmaceutical to overcome an inherited genetic predisposition, could such therapy be considered growth in the spirit?

Flesh and Spirit vs. Body and Soul

Before we proceed further, I'd like to introduce a theological clarification. The struggle between flesh and spirit ought not to be equated simply with the distinction between body and soul, even though many have lived vibrantly with this partially misleading equation. In St. Paul's theology, both body and soul are caught up in the war between flesh and spirit. Flesh and spirit are forces exerted on body and soul, even if it seems at first glance that flesh wells up out of the body to contaminate the soul while spirit strengthens the soul so it can gain control over the body. Therefore, by "flesh" we mean the body at war with the Spirit of God; fleshly forces can dim the soul, coercing it into doing their bidding. The countervailing force of the divine Spirit liberates the self, both body and soul, from fleshly degradation.

Despite the above clarification, Stoics and ancient Christian theologians tended to associate flesh with body and spirit with soul. They dubbed the former our "lower nature" and the latter our "higher nature." The spiritual task, they said, was to cultivate the life of the mind or soul so that our higher nature could gain control over our lower nature. We are born dominated by our body; we should die victoriously free in the life of the liberated mind. Our higher natures cleave to sublime thoughts about God, to virtuous ideals such as justice and beauty, to moral integrity, and to mental disciplines such as prayer and meditation. These higher thoughts are eternal, whereas thoughts about cravings dictated by the body are ephemeral. Strength in the soul enables the higher or spiritual dimension to gain freedom from our bodies through control over the source of fleshly desire. Whether they used the word "soul" or "mind," they were actually seeking victory for the spirit. The result of such thinking led to centuries of spiritual practices where the goal was to gain mental control over the physical, immaterial control over the material, and hence spiritual control over the flesh.

Biological Reductionism vs. Human Freedom

This history of spiritual thought provides a valuable resource for assessing the rapid pace of developing knowledge about human nature rising out of research in molecular biology and the neurosciences. Although to date the experiments have been few and empirically reliable information remains fractional at best, a mood of genetic determinism and biological reductionism is beginning to emerge. Researchers are looking for genetic predispositions to mental states and propensities toward antisocial behavior, and brain researchers are looking for the roots of intellectual and emotional processes in neuronal activity. Yet, even as the specters of genetic determinism and biological reductionism are looming on the horizon, religious reactions to such thinking could be plastic and protean, given what we have just noted regarding the tradition of theological thinking about the struggle between flesh and spirit.

Is contemporary science about to take away our freedom? Are biologists about to imprison the human spirit in a fleshly jail? Is our higher nature reducible to our lower nature, so that the spirit no longer has leverage to deal with our fleshly desires?

The level of alarm need not be this shrill. There is no need to react like Pavlov's dogs in defense of human freedom against the alleged scientific jailers. There is no need to avoid the science on the grounds that it is irrelevant to truths already firmly and independently established by religion.

Genes, Nurture, and Antisocial Behavior

Let us take a brief look at a single scientific study, the kind we would expect from those seeking biological explanations for human behavior. Under the hypothesis of genetic determinism or, perhaps more modestly, genetic influence, questions are being asked about biological factors in human behavior. This becomes especially relevant to theology when the behavior in question is either sinful or virtuous. Do genes make us sin? If so, does this contradict or complement what Christian theologians have previously thought about our bodily inheritance and its influence on the soul, or even on the spiritual dimension of who we are?

Our sample study—we will nickname it the "X chromosome study"—addresses the question of genetic influence in moderating environmental factors affecting human behavior, specifically antisocial or criminal behavior. The conclusion is that if a certain gene regulator on the X chromosome permits only a low level of expression of the monoamine oxidase A (MAOA) gene, which governs a neurotransmitter-metabolizing enzyme in the brain, then young boys have an increased risk of going to jail; conversely, a higher level of this gene's expression reduces the risk of engaging in the kind of antisocial behavior that makes a young man jail bound.

The X chromosome study looked at young boys, maltreated in their youth, whom we would expect to grow up to become criminals. Yet, an identifiable level of a certain gene's activity seems to reduce the otherwise fatalistic power of a family environment of abuse (Caspi et al. 2002). The research question was formulated thus: Why do some male children who are maltreated in their homes grow up to develop antisocial behavior traits while others do not?

The assumptions orienting the research question are worth noting. First, male children rather than female children were selected because the researchers were already looking for a factor that only the male gender carries on the X chromosome —that is, they assumed that the antisocial behavior in question is a gender-specific phenomenon. Second, the researchers assumed that maltreatment of young boys increases the risk that they will grow up exhibiting antisocial personality symptoms and conduct disorders and will become violent offenders—that is, they assumed that a social environment of victimization exerts a strong influence toward becoming a victimizer.

With these assumptions in hand, the researchers built their experiment on top of a previous study of one thousand children, half boys and half girls, who were assessed for maltreatment at ages 3, 5, 7, 9, 11, 13, 15, 18, 21, and 26. Of these, 8 percent were categorized as having experienced "severe maltreatment" between years 3 and 11; 28 percent were dubbed as "probable maltreatment" cases; and 64 percent experienced no maltreatment. The researchers focused on the first category, 26-year-old males who had been severely maltreated between the ages of 3 and 11, and slated them for genetic testing. Then on the X chromosome they examined the gene for MAOA, or actually the promoter or regulatory sequence for this gene expression. They found a polymorphism that down-regulates gene activity. Those young men whose MAOA gene exhibited low expression levels were much more likely to exhibit aggressive antisocial behavior and become incarcerated for violent crimes than those whose gene exhibited a high level of expression.

The research team noted that the effect of childhood maltreatment on antisocial behavior was significantly weaker among males with high MAOA activity. More broadly, they noted that maltreated males with a low MAOA-activity genotype were more likely than nonmaltreated males with this genotype to be convicted of a violent crime by a significant ratio, thereby reinforcing the environmental assumption identified above. Finally, the scientists concluded that the association between maltreatment and antisocial behavior is conditional, depending on a child's MAOA genotype. In sum, environmental or social influences are relevant but insufficient to explain antisocial behavior. Genotype must be factored in. DNA is decisive.

As we tease out the significance of this X chromosome research, we note that both assumptions and conclusions are deterministic in structure. They begin with the assumption of environmental determinism—if young boys are maltreated, then they will grow up antisocial—and then shift to genetic determinism—gene expression exacerbates or mitigates environmental influence. The net effect of both the assumptions and the conclusions is that some boys are born into situations in which the combination of gene expression and social context heavily determine what kind of person they will be in adult society.

Are We Born Morally Neutral?

Do such findings by contemporary science contradict or complement what theologians have traditionally believed? We could imagine that a modern Pelagian
might want to defy the science of the X chromosome study by asserting that we are
born morally neutral, that we enter the world and grow up with the capacity to
decide equally between right and wrong. In the fifth century, Pelagius himself actually showed little interest in the concept of original sin; his thesis was that human
beings could take initiative toward salvation from our natural state without the aid
of divine grace. Yet the Pelagian tradition down to modern humanism emphasizes
original neutrality over original sin. Good and evil here are thought to be equal
options standing before a freely deciding human psyche. So, assumptions about
determinism, either biological or social, would have to be dismissed as compro-
mising this morally neutral anthropology. Science must be mistaken if it asserts
that some, if not all, of us are driven by birth or by rearing toward an ineluctable
propensity for evil behavior. The theological position that we are born morally neutral will find rough sledding in this scientific environment.

An Augustinian, in contrast, might see such scientific research as partially demonstrating what Christians have known all along—that we emerge from our mother's
womb with a self-orientation that makes loving God and loving neighbor contradictory to our innate propensity. We are born *homo incurvatus in se,* curved in on
ourselves. It takes an act of divine grace to reorient us toward loving God and loving our neighbor as we would love ourselves. It takes the inspiration of the Holy
Spirit to orient our hearts and wills and minds toward expressing the fruits of the
Spirit.

Now, what we have in theology is much broader and more sweeping in scope
than what appears in such a scientific study, to be sure. Such research does not even
ask about the total orientation of the human self. It deals only with one segment of
human behavior and a pattern of behavior that applies to some, but not all, of us.
Does this obviate the value of comparing science and theology? By no means. Such
science is still quite relevant to theological anthropology. If genetic inheritance and
social inheritance combine to predispose us to behavior with moral valence in some
cases, then we can hypothesize that some level of genetic and environmental determinism has an effect on everyone's life. Our genes and our family experience provide both opportunity and constraint for us to become the kind of person we will
grow up to be.

Further, although we are focusing here on the predisposition toward sinful behavior, in another setting we might provide a parallel analysis of caring behavior. I
believe we can safely assume that favorable genotypes and certainly loving family
contexts increase a child's opportunity to grow up with high-minded values and
an increased capacity for loving his or her neighbor.

Further still, a nuance related to the X chromosome study might be worth pondering here. The young men studied were victims of maltreatment. We might wish
to ask: Do they love themselves? Does their overwhelming experience of abuse permit the emergence of self-love, or might maltreatment more likely retard the growth

of self-worth and leave the child with self-loathing? Might the antisocial behavior in question be an expression of self-hatred rather than a self-love unable to expand to include others? If the Augustinian lens through which sin is interpreted is this—sin is too much love for self and not enough love for God or neighbor—then perhaps we need a more subtle analysis of the young men in the X chromosome study. If scripture is right that we love because God first loved us (1 John 4:19), then perhaps all of us, these young men included, need first to experience love before the capacity to love either self or neighbor can develop. Perhaps we need to experience unconditional love before we can develop the capacity to love others unconditionally. This may be the way grace works in a redemptive way.

Original Sin as Inherited Sin

The theological language of original sin creates discordant sounds in the ears of modern intellectuals. The concept is unwelcome, even shunned. Perhaps this shunning is due to the historical connotations of the term "original." The picture painted by Augustine is that Adam and Eve committed the first sin, the original sin, in the Garden of Eden; and through procreation they have passed this fallen state on to each subsequent generation. We all inherit—and participate—in Adam's sin.

This prompts two contemporary objections. First, our modern notions of justice would limit our responsibility to our own sins; we should not be held accountable for an action of someone else, such as Adam or Eve. This is a Pelagian objection built on the assumptions that we are born as isolated individuals disconnected to humanity as a whole and born with moral neutrality accompanied by the freedom to choose between two equal options, good and evil. The second objection is that the Augustinian history is apparently no longer acceptable in a Darwinian era. The dominance of the theory of evolution with its deep time and epic of human emergence from previous species has no room for a myth of origin that places the human race in a prior state of grace. The Garden of Eden cannot be located geographically or geologically. Rather than a fall from a pristine state, modern science sees the human race arising from a long struggle characterized by natural selection and survival of the fittest.

It seems to me that the concept of "original" in the context of sin does not require a history that includes a past Garden of Eden with a now-lost perfection; nor does it require blaming Adam and Eve for our own moral condition. Rather, it is sufficient for "original" to refer to the "origin" of each one of us. Our own individual origin is characterized by conditioning—genetic conditioning and family-context conditioning. We are born with opportunities and constraints over which we had no original control, and some of this conditioning influences our predisposition to behavior toward others.

Perhaps we might retrieve here the theological term "inherited sin." When the Augsburg Confession discusses "original sin," we read that all of us who are conceived according to nature are born into sin, that we are "full of evil lust and inclinations" from our mothers' wombs onward, that we are unable by nature to have true fear of God and true faith in God. This state is referred to as *Erbsunde,* "inborn sickness and hereditary sin" (Article II). In *Institutes of the Christian Religion*, John Calvin similarly interprets the concept of original sin so that what we inherit becomes prominent: "Original sin, therefore, seems to be a hereditary depravity and corruption of our nature, diffused into all parts of the soul, which first makes us liable to God's wrath, then also brings forth in us those works which Scripture calls 'works of the flesh'" (II:i:8).

Much is being said here. The single item I would like to lift up is the ease with which such theological thinking accepts the notion of inheritance. When we are born, we find ourselves already conditioned, already predisposed toward a life that is alienated from God's will, even alienated from faith in God. Although the presumption here is that this inheritance is physical—that is, passed on through conception and birth—the point is that we begin our life of moral responsibility already conditioned by factors beyond our control. It is certainly consistent, then, for Social Gospel theologians such as Walter Rauschenbusch early in the last century to observe how prejudice and social discrimination are passed down from one generation to the next; and it is consistent for liberal theologians today to incorporate observations about social inheritance—what liberation theologians and feminist theologians call "social location" or "systemic evil"—into our understanding of the human condition. Whether biological or social, innate or environmental, we begin our morally responsible life with a specific inheritance and a predisposition toward behaving in specific ways.

Fruits of the Spirit

Let us speculate. Suppose a clever medical scientist could invent a pharmaceutical capable of up-regulating the expression of MAOA. Suppose the young boys subjected to family abuse could have access to MAOA therapy. And suppose that this genetic therapy strengthens the influence of genetic determinants over environmental determinants. Suppose the result would be that when attaining adulthood these young men would possess a greater sense of social responsibility exercised through greater self-control. Theologically speaking, should we consider this to be a fruit of the spirit?

Let me offer a qualified "yes" in answer. As Augustine sorts out the dialectic of sin and grace in *Enchiridion*, he begins with bondage to sin and then moves to liberty from it: "He who is the servant of sin is free to sin. And, hence, he will not be free to do right, until, being freed from sin, he shall begin to be the servant of righteousness. And this is true liberty" (chapter XXX). Might we think of the combination of genetic predisposition and maltreatment in youth as a form of bondage? And might we think of medical therapy that readies a person for increased self-control a form of liberation?

Note a pitfall I am trying to avoid here: that of defining the question in terms of metaphysics. If we are assuming that the distinction between body and soul, or the conflict between flesh and spirit, are metaphysical divisions, then the situation would be conceptually hopeless. If we would assume that body and soul are different substances and that flesh and spirit are metaphysical opposites, then the spiritual conflict precipitated by gene function would be unanalyzable. However, if we presume that a person is a psychosomatic unity, that who we are as persons is inclusive of both body and soul, then their interaction at the level of the human self becomes accessible.

Recall that earlier I suggested that we can best understand flesh and spirit as forces, not merely as alternative terms for body and soul. One of the fruits of the spirit in St. Paul's list is "self-control." No matter what genotype we are born with or what family pattern of rearing we experience, self-control remains an achievement that each self must attain in the maturing process. In common parlance, "self-control" means what it says, namely, the self takes over a level of control that was previously under the hegemony of bodily cravings and social influences. If a pharmaceutical could enhance one's capacity for self-control, such therapy could very well be thought of as a spiritual force. That such therapy works on the body does not make it any less spiritual. Nor does it make medical therapy anything less than an expression of God's grace in the life of a person who benefits from it.

Need we theologians become anxious that modern medicine will put us out of a job? No worry is fitting here. The struggle between flesh and spirit is a big one, and winning one little battle over genetic expression of MAOA does not in itself indicate that we are ready to declare total victory in the war against the flesh. The spirit's orchard covers many acres, and there are many more fruits of empowering grace that the Holy Spirit can cultivate through either our body or our soul.

✍

TED PETERS, PH.D., received his doctorate from the University of Chicago in 1973 and is an ordained pastor in the Evangelical Lutheran Church of America. Currently, he serves as Professor of Systematic Theology at Pacific Lutheran Theological Seminary, of which he is the former president, and at the Graduate Theological Union in Berkeley, California. Professor Peters is editor of *Dialog, A Journal of Theology* and co-editor of *Theology and Science*. He is author of *GOD—The World's Future* (Fortress, 2000); *Playing God? Genetic Determinism and Human Freedom* (Routledge, 2002); and *Science, Theology, and Ethics* (Ashgate, 2003). He is also co-editor of *Bridging Science and Religion* (Fortress, 2003). From 1990 to 1994, Professor Peters worked as Principal Investigator on a research grant from the U.S. National Institutes of Health, "Theological and Ethical Questions Raised by the Human Genome Project." From 1998 to 2002, he directed the "Science and Religion Course Program" at the Center for Theology and the Natural Sciences.

REFERENCES

The Augsburg Confession, in *The Book of Concord: The Confessions of the Evangelical Lutheran Church*, edited by Robert Kolb and Timothy J. Wengert. Minneapolis: Fortress Press, 2000.

Augustine, *The Enchiridion on Faith, Hope, and Love*. Washington: Gateway, 1961.

Calvin, John, *Institutes of the Christian Religion*, translated and annotated by Ford Lewis Battles. Atlanta: John Knox Press, 1975.

Calvin, John, *Institutes of the Christian Religion*, edited by John T. McNeill, *Library of Christian Classics* XX, XXI. Philadelphia: The Westminster Press, 1960.

Caspi, Avshalom, Joseph McClay, Terrie E. Moffitt, Jonathan Mill, Judy Martin, Ian W. Craig, Alan Taylor, and Richie Poulton, "Role of Genotype in the Cycle of Violence in Maltreated Children," *Science* 297 (2 August 2002): 851–54.

Mental Health, Spiritual Information, and the Power of the Mind to Shape the Brain 65

Jeffrey M. Schwartz

Suppose I say of a friend: "He isn't an automaton."

What information is conveyed by this, and to whom would it be information? To a human being who meets him in ordinary circumstances? What information could it give him? (At the very most that this man always behaves like a human being, and not occasionally like a machine.)

"I believe that he is not an automaton," just like that, so far makes no sense.
—*Ludwig Wittgenstein*, Philosophical Investigations, Part II, Section IV

THE NEW SCIENCE of brain imaging has already amply demonstrated that, with appropriate training and effort, people are capable of rewiring brain circuitry associated with a variety of mental and physical states. For example, people suffering from obsessive-compulsive disorder (OCD), a neuropsychiatric condition that causes thoughts and urges to intrude into the stream of daily experience, can change the brain activity associated with that condition (see Figures 1a and 1b). This is done by applying basic principles of mental training developed in the course of my work at the University of California, Los Angeles, over the past decade.

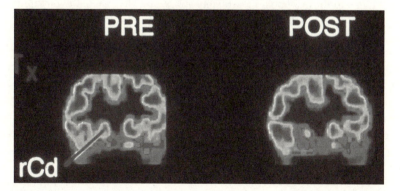

FIGURES 1A AND 1B. PET scan of a person with OCD before and after treatment. Figure 1a (PRE) shows the brain before and Figure 1b (POST) shows the brain ten weeks after behavioral therapy with no medication. Note in Figure 1b the decrease in "size," which signifies decreased energy use in the right caudate (rCd) nucleus (which appears on the left side of a PET scan) after treatment. Reprinted with permission from *Archives of General Psychiatry*, February 1996, Volume 53, page 112. © 1996, American Medical Association. All rights reserved.[1]

Further, and quite importantly, studies have demonstrated that directed mental effort can alter brain function in normal people undergoing stressful situations. The brain's responses even to experiences as basic as sexual arousal can be readily modified by simple willfully applied acts of the mind. In my recent book *The Mind and The Brain*, co-authored with Sharon Begley, we coined the term "self-directed neuroplasticity" to serve as a general description of the principle that focused training and effort can change brain function in ways that permit people to potentially become active participants in the treatment of their own medical and psychological conditions.

The possible application of this recent work to the design and discovery of new approaches to the treatment of brain-related diseases is obviously of great practical importance. Because this approach to treatment carries with it the explicit message that people can change their own brain function, it can have a potentially profound impact on issues concerning the culture of public health. Further, and crucially, these findings can help us shed new light on the critical question of the relationship of the striving human spirit to the biological matter of the human body.

Beyond the obvious clinical significance of scientifically demonstrating that humans can, with appropriate effort and training, rewire their own brain circuitry, perhaps the most important aspect of this research is its implications for our understanding of the role of willfully directed attention in shaping brain activity. Scientific research on the workings of the human brain tends to assume that what the brain does in any given situation is understandable in ways that view people as basically no different than machines. For instance, a person, let's call her Susan, is shown pictures depicting emotionally or perhaps sexually arousing scenes while images are made of the inner workings of her brain. Certain brain areas are noted to be activated. The scientist generally concludes that the observed brain activity is the cause of the emotional and other responses Susan is observed to have. All well and good, as far as it goes. And all quite passive and machinelike from Susan's point of view; all she had to do was remain reasonably awake and alert while the pictures were shown to her. What was being studied was how her brain machinery operates in that situation.

While this may be quite interesting to know for a scientist, it doesn't tell us very much about Susan as a person, and tells us close to nothing at all about her as a striving and willfully directed spiritual being. But if, as happens in a growing number of studies, Susan were encouraged to make an active response aimed at systematically *altering* the nature of her emotional response to what she was being shown—for example, by actively performing a new therapy skill she had been taught—understanding the experiment merely as a study of her brain's machinery would actually miss the basic point of the whole experiment. For in such a situation the point would be to show that Susan was able to *change how her brain works* by applying her new knowledge. This is especially true when one is doing medical research on how to develop improved methods for altering the emotional and brain responses to stressful stimuli. In such a case, we would not merely be studying Susan the human machine. We would be working together with Susan, a human person who was applying her new knowledge to help us discover better ways to treat brain-related emotional problems. By doing that she would also be proving that by using her mind she could change how her brain works. And this is an action that, beyond doubt, has true spiritual content, insofar as it empowers the value-laden inner life of a person to transcend the merely mechanical aspects of the material machinery of the brain. It thus provides a scientifically accessible context in which to demonstrate the capacity of self-aware and knowledge-seeking spiritual beings to reshape, through directed effort, their most deeply entrenched biological processes.

Simply stated, confusion concerning the relative importance of physical and mental aspects of the human condition can lead literally to fatal confusion about causes and effects in the study of human behavior. Tricky though it sometimes is to sort out these kinds of "chicken and egg" questions, serious investigators of the human condition must make a good-faith effort to do so. This is especially so when the investigation involves facts that are value-laden and can critically influence ethical choices we make about the world we live in.

In the case of studying psychological treatments and their physical effects, the distinction between mind and brain becomes absolutely critical. That's because if one simply assumes the most common belief of our era of medical research, namely that all aspects of emotional response are passively determined by biological (and especially brain) mechanisms, then developing genuinely effective self-directed psychological strategies that cause real changes in how the brain works becomes, in principle, impossible. The treating clinician thus becomes locked into the view, often without even realizing it, that the psychological treatment of ailments caused by physical brain-based problems is not a realistic goal.

There is already a wealth of data arguing against this view. For instance, the work in the 1990s on patients with OCD referred to above demonstrated significant brain changes in those who responded to psychological treatment. More recently, work by Mario Beauregard and colleagues at the University of Montreal have demonstrated brain changes after psychological therapy for spider phobia. There are now many scientific reports on the effects of self-directed regulation of emotional responses in conditions such as depression, panic anxiety, pathological shyness, and so on; the list continues to grow. Similar findings showing that self-directed effort can help heal the brain have even been made in such serious medical conditions as stroke and some forms of paralysis. Thus, the limitations and restrictions caused by even profoundly damaged biological matter can be transcended, and the brain itself reformed, by the directed striving that epitomizes the capacity of a the human spirit to prevail over adversity.

One aspect of willful mental activity seems particularly critical to the effective application of self-directed therapy: dispassionate self-observation, frequently called "mindfulness" or "mindful awareness." This mental act of clear-minded contemplation and scrutiny has a long and distinguished history in the description of human mental states. The most systematic and extensive description is in the canonical texts of classical Buddhism. Because of the critical importance of this type of close attentiveness in the practice of Buddhist meditation, some of its most refined descriptions in English are in texts concerned with meditative practice (although it is of critical importance to realize that the mindful mental state does not require any specific meditation practice to acquire and is *certainly not* in any sense a "trancelike" state). One particularly well-established description, referred to as "bare attention," is as follows:

> Bare attention is the clear and single-minded awareness of what actually happens *to* us and *in* us at the successive moments of perception. It is called "Bare" because it attends just to the bare facts of a perception as presented either through the five physical senses or through the mind . . . without reacting to them.[2]

Perhaps the essential aspect of mindful observation is that you are just watching, observing all facts, both inner and outer, very calmly, clearly, and closely.

This mental action is the core aspect of all self-regulation, for it is the means by which self-regulating strategies are performed. It is the essential ingredient of what the ancient Stoics called "self-command," the core element of controlling one's own responses to life's ups and downs. That is because mindful awareness is the mental act whereby one monitors whether the act of regulating one's responses is actually being effectively performed; that is, mindfulness is the way in which one evaluates whether one is, in fact, coping more successfully with stress. In a nutshell, bare attention is the key to putting self-regulating strategies into practice.

When observing and modulating one's own mental states, the mind plays a willful role in which it actively *affects* the brain and is not merely *affected by* it. Highlighting the active role of the mind in self-regulation is critical for a proper understanding of what is actually happening when a person directs his or her inner resources to the challenging task of modifying emotional responses. It takes *effort* for people to do this. That is because it requires a redirection of the brain's resources away from responses controlled largely by lower brain centers and toward higher-level functions that are associated with parts of the brain unique to human beings. This does not happen automatically. Rather, it requires willful training and directed effort. This is precisely why the Scottish philosopher Adam Smith, following the ancient Stoics, so extolled the development of self-command as the source of all human greatness. As he put it, "Self-command is not only itself a great virtue, but from it all other virtues seem to derive their principal lustre." The use of mindful awareness is the practical key that opens up the human capacity for self-regulation. The application of bare attention to one's own mental processes is the activity that leads to the development of the human mind's full potential. And as we now know, because of advances in scientific understanding, it is an act of the mind that is capable of rewiring the brain. The fact that immaterial mental states can causally influence the material workings of the brain is thus becoming established within the paradigmatic realm of mainstream science. As described in detail in a recent publication co-authored with theoretical physicist Henry Stapp, "the effects of *mentalistically described human intentional actions upon the physically described systems*" of the brain (Schwartz et al., 2004, italic in original),[3] is now something all scientifically oriented investigators, whatever their spiritual inclinations, must take into account.

Scientists and other technocratic elites pride themselves on being precise, yet when it comes to questions concerning the ethical and spiritual nature of human beings they too frequently use language glibly. They refer to willfully acting people with words that are more appropriate to the description of machines. As the philosopher Ludwig Wittgenstein so lucidly pointed out in the quotation with which we began this discussion, the string of words "I believe that he is not an automaton," just like that, so far makes no sense. This is so because of the plain fact that statements about the motives and ethics of people we interact with on a regular basis always convey spiritual information. Our intrinsic capacity to connect empathically with people we genuinely respect and love conveys real information to both them and us, information that is an inextricable aspect of both their and our spiritual natures. This is a core truth that exists prior to and is a requirement for genuinely intimate communication among humans in the real world. There is no need to prove that my best friend is not a machine—that the word "friend" has clear meaning is proof enough. Even so, it seems somehow reassuring that twenty-first-century brain science is now ready to reaffirm that fact.

✍

JEFFREY M. SCHWARTZ, M.D., Research Professor of Psychiatry at the University of California, Los Angeles, is a seminal thinker in the field of self-directed neuroplasticity. His major interest has been brain imaging/functional neuroanatomy and cognitive-behavioral therapy, with a focus on the pathological mechanisms and psychological treatment of obsessive-compulsive disorder. Dr. Schwartz is the author of *The Mind and the Brain: Neuroplasticity and the Power of Mental Force*, more than one hundred scientific publications, and two popular books: *Brain Lock: Free Yourself from Obsessive-Compulsive Behavior* and *Dear Patrick: Letters to a Young Man*. He received an honors degree in philosophy from the University of Rochester. In the 1970s, he began to immerse himself in Buddhist philosophy—in particular, the philosophy of mindfulness, or conscious awareness—and it became his goal to find a scientific underpinning for the belief that mindfulness affects how the brain works. In the 1990s, he made his key discovery: that cognitive behavioral therapy is capable of changing the activity in a specific brain circuit of patients with obsessive-compulsive disorder. This breakthrough provided hard evidence that the mind can systematically change the brain's chemistry and that it can do so through the classic Buddhist idea of mindfulness.

NOTES

1   Schwartz, J. M., Stoessel, P. W., Baxter, L. R., et al. (1996). Systematic changes in cerebral glucose metabolic rate after successful behavior modification treatment of obsessive-compulsive disorder. *Archives of General Psychiatry* 53: 109–13.

NATIVE AMERICAN WISDOM AND HEALING IN THE MODERN WORLD

Lori Arviso Alvord

I AM A MEMBER of the Navajo Tribe, and the first Navajo woman to become a surgeon. Currently, I practice at Dartmouth Medical School. My surgical practice is based on years of the careful, disciplined, and difficult training of the U.S. medical school system to master the art and science of medicine and my specialty in general surgery. In my professional life, I am able to bring healing to my patients using the benefits of this long training, drawing together the best of medical research and surgical innovation gained over the last century of medical progress. Yet I also carry with me another kind of long learning as a person, which comes from my people, the Navajo. This learning cannot be dated. It includes senses of the word "healing" that are quite different from what the term usually connotes in the halls of Dartmouth Medical School.

Part of my vision of life is to combine what is best from both worlds—as different as they are. And, even more ambitiously, I hope that the dynamism of the world of medical research will understand the insights that we Navajo cherish and will expand and multiply them. Spirituality and healing are intertwined in our ceremonies. An examination of some of the principles of our ceremonies may be one vision of what "expanding spiritual information" can be.

If we contemplate the existence of our Creator, it would stand to reason that our Creator would provide a spirituality that would mirror the beauty and vastness of the world that S/He created. And this spirituality would not be separate from the rest of daily living, but rather, interwoven, united with all things.

When Europeans first encountered Native American cultures, they dismissed much of it as inferior. Indigenous religions were considered primitive compared with other theologies. Yet a deeper look reveals a connectedness and complexity that rivals that of the universe itself. In the belief system of my tribe, we use ceremonies that are blueprints for how to live a life that is whole and balanced, a life connected to all of Creation, a life that honors all living things. All wisdom, all life, arises from one source: *Sa'a naghaii bik'e hozho*, which literally means "To travel along life's path with spiritual beauty." This is also the name of a unifying force that is within all things, connects all things, and creates all things. Healers, medicine men in our tribe, have described it as "Universal Mind," indicating that this force has consciousness and exists throughout the universe. Because it is within all things, we learn that we, as humans, are not separate from other humans or the rest of our world. It is said that the First Man carried this force up through four previous worlds in his medicine bundle. This journey, by the way, mirrors evolution. The First World was filled with "mist beings"; the Second, with insects and small animals; the Third, with larger animals; and the Fourth, with humans.

Our ceremonies teach us to live in *hozho*, a word that describes a combination of beauty, balance, and harmony. It includes the teaching that humans should honor and respect other humans, a practice that is capable of creating family and work-place stability. This reduces the likelihood of destructive relationships. When others are honored and respected, the self-esteem of all rises, and the byproducts of low self-esteem—hatred of self and others, depression, and fear—are diminished. Strong interpersonal relationships help build strong families and communities. An inter-generational approach to raising children creates a safety net that protects them in the event that the "nuclear family" is ineffective. We also learn that elders should be respected for their wisdom; this helps counteract elder abuse or neglect.

Hozho is extended to the realm of thoughts. In this world, it is possible to "speak something into existence." Therefore, Navajos avoid speaking in a negative way about the future. The expectation of good outcomes, also known as "positive think-ing," is a cornerstone of Navajo culture. Positive thinking has been embraced by Western civilization and shown to produce positive outcomes. Optimists live longer; athletes who visualize success are more likely to achieve it. It actually *is* possible to think something into existence.

Hozho and positive thinking have another benefit. The practice of seeking to reduce conflict and produce positive outcomes reduces stress, and stress reduction has been found to have healthy side effects. The field of psychoneuroimmunology has shown that stress and depression are capable of suppressing the immune system, which in turn interferes with our ability to fight infections and to defend against cancer. Ceremonies encourage this process as well through physical and mental/spir-itual purification. The prayers and chants are vivid examples of guided imagery and create powerful images for the mind to use for rebalancing. Here is an example excerpted from "The Night Chant," our winter ceremony, which includes more than 750 chants, including this one:

> House made of Dawn
> House made of Morning Light
> House made of Evening Light,
> With the light fall of the she-rain,
> With the jagged lightning high above,
> On the trail of pollen,
> With Beauty (*Hozho*) before me,
> There may I walk.
> With Beauty behind me,
> There may I walk.
> With Beauty above me,
> There may I walk,
> With Beauty below me,
> There may I walk,
> With Beauty all around me, there may I walk.
> In Beauty (*Hozho*) it is finished.

Recently, art has been shown to be a healing force. When the mind encounters certain forms of art, the joy, delight, or awe it experiences is capable of relieving stress, of counteracting depression, and through psychoneuroimmunology (mind-body medicine) of possibly helping the immune system. Those who produce art sometimes say that it comes through them, rather than from them. The creation process has its own energy. Navajo ceremonies include layers upon layers of art—from multiple sources, but designed to be woven together, integrated. From the power and beauty of the chants and the images they evoke to the powerful rhythms of the drums and the music that carries the words forward, art moves through ceremonies as both the background and the foreground, as both the earth and the air. Art is expressed in paintings created with sand. The Yeii'is (katchinas), our spiritual guardians, are represented in the sandpainting images (see Photo 1), visual metaphors of the stories the ceremonies describe. These intricate designs are created with great attention to detail, but their images are returned back to Mother Earth at the end of the ceremony. In the same way, art is made manifest by dancers who represent the spiritual beings and animal guardians described by the ceremonies. Headdresses (of deerskin, buffalo skins, eagle feathers, and spruce branches), buck-skin clothing, and moccasins are created. Beauty and art are present in even the smallest objects used in ceremonies. Medicine bundles contain beautiful buckskin bags of corn pollen, prayer feathers, small carved animal spiritual guardians, and bundles of earth from the four sacred mountains. The combined effect is a tapestry that deeply endorses the belief that art has the power to heal, that art is not separate from spirituality (see Photo 2).

Photo 1. Medicine man and large sand-painting of Yeii'is, or spiritual guardians.

[From Navajo (New York: Harry N. Abrams, Inc., 1995). Copyright 1995 Susanne Page and Jake Page.]

This spirituality goes beyond the individual to elements that strengthen the health of entire communities and the natural world. Ceremonies reinforce the belief that we live in harmony with the animal world and the natural world. Humans have valued many things, but they often assign greatest value to those they consider family, or that which they consider sacred. Many Native American tribes have assigned both a spiritual and a familial value to the animal world and the environment. The earth is "Mother," the sky "Father." The eagle and bear are "Brother." Mother Earth is sacred in her mountains and valleys. The relationship of humans and their environment is therefore one of deep respect, a desire to protect and defend the animal world and the environment. The protective element provided by spirituality has direct healing effects on human beings: By keeping the environment protected, we have clean air to breathe, clean water to drink, clean earth in which to grow plants. We are shielded from the illness that results when our world becomes toxified.

PHOTO 2.
"Sacred mountain" tapestry showing that art is not separate from spirituality.

[Courtesy of Museum of Northern Arizona Photo Archives, (81C.24).

A message of sustainable living is found within our ceremonies. The "Night Chant" carries a warning within it, in a story known as "The Dream of the Blue Rams." Ages ago, it is said, a boy had a dream. In the dream, rams with blue faces came and told the boy that the men of the tribe who hunted game had taken more food than they needed and that this had thrown the world off balance. They added that if this continued, the rams would make the game scarce, and the people would starve. The boy awoke and went to the men who led the hunting and told them about the dream. The men told him, "Go back to your dreaming, and let us do the hunting." And what the rams predicted came to pass, and the people suffered greatly. They then remembered, and they listened. Even today, Navajos remember and practice the teachings of the "Night Chant": "Never take more than you need, use everything fully, give some of what you have to those who cannot hunt for themselves, and leave everything the way it was found—there should be no sign that a human has passed this way." We are taught that the natural world has spirit and life. These teachings contain powerful principles for how we use the resources of the natural world.

Luther Standing Bear, an Oglala Sioux chief, expressed this concept well: "I am going to venture that the man who sat on the ground in his tipi meditating on life and its meaning, accepting the kinship of all creatures, and acknowledging unity with the universe of things, was infusing into his being the true essence of civilization."

Ceremonies are often performed for the purposes of healing, as described earlier. The effects of stress and depression on the immune system are better understood, and the effects of ceremonies are easily understood in this context. These principles are now beginning to be used by other healing systems as well. Western medicine is waking up. It has started to realize the power of healing that exists beyond the realms of procedures and medications. Studies have started to prove the healing power of such realms as spirituality, support group therapy, art and music therapy, pet therapy, massage therapy, aromatherapy, and so on. The research is still in its beginning stages, but points to the fact that healing can be influenced by multiple forces within our lives, that we are deeply interconnected to all aspects of our lives, and that we can immerse ourselves in many areas to achieve healing.

During my training as a surgeon, I was unable to harmonize my background as a Navajo with my medical world. Initially, I encountered not a healing environment, but a place that needed as much healing as the patients it treated. I hope that healing environments can be created that incorporate many "ceremonial" aspects. Among these are creating a space of trust and deep support for patients, developing an environment for staff that is supportive and that encourages building teams that have good working relationships, and encouraging spaces that are visually beautiful and comfortable for both patients and families. We have moved away from cold, sterile medical surroundings, but we still have worlds of healing that are waiting to be included in medical models of the future.

By examining the extraordinary complexity and interrelatedness of our natural world, we may begin to understand that, in much the same way, the forces of art, ceremonies, sustainability, and healing are deeply woven and interconnected. The cultures of Native people encourage the recognition of interconnectedness, a "systems dynamics" interpretation of the world. The beauty and complexity of our world are not accidents. It is the mirror of a universal spirituality.

✐♥

LORI ARVISO ALVORD, M.D., is Associate Dean of Student and Multicultural Affairs at Dartmouth Medical School, as well as a practicing board-certified general surgeon and Assistant Professor of Surgery at Dartmouth-Hitchcock Medical Center. She earned her undergraduate degree at Dartmouth College and her M.D. at Stanford University, where she completed her surgical residency. For the next six years, she worked for the Indian Health Service in Gallup, New Mexico, providing healthcare to members of the Navajo and Zuni tribes. *The Scalpel and the Silver Bear* (Bantam, 1999), her autobiography, tells the story of her journey from a Navajo reservation to the world of surgery and her efforts to combine Navajo with Western medicine. Her lectures describe how she has incorporated this wisdom into her surgical practice and how others can apply these principles to their own lives and communities. Dr. Alvord has received numerous awards, including an honorary Doctor of Science Honoris Causa from Albany Medical College (2001) and the Governor's Award for Outstanding Women from the State of New Mexico (1992).

OF MONOCYTES
AND THE SPIRITUAL MAN 67

Gregory L. Fricchione

I N THE LABORATORY, white blood cells called monocytes, when separated out from other blood products, sit placidly in well-rounded repose on a slide. It takes the addition of a chemical attractant at the edge of the cover slip to activate the monocytes. These macrophages, as they are also called, then elongate and move toward the chemotactic agent in a process essential to life called chemotaxis. If morphine is applied, the cells will "round up and stone out," becoming unresponsive to the chemoattractants. This is a miracle of evolutionary engineering I find enjoyable to watch.

More than ten years ago, I was called to see a man in the intensive care unit. As a medical psychiatrist, my job was to evaluate him for depression in the wake of his receiving an unusual diagnosis. This unfortunate sixty-five-year-old man, someone's husband and father, had a rare cancer of his macrophages, something called malignant histiocytosis (Mongkonsritragoon et al. 1998). This is a death sentence in most instances. Macrophages become voracious "pac-man-like" organisms, gobbling up platelets, red blood cells, other white blood cells, and anything they can get their pseudopods on. Patients succumb to bleeding, infection, and multiorgan failure. I find this very hard to witness.

That this can be hard to witness is because of something called empathy—our ability to, in varying degrees, feel the anguish of others. Fortunately for the human race, empathy can be exercised into compassionate love, although this occurs less frequently than one would like. There are several ways to understand empathy (Brothers 1989). It could be an unconscious somatic mimicry capability that produces a feeling in the subject akin to that observed in the object, or it could also be an unconscious psychological identification with another's feelings. Perhaps it is the sensory experience of witnessing another's suffering state, processing it, and matching it with one's own experience, resulting in a cascade of brain changes culminating in an empathic response.

It turns out that the brain has both fast and slow analysis systems. The former mode takes advantage of a fast, single-synapse connection that has been delineated between the sensory nucleus called the thalamus and a limbic emotion processor called the amygdala (LeDoux 1996). The amygdala is then connected with the autonomic nervous system responder, which can increase pulse and blood pressure and cause other bodily changes. The slower mode involves cortical processing in a multisynaptic, multimodal, more refined analysis of incoming information. This latter "cognitive" appraisal will eventually match the former "emotional" appraisal, and an empathic response can then result.

We think the selection of such a response takes place in the so-called paralimbic circuit that includes the anterior cingulate cortex (Devinsky et al. 1995). This particular circuit, like several other circuits that are integrated yet segregated in the brain, contains a motor area (the basal ganglia), a sensory locus (the thalamus), and an analyzer-effector section (the cortex) (Alexander et al. 1990). It evolved in mammals to enable us to employ parent-offspring and social attachments as our survival strategies (MacLean 1990). The paralimbic zones are tightly connected with the prefrontal cortex, which enables us to plan and execute our attachment behaviors. Empathy then can be described as the afterglow of what burns in the furnace of our brain's attachment area.

Our empathic brain is an organ evolved from unicellular life as represented in the amoeboid existence of the monocyte inside of us. The monocyte can be said to possess a primordial intelligence as it optimizes its behavior in light of incoming data. Cell surface sensory receptors are attached to machinery inside the cell, which effects a cytoskeletal motor change (Cairns-Smith 1996). What is the brain for? It uses its sensory thalamus, its motor basal ganglia, and its analyzer-effector cortex to make optimal immobilization-mobilization, avoidance-approach, and separation-attachment response selections in an environment of much noisy information. The body is the apparatus available to immobilize or mobilize, avoid or approach, separate or attach. The mind is what the brain produces in interaction with its internal and external environments in order to accomplish what the brain is for.

Decision making in the brain is informed not only by sensory data, but also by memory and foresight. A mind that can "leave" the body in order to picture it in some future desirable setting can make plans on how to get there, using what David Ingvar called "a memory of the future" (Ingvar 1985). As mentioned, processing of these cognitive and emotional sources of information takes place so that appropriate responses can be selected. Such information is evolutionarily important only in proportion to what it tells us about human separation from or attachment to the needs of existence or the desiderata of life.

Against this backdrop, it may become clearer why the conceptual network of physical terms and the conceptual network of mental terms—or, for that matter, spiritual terms—evolved and are delimited by the dialectical language of separation and attachment (Fricchione 2002). This is especially clear in the parlance of psychology in general and object relations theory in particular, where separation-individuation challenges and attachment to a secure base are the dipoles of development (Bowlby 1969). But the cosmologist, too, must use similar dipolar language to describe the moment of creation in the Big Bang by assuming a gravitational separation energy surge to overcome the initial gravitational moment. And what is the cosmological constant, if not an attempt to understand the fate of the universe based on the ratio of repulsive (separative) forces and attractive (attachment) forces (Weinberg 1992)? The chemist speaks to us of the separation of electrons (oxidation) or their attachment (reduction), while the poet laments "The Stolen Child" as one taken from us too young (Yeats 1968). Poets suffer from the metaphorical imperative—the need to bind up two separated objects; but so do scientists. Poets and scientists are both moved from theoretical sources by their attractions to hypothetical targets (Holland 1998). And for the theologian, of course, there is the matter of sin or separation from God. And then there is communion.

Human language must give vent to this dialectic of separation and attachment, no matter what discipline is used to provide information and regardless of whether matter or spirit is being expressed. In this way, all expressed information flows from the same source, and fields as diverse as science and theology share an extensional identity in terms of knowledge. Examining the source of the common language of separation and attachment may provide the vehicle for consilience (Fricchione 2002; Wilson 1997).

Information then can be thought of as the ratio of separation to attachment. This ratio allows us to depict the complexity of the world around us. Thus, a cosmological constant that is a small number reflects a physical universe that is slowly expanding. And a biological organ like the brain is complex inasmuch as it has components that are simultaneously segregated and integrated (Tononi et al. 1994). And Jesus can inform us all that he has come not to bring peace, but to separate mothers from daughters and to pronounce that he who loses his life will gain it—and with it, peace.

Yes, indeed. But my patient lies in bed destined to die soon. We talk about macrophages and how they need chemical information to do their chemotaxis. He gives me a blood sample so we can analyze in the lab why his particular macrophages have become voracious and treacherous. He is happy to do this. "Maybe it will help someone someday," he says. Yet he is locked in his own more inexplicable mystery, which no lab can help him understand, and all he really wants is to be back with his wife and family. We talk about the *Odyssey*, how he is a modern-day Odysseus fighting to return home. And we talk about the Christian paradox as well. Often at the bedside my hand is on his arm as he reminisces about Christmas mornings with his smiling children and other such reveries. He is proud of them and the college educations they have all earned. "I used to read to them all the time," he remembers. I picture him reading the Christopher Robin stories to them when they were young, helping them face the separation challenge of sleep and the monsters that inhabit the night. He acknowledges with his tears how painful it is to be away and to be drifting further away with the current of the days. This is the time of spiritual man, and this particular man needs his spiritual separation and attachment information to select the responses most important for his life . . . even as he loses it.

As there is a chemical concentration gradient that enables the monocyte to make a response selection, so too there is a spiritual concentration gradient for the human being, which enables him to do his "spiritotaxis."

God can be the strongest attractant for those who are suffering. Even Freud recognized (and lamented) the supremacy of God's attractiveness for us. It is stronger than the "intoxicating substances," or the "substitutive satisfactions" of "illusions in contrast to reality" to be found in pursuit of the arts or the "powerful deflections" of the scientific project (Freud 1961).

I have felt him at the bedside. He is in the ether, the surround, at the edge of the "universal cover slip"—whatever you want to call it—and most strongly at the spiritual time in the clarity of the moment of serious illness. Is he really there? I don't know for sure. As a scientist, I do know that there needs to be a chemotactic agent at the edge of the cover slip for the amoeboid cell to move in the agent's direction. And as a physician at the bedside, I do know that we are all potentially drawn along by the spiritual information inherent in the moment of suffering when we experience serious illness. I also think sufferers, by the way, can themselves serve as attractants for those with compassionate love, perhaps because those with compassion are themselves drawn nearer to God in their accompaniment of the suffering ones.

The macrophages of my patient were examined in the lab of my friend and collaborator, George Stefano. We thought we could cause them to round up by applying morphine. But his cells kept on moving in random, nondirected, chemokinetic frenzy. We discovered they had lost their ability to do chemotaxis, partly, perhaps, because of the disappearance of a cell-surface morphine receptor.

I recall thinking at the time about Albert Schweitzer in Gabon peering in with his microscope at *Trypanosoma brucei gambiense*, the dreaded cause of the West African sleeping sickness. He felt bad for the little microbe going about the basic life rhythms of avoidance/approach in an ever-present foreshadowing of our evolved separation/attachment mystery. He describes this in the elucidation of his "Reverence for Life" philosophy. "But every time I put the germ that causes the disease under the microscope, I cannot but reflect that I have to sacrifice this life in order to save another" (Schweitzer quoted in Cousins 1985, 236).

I felt no such empathic bond with the delinquent unicells seen under our microscope. These mutated little monsters, although themselves part of my patient, were, in a basic physical way, unrelenting in devouring important parts of him. It was difficult to revere the destructive "greed" in these forms, which took on lives all their own, separate from the whole.

The trouble is: Here the monsters win, and it is very hard to witness. My patient had one remission. He was worried and sad, but became reconciled to his fate when the disease recurred. He inquired about the study we had done on his macrophages. I told him about the lack of morphine effect and the receptor loss and the resultant maniacal cell activity. He said that maybe the new information might help someone down the road someday. I said, "Yes." He thanked God for the time he had at home with his family during his remission. He had shared moments with his wife and his children and grandchildren "that will last forever." He really didn't need me much toward the end. I believe he was a man who had loved and been loved, and in that way he had felt God's presence. And with that secure attachment attracting him, he could face the ultimate separation challenge.

I read recently about AIDS mothers in Uganda facing death, or as they call it the "final separation." They are spending time putting together "memory books" for their soon-to-be orphaned children, filled with photos of loved ones and of happy times. Wisdom is passed on in the form of motherly advice and biblical sayings. These memory books will have the power to transubstantiate into love for these children as they grow and develop. At each transition in their lives, the books will kindle the love that will entangle them back with their mothers, who have gone before them out past the boundary.

Perhaps the concept of love is indeed unlimited as it slips past the dialectical boundary. As the process theologian Daniel Day Williams pointed out in his classic description, love is in essence mutuality (Williams 1968). Self-affirming love and self-giving love are entangled and harmonious. One individuates only in community. True community requires individuals with the freedom to select it.

According to Williams, self-asserting love contains "both the pole of autonomy, the affirmation of self-integrity and independence, and the pole of symbiosis, which requires conformity and relatedness to the other" (Williams 1968, 206). And with this separation-attachment-based understanding, "We now see human loves in a new light. Agape is not another love, which is added to the others. Neither is it their contradiction. It is the love which underlies all others, leads them towards the discovery of their limits, and releases a new possibility in the self, which is created for communion" (Williams 1968, 210).

"Agape indeed bears an assurance for every future. It overcomes the fear of death and defeat. 'Nothing can separate us from the love of God.' Love never disappears. But what love may do and will do, what creative and redemptive work lies ahead, can only be known partially in the history of love until the 'end'" (Williams 1968, 212).

God's love can overcome the "permanent separation" my patient faced as it can overcome the permanent separation of the AIDS mother from her child. Nothing can separate us from the love of God, which "releases a new possibility in the self, which was created for communion."

We went on to publish an article in the *American Journal of Hematology* on this case, detailing the computerized microscopic analysis of the behavior of the macrophages in question (Fricchione et al. 1997). The article was more about the monocytes than the man. But he was a good man, and he had a spirit. And I believe he was being attracted to Someone who loved him.

✒

GREGORY L. FRICCHIONE, M.D., is Associate Professor of Psychiatry at Harvard Medical School and Associate Chief of Psychiatry and Director of Psychiatry in Medicine at Massachusetts General Hospital. Recently, he spent two and a half years directing the Mental Health Program at The Carter Center in Atlanta, Georgia, and continues on the board of the Rosalynn Carter Institute for Human Development. Dr. Fricchione provides care for patients with problems at the interface of the body and the mind. His research includes studies on neuroimmunology, catatonia, and the relationship between mood dysfunction and cardiac disease. He is a consultant for the Institute for Research on Unlimited Love at Case Western Reserve University School of Medicine. Dr. Fricchione is an associate editor of *Medical Science Monitor* and *Acta Pharmacologica Sinica*, as well as a reviewer for many other medical and psychiatric journals.

REFERENCES

Alexander, G. E., Crutcher, M. D., DeLong, M. R. Basal ganglia-thalamo-cortical circuits: parallel substrates for motor, oculomotor, "prefrontal" and "limbic" functions. *Prog Brain Res* 1990; 85: 119–46.

Bowlby, J. *Attachment and loss.* Vols I and II. Basic Books, NY, 1969.

Brothers, L. A biological perspective on empathy. *Am J Psychiatry* 1989; 146: 10–19.

Cairns-Smith, A. G. *Evolving the mind: On the matter and the origin of consciousness.* Cambridge University Press, NY, 1996.

Devinsky, O., Morrell, M. J., Vogt, B. A. Contributions of the anterior cingulate cortex to behavior. *Brain* 1995; 118: 279–306.

Freud, S. *Civilization and its discontents.* Trans. by James Strachey. W.W. Norton and Co., NY, 1961.

Fricchione, G. Separation, attachment and altruistic love: the evolutionary basis for medical caring. In: S. G. Post, L. G. Underwood, J. F. Schloss, W. Hurlbut (eds). *Altruism and Altruistic Love: Science, Philosophy and Religion in Dialogue.* Oxford University Press, Oxford, 2002.

Fricchione, G. L., Cytryn, L., Bilfinger, T. V., Stefano, G. B. Cell behavior and signal molecule involvement in a case study of malignant histiocytosis: a negative model of morphine as an immunoregulator. *Am J Hematol* 1997; 56; 197–205.

Holland, J. H. *Emergence: From chaos to order.* Addison-Wesley, Reading, MA, 1998.

Ingvar, D. Memory of the future: an essay on the temporal organization of conscious awareness. *Human Neurobiol* 1985; 4: 127–36.

LeDoux, J. *The emotional brain.* Simon and Schuster, NY, 1996.

MacLean P. D. *The triune brain in evolution: Role in paleocerebral functions.* Plenum Press, NY, 1990.

Mongkonsritragoon, W., Li, C. Y., Phyliky, R. L. True malignant histiocytosis. *Mayo Clin Proc* 1998; 73: 520–28.

Schweitzer, A. Out of my life and thoughts. Quoted in Cousins, N. *Albert Schweitzer's mission: healing and peace.* W. W. Norton and Co., NY, 1985.

Tononi, G., Sporns, O., Edelman, G. M. A measure for brain complexity: relating functional segregation and integration in the nervous system. *Proc Natl Acad Sci USA* 1994; 91: 5033–37.

Weinberg, S. *Dreams of a final theory: The search for the fundamental laws of nature.* Pantheon Books, NY, 1992.

Williams, D. D. *The spirit and forms of love.* Harper and Row, NY, 1968.

Wilson, E. O. *Consilience. The unity of knowledge.* Alfred A. Knopf, NY, 1997.

Yeats, W. B. The stolen child. In: M. H. Abrams (ed). *The Norton Anthology of English Literature,* Vol 2. W. W. Norton and Co., NY, 1968.

A Scientist Reflects on the Life of Christian Healer Dorothy Kerin

Stevens Heckscher

Is science the only valid way to knowledge? Is all knowledge limited, or reducible, to what rationality and science can tell us? Or does scientific fidelity to the full testimony of reality lead us away from philosophical materialism? Many—but by no means all—scientists would answer "yes" to the first two questions and "no" to the third. As a scientist, I respond contrariwise: "no" to the first two and "yes" to the third.

In the following essay, I adduce several modern case studies that, I argue, present a robust challenge to materialistic philosophy, much as other numerous, carefully studied, similar events have done. On this basis, I set forth the hypothesis that the foundations of the world's great religions are firmer than many believe today. Thus, I suggest that reality is too rich and strange to be blithely dismissed as containing no basis for eternal hope and that science is not the only valid way of knowing: There is a reality beyond the purview of science that can only be known by following other pathways. To illuminate those other pathways for scientists and other critical thinkers, I urge debate on, and serious research into, examples such as those I discuss below.

"London's Modern Miracle"

Greater London, 1912. Late on a winter's evening, family, relatives, and friends are standing around the deathbed of a young woman. Emaciated, almost without flesh on her limbs, she has been nearly comatose for two weeks; and for the past five years, she has been bed-ridden, suffering from tuberculosis with many complications, her whole body filled with infection. For nearly eight minutes now, there has been no sign of life—no breath, no pulse, no discernible heartbeat. To all appearances, she has died. Suddenly, she sighs and resumes weak breathing. Her mother, one of a number of witnesses, tells us:

> . . . we distinctly heard Dorothy say to some unseen being, "Yes, I am listening." Her face was radiant with a beautiful smile. . . . As we looked we saw her raised up in bed, and her arms were gracefully raised, as though she were being lifted up bodily. She turned her head round and faced us, at first squinting horribly; but almost instantaneously her eyes returned to their natural beauty. . . . Holding her head up as if in prayer, she said, "Mother, I am well; I am to get up now," at the same time asking her sister for her dressing-gown. . . . She put it on, got out of bed, and walked quite steadily across

the room. She went to the door, and advanced along the passage, saying, "Don't touch me, I am following the light." She had apparently not the least difficulty in walking, and on returning to the room she said, "Why are you all here, and why are you so frightened? I am quite well." She was the calmest person in the house, and seemed so surprised at our wonder and excitement. (E. J. Kerin, quoted by D. Kerin 1914a)

The young Englishwoman was named Dorothy Kerin. Following her walk, she asked for food and descended two flights of stairs by herself to prepare a cold meal, the first solid food she had taken for years. She ate this meal with relish and suffered no ill aftereffects. The next morning on her awakening, it was found that her normal body weight had been restored overnight, her arms and legs fully fleshed out. From that moment, she enjoyed perfect health for nearly two years. In spite of several later illnesses, X-ray examinations showed no evidence of recurrence of her tuberculosis (Arnold 1965).

During her fortnight of apparent unconsciousness, Dorothy reported, she "seemed to drift into space," where, according to her account, she met angels and then Christ himself, who asked her to return to earthly life to perform a mission.

At the time, this event was reported in the press worldwide, and sometimes referred to as "London's modern miracle." Today it would be termed a "near-death experience." While thousands of such events have been carefully studied, this one appears to be especially worthy of note, as it contains not only what appears to be an encounter with Christ (as in many such experiences), but his prediction, later fulfilled in an astonishing way, that she would do something important for him, followed by her revival and complete and nearly immediate physical restoration after eight minutes of what, as far as can be determined today, was total lifelessness (D. Kerin 1914b).

She also had seemingly miraculous recoveries from two subsequent grave threats to her life and health. Thereafter, Dorothy entered spiritual direction under one of the few priests in the Church of England at that time sufficiently learned in mystical or ascetical theology to be able to guide her. In 1929, she established a nursing home in London, which she removed to the country following World War II, eventually locating all her work at the Burrswood estate in Kent. She brought to this labor a saintly life and a gift for healing of body, emotions, and spirit. By the time she died in 1963, this petite Anglican woman had brought religious faith and bodily and inner healing to thousands. A number of apparently miraculous recoveries resulted from her ministrations, and to two of these we shall shortly turn our attention.

First, it must be emphasized that she never showed signs of hysteria, instability, or idiosyncrasy. She was a serene but energetic Christian woman who spent much time in contemplative prayer, who brought comfort to many in sorrow, and who was sought for her reputed wisdom. She stressed the importance of religion and medicine working together, and her centers always had the finest medical resources available. The healing ministry growing today in the Anglican Church and beyond owes much to her pioneering work.

I should also remark that the annals of Christianity and of all the great religions contain many instances of modern "saints" who performed well-attested miraculous works often reminiscent of biblical accounts (e.g., Treece 2001). St. Seraphim of Sarov (Russian Orthodox, nineteenth century) and Padre Pio (Roman Catholic, twentieth century) are two famous Christian examples. Dorothy Kerin is one modern "saint" whose remarkable life is especially well documented and whose memory still lies fresh in many people's minds, especially in England and Western Europe.

I want now to examine scientifically—that is, in as disciplined a manner as possible from careful and detailed accounts—two of many apparently miraculous events in Dorothy Kerin's life. I offer two criteria of authenticity, namely, *reliability* and *objectivity* in the form of detailed eyewitness accounts by several trustworthy persons. In this essay, I advance no formal explanation for the events. *I propose only that they, and the many others like them, present a serious challenge to a naturalistic or materialistic worldview.* Science is limited mostly to investigation of replicable or repeatedly observable events, while of course the episodes presented here cannot be replicated. Despite this limitation, I hope that the disciplined reflections of a scientist on the matter at hand may lend conviction to the findings. I also urge that a systematic and disciplined project be undertaken to attempt to catalog in one place, under stringent guidelines to avoid fraud and deception, the gamut of all recent and well-attested phenomena of the kind we are discussing.

Report I

The following account by Peta Pare (Pare n.d.) is reproduced here in full for its richness of detail.

> In 1961 a man of 47 went to see his doctor about his troublesome "piles." During the examination the doctor discovered some enlarged abdominal glands. A subsequent visit to a surgeon, an abdominal operation, and a depressing prognosis followed. Robert, a highly intelligent and sensitive man, was shocked, and anxious for his wife and two young children. The deep X-ray therapy which followed the operation did nothing to cure his depression. When his wife asked the doctor how long he might have to live, she was told 18 months would see him facing another major operation. And then? . . . [ellipsis in original].
>
> Robert improved, and went back to his academic job of working on ancient manuscripts. His wife started to train as a teacher.
>
> Twenty months later, Robert became ill with what was clearly an acute obstruction. There was no possibility of admission to hospital until the following day. The Doctor gave him a pain-killer, and a friend rang up Dorothy Kerin to ask for her prayers. She was unable to come over to see him, and she sent back this message, "Give him my love and tell him I am thinking of him especially." A priest took the message to Robert, explaining very briefly about Dorothy, and her capacity for lifting people into the presence of God by her prayers. He laid his hands on Robert's head, and prayed the Burr-

swood prayer, "May new life quicken thy mortal body . . .", because as he said afterwards, "I thought that's what she would have wanted me to do."

That night, Robert slept soundly, and opened the front door when the friend called early the next morning. He went into hospital later that day, and was operated on. There was no sign of disease, and his wife had to wait ten days before the laboratory report showed that this time there was no cancer. The doctors stood round his bed, astonished and unbelieving.

That was years ago, and Robert and his family thrive.

Report II

Following is another report of a dramatic, instantaneous physical healing (Chavchavadze 1995) associated with Dorothy Kerin. This occurred after the end of World War II:

> Jummie [the head of the community nursing staff] fell down the main stairs and lay unconscious in a pool of blood. Dr. Elliott [the Visiting Physician] ascertained that she had a deep gash in her head, over four inches long, a compound fracture of her right arm, and broken ribs; and immediately rang for an ambulance. He then telephoned the surgeon who was having his Sunday rest in the country. In view of the emergency the surgeon agreed to drive straight to the hospital. Dorothy [Kerin] accompanied Jummie in the ambulance and in the hospital they were met by the theatre Sister [nurse] who took them to the X-ray room. Before going in, Dorothy was able to pray over Jummie and give her the laying-on of hands [a form of ministration to the sick frequently used in the Church], and when the Sister re-examined her she was amazed to find no trace of *any kind of injury* [emphasis mine]; only blood in the hair where the gash had been. Fortunately for John Elliott [i.e., for his professional surgical reputation], the Sister confirmed the accuracy of his diagnosis.

Several comments are in order. First, these episodes are only two of numerous such occurrences in Dorothy Kerin's life. Many of them, including these two, satisfy both of our criteria, reliability and objectivity (multiplicity and agreement) of witness. However, Dorothy herself, who possessed great humility and modesty, did not emphasize these miraculous or spectacular events. Rather, she continually taught that healing of mind and spirit was the most important part of her and the church's ministry. Second, and contrary to most popular belief, in addition to the works performed by Dorothy, ample reliable testimony describes the occurrence in modern times, inside as well as outside the Christian orbit, of what to all appearances are interventions in the material world by supernatural agency. Of course, I am emphasizing here well-documented instances within Christianity, such as visions shared by more than one person, healings witnessed by several reliable observers, messages that are independently corroborated, and the like. While almost all of these events individually could be argued away, although sometimes only with special pleading, collectively the number, variety, and verifiability of so many of them pose a serious problem for materialist philosophy. Third, so much scope for both fraud and self-deception exists in this area that the entire subject does need to be approached with great care. The skepticism that protects scientific investigation from much error must remain part of the investigator's equipment. Many careful investigations have exposed charlatans and credulous practitioners, and we do well to keep that in mind, remembering that the existence of fraud and gullibility does not prove that all supposed supernatural interventions are hoax or illusion.

In Western culture, a swing away from the gullible to the skeptical has been the trend since the Enlightenment. This has resulted in great loss of religious faith, but it has also taught us to be circumspect, to examine minutely claims of supernatural intervention, and always to look first for natural causes. In these matters, one extreme, gullibility, is as dangerous as the other, a priori skepticism. I am arguing here for a middle pathway.

The nature of faith has always been a mystery. It is not mere acceptance of an attractive belief system. Rather, religious faith, beginning with the Kierkegaardian leap into a largely unknown realm, often leads to a state of knowing that those in that state claim, sometimes with great conviction, is illuminated either from deep within the self—or from without. Those who have this experience can never rigorously prove that the illumination is real; they can only invite us to make the leap and to see for ourselves. Dorothy Kerin claimed that her life was so permeated by this illumination that she was able to insist that she had passed beyond faith to knowledge, to a state that is known as mystical (cf. Underhill 2002; Clement 1995). "I do not believe," she sometimes said, "I know."

I began the journey that led to my faith equipped both with the scientific skepticism that requires strong evidence before acceptance of a hypothesis and with hope that I could believe in a world beyond, and more glorious than, the material world. I had heard the Christian message and longed to be able to accept it. Although well versed in the New Testament accounts of Christ, I was haunted by the dread that—ancient, remote, and filtered through many chroniclers as they then seemed to be—I could not put my trust in them. I took the Kierkegaardian leap, retaining the scientific skepticism of my professional training. A long pilgrimage led me to examine the lives of modern saints, among whom Dorothy Kerin stood out because, only a few years after her death, I met and talked with persons who had known her well. Accounts of her life, like those of other contemporary saints, were so well attested, and so resembled those arresting New Testament stories of Christ, that the proper demands of my professional skepticism had gradually to yield to the conviction that interventions from a world beyond the material do occur.

Although the well-documented, seemingly miraculous events in the lives of modern saints are congruous with the supernatural events reported in the New Testament, Christ himself is recorded as saying that marvelous works will not of themselves compel religious belief (Luke 16:31). Rather, he invited his hearers to look at him, listen to his message, and consider his works. Thus, striking occurrences such as those discussed in this essay will not convince skeptics. But I think that they do present gainsayers with a serious challenge to the foundations of naturalistic belief. And they invite us to look deeply and questioningly at the supernatural interventions reported in the New Testament and in times past, undertaking systematic, directed research into recent occurrences, across the boundaries of denominations and religious systems, asking whether it is as easy to dismiss these interventions as "myth," as many contemporary critics have asserted. I propose that such research would result in strengthening the challenge to materialism—and, like Dorothy herself, might point to what is beyond.

𝒵♥

STEVENS HECKSCHER, PH.D., received his doctorate in Mathematics from Harvard University in 1960. He taught in the Mathematics Department of Swarthmore College until 1980, when he left to take a position with the Natural Lands Trust, a regional land conservancy in the Delaware Valley. Currently, he is Conservation Biologist with that organization and Lecturer in Earth and Environmental Science at the University of Pennsylvania. His research interests are mathematical and plant community ecology and spiritual theology. He is the author of a number of scientific and theological papers and senior author of *The Good Shepherd Manifesto*, a document recently published on the Internet calling for fundamental reforms and renewal in the Anglican Church. He is also Lay Associate for Spiritual Direction at the Episcopal Church of the Good Shepherd in Rosemont, PA.

REFERENCES

Arnold, Dorothy, 1965. *Dorothy Kerin, Called by Christ to Heal.* First published 1965; fourth impression 1972 by K&SC (Printers) Ltd., High Brooms, Tunbridge Wells, Kent, U.K., 59–60.

Chavchavadze, Marina, 1995. *Dorothy Kerin As I Knew Her.* K&SC (Printers) Ltd., High Brooms, Tunbridge Wells, Kent, U.K., 61–62.

Clement, Olivier, 1995. *The Roots of Christian Mysticism.* New City Press, NY.

Kerin, Dorothy, 1914a. *The Living Touch.* First published 1914. 1987 printing by K&SC (Printers) Ltd., High Brooms, Tunbridge Wells, Kent, U.K., 49–57. Numerous other accounts of this event have been published.

Kerin, Dorothy, 1914b. Ibid., 54.

————, 1960. *Fulfilling: A Sequel to The Living Touch.* First published 1952. Third edition 1960 by K&SC (Printers) Ltd., High Brooms, Tunbridge Wells, Kent, U.K., 149–51.

Pare, Peta, n.d. *Chosen Vessel: A Story of Dorothy Kerin and Burrswood.* Printed privately by the Dorothy Kerin Trust, Burrswood, Kent, U.K.

Treece, Patricia, 2001. *Apparitions of Modern Saints.* Charis, Servant Publications, Ann Arbor, MI.

Underhill, Evelyn, 2002. *Mysticism: A Study in the Nature and Development of Spiritual Consciousness.* First published 1911; 1930 New York edition reprinted by Dover Publications, Mineola, NY.

PART EIGHT

Perspectives on Contemplation and the Virtues

FROM SCIENCE TO MEDITATION

Hendrik P. Barendregt

Reflection plays a fundamental role in our existence in several ways. Among the areas in which the phenomenon occurs are biology, language, computing, and mathematics. A fifth area in which reflection occurs is spiritual development. In all of these cases, the effects of reflection are powerful, even downright dramatic. We should be aware of these effects and use them in a responsible way. In this essay, I introduce the notion of reflection and expand and clarify it with examples.

Reflection: Domains, Coding, and Interaction

Reflection occurs in situations in which there is a domain of objects that all have active meaning—that is, specific functions within the right context. Before turning to the definition of *reflection*, let us present the domains relevant to the four examples. The first domain is the class of molecules occurring in biology known as *proteins*, which have very specific functions within living organisms, from bacteria to Homo sapiens. The second domain consists of sentences in *natural language* that are intended, among other things, to make statements, ask questions, or influence others. The third domain consists of (implemented) *computable functions*, which perform computations—sometimes stand-alone, sometimes interactive—that produce output that usually serves users in one way or another. The fourth domain consists of *mathematical theorems*, which express valid phenomena about numbers, geometric figures, or other abstract entities that, when interpreted in the right way, enable us to make correct predictions.

Now let us turn to reflection itself. Besides having a domain of meaningful objects, it needs coding and interaction. Coding means that for every object of the domain there is another object, the (not necessarily unique) *code*, from which the original object can be reconstructed exactly. This process of reconstruction is called *decoding*. The code *C* of object *O* does not directly possess the active meaning of *O* itself; this happens only after decoding. Therefore, the codes are outside the domain, and form the *code set*. Finally, the interaction needed for reflection consists of an encounter of objects with their codes. Hereby, some objects may change the codes and, after decoding, give rise to modified objects. This process of *global* feedback (in principle on the *whole* domain through codes) is the essence of reflection.

It should be emphasized that just the coding of elements of a domain is not sufficient for reflection. A music score may code for a symphony, but the two are on different levels: Playing a symphony usually does not alter the written music.[1]

Examples of Reflection

Given this definition, I present four examples of reflection.

1. *Proteins*: The first domain consists of proteins, each protein being essentially a linear sequence of a set of twenty amino acids. Because some of these amino acids attract one another, the protein assumes, with the help of proteins already present, a three-dimensional shape that provides its specific chemical meaning (see Figure 1).

FIGURE 1. A schematic display of the protein NGF_Homo_Sapiens, a nerve growth factor. Its three-dimensional structure can be perceived by looking at the picture with crossed eyes such that the left and right images overlap. Courtesy of the Swiss Institute of Bioinformatics, Peitsch et al. [1995] (see ftp://ftp.expasy.org/databases/swiss-3dimage/IMAGES/JPEG/S3D00467.jpg).

To mention just two possibilities, some proteins may be building blocks for structures within or between cells, while others may be enzymes that enable life-sustaining reactions. The code-set of the proteins consists of pieces of DNA, a string of elements from a set of four "chemical letters," or nucleotides. Three such letters uniquely determine a specific amino acid, and hence a string of amino acids is uniquely determined by a sequence of nucleotides (see Table 1 and Alberts et al. 1994). A DNA string does not have the meaning that the protein counterparts have, for one thing because it does not have the specific three-dimensional folding (see Table 2).

The first advantage of coding is that DNA is much easier to store and duplicate than the protein itself. The interaction in this example is caused by a modifying effect of the proteins on the DNA. This is also a second advantage of the protein coding, providing the possibility of change, to be described later.

TABLE 1. Amino acid sequence of NGF_Homo_Sapiens

```
Protein: 241 amino acids; molecular weight 26987 Da.
www.ebi.ac.uk/cgi-bin/expasyfetch?X52599

MSMLFYTLIT  AFLIGIQAEP  HSESNVPAGH  TIPQVHWTKL  QHSLDFTTALRR  ARSAPAAAIA   60
ARVAGQTRNI  TVDPRLFKKR  RLRSPRVLFS  TQPPREAADT  QDLDFTFEVGGA  APFNRTHRSK  120
RSSSHPIFHR  GEFSVCDSVS  VWVGDKTTAT  DIKGKEVMVL  GEVFTNINNSVF  KQYFFETKCR  180
DPNPVDSGCR  GIDSKHWNSY  CTTTHTFVKA  LTMDGKQAAW  RFFTIRIDTACV  CVLSRKAVRR  240
A                                                                         241
```

TABLE 2. DNA code of NGF_Homo_Sapiens

```
ACGT-chain: Length 1047 base pairs.
www.ebi.ac.uk/cgi-bin/expasyfetch?X52599
```

```
agagagcgct  gggagccgga  ggggagcgca  gcgagttttg  gccagtggtc  gtgcagtcca    60
aggggctgga  tggcatgctg  gacccaagct  cagctcagcg  tccggaccca  ataacagttt   120
taccaaggga  gcagctttct  atcctgggca  cactgaggtg  catagcgtaa  tgtccatgtt   180
gttctacact  ctgatcacag  cttttctgat  cggcatacag  gcggaaccac  actcagagag   240
caatgtccct  gcaggacaca  ccatccccca  agtccactgg  actaaacttc  agcattccct   300
tgacactgcc  cttcgcagag  cccgcagcgc  cccggcagcg  gcgatagctg  cacgcgtggc   360
ggggcagacc  cgcaacatta  ctgtggaccc  caggctgttt  aaaaagcggc  gactccgttc   420
accccgtgtg  ctgtttagca  cccagcctcc  ccgtgaagct  gcagacactc  aggatctgga   480
cttcgaggtc  ggtggtgctg  cccccttcaa  caggactcac  aggagcaagc  ggtcatcatc   540
ccatcccatc  ttccacaggg  gcgaattctc  ggtgtgtgac  agtgtcagcg  tgtgggttgg   600
ggataagacc  accgccacag  acatcaaggg  caaggaggtg  atggtgttgg  gagaggtgaa   660
cattaacaac  agtgtattca  aacagtactt  ttttgagacc  aagtgccggg  acccaaatcc   720
cgttgacagc  gggtgccggg  gcattgactc  aaagcactgg  aactcatatt  gtaccacgac   780
tcacaccttt  gtcaaggcgc  tgaccatgga  tggcaagcag  gctgcctggc  ggtttatccg   840
gatagatacg  gcctgtgtgt  gtgtgctcag  caggaaggct  gtgagaagag  cctgacctgc   900
cgacacgctc  cctccccctg  cccttctac  actctcctgg  gcccctccct  acctcaacct   960
gtaaattatt  ttaaattata  aggactgcat  ggtaatttat  agtttataca  gttttaaaga  1020
atcattattt  attaaatttt  tggaagc                                         1047
```

A simple calculation ($1047/3 \neq 241$) shows that not all the letters in the DNA sequence are used. In fact, some proteins (RNA splicing complex) make a selection as to what substring should be used in the decoding toward a new protein.

2. *Natural language*: The domain of the English language is well known. It consists of strings of elements of the Roman alphabet extended by numerals and punctuation marks. This domain has a mechanism of coding, called *quoting* in this context, that is so simple that it may seem superfluous. A string in English, for example, might look like this:

> Maria

This has as its code the quote of that string:

> "Maria"

In Tarski (1933/1995), it is explained that of the following sentences

Maria is a nice girl.
Maria consists of five letters.
"Maria" is a nice girl.
"Maria" consists of five letters.

the first and last one are meaningful and possibly valid, whereas the second and third are always incorrect, because a confusion of categories has been made (Maria consists of cells, not of letters; "Maria" is not a girl, but a proper name). We see the simple mechanism of coding and its interaction with ordinary language. Again, we see that the codes of the words do not possess the meaning that the words themselves do.

3. *Computable functions*: The third domain comes from computing. The first computers made during World War II were ad hoc machines, each built for a specific

use. As hardware at that time was a huge investment, it was recycled after each completed job by rewiring the parts. Based on ideas of Turing, this procedure was changed. One particular computer was constructed, the *universal machine* (see Figures 2 and 3), and for each particular computing job one had to provide two inputs: the instructions (the software) and the data that the instructions act on. This has become the standard for all subsequent computers.

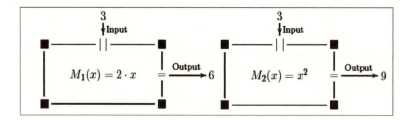

FIGURE 2. Two ad hoc machines: M1 for doubling and M2 for squaring a number.

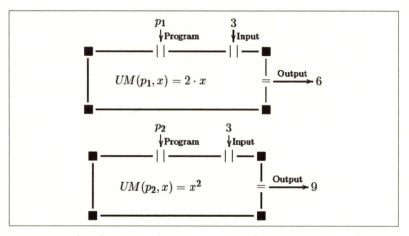

FIGURE 3. Universal Machine (UM) with programs p1, p2 simulating M1, M2, respectively. So p1 is a code for M1 and p2 for M2. Because we can consider M1 (p2) (i.e., M1 acting on p2) and M2 (p2), there is interaction: agents acting on a code, in the second case even their own code.

The domain in this case consists of implemented computable functions—that is, machines ready for a specific computing job to be performed. A code for an element of this domain consists of a program that simulates the job on a universal machine. The program of a computable function is not yet active, not yet *executable* in computer science terminology. Only after decoding does a program come into action. Besides coding, interaction is also present. In the universal machine the program and the data are usually kept strictly separate. But this is not obligatory. One can make the program and the input data overlap so that after running for a while on the universal computer the initial program is modified.

4. Mathematical theorems: A final example in this section is concerned with mathematics. A mathematical theorem is usually about numbers or other abstract entities. Gödel introduced codes for mathematical statements and used as a code-set the collection {0, 1, 2, 3,...} of natural numbers that do not have any assertive power. As a consequence, one can formulate in mathematics not only statements about numbers, but, through coding, also about other such statements. There are even statements that speak about themselves. Again, we see that both the coding and interaction aspects of reflection are present.

The Power of Reflection

The mentioned examples of reflection all have quite powerful consequences.

We know how dramatically life has transformed our planet. Life essentially depends on the DNA coding of proteins and the fact that these proteins can modify DNA. This modification is necessary in order to replicate DNA or to "proofread" it to prevent fatal errors.

One particular species, Homo sapiens, possesses language. We know its dramatic effects. Reflection using quoting is an essential element in language acquisition. It enables a child to ask questions such as: "Mom, what is the meaning of the word 'curious'?"

Reflection in computing has given us the universal machine, just one design[2] with possible variations through software. This has had a multitrillion-dollar (US) impact on the present stage of the Industrial Revolution of which we cannot yet see all the consequences.

The effects of reflection in mathematics are less well known. In this discipline, there are statements that one can see intuitively are true, but a formal proof is not immediate. Using reflection, however, proofs using intuition can be replaced by formal proofs[3] (see Howe 1992 and Barendregt 1997, 21–23). Formal provability is important for the emerging technology of an interactive (human-computer) theorem for proving and proof verification. Such formal and machine-checked proofs are already changing the way hardware is being constructed[4] and may in the future also affect the way software is developed. As to the art of mathematics itself, it will bring the technology of computer algebra (dealing exactly with equations between symbolic expressions involving elements such as $\sqrt{2}$ and ≠) to the level of arbitrary mathematical statements (involving more complex relations than just equalities between arbitrary mathematical concepts).

The Other Side of Reflection

Anything that is useful and powerful (like fire) also can be applied to negative effect (such as arson). Similarly, the power of reflection in the four given examples can be used in different ways.

Reflection in the chemistry of life has produced proteins, but it also has produced viruses. Within natural language, reflection gives rise to learning, but also to paradox.[5] The universal machine provides useful output, but it also produces unsolvable problems, notably the ones in which we are most interested.[6] Reflection within mathematics means that for almost all interesting consistent axiomatic theories, there are statements that cannot be settled (proved or refuted) within that theory (e.g., Gödel's incompleteness result).

We see that reflection can be compared with the forbidden fruit: It can seem an appealing and powerful agent for good, but at the same time it presents dangers and limitations. A proper view of these latter aspects will make us more modest.

Reflection in Spirituality

Insight (*vipassana*) meditation, which stems from classical Buddhism, concerns itself with consciousness. When impressions come to us through our senses, we obtain a mental representation (e.g., an object in front of us). Now this mental image may be *recollected*: This means that we obtain the awareness of the awareness, also called *mindfulness*. To develop the right mindfulness, awareness should be applied to all aspects of consciousness. Parts that usually are not seen as the content of consciousness, but rather as a "coloring" of it, become just as important as the object of meditation. If a leg hurts during meditation, one should be mindful of it. Moreover, one learns not only to see the pain, but also the feelings and reactions in connection to that pain. This fine-grained mindfulness will have an "intuitive analytic" effect: Our mind becomes decomposed into its constituents (input, feeling, cognition, conditioning, and awareness). Seeing this, we become less subject to various possible vicious circles in our mind-body system that often push us into greed, hatred, or compulsive thinking.

Because mindfulness brings the components of consciousness to the open in a disconnected, bare form, they are devoid of their usual meaning. The total information of ordinary mental states can be reconstructed from mindfulness. That is why it works like coding with the contents of our consciousness as domain.

The reflective role of mindfulness in our consciousness is quite similar to that of quoting in ordinary language. As proteins can purify part of our DNA, the insight into the constituents of consciousness can purify our mind. Mindfulness makes visible processes within consciousness, hitherto unseen. After that, mindfulness serves as a protection by not letting the components of consciousness exercise their usual meaning. Finally, the presence of mindfulness reorganizes consciousness, giving it a degree of freedom greater than before. Using mindfulness, one may act, even if one does not dare; or one may abstain from acting, even if one is urged. Then wisdom will result: morality not based on duty, but on virtue. This is the interaction of consciousness and mindfulness. Therefore, by our definition, one can speak of reflection.

This power of reflection through mindfulness also has another side. The splitting of our consciousness into components causes a vanishing of the usual view we hold of ourselves and the world. If these phenomena are not àccompanied in a proper way, they may become disturbing. But during intensive meditation retreats, the teacher pays proper attention to this. With the right understanding and reorganization, the meditator obtains a new stable balance, as soon as one knows and has incorporated the phenomena.

Mental disorders related to stress can cause similar dissociations. Although the sufferers appear to function normally, to them the world—or worse, their person—does not seem real. This may be viewed as an incomplete and unsystematic use of mindfulness. Perhaps this explains the enigma of why some sufferers become "weller than well," as Menninger et al have observed (1963). These cured patients might very well have obtained the mental purification that is the objective of *vipassana* meditation.

Pure Consciousness

In Hofstadter (1979), the notion of the "strange loop" is introduced: Something that contains a part that becomes a copy of the total when zoomed out. In the present paper, reflection is inspired by that notion, but focuses on a special aspect: Zooming out in reflection works through the mechanism of coding. The main thesis of Hofstadter is that "strange loops" are at the basis of self-consciousness. I partly agree with this thesis and would like to add that mindfulness serves as the necessary zooming mechanism in the strange loop of self-consciousness. On the other hand, the thesis only explains the "self" aspect; the "consciousness" part remains obscure. I disagree with the title of Dennet (1993): *Consciousness Explained.* No matter how many levels of cognition and feedback we place on top of sensory input in a model of the mind, a priori it seems not able to account for experiences. We always could simulate these processes on an old-fashioned computer consisting of relays, or even play it as a social game with cards. It is not that I object to basing our consciousness on outer agents such as card players (we depend on Nature in a similar way). It is the claimed emergence of consciousness as a side effect of the card game that seems absurd.

Spiritual reflection introduces us to awareness beyond ordinary consciousness, which is without content, but is nevertheless conscious. It is called *pure consciousness.* This phenomenon may be explained by comparing our personality with the images on a celluloid film, in which we are playing the title role in the story of our own life. Although everything that is familiar to us is depicted on the film, it is dark. We need light to see the film as a movie. It may be the case that this pure consciousness is the missing explanatory link between the purely neurophysiologic activity of our brain and the conscious mind that we (at least think to) possess. This pure light is believed to transcend the person. The difference between you and me is in the matter (cf. the celluloid of the film). What gives us awareness is said to come from a common source: the pure consciousness acting as the necessary "light."

To understand where this pure consciousness (our inner light) comes from, we may have to look better into Nature (through a new kind of physics; see, for example, Chalmers [1996] or Stapp [1996]) or better into ourselves (through insight meditation; see for example Goldstein [1983]). Probably, we will need to do both.

ℒ♥

HENDRIK P. BARENDREGT received his Ph.D. for a thesis in Mathematical Logic in 1971 from Utrecht University. From 1972 to 1979, he studied Zen meditation with Kobun Chino Roshi (1938–2002) in California, and from 1977 to the present he has been studying *Vipasssana* meditation with Most Venerable Phra Mettavihari in Amsterdam. His publications in the field of mathematical logic and theoretical computer science are frequently cited; among the best known are *The Lambda Calculus, Its Syntax and Semantics* (Elsevier, 1984) and "Lambda Calculi with Types," in *Handbook of Logic in Computer Science*, Vol. II (Oxford University Press, 1992), 117–309. He has received substantial personal research funds from Nijmegen University (1997) and also the Spinoza award in 2002 given by the Dutch National Science Foundation (NWO). He holds memberships in the Academia Europaea, the Hollandsche Maatschappij der Wetenschappen, and, since 1997, the Royal Dutch Academy of Sciences. Currently, Dr. Barendregt occupies the Chair for Foundations of Mathematics and Computer Science at Radboud University, Nijmegen, The Netherlands.

NOTES

1 However, in aleatory music—the deliberate inclusion of chance elements as part of a composition—the performance depends on dice that the players throw. In most cases, the score (the grand plan of the composition) will not alter. But music in which it really does alter is a slight extension of this idea—that is, a score on a computer and electronic alterations in the score induced by the dice, or even by the playing, would involve an interaction, and hence reflection.

2 That there are several kinds of computers on the market is a minor detail; this has to do with speed and user-friendliness.

3 Often an opposite claim is based on Gödel's incompleteness result. Given a mathematical theory T containing arithmetic that is at least consistent [expressed as Con(T)], incompleteness states the following: There is a statement G (equivalent to "G is not provable") within the language of T that is neither provable nor refutable in T, but nevertheless is valid (see Smullyan 1992). It is easy to show that G is improvable if T is consistent; hence, by construction, G is true. So we have informally proved that G follows from Con(T). Our (to some unconventional) view on Gödel's theorem is based on the following: By reflection, one also can show formally that Con(T) $\Rightarrow G$. Hence, it does not come as a surprise that G is valid on the basis of the assumed consistency. This has nothing to do with the special quality of the human mind, in which we believe, but on different grounds (see the section "Reflection in Spirituality").

4 That is, making it much more reliable.

5 That is, as in "This sentence is false."

6 "Is this computation going to halt or run forever?" (See Yates 1998.)

References

Alberts, B. et al. [1994] *The Cell.* Garland.

Barendregt, H. [1997] The impact of the lambda calculus. *Bulletin of Symbolic Logic* 3, no. 2: 181–215.

Chalmers, D. [1996] *The Conscious Mind, Towards a Fundamental Theory,* Oxford University Press.

Dennet, D. C. [1993] *Consciousness Explained.* Penguin Books.

Goldstein, J. [1983] *The Experience of Insight.* Shambhala.

Harrison, J. [1995] *Metatheory and Reflection in Theorem Proving: A Survey and Critique,* available at http://www.cl.cam.ac.uk/users/jrh/papers/reflect.dvi.gz.

Hofstadter, D. [1979] *Gödel Escher Bach.* Harvester Press.

Howe, D. J. [1992] Reflecting the semantics of reflected proof, in: *Proof Theory,* Aczel et al. (eds.). Cambridge University Press, 229–50.

Menninger, K., M. Mayman, and P. Pruyser. [1963] *The Vital Balance: The Life Process in Mental Health and Illness.* Viking.

Peitsch, M. C., D. R. Stampf, T. N. C. Wells, and J. L. Sussman. The Swiss-3D Image Collection and PDB-Browser on the World-Wide Web. *Trends in Biochemical Sciences* 20 1995): 82–84, available at http://www.expasy.org.

Smullyan, R. [1992] *Gödel's Incompleteness Theorems.* Oxford University Press.

Stapp, H. [1996] The Hard Problem: A Quantum Approach. *Journal of Consciousness Studies* 3 (3): 194–210.

Tarski, A. [1933/1995] *Introduction to Logic.* Dover.

Yates, M. [1998] What computers can't do. *+Plus,* issue 5, available at http://plus.maths.org/issue5/index.html.

OPPOSING SOURCES OF SPIRITUAL INFORMATION

Jonathan Haidt

I F EMOTIONS evolved to make us care about and respond to important events in our lives, then what are the emotions that underlie spiritual life? And what exactly are these emotions telling us?

Some emotions tell us that we live in a world of enormous beauty and complexity, a world that *feels* to us to be full of meaning and design. The emotion of awe, for example, seems to be a response both to direct encounters with divinity and to encounters with nature, art, or music, in which we are transported out of our everyday selves and feel in some way nearer to heaven (Keltner and Haidt 2003).

Other emotions tell us that we live in a world of bounty and generosity. Gratitude may have evolved as part of a suite of emotions that help humans engage in trade and long-term reciprocal alliances (Trivers 1971), but many people feel what McCullough et al. (2001) call "cosmic gratitude," that is, gratitude for the simple gift of life and for all the good things in it.

Still other emotions tell us that we live in a world where people show greater or lesser degrees of divinity in their actions. This essay is about a pair of opposing but related emotions—disgust and elevation—that help us navigate the social world by providing us with spiritual information about our fellow human beings and what is noble, decent, and virtuous in ourselves and others.

Disgust and the "Wisdom of Repugnance"

Disgust is a fascinating and underappreciated emotion. It appears to have been shaped by evolution to help our omnivorous ancestors figure out what to eat while simultaneously avoiding various sources of bacterial and parasitic infection (e.g., from corpses, waste products, certain animals, and each other). Disgust allowed our ancestors to go beyond immediate sensory information and to reject foods (or people) based on what these foods (or people) had touched previously. Since bacteria and parasites spread by contact, this kind of contamination sensitivity makes good evolutionary sense.

But somewhere along the line, disgust became a social emotion, too. My colleagues and I have studied disgust in several cultures, and, while the specific elicitors of disgust may vary, all cultures we looked at have a concept of an emotion that responds both to physical things (including certain foods, animals, body products, corpses, and violations of the external envelope of the body) as well as to a subset of social violations. A study we did in Japan and the United States (Haidt et al.

1997) indicated a great deal of similarity for the physical elicitors, but a larger degree of difference for the social elicitors. For Americans, social disgust was a response to cruelty, racism, and other cases where one person stripped away the dignity of another. The Japanese, however, extended the word *ken'o* from the physical world into the social world to apply to cases where the self had failed to achieve the proper fit into society, either because of a personal failure or because others were treating the person as a nonentity.

Thus, the emotion of disgust seems to work in both cultures to provide moral information about violations of some of the culture's most important values. American morality, with its extreme emphasis on rights and individuality, seems to use social disgust as a way to reinforce the importance of the person, while Japanese morality, with its greater emphasis on harmony and interdependence, may use social disgust to support the importance of the group.

The idea that disgust provides moral information has been discussed recently by the ethicist Leon Kass (chairman of President Bush's Council on Bioethics). Kass is concerned about the continual encroachment of a utilitarian and technocratic ethos into medical decision making in which the sacredness and dignity of human life is ignored. In discussing human cloning, Kass (2001) writes:

> In some crucial cases, however, repugnance is the emotional expression of deep wisdom, beyond reason's power completely to articulate it. Can anyone really give an argument fully adequate to the horror that is father-daughter incest (even with consent), or bestiality, or the mutilation of a corpse, or the eating of human flesh, or the rape or murder of another human being?

Kass argues that we should take our feelings of disgust into account when thinking about matters such as cloning, assisted suicide, and reproductive technologies. We should not follow these feelings blindly—indeed, some practices that used to trigger disgust (such as interracial marriage) we have now come to fully accept. But, as Kass says, "Shallow are the souls that have forgotten how to shudder."

The Spiritual Dimension of Social Cognition

My colleagues and I have been trying to understand the "wisdom of repugnance" for many years. Why do certain social violations trigger disgust, while others trigger anger, or contempt, or indifference? From our review of both anthropological and psychological sources, our best explanation is this: Human cultures generally order their social space in terms of a vertical dimension, running from God and moral perfection above to demons and moral evil below. Human beings are generally seen as being suspended precariously somewhere in the middle, capable of rising to godly sainthood or falling to bestiality or "subhuman" behavior. The medieval *scala natura* and the Hindu notion of reincarnation at higher or lower levels, depending on one's actions in life (karma), illustrate this vertical dimension. Social disgust can then be understood as the emotional reaction people have to witnessing others moving "down," or exhibiting their lower, baser, less God-like nature. We feel revolted by moral depravity, and this revulsion has some overlap, and also some difference, with the revulsion we feel toward rotten food and cockroaches (Rozin et al. 2000).

But if this powerful negative emotion can be triggered by seeing people move "down" on the vertical dimension, then what happens when we see people move "up"? Is there a corresponding positive emotion triggered by seeing people manifesting their higher, better, more saintly nature?

Elevation and the Wisdom of Thomas Jefferson

I believe that there is such an emotion, and that it was best described more than two hundred years ago by Thomas Jefferson. In 1771, Jefferson's friend Robert Skipwith wrote to him asking for advice on what books to buy for his own library. Jefferson loved to give advice and he loved books, so he embraced the chance to give advice about books. Along with a list of suggested titles in history, philosophy, and other branches of learning, he sent a letter making the case for the inclusion of literature. Great works of fiction, he said, contribute to our moral education by making us feel the right feelings:

> [E]very thing is useful which contributes to fix us in the principles and practice of virtue. When any . . . act of charity or of gratitude, for instance, is presented either to our sight or imagination, we are deeply impressed with its beauty and feel a strong desire in ourselves of doing charitable and grateful acts also. On the contrary when we see or read of any atrocious deed, we are disgusted with its deformity and conceive an abhorrence of vice. Now every emotion of this kind is an exercise of our virtuous dispositions; and dispositions of the mind, like limbs of the body, acquire strength by exercise. (Jefferson 1771/1975, 350)

Jefferson went on to say that the physical feelings and motivational effects caused by a good novel are as powerful as those caused by real episodes:

> [I ask whether] the fidelity of Nelson, and generosity of Blandford in *Marmontel* do not dilate [the reader's] breast, and elevate his sentiments as much as any similar incident which real history can furnish? Does he not in fact feel himself a better man while reading them, and privately covenant to copy the fair example?

Jefferson was saying quite explicitly that emotions give us moral information. He specifically cites "disgust" as giving us an "abhorrence of vice," and he describes an unnamed emotion that impresses us with the beauty of virtuous deeds and makes us want to do "charitable and grateful acts also." Jefferson then goes on to describe this emotion in much the same way that a modern emotion theorist would—by breaking it down into its component parts: elicitors, physiological changes, motivations, and subjective feelings. The elicitors of this moral emotion include acts of charity, gratitude, fidelity, and generosity. The physiological effects are said to be in the chest, a feeling of dilation (opening). The motivation is clearly moral self-improvement, wanting to copy the virtuous exemplar. The subjective feelings of this emotional state include elevated sentiments and feeling oneself to be a better person.

It is this last component that suggests to me that this moral information is also spiritual information. Jefferson's unnamed emotion tells us about what is best in life, and gives us a glimpse of a higher and nobler way of being.

Moral Information Is Spiritual Information

It is a lovely coincidence that I happen to work at Jefferson's university—the University of Virginia—where statues of Jefferson and inscriptions bearing his words surround students and faculty alike, inspiring us even as we exercise in the gymnasium. The coincidence is particularly lovely because my recent research has begun to prove Jefferson right.

For the last few years, I have been studying Jefferson's emotion, which I call "elevation" (both because of Jefferson's phrase "elevated sentiments" and because of its fit with the vertical spiritual dimension of social cognition I described earlier). I have asked people to recall times when they witnessed a good deed and compared what they wrote to times when they got something good for themselves. I have shown people video clips about Mother Teresa and about an eleven-year-old boy who founded a shelter for the homeless, and I have compared their responses to those of people who watched video clips of comedians. I have found that viewing or thinking about acts of moral beauty causes the set of responses that Jefferson described: feelings in the chest (sometimes described as a warm or open feeling) coupled with a motivation to help others and a feeling of being uplifted oneself (Haidt 2003). I am now looking into the possibility that elevation can be used in moral education programs, inspiring young people in ways that more traditional teaching techniques cannot.

I believe that elevation is one of the most important emotions underlying human spiritual life and spiritual growth. It is a surprising and very beautiful fact about our species that each of us can be moved to tears by the sight of a stranger helping another stranger. It is an even more beautiful fact that these feelings sometimes motivate us to change our own behavior, values, and goals. Narratives of the lives of Jesus, Buddha, Mother Teresa, and other inspiring figures are full of stories of people who, upon meeting the saintly figure, dropped their former materialistic pursuits and devoted themselves to advancing the mission of the one who elevated them.

If elevation is an emotion that creates disciples and helps moral visions to spread, then elevation has changed our world. Elevation and its opposing emotion, disgust, provide us with a constant stream of emotionally charged spiritual information, telling us not just who is good, but what is good.

JONATHAN D. HAIDT, PH.D., is Associate Professor in the Department of Psychology at the University of Virginia. He studies morality, emotion, and culture. Professor Haidt has been awarded three teaching awards by the University of Virginia and one by the State of Virginia. His recent publications include: "The Emotional Dog and Its Rational Tail: A Social Intuitionist Approach to Moral Judgment," *Psychological Review* (2001); and "Appreciation," in C. Peterson and M. E. P. Seligman (Eds.) *Character Strengths and Virtues*. (American Psychological Association Press.

REFERENCES

Haidt, J. (2003). "Elevation and the Positive Psychology of Morality." In C. L. M. Keyes and J. Haidt (Eds.), *Flourishing: Positive Psychology and the Life Well-lived* (275–89). Washington DC: American Psychological Association Press.

Haidt, J., Rozin, P., McCauley, C. R., and Imada, S. (1997). "Body, Psyche, and Culture: The Relationship between Disgust and Morality." *Psychology and Developing Societies* 9: 107–31.

Jefferson, T. (1975). Letter to Robert Skipwith. In M. D. Peterson (Ed.), *The Portable Thomas Jefferson* (349–51). New York: Penguin.

Kass, L. (2001). "Preventing a Brave New World," *The New Republic*, May 21, 30–39.

Keltner, D., and Haidt, J. (2003). "Approaching Awe, a Moral, Spiritual, and Aesthetic Emotion," *Cognition and Emotion* 17: 297–314.

McCullough, M. E., Kilpatrick, S. D., Emmons, R. A., and Larson, D. B. (2001). "Is Gratitude a Moral Affect?" *Psychological Bulletin* 127: 249–66.

Rozin, P., Haidt, J., and McCauley, C. R. (2000). "Disgust." In M. Lewis and J. M. Haviland-Jones (Eds.), *Handbook of Emotions*, 2nd ed. (637–53). New York: Guilford Press.

Trivers, R. L. (1971). "The Evolution of Reciprocal Altruism." *Quarterly Review of Biology* 46: 35–57.

Barbara L. Fredrickson

AMERICANS today face prospects of war, further terrorist attacks, and other untold bloodshed. Sometimes the world gives us one bad thing after another. In the face of all this bad, what good is it to think about the good in the world? What good is it to feel good? Won't the world be the same no matter what you think or feel?

Think back to people's emotional reactions to the September 11 attacks. Most Americans (and many others) were horrified by them. Yet some people, amidst their feelings of horror, also felt profound gratitude. Why? Because they were still alive. Still able to hold their loved ones close. Did it do any good to think about the good side of this tragedy? Did it do any good to feel grateful? Surprisingly, it did. New psychological science tells us that goodness matters.

A recent landmark study sounds a wake-up call about the profound benefits that a focus on goodness holds. This was a study of 180 Catholic nuns who pledged their lives not only to God but also to science. As part of a larger study of aging and Alzheimer's disease, these nuns agreed to give scientists access to their archived work and medical records (and to donate their brains at death). The work archives included autobiographies handwritten when the nuns were in their early twenties and about to take their final vows, which was in the 1930s and 1940s. Researchers scored these essays for emotional content, recording instances of positive emotions, such as happiness, interest, love, and hope, and negative emotions, such as sadness, fear, and lack of interest. No association was found between negative emotional content and mortality, perhaps because negative emotional content was rather rare in these essays. But a strong association was found between positive emotional content and mortality: Those nuns who expressed the most positive emotions lived up to ten years longer than those who expressed the least positive emotions (Danner, Snowdon, and Friesen 2001). This gain in life expectancy is considerably larger than the gain you'd get from quitting smoking. Imagine how long you'd live if you both quit smoking and accentuated the positive!

Although this study of nuns is compelling, it does not address *how* positive thinking and pleasant feelings help people live longer, or whether they help people live better—or thrive—as well. My own scientific research targets the possible pathways for many life-enhancing effects of positive emotions. I've distilled this research into what I call the *broaden-and-build theory* of positive emotions, because positive emotions both *broaden* people's mindsets and *build* their enduring resources.

Like many scientists and scholars, I see emotions as products of evolution. They are time-tested solutions to recurrent life problems. Problems such as facing a snake, a bear, or any other clear-and-present danger spark fear. And along with feelings of fear come a whole set of useful responses: an adrenaline surge, the urge to run, and a scream or look on your face that warns others nearby of the danger as well. This package of reactions makes fear (and other negative emotions such as anger and disgust) a useful or adaptive response to threatening situations. Emotions, this view holds, are creative and efficient solutions to recurrent problems our ancestors faced over the ages.

Yet positive emotions posed a puzzle to scientists. From the vantage point of evolutionary theory, joy, serenity, gratitude, and other positive emotions didn't seem as useful as fear, anger, or disgust. These good feelings don't spark specific bodily changes, action urges, or facial expressions. Your smile, after all, doesn't tell *which* positive emotion you feel or why. If positive emotions didn't promote our ancestors' survival in life-threatening situations, then what good were they? Did they carry any adaptive value at all? Perhaps they merely signaled the absence of threats.

Yet the puzzle of pleasant feelings stems from trying to squeeze positive emotions into the same mold as negative emotions. We can solve the puzzle by allowing positive emotions to solve different sorts of ancestral problems than those solved by negative emotions. I argue that instead of solving problems of self-survival, positive emotions solved problems of self-improvement (Fredrickson 1998). For example, when and how should individuals better themselves so that down the road they are better equipped to survive life's challenges? It turns out that situations that spark positive emotions seem to lead naturally to self-improvement. To see why this is so, it's useful to look closer at how positive emotions change people's thinking and actions.

As we've seen, one virtue of negative emotions is that they spark strong urges to act in specific ways: to fight when angry, to flee when afraid, or to spit when disgusted. Put differently, negative emotions narrow your action urges toward those that worked best in getting our ancestors out of life-or-death situations. Positive emotions, by contrast, have a complementary effect. They broaden your thinking and actions. Joy creates the urge to play, serenity the urge to savor, and gratitude the urge to repay kindness in creative ways. The virtue here is that positive emotions expand your typical ways of thinking and being in the world. They push you to be more creative, more curious, or more connected to others than you otherwise would be. This *broadening* effect of positive emotions has been tested scientifically. My colleagues and I find that when we induce people to feel negative, neutral, or positive states, only those who feel positive emotions—joy, serenity—show broader scopes of attention and thinking, as well as more socially connected views of themselves (Fredrickson 2001).

What good is a broader scope of attention or thinking? Even though positive emotions and these broadened mindsets are themselves short-lived, they can have lasting effects. By momentarily broadening your attention and thinking, positive emotions can lead you to discover novel and creative ideas, actions, and social bonds. Playing, for instance, can build your physical, social, and intellectual resources; savoring can solidify your life priorities; and creatively repaying kindnesses can strengthen your social ties and build your skills for expressing love and care. Importantly, these outcomes often endure long after the initial positive emotion has vanished. In this way, positive emotions build up your store of resources to draw on in times of trouble, including physical resources (e.g., health), intellectual resources (e.g., problem-solving skills), psychological resources (e.g., resilience, optimism), and social resources (e.g., someone to turn to for help).

These *building* effects of positive emotions have also been tested scientifically. My colleagues and I surveyed a group of people early in 2001 and learned how resilient and optimistic they were relative to their peers. In the days after the September 11 attacks, we surveyed these same people again, asking them the emotions they were feeling, what they had learned from the attacks, and how optimistic they were about the future. We learned that, after September 11, nearly everyone felt sad, angry, and to a lesser degree afraid, and that overall more than 70 percent were depressed. Yet resilient people (as identified earlier in 2001) felt positive emotions strongly as well, and they were half as likely to be depressed. Plus, statistical tests showed that resilient people's greater positive emotions were what buffered them from depression (Fredrickson, Tugade, Waugh, and Larkin 2003).

It turned out that feeling grateful was particularly common after the attacks. And in turn, gratitude was associated with both learning many good things from the crisis (e.g., "I learned that most people in the world are inherently good") and to increased levels of optimism. Put differently, feeling grateful *broadened* positive learning, which in turn *built* optimism, just as the broaden-and-build theory suggests.

So feeling good, this new scientific evidence suggests, does far more than signal the absence of threats. Feeling good can actually transform people for the better, making them more optimistic, resilient, socially connected, and healthy versions of themselves.

Indeed, this insight solves the evolutionary mystery of positive emotions: Simply by experiencing positive emotions, our ancestors would have naturally accrued more personal resources. And when later faced with threats to life or limb, these greater resources translated into greater odds of survival, and greater odds of living long enough to reproduce. The good in feeling good, then, lies in automatic self-improvement. This begins to explain *how* those nuns got to live ten years longer: People who regularly feel positive emotions will not be stagnant. Instead, they will be automatically lifted on an upward spiral of continued growth and thriving.

But that's not all. Positive emotions don't just transform individual people. They can also transform groups of people, within communities and organizations. Community transformation becomes possible because each person's positive emotion can resound through others. Take helpful, compassionate acts as an example. Classic research demonstrates that feeling good means doing good: People who feel good become more helpful to others. Yet being helpful not only springs from positive emotions, but also produces positive emotions. People who give help, for instance, can feel proud of their good deeds, and so experience continued good feelings. Plus, people who receive help can feel grateful, and those who merely witness good deeds can feel elevated. Each of these positive emotions—pride, gratitude, and elevation—can in turn broaden people's mindsets and inspire further compassionate acts. So, by creating chains of events that carry positive meaning for others, positive emotions can trigger upward spirals that transform communities into more cohesive, moral, and harmonious social organizations.

Return now to the question posed at the start "… what good is it to think about the good in the world?" Our minds are powerful allies. As John Milton told us, they "can make a heaven into a hell, or a hell into a heaven." The new psychological science that I've described begins to unravel how such stunning transformations occur. Think about the good in the world, or otherwise finding positive meaning, and you seed your own positive emotions. Positive emotions, in turn, *broaden* your mind-sets and *build* your enduring personal resources. Finding the good, and feeling it emotionally within you—in terms of gratitude, love, or joy—can transform you for the better. A focus on goodness, then, can not only change your life and your community, but perhaps also the world, and—over time—create a heaven on earth.

✍

BARBARA L. FREDRICKSON, PH.D., is Associate Professor of Psychology at the University of Michigan and a Faculty Associate at the Research Center for Group Dynamics at UM's Institute for Social Research. Dr. Fredrickson's research centers on positive emotions. She has won numerous academic prizes, and in 2000 she was awarded the first-ever, first-place Templeton Prize in Positive Psychology (the largest prize awarded in psychology) for her original research on how positive emotions cultivate and build human strengths. Dr. Fredrickson is the author of forty articles and book chapters on emotions. Her research is supported by the National Institute of Mental Health, and she directs the Positive Emotion and Psychophysiology Laboratory at UM's Department of Psychology (PEPLab).

REFERENCES

Danner, D. D., Snowdon, D. A., Friesen, W. V. (2001). Positive emotions in early life and longevity: Findings from the nun study. *Journal of Personality and Social Psychology* 80: 804–13.

Fredrickson, B. L. (1998). What good are positive emotions? *Review of General Psychology* 2: 300–319.

———. (2001). The role of positive emotions in positive psychology: The broaden-and-build theory of positive emotions. *American Psychologist* 56: 218–26.

Fredrickson, B. L., Tugade, M. M., Waugh, C. E., and Larkin, G. R. (2003). What Good Are Positive Emotions in Crises? A Prospective Study of Resilience and Emotions Following the Terrorist Attacks on the United States on September 11th, 2001. *Journal of Personality and Social Psychology* 84(2):365-76.

PSYCHOLOGICAL SCIENCE AND SPIRITUAL PURSUITS 72

David G. Myers

A S I EXPLAIN in *Intuition: Its Powers and Perils*,[1] today's cognitive science reveals some astounding powers (and notable perils) of human intuition. This growing scientific appreciation of nonrational, intuitive forms of knowing lends credence to spirituality. Great activity lies beneath the ocean's surface, and perhaps untapped wisdom resides beneath our conscious, rational mind. Hamlet was surely right: "There are more things in heaven and earth, Horatio, than are dreamt of in your philosophy."

Science also informs the spiritual quest as it helps us winnow genuine from pseudo-spirituality. When people make certain claims of spiritual intuition, science can test them. Putting spiritual claims to the test may sound like letting the scientific fox into the spiritual chicken coop, but actually a religious mandate for science exists—even science applied to religion.

The Religious Mandate for Science and Skepticism

Religion and spirituality come in two forms: (1) Dogmatic faith—absolute certainty in one's convictions—feeds fanaticism: "I am right; if others disagree, they are wrong." (2) Humble faith feeds openness, dialog, and searching: "As a finite and fallible human, I am sometimes wrong; if others disagree, we may each have something to learn. 'Judge not.'"

Humility lies at the heart of theology. Biblical monotheism, someone has said, offers two simple axioms: (1) There is a God. (2) It's not you. These axioms mandate humility, and humility lies at the heart of science. "LORD, I have given up my pride and turned away from my arrogance," wrote the author of Psalm 131.[2] Biblical spirituality understands the Psalmist's humility, views human reason as limited, and implies that our most confident belief can, therefore, be the conviction that some of our beliefs are in error. In the Reformation tradition, theology itself must be ever-reforming its always imperfect understandings. In principle if not always in practice, people of faith can readily accept Cromwell's plea to "think it possible you may be mistaken."[3] They can test their ideas against the axioms of their faith, against the historic convictions of their community, and against the insights of science.

Humility also lies at the heart of science. What matters in science is not my opinion or yours, but whatever truths nature reveals in response to our questions. If people don't behave as our ideas predict, then so much the worse for our ideas. Historians of science remind us that many of the pioneers of modern science were people whose faith made them humble before nature and skeptical of human authority.

One of psychology's early mottos expressed this humble attitude: "The rat is always right." It is also the testing attitude commended by both Moses—"If a prophet speaks in the name of the Lord and what he says does not come true, then it is not the Lord's message" (Deut 18:22);[4] and St. Paul—"All must test their own work" (Gal 6:3–4a).[5]

Humility, that synthesis of faith in God and skepticism of human presumption, helps us critique certain spiritual claims, challenging some and affirming others.

Near-Death Experiences

"A man ... hears himself pronounced dead by his doctor. He begins to hear an uncomfortable noise, a loud ringing or buzzing, and at the same time feels himself moving very rapidly through a long dark tunnel. After this, he suddenly finds himself outside of his own physical body ... and sees his own body from a distance, as though he is a spectator. ... Soon other things begin to happen. Others come to meet and to help him. He glimpses the spirits of relatives and friends who have already died, and a loving, warm spirit of a kind he has never encountered before—a being of light—appears before him. ... He is overwhelmed by intense feelings of joy, love, and peace. Despite his attitude, though, he somehow reunites with his physical body and lives."

This passage from Raymond Moody's bestselling book *Life after Life* is a composite near-death experience.[6] Near-death experiences are more common than one might suspect. Several investigators each interviewed a hundred or more people who had come close to death through physical traumas such as cardiac arrest.[7] In each study, 30 percent to 40 percent of such patients recalled a near-death experience. When George Gallup Jr. (who contributed an essay to this volume) interviewed a national sample of Americans, 15 percent reported having experienced a close brush with death. One-third of these people—representing eight million people by Gallup's estimate—reported an accompanying mystical experience.[8] Some claimed to recall things said while they lay unconscious and near death. (But then, anesthetized surgical patients in a "controlled coma" are sometimes not as out for the count as surgical teams might suppose. Occasionally, they can later recall operating room conversation or obscure facts or words presented over headphones.)[9]

Moody's description of the "complete" near-death experience sounds peculiarly like psychiatric researcher Ronald Siegel's descriptions of the typical hallucinogenic experience.[10] Both offer a replay of old memories, out-of-body sensations, and visions of tunnels or funnels and bright lights or beings of light. Patients who have experienced temporal lobe seizures also reported profound mystical experiences, as have solitary sailors and polar explorers while enduring monotony, isolation, and cold.[11] Oxygen deprivation can produce such hallucinations. As lack of oxygen turns off the brain's inhibitory cells, neural activity increases in the visual cortex, notes Susan Blackmore.[12] The result is a growing patch of light, which looks much like what one would see moving through a tunnel.

Perhaps, then, the bored or stressed brain manufactures the near-death experience, which, argued Siegel, is best understood as "hallucinatory activity of the brain."[13] It's like gazing out a window at dusk: We begin to see the reflected interior of the room as if it were outside, either because the light from outside is dimming (as in the near-death experience) or because the light inside is being amplified (as with an LSD trip).

Some near-death investigators object. They report that those who have experienced both hallucinations and the near-death phenomenon typically deny their similarity. Moreover, a near-death experience may change people in different ways than a drug trip. Those who have been "embraced by the light" may become kinder, more spiritual, and more devout in their life-after-death belief. And even if the near-death experience is hallucinatory, might it not also be a genuinely mystical, authentic, and rare opportunity for spiritual insight? Skeptics reply that these effects stem from the death-related context of the experience. When near death, people worldwide sometimes report intuitions of another world, although their content varies with the culture.[14] Under stress, the brain draws on what it knows.

Spirituality and the Good Life

Scientists have similarly challenged spiritual claims of conversations with the dead, reincarnation, and miracles called up by people with a supposed hotline to God. After discarding spiritual "bath water," does a spiritual "baby" remain? Can one challenge the sort of spirituality that gives spirituality a bad reputation without expressing a condescending cynicism toward all spirituality?

Medicine, twisted, can kill people. But far more often, medicine enhances life. Can the same be said of religion? In both *The Pursuit of Happiness* and *The American Paradox*,[15] I explore evidence pertinent to religion's adaptiveness. Here is a quick synopsis of four links between an active faith and health, well-being, and goodness.

HEALTH

Recent epidemiological studies comparing health and longevity in secular and religious Israeli kibbutzim, and among religiously active and inactive Americans, find consistent correlations between religion and health. One recent national health study following twenty-one thousand lives through time revealed that life expectancy among those never attending church is seventy-five years, but eighty-three years among those attending church more than weekly. For several reasons, an active faith is nearly as strongly associated with longevity as is nonsmoking.[16]

HAPPINESS

Many studies have also found correlations between faith and "subjective well-being" (happiness and satisfaction with life). For example, in National Opinion Research Center surveys of 40,167 Americans since 1972, 26 percent of those never attending religious services reported being "very happy," as did 47 percent of those participating in services more than weekly. Faith, it seems, connects us with others, engenders meaning and purpose beyond self, provides a grace-filled basis for self-acceptance, and sustains our hope that, in the end, the very end, all shall indeed be well.

COPING

One national survey found that people who had recently suffered divorce, unemployment, bereavement, or serious illness or disability retained greater joy if they also had a strong faith.[17] Compared with religiously inactive widows, recently widowed women who worship at their church or synagogue report greater well-being.[18] Compared with irreligious mothers of children with developmental disabilities, those with a deep religious faith are less vulnerable to depression.[19] "Religious faith buffers the negative effects of trauma on well-being," concluded University of Texas sociologist Christopher Ellison.[20]

GOODNESS

Does faith feed morality and compassion, as Senator Lieberman argued during the 2000 presidential campaign? No way, said *New York Times* columnist Natalie Angier: "No evidence supports . . . the canard that godliness and goodliness are linked in any way but typographically."[21] But Angier is demonstrably wrong: The 24 percent of Americans who attend church weekly give 48 percent of all charitable contributions to all causes in the United States and are twice as likely as the irreligious to volunteer among the poor, infirm, and elderly. Moreover, in areas where churchgoing is high, crime rates are low. Even the unbelieving skeptic Voltaire recognized the faith-morality connection: "I want my attorney, my tailor, my servants, even my wife to believe in God," he said. "Then I shall be robbed and cuckolded less often."[22] And consider: Who is most likely to sponsor food pantries and soup kitchens? Who took medicine into the Third World and opened hospitals? Who sheltered orphans? Who spread literacy and established schools and universities? Who led movements to abolish the slave trade, end apartheid, and establish civil rights? Who most often adopts children? The answer to all these questions is the same.

Let no one get smug. As Steven Pinker noted, faith sometimes provides justification for greed, war, bigotry, and terrorism. The Christian writer Madeleine L'Engle acknowledged as much: "Christians have given Christianity a bad name" (and some Muslims and Jews have done the same for their faiths).[23] No wonder that Stephen Jay Gould could write that much of his "fascination" with religion "lies in the stunning historical paradox that organized religion has fostered, throughout Western history, both the most unspeakable horrors and the most heartrending examples of human goodness."[24] The "insane courage" that enabled the horror of 9/11 "came from religion," noted Richard Dawkins.[25] If "a martyr's death is equivalent to pressing the hyperspace button and zooming through a wormhole to another universe, it can make the world a very dangerous place," he concluded. Although the worst genocides have mostly come from irreligious tyrants (Mao, Stalin, and Pol Pot) who did not value fellow humans as "God's children," religion's record is indeed mixed. Still, on balance, the evidence now suggests that faith more often breeds health, happiness, coping, character, and compassion.

All this cannot tell us whether spirituality pursues an illusion or a deep truth. Is "God" merely a word we use to cover our ignorance? Is spirituality an opiate of the people? Or is it human ignorance to presume God's absence from the fabric of the universe? If we are honest with ourselves, we cannot know which is right. In the dark of the night, the theist and atheist will each have moments when they wonder whether the other might be right. Perhaps all spiritual intuitions are illusions. Or, perhaps those missing a spiritual dimension are flatlanders who miss another realm of existence. If we could prove the nature of ultimate reality, we would not need faith to bet on God's existence.

Lacking proof or certainty, should we straddle the fence with perfect indecision? Sometimes, said Albert Camus, life beckons us to make a 100 percent commitment to something about which we are 51 percent sure. Credit Dawkins for the courage to get off the fence and stir the debate. It is understandable that the successes of scientific explanation combined with the superstition and inhumanity sometimes practiced in religion's name might push some people off the fence toward skepticism. And credit people of faith, including those who practice faith-based skepticism, for venturing a leap. Many do so mindful that they might be wrong, yet bet their lives on a humble spirituality, on a fourth alternative to purposeless scientism, gullible spiritualism, and dogmatic fundamentalism. They can root themselves in a spirituality that helps make sense of the universe, gives meaning to life, opens them to the transcendent, connects them in supportive communities, provides a foundation for morality and selfless compassion, and offers hope in the face of adversity and death.

Although we're all surely wrong to some extent—we glimpse ultimate reality only dimly, both skeptics and faithful agree—perhaps we can draw wisdom from both skepticism and spirituality. Perhaps we can anchor our lives in a rationality and humility that restrains spiritual intuition with critical analysis and in a spirituality that nurtures purpose, love, and joy.

✐♥

DAVID G. MYERS, PH.D., is a social psychologist and communicator of psychological science to college students and the general public. His scientific writings, supported by National Science Foundation grants and fellowships and recognized by the Gordon Allport Prize, have appeared in two dozen periodicals, including *Science*, the *American Scientist*, the *American Psychologist*, and *Psychological Science*. Professor Myers has digested psychological research for the public through articles in more than three dozen magazines, from *Scientific American* to *Christian Century*, and through fifteen books, including *The Pursuit of Happiness: Who Is Happy—and Why* (Morrow, 1992; Avon, 1993), *The American Paradox: Spiritual Hunger in an Age of Plenty* (Yale University Press, 2000), and *Intuition: Its Powers and Perils* (Yale University Press, 2002). His textbooks, including *Psychology*, 7th ed., *Exploring Psychology*, 6th ed., *Social Psychology*, 8th ed., and *Exploring Social Psychology*, 3rd ed.

are studied by students at one thousand colleges and universities and translated into twelve languages. Professor Myers is also the author of books relating psychological science to religious faith.

NOTES

1 Myers, D.G. *Intuition: Its Powers and Perils.* Yale University Press, 2002.

2 Psalm 131:1, Today's English Version.

3 Cromwell, O. Letter, Aug. 3, 1650, to the General Assembly of the Scottish Kirk. In: Carlyle, T., *Oliver Cromwell's Letters and Speeches,* 1845.

4 Today's English Version.

5 New Revised Standard Version.

6 Moody, R. *Life after Life.* Harrisburg, PA: Stackpole Books, 1976, 23–24.

7 Ring, K. *Life at Death: A Scientific Investigation of the Near-Death Experience.* New York: Coward, McCann and Geoghegan, 1980; Schnaper, N. "Comments Germane to the Paper Entitled 'The Reality of Death Experiences' by Ernst Rodin," *Journal of Nervous and Mental Disease* 168 (1980): 268–70.

8 Gallup, G. H., Jr., and O'Connell, G. *Who Do Americans Say That I Am?* Philadelphia: Westminster Press, 1986; Gallup, G. H., Jr. *Adventures in Immortality.* New York: McGraw-Hill, 1982.

9 Bonke, B., Schmitz, P. I. M., Verhage, F., and Zwaverling, A. "Clinical Study of So-Called Unconscious Perception During General Anaesthesia," *British Journal of Anaesthesia* 58 (1986): 957–64; Jelicic, M., De Roode, A., Bovill, J.G., and Bonke, B. "Unconscious Learning During Anaesthesia," *Anaesthesia* 47 (1992): 835–37; Merikle, P, and Daneman, M. "Memory for Unconsciously Perceived Events: Evidence from Anesthetized Patients," *Consciousness and Cognition* 5 (1996): 525–41.

10 Siegel, R. "Hallucinations," *Scientific American* (Oct. 1977): 132–40.

11 Suedfeld, P., and Mocellin, J. S. P. "The 'sensed presence' in unusual environments," *Environment and Behavior* 19 (1987): 33–52.

12 Blackmore, S. "Near-Death Experiences: In or Out of the Body?" *Skeptical Inquirer* (Fall 1991): 34–45; *Dying to Live.* Amherst, NY: Prometheus Books, 1993.

13 Siegel, R. "Of the Brain: The Psychology of Life after Death," *American Psychologist* 35 (1980): 911–31.

14 Kellehear, A. *Experiences Near Death: Beyond Medicine and Religion.* New York: Oxford University Press, 1996.

15 *The Pursuit of Happiness: Who Is Happy, and Why?* Morrow, 1992, Avon, 1993; *The American Paradox: Spiritual Hunger in an Age of Plenty.* Yale University Press, 2000.

16 Hummer, R. A., Rogers, R. G., Nam, C. B., and Ellison, C. G. The National Health Interview Survey Study: "Religious Involvement and U.S. Adult Mortality," *Demography* 36 (1999): 273–85. I summarize this evidence in my *Psychology*, 6th edition. New York: Worth, 2000.

17 Park, C., Cohen, L. H., and Herb, L. "Intrinsic Religiousness and Religious Coping as Life Stress Moderators for Catholics Versus Protestants," *Journal of Personality and Social Psychology* 59 (1990): 562–74.

18 McGloshen, T. H., and O'Bryant, S. L. "The Psychological Well-being of Older, Recent Widows," *Psychology of Women Quarterly* 12 (1988): 99–116; Harvey, C.D., Barnes, G.E., and Greenwood, L. "Correlates of Morale Among Canadian Widowed Persons," *Social Psychiatry* 22(1987): 65–72.

19 Friedrich, W. N., Cohen, D. S., and Wilturner, L. T. "Specific Beliefs as Moderator Variables in Maternal Coping with Mental Retardation," *Children's Health Care* 17 (1988): 40–44.

20 Ellison, C. "Religious Involvement and Subjective Well-Being," *Journal of Health and Social Behavior* 32 (1991): 80–99.

21 Angier, N. "Confessions of a Lonely Atheist," *New York Times Magazine*, Jan. 14, 2001.

22 Voltaire, quoted by Wilson, J. Q. *The Moral Sense*. New York: The Free Press, 1993, 219.

23 L'Engle, M. *Walking on Water: Reflections on Faith and Art*. Wheaton, IL: Harold Shaw, 1980, 59.

24 Gould, S. J. *Rocks of Ages*, New York: Ballantine, 1999.

25 Dawkins, R. "Discussion: That's religion for you," *The Guardian*, September 15, 2001.

Identifying and Measuring "Religious Genius"

Arthur J. Schwartz

> After three days Joseph and Mary found Jesus in the Temple courts, sitting among the teachers, listening and asking them questions. Everyone who heard Jesus was amazed at his understanding and his answers.
>
> *—Luke 2:46–47*

B IBLICAL SCHOLARS, in their efforts to discern the significance of Luke's story about the twelve-year-old Jesus in the Temple, have debated for centuries what so "amazed" the rabbis. One group of scholars posit that Jesus was simply profoundly "learned" in the traditional sense, possessing an uncommonly mature intellectual grasp of Torah, especially for a twelve-year-old. Other scholars suggest that the rabbis (as well as Joseph and Mary) were "amazed" because this pre-adolescent from Bethlehem was communicating a new—if not revolutionary—understanding of God and God's nature.

Although this debate may rage on for centuries to come, what is clear is that Luke sought to portray Jesus as a religious or spiritual prodigy. The notion of spiritual prodigies is well established in many religions. In Judaism, for example, the Baal Shem Tov, founder of Hasidim, was widely acknowledged as a religious prodigy, especially his mystical (and nonrational) orientation to God and Torah. And it is difficult to understand the theology of Buddhism, especially Tibetan Buddhism, without recognizing that each of the fourteen Dalai Lamas possessed at birth and throughout childhood extraordinary spiritual gifts and proclivities.

This essay seeks to explore the nature and nurturing of spiritual giftedness. Does it exist? If so, how might it be identified and measured? And even if research could develop an empirically valid measurement tool to examine this aspect of human difference, why undertake such an effort? Don't we all have the capacity to be spiritual prodigies in different ways or according to our "callings"? Hasn't God provided each one of us with our own unique spiritual gifts? And in this age where the pervasive yoke of radical egalitarianism abounds, is it problematic to suggest that some of us are more spiritually gifted than others?

Yet if we examine other domains, it is clear that individual differences do exist. And quite frequently these God-given attributes, qualities, and skills are exuberantly praised and celebrated. Tiger Woods made a guest appearance on *The Tonight Show* with Johnny Carson at age six because of his extraordinary ability to hit a golf ball. And most of us, I would venture to say, if asked to define the term "prodigy" conjure up the genius of Mozart and the manifestation of his musical gifts at such a tender age. History is replete, moreover, with examples of gifted chess players and mathematical virtuosi whose profound talents and skills became apparent during their first decade of life.

Indeed, whether it is in the academic classroom or on the athletic field, educators and coaches are identifying and nurturing *individual differences.* Throughout much of the world, gifted education has become a well-established and significantly funded component of schools, whereby students who possess even "moderate" academic talents (in disciplines ranging from science to history to the arts) are offered a smorgasbord of enrichment programs and challenging curricula. And who can deny that coaches in almost all sports have become adept at identifying and cultivating athletic "giftedness" in very young children? My own son, along with 150 peers, was evaluated at age eight for his ability as a soccer player. After assessing his soccer ability, he was placed on the township's "A" team. For the past five years, his team has practiced more frequently than teams deemed less "gifted," and the team has been given the opportunity to learn from highly knowledgeable and expert soccer coaches. Is there any doubt that these highly structured "interventions" have helped to maximize my child's athletic gifts?

Perhaps the reader has already raised in his or her mind the following question: Why is it necessary to identify and measure "giftedness" in any domain? Indeed, readers may be recalling stories they've read about talented tennis players or piano prodigies who suffer burnout before they are old enough to drive a car. Why must we be so focused on identifying and nurturing the skills and talents of our young people? It is a fair question to ask.

The answer is deceptively simple: Research has shown that we soar with our strengths. While the risk of burnout is real, the reality is that young people who are gifted in a particular domain often *want* to exercise and strengthen their talent. Scholars from a wide variety of research disciplines have demonstrated a strong correlation between what we're good at and what we like doing. That is to say, kids who are especially talented at solving mathematical problems tend to *enjoy* math and readily seek out opportunities to improve their math skills. In the realm of athletics, scores of articles have been written about talented basketball players, labeled "gym rats" at an early age because of their love and passion for the game.

In other words, no matter how much raw talent and innate skills a young person may exhibit, these abilities will wither unless there exists what researchers describe as a "rage to master." Once again, the research is clear: There is no substitute for hard work and the intrinsic motivation to excel at a particular task or domain of activity, no matter how much natural ability is prevalent. While it may be stretching the research to suggest that high achievement is more a function of tenacity than talent, deliberate practice is a critical and necessary ingredient. Prodigies practice—and often quite a bit. For example, while Mozart could play the clavier by his fourth birthday and began to compose little keyboard pieces by age five, it wasn't until he was fifteen that he began to produce significant musical creations.

It is doubtful that Mozart thought of practicing as an arduous or painful enterprise; rather, it is more likely that he found his time at the piano a positive (if not joyful) experience. Indeed, a considerable body of contemporary research shows that children like to practice and strengthen their God-given "gift"—especially when their practices are viewed as preparation for a "performance" or "final project" (whether it be an athletic competition or building a model rocket). Professor Mihaly Csikszentmihalyi suggests that during these practices and performances individuals may experience what he calls "flow," a biological term to describe how people feel when they are involved in a sustained activity worth doing for its own sake. Flow occurs, he suggests, when an activity challenges the individual to *fully* engage his or her capacities. Furthermore, as these capacities grow, staying in flow requires taking on increasingly greater challenges (e.g., more complex equations or rocket designs).

In sum, while there may be multiple reasons that societies focus on identifying and nurturing the skills and talents of our young people, one very compelling reason may be that parents and educators clearly recognize that children *thrive* when they have the opportunity to develop their God-given skills and talents. It's a simple calculus: Kids like to do what they're good at, and what they're good at they tend to like to do. Furthermore, ample research suggests that when given the opportunity to soar with their strengths, kids are more intrinsically motivated, happier, less at risk, and—if you ask almost any educator—fun to teach!

It is clear as well that contemporary educators utilize, whether within the domain of science or soccer, roughly the same set of pedagogical strategies: (1) identify a "gifted" child through a range of assessment tools; (2) determine whether the child has an intrinsic motivation to acquire new skills in that domain; if so, (3) provide opportunities, through sustained practice, for the child to strengthen his or her natural talents and skills in that domain; and (4) offer a scaffolding of increasingly more difficult challenges, such as performances or projects, whereby the child can self-assess his or her acquisition and mastery of skills compared with the recognized "experts" in the domain.

The question that frames the final section of this essay is whether the principles and pedagogical strategies outlined above can be applied to religion and spirituality. First, I recognize that developing a range of assessment tools to measure spiritual giftedness is a challenging task. It is difficult to envision a pencil-and-paper test that captures the validity and essence of a young person's religiosity or spirituality, although a number of researchers have begun to develop and refine such empirical instruments.

Perhaps the first step is to identify more precisely what I mean when I suggest that someone is religiously or spiritually "gifted." Am I referring to his or her religious piety? Or should we measure selfless acts of compassion for those less fortunate? What about those children who possess extraordinary knowledge of sacred texts? While these are clearly elements of religiosity that need to be more closely investigated and measured, none of these dimensions exemplify, for me, spiritual giftedness.

Research by Professor Ralph Piedmont suggests that the domain of spiritual giftedness consists of three independent dimensions. First is *prayer fulfillment*, which is a feeling of joy and contentment that results from personal encounters with a transcendent reality (e.g., "I find inner strength and/or peace from my prayers"). The second dimension is *universality*, a belief in the unitive nature of life (e.g., "I feel that on a higher level all of us share a common bond"). The final dimension is *connectedness*, a belief that one is part of a larger human reality that cuts across generations and across groups (e.g., "I am concerned about those who will come after me in life").

These three dimensions are clearly principles that animate the world's faith traditions and theological literature. Furthermore, we know from the writings of spiritual geniuses, ranging from Meister Eckhart to Maimonides, that these three principles are at the core of the religious experience. Yet how might religious educators and parents assess these dimensions in young people? How might we begin to measure "prayer fulfillment" in children?

Certainly this challenge is not as simple as denoting how far a golf ball is hit or how fast and elegantly a complex algebraic equation is completed. Perhaps we ought to be guided by the maxim that George Gallup once shared with me: "Just because we don't yet know how to measure something, doesn't mean it doesn't exist."

Therefore, let's begin by acknowledging that some young people have (statistically) more meaningful "prayer lives" than others. And would any religious educator disagree that some kids simply have a stronger or more deeply felt understanding of the universality and connectedness of life? In sum, there is a phenomenological truth to the reality of "spiritual giftedness" that simply has never been researched. For example, in my review of the literature, I have yet to identify a single book or article (in any religion) that explores the concept of spiritual giftedness in ways analogous to mathematical or athletic giftedness. As Sir John Templeton might put it, we are at a point of "maximum pessimism."

Perhaps during the twenty-first century we will witness the radical acceleration of interest and enthusiasm for discovering new methods to identify and measure spiritual giftedness in young people. This is not to say that I am suggesting that only spiritually gifted children should learn how to pray, any more than I would advocate that only mathematically precocious children learn geometry. However, in a spirit of humility, let me forward the possibility that by taking more seriously the identification and nurturing of the spiritually gifted, we may be entering a century in which spiritual adepts are as cherished and praised as mathematical prodigies, a century in which houses of worship (across religious traditions) provide sustained opportunities for spiritually gifted children to practice and strengthen their innate ability to communicate with God, a century in which it will be commonplace for spiritually gifted children to learn from "experts" and "masters" about the practices and methods by which to develop a deeper relationship with God. In many ways, the novelist Chaim Potok captures this vision, within my own religious tradition, in his classic book *The Chosen*.

If a spiritually accelerating society can encourage and support this level of advancement, we may one day educate an "Einstein of the Spirit" who radically revolutionizes our understanding of God and of God's divine purposes.

RESEARCH ON FORGIVENESS 74

TEN LESSONS LEARNED (SO FAR)

Everett L. Worthington Jr.

I F YOU ASKED one hundred people to name a word they associate with religion
or spirituality, many would answer "forgiveness." "Forgiveness is what Christians
must practice," Christians might say. "God is forgiving, and Mohammed forgave
his enemies," Muslims might suggest. Jewish scholars have described forgiveness as
a necessary response when one transgresses and returns to the path of God, or
engages in *teshuva*.

Forgiveness has been both lauded and maligned throughout the ages. But in
recent times, world events have brought forgiveness to a different degree of attention than ever before. Forgiveness has been examined under the microscope of scientists. But can a topic so thoroughly associated with religion and spirituality be
scientifically investigated? Will its study yield new information about religion, spirituality, and the way we live our daily lives?

Since September 11, 2001, I have visited Nassau, Canada, the Philippines, Brazil,
Singapore, and Malaysia. In every country, people have asked: "Can the USA forgive
the terrorists?" This is an important question. The events of 9/11 have already influenced U.S. policy in the Philippines, Iraq, Israel, and elsewhere.

A more accurate question would be: "Can the *people* of the USA forgive terrorists?" A country cannot forgive. Only people can forgive. The policy of the United
States toward terrorists depends on what the politicians sense the collective will of
the people to be. So, ultimately, we will answer the question as to whether the United
States can forgive by understanding how forgiveness is practiced by individuals.

Since early 1998, researchers have been studying forgiveness by individuals. A
grant program was initiated by the John Templeton Foundation (JTF), which put
up $3 million to fund research. *A Campaign for Forgiveness Research* was later estab-
lished and raised an additional $3.4 million. Altogether, twenty-nine research proj-
ects have been funded, and countless other researchers have been galvanized into
action by this grant program.

World events made studies of forgiveness a hot topic. In 1989, when communism
fell, former enemies had to figure out how to coexist. In the early 1990s, spectacular examples of forgiveness and reconciliation—such as in Northern Ireland and
South Africa—contributed to optimism. Tragic examples of human cruelty—in
Rwanda, Kosovo, Bosnia-Serbia—added an urgency of need. The promise and need
are no less today. The events of nations trickle, and sometimes cascade, down into
the lives of individuals.

What have researchers learned from scientific studies of forgiveness? Religions have advocated forgiveness for millennia, and each major religion has taught people different lessons. Scientific researchers have typically asked different questions than religious theologians have asked. Below, I briefly examine only ten of the many findings from the research on forgiveness.

Finding 1: Forgiveness involves changes in thinking, feeling, motivation to act, and acting.

Researchers have adopted different ideas about what is important in forgiving. They have pursued different definitions of forgiveness. Author Beverly Flanagan studied hard-to-handle hurts and believes that when people forgive they re-form their worldview. Leslie Greenberg, professor at Toronto's York University, believes that forgiveness entails resolving feelings against the offender. Michael McCullough, health psychologist at the University of Miami, believes that forgiveness means giving up on revenge and avoidance motivations for behavior. Social worker Fred DiBlasio, researcher at the University of Maryland–Baltimore County, believes that forgiveness is a decision. Indeed, sometimes it is. We might give up seeking revenge against or avoiding our transgressor. But although that decision affects our future behavior, it doesn't necessarily change our internal experience. Robert Enright, pioneer of research into forgiveness and professor at the University at Wisconsin–Madison, believes that forgiveness involves thinking, feeling, and acting differently. These researchers have turned up evidence that forgiveness can begin with thoughts, feelings, motivations, decisions, or actions. I believe that forgiveness is complete, however, when a person has changed both his or her emotions and motivations toward the person who has offended.

Finding 2: Forgiveness is related to justice.

After 9/11, when General Norman Schwarzkopf was asked whether the United States could forgive the terrorists, he said: "I believe that forgiving them is God's function. Our job is simply to arrange the meeting."

When a person transgresses against another, the relationship is thrown out of balance. The icon of justice is portrayed as blindfolded with scales in her hand. Justice seeks to restore financial and social equanimity. When an injustice occurs, there is always a gap between what a person believes should transpire to restore the relationship and where the person believes the relationship is currently. I call this the "injustice gap." People can fill this injustice gap with both unforgiveness and motivations to achieve a just solution. When that injustice gap is huge, people have difficulty forgiving.

Many things can reduce the injustice gap and allow people to at least consider forgiving. In the attack on the World Trade Center, people lost loved ones and possessions, a sense of safety and security, a sense of a just world, a sense of pride, and a stable worldview. For many, the injustice gap is so cavernous that forgiveness might not be an option. The person might want justice alone, as the quotation from General Schwarzkopf illustrates.

Over time, justice will be attained. More terrorists will be caught. More will be punished. The United States will rebuild its sense of national self-esteem, security, and a sense of a just world. The injustice gap will narrow. Eventually, some people will forgive. As time ticks by, others may forgive. Perhaps U.S. national policy might change to reflect a shift in public opinion. In 1942, no one would have predicted that the America would ever have friendly relations with Japan.

Finding 3: People don't have to forgive. There are alternatives to forgiveness.

There are many ways to deal with transgressions besides forgiving. We've already mentioned legal or political justice, but other avenues to obtaining justice also exist. Obviously, seeking revenge—what Francis Bacon called "wild justice"—is an alternative to forgiving. Also, a perpetrator's apology is a form of justice. Apologies balance the social books. A person who harms me places himself or herself above me. If he or she apologizes, it brings the person back to my level. If the person makes restitution—particularly if it involves punitive payments—then financial justice can be obtained.

People can close the injustice gap by excusing or justifying the transgression. They can simply accept the tragedy and move on with their lives. Sometimes they merely forget what happened. Many in the current generation of youth do not know what happened in Vietnam. In time, many people will forget what happened at the World Trade Center. In twenty years, many youth might think of 9/11 as just old television footage.

Finding 4: Forgiveness is related to predictable personality traits.

In 1992, psychologist Paul Mauger began to study people with a forgiving personality. Since then, others have carried forth the work. McCullough has looked at vengeful personalities—what we might term "Type V." Type V people seem to be highly reactive to disturbances. They ruminate about problems, mulling the events, consequences, and potential vengeful responses. Type V people might also have generally high levels of negative emotions, such as anxiety, depression, and anger. In fact, other scientists have found trait anger, hostility, and narcissism to be associated with this Type V personality.

On the contrary, Jack Berry, research professor at Virginia Commonwealth University, has studied what we might term a forgiving personality type, or "Type F." Type F people generally get along with others easily. They dissipate negative events, allowing them to simply roll off their shoulders. Type F people are empathic. They can see things from other people's points of view, even in emotionally taxing situations. Some research has tied qualities of gratitude and humility to the Type F personality. Type F people are not doormats who forgive out of "wimpiness." Rather, they have deep respect for fellow humans and are willing to look at things from others' points of view. They try to get along—but not by giving up their sense of self.

Finding 5: Forgiveness is good for your mental health.

If we forgive, we often feel more hope in our interactions with a person. Enright has shown that forgiving can reduce people's depression and anxiety and increase their hope and sense of well-being.

Of course, holding onto a sense of injustice can also have positive effects. It can restore people's sense of control and give them inspiration to right the injustices. Some people have "proactively reacted" to horrid events, such as Carolyn Swinson, past president of Mothers Against Drunk Driving Canada. She suffered the loss of her father and a child to drunk-driver-related accidents within a short time. She turned her sense of injustice into dedication to reduce drunk driving in Canada.

Finding 6: Forgiveness is good for your relationship.

Frank Fincham, professor at Florida State University's Family Institute, has studied forgiveness in families in both the United States and Italy. When family tensions rise, he says, making up is like two porcupines kissing: It must be done carefully. DiBlasio and three other researchers—Donald Baucom, Douglas Snyder, and Kristina Gordon—have looked at how to promote healing in couples that have suffered an infidelity. They conclude that forgiveness is a long process, but can result in eventual healing.

Finding 7: Forgiveness is good for your physical health.

Several scientists have studied how forgiveness or unforgiveness affects health. For example, Loren Toussaint headed a group that conducted a national probability survey in the United States. They found that forgiving people have fewer health problems. Why might this happen? Health psychologists have taken several paths to understanding why this might occur. For some, like Italian researcher Pietro Pietrini and British researcher Thomas Farrow, the answer is in brain structures. They have found that the emotional brain takes over from the reasoning brain when people are upset. Charlotte van Oyen Witvliet, at Hope College in Michigan, has shown that when people imagine holding a grudge, their bodies respond in a stress pattern. Jack Berry and I have shown that people who are unforgiving toward a spouse or relational partner produce additional cortisol, a stress hormone. From many laboratories, the results have converged to show that unforgiveness is stressful. The negative health effects accumulate, so the elderly are most likely to show physical symptoms.

Finding 8: Forgiveness may be good for your spirituality.

Sometimes people are called on to forgive others, but they have experienced little forgiveness from people in their own lives. Richard Gorsuch of Fuller Theological Seminary has shown that people who believe that God has forgiven them are more likely to forgive other people. Some people blame God when things go wrong. When that occurs often, people experience many ill effects on their physical and mental health, as Julie Exline, a professor at Case Western Reserve in Cleveland, has found.

Forgiveness does not have to occur within a formal religious setting, but it seems that forgiveness is tied to people's spiritual existence. Friends can help each other forgive. Robert Wuthnow, from Princeton University (who has a contribution in this volume), has found that people receiving support from friends in church groups report being able to forgive harms more than church people who do not participate in groups.

Neal Krause and Berit Ingersoll-Dayton of the University of Michigan interviewed elderly Christians about their experiences with forgiveness. Not everyone experienced forgiveness similarly. Some were inclined to forgive instantly. Others forgave reluctantly or intentionally held grudges. Still others believed that transgressors had to earn forgiveness through apologizing, groveling, suffering, or making restitution.

Finding 9: Psychologists can help people forgive.

Enright has developed a twenty-step forgiveness method to help people who have been seriously harmed. He and several colleagues have applied his method to incest survivors, men whose wives have had abortions, elderly women, and adolescents who feel that their parents have deprived them of love. Others have applied Enright's methods. Ken Hart, a researcher from Canada, studied forgiveness as an adjunct to twelve-step methods in drug and alcohol rehabilitation. Enright's methods have been found to be effective even in very severe cases.

In my own research, my colleagues and I have developed a five-step process to help people forgive. In seven studies, this has also been found to be effective. Other investigators, such as Carl Thoresen and Fred Luskin in the Stanford Forgiveness Project and Mark Rye and Ken Pargament in Ohio, have developed effective forgiveness groups.

Finding 10: Forgiveness usually takes time.

Here's one eye-catching fact: There are no quick forgiveness solutions. The best interventions typically take six to ten hours to help people forgive. In severe cases, such as incest survivors, Enright and colleague Suzanne Freedman found that an average of sixty hours was required before people had forgiven the perpetrators.

Let's reconsider the question: "Can people in the United States forgive the terrorists?" We see that this will take time. People might need to spend as many as fifty hours intentionally trying to forgive. It will take years for many people to accumulate such effort trying to forgive.

Meanwhile, the injustice gap caused by 9/11 is still huge. As a nation, we are attempting to re-establish social, political, and legal justice. Until we do, the events will weigh on our minds, our relationships, our bodies, and our spirits. We don't have to forgive the terrorists, but research in the last five years suggests that some day it might be a good idea.

ℒ♥

EVERETT L. WORTHINGTON JR., PH.D., is Professor and Chair of the Department of Psychology at Virginia Commonwealth University (VCU) and also a licensed clinical psychologist. He has published 20 books and more than 200 articles and chapters, mostly on forgiveness, marriage, and family topics. The most recent books are *Five Steps to Forgiveness: The Art and Science of Forgiving* (Crown Publishers, 2001) and *Forgiving and Reconciling* (InterVarsity Press, 2003). He directs *A Campaign for Forgiveness Research* (www.forgiving.org), which sought from 1998 to 2001 to raise money to support research into forgiving, and since December 2001 has sought to disseminate findings about forgiveness arising from research. He was founding editor of *Marriage and Family: A Christian Journal.* He has received awards for overall professional contributions from the American Association of Christian Counselors (Gary R. Collins Award for Excellence in Christian Counseling, 1999) and Christian Association for Psychological Studies (Distinguished Member Award, 2001), as well as awards for teaching, scholarship, and leadership from several organizations. An international speaker, Dr. Worthington's mission is "to bring forgiveness into every willing heart, home, and homeland."

PSYCHOLOGICAL RESEARCH ON GRATITUDE AND PRAISE

Robert A. Emmons

"IN ORDINARY LIFE we hardly realize that we receive a great deal more than we give, and that it is only with gratitude that life becomes rich," wrote German theologian Dietrich Bonhoeffer. Religions and philosophies around the world would agree. They have long acclaimed the inner state of gratitude and its outward manifestation of thanksgiving to be indispensable aspects of virtue and an integral component of health, wholeness, and well-being. Gratitude is an expression of a fundamental value of human existence that has been known and acknowledged by thinkers from the Roman philosopher Seneca to contemporary writers, from the oldest religions and cultures to modern expressions of thanksgiving customs and rituals around the world.

What exactly is gratitude? Derived from the Latin *gratia*, it means "grace, graciousness, or gratefulness." All derivatives from this Latin root have to do with kindness, generosity, gifts, and the beauty of giving and receiving. At the cornerstone of gratitude is the notion of *undeserved merit*. This is reflected in one definition of gratitude as "the willingness to recognize the unearned increments of value in one's experience." There is also a cosmic gratitude that is felt in the form of awe and wonder elicited by the grandeur of natural beauty. Whatever the source of gratitude, in this attitude people recognize that they are connected to one another, their God, and their world in a mysterious and miraculous way that is not fully determined by physical forces, but is part of a wider, or transcendent, context.

Gratitude and Religion: A View from Tradition

As far as we know, there has never been a religion that has not embraced the concept of gratitude. From the beginning of time, those who have entered into a relationship with God have expressed their gratitude to that God. In the great monotheistic religions of the world, gratitude permeates texts, prayers, and teachings. The word "thank" and its various cognates appears more than 150 times in the Hebrew Bible and in the New Testament and 71 times in the Koran. Worship is praising God for who he is, and gratitude is thanks directed toward God for the many gifts he has bestowed. What begins as thanking God for specific things culminates in praising God for his goodness, steadfast love, and mercy. Furthermore, entire theologies have been built around the concept of gratitude. In his doxological theology, John Wesley stated:

[T]rue religion is right tempers toward God and right tempers toward man. It is, in two words, gratitude and benevolence—gratitude to our Creator and supreme Benefactor, and benevolence to our fellow creatures. (Wesley 1987, 66–67)

Gratitude was also central to the religious affections of theologians such as Jonathan Edwards, who wrote of the "gracious stirrings of grateful affection toward God," and Karl Barth, who noted that "grace and gratitude belong together like heaven and earth." From these perspectives, gratitude begins with God, is made possible by God, and reveals to humanity the purposes of God.

Religious narratives provide methods and models for affirming the goodness in one's life and for recognizing that the sources of this goodness lie outside oneself. Many religiously oriented events, such as reflection days or scheduled weeklong retreats (for example, those influenced by Jesuit spirituality), have as a recurring theme the notion of "gift." Similarly, many self-help groups and organizations, such as Alcoholics Anonymous, make use of the theme of gratefulness. Religions remind us that gratefulness is not just a positive-thinking veneer, but is a deep and abiding sense that goodness and hope dwell even under devastation and despair.

Do only the monotheistic faiths commend gratitude? Or, to phrase it differently, does one have to believe in a *personal* God in order to be grateful? The available evidence suggests not. A positive affirmation of life comes from a deep sense of gratitude to all forms of existence, a gratitude rooted in the essence of being itself, which permeates one's every thought, speech, and action. Gratitude, in this profound sense, is not simply a mere attitude, a deep feeling, or even a desirable virtue. It is as elemental as life itself. In many world ethical systems, gratitude is *the* compelling force behind acts of compassion because life is seen as a vast network of interdependence, interpenetration, and mutuality that constitutes being. In Indian Buddhism, for example, gratefulness, humbleness, and compassion are the natural flowerings of life.

Gratitude and the Human Person: Effects on Well-Being and Health

PSYCHOLOGICAL WELL-BEING

Does the conscious practice of gratefulness matter for human well-being? Devotional writers have long assumed that an effective strategy for enhancing one's spiritual and emotional life is to count one's blessings. At the same time, current psychological dogma states that one's capacity for joy is biologically set. Psychological research has begun to put these conflicting assertions to rigorous test. Preliminary findings suggest that those who regularly practice grateful thinking do reap emotional, physical, and interpersonal benefits. Studies have shown that adults who keep gratitude journals exercise more regularly, report fewer illness symptoms, feel better about their lives as a whole, and are more optimistic about the future. These benefits were observed in experimental studies when comparisons were made with those who were asked to chronicle their daily travails or to reflect on ways in which they were better off than others. In daily studies of emotional experience, when people report feeling grateful, thankful, and appreciative, they also feel more loving, forgiving, joyful, and enthusiastic. These deep affections appear to be formed through the discipline of gratitude. In this regard, it is interesting that the Greek root of the word enthusiasm, *entheos*, means "inspired by or possessed by a god."

Other research has found that adopting an attitude of gratitude results in higher reported levels of alertness and energy, better sleep quality, a greater sense of interpersonal connectedness, and more helpfulness toward others. In other words, gratitude leads not only to feeling good, but also to doing good, lending empirical support to Albert Schweitzer's claim that "the gratitude that we encounter helps us believe in the goodness of the world, and strengthens us thereby to do what is good."

How does one explain these findings? Grateful thinking may become a form of positive, automatic thought for those who train their minds in this fashion. For these individuals, a grateful response to life circumstances might be an adaptive psychological strategy and an important process by which they positively interpret everyday experiences. Focusing on the gifts one has been given is an antidote to envy, resentment, regret, and other negative states that undermine long-term happiness. The experience of gratitude, and the actions stimulated by it, also build and strengthen social bonds and friendships. We know that social support is vital to physical and psychological well-being. Encouraging people to focus on the benefits they have received from others leads them to feel loved and cared for.

Physical Health

In addition to the psychological and interpersonal benefits of gratitude, there appears to be growing evidence that gratitude and related states can positively affect physiological functioning and physical health. Studies of the physiological effects of positive emotions closely related to gratitude—namely, appreciation and compassion—suggest that reliable changes in cardiovascular and immune functioning may confirm these findings. Rollin McCraty and his colleagues at the HeartMath Institute in Boulder Creek, California, have found that consciously experiencing appreciation increases parasympathetic activity, a change thought to be beneficial in controlling stress and hypertension. A grateful heart, then, might be a healthy heart.

In research conducted at the University of Pittsburgh, thankfulness and appreciation as aspects of religious faith in heart recipients were positively related to perceived physical and mental health one year after transplant, with greater compliance to medical regimens and with fewer difficulties with diet and medications. Another study found that medical patients with higher levels of gratitude for their medical care reported greater levels of satisfaction and fewer emotional problems.

Can gratitude add years to one's life? In what might be the most significant study to date on positive emotions and health, University of Kentucky researchers have found a strong inverse association between positive emotional content in autobiographies from 180 Catholic nuns written at age twenty-two and risk of mortality in later life. The more positive emotions expressed in their life stories (contentment, gratitude, happiness, hope, love), the more likely they were to be alive six decades later. Specifically, the study found a 6.9-year difference in longevity in the "happiest" compared with the "least happy" nuns.

Scientific and medical research showing the beneficial effects of religious involvement on health has been rapidly accelerating. Researchers are just beginning to unravel the complex causal mechanisms responsible for these relationships. One particularly promising explanation might involve the experience of the religious affections: hope, love, forgiveness, joy, and gratitude. Psychoneuroimmunologists are beginning to explore the pathways by which these and other positive emotions influence the immune system. Given that expressions of praise and thanksgiving are key components of religious worship, the physiological effects of gratitude hold promise for understanding religion's impact on health. We know that prayer is associated with improved health outcomes. A plausible hypothesis is that prayers saturated with praise and thanksgiving lead to neurochemical changes that produce beneficial physical outcomes over time.

Religion and Spirituality: A Lifelong Pursuit

What does research tell us about the link between gratitude and religion/spirituality? People who describe themselves as either religious or spiritual are more likely to be grateful than those who describe themselves as neither. A Gallup survey reported that 54 percent of adults and 37 percent of teens said they express thanks to a God or Creator "all of the time." Two-thirds of those surveyed said they express gratitude to God by saying grace before meals, and three out of four reported expressing thanks to God through worship or prayer. In a classic study conducted over a half-century ago, gratitude was one of the main motivations for religious conversion in college students. We have found that those who regularly attend religious services and engage in religious activities such as prayer or reading religious material are more likely to be grateful. Grateful people are more likely to acknowledge a belief in the interconnectedness of all life and a commitment and responsibility to others. In addition, grateful individuals place less importance on material goods; they are less likely to judge success in terms of possessions accumulated.

How can people, young and old, be guided toward a life of thanksgiving? As an attitude, gratitude does not emerge spontaneously in children. As with other virtues, it is acquired only through sustained focus and effort. Nearly seventy years ago, one developmental psychologist suggested that parents emphasize the sense of community created or strengthened through gratefulness—and diminished or destroyed through ingratitude—rather than appeal to a child's sense of politeness or obligation. Today, children's books and articles in parenting magazines regularly encourage the cultivation of gratitude and thankfulness in children and offer strategies for parental inculcation. The essence of these approaches is that gratitude is taught as a form of unlimited love, rather than as a baptism into moral recordkeeping.

Yet practically no scientific research has been conducted on the emergence of gratitude in children. In this regard, programmatic, developmental research stands out as a critical priority. What are the most promising means for increasing *gratitude literacy* in our children? The Thanksgiving Leadership Forum of Dallas, comprising business and civic leaders, has sponsored essay-writing contests for high-school students in which they write thousand-word essays on gratitude and thanksgiving as a way of life. College scholarships are awarded for the best essays. Others have developed curricula and gratitude activities for use in schools and in parenting. A sustained research commitment to reveal the most effective strategies for increasing thanksgiving literacy would enable parents and educators to guide more effectively their child's passage into responsible and grateful adulthood. In these efforts, psychologists would be wise to enlist the assistance of schools, religious organizations, and parenting groups to develop climates that educate for gratitude.

Conclusion

John Calvin stated, "we are . . . overwhelmed by so great and so plenteous an out-pouring of benefactions . . . that we never lack reason for praise and thanksgiving." Through modern research we are beginning to recognize this basic truth and dis-cover how this attitude can be cultivated for the betterment of individuals and com-munities.

Unquestionably, there are limits to the power of gratitude. Grateful thinking will not in and of itself cause tumor cells to shrink, nor will individuals whose depres-sion is caused by a biochemical imbalance necessarily profit from gratitude train-ing. Yet one thing is clear: People who live under an "aura of pervasive thankfulness" reap the rewards of grateful living. Conversely, those who fail to feel gratitude cheat themselves out of their experience of life.

The significance of gratitude lies in its ability to enrich human experience. Grat-itude elevates, energizes, inspires, and transforms. People are moved, opened, and humbled through expressions of praise and gratitude. By embracing life itself as a gift, gratitude provides our lives with meaning. Within such a framework, gratitude can come to dominate one's entire life outlook, or even the outlook of entire nations.

By cultivating a thankful perspective on life, the grateful person sees himself or herself in a transcendent context, opening one's soul to an endless stream of divine blessings.

✍❦

ROBERT A. EMMONS, PH.D., is Professor of Psychology at the University of Cali-fornia, Davis. He was formerly an affiliated scientist with the Duke University Center for Religion/Spirituality and Health and a research fellow for the Interna-tional Center for the Integration of Health and Spirituality. Professor Emmons served as 2003–2004 President of the American Psychological Association's Divi-sion 36, The Psychology of Religion. He is the author of nearly 80 original publi-cations in peer-reviewed journals or chapters in edited volumes and is an associate editor for the *Journal of Personality and Social Psychology* and the *International Journal for the Psychology of Religion*. Professor Emmons is the author of the acclaimed *The Psychology of Ultimate Concerns* (Guilford Press), and he also co-edited with Michael McCullough the newly released *The Psychology of Gratitude* (Oxford University Press).

REFERENCES

Danner, D. D., Snowdon, D. A., and Friesen, W. V. Positive emotions in early life and longevity: Findings from the nun study. *Journal of Personality and Social Psychology* 80 (2001): 804–13.

Emmons, R. A., and Hill, J. *Words of Gratitude for Mind, Body, and Soul.* Radnor, PA: Templeton Foundation Press, 2001.

Emmons, R. A., and McCullough, M.E. "Counting blessings versus burdens: Experimental studies of gratitude and subjective well-being in daily life." *Journal of Personality and Social Psychology* 84 (2003): 377–89.

Emmons, R. A., and Shelton, C. S. "Gratitude and the science of positive psychology." In *Handbook of Positive Psychology*, edited by C. R. Snyder and S. J. Lopez, 459–71. New York: Oxford University Press, 2002.

Gallup, G. H., Jr. "Thankfulness: America's saving grace." Paper presented at the National Day of Prayer Breakfast, Thanks-Giving Square, Dallas, 1998.

McCraty, R., Atkinson, M., Tiller, W., Rein, G., and Watkins, A. D. "The effects of emotions on short-term power spectrum analysis of heart rate variability." *The American Journal of Cardiology* 76 (1995): 1089–93.

Wesley, J. *The Works of John Wesley.* Vol. 4 (Sermons IV: 115–51). A. C. Outler (Ed.). Nashville: Abingdon Press, 1987.

"Ecce Homo" 76

To Welcome the Suffering Is the Sign of Our Humanity[1]

Xavier Le Pichon

T HE REMARKABLE interest of Sir John Templeton in what he calls progress in acquiring spiritual information is similar to the spiritual quest that has been close to my heart. This quest has led me to share the life of mentally handicapped people. My life is built on two anchor points—science, with my passion for earth sciences, and the community of L'Arche,[2] where I have lived since 1976 with mentally handicapped people. This link between science and suffering people may seem strange, but I feel that such a connection is crucial in the development of humanity.

Science has to be humane, and it cannot be so if scientists do not integrate their scientific vision and their love for humanity. Teilhard de Chardin is my role model in this respect. This mystic was also a great specialist in earth sciences. He knew that the history of the Earth and the universe and the history of humanity are inextricably linked; he contemplated the best scientific conclusions as a Christian believer in order to reflect on evolution in human societies. Like me, Teilhard de Chardin was offered a chair at the College of France, but he was not permitted to accept this offer. I owe it to his memory to emphasize the importance of the type of reflection that he inaugurated and that I have tried, in a more modest way, to pursue in a recent book.[3]

I often use the term "human/humane." In French, "humain" is used to denote someone who is both human and humane; that is, someone who is sensitive to the suffering of others and tries to alleviate that suffering. In the same way, a society is "humain" to the degree that it takes care of those who suffer most without either rejecting or marginalizing them. In 2000, I organized a conference of specialists at the College of France to discuss "The Unhappiness of Others: Suffering and Culture." A dozen of us shared our thoughts about the way in which different cultures understand this situation.

The first paper was given by Yves Coppens, a specialist in prehistoric human fossil evidence.[4] He reported that an adult skeleton had been found in Iraq in a tomb dating back sixty thousand to one hundred thousand years. It was the skeleton of a crippled adult man that showed multiple fractures that had healed long before his death. Examination of the skeleton showed that, during a major traumatic event, the man had lost the use of his right arm, that he was partially blind, and that he would have had serious difficulty with mobility. In other words, he was unable to take care of himself. For him to have been able to continue living for many years (as the healed bones showed he did), it would have been necessary for him to be entirely taken care of by his community. This community would have consisted of perhaps twenty or thirty people living by hunting and gathering, with no permanent camp. Every day, the community would have moved on in search of new resources. We can only imagine the considerable effort this group had to make over many years to transport this person from camp to camp, to care for him, and to allow him to live. In the past, the mere fact of being buried showed the great respect shown by the community for that person; internment became common only around ten thousand years ago. Thus, caring for a living person in such a manner was extraordinary, although by no means is this the only such example.

We are therefore faced with a phenomenon as old as humanity itself: In the face of the utilitarian logic that dominates the world, humankind devised a way to put someone who no longer had any "utility" at the center of his community, thus allowing him to continue occupying his place in society. Such a choice inevitably leads to a reorganization of society. As soon as such a seemingly foolish choice is made, everything must be reorganized around the person who is the most wounded and handicapped. That person becomes the center of everyone's attention, and something completely different is created: This person becomes the new focus of society.

The practice of protecting the weakest members of society certainly existed before this, as the very young were always taken care of; without them there would be no future. But many animal societies are organized in the same way to ensure the protection of their offspring. Putting those who are suffering at the center of society in a systematic way is specific to humanity, so that those who are at the end of life or who no longer lead a productive and useful life are looked after. This is at the heart of human culture. Scientists have been looking for and discovering signs of "compassion" in other animal societies, but compassion is not integrated in a systematic way within the cultures of other animal societies. Most research today seems to be driven by the view that no fundamental differences exist between humans and other living beings. Yet this difference seems to be fundamental, and I make the plea that it be investigated in a more systematic manner.

We are dealing with a species *par excellence*, a human group that is discovering the true and full meaning of its humanity. In a way, one can say that since humankind's beginnings we have not ceased to reinvent our humanity. When faced with the suffering of a sick, wounded, aging, or handicapped person, we are confronted with an extremely difficult and painful choice: We may say, "I cannot" or "I don't want to" or "I don't want anymore" to care for this person. This is rejection. Either society becomes hardened by concentrating on only those who are productive or who will be so in the future, or it opens up by refocusing on new avenues, new dialogs, and new ways of life. In this way, people will invent new benefits for society, such as communication, openness, and sharing. Those who are no longer capable of direct contribution to society discover that they are nevertheless welcomed as full participants in that society. And this profoundly changes the community that practices it.

Society must continually reinvent its humanity by responding to new challenges. It would be a remarkable undertaking for the John Templeton Foundation to help show how different cultures have "reinvented their humanity," how they were able to take a seemingly foolish gamble on their weakest members. This gamble would not pay off if this were about a one-way relationship. Something must be received in return. I believe that what societies receive in return for opening their hearts to the suffering is an increase in their humanity. This is the discovery that the person whom we have welcomed changes us and raises us up.

I have certainly experienced this in the community of L'Arche co-founded by Jean Vanier and Father Thomas Philippe. My family and I live there with mentally handicapped people who are placed at the center of the community. Together, we are discovering our humanity. Often, when people arrive who want to live with the community, usually the young, they explain that they have come to help the handicapped. But as time passes and they find that they themselves have been truly welcomed by those they came to help, they acquire a new perspective about life and live fuller lives with their hearts more open to the possibility of growth. They discover new paths leading to communication and communion. They no longer say, "I am here to help," but "I have discovered friends who have taught me something entirely new about who I am."

Our friends at L'Arche love to receive postcards and letters, even though they cannot read or write. They understand the deepest and most basic meaning of a letter: "You have written to me, therefore you have not forgotten me." They attach themselves to us first as people, and they know that when we welcome them we accept who *they* are as people. They have no idea what kind of work I do. They sometimes say to me, "You seem very tired. Were your students acting up today?" Although they have no idea of what I do in my work, they notice immediately when I have ceased to be "present." It is my person that interests them, not my social position or my job. The steps that we are taking at L'Arche are not so different from those that our ancestors took a hundred thousand years ago. As soon as we welcome anyone who is marked by their difficulties in life, someone who may no longer be "productive," a transformation is operative in both the one who welcomes and the one who is welcomed.

To explain the nature of this transformation, I will use the example of my parents at the end of their lives. I have written about this in a little book on death.[5] My mother was affected by Alzheimer's disease, and my father chose to stay with her until the end. Alzheimer's is a terrible illness that progressively destroys the neurons. It results first in loss of short-term memory, leads progressively to deterioration, and then finally ends in dementia. The choice my father made led him to accept a radical change in his life: He had been a man of action; he became a man of service.

When Alzheimer's affects someone, the little memory and security that they retain must be protected because our sense of security depends on our memory. Each one of us has experienced the feeling of waking up in the morning and not knowing where we are, no doubt recalling the fright that accompanies this sensation. Mother lived permanently with this fright. "Where am I?" "Who are you?" Father structured their days in order for them to lead a life that was as consistent as possible, with unchanging rituals: morning and evening prayers (said in Latin because those were the prayers Mother remembered), regular mealtimes, afternoon tea, Mass at the end of the day. This meant that Father always had to be present and give her his continuous attention, and it also demanded what I would call an "inventive heart." Mother, to whom he devoted all his time, became the center and source of his life. This new phase of his life gave him a new name. Although Mother had forgotten that Father was her husband, for her he became "Jean," the person who was always there when she needed him. Mother had never had so much influence on her husband, had never changed him so much than during this time when she was at her weakest and poorest. But she greatly benefited from the change in her husband. Until her death, she was able to keep in touch with reality, keep her faith by continuing to pray and participate in the Eucharist. Father said at her death: "I have never loved her so much. And I am only discovering now what the Sacrament of Marriage really is."

The experimental L'Arche community and what my mother and father experienced together during her long and painful illness help us to better understand the nature of this mysterious transformation of relationships that comes when we welcome handicap, suffering, and illness. If this welcome is made with dignity and love, the person we welcome becomes the one who leads us into a new deepening of our true humanity. That person changes us deeply as they also change the nature of the community around them.

The community and the society become more human in the deepest sense of the word. But this humanity is not acquired in a single moment. We must be constantly inventive in order to respond to new handicaps and new suffering. And even if this inventiveness demands all our technical and scientific resources, it remains fundamentally an inventiveness of the heart. In the end, the humanization of society comes through the way in which it welcomes its most wounded members. It is, in fact, the response society brings to such a challenge that makes it more, or less, human/humane.

This brings us directly to the teaching that Jesus gave us on how to enter his Father's Kingdom. As is true for all that he taught us, we are not given cut-and-dried directions. We have signposts pointing the way, following in Jesus's footsteps. Whom did he welcome? Toward whom did he go? Those who were most rejected by society, the suffering, the wounded, the mistrusted, the avoided. In one of his key teachings, Jesus deals with the Last Judgment. Here, he tells us that those who live their earthly life in poverty and rejection are the ones who hold the keys to his Father's Kingdom:

> Come, you that are blessed by my Father,
> inherit the kingdom prepared for you
> from the foundation of the world;
> For I was hungry and you gave me food,
> I was thirsty and you gave me something to drink,
> I was a stranger and you welcomed me,
> I was naked and you gave me clothing,
> I was sick and you took care of me,
> I was in prison and you visited me.[6]

It is those who are fed, welcomed, clothed, cared for, and visited who open the door of heaven to those who come toward them. Note that we are talking in each case about services to the body, services that imply our presence and therefore the gift of our time. Finally, Jesus speaks to us in this passage of welcoming the "poor." The poor person we welcome on Earth is the one who welcomes us in Heaven. Christians have speculated on the interpretation of the Last Judgment throughout the history of the church. What is Jesus saying to us when he affirms that he is present in the person who is rejected, suffering, or wounded? These days, more and more people are discovering in this teaching the sacrament of the poor, which is a sign of God's presence. But have we really entered into the mystery of this sacrament? Have we understood that the poor really possess the keys of the Kingdom? What is the Kingdom? "The Kingdom of God is in your midst,"[7] said Jesus. It is the Kingdom of God where peace, fraternity, and love reign. And, in fact, these people hold the keys to the Kingdom, for if we do not welcome them, how can there be peace, love, and fraternity? How can we take possession of God's Kingdom on Earth?

Something very mysterious and very profound is found in this welcome. Jesus says, "I am showing you these people. They have a secret, the secret of my Kingdom. It is up to you to discover this secret with them and through them." Again, he does not give us directions. He invites us to share in suffering, but suffering shared in community. Without us, the suffering cannot get away from their unhappiness and risk falling into despair. But without them, we cannot enter the Kingdom of Heaven. Father Thomas Philippe, co-founder of L'Arche with Jean Vanier, said: "If we take away from someone who is suffering, any meaning to his suffering, if we make them feel even indirectly that their suffering is useless and is a burden to the community, what is left for them? Despair." We must welcome each person in such a way that they retain their full dignity and still have a sense of having something to offer to the community.

I conclude by citing another paper from the 2000 conference, this one given by Claude Birman. The theme was suffering in the Jewish tradition.[8] The speaker concentrated particularly on a very beautiful commentary from Talmud Babli, written in the fifth century CE. Rabbi Anan comments on verse 4 of Psalm 41:

> He who comes to visit someone who is sick must not sit on the edge of the bed nor on a chair; he must cover himself entirely and sit in front of the one who is sick, because the divine presence is over the head of the sick person. This is because the psalm says "The Eternal, who is above the bed of the one who is sick, upholds him."

Claude Birman explained that the divine presence manifests itself particularly to those who suffer:

> To be in the presence of suffering, he says, is to be in the presence of God. The visitor, parent, friend, carer, consoler is in the image of God. He is present to the sick person in the same way that God is there, bending over him. But this resemblance remains respectful and leaves the divine presence its rightful place; no one takes the place of God.

What suffering does for the one who is sick is in some way to lay bare his humanity and reveal him as a child of God. Everything else is of lesser importance.

In this commentary, we touch on what Pontius Pilate reveals when he presents Jesus to the crowd, Jesus who is suffering, scorned and humiliated: "Ecce Homo" (Behold the man).[9] Man in his suffering, man wounded and tortured, at this moment more than any other reveals the mystery of his humanity, the mystery that renders him in the image of God. Let us not forget that it is as the Suffering Servant that Jesus chose to reveal his humanity to us.

In the same way as the sick person is supported in his bed by the presence of God and becomes a sign of God, Jesus in his extreme agony reveals to us his humanity as "God-Man." Rabbi Anan made the discovery long ago of the mystery hidden in the hearts of those who suffer. Following them, following so many people who have approached the mystery of suffering, and of course, following Jesus who invites us to engage ourselves fully, we must now respond to this call to deepen our humanity. The only way is to go the way of the suffering person, as John Paul II has written: "The suffering person is in a special way the path of the Church."[10] The rejected, the suffering, the handicapped are put on our path so that we will welcome them, and thereby find our way to Heaven.

The inventive heart permits each of us to freely discover our own humanity—and the humanity of the whole of society. It seems to me that this call is more urgent than ever because we see new challenges continually arising among certain of society's members: the aging, the mentally ill, the disadvantaged—all those who feel lost and abandoned.

The challenges we face are perhaps not so different from those faced by our ancestors millennia ago. Did they not need just as much, if not more, courage to accept what appears to be an intolerable burden? The burden of taking long-term care of a disabled person in their small group of hunter-gatherers with no permanent home? In caring for him, in putting him at the center of their lives, they discovered that they were creating a new way of life. They did not know that it was a human/humane way, but they invented it just the same. Is it more difficult for us today? Perhaps. But we have to take up the challenge in the same way. In order to do this, we must change the way we look at the "other," the one who is suffering, the one Jesus calls our "neighbor." Those who have never had contact with the mentally handicapped are often afraid at the first contact. But in visiting the L'Arche communities, they lose their fear because they see how the people who live there are loved and regarded. Their ideas change because their heart is touched.

The changed discover what Father Thomas Philippe said, that the poor who are accepted become "peacemakers."[11] This radiated peace is visible to all hearts that allow themselves to be touched. Thus, through the disfigured features of the Suffering Servant, we begin to see his true essence: "Ecce Homo." Jesus chose to be presented by Pilate as "man" at the mock tribunal, in all his derisory finery, so that we would discover the secret of humanity: Welcoming the suffering enables us to enter the Kingdom of Heaven.

&

XAVIER LE PICHON, PH.D., is Professor and Chair of Geodynamics at the Collège de France. He received his doctorate in Geophysics at Strasbourg in 1966. A major contributor to Plate Tectonics Theory, he was the first to develop a global model based on quantitative analysis, which has become the basis for a better under-standing of the distribution of earthquakes and the large-scale reconstruction of the configuration of continents and ocean basins in the past. Professor Le Pichon's book *Plate Tectonics* (with Jean Bonnin and Jean Francheteau 1973) became the stan-dard reference work in the field for many years, and he was the most-cited author in *Earth Sciences* between 1965 and 1978. Since the late 1990s, geodetic methods using satellites have allowed him to shed light on interseismic deformation. By combining mathematics, geophysics, and geology, Professor Le Pichon has played a leading role in the development of marine geology in France and in many inter-national programs. Among his awards are the Maurice Ewing Medal (1984), the Huntsman Prize (1987), the Japan Prize (1990), the Wollaston Medal (1991), the Balzan Prize (2002), and the Wegener Medal (2003). He is a member of the French (1985) and American (1995) academies of science. Since 1976, Professor Le Pichon has also been a member of L'Arche, which brings together people that have learn-ing disabilities with others who choose to live in the same community (see http://www.larche.org/).

NOTES

1 Address to the 76th session of the Semaines Sociales de France, November 23–25, 2001: *Que ferons-nous de l'homme?* Published by Bayard Ed., Paris, 2002: 51–66. Current essay translated and adapted with permission from the publisher.

2 The first L'Arche community was founded at Trosly-Breuil near Compiegne in 1964 by Jean Vanier and Father Thomas Phillipe to welcome mentally handicapped people as full human persons. It has since become an international federation of communities, which share a common charter inspired by the Beatitudes of the Gospels (see http://www.larche.org/). The author has lived at Trosly-Breuil with his family since 1976.

3 Xavier Le Pichon, *Aux Racines de l'Homme, de la Mort à l'Amour*, Presses de la Renais-sance, 1997.

4 Yves Coppens, "La Conscience et le rapport à la souffrance et à la Mort dans la Préhis-toire." Coppens was referring to the discovery of Ralph Solecki in the Shanidar cave of a Neanderthal Mousterian cemetery. Solecki considered that his discovery demon-strated that Neanderthals were "human, humane, compassionate, and caring."

5 Tang Yi Jie and Xavier Le Pichon, *La Mort* (Paris: Desclee de Brouwer, 1999).

6 Matthew 25:34–36. Scripture quotations are from the New Revised Standard Version.

7 Matthew 12:28.

8 Claude Birman, "Souffrance et signification dans la Tradition Juive," Colloquium *Le malheur de l'autre: souffrance et culture*, 22–23 September 2000 à la Fondation Hugot du Collège de France.

9 John 19:5.

10 John Paul II, *Le Sens Chrétien de la Souffrance Humaine* (Paris: Le Cerf, 1984), 89.

11 Matthew 5:9.

Stephen G. Post

SPIRITUAL EXPERIENCE is typically envisioned as a mystical vision of God, a worshipful quietude, or an existential sense of awe before a presence in the universe that is greater than our own. Yet it can also be said that whenever human beings move through everyday life with loving-kindness, they are one with God. The New Testament reads, "God is love, and those who abide in love abide in God, and God abides in them" (1 John 7–8). Can this be true? And is it true that when we love our neighbor we are "participating in God" on the levels of both human nature and God's grace? If so, what does this entail?

In the tradition of Sir John Templeton, we can ask: What new information might be learned about such love, which rests at the center of all true spirituality? Can focused research on love lead to spiritual progress and important new insights? Ours is an age seriously beginning to consider "transhuman" possibilities through biotechnological enhancements in human biological capacities such as lifespan, personality type, and intelligence. But what will be the status of love as adventurous human beings begin to experiment with efforts to alter their own biology and that of their descendants? Will altruistic love be left behind in favor of the biotechnological pursuit of bigger muscles, happy dispositions, and unfading beauty? Or is love the "ultimate human enhancement"? What can science do to move us forward toward a better future? The remarkable powers of science very likely can help humanity to discover and illuminate the "ways and power of love" (Sorokin 1954/2002).

Unlimited Love

Unselfish love for all people, without exception, is the most important point of convergence between all significant religions and spiritual pursuits. We often marvel at the ways and power of love and may consider it the best reason to hope for a far better human future. Innumerable everyday people excel in demonstrating loving-kindness, not only toward their nearest and dearest, but frequently in service to the neediest or most imperiled. But how do our complex brains—our unique imaginations, communicative abilities, reasoning powers, moral sense, and spiritual promptings—give rise to the remarkable and not at all uncommon practice of showing unselfish love for our neighbors, or for those we do not even know? It is natural to love one's children and friends. But it is less so to love strangers, enemies, or those made unattractive by an illness that robs them of normal functioning. Yet most of us have encountered unselfish, genuinely kind, and deeply generous individuals, some of whom have put themselves at considerable risk in service to perfect strangers.

If we could answer this question and harness the power of love, the world would indeed be a place of great hope. It is in reaching outward to all humanity that one transmits to children and friends the higher purpose that can elevate their lives beyond the confines of fulfilling their own immediate needs. Tapping the love that resides within us is an unambiguous source of good in a world that otherwise engages in a battle between "right and wrong."

Sir John Templeton's term "unlimited love" is intriguing.[1] What other term could describe the scope of unselfish love for every person without exception? Such love might take many forms, ranging from compassion to correction—sometimes it might have to be constructively "tough" to be effective. But underlying all the expressions of love is an affirmation of the goodness and potential in every life. Sir John understands that "unlimited love" at its highest is God's love for humanity and that we can participate in this love to varying degrees.

One alternative to unlimited love is reasonable, law-abiding self-interest. Such moral minimalism does not abide by the positive version of the Golden Rule, "Do unto others as you would have them do unto you," but rather by the less demanding negative version, "Do not do unto others as you would not have them do unto you." In a culture of moral minimalism, the principle of nonmaleficence ("do no harm") stands alone, enforced by law and contract. Yet there is no elevating call for kindness, generosity, compassion, and beneficent love. It might easily be argued that without the influence of love and beneficence in the form of forgiveness, even such minimalism would be unsustainable.

Another alternative to unlimited love, in addition to the pursuit of ultimately meaningless selfish goals connected with narrow ambitions and materialism, is the descent into hatred. Before September 11, 2001, there was April 20, 1999, when thirteen students were gunned down by two of their peers at Columbine High School in Littleton, Colorado,. We are astounded at the downward spiral of relatively young people of all creeds and nationalities into a vortex of hatred and murderous suicide. To some extent, we can study the opposites of love in order to understand what love requires. For example, Paul Connolly surveyed 352 children between three and six years of age from across Northern Ireland. Through the influence of the family, the local community, and the school, Roman Catholic and Protestant children have learned to loathe and fear one another even at these very young ages; by age five they have absorbed hatred and prejudice. This early inculcation of hatred mirrors studies of the attitudes of Israeli and Palestinian children (Connolly 2002). Yet such attitudes do not imply that loving-kindness is not within the repertoire of human nature.

How can love penetrate and transform young and old from emptiness to fullness? Faith in love can prevail despite the turbulence of our lives. How can a world in which we not only respect, but actually cherish, one another be achieved? This would require that every scientific, educational, spiritual, ethical, and religious insight be brought to this endeavor, along with an evidence-based shift in our perceptions of human motivational structure and a renewed confidence in the genuineness of our helping inclinations. We owe this to humanity, our dignity, our future, and our Creator.

The Science of Unlimited Love

Anders Nygren was, perhaps, the foremost theologian of *agape* (selfless love) in the twentieth century. However, in hindsight, it is clear that his analysis was wrong in two ways. First, Nygren argued that generous, unselfish love is entirely a divine gift. Correspondingly, he argued that the human creature is by nature locked in an egoistic or *eros* motivational structure, contrary in all respects to the spirit of *agape*. However, empirical research, particularly the work of C. Daniel Batson, paints a different picture, one that is consistent with the existence of an "empathy-altruism axis." Even with regard to non-kin, Batson's work shows that human motivational structure includes something beyond *eros*—that is, acquisitive desire and longing. Science makes it more plausible to believe that our natural capacity for generous, unselfish love (non-*eros*) is richly elevated, strengthened, and universalized by divine grace—that is, transmuted into *agape*.

Second, if Batson is correct, Nygren was partly mistaken in thinking of the human agent as a passive conduit through which *agape* merely flows. The energy of divine unlimited love does flow, but not through a passive or empty vessel. Rather, it is the enlivening, quickening, and transposing non-*eros* capacities that are already part of human motivational structure. We are not just the empty conduit through which *agape* "comes down" (Batson 1991, 210); within each person is a capacity for generous and unselfish love that combines with *agape* to make us more and more "unlimited." A better image might be a flask that contains a base chemical with which some much grander substance from above will be bonded in a process of elevating transformation.

It is this potential for transformation that underlies the great paradoxical law of life associated with all wisdom traditions: In the giving of self lies the unsought-for discovery of self. Nygren misses the paradoxical nature of a passage such as this: "Those who find their life will lose it, and those who lose their life for my sake will find it" (Matt 10:39). In the losing lies the unintended finding. This may be true even when the giving of self requires the "tough love" of skillful confrontation with evil: *Agape* does not seek the cross, but sometimes the cross comes, and *agape* is "open" to it (Jackson 1999). It is noteworthy that in the Translator's Preface to Nygren's great work, Phillip S. Watson, a Methodist thinker, acknowledges the theme of self-discovery in a way that Nygren himself never could:

> *Agape* is by nature so utterly self-forgetful and self-sacrificial that it may well seem (from an egocentric point of view at any rate) to involve the supreme irrationality of the destruction of the self, as some critics have alleged that it does. But in fact, *agape* means the death, not of the self, but of selfishness, which is the deadliest enemy of true selfhood. Man realizes his true self just in so far as he lives by and in *agape*. That is what he was created for by God, who is *agape*. (xxii)

There is no need, when reflecting on *agape*, to confuse the valid norm of unselfishness with selflessness, its exaggeration. While the idea of "no self" has a role in Buddhist thought and deserves serious attention, it is more ontologically valid to speak of a transformation from an old self to a higher, unselfish self.

Unlimited Love as a Law of Life

Giving ourselves in unselfish love is transformative. Religious traditions have always captured this insight in their narratives. For example, Christianity speaks of *kenosis*, a Greek word that means literally "emptying" in spiritual generosity to open the heart of another (Phil 2:6–10). And the Rig-Veda, a foundational Hindu text, introduces the concept of Rita, or self-sacrifice, into both cosmology and human growth—sacrifice of the old is a prerequisite to subsequent development.

Perhaps unlimited love is the Master Poet behind the universe, fostering altruistic behavior in a still incomplete and chaotic human world. Unlimited love may be a real energy that draws forth latent human possibilities. Is our human potentiality for love much greater than most of us think? Is there evidence that the direction of human development has been toward greater cooperation and that love is an evolutionary necessity (Montagu 1955; Wright 2002)?

In the giving of self lies the unsought discovery of self. This fundamental law of life is simple and intuitive, yet it is not clearly acknowledged. In essence, the law is simple: To give is to live. And the root experience of love is, I think, the amazing realization that another person actually means as much or more to me than myself.

Love can take so many forms. As a teacher, I am always impressed at graduation ceremonies when family members and friends gather joyfully around a loved one who has a new degree in hand. Their loving delight in his or her successful completion of studies and in the start of a new stage of life is unmistakable. Such joy is palpable and easily observed and felt by anyone around them. Here love takes the form of celebration, something we need to remind ourselves that life is a blessing. *In times of celebration, we give ourselves and we discover ourselves.*

Love can take the form of active compassion when someone is suffering and needs support. Compassion includes responsive, helping behavior. It is an emotional state with practical consequences. *In times of compassion, we give ourselves and we discover ourselves.*

Love can take the form of forgiveness when someone needs to be reconciled with the community, a loved one, or a nation after making a significant mistake. Everyone who is truly apologetic deserves to be forgiven. *In times of forgiveness, we give ourselves and we discover ourselves.*

Love can take the form of caregiving when someone falls ill or infirm and has needs that must be met by others. Every day, family caregivers tend to the needs of children, older adults, and other loved ones. Professional caregivers, from health professionals to social workers, are trained to give competent care as needed. *In times of caregiving, we give ourselves and we discover ourselves.*

Love can take the form of companionship when solitude becomes burdensome. The simple experience of being with another in friendship is a form of love, whether breaking bread, sharing wisdom in quiet conversation, or attentively and actively listening. *In times of companionship, we give ourselves and we discover ourselves.*

Love can take the form of correction, or tough love. At the deepest level, love always affirms the value of all others; but it will not affirm hatred and harmful actions. Only a cowardly love is unwilling to confront maleficence. In an informed and beneficent way, love is ready to skillfully confront behaviors that are destructive of both self and others. Thus do we honor the memories of Bonhoeffer and King. As psychiatrist M. Scott Peck writes, love must be willing to take "the risk of confrontation" (1978, 150–55). But love must never give way to malice when confronting harmful motivations and behaviors. *In times of tough love, we give ourselves and we discover ourselves.*

Visionary Philanthropy

How do we approach the study of unlimited love? Just as we investigate the force of gravity or the energy of the atom, we can scientifically examine the power of unlimited love in human moral and spiritual experience. Even though thousands of books have been written about this love, they have focused on the history of religious and philosophical ideas without considering scientific research. How can we better understand unlimited love in a way that brings together evolution, genetics, human development, neurology, social science, positive psychology, philanthropy, marriage and family studies, and leadership with great religious thought and practice, affirming the moral vision of a common humanity to which deep spiritual traditions give rise? Without that vision, the future of humankind is increasingly compromised.

Philanthropists typically support programs that implement helping behavior and service in practical ways. This emphasis is entirely correct, for the practice of love is essential to society, and especially to the most needful. Yet if only a small portion of this philanthropic support were focused on the scientific study of such helping behavior, the benefits to society would be very great. Leading-edge science can demonstrate the benefits of such kindness not only for recipients, but also for those who live unselfishly, and thereby convey to the wider culture in concrete terms an empowering image of human good. Because love is so central to human moral, spiritual, and political concerns, and because science continues to have a dominant impact on our images of human flourishing, those probing the contemporary love-and-science symbiosis are engaging in matters of vast importance to our future.

For these reasons, the Institute for Research on Unlimited Love, a nonprofit organization, was formed in 2001 with initial funding from the John Templeton Foundation to conduct high-level empirical research on topics such as unselfish love, compassion, caregiving, loving-kindness, and altruism, as well as to encourage scientifically informed pedagogy.[2] Devoted to progress in the scientific understanding and practice of such remarkable phenomena as altruism, compassion, and service, the Institute's mission is chiefly focused on supporting leading-edge and visionary scientific research. It offers the following definition of unlimited love:

The essence of love is to affectively affirm, as well as to unselfishly delight in, the well-being of others and to engage in acts of care and service on their behalf. Unlimited love extends this love to all others without exception in an enduring and constant way. Widely considered the highest form of virtue, unlimited love is often deemed a Creative Presence underlying and integral to all of reality: Participation in unlimited love constitutes the fullest experience of spirituality. Unlimited love may result in new relationships, and deep community may emerge around helping behavior. But these are secondary goals. Even if connections and relations do not emerge, love endures.

The Institute has initiated collaborations with major national foundations and institutions to explore how unlimited love and creative altruism fit into every aspect of positive human experience. Ideas are encouraged from all people, from all walks of life, who wish to assist us in enhancing our understanding of loving-kindness and service to humanity without exception. Such understanding has the potential to shape science, thought, education, spirituality, and culture globally in the twenty-first century. Researchers currently are conducting groundbreaking investigations into the nature of unselfish and unlimited love, exploring topics as varied as the impact of compassionate love on the therapeutic relationship in healthcare settings, the role of benevolent love in marriage, the protective effects of love with respect to mental illness, the impact of spiritual commitment on civic engagement and public service, and the ways in which subjects both perceive and are inspired by divine love, which prompts them to extend love to their neighbors and to their neediest community members.

In summary, our goal is to shed scientific light on the human substrate of generosity and love and to better understand how that substrate can be elevated and enhanced through the perfect unlimited love that is perennially associated with Divine Nature. This is no short-term project. But through the Institute for Research on Unlimited Love, we hope to make the world a more loving place in the long term.

❧

STEPHEN G. POST, PH.D., is Professor in the Department of Bioethics at Case Western Reserve University School of Medicine. He received his Ph.D. from the University of Chicago Divinity School (1983), where he was an elected doctoral fellow in the Institute for the Advanced Study of Religion. He is also Senior Research Scholar at the Becket Institute at St. Hugh's College, University of Oxford. Since 2001, he has served as President of the Institute for Research on Unlimited Love, which focuses on the scientific study of altruism and theological concepts of unselfish love. Professor Post has written extensively on these topics, most recently as co-editor of *Altruism and Altruistic Love: Science, Philosophy, and Religion in Dialogue* (Oxford University Press, 2002), and also as author of *Unlimited Love: Altruism, Compas-*

sion, and Service (Templeton Foundation Press, 2003). He is also editor-in-chief of the *Encyclopedia of Bioethics, 3rd edition* (Macmillan Reference Division, 2003), and co-editor of *The Fountain of Youth: Cultural, Scientific, and Ethical Perspectives on a Biomedical Goal* (Oxford University Press, 2004). Professor Post is the author of more than 130 articles in a number of leading peer-reviewed journals representing the sciences and humanities, ranging from *The Journal of the American Medical Association* to *The Journal of the American Academy of Religion.* He has received funding from the National Institutes of Health Human Genome Research Institute and from the National Institute on Aging.

NOTES

1 See *Pure Unlimited Love: An Eternal Creative Force and Blessing Taught by All Religions,* Templeton Foundation Press, 2000.

2 See http://www.unlimitedloveinstitute.org/.

REFERENCES

Batson, C. Daniel. *The Altruism Question: Toward a Social Psychological Answer.* Hillsdale, NJ: Lawrence Erlbaum Associates, 1991.

Connolly, Paul, Smith, A., and Kelly, B. "Too Young to Notice? The Cultural and Political Awareness of 3-6 Year Olds in Northern Ireland." Belfast: Northern Ireland Community Relations Council, 2002.

Heschel, Abraham Joshua. *God in Search of Man: A Philosophy of Judaism.* New York: Farrar, Straus and Giroux, 1955.

Jackson, Timothy P. *Love Disconsoled: Meditations on Christian Charity.* Cambridge: Cambridge University Press, 1999.

Montagu, Ashley M. F. *The Direction of Human Development: Biological and Social Bases.* New York: Harper and Brothers, 1955.

Nygren, Anders. *Agape & Eros,* trans. Philip S. Watson. Chicago: University of Chicago Press, 1982 [original 1932].

Peck, M. Scott. *The Road Less Traveled.* New York: Simon and Schuster, 1978.

Rilling, James K., Gutman, David A., and Zeh, Thorston R. "A Neural Basis for Social Cooperation," *Neuron* 35 (July 2002): 395–405.

Sorokin, Pitirim A. *The Ways and Power of Love: Types, Factors, and Techniques of Moral Transformation,* with a Foreword by Stephen G. Post. Philadelphia, PA: Templeton Foundation Press, 2002 [original 1954].

Wright, Robert. *Nonzero: The Logic of Human Development.* New York: Vintage, 2002.

PART NINE

Perspectives from Theology and Philosophy

RULES FOR ACQUIRING SPIRITUAL INFORMATION

Martin E. Marty

EUNOMIUS of Cyzicus, bishop and scholar of early Christianity, gets my vote as Fool Number One in the crowded gallery of theological absurdists. He would have failed "Humility Theology 101" because of his contention that he knew God better than God did, concluding that God was evidently busy realizing all of his commitments. Eunomius, in contrast, had the freedom and mandate to specialize. He chose to refine his discipline and focus his inquiry on the nature and action of God, with results that his contemporaries found to be heretical. His claim about knowledge, it turns out, succeeded in informing us *not at all* about God. But it did provide information about Eunomius that we might wish to forget. His efforts showed how an errant individual can block progress in acquiring spiritual information.

To the scientists in our company, I leave the task of nominating Fool Number One in their similarly crowded gallery. Nominees must include those who, through the scientific method, either claim to prove that non-God is the only reality, or that this God or that God is *the* God. There had better be a course called "Humility Science 101," which such characters can fail as they in their own way block progress in spiritual information.

The pursuits of progress have to include better ways than those just mentioned. Among the dictionary meanings of the word "progress," the most congenial for present purposes is "to go or move forward." A second dictionary definition, "to proceed to a further or higher stage," or "to further a higher stage continuously," is, of course, the outcome one hopes for from such movement. Both those devoted to the scientific and to the spiritual should know enough to withhold judgment about whether some measurable results even exist for the steps to such a stage.

This project also focuses on the word "information," which signals what people who are devoted to the spiritual would advance. The word "information" is "knowledge communicated concerning some particular fact, subject, or event," and it is "that of which one is apprised or told; intelligence." One derives information from investigation, study, or instruction.

Freedom from the Tug of the Past

We historians are not alone in our ability to observe and document the fact that activity in respect to progress in acquiring spiritual information is inhibited when the self is captive of the past, which includes earlier formulations in science or theology. While scientists may often be retarded because of their bondage to obsolete paradigms, the temptation for theologians to "move backward" is greater. Theologians, who must work with the word (*logos*) or words in respect to God (*theos*), belong to traditions. These are based on revelations that religious thinkers ordinarily perceive as having shaped the experience and witness of people in the past. These theological scholars then characteristically study ancient sacred texts.

To "move forward," however, does not and need not mean rejecting the past; it indeed may imply a reworking of the heritage. The old books and traditions, one remembers, had themselves challenged and often replaced older books and traditions. The prophets who came newly onto the scene often referred positively to covenants older than those cherished in the earlier texts they criticized as idolatrous or deceptive. Consequently, they could celebrate newness. Only someone not fully alert to irony, which may mean the majority of religious people, would suggest that they are continually doing justice to what they think of as *The* Tradition while they are actually ossifying it.

Everyone devoted to progress in acquiring spiritual information has to use concepts, symbols, and words. If these are to communicate at all, they must come from a past that has to be transmuted in present-day exchanges. Many religious scholars justify their attention to older texts and concepts for quite other than antiquarian reasons. Instead, they suggest that when the texts were originally written and the concepts developed, the people "back there" knew some things that we do not know "as yet." In that spirit, whenever I am invited as a historian or theologian to participate in conversations on progress in acquiring spiritual information, I not only do not feel marginal or retarded, but I feel—I hope "humbly"—at home in the central activities. To make that claim is one thing. To confront the books and records and demonstrate that one can make contributions to progress using them as a basis is another.

Yet Voices from the Past Can Address Us Afresh

My personal experiment in "moving forward" is grounded in my recent studies of one historic figure out of one tradition. Martin Luther was listed near the very top of the list of those who left a mark on the past millennium, and I just published his biography for the *Penguin Lives* series.[1] Luther was not like men of our times, but was in almost all respects a medieval person. He believed, moderately, in witches and poltergeists, in omens and signs in the sky. Scientifically, the formulators who were called "Lutheran" put into their doctrinal book folk beliefs such as this: that rubbing a magnet with garlic would have an effect on the magnetic power. They could have served as scientists and checked such a claim empirically; but they didn't. Luther himself held medieval views of patriarchy and governance and would resist the attempts of some scholars and devotees to turn him into a modern.

At the same time, among people seeking to make progress in acquiring spiritual information, it is possible to successfully defend the idea that on some issues Luther "knew some things already that we do not know as yet."[2] This means that in talks between scientists and theologians, when the former nudge the latter to come up with something larger than conventional references in respect to God-talk, the voice of Luther the grand cosmologist as well as the miniaturist can inform the discussion with this kind of word, chosen from among many possibilities:

> Nothing is so small but God is still smaller, nothing is so large but God is still larger, nothing is so short but God is still shorter, nothing is so long but God is still longer, nothing is so broad, but God is still broader, nothing is so narrow but God is still narrower, and so on. [God] is an inexpressible being, above and beyond all that can be described or imagined. (Pelikan and Lehmann 1955; 37:228)

Accept that—and it is hard to reject it, if one listens to major religious traditions—and another barrier against making progress in acquiring spiritual information will have fallen. Whether in nature, in the human heart, in revelation received as somehow divine, or in the laboratory, the question arises: While moving forward, what or who do you seek that can go by the name of God?

In Sir John Templeton's vision, the final word has to be "Infinity," which, by definition, the finite can never reach. Still, humans seek language to describe the boundaries of what they might come to know and what will always go beyond information as facts. Once more, Luther strikes me as still being ahead of us by speaking of *deus nudus*, the nude, naked God, who is always beyond what human vision or discovery can gain or sustain. True, for him God is somehow and partly revealed in nature and human witness. At the same time, however, this revealed God, *deus revelatus*, remains hidden, *deus absconditus*. Whoever would claim that there are not hidden dimensions to God or, conversely, that one has fully exposed the revealed God would not likely qualify to be in the ranks of those who cherish "humility theology," like Sir John Templeton.[3]

Luther became radical on this point. God is hidden, he says, masked "in" his revelation, which in the particular Christian perception meant in sacraments and scriptures, religious speech and action. But God is also hidden "behind" his revelation. Some dimensions of God's reality, in this understanding, will always remain masked, elusive, and beyond reach. God is larger than God's revelation and does not disclose all dimensions of God's being in it. One cannot exhaust this partly inscrutable God.

To affirm something about limits along that line need not mean that scientific and theological efforts to "move forward" in acquiring spiritual information are futile. It does not mean that current boundaries of knowledge are to be frozen and set as inhibitors in the search. It need not mean that scientists or theologians have to fall into relativism and cynicism, as if *nothing* can be known because *not all* can be known. Instead, humility theology uses this recognition of both temporary limits, which are known, and final or ultimate limits, which can never be known, as a dual impetus for inquiry, for experiment, for study of the human subject who experiences and speaks of God and nature.

Humility Theology Invites Conversation

Throughout this essay, I have used the words "science" and "theology" to refer to two ways of moving forward through two discourses about the goal of acquiring spiritual information, code-named "God." I have been among those who have welcomed the Templeton effort to refine the languages and to bring the various voices of the disciplines together. At their best, these conversations have demonstrated that no single "mode" or "voice" has or should have a monopoly and, at the same time, that no two "modes" or "voices" should be confused.

The voice of the scientist, philosopher Michael Oakeshott reminds us, is exercised *sub specie quantitatis*. That is, whatever else the scientist does, he or she measures. Scientists may measure the cosmos in search of the "theory of everything" and seek to measure human consciousness, something that most philosophers who are devoted to the subject say cannot by definition be finally done. "How do I know that my 'blue,' the 'blue' of which I am conscious, is your 'blue'?" The scientist will always be pushing back the boundaries in studying the universe "out there" and the universes "in here." Yet measurement and quantification, so useful in natural and human affairs, fail when one deals with *deus nudus,* the God hidden not only "in," but "behind," revelation.

Similarly, the theologians, who listen to and analyze the voice of those who speak of the experience of God, operate with other modes than those used to measure. They may speak *sub specie moris,* or *sub specie voluntatis,* or *sub specie imaginationis,* which, in practical terms, means setting out to alter the world in respect to morals, the will, or the act of imagining. The social scientist cannot meet the pope and announce that, having measured this or that human practice or perception, the religious leader must change a particular doctrine. Well, one could make the announcement, but it would have no effect. Such witness might be influential, but it is not determinative. To confuse the languages, one would be guilty of *ignoratio elenchi,* category mistakes.

This notion of science as a mode whose differentia is measurement and quantification, while the mode of theology is *not* that, deserves careful attention, some of it directed at the John Templeton Foundation agenda and enterprises. When invited to contribute to a book edited by John Marks Templeton entitled *How Large Is God?* (1997), I asked, half playfully but also half seriously: When I wear my theologian's hat, "If I don't measure, do I measure up?"

The notion that God, the subject of theology and of most religious reflection, can be grasped by or reduced to questions of size and measurement can sound bizarre. There is no question that much of what the Foundation encourages does, indeed, measure. What it measures, however, is not God, but the human subject, whether by the relaxation response, quantifications of healing successes and failures, the state of the brain when a subject is meditating, or the size of the universe. A safeguard against "reduction" is the regular reminder by the editor of that book and most of those who associate with him that God is infinite and thus beyond measurement. One might also note that when the human subject receiving or reaching God is being measured, theologians do not have to be ignored. "Infinity" is by definition beyond the reach of theologians and scientists alike. Still, differences exist that representatives among them in both sets of disciplines must remember and respect.

Oakeshott's Voice in the Conversation

Scientists and theologians operate within distinctive modes and speak with distinctive voices. That assertion could imply to some critics that there can be no communication, only two voices given to solipsism and then to nihilism. Instead, as the Templeton venture has shown, these voices do meet, in what philosopher Michael Oakeshott formally defined as "conversation." As Oakeshott contended, "the image of this meeting place is not an inquiry or an argument, but a conversation." For here "the diverse idioms of utterance which make up current human intercourse have some meeting-place and compose a manifold of some sort." Conversing, in this sense, has been one of the main Templeton contributions to spiritual progress.

I agree with Oakeshott that one cannot transport information in the form of "facts" from one mode to the other. Instead, this exchange occurs:

> In conversation, "facts" appear only to be resolved once more into the possibilities from which they were made; "certainties" are shown to be combustible, not by being brought in contact with other "certainties" or with doubt, but by being kindled by the presence of ideas of another order; approximations are revealed between notions normally remote from one another. Thoughts of different species take wing and play around one another, responding to each other's movements and provoking one another to fresh exertions. There is, we are told, no hierarchical order among these voices, there is no symposiarch or arbiter; not even a doorkeeper to check credentials.

Admittedly, to encourage progress toward coherence, the John Templeton Foundation *does* check credentials of participating scholars. But once at the table, they are called "in humility" to listen to one another's distinctive voices, to be willing to change and thus to be more ready than they would have been, apart from the conversation, to contribute to progress in acquiring spiritual information.

✒

MARTIN E. MARTY is Fairfax M. Cone Distinguished Service Professor Emeritus of the History of Modern Christianity in the Divinity School at the University of Chicago and a member of the Committee on the History of Culture. He is also the original director of the Institute for the Advanced Study of Religion, which officially opened at the University of Chicago in October 1979 and was renamed "The Martin Marty Center" after his retirement. Professor Marty has received the National Medal for Humanities, the Medal of the American Academy for Arts and Sciences, and the National Book Award. A prolific author who has written or edited more than fifty books on religious subjects, his foremost field of expertise is religious history. Professor Marty's most recent book, *Martin Luther: A Penguin Life* (2004), describes Luther as a seminal Christian figure, his place in history, and his relevance to our times.

NOTES

1 *Martin Luther: A Penguin Life.* New York: Viking Penguin, 2004.

2 I suppose one would have to define "we" or acknowledge that he is speaking for himself. I here refer to the observation that in cultures tinged by religion the temptation is strong to cut God down to congenial size.

3 See References.

REFERENCES

Fuller, Timothy, ed., Michael Oakeshott. *Rationalism in Politics and Other Essays.* Indianapolis, Indiana: Liberty Press, 1991, 489.

Marty, Martin E. *Martin Luther: A Penguin Life.* New York: Viking Penguin, *Penguin Lives* series, 2004.

Pelikan, Jaroslav, and Lehmann, Helmut T., eds. *Luther's Works. 56 vols.* St. Louis: Concordia Publishing House. Philadelphia: Fortress Press, 1955: 37:228.

Templeton, John M. *Possibilities for Over One Hundredfold More Spiritual Information: The Humble Approach in Theology and Science.* Philadelphia: Templeton Foundation Press, 2000.

Templeton, John M., ed. *The Humble Approach: Scientists Discover God.* Philadelphia: Templeton Foundation Press, 1998.

———. *How Large Is God? The Voices of Scientists and Theologians.* Philadelphia: Templeton Foundation Press, 1997.

God, Spiritual Information, and Downward Causation[1] 79

John W. Bowker

In recent years, the notion of "downward" or "backward causation" has become increasingly important in the natural sciences, especially in biology. It is equally important in religions: Without it, it is impossible to understand a major way in which spiritual information acts causatively in human life.

At first sight, the idea of downward or backward causation seems counterintuitive because we tend to think of causes as sequential. One event leads to a second event in such a way that the second is a consequence, direct or indirect, of the first: If I push a book, it moves in that sequence of two events, the one earlier than the other. It seems, therefore, paradoxical to think of future states being causative in relation to the present.

But the trouble here lies in the word "cause." What is meant by "downward" or "backward causation" becomes much clearer if we use the word "constraint." In my book *Is God a Virus? Genes, Culture and Religion,*[2] I have summarized why the word "constraint" is a far wiser choice than the word "cause." The point about constraint is that it *includes* active causes of a direct or indirect kind, but it also alerts us to a far wider network of what has brought an eventuality into being, including passive and domain constraints. The fact that the book moves is indeed because I pushed it, but also because both I and the book are constrained by (among many other influences) the laws of motion.

Of course, in the ordinary business of life, and especially in the business of offering scientific explanations, we do not have time to specify *all* the constraints that have controlled an eventuality into its outcome, into its being what it is. In explaining, therefore, any phenomenon, we choose from the whole range of actual constraints those that relate most closely and immediately to our concern and leave the others as an unspoken assumption. But the fact remains that we do have to choose. If, as loss adjusters for an insurance firm, we ask, "What caused that fire?" we are unlikely to specify, "The presence of oxygen." Yet, if we are seeking to explain the outbreak of fire in a space capsule, we undoubtedly want to include the presence of oxygen in the specification of constraints.

So how do we choose? It is at this point that a version of Occam's razor is usually wielded ("where one explanation will do, don't multiply explanations"); but Occam's razor has virtue only so long as you do not use it to cut off your own head. As I put it in *Is God a Virus?*

> Where additional constraints must be specified in order to account for an eventuality, nothing is gained by insisting, in the name of Occam, on only

one. A better principle is this: be sufficiently, but not recklessly, generous in the specification of constraints; or at least otherwise be modest in what you claim to be "the true and only explanation."[3]

If, then, we think of constraints instead of causes, we can avoid the futile battles of reductionism that so vitiated the exposition of science in the last century. To repeat: Nothing is brought into being by one single cause. Eventualities are brought into their outcomes (into their being what they are) by networks of constraint. We can obviously continue to recognize and specify that active and proximate causes of eventualities exist while still insisting on the fact that, in the case of complex transformations of energy, many contingent constraints would need to be specified if a full account were to be given of what has brought them into being.

In that context, it becomes straightforward to see how the future acts as a constraint over eventualities in the present. Consider the case of the little brown bat (*Myotis lucifugus*), which has a wide distribution in North America, at the moment almost entirely in the United States. It is one of the tasks of ecology to explain the geographic distribution of organisms.[4] In the case of the little brown bat, ecology will specify constraints that set a limit on its possible habitats. Some of these will be from the past (e.g., an inherited biology that enables it to occupy a particular ecological niche, above all in terms of its intake of sufficient food to secure hibernation through the winter).

But clearly the resource of sufficient food is dependent on climate, and climate is not stable. Climatic change will set new boundaries on feasible habitats, so that in this case the future condition acts as a constraint over the unfolding behaviors of the bat. The distribution of the bat will change as it conforms to the conditions set by climate change. It is thus possible to produce a bioenergetics model to predict the feasibility of mammalian hibernation under different climatic conditions:

Our model predicts pronounced effects of ambient temperature on total winter energy requirements, and a relatively narrow combination of hibernaculum temperatures and winter lengths permitting successful hibernation.[5]

The model, therefore, is able to predict the consequence of future climatic conditions acting as a constraint on successful hibernation. Climate change acts as a constraint over the exploration of ecological niches, and on this basis the authors predict that the little brown bat will be found by 2080 almost entirely in Canada. It is noteworthy that in doing so the language used is that of constraint, not of cause:

The pronounced increase in hibernation energy requirements at low ambient temperatures, combined with constraints on the size of fat reserves at the onset of hibernation and the length of the hibernation season, permits application of our model to predict the northern biogeographical limit for *Myotis lucifugus* hibernation. . . . Energetic constraints at higher latitudes should be especially severe for juveniles, owing to their limited capacity to grow and fatten during a short active season.[6]

Conditions that lie in the future (from the point of view of the organism) set limits on possible behaviors, particularly when projected behavior is (or is not) rewarded by survival. In the whole evolutionary process, future conditions act as a constraint on the bearers of mutations; as they move into those conditions, some survive and flourish, but many do not.

The importance of backward or downward causation, understood as constraint, becomes even more obvious in the case of motivated and conscious behavior, because the future can be internalized as a relevant and positive constraint. Anyone playing a game of patience knows what the future outcome should be. That future outcome acts as a constraint over the ways in which the cards are played in the present. In general terms, this is true of any homeostatic system, such as a guided missile or a mechanical governor. The future state (for example, the target) acts as a constraint: If the feedback loop regulates the matrix of transition probabilities and controls future states of the system, and if the set of stable system states is limited, then the system will tend to oscillate around and converge on successive stable states.[7]

The consequences of constraint in this sense are immense for our understanding of God's relation to the universe and to the human lives within it.[8] They are equally important for the forming of spiritual life; it is obvious that religions map the future, often with considerable precision, and that they clearly expect those future states to act as a constraint over present behaviors. Thus, the Qur'an describes the ultimate future states in detail:

> Surely, those who reject our signs we will soon roast at the fire. As often as their skins are burnt through, we change them for other skins, that they may taste the penalty. Surely, God is powerful, wise. And those who believe and do deeds of righteousness we will cause to enter gardens with rivers flowing beneath, dwellers there forever. There they will have companions unsullied, and we will bring them into the shade of shades.[9]

Few Muslims allow that these descriptions might be metaphorical. In *The Islamic Book of the Dead*, al-Qadi insists that it is "not acceptable to reduce the descriptive content of the after-death states to the realm of myth."[10] Not surprisingly, therefore, observant Muslims allow those future states to constrain their lives in the present; otherwise, they may, in the final judgment, fail what Mohammad Jamali called "the examination of life":

> My view is that all life is an examination and that Allah created man in order to examine him in this world. . . . Success is required not only in mathematics and chemistry but in everything, and we must seek the help of the Holy Koran every day for success in the examinations of life.[11]

Other religions may look to the future in far less literalistic ways, in terms, for example, of union with God or of the realization of enlightenment or of the Buddha-nature. Even so, it will be equally the case that those futures will constrain behaviors in the present—or should do so, if the goal is to be attained.

Within that broad understanding of downward causation and constraint, we can then see many specific ways in which downward causation operates in the detail of life as projected into an acknowledged and hoped-for future. Think of El Greco sitting in Rome and gaining few commissions because of the prejudice against foreign artists. Then in 1756 came the invitation from Don Diego de Castilla to paint appropriate pictures for the altarpieces of the Church of the Convent of Santo Domingo in Toledo. El Greco returned to Spain, and his genius was let loose, culminating in the brilliant and moving "Apocalyptic Vision" (now in the Metropolitan Museum of Art, New York).

Both the commission and the art demonstrate the profound importance of downward causation in spiritual life. Don Diego believed that the future state includes a period in purgatory when the deserved penalties of sinners are alleviated by the prayers of the faithful.[12] The future constrained him into rebuilding the Church in Toledo to serve as burial place for himself and his son where priests would pray for their souls. The same constraint from the future led to the widespread endowment of chantry priests and chapels for that purpose.

Where El Greco was concerned, the painting "Apocalyptic Vision" exhibits how the future constrained the artist's work in the present—his vision, his technique, and his design—because El Greco attempted to convey the final resurrection.[13] Downward causation constrains the artist into producing a work of art that otherwise would not exist.

Spiritual information, therefore, enters human lives, not only from the past (from revelation, teachers, etc.), but also from the future, from the One to whom they offer their lives in faith and hope. The consequence of that downward causation can be seen in the extent to which it constrains lives in the present. It is therefore appropriate that this paper is offered to John Templeton, in whose life the consequence of grace and truth is so abundantly clear.

ℐ❤

JOHN WESTERDALE BOWKER has served as Dean of Trinity College of Cambridge University and is an Honorary Canon of Canterbury Cathedral. Currently, he is a Fellow of Gresham College, London. He has written numerous books on religion, including *The Oxford Dictionary of World Religions, The Meanings of Death, Is God a Virus? Genes, Culture and Religion,* and, most recently, *God: A Brief History.*

NOTES

1 An expanded version of this article appeared in *Theology* (March/April 2004): 81–88.

2 *Is God a Virus?* London, SPCK, 1995.

3 Ibid., 104.

4 See, e.g., D. M. Gates, *Climate Change and its Biological Consequences,* Sunderland, Sinauer, MA, 1993, 162–201.

5 M. M. Humphries, D. W. Thomas, and J. R. Speakman, "Climate-mediated energetic constraints on the distribution of hibernating mammals," *Nature* 418, no. 6895 (2002): 313.

6 Ibid., 315.

7 See Bowker, *The Sense of God: Sociological, Anthropological and Psychological Approaches to the Origin of the Sense of God*, Oxford, Oneworld, 1995, 50.

8 See my "Prayer for Others: The Language of Love," *A Year to Live*, London, SPCK, 1991, 52.

9 iv.59f/56f.; cf. xx.20ff.

10 *The Islamic Book of The Dead*, Wood Dalling, Diwan Press, 1977, 9.

11 *Letters on Islam*, London, Oxford University Press, 1965, 3.

12 See my *God: A Brief History*, New York, Dorling Kindersley, 2002, 290.

13 Some argue that the painting is of the breaking of the fifth seal, Revelation 6:9–11, but Richard Mann, *El Greco and His Patrons*, Cambridge, Cambridge University Press, 1989, has shown why the final resurrection is more likely; but in either case, the conceptualized future is acting as a downward constraint, producing a unique consequence.

HUMAN EVOLUTION AND THE LOVE OF GOD

Niels Henrik Gregersen

SINCE THE ADVENT of Charles Darwin's theory of evolution, religious thinkers from all faith traditions have continued to discuss the implications of Darwinian biology for the truth-claims of theism. Today, we have achieved a consensus about the compatibility between Darwinian biology and theism—provided that theists do not slide back into scriptural literalism or think of God as predetermining the course of biological evolution from the beginning. Quite a few scholars, both biologists and theologians (like myself), even believe that Darwinian biology and Judeo-Christian belief are highly congenial. Both suggest a picture of a world developing through trial and error, through labor and work.

One might say that a "law of life" pertains, albeit in different ways, both to the world of biology and to the world of human culture: Important results of evolutionary ascent can be obtained only by trying out new possibilities—and thereby incurring the risk of failure. But sometimes gain comes only through pain. This law may be said to constitute spiritual information that is of central importance to understanding the evolving place of humanity in God's creation. However, it also raises critical ethical concerns. What are the ethical limits of risk-taking? Human risk-taking often involves third parties who do not bear the potential cost of the adventure. But what ethical concerns will an adventurous Creator, Giver of the very laws of life that include a demand to try out new possibilities even in the face of potential loss, have to respond to?

Certainly, the debate still rages about how far evolutionary theory can explain specific cultural developments within human history, such as the emergence of novel moral insights, religious belief systems, and scientific discoveries. Culture is constrained by biology insofar as any cultural development needs to be biologically sustainable. But the world of biology seems to afford a wide variety of cultural options. In fact, one can well argue that the present state of our multicultural civilization is a sign of the inexhaustible flexibility of the human species.

Evolutionary biology, nonetheless, may inspire both philosophers and theologians to reevaluate the importance of specific features of human culture. This essay on risk and risk-taking is but one example of an ethics and a theology inspired by the Darwinian discovery of the constructive role of chance in evolution. Indeed, although an understanding of the productive role of risk in human culture cannot be reduced to biological explanations, a parallel exists between the biological principles of trial and error and the human discovery of the value of risk-taking as it emerged during the Renaissance.

Risk = Danger + Adventure

Life is a risky affair. It is risky to fly. It is risky to drive. Stay home, however, and you risk becoming dull and fearful. Playing it safe is not easy in the world we inhabit. This risk awareness is so self-evident that it is hard to believe the logic of risk-taking is a rather late discovery in human history. Historians tell us that the concept of risk first appeared in the mercantile world of the Renaissance, when sailors embarked on adventurous expeditions. "Risk" is probably derived from the Greek *riza,* which means both "root" and "cliff." If so, the Latin *risicare* means something like "sailing around dangerous cliffs," and *riscum* is the result of such a venture. Thus, the word itself tells us that risks are not "things" that wait on the horizon, but are the result of our engagement with the world.

Living with danger is one thing; living with risk something else. Danger is that which comes to us from outside in the form of accident, illness, war, and other negative events. Such dangers were much more imminent in ancient times than they are today. Thanks to progress in science, technology, and our political institutions, today we are less vulnerable to external dangers. At the same time, however, we are becoming acutely aware that we ourselves are the co-creators of risk. Danger exists "out there," but risk is prompted by our method of coping with danger in a spirit of adventure. Even preventing risk creates new risks. For example, the use of antibiotics to defeat infections has slowly made many forms of bacteria resistant to antibiotics, so that future infections may not be curable with today's drugs. Paradoxically, we find ourselves placed in an evolutionary race in which we face great risk because we happily incur ever-greater risk.

The Value and Limit of Risk-Taking

The road back to Paradise is blocked, yet there seems only one way to proceed: forward. As we move forward, we discover the value of risk-taking: Important advances can be made only by accepting certain risks. By taking a chance, we also run the risk of being harmed or of imposing harm on others. This leads to new questions: What are the risks that are worth taking? And what are the conditions under which risks are acceptable? These questions will hardly find a general answer, for risks are as numerous as are the array of future possibilities multiplied by the number of our possible interactions with these possibilities—indeed, an astronomical number!

Here an important distinction in types of risk comes to the fore. *Existential* risks are those in which we put everything at stake for one desired purpose. *Distributed* risks are those whose outcomes do not bring an irreversible impact, either positively or negatively, and we can live comfortably with a variety of outcomes. Existential risk-taking involves matters of ultimate significance. Proposing marriage— laying bare one's intentions, declaring one's love to the beloved other—entails the risk of rejection. Avoiding this risk, however, also entails the further risk that the moment of opportunity will be lost forever. In this case, risk-taking is a matter of winning or losing it all. There are no mean values to be calculated. The result is purely yes/no and depends ultimately on the response of the other person.

It is different in the case of distributed risk-taking, which is about apportioning the risks. For example, provided that one has trust in the growth of the stock market over a significant period of time, it is prudent to spread one's investments across issues, markets, and regions. The potential for large losses in any one sector is offset by the exposure to numerous other sectors that may result in significant gains. Here the averaging "Law of Large Numbers" applies: The greater the risk-tolerance an individual possesses, the greater the possible long-term reward for that individual.

Thus, risk-avoidance cannot be our highest value. Neither, however, can risk-taking be a value in itself. It all depends on the reasonableness of the goals that one seeks. There also are ethical limits to risk-taking because we, for better or for worse, share the risks with one another. There may thus be a *catastrophe threshold* to risk-taking.

In the case of nuclear power plants, experts provide us with various risk assessments about potential breakdowns, such as those in Chernobyl. Even if the probabilities of such disasters can be significantly reduced by improved technology, one can well argue that an outcome above a catastrophe threshold should be avoided, even if the probability of such an outcome is very low. In addition, we have to ask, *Whose risks are we talking about?* There is a paramount distinction to be made between incurring a risk on behalf of oneself and imposing a risk on others. Here a distinction is clear between taking a risk and creating a risk: Enjoying skydiving and cajoling scared friends into jumping are two very different actions.

An ethically informed risk-taker acts differently (1) in cases of ultimate importance, where only one end is desired; (2) in cases of distributed risk-taking, where many options are possible; and (3) in the face of potential catastrophes, where one particular outcome would be fatal. In the first case, one has to cast one's lot unreservedly and be willing to lose everything. In the second and most frequent case, one seeks to maximize benefits while accepting certain losses along the way. In the third case, one follows the precautionary principle of minimizing the risks of the worst possible scenario.

Does God Take Risks?

Does the logic of risk have any bearing on the relationship between God and the world? I believe so, although the point is contestable. In classical Jewish, Christian, and Muslim theism, God was seen as directing every movement within the world. As the "Cosmic Controller," God certainly did not take risks and did not provide room for risk-taking. Accordingly, the gateway to God was to stay within the unchangeable boundaries of the Torah, the Law, and the Sharia.

This view is still a living option in the Abrahamic traditions. But perhaps God is forever greater than our inherited images of him? In fact, there is an alternative notion. This idea is sometimes called *kenosis*, or "divine self-emptying." The largesse of God may imply setting free and handing over power to his creatures. Let me suggest a picture from my own faith tradition by offering a view that combines kenosis and risk-taking.

The teachings of Jesus often suggest a dauntingly positive view of human risk-taking. In the parable of the talents (Matt 25:14–30; Luke 19:11–27), a master hands over to his servants a certain amount of money (talents). Some went out to trade with it and came back with even more money. One of the servants, however, was so terrified of his master that he immediately went off to dig a hole in the ground; there he hid the talent entrusted to him. As the story goes, the master, who took the one talent given to the fearful servant and handed it over to the most risk-taking servant, thus punished this strategy of safety. It is in this context that the general maxim "to those who have, more will be given, and they will have an abundance; but from those who have nothing, even what they have will be taken away" applies. The point is clearly that the strategy of safety fails for certain, whereas risk-taking may pay off—and may do so abundantly.

Positive views of risk-taking can be found in many other strands of the Jesus tradition, especially in relation to the need for giving up everything for one purpose: entering the Kingdom of God. The followers of Jesus were after all those who had left the safe routines of work and family life. Accordingly, the early church understood itself as nomadic, composed of a wandering people of God who had no temple or sanctuary on Earth in which to dwell. Yet, only the one who is willing to face uncertainty on the streets of life will find the pathway to God. The basic idea is that the world is created to favor and reward a risk-taking attitude. Even death cannot put an end to the logic of abundance: "Unless a grain of wheat falls into the earth and dies, it remains just a single grain. But if it dies, it produces much grain" (John 12:24).

However, the concept of risk may also apply to God. It seems to me that God takes substantial risks both by creating a world of autonomous agents and by loving a world that does not love him. First, if God establishes a creation endowed with freedom, he is a risk-taker: Freedom includes the liberty to explore as well as the ability to say no. Admittedly, the freedom of creatures is never absolute. They are bounded by natural laws and informed by moral principles. However, the freedom of creation suggests that divine power is not a commodity that God wants to possess in peaceful isolation. Rather, God continuously reaches into the matrix of creation; the loftiness of divine creativity is not the least displayed by the Creator's ability to make creatures that make themselves.

Second, God shares the risks involved in love. According to Christian faith, God not only bestows the gift of existence on the world, but also is the paragon of self-giving love: "God loved us first" (1 John 4:19). As with proposing marriage, loving with no guarantee of being loved in return inevitably involves a twofold risk: the risk of being misunderstood and the risk of being rejected. By revealing his love to human beings, God is both exposed to the *risk of negligence* and to the risk of *not being accepted.* God's exposure to vulnerability reveals the generosity of divine love.

The Threefold Risk of Divine Love

A theology of risk will thus emphasize Love as the divine matrix for risk-taking. First, as the Father, God is the *prime initiator* of risks. If God had a definite plan or design for the world, he would be infringing on the respect for otherness provided by divine love. Instead, God seems to be "building" His creatures in small steps in accordance with their own self-development. Moral freedom can be exercised only by human beings; however, an exploratory freedom is also exercised by biological life forms that are able to learn from and adapt to their environments. The pathways of creation are thus laid down, for example, in the process of walking. God is both setting creation free "in the beginning" and awaiting its achievements "at the end" of the journey.

However, God is not only taking a risk by giving autonomy to his creatures. God is also *bearing the risks* incurred by his unfinished creation. In Christian symbolism, the Divine Spirit is the One who insists on the goals of creation while patiently offering the time needed to complete the process. Here, God is not only active in, but also responsive to, the sighs, pains, and laments of creation (cf. Rom 8:22–23). In helping us overcome our shortcomings within an ever-evolving creation, the Holy Spirit bears the mark of the resourcefulness and proficiency of God.

In the third step of divine risk-taking, God is also *assuming the victim's role* through incarnation. The story of Jesus tells us that God is not only the author but also the bearer of risk. The crucifixion and resurrection demonstrate how God the Creator of risk is also the co-bearer of risk. On the cross, God is self-giving, even while crumbling under the great burden of having taken on risk. As he had no off-spring, Jesus is the iconic "loser" in the evolutionary arms race. As he did not have the protection of social networks, Jesus is also the iconic "outlaw" who refused to play the game of success in social competition.

Thus, the limits of risk-taking—to the catastrophic threshold—apply even to God. In an interconnected world, risks are shared. God did not withdraw from the ethical act of sharing risks, even to the point of death. In fact, if God imposed risks on his creatures without also absorbing them, his creation would be morally tainted. The more risks God is willing to take in ordering creation, the more risks he must be able to absorb. If not, divine risk-taking falls outside the logic of love.

From this perspective, the classic question of theodicy may be seen in a new light. The question is no longer, How can God permit suffering at all? The question now is, How can God permit *so much* suffering? Could the grandeur of life, of which Darwin himself spoke in the concluding paragraph of *On the Origin of Species*, be achieved at a cheaper price? Could human civilizations have been brought about without so much suffering of individuals, who were forced into carrying the risks that others heaped on them? What is the responsibility of God? Of human beings? The theodicy question may thus be translated from a simple affirmation or negation of God's fairness to a much more subtle question concerning the *extent* of responsible divine risk-taking.

Thus, acts of both taking and bearing risks belong together and must be affirmed together. In acknowledging this law of life, a Christian theology and a philosophical reflection on the implications of Darwinian theory might be able to concur. This notion in principle is open to the quantitative approaches of the natural and social sciences. New approaches to this old problem should be explored in the future interaction between theology and the sciences. It's worth the risk.

✌

NIELS HENRIK GREGERSEN, PH.D., obtained his doctorate from Copenhagen University. Previously Research Professor in Theology and Science at the University of Aarhus, Denmark, in 2004 he became Professor of Systematic Theology at the University of Copenhagen, Denmark. From 1992 to 2003, Professor Gregersen was a leader of the Danish Science-Theology Forum. From 1998 to 2002, he was Vice-President of The European Society for the Study of Science and Theology (ESS-SAT) and responsible for its publication program. In 2002, Professor Gregersen was elected president of The Learned Society, Denmark, and served through 2003. His most recent publications include *From Complexity to Life: On the Emergence of Life and Meaning* (Oxford University Press, 2003) and *Design and Disorder: Perspectives from Science & Theology* (T & T Clark, 2002). He is associate editor of the *Encyclopedia of Science and Religion*, Volumes I-II (MacMillan Reference, 2003), and systematic theological editor of *Dansk teologisk Tidsskrift*.

REFERENCES

Bernstein, Peter L. 1998. *Against the Gods: The Remarkable Story of Risk* (New York: John Wiley & Sons).

Gigerenzer, Gerd. 2002. *Reckoning with Risk: Learning to Live with Uncertainty* (London: Allen Lane/Penguin Press).

Gregersen, Niels Henrik. 2002. "Faith in a World of Risks," in *For All People: Theology and Globalization*, Else Marie Wiberg Pedersen and Peter Lodberg, eds. (Grand Rapids: Eerdmans).

———. 2003. "Risk and Religion: Toward a Theology of Risk Taking," *Zygon: A Journal of Theology* 38, no. 2 (June).

Saunders, John. 1998. *The God Who Risks: A Theology of Providence* (Downer's Grove, IL: InterVarsity Press).

Vanstone, W. H. 1978. *The Risk of Love* (New York: Oxford University Press).

A New Relationship between Theology and Science?

81

One Theologian's Reflections

Anna Case-Winters

A NEW DAY is dawning in the relationship between theology and science. Emblematic of the change is a 1998 cover of *Newsweek* announcing "Science Finds God."[1] After the conflict-ridden decades that followed publication of Darwin's discoveries, an uneasy truce was declared. Science and theology were described notably by Harvard paleontologist Stephen Jay Gould as "non-overlapping magisteria"[2] having different questions, different methods, and different domains that in no way meet on common ground. At least for those willing to entertain this "good fences make good neighbors" solution, there was an advance from conflict into the partitioned safety of isolation.

The Dialog Reopened: A Dual Crisis of Authority

What has changed? Why do theology and science once again find themselves in conversation? Part of the story may be that, of late, both dialog partners have undergone some changes. With the entry into the postmodern era, each in its own way has faced a crisis of authority.

In days gone by, theology conducted its work under the shelter of the "house of authority."[3] Scripture and tradition were treated as a kind of ahistorical, immutable deposit of truth needing no explanation and no defense. Under the weight of historical criticism and the disturbing accusations of ideological abuse of scripture and tradition, this "house of authority" that once seemed solid has collapsed.

A parallel crisis of authority has occurred in science. The naive realism of the nineteenth century has been largely discredited. The sociology of knowledge has posed probing questions about the extent to which what appears to be "hard," objective information about the world may be, in some cases, socially constructed. It is now well appreciated that previous understandings of the world and its processes often have undergone radical revision. For example, the Euclidean and lawful world of Newton gave way to the relativistic frameworks of Einstein, dismantling concepts of absolute time and space. Now, quantum mechanics proclaims a fundamental indeterminacy at the heart of things. With such rapid and radical shifts, science has observed in some of its most spectacular advances that its sureties can be readily overturned by new breakthrough insights.

The crisis of authority has produced a humbling effect in both fields. Both admit that their respective claims are to some extent "socially constructed," or, as the scientists say, "underdetermined by the data." Humility has made both fields to some degree more open and teachable, and a new space for dialog has been created. Interestingly, some common ground seems to be emerging. For example, both are admitting that there is a distance between "referents" and verbal representations of them (whether we are talking about physical reality in science or ultimate reality in theology). Both have moved beyond terms of un-nuanced epistemic dogmatism and realist literalism. Moreover, neither science nor theology is willing to placidly adopt the bland relativism urged on us by the dominant postmodern ethos. Both are unwilling to collapse into a cynicism of seeing knowledge as "nothing but" power. Both continue in the quest for truth. Both continue to make claims and argue for them. A kind of alliance of stubborn truth-seeking is formed here.

Beyond the crisis of authority that both fields have experienced, another factor may be at work. From the longer historical view, this present engagement is not so much a "new day dawning" as it is a normalization of relations. Even the briefest review of the context of history shows that neither conflict nor indifference is really characteristic of the science-theology relationship. The evidence of history reveals that (speaking broadly) all the great theologians were fully conversant with the intellectual currents of their day and allowed those currents to significantly shape their work. This is certainly the case for Augustine, Aquinas, and Calvin (and indeed for countless others). The fearful isolation of theology from the wider human quest for truth is truly an anomaly. As theologian Ulrich Zwingli affirmed, "The truth, wherever it is found and by whomever it is brought to light, is from the Holy Spirit" (*Treatise on Providence*, 1530). In his Commentary on Titus (1:2), he says, "All truth is from God, who is the fountain of all truth." In such a view, theology should have nothing to fear from the pursuit of truth, whether in science or anywhere else. In this sense, the new relationship can be viewed as really the old relationship restored.

The "New Old" Relationship: Changing Patterns of Interaction

Yet, if contemporary theology is to be relevant and intelligible today, very clearly it needs to be fully conversant with the scientific picture of the natural world. This does not necessarily mean that, with every new theory in science, theology must somehow be reinvented. As William Ralph Inge, dean of St. Paul's, famously remarked: "Whoever marries the spirit of this age will find himself a widower in the next." Rather, theology should be in a situation where it can engage intelligently with scientific pictures of the world and in an informed manner be able to reflect theologically on substantive issues in a process of dialogical learning.

Here, I have listed some elements that characterize an enhanced quality of interaction between theology and science (this vision of the dialog is significantly shaped by the work of Ian Barbour, Arthur Peacocke, and John Polkinghorne):

✦ *Mutual respect.* The conversation is more likely to be beneficial for mutual learning if there is mutual respect. Perhaps the science and theology dialog can build on learnings from cross-cultural conversations. Sometimes, for example, one side is the "dominant culture," and power differentials result. One party is in the position of always accommodating the other, needing to learn the language of, and to put things in the terms of, the other. Mutual respect would require that there be reciprocity in which each party tries to learn the other's language, to hear the other in his/her own terms.

✦ *Willingness to challenge.* Those already committed to the dialog seem more comfortable with listening respectfully than with offering challenge and critique. This may be a second step, but it is a necessary one. There are salutary admonitions that each has to offer the other. For example, theology might challenge science where it falls into crude ontological reductionism. Or science might challenge theology where it relies on habituated tradition for its best argument in areas where scientific facts and trends are substantively involved.

✦ *A stance of critical realism.* This is a point of view that takes empirical phenomena seriously, but does not assume that reality is always straightforwardly apparent from the phenomena observed.

✦ *A spirit of forbearance and humility in the face of limitations.* The limitations to be acknowledged would include not only those of the respective disciplines, but also personal limitations as each scientist/theologian is gifted and limited by his/her particular historical, cultural, and social location.

✦ *A valuing of both knowledge* ("scientia") *and wisdom* ("sapientia"). Neither of these should have a privileged position over the other. Nor, of course, should it be assumed that science has all the knowledge while theology has all the wisdom.

✦ *Hope for consonance*[4] *and an ability to recognize it when it happens.* For example, speaking theologically, it sometimes is said that all things are "utterly connected" in Divine Reality. In this light, it is fascinating to discover that the phenomenon of quantum "nonlocality" implies a kind of transcendent togetherness-in-separation with respect to causal relationships in space and time. This seems prima facie to be a stunning instance of consonance. Theologians talk about how we are created for relation, socially constituted, interdependent, and connected with one another. Hence, science appears to demonstrate (something like) relationality at the level of particle physics.[5]

✦ *Recognition of the "benign circularity" of the interplay between interpretation and data/experience.* This dynamic is present in both science and theology. Interpretations of reality shape hypotheses. Hypotheses shape experiments. Experiments yield data. Data illuminates the interpretation of reality. And the process begins again. In this way, knowledge progresses, spiraling more than simply circling. Interpretation and data inevitably and appropriately influence each other.[6] This phenomenon of the *vorverstehung* (fore-understanding)[7] is a common, deep insight in both fields and can be self-critically employed.

✦ *Recognition of the line between descriptive work (the data of experience) and interpretation at the level of metaquestions/metaphysics.* Scientists might agree, for example, that the cosmos demonstrates a phenomenon of temporal evolution toward ordered complexity.[8] However, it is an interpretive, rather than a factual, leap if a theologian concludes that this is because there is a conscious/purposive Creator working in the process.

✦ *Recognition of the limits of the dialog.* As it is unlikely that science would prove the existence of God, it similarly is impossible that theologians could develop interpretive "knock-down answers of a logically coercive kind." In the history of "proofs" for the existence of God, it has usually been the case that they are compelling only to those who already believe on other grounds. Such logical "proofs" do not remove the necessity for a rationally underdetermined "leap of faith." The way one construes relevant evidence is a conscious decision, not a foregone conclusion: "The most we can require is an interpretation that is coherent and persuasive."[9] At most, perhaps, the discoveries of science may now and then give evidence that seems like confirmation—a reason to believe that it is not unreasonable to believe. Theologians, therefore, should not expect to derive a natural theology from science. However, they may find science helpful as an aid to constructing a theology of nature.[10]

✦ *Avoidance of the bad habit of the "God of the gaps" thinking.* This is a habit of thought that is generically tempting to religious thinkers wherein God inhabits the domain of mystery corresponding to whatever the science of the day cannot explain or predict, thus offering the "hypothesis of God" as an explanation.[11] The problem is, of course, that as knowledge expands, the "gaps" shrink. It is good theology to avoid such bad habits!

✦ *Caution regarding easy resolution of differences.* Sometimes it will be important to let differences stand rather than to seek easy (but false) resolutions. "There are times when one must cling to the strangeness of experience, resisting the temptation to deny part of that experience in order to achieve a facile, but unsatisfactory relief from perplexity."[12]

Furthering the Relationship: A Model for Proceeding

There are, it seems to me, three basic "movements" in any dialog between theology and science: listening, clarifying, and rethinking. The example of scientific accountings of the operation of the universe as they relate to traditional understandings of Divine Providence help to illustrate these movements.

Listening

A first step is in listening carefully to what scientists say about the way the world works. This listening requires learning the language of science. Discussions of the laws of nature, cause-and-effect relations, the interplay of chance and necessity, etc., need to be attended to carefully. Scientific accountings pose a question of whether and in what sense God may be said to "act" in the world. Traditional ways of picturing this as intervention from outside the system may be difficult to incorporate within current scientific understandings. Listening is an important skill because the specific arguments may scientifically be both technical and nuanced. It is important for a theologian to have a clear understanding of what the technical issues actually are. If the issue is one of lower-level description, the scientific issue may be an inability to conceptualize a "personal cause" in general.

CLARIFYING

Among other steps of clarifying, one may ask, "What really is at stake theologically in this?" The traditional doctrine of Providence has affirmed that God in some sense governs world process, acting in the world with personal and particular care to accomplish good purposes. This much seems important to affirm. But how important is it to view this as intervention from outside world process? Can God work *within* the ordinary processes of nature? Interestingly, some scientists working in quantum physics and chaos theory speak of "openness" at the heart of things. This prospect raises all kinds of interesting questions. How closed is this system, really? How do the detailed technical debates actually work?

Clarification is also needed in what we mean by "miracle." Not all theologians view "miracle" in the same way. In the view of Thomas Aquinas, for example, the meaning of miracle is an act of God that overrides laws of nature; it is this overriding that makes a miracle a miracle. Here we may have a conflict with the typical scientific picture. However, another theologian, John Calvin, thinks of "miracle" in terms of God's working everywhere and always. It does not imply an occasional intervention from the outside that overturns laws of nature. And, more basically, how do living beings such as we act as causes within the physical world? He related the laws of nature to God's own self-consistency; they were not external to God. (To multiply loaves and fishes is not qualitatively different from providing daily bread. It is just more calculated to strike the eye.) Other differences among theologians on how we may think of God acting in the world can be highlighted. There are ranges of substantive nuance on both sides.

RETHINKING

Along the way, it might be noted that some of the more telling objections to "miracle" (as occasional intervention from outside) are theological. Affirming an occasional intervention from outside brings in its wake an unwanted affirmation of the ordinary absence of God. Are there ways to maintain Divine activity in world process without this kind of interventionist thinking? Might we imagine God as present and active in world process without being the sole causal element? This would require rethinking notions of God's activity as coercive exercise of unidirectional power and articulating visions of God as Creator of a self-creating Creation. In fact, there are a number of good candidates for expression of an alternative vision. Process theology sees God as presenting "initial aims" that lure Creation persuasively toward its best possibilities, but that do not coerce. Polkinghorne talks about "active information" functioning within an open physical ontology from the top down. This concept engages the idea of possible scientific support for an underlying ontological openness in Creation. As he says, the concept of active information "might prove to be the scientific equivalent of the immanent working of the Spirit on the inside of creation."[14]

All these functions have the advantage of maintaining God's presence and activity in world process and doing so in such a way that seems consistent with a reasonable understanding of scientific constraint. "God acts but does not overrule. The Spirit guides, but with a gentle respect for the integrity of creation."[15] "God can indeed do anything that is in accordance with the Divine Will, but it would not be consonant with that will to create a world as a kind of puppet theater. Instead, there is a Divine 'letting-be,' a making room for the created-other, together with the acceptance of the consequences that will flow from free process and from the exercise of human free will."[16] In fact, the quest to understand freedom may represent an exciting joint adventure for both science and theology.

Theologically, what is needed is a more comprehensive picture of God's activity in world process. When science observes that there is both chance and necessity in the way the world works, it would seem important theologically to think through God's activity in terms of both—not just one or the other. Polkinghorne invites us to look for God's presence in the historical contingency (chance), as well as in the regularity (necessity), of what is happening. "Historical contingency is God's gift to creation of the power to make itself; lawful necessity is God's gift of dependability. Fruitfulness and frustration are both consequences of the resulting interplay."[17]

Conclusion

Let me reiterate that a new day is dawning in the relationship between theology and science. Again, this signals restoration of a longstanding relationship, lately interrupted by conflict and isolation. In these decades of re-engagement, it is essential to find patterns for interaction and models for proceeding that will enhance and strengthen this resumed relationship. Possibly, such efforts at serious dialog will be richly rewarded with new insight. I certainly hope so!

☙

ANNA CASE-WINTERS, PH.D., M.DIV., is Associate Professor of Theology at McCormick Theological Seminary in Chicago and an ordained minister in the Presbyterian Church (U.S.A.). She obtained her M.Div. from Columbia Theological Seminary and her Ph.D. in theology from Vanderbilt University. Dr. Case-Winters was recipient of the John H. Smith Fellowship. She is a member of the American Academy of Religion and past president of the American Theological Society. Dr. Case-Winters is currently serving as Moderator of the Theology Committee of the World Alliance of Reformed Churches (Caribbean and North American Area). She is also the Chair for Christian Unity on the Ecumenical Relations Committee of the Presbyterian Church (U.S.A.) and has been a representative at several international ecumenical dialogs. Dr. Case-Winters is regularly engaged in research and writing on the topic of theology and science. She is the author of *Divine Power: Traditional Understandings and Contemporary Challenges* (Westminster Press, 1990) and currently is completing *Reconstructing a Christian Theology of Nature*.

NOTES

1 Sharon Begley, "Science Finds God," *Newsweek*, July 20, 1998.

2 Stephen Jay Gould, "Nonoverlapping Magisteria," *Natural History*. March 1997, 1.

3 Edward Farley, *Ecclesial Reflection: An Anatomy of Theological Method* (Philadelphia: Fortress), 165–68.

4 John Polkinghorne opts for what he calls "consonance" that admits more independence for theology, but insists that there should be consistent fit with science where there is overlapping concern. I prefer a position more like what he calls "assimilation," the search for as close a conceptual relationship between the two subjects as can be achieved without the surrender of one to the other (Polkinghorne 1998, 118). I think "assimilation" is a bit of a misnomer here and really implies surrender.

5 Ibid., 31–32.

6 Ibid., 102.

7 Fore-understanding is a concept that is helpfully treated by Martin Heidegger in *Being and Time* and is also taken up by Hans-Georg Gadamer in *Truth and Method*.

8 "The whole history of the universe, and particularly the history of biological life on Earth, has been characterized by the steady emergence of complexity. The story moves from an initial cosmos that was just a ball of expanding energy to a universe of stars and galaxies; then on to at least one planet, to replicating molecules, to cellular organisms, to multicellular life, to conscious life, and to humankind" (Polkinghorne 1998, 44).

9 Ibid., 73.

10 Barbour 2002, 2.

11 We still have a bit of a holdover in popular language here when insurance companies refer to tornadoes and the like as "acts of God."

12 Polkinghorne 1998, 108–9.

13 Ibid., 84.

14 Ibid., 89.

15 Ibid., 95.

16 Ibid.

17 Ibid., 84.

REFERENCES

Barbour, Ian. 2002. *Nature, Human Nature, and God*. Minneapolis: Fortress.

———. 1990. *Religion in an Age of Science*. San Francisco: Harper & Row.

Case-Winters, Anna. 1990. *God's Power: Traditional Understandings and Contemporary Challenges*. Louisville: Westminster Press.

Farley, Edward. 1982. *Ecclesial Reflections: Anatomy of Theological Method.* Fortress: Philadelphia.

Hartshorne, Charles. 1948. *The Divine Relativity: A Social Conception of God.* New Haven, CT: Yale University Press.

———. 1984. *Omnipotence and Other Theological Mistakes.* Albany: SUNY Press.

Kaufman, Gordon. 1993. *In Face of Mystery: A Constructive Theology.* Cambridge, MA: Harvard University Press.

Peacocke, Arthur. 1990. *Theology for a Scientific Age.* Oxford: Basil Blackwell.

Polkinghorne, John. 1998. *Science and Theology.* Minneapolis: Fortress Press.

Thomas, Owen. 1983. *God's Activity in the World.* Chico, CA: Scholars Press.

Ward, Keith. 1996. *God, Chance and Necessity.* Oxford: One World.

Whitehead, Alfred North. 1933. *Adventures of Ideas.* New York: Macmillan Co.

———. 1926. *Science and the Modern World.* New York: Macmillan Co.

The Emergence of Spirit 82

Philip D. Clayton

I
T IS NOT TYPICAL for theologians to learn much from investors. Recently, however, one renegade investment entrepreneur and mutual funds manager, Sir John Templeton, has been making some strange recommendations for theology that at least some theologians are heeding—and not only because he has put the rather substantial resources of the John Templeton Foundation behind his ideas.

Spiritual Information

Sir John's recommendations are based on the notion of spiritual information. Readers need no reminding of exactly how unfashionable this notion is. After all, we live in the age of hermeneutics, in which the idea and ideals of objectivity often take a back seat to the intricacies of interpretation. Beyond hermeneutical sensitivity, however, some postmodern theologians proclaim that theology is *only* about the feelings and subjective perceptions of the speaker, writer, or religious community. Thinkers such as the British theologian Don Cupitt promote the vision of a theology set free from any object of reference outside itself. On this view, theological statements cannot provide information about anything more than the mental states of the speaker or the linguistic and political systems in which he or she is embedded.

Sir John, by contrast, means information about spiritual realities. For Christians, that would mean, among other things, information about God and God's actions in the world.

This controversial notion of pursuing new spiritual information has a second implication, which is also *contra temps*. It suggests that one look to areas of the human intellectual quest where new information is becoming available, where knowledge is increasing. In our current intellectual world, that means, paradigmatically, looking to the sciences as allies in the theological project. Herein lies the real controversy of Sir John's suggestion and the focus of this essay: What does it mean to speculate about the nature of God based on the most recent scientific breakthroughs?

Much has already been written about the exploding religion-science discussion and its growing impact on the self-understanding of theology; those roads don't need to be retraveled here. Suffice it to say by way of summary that the religion-science movement is having an impact on pastors, theological educators, and congregations akin to the huge influence of "spirituality and science" discussions in the broader society.

Instead of chronicling the impact of the movement, I would like to make a somewhat daring proposal about what might happen to the doctrine of God if we indeed trace out the speculative lines suggested by the most recent breakthroughs in natural science. Theologically trained readers will recognize the influence of my *Doktorvater*, Wolfhart Pannenberg, in what follows. (The following paragraphs are nontechnical, and unashamedly so; those interested in the full theories and further references can find a fuller account in *Mind and Emergence: From Quantum to Consciousness* (2004).

The Divorce That Never Existed

Natural science (or "natural philosophy"), it turns out, has always offered a framework for conceiving God—or for dispensing with the concept of God, as the case may be. Consider just a few brief examples. As Augustine realized, Plato's forms needed to be located *somewhere*, and the mind of God was the natural place to put them. Hence, Augustine could argue, since any successful science requires the existence of forms, there must be a God to eternally think them. No God, no science.

Aristotelian science, dominant in the West for nearly fifteen hundred years, just as clearly required a God, at least according to St. Thomas's masterful interpretation. Consider, for example, the famous doctrine of the "four causes." From Aristotle to (roughly) Galileo, to "do science" just meant to discover the four causes of a thing. As we saw above, the forms (*formal causes*) require a divine mind in which they can be located. Assuming that matter, or the *material cause* of a thing, is not eternal, it must be created—by God, of course. *Efficient causes*—say, the sculptor who transforms a block of marble into a statue of Athena—exist as separate from God; but since they are contingent, they too require God as their ultimate cause. And the *final cause*, or goal toward which everything develops, is of course God, for God must be the one who brings about the final outcome of the earthly process in accordance with the divine aims. Hence, again: no God, no science.

I have mentioned only St. Augustine and St. Thomas, but dozens of other examples of the intimate union of science and theology could be listed—nearly as many as there are theologians!

Admittedly, connecting science (or natural philosophy) and theology became progressively more difficult as the modern era progressed. Yet even as late as Newton, a compelling line of speculation still seemed to lead from science to God. Or, to use that controversial phrase again, the science of the day provided "spiritual information" about the nature of God. It appeared that Newton's laws could account for the interactions of all bodies in the universe. But, as Newton saw, applying these laws required an ultimate, unchanging framework of "absolute space" and "absolute time" within which bodies moved. This framework could only be located within God, or as the eternal object of God's thought—or at least it could only exist with the concurrence of God's will and as a reflection of the divine nature. Hence, it seemed, the greatest insight in the history of physics, Newton's laws, still communicated something of the nature of God.

The New Science of Emergence

With this background in place, it is now possible to state my central thesis. It comes in two parts. First, beginning shortly after Newton and continuing until very recently, most of the dominant scientific models left precious little place for the sort of theological connections we have been considering. The explosion of scientific knowledge, the predictive accuracy of mathematical physics, the emergence of evolutionary science based on random variation rather than on purpose, the controlling paradigm of reductionism, the dominance of materialist explanations and assumptions—all of these made science-based theological speculations difficult and even, in the eyes of many, impossible. The story of the modern warfare between science and theology has been well told elsewhere (see, among others, the works by John Hedley Brooke) and need not be repeated here.

Let us focus instead on the more controversial second half of the thesis: *The last few decades have brought an important new opening for science-based reflection on the nature of God.* This opening lies in the ascendance of the concept of *emergence,* and more recently in the development of the new field of emergence studies. What is this new concept, and why does it so clearly give rise to speculation about God? Finally, assuming that it does, what might one conclude about the nature of God based on the new science of emergence?

In one sense, it is a truism to note that things emerge. Once there was no universe and then, after the Big Bang, there was an exploding world of stars and galaxies; once the Earth was unpopulated, and later it was teeming with primitive life forms; once there were apes living in trees, and then there were Mozart, Einstein, and Gandhi. But the new empirical studies of emergence move far beyond truisms. A growing number of scientists and theorists of science are working to formulate the fundamental laws that explain why cosmic evolution produces more and more complex things and behaviors, perhaps even by necessity. Especially significant for religionists, they are also arguing that the resulting sciences of emergence will break the stranglehold that reductionist explanations have had on science. Attention is turning to what we might call *the laws of becoming:* the inherent tendency toward an increase in complexity, toward self-organization, and toward the production of new emergent wholes that are more than the sum of their parts. Perhaps, many now suggest, it is a basic rule or pattern of this universe that it give rise to ever-more complex states of affairs, ever-new and different emergent realities. (See, among many recent works, Stuart Kauffman's *Investigations* and Harold Morowitz's *The Emergence of Everything.*)

The Theological Bottom Line

Assume for a moment that these theorists are right and that it is an inherent feature of our universe to produce new types of entities and new levels of complexity. What might this fact tell us about the existence and the nature of God?

Traditional theology looked backward; it postulated God as the cause of all things. Emergentist theology looks forward; it postulates God as the goal toward which all things are heading. Moreover, if God stood at the beginning and designed a universe intended to produce, for example, Jesus, then God would have to use deterministic laws to reliably bring about the desired outcome. Where the deterministic processes, left on their own, are insufficient to produce a theologically acceptable world, God would have to intervene into the natural order, setting aside the original laws to bring about a different, non-lawlike outcome. Divine action then becomes the working of miracles, the breaking of laws; and God becomes, paradigmatically, the being whose nature and actions are opposed to Nature. Of the results of this disastrous dualism, the opposition of God and Nature, readers are well enough aware.

By contrast, emergence suggests a very different model of the God-world relationship. In this model, God sets in motion a process of ongoing creativity. The laws are not deterministic laws. Instead, they are "stochastic" or probabilistic: Although regularities still exist, the exact outcomes are not determined in advance. More and more complex states of affairs arise in the course of natural history through an open-ended process. With the increase in complexity, new entities emerge—the classical world out of the quantum world; molecules and chemical processes out of atomic structures; simple living organisms out of complex molecular structures. And then gradually emerge complex multicellular organisms; societies of animals with new emergent properties at the ecosystem level; and, finally, conscious beings that create culture, use symbolic language, and experience the first intimations of transcendence.

As conceived of according to the model of emergence, God is no longer the cosmic lawgiver. Thus, the result is a far cry from Calvin's God, who must predestine all outcomes "before the foundation of the world." Instead, God guides the process of creativity; *God and creatures together* compose the melodies of the unfolding world, as it were, without pre-ordaining the outcome. Emergentists note that this God must rejoice in the unfolding richness and variety, apparently willing to affirm the openness of the process and the uncertainty of particular outcomes. In this model, God's finite partners are the sum total of agents in the world, and all join in the process of creation. In theologian Philip Hefner's (editor of *Zygon*) beautiful phrase, we become "created co-creators" with God.

Finally, in the emergence model, God does not sit impassively above the process, untouched and unchanged by the vicissitudes of cosmic history. Instead, there must be emergence within God as well. God is affected by the pain of creatures, is genuinely responsive to their calls, acquires experiences as a result of these interactions that were not present beforehand—all ideas familiar to readers of process theology or (to cite only one example) Jürgen Moltmann's *The Crucified God*. Ultimately, is not such a picture of God closer to the biblical witness than the distant God-above-time of classical philosophical theism?

Emergence and Panentheism

How radical should God's closeness to the world be thought? Should emergence-based reflection on the nature of God be allowed even to cast the very separation between God and world into question? A major school of late-twentieth-century theology known as *panentheism* argues that the world is more correctly understood as located *within* the divine being rather than as separate from it (see Arthur Peacocke and Philip Clayton, eds., *In Whom We Live and Move and Have Our Being*, 2004). Panentheists, reflecting on the scientific evidence and willing to explore the intimate interdependence of God and world, now conceive of the world as "within" God and God as "in, with, and under" all existing things (to adapt Luther's language for the sacraments).

Does all this mean that, given the turn to emergence, the transcendence of God will be lost and the Divine will be completely "immanentized"? Such was the famous claim of Samuel Alexander in *Space, Time and Deity.* As the world gradually develops more and more complex structures, it becomes more God-like or (in Alexander's atrocious neologism) it "deisms." On such a view, "divinity" is a property that *the world* develops in the course of emergent evolution. There is no longer a transcendent God—only an emerging, fully immanent one.

Some may wish to go this far, but emergence in the natural world does not require it. As a theological model, panentheism is responsive to the emergentist turn, yet is able to preserve a basic (and highly desirable!) feature of traditional theology: the transcendence of God. For panentheists, the world is in God, but God is also more than the world. Fundamental differences in the natures of the two remain: God is necessary, the world contingent; God is eternal, the world limited in duration; God is infinite, the world finite; God is by nature morally perfect, the world . . . well, that's obvious.

The Political Agenda of Emergentist Theologians

With this last subheading, we finally reach the social and political implications of emergentist panentheism—the dimension that for many of us is the real motivation for the position. The first implication was already implicit in the opening paragraphs: A doctrine of God inspired by emerging scientific models is speculative rather than dogmatic, not fixed in stone but open to new information and revisions. It is a dialog partner in the political process, not a final authority or arbiter of all truth. Moreover, a God who is intimately involved in the world, who is responsive to its joys and its suffering, can never be apathetic to the injustices in the world. And if each of us is in some sense "within" the Divine, then our striving for justice is itself part of the unfolding purposes of God.

There is no moral triumphalism here, however. The mystery of evil is pervasive: How can God allow evil actions when these now take place not "at the far ends of the earth," but within the divine being itself? No less decidedly, however, emergentist panentheism also testifies to the mystery of grace: Somehow the divine love is such that it even tolerates imperfection within itself—presumably, because of some metaphysical necessity beyond our ken, it is not possible to create finite, limited agents without their engaging in actions that are imperfect, short-sighted, self-serving. That evil exists in our societal structures and in our very souls is for panentheists not an invitation to quietism, but rather a clarion call to action. Because we live "in, through, and under" the divine presence, it behooves us to do everything that lies within our power to make the world around us reflect more clearly the divine source and presence to which it owes its very existence.

✍

PHILIP D. CLAYTON, PH. D., holds a doctorate in both philosophy and religious studies from Yale University. He has taught at Haverford College, Williams College, and California State University and is currently the Ingraham Chair at the Claremont School of Theology. Dr. Clayton has been guest professor at the Harvard Divinity School, Humboldt Professor at the University of Munich, and Senior Fulbright Professor, also at the University of Munich. Dr. Clayton is currently Principal Investigator of the "Science and the Spiritual Quest" (SSQ) project at the Center for Theology and the Natural Sciences in Berkeley, California. SSQ has brought together more than one hundred top scientists from around the world to explore the connections between science, ethics, religion, and spirituality. As author of numerous books in science and religion, he has edited and translated several other volumes and published forty articles in the philosophy of science, ethics, and the world's religious traditions. His current research interest lies in developing a theology of emergence, published as *Mind and Emergency: From Quantum to Consciousness* (Oxford University Press, 2004).

A Sense of Calling as a Clue to the Character of the Universe 83

C. Stephen Evans

Many persons throughout history have had a sense that they had a "calling" to some particular task. Notable examples include, of course, the Hebrew prophets who had a sense that they were called by "Yahweh" to "speak the word of the Lord." However, such a sense of calling is by no means unique to Judaism and Christianity. In the ancient Greek world, Socrates provides a powerful example of an individual with a sense of calling.

Those who have at least a modest knowledge of the history of philosophy will remember that in Plato's *Apology*, Socrates defends his life as a philosopher in a powerful, memorable way. On trial for his life for corrupting the youth and undermining religious belief, Socrates testifies that he has been called by "the god" to the task of philosophizing. (Interestingly, to a monotheist at least, when Socrates discusses the beliefs of the community, he speaks of "the gods," but when he speaks of his own convictions he usually switches to the singular form of the expression, "the god.") Socrates' critical examination of the leading politicians and poets and self-proclaimed wise men is not, he says, a task undertaken lightly. Rather, when the Oracle at Delphi told Socrates' friend that there was no one wiser than Socrates, Socrates set out to prove the Oracle wrong. When he discovered that true wisdom was not to be found among humans, Socrates realized the truth of the god's utterance. Socrates and his contemporaries all lack wisdom, but Socrates is at least wise enough—and perhaps humble enough—to recognize his ignorance. Far from undermining religious faith, Socrates thinks the upshot of his philosophical work is to drive home the realization that true wisdom belongs to God alone, and that human wisdom is worth little or nothing. God has placed Socrates in Athens as a gadfly to prod the Athenians to a concern with virtue, in much the same way that a commanding officer places a soldier at a post in wartime. Socrates must not desert his calling, even if it costs him his life.

Socrates is, of course, a notable figure in human history. However, many ordinary people, both past and present, have had a sense that they were, like Socrates, called to a certain kind of life, and even to particular activities or work. Recently, this sense of calling has been made the subject of scientific investigation. Psychologists such as Amy Wrzesniewski of New York University have developed empirical criteria for discovering how people approach their work. Building on the seminal thinking of sociologist Robert Bellah in *Habits of the Heart*, Wrzesniewski and her colleagues developed ways of distinguishing between people who think of their work simply as a job, those who think of their work as a career, and those who think of it as a calling.[1] Roughly, those who think in terms of a job are motivated primarily by material benefits, while those who think of their work in terms of career are motivated not simply by financial rewards but by a sense of accomplishment and prestige as they advance through the occupational ladder. Those who think of their work as a calling, however, find intrinsic fulfillment in the work, not necessarily because the work is inherently enjoyable or interesting, but because they see themselves as thereby doing something of significance to others.

The interesting thing about this psychological research is that it turns out that people who have this sense of calling are in fact happier and more contented than others. This is true not merely for people who have interesting and prestigious jobs, such as physicians and professors, but people who have jobs with low status and menial tasks. Psychologist Martin E. P. Seligman (who has contributed an essay to this volume) nicely summarizes these findings:

> People with callings are consistently happier than those with mere jobs or careers. And if you think callings are only for artists and healers, think again. Recent studies suggest that any line of work can rise to that level.

In one seminal study, researchers led by Amy Wrzesniewski studied twenty-eight hospital cleaners. Some viewed their work as drudgery, but others had found ways to make it meaningful. Researchers have seen the same phenomenon among secretaries, engineers, nurses, kitchen workers, and haircutters.[2]

What conclusions can we draw from these findings? There is, of course, the obvious practical conclusion that those of us who wish to be happy should seek to view our own work in this way. However, I wonder whether there are not deeper lessons to be drawn from these findings. As I thought about them, I tried to apply these findings to my own life.

I myself am a philosopher, and I do indeed have a sense that I am called to work as a philosopher. I believe that my work can be of value to my fellow human beings and even to my religious community. What implications might this sense of calling have for the work I do as a philosopher? Can a philosopher have a calling? Must a true philosopher have a calling? If a philosopher has a calling, should this fact shape in some way the content of the philosophy of that individual? To ask such questions is to raise the issue of the relation between the life of the philosopher and philosophy itself. For some philosophers, such questions are illegitimate. Hegel warns us against mixing the personal and the philosophical when he advises us, "Philosophy must beware of the wish to be edifying," an admonition that is directly opposed by Kierkegaard in *Either-Or,* who ends the book by having one of his pseudonyms tell us that "Only the truth that edifies is truth for you."

David Hume, perhaps implicitly taking what was later to be Hegel's side in this controversy (although, of course, Hume wrote before Hegel), recommends personal life as a kind of cure or antidote for philosophy. When doing philosophy, says Hume, he winds up in a dreadful skepticism, "ready to reject all belief and reasoning," and in a state where he "can look upon no opinion as more probable or likely than another."[3] This deplorable state of "philosophical melancholy" cannot be dispelled by reason, says Hume, but only by what we might call "real life," which seems to be something that cannot be combined with philosophy:

I dine, I play a game of back-gammon, I converse, and am merry with my friends; and when after three or four hours' amusement, I wou'd return to these speculations, they appear so cold, and strain'd, and ridiculous, that I cannot find in my heart to enter upon them any farther.[4]

These innocent amusements rescue Hume from philosophy and make it possible for him "to live, and talk, and act like other people in the common affairs of life."

Is it a merit or a defect if a philosopher's thought be such that it is impossible to combine that thought with human life? Some would doubtless consider it a meritorious thing, a sign of the heroic path the philosopher has followed to the truth, impervious to the personal distress the bitter truth has brought in its train. William James, for example, quotes poet Clough (although James does not agree with the quoted sentiment), who writes:

It fortifies my soul to know
That, though I perish, Truth is so:[5]

Kierkegaard, however, once more takes a different perspective. While praising ancient Greek philosophers for their attempts to embody their lives in their philosophy, he finds it comical that modern philosophers have constructed grand theories that make no contact with their own existence: "A thinker erects a huge building, a system, a system embracing the whole of existence, world history, etc., and if his personal life is considered, to our amazement the appalling and ludicrous discovery is made that he himself does not personally live in this huge, domed palace but in a shed alongside it, or in a doghouse, or at best in the janitor's quarters."[6]

I side with Kierkegaard here. It has always struck me that if a philosophy cannot be lived, that this is a problem for that philosophy. It is true that there is something in our nature that fears that the ultimate truth will be something terrible, and we are tempted to see the individual who faces up to an unlivable bitter truth as heroic. However, fear fulfillment is no more rational than wish fulfillment, and we have no a priori reason for thinking that the ultimate truth is something that humans cannot live with. To the contrary, it seems plausible to me that the reality that has produced human beings, whatever the ultimate nature of that reality might be, would in some way fit the aspirations and lives of the humans it has produced. If that is so, and we have a need to think of our lives as a calling, then perhaps we should also try to interpret the world as a place where the notion of "calling" makes sense.

According to this line of thought, if a philosopher takes himself or herself to have a calling to do philosophy, then the philosophy this individual produces should be one that can make sense of the idea that a human being has a calling. It is perhaps natural for a religious philosopher, particularly a believer in God, to see philosophy in this way; after all, many religious believers think that every human has a calling. Each of us is called to become the unique individual God intends and make a contribution to God's Creation. Curiously, however, among philosophers I have known it is not just the religious ones who tend to think this way about philosophy. I am confident that a great many nontheists I have known would also say that philosophy is for them a calling. Perhaps they would apply the term only metaphorically, as a symbol of the sense of satisfaction they gain from philosophy, or to express their enthusiasm and love for the discipline. However, I suspect that for many the sense of "call" goes deeper than that. Perhaps if they thought more deeply and honestly about this they would be open to the possibility that if they really do hear a call, there must be someone who has called them.

Having a sense of calling as a philosopher pushes us toward philosophizing in a particular way. Perhaps it should suggest to us that we ought to think of God in personal terms, as the kind of being who can call us to a task, offer us assistance in carrying out that task, and hold us responsible for performing that task. There is a certain kind of piety, often seen in philosophy, that resists such views of God. Thinking of God in personal terms, we might imagine someone saying, is too limiting. Surely God far exceeds our human conceptions, including our human concept of personhood. When in the grip of this mode of thinking, we are tempted to agree with Tillich that God must not be thought of as a being, but as being itself, or the ground of being, or that which is simply beyond all being or thought of being.

Certainly there is something right about this way of thinking. In relation to God, we are like the grass that is here today and tomorrow is thrown into the oven, (Matthew 6:30, KJV) and such a God must far surpass any human concepts of God. If we say that God is personal or is a person, we must recognize that the personal life of God must differ vastly from our own lives as persons. However, it is all too easy, when we try to safeguard God's transcendence and guard against anthropomorphism, subtly to reduce God's majesty. In attempting to conceive of God as more than personal, we may easily fall into the trap of thinking of him as less than personal, as C. S. Lewis wisely noted many years ago.[7] Instead of picturing God as a parent, friend, or lover, we picture God as "ground of being" or "power of being," nonpersonal images that lack both specificity and power.

When I remind myself that God is the one who has called me to do philosophy, I am aware in a powerful way of the personal character of God. This was certainly true for Socrates himself. His conception of God was doubtless far from a Christian conception, but Socrates thought of God as the Commander with authority who had placed Socrates at his philosophical post. Religious philosophers could do worse than to follow Socrates here. Whatever else God may be like, God is a being who can act, for he has performed the act of calling me to practice philosophy. God is enough like a person to enable me to have a relationship with him. I may look to God for guidance, pray to him for assistance in my task, ask him for forgiveness for my failings. If I really take my vocation as a philosopher seriously, I must not fall into a practical contradiction by denying in my philosophy what is presupposed in my life. This has been important to me in my work in philosophy of religion and philosophical theology. The God who is the object of my reflection is also the one who has called me to reflect. If I am going to err in my conception of God, as I surely will, let it not be an error that makes nonsense of the calling that sustains me by making God into a being who is incapable of calling anyone to do anything. If I said that I was called by God to philosophize about a God who does not and cannot call anyone, I would testify not to God's call, but to my own confusion.

In any case, I find the discoveries of contemporary psychology with respect to the notion of calling to be interesting and provocative. For these findings imply that it is not just a personal idiosyncrasy on my part when I think of my work as part of a calling; rather, this is something many humans do naturally. And when humans do think of their lives in this way, they find happiness and a sense of satisfaction, as I do myself. It appears, one might say, that humans are made such that they flourish when they think about themselves in this way. That seems to be a fact about human nature. And such facts about human nature may give us insight into the character of the universe that has produced that human nature.

Of course, one may argue here that humans who think of their lives in terms of a calling do not necessarily think of themselves as having a literal calling. Rather, they think of their lives as ones that can serve others; we might say they may live *as if* they have been called to live in a certain way. And that is certainly true for many nonreligious persons. However, it is also possible that these people may in fact have a calling in a literal sense, even if they do not recognize it. Perhaps their sense that they are called to live in an unselfish and loving way for the good of others really does stem from a loving creator. For it is quite possible to be aware of a call from God without being aware that such a call is a call from him. The way in which a sense of call is embedded in our human nature may be one of the clues that God has implanted within that nature, a clue that points in a non-coercive manner to God's reality and character—and toward the ultimate purpose of human existence.

ℒ♥

C. STEPHEN EVANS is currently University Professor of Philosophy and Humanities at Baylor University. His published works include fifteen books, among which are *Faith Beyond Reason; The Historical Christ and the Jesus of Faith: The Incarnational Narrative as History;* and *Passionate Reason: Making Sense of Kierkegaard's Philosophical Fragments.* More popular recent works include *Why Believe?* and *Pocket Dictionary of Philosophy of Religion and Apologetics.* Evans has published many professional articles and has received two Fellowships from the National Endowment for the Humanities, as well as a major grant from the Pew Charitable Trusts. Before going to Baylor, Evans taught at Wheaton College; St. Olaf College, where he served as Curator of the Howard and Edna Hong Kierkegaard Library, as well as being a member of the Philosophy Department; and at Calvin College, where, besides teaching philosophy, he served as Dean for Research and Scholarship and was the inaugural holder of the William Spoelhof Teacher-Scholar Chair. He is a past president of the Society of Christian Philosophers and the Søren Kierkegaard Society.

NOTES

1 Amy Wrzesniewski et al., "Jobs, Careers, and Callings: People's Relations to Their Work," *Journal of Research in Personality* 31 (1997): 21–33.

2 "How to See the Glass Half Full," *Newsweek,* September 16, 2002, 49.

3 David Hume, *A Treatise of Human Nature*, ed. L. A. Selby-Bigge (Oxford: Clarendon Press, 1888), 268–69.

4 Ibid., 269.

5 Clough, Hugh, "With Whom Is No Variableness, Neither Shadow of Turning," from *Poems, with a Memoir* (New York: Macmillan, 1862). Quoted in William James, "The Will to Believe," in *Essays in Pragmatism*, ed. Alburey Castell (New York: Hafner Publishing Co., 1948), 92.

6 Søren Kierkegaard, *The Sickness Unto Death*, trans. and ed. by Howard V. Hong and Edna H. Hong (Princeton: Princeton University Press, 1980), 43–44.

7 *Mere Christianity* (New York: MacMillan, 1952), 141.

THE ROLE OF DISCERNMENT
IN SEEKING SPIRITUAL KNOWLEDGE 84

Nancey C. Murphy

Does RELIGIOUS experience contribute to new spiritual knowledge? Scientific research could tell us whether it does or not.

While many fine works have been written on what can be learned from scientific methods for the pursuit of spiritual knowledge (Barbour 1974, 1990; Pannenberg 1976), the objection critics will raise is that theology, unlike science, has no data. Christian theologians might reply that they treat the Scriptures as data, and other data are gathered from history and religious experience. So, the problem is not the absence of anything that functions as data; it is rather that Scriptural texts and religious experiences seem defective when compared with scientific data. Religious experience seems too subjective. And how do we know that Scripture tells us anything reliable about God and not just about Jews' and Christians' beliefs about God?

I concentrate here not on Scripture, but on religious experience. The puzzle of how religious experience can be used as a source of valid data for new spiritual knowledge can be solved by putting together two pieces—theories of instrumentation (a concept from the philosophy of science) and the Christian practice of spiritual discernment.

An important component of scientific research programs is what philosophers call *theories of instrumentation*. Consider the measurement of temperature. We have a variety of instruments: mercury and alcohol thermometers, procedures based on the thermoelectric effect, and others. The confidence we place in any of these is based, first, on the consistency of results obtained by the various methods. But, more important to my purposes here, the operation of each of these instruments is explained by, and thus validated in part by, scientific theory. For example, the kinetic theory of heat, which defines heat in terms of movement of particles, partially explains the expansion of liquids when heated, and so supports the use of ordinary thermometers.

Thus, an entire network of theory, laws, and experimental results is accepted as a whole because of its consistency and its explanatory power. There is always a degree of circular reasoning involved—as when a thermometer is used in confirming certain consequences of the kinetic theory—but it might be called "virtuous" rather than "vicious" circularity because it is part of what goes into showing the consistency of the entire network.

Now, what about religious experience? We surely do not want to count all so-called religious experiences as data for theology. Nor do we want to count all sensory experiences as data for science. If we did we would have to explain, for instance, how oars bend when put into water and straighten immediately when taken out.

The relevant parallel in theology to a theory of instrumentation is the theory of discernment. The Christian tradition offers a treasury of answers to the question of how it is possible to distinguish between "religious experiences" that represent encounters with God and those that do not. So, here we have a theory that states that it is possible to recognize the activity of God in human life by means of signs or criteria, some of which are public and relatively objective. I claim that the theory of discernment functions in Christian theology in exactly the same way as theories of instrumentation do in science.

The criteria for discernment can be grouped under two headings: consistency and fruits. "Consistency" for Protestants means consistency with Scripture. For Catholics, consistency with church teaching is also important. Use of the consistency criterion, of course, raises all of the problems of interpretation involved in using the Bible for any purpose—problems I shall not address here except to note the following: A wooden application of this criterion would mean that no religious experience could ever challenge traditional teaching because such an experience would automatically be judged inauthentic. However, if this criterion is used in conjunction with others, there will be cases where an experience, attested on the grounds of other signs, conflicts with a traditional *interpretation* of Scripture. The experience, together with critical reflection on the received interpretation, may then result in the overturning of an interpretation. So there is room for a dynamic interplay among texts, interpretations, and religious experiences.

If this is the case, a clear parallel exists with science, where an observation or experimental result that conflicts with accepted theory will be regarded with suspicion. The decision either to ignore the datum or to revise the theory can go either way and will only be made after reevaluating the theory and performing additional experiments.

The criterion of "fruits" refers to various effects in people's lives and in their community. Jesus declared that false prophets could be known by their fruits (Matt 7:16). Paul listed the fruits of the Holy Spirit as love, joy, peace, patience, kindness, generosity, faithfulness, gentleness, and self-control (Gal 5:22–23). Other spiritual writers would add humility, contrition for sin, and the consensus of the church.

Consider this example: Catherine of Siena, a fourteenth-century mystic, posed questions to God and then wrote (or recorded) passages that were supposed to be God's replies. One of these is about how to distinguish between experiences that come from God and those that do not:

> Now, dearest daughter . . . I told you how she could discern whether or not these [visions] were from me. The sign is the gladness and hunger for virtue that remain in the soul after the visitation, especially if she is anointed with the virtue of true humility and set ablaze with divine charity. (Noffke 1980)

So Catherine would say that she could recognize when a religious experience is from God by these signs: if it is from God, it produces gladness, hunger for virtue, humility, and charity.

Now, the critic would ask Catherine:

Critic: "How do you know that those are reliable signs?"
Catherine: "Because God told me so."
Critic: "How do you know it was God who told you that?"
Catherine: "Well, the experience produced gladness, humility, charity. . . ."

So you see the problem.

In the case of science, theories of instrumentation are confirmed by two factors: One is the experienced reliability of the instrument; it produces similar or identical readings again and again under similar circumstances, and these results correlate with those produced by other measuring devices. The other is that a theory of instrumentation follows from theoretical beliefs that we have no good reason to call into question. In other words, the truth of the theory of instrumentation is supported by its consistency with a network of other experiential and theoretical statements.

The Christian theory of discernment is likewise supported by its connections to a variety of other statements, some based on experience, others of a theoretical (or theological) nature. For example, the great American theologian Jonathan Edwards presents a simple theoretical account of why the fruits of the Spirit should provide valid signs of God at work in a human life. The fruits of the Spirit jointly constitute a particular kind of character—what Edwards calls the "lamb-like, dove-like character" of Christ (Edwards 1746/1959). In light of Christian theology, this is exactly what is to be expected. The fruits are signs that the Holy Spirit is at work in a person's life; the Holy Spirit is otherwise known as the Spirit of Christ; Christ's spirit should manifest itself in a Christ-like character.

The second kind of support for the theory of discernment needs to be experiential—does it work reliably, and is it connected in a consistent way with other experiences? As we saw above, the process of discernment is exactly the test of whether the inner experience, putatively of God, is correlated with the other sorts of experiences that our theories lead us to expect. Reliability means, simply, that a measurement or process results in roughly or exactly the same results under similar circumstances. Reliability is always a matter of degree; different degrees are required, depending on the complexity of the matter under study. Measurements with a ruler are highly reliable; measurements with an I.Q. test are only moderately reliable.

We have anecdotal data on the reliability of believers' judgments regarding the presence or absence of God's agency in certain events. However, it would seem to be possible to design research to measure the reliability of these practices. I anticipate that the development of an adequate methodology would be difficult, but not impossible. Were such a study to be done, positive results of this second-order investigation would provide valuable tools for the search for new spiritual knowledge. Just as scientific instruments are tested before being used in a laboratory, this "instrument" for detecting the presence and activity of the Spirit of God might be validated for future first-order research on spiritual subjects. Thus, we could have scientific evidence for the reliability of religious experience.

✒

NANCEY C. MURPHY, PH.D., TH.D., has been Professor of Christian Philosophy at Fuller Theological Seminary in Pasadena since 1989 and is an ordained minister in the Church of the Brethren. She received her doctorate in Philosophy from the University of California, Berkeley and her theology degree from the Graduate Theological Union, Berkeley. Her research focuses on the role of modern and postmodern philosophy in shaping Christian theology and on relations between theology and science. Professor Murphy speaks internationally on these topics and has published numerous books. Her first book, *Theology in the Age of Scientific Reasoning* (1990), won the American Academy of Religion award for excellence. She is the author of six other books, including *On the Moral Nature of the Universe* with George F. R. Ellis, and is co-editor of six. Her book with Warren Brown and Newton Malony, *Whatever Happened to the Soul?* was awarded the 1999 Templeton Prize for Outstanding Books in Theology and the Natural Sciences. She also serves as a corresponding editor for *Christianity Today*. Professor Murphy is former Chair of the Board of Directors of the Center for Theology and the Natural Sciences, Berkeley, where she still serves on the Board, and is also is a member of the Planning Committee for conferences on science and theology sponsored by the Vatican Observatory.

REFERENCES

Barbour, Ian, *Myths, Models, and Paradigms.* New York. Harper and Row, 1974.

———. *Religion in an Age of Science: The Gifford Lectures 1989-91, vol. 1.* New York. Harper and Row, 1990.

Edwards, Jonathan, "A Treatise Concerning Religious Affections." Reprinted in Perry Miller, ed., *The Works of Jonathan Edwards,* vol. 2. New Haven. Yale University Press, 1746/1959.

Noffke, Suzanne, trans. and ed., *Catherine of Siena: The Dialogue.* New York. Paulist Press, 1980.

Pannenberg, Wolfhart, *Theology and the Philosophy of Science.* Philadelphia. Westminster Press, 1976.

Kuruvilla Pandikattu

The Crises in Humanity

J OHN F. KENNEDY, in his inaugural address, promised Americans two things: to
take human beings to the Moon and to eliminate world poverty. The former was
a technical feat, which was accomplished spectacularly. It required scientific information and led to technical success. It could also have led to transformation of the
country's identity. But the latter is a moral feat that requires one important element
before it can be achieved: spiritual information.

Information, like knowledge, is power. It changes both the individual and the
larger society. That is why Paul Ricoeur maintains, "Every understanding is self-
understanding." Every bit of information acquired leads to a better understanding of the self and therefore inevitably to transformation, both at the level of
consciousness. As G. K. Chesterton put it, "The most practical thing is a good
theory."

In this essay, I deal concisely with the primary sources of information and transformation in our modern society: science and religion. I briefly examine the crises—
the challenges and the opportunities—created by these two primary sources of
information based on my perspective that a healthy and enterprising collaboration
between them leads to a total, integrative transformation of society at the level of
human consciousness. That, I believe, is crucial for the survival and progress of
humanity.

The Sources of Information

The primary sources of information could be generally classified as *rational* (the
intellectual challenge of science) and *intuitive* (the spiritual creativity of religion),
both of which have personal and institutional dimensions. Although they have unal-
terably affected human life and promise to continue to do so, we cannot ignore the
threats they pose.

THE INTELLECTUAL CHALLENGE OF SCIENCE

The empirical knowledge and technical information provided by science have led
to marvelous progress. Not only has science taken humans to the Moon, it has
enabled the whole of humankind to be connected—through communication, trans-
portation, information technology, and so forth. Paradoxically, science also has

taken the world to the brink of extinction. The threat of nuclear explosions, chemical and biological weapons, depletion of the ozone layer, and other human-made catastrophes also are destructive possibilities produced by our technological "marvels." Survival of the human species—and life itself—is at stake!

Such a crisis was predicted by Albert Einstein, the greatest scientist humanity has yet produced, who maintained that "all our lauded technological progress—our very civilization—is like the axe in the hands of the pathological criminal." While this is a strong indictment, indeed, he further stated: "It has become appallingly obvious that our technology has exceeded our humanity."

Much more than fostering technological comforts and dangers, science has irrevocably altered our worldview, lifestyle, and, through the Human Genome Project, our very understanding of life. Science has led to arguments that states of nihilism and absolute relativism are plausible, making despair an irrevocable burden of humanity exacerbated by an increasingly pervasive reductionistic, mechanistic interpretation of life.

THE SPIRITUAL CREATIVITY OF RELIGION

Confronted with these challenges, it is reassuring to refer to another assertion by John F. Kennedy: "Every problem created by humans has a human solution." While we may totally agree with this, we need to remember the caveat put forward by Einstein: "The significant problems we face cannot be solved at the same level of thinking we were at when we created them."

Fortunately, we have recourse in religion. If anything can inspire a new vision and provide a new worldview, it is the creative commitment and innovative motivation offered by the world's spiritual traditions. They enable us to discover the harmony and beauty in life. Religions—or, may I say *religion?*—can offer us an all-encompassing worldview that can stand up to the hubris of technology and the nihilism of destructive science. At the same time, religion can promote constructive technology and cooperative science for the progress of humanity. What we need is a worldview that can help us cope with the conflicts and possibilities offered by science and technology, neither rejecting them totally nor accepting them unconditionally, but rather affirming them cautiously, creatively, and ingeniously.

To quote Einstein again: "The release of atomic power has changed everything except our way of thinking. . . . The solution to this problem lies in the heart of mankind." What truly touches the human heart is religion. Yet religions, particularly the institutional varieties, have been responsible for promoting violence, hatred, and inhuman behavior toward the "out-groups." The negative aspects of institutional religion, like the potentially destructive power of science, cannot be denied. However, we can assert that religion provides humanity with the most precious— although fallible—knowledge we possess. Religion has given humans a sense of meaning, dignity, and a reason to live, which is tremendously reassuring and enriching for humanity. When brought to bear on the realms of values and ethics, religions help us to respond positively to the challenges posed by modern science and the worldviews it inaugurates.

Need for Constructive Collaboration between Science and Religion

The crises that confront us can be viewed either as the result of a relentless human quest for self-annihilation or as an opportunity provided by life to transcend itself. We prefer to look at today's moral, spiritual, and technological threats—which are definitely grave—as chances for the forces of life to recuperate, so that humanity can forge ahead to unexplored territories. Seen as the birth pangs of a new generation— a new way of life—the crises of the world should be perceived as fresh challenges for science and religion to come together in close and imaginative collaboration.

FROM A PRAGMATIC PERSPECTIVE: PRESERVE PRECIOUS LIFE

The close collaboration between science and religion is necessary to counter the most obvious problem threatening us: the extinction of life from the planet. Many critical observers are convinced that the world's progression will inevitably lead to self-destruction. Yet the situation is not hopeless. The essential human spirit is tenaciously open to inexhaustible creativity and boundless innovation. Where there is a collective will, there is a collective way to overcome the crucial problems confronting us.

Science cannot handle the threat of self-annihilation alone. Neither can religion deal with it on its own. We need a concerted effort, pooling all the resources at our disposal. What threatens us is not "just" the destruction of the soul, but the whole of life. Thus, for the most pragmatic of all purposes—saving precious life on planet Earth—religion and science must collaborate with urgency and creativity.

Although many people are aware of these concerns, they do not always undertake concerted, unified action. However, it is encouraging that so many individuals and groups are addressing the problem in their own ways. We can very well hope that the larger problems of hunger, sickness, violence, terrorism, and poverty will be reduced, although not totally eliminated. We can hope that life-threatening forces such as nuclear war, biological and chemical weapons, and ecological disasters will be managed innovatively and ingeniously. Once humans have the will, they will find the way. Friedrich Nietzsche's slogan, "If you have a why, then you can cope with any how," is apt. Once the "why" for protecting human life is provided (primarily by religion), we can cope with the "how" to accomplish the task (primarily through science). Therefore, once the issue is saving the world, and saving precious human life on this planet, no force on Earth can really stop the constructive collaboration between science and religion.

FROM A HUMAN PERSPECTIVE:
RETAIN HUMANNESS AND HUMANENESS

It is a fundamental "law" that life progresses unhindered. Human beings, following this law, become more progressive technologically, morally, psychologically, and spiritually.

All religious traditions affirm that life is worthy and meaningful. Worth and meaning are found in being true to oneself and in realizing the truth of oneself. In this process of realization, love for oneself and openness to others are imperative.

It is a universal spiritual insight that in humility and gentleness human beings become authentic, genuine, transparent, and joyful. By getting in touch with our own humanity, grasping the enigma of human existence, grappling with the questions of life, and rejoicing in day-to-day experience, we become more human—and more humane.

To be authentic and complete, scientific progress, both in terms of technology and worldview, has to permeate the spiritual domain, too. The true realization of our humanness and humaneness causes a gradual spiritual evolution in which we get more and more in touch with our deepest selves through listening, awareness, gentleness, and compassion. Therefore, at the human level, science and religion foster our humaneness by helping us to realize ourselves truly, to enable us to be authentic, to open our hearts so we can connect with others.

FROM A COSMIC PERSPECTIVE:
WIDEN CONSCIOUSNESS TO BE CO-CREATORS

At a deeper level, when we look at the flow of evolution and the progress of life, we realize that we humans have reached the highest level of consciousness. Our consciousness—the integration of our intellectual, moral, spiritual, and metaphysical selves—has emerged, evolves, and will develop further. This growth of consciousness is integral to life. It is here that our world within converges on the world without.

Today, we have passed beyond the stage of "evolution becoming conscious of itself." We have become capable of guiding the evolutionary process forward, in and through us. We are at the juncture where we can influence evolution—and with it the whole of life—dynamically, even at the level of consciousness.

Are we not today at such a level, where we are open to the whole cosmos, transcending the limits of our tribal, linguistic, national, religious—and even human—identities? We are possessed by life and also further it by expanding our own consciousness—toward a mystical, numinous, or liminal level! Thus, we are not just widening our horizons—our consciousness—to include everything, but we are actually becoming part of "everything," and thus merging with the whole of creation.

Spiritual information—obtained through genuine scientific enterprise and true religious dynamism—promotes this sense of oneness. In such a noble, all-embracing, ever-widening endeavor, science and religion cannot stand apart as two distinct disciplines, but must creatively and innovatively contribute to a grander vision of the whole of which they are an integral part. This is the life-fostering *sat-cit-ananda* (being-consciousness-bliss) described in the Indian traditions.

Opportunity to "Outgrow" Ourselves

Albert Einstein and Mahatma Gandhi were two people who contributed significantly to the collaboration between science and religion in an effort to protect life, promote humanness (and humaneness), and extend our consciousness. Although different in personal history and field of engagement, both were genuine and humble seekers of truth. They strove to liberate humanity from the clutches of narrow self-interest. Both were spiritually informed people who were key figures in the quest to widen human consciousness in their respective disciplines of science and religion.

Information—especially the spiritual information that results from a collective, collaborative, creative quest between science and religion at the deepest human level—integrates, transforms, and leads to an integral and total transformation of humanity. The result is a nobler, deeper, and wider consciousness that is both compassionate and all encompassing. This is both the challenge and the opportunity facing humanity today.

We can aptly conclude by quoting what Einstein said of Gandhi, hoping that future generations will express similar sentiments about themselves as a community: "Generations to come, it may be, will scarcely believe that such a one as this ever in flesh and blood walked upon this earth."[1]

ℒ♥

KURUVILLA PANDIKATTU, S.J., PH.D., is a Catholic priest whose area of specialization is the dialog between science and religion and between religion and hermeneutics. He obtained two doctorates in Philosophy and Christian Theology, both from the University of Innsbruck. Fr. Pandikattu teaches science, philosophy, and religion at Jnana-Deepa Vidyapeeth, Pune, India, and is a visiting professor at many other universities and colleges. He is a founding member of the Association of Science, Society, and Religion, the first organization of its kind in India, and is an active member of various other learned associations and societies. Author of more than thirty scholarly articles and secretary to two scholarly journals, Fr. Pandikattu writes a regular column in the local newspapers. Among his numerous books are: *Dialogue as Way of Life* (with an American edition); *Idols to Die, Symbols to Live*; and *It's Time! Science, Religion and Philosophy on Time*. He has edited seven books, including *Hopefully Yours*; *Meaning of Mahatma for the Millennium* (with an American edition); and *Human Longing and Fulfillment*. Fr. Pandikattu has organized and participated in many national and international symposia on science and religion.

NOTE

1 Einstein, A. From "Out of My Later Years," New York: Philosophical Library, 1950. New translations and revisions by Sonja Bargmann, based on *Mein Weltbild*, edited by Carl Seelig, Laurel Edition, Dell Publishing Co. Written on the occasion of Gandhi's 70th birthday in 1939. Note the several other essays in this volume discuss Einstein and Gandhi; see especially the essay by Ramanath Cowsik.

SCIENCE AND THE QUESTION OF COSMIC PURPOSE

John F. Haught

B EFORE MODERN times, most people thought the universe had a purpose. The natural world existed for a reason, although it was not always easy to say exactly what this was. Philosophies and religions were aware of Nature's flaws, of course, but they viewed the cosmos as a "great teaching," at times even as a sacred text. By approaching it reverently, one could read beneath its surface and discover a profound message hidden from ordinary awareness. Pythagoreans, for example, found in the depths of Nature a mystical realm of musical and numerical enchantment. Ancient Israelites read the universe as an expression of Divine Wisdom. Egyptians delved beneath the surface of Nature to the realm of Maat, Indians to the domain of Dharma, and Taoists to the Tao. Stoics read the cosmos as the outward manifestation of an inner rationality that they called Logos. And the Gospel of John pierced beneath all things to an eternal Word that was in the beginning with God, and that was God.

Traditionally, almost all religions and philosophies read the universe as a revelation of order or purpose. Reading the universe, however, was not an exercise to be undertaken lightly, for beneath Nature's surface lurked layer upon layer of challenging mystery and meaning. In the process of penetrating to the world's inner substance, the interpreter would have to undergo a purifying transformation. One could not really come to know the universe without being deeply changed in the process.

The universe no longer works this way for most of us. With the help of science we can now read it quite competently—or so it seems—but we are seldom significantly changed in the process. We have laid bare Nature's atomic and molecular alphabet, its genetic lexicon, and its evolutionary grammar; but we are less confident than ever that any profound teaching lies beneath its surface. While scientific understanding of the universe progresses at an accelerating rate, our lives do not necessarily become deeper, better, or happier. Transformation does not keep pace with information.

Scientifically educated people today, generally speaking, do not read the cosmos as a text bearing any deep meaning at all. To some, the universe is a swirl of meaningless matter on which a patina of life and mind glimmers for a cosmic instant before fading out forever. To others, it is a blank tablet onto which we may inscribe our own human meanings. "I, for one, am glad that the universe has no meaning," says philosopher E. D. Klemke, "for thereby is man all the more glorious." A meaningless universe, he testifies, "leaves me free to forge my own meaning." Likewise, the late paleontologist Stephen Jay Gould claimed that a pointless universe is a great new opportunity for humans. We can now fill it, he counseled us, with our own meanings. Yet both Klemke and Gould would agree that, in the end, all meaning will vanish along with our lives.

Today, "cosmic purpose" is scarcely mentioned in learned circles—a hush not only tolerated but at times even celebrated in the academic world. After Darwin, any claim that the universe is the unfolding of a profound meaning sounds especially strained. The randomness and impersonality of life's evolutionary epic have made Nature seem forever incompliant to the human heart's habitual longing for a purposive universe. Commenting on neo-Darwinism, the philosopher Daniel Dennett has confidently declared that the only message in evolution is that "the universe has no message."

Science and Purpose

If the idea is to make sense at all today, therefore, what could it possibly mean to say that the universe has a purpose? "Purpose" usually means the "goal" or "end" toward which a particular set of events is oriented. Deeper yet, purpose implies that something of great value is in the process of being realized. Our own lives, for example, are said to have purpose if we dedicate them to bringing about something of lasting importance. By surrendering ourselves to causes that embody imperishable values, we discover a coherence to our lives, a backbone to our commitments, and at times even a reason to die. But what value could the *universe* possibly be in the process of realizing? And how might we understand the entire cosmic process disclosed by modern science as purposeful?

Parallel to a meaningful human life, a purposeful universe would have to possess at least a loosely directional aim toward bringing about something of great and lasting consequence. But what could this possibly be? What is really going on in the universe? And can science help us find out?

Science, it is true, does not deal formally with the question of purpose or value. It is concerned with physical, not final, causes. However, any answer we give to the question of what's going on in the universe requires our taking into account the undeniable *discoveries* of science. Since it is primarily through scientific exploration that we learn about the universe, any coherent quest for cosmic purpose today cannot ignore what science has seen. This means also that such a quest cannot truthfully disregard the ambiguities in evolution and the prospect of an eventual physical dissolution of the entire universe.

What pillars of certainty, then, could we possibly uncover in the burgeoning mound of scientific information that might render it at least conceivable that the universe has some overall point to it? I would suggest that there are at least two. These two scientific fixtures do not by themselves prove that purpose pervades the universe, but they give us something to stand on as we speculate about what might be going on in the cosmic depths. They were entirely unknown to ancient religions and philosophies, and they have altered forever the rules for reading the universe.

The first pillar is our new certainty that the physical universe is unfinished. Evolutionary biology, geology, and cosmology have now established as fact that the cosmos is still emerging and that it remains incomplete. As a work in progress, an unfinished universe is a book still being written. The incontestable fact of an unfinished universe may not seem like much of a footing on which to erect a sense of cosmic meaning, but at least it invites us to keep on reading. And if a plot is still unfolding there, we cannot expect it to be fully manifest to us yet. Any meaning it may have will be at least partially hidden from us—at least for now.

Our second pillar is the new scientific disclosure of a universe that has evolved over the course of an unimaginably prolonged history into a stupendous array of *beauty*. By beauty I mean the harmony of contrasts, the ordering of complexity, the fragile combining of what is new with what is stable, of fresh nuance with persistent pattern. The cosmos, to be specific, has made its way gradually from a monotonous primordial sea of subatomic mist, through the emergence of atoms, galaxies, stars, planets, and life, to the bursting forth of sentience, mentality, self-consciousness, language, ethics, art, religion, and science. Surely, by any objective standard of measurement, something momentous has been going on here. For all we know, a deeply meaningful story is in the process of unfolding. But how are we to read a narrative that is still being written? And what is the story really all about?

The Aim toward Beauty

As with any book in progress, we cannot yet read the universe all the way down to its ultimate depths, either through science or theology. The vast distances below, above, behind, and ahead of us extinguish any such pretense. However, we may still approach the emerging cosmos in a spirit of expectation. Now that we know for sure that the universe is an incomplete story, we may find there the kind of dramatic tension that compels us to keep on reading.

It simply cannot be unremarkable, for example, that the universe eventually abandoned the relative simplicity of its earliest moments and flowered, over the course of billions of years, into an astounding array of complexity and diversity, including human consciousness and moral aspiration. Something other than just the mere reshuffling of atoms has been going on here. And while the journey from primordial cosmic monotony to the intense beauty of life, mind, and culture is no hard proof of an intentional cosmic director, this itinerary is at least open to the kind of "ultimate" explanation that religions seek to provide.

The universe, in any case, has an overarching inclination to make its way from trivial toward more intense versions of beauty. This aesthetic directionality was enough finally to convince the great philosopher Alfred North Whitehead, after a long period of skepticism, that there is indeed a point to the universe. Purpose means the "realizing of value," and to Whitehead beauty is the queen of all values. Cosmic purpose, he argued in *Adventures of Ideas*, consists of an overall aim—not always successful—toward the heightening of beauty.

But what about the dark side of things—the tragedy in life's evolution and the moral evil in human existence? And what sense can we make of the dismal scenarios that cosmologists are now entertaining about the eventual, although certainly far-off, demise of the universe? How do we know that all things will not finally trail off into lifeless and mindless oblivion?

Whitehead speculated that the problem of evil comes down, in the end, to the plain fact that "things perish," and he was acutely aware that the most beautiful entities and ideals last least long of all. Organisms all die, and great civilizations sooner or later decay. Hence, if there is any purpose to the universe, perishing must be redeemed—not only our own but *all* perishing. At one time an atheist, Whitehead eventually concluded that there is something in the depths of the world-process that redresses the fact that nothing lasts. His own suffering and searching led him to reach beneath the transient flux of immediate things to something that endures everlastingly, and in whose embrace all actualities attain a kind of immortality.

In arriving at his sense of the permanence beneath all perishing, unlike most other academic philosophers in the twentieth century, Whitehead took religious experience as seriously as he took science. Although religions are imprecise and inconsistent, he thought they could read more penetratingly into the fabric of universe than can the clearer abstractions of science. Science deals well with the surface of Nature, but only religious intuition can carry us beneath the temporal flux to a "tender care that nothing be lost"; that is, to God. In God's experience, the entire sweep of events that we call the universe is endowed with permanence along with purpose. Even the passing of an entire cosmic epoch—such as the predicted dissolution of our own expanding universe—would not entail its absolute disappearance. Its history, down to the last detail, is internalized forever in the life of God.

God, therefore, is not only the lure that summons the world to realize more intense beauty, but also the compassionate "fellow sufferer" who preserves everlastingly all of the transient value that the evolving cosmos achieves. God, in Whitehead's interpretation of religion, has the breadth and depth of feeling to take into the divine life the entire cosmic story, including its episodes of tragedy and its final expiration. Within God, the whole universe and its finite history are transformed into an everlasting beauty. The ever-expanding divine beauty, in turn, becomes the ultimate context for the ongoing world-process, adding new definition to what has already become. In God, the world remains eternally new, even if many of its temporal epochs are now over.

Is such a proposal believable? We can't know for sure. Here, as Whitehead also understood, the risk of faith accompanies the certainties of science. But before complaining that faith is an escape from reason or reality, we might reflect on an observation made by Whitehead's contemporary, the Jesuit geologist Teilhard de Chardin. That we have to walk by faith and not by sight, Teilhard noted, is one more corollary of the fact that we and our religions are also part of an unfinished universe. Can we realistically expect our faith traditions to answer with climactic clarity the truly big questions as long as the universe itself is still *in via*—and we along with it? Faith reads the universe now only "through a glass darkly," and the darkness that goes with faith, Teilhard instructed us, is somehow inseparable from the incompleteness of the cosmos.

Finally, however, both Whitehead and Teilhard would not let us forget that the incompleteness of the cosmos, our first scientific pillar, is inseparable from the second—that out of nothingness a world rich in beauty and consciousness has already awakened. If the cosmos is an unfinished story, it is also a story that at least up until now has been open to surprising and momentous outcomes. For fifteen billion years, our universe has shown itself to possess a fathomless reserve of creativity. It has not only been winning the war against nothingness, but in its emergent beauty, feeling, and "thought" it has triumphed. If the unfinished universe has something to do with the uncertainty in our faith, then the creative resourcefulness embedded in the universe cannot fail to give us "a reason for our hope."

✐

JOHN F. HAUGHT, PH. D., is the Healey Distinguished Professor at Georgetown University and a member of the theology faculty. He is also the founding director of Georgetown's Center for the Study of Science and Religion. Dr. Haught is the author of more than fifty articles and book chapters and has published twelve books, including *The Promise of Nature: Ecology and Cosmic Purpose* (1993); *Science and Religion: From Conflict to Conversation* (1995); and *God after Darwin: A Theology of Evolution* (1999). He is also the author of *Deeper Than Darwin: The Prospect for Religion in the Age of Evolution* (2003).

WHERE MIGHT WISDOM BE FOUND?

Celia Deane-Drummond

THE WAVE of publicity surrounding the birth of Dolly the cloned sheep in 1997 betrayed the fear that human beings might eventually be able to make copies of themselves, evoking the specter of Frankenstein and images of a new eugenicized race. At the time, scientists claimed that, as far as they could tell, Dolly was simply a normal sheep. However, she subsequently developed arthritis, unexpected for a sheep of her age, and then died prematurely early in February 2003. Her death, according to her "creators" at the Roslin Institute in Scotland, vindicated their earlier decision to argue against human reproductive cloning. But this has not stopped heated debates in the last six years about whether human cloning is permissible. The somewhat bizarre American-based Raelian cult, for example, believes that the human species first appeared on Earth through a cloning process devised by aliens, who had arrived here from outer space. For Raelians, cloning is simply the next step in the advancement of the human race.

Raelians are also highly successful at fundraising, acting as brokers between couples desperate to have children and between scientists eager to break the boundaries of knowledge. They have established a service called "Clonaid," which offers opportunities to become involved in the experimental process of cloning humans. In July 2002, a criminal investigation began in Korea against a woman who was supposedly two months pregnant with a cloned embryo obtained through Clonaid, who claimed that they were not breaking the law. If the pregnancy was successful, then the couple would have been in debt to the company (Valiant Venture) to the tune of hundreds of thousands of dollars. But, interestingly, there have been no further reports on the case. Subsequently, legislation banning human cloning was rushed through the Korean government. By September 25, 2002, a bill was in place; by November 2002, the law had been passed. Korean public opinion favored the ban, apparently based on the belief that allowing a human clone to be born would make Korea "an international disgrace."

The Uses and Limits of Human Cloning

Most Christian theologians oppose the use of human cloning for reproductive purposes, although some support its more limited use for treating human diseases. Other secular philosophers argue in favor of human reproductive cloning, including allowing a cloned egg to implant in a woman's womb. According to their thinking, as long as the risks are sufficiently reduced and as long as it can do some good (e.g., treating infertility), why not permit it?

The issue of cloning raises a number of fascinating questions, some of which apply more generally to biotechnology. General questions include: What are the limits, if any, to the freedom of scientific investigation? What are the risks involved? Who benefits from the procedure? What is the motivation behind the process? What are the sociopolitical implications? What are the costs? More specific questions that relate to the fact that this is *human* cloning include: Can the cloned embryo be thought of in any sense as a person having a soul? Does cloning infringe on human dignity? What might be the psychological outcomes for a child born through cloning? What are the implications for social and family relationships? All these questions have become the subject of intense debate.

The limits to scientific freedom are, more often than not, couched in terms of legal restrictions on scientific activity. However, so far no international agreement on cloning has been reached regarding what is permissible and what is not. Cloning animals is currently legal, although the degree of suffering caused through the cloning process is a matter for serious ethical debate. Sadly, perhaps, scientists are more inclined to work within the legal framework rather than listen to ethical arguments, which frequently seem to be confused and may be biased against their work. As far as the legal situation is concerned, laws and treatises on human cloning have developed very quickly in some countries where strong public opinion has fueled the debates. The Council of Europe's Convention on Human Rights and Biomedicine added an Additional Protocol in 1998 outlawing human reproductive cloning. Germany and Switzerland have banned all cloning technology in humans, including "therapeutic" cloning, and Canada is set to follow suit. Greece and Ireland have effectively banned cloning through general legislation against experimentation with human embryos. In the United States, a bill is in place to ban the creation of embryos for therapeutic purposes; although existing cell lines can be used, considerable debate continues about the extent of availability of embryonic stem cells for research. In the United Kingdom, a law has been in place since 2001 that prohibits reproductive cloning; however, it is still possible to engage in therapeutic cloning as long as proper procedures are followed, including obtaining a license for the research through the Human Fertilization and Embryology Authority. In other countries, such as Israel and Russia, a five-year moratorium on reproductive cloning is in place. Although Korea banned all human cloning in 2002, in other nations, including most countries in Africa, Asia, and Central and Eastern Europe, a legal vacuum exists; no laws have been passed.

Korean scientists were frustrated by the blanket ban on all human cloning, including therapeutic cloning, which for them amounted to an unwarranted restriction on their freedom because, from their perspective, such techniques would do good. Such restriction echoes those times in history when the church condemned scientific work, largely out of ignorance. But, from a theological perspective, freedom is not simply what we are allowed to do from a legal perspective as individuals, but also how far and to what extent our actions may impinge on others. Freedom seems like a natural gift, but if it is orientated toward selfish ends it is no longer serving a high purpose. When considered correctly, freedom exists for the good of individuals, of communities, and of society.

Many scientists strongly support the use of human cloning to produce embryonic stem cells for therapeutic purposes because they foresee the potential for positive outcomes in treating human ailments such as Parkinson's disease and diabetes. Yet for some Christian believers those early embryonic cells are not simply "tissue" to be used for particular purposes, but are the stuff of human life that has a special dignity from the moment of its beginning. Treating such cells as "material" to be used for the benefit of another human life is unacceptable for those who have a strong sense that *all* human life requires protection. The added danger, for those opposed to human cloning, is that therapeutic cloning would then open the door for the use of reproductive cloning to create "designer" babies, evoking memories of the desire for a "pure" race that led to the horrific eugenics practiced in Nazi Germany, even though this is a somewhat remote scientific possibility.

We are left, then, with two broad questions for humankind: Are we masters of the universe, and so able to use our technology and skill for the benefit of humanity in any way that we choose? Or are we subject to a certain ordering in Nature, put here by God, and hence subject to particular limits with respect to such an order? Neither extreme seems very helpful. How might we mediate between them?

Seeking Wisdom in Two Thought Systems: Neo-Confucian and Christian

Cloning represents a global issue for humanity. What might religious traditions contribute to the debate? I suggest that, contrary to expectation, a common search for wisdom can offer ethical perspectives grounded in spiritual information. Asian religious traditions often seem far removed from Christian traditions in the Western world. However, I suggest that commonality does exist and can become the basis of a search for a global ethic. For example, one of the main strands in the teachings of Confucius is that humans need to cultivate a moral sense. In Confucian times, everyone who sought to acquire morality tried to fit in with the patterns found in the universe itself, leading to a peaceful, flourishing society.

In the Judeo/Christian tradition, wisdom is also embedded in the creative processes of the world, so that to observe the natural world in one sense is also to find wisdom. In the Christian tradition, Christ becomes the exemplar of wisdom. However, a tension exists between the old and new nature in Christian teaching. Virtues are not just "acquired" through learning; they are also "received" as gifts from God. The closest that Confucian thought comes to this is in the strands of teaching suggesting the possibility of acquiring a new nature, although such a nature does not come from "God" as such. Confucian thinkers also affirmed the role of the "heart and mind" in making decisions. The term they used for this (*xin*) contained the cognitive and the emotional faculties, as well as the moral sense. Christian theology has tended to separate these two functions. For example, Aquinas distinguished the intellectual virtues of understanding, *scientia* (science), and wisdom from the theological virtues of faith, hope, and charity. However, he strongly believed in the unity of virtues, so that wisdom was necessarily rooted in charity. Thus, the end result was similar to Confucian reflection. Both Confucian and Christian virtues were orientated toward the good, understood in terms of what is best for individuals and for society, and both led to feelings of deep joy. Both argued for purgation of all forms of selfish behavior or self-seeking.

Both Neo-Confucian and Christian traditions stress that theoretical knowledge without action fails to lead to progress in moral life, with some writers putting particular emphasis on the primary importance of daily practice. For Aquinas, prudence, or practical wisdom, is the correct discernment of a particular course of action, a way of expressing a particular virtue. This combination of judgment-with-action is also integral to Confucian thought. For Neo-Confucian thinkers, there was a grand design for individuals, families, and society. Moral self-cultivation was the way to bring human needs into harmony with the natural world and Nature's capacity for producing practical goods. Medieval Christian writers, such as Aquinas, also believed in an ordered universe, but it was one that placed humanity in charge of the natural world. There is less a sense of finding harmony with Nature than of becoming masters of it for human benefit. The wisdom traditions remind us of the paramount importance of looking to our own human attitudes and dispositions. While for Christian wisdom the source of such insight ultimately comes from God, Neo-Confucian wisdom reinforces the holistic nature of such a task. In other words, it is not just about an individual's journey, but who a person is in relation to others and in relation to the natural world. For those following the Neo-Confucian tradition, this amounts to an expression of "The Way" (Tao). For Christian writers, such an orientation is impossible without reference to Christ, who is also "The Way, the Truth, and the Life"—and one might also say "Wisdom incarnate."

Where might this take us in making complex decisions about the future of biotechnology, the dawn of the clone age? The wisdom traditions remind us of the importance of developing character, of seeking to instill ingrained habitual attitudes so that virtues become part of who we are as persons. It is from within such a pursuit, gained through openness to the gifts of the Holy Spirit in the Christian tradition or through moral self-cultivation in Confucianism, that discernment for the good of the whole community becomes possible and practical. Science can then exist not so much in detachment from religious concerns, or in opposition to them, but in partnership for the wider good of society. Seeking such wisdom takes time and involves the whole community. Yet the beatitude most commonly associated with wisdom is peacemaking. Hence, the task becomes one of dialog, mutual respect, and fostering of right relationships. Only in this spirit will contested issues over biotechnology begin to be resolved.

✍

CELIA DEANE-DRUMMOND, PH.D., Director of the Centre for Religion and the Biosciences at University College Chester, received her doctorate in plant physiology from Reading University. After working at the International Consultancy on Religion, Education, and Culture in Manchester, she obtained a doctorate in theology from Manchester University and then took the teaching post at Chester. Professor

Deane-Drummond's research has focused particularly on the interrelationship between Christian theology and the biological sciences, for which she received a personal Chair in Theology and the Biological Sciences in 2000. She previously held postdoctoral fellowships at the University of British Columbia (Canada) and the University of Cambridge and a lecturing post in plant physiology in the Botany department at Durham University. Professor Deane-Drummond has published more than thirty articles in science journals and has continued to be active in research relating science to theology. She has published a number of books, including *A Handbook in Theology and Ecology* (SCM, 1996), *Ecology in Jurgen Moltmann's Theology* (Mellen, 1997), *Theology and Biotechnology* (Chapman, 1997), and *Creation through Wisdom: Theology and the New Biology* (T&T Clark, 2000). She is joint editor of *Reordering Nature: Theology, Society and the New Genetics* (2003) and editor of *Brave New World: Theology, Ethics, and the Human Genome* (2003). Her most recent book is *The Ethics of Nature* (Blackwells, 2004).

MUSIC, METER, SILENCE, AND HOPE

Jeremy Begbie

How does music keep our attention? Although we may rarely stop to think about it, one of the great mysteries of music is that it can keep us interested and involved—even when it comes without words or images. Once a piece starts, if it is the kind of music we like, we want it to carry on. Why? It doesn't "tell" us things—like a novel; it doesn't picture things—like a painting. On the face of it, it just chugs along, one sound after another. And yet we're caught up in it, captured in its movement. We don't want it to stop. It makes us hope for more. How?

Asking and answering this question, I believe, takes us close to the heart of what it means for humans to have hope. More than this, we can learn much about the way hope is created and sustained by God. This might seem like an outrageous claim, but it is a defensible one, as I hope to show. And if it is true, then something remarkable about music begins to emerge: It can be a vehicle not just for human expression (which few would dispute), but also a means of *discovery*, with unique powers to open up the world we live in, in its physical as well as well as its theological dimensions.[1] As such, it may well have a key role to play in the dialog between the natural sciences and theology.

But this all sounds rather grand. We need to begin more modestly by going into the engine room of music, to find out what drives it along. In particular, we need to examine *meter*, the pattern of beats underlying musical sounds. In a score, it is indicated by a "time signature" (e.g., 2/4, 3/4). When you tap your feet to music, you're tapping your feet to meter. The conductor of an orchestra beats to meter. When you dance, the chances are you are dancing to meter.

Metrical beats are grouped into measures, or bars. A waltz has three beats to a measure, and the beats are not of the same strength—as you will know if you have ever tried to dance to one. The first beat is strongest, the second is weaker and sets up a tension, and the third is weaker still, "moving toward" a release of the tension on the first beat of the next bar. A wave of tension and resolution is set up, repeated bar after bar:

Now comes the interesting part. Meter operates at different levels. The successive downbeats of each bar are themselves of a different strength. In many pieces, beats are grouped in twos or fours—the first of each group the strongest, the last of each group the weakest. Together, then, they build up a wave of tension and resolution at a higher level. And the downbeats of *that* wave are also of a different strength, setting up a further wave, and so on. The process continues up, level after level, higher and higher, until the whole piece is covered:

A pattern something like this applies to virtually all types of Western music, from Bach to Brahms, REM to Eminem. It is basic to the way most of the music we hear operates.

The key point is this: Every downbeat kicks forward a wave on another level. One level's return is always another's advance. Every return closes *and* opens, completes *and* extends, resolves *and* intensifies. In short—*there is always hope on another level.* Music keeps our attention because, as along as the piece is running, we are aware that there is at least one wave at a higher level that is not yet closed. And so we expect—and want—more. (Try singing "The Star-Spangled Banner" and stopping after the words "through the perilous fight." The musical phrase has ended [on the lower level], but the music sounds incomplete, because many upper waves still have to close. You expect—and want—more.)

The God of the Jewish and Christian faiths, I would suggest, moves not just in mysterious *ways*, but in mysterious *waves.* God invites people to live on more than one level; that is how he keeps them hoping. So, typically, God makes a promise—for example, he promises his people a Saviour-figure and that they will be part of a vast, new community. This generates hope. The coming of Jesus, so the New Testament claims, is the climactic fulfillment of this promise and hope—"the hopes and fears of all the years are met in thee tonight." Yet the fulfillment does not kill the hope. Just the opposite. The original promise is widened and intensified. The coming of Christ makes the writers of the New Testament hope all the more, and for more—for a final, ultimate fulfilment of the promise, when a huge, multi-ethnic community will inhabit the new Heaven and the new Earth. The closing of one wave pushes a higher wave forward, and hope is regenerated.

Time and time again, the Jewish and Christian Scriptures seem to be saying, in effect: "Stay on the one level, and your hope will die. Tune into the upper waves of what God is doing, and you'll never stop hoping."

Our so-called postmodern culture encourages us to live on the lowest level—as Frederic Jameson has put it, in "flat time"—typically with only little short-term "micro-hopes," one day at a time. We dare not hope for anything too great in the long term, nor do we know how to hope like this. With no comforting grand story to hold together our view of the world, we settle for mini-hopes, a lifespan at the most. But to be drawn into the waves of God means that our lives are set in the context of a multilevel hope, covering different time scales. Within the vast hope stretching into God's eternity, many shorter-term waves are operating, right down to the micro-level. And these can all get drawn into the larger hope. So, for example, it may be that out of the little short-term routines of our lives, something wonderful is being crafted, the thought of which will make hope live again.

Fundamentalism is music on the lowest level. It tends to read Scripture in the "flat." Every word is treated as if it were literal, plodding prose about events on one level. So every prophecy has to come true at only one single time and in one unambiguous way. Often, when the fulfillment doesn't appear exactly as expected, there is a huge panic, and strenuous efforts are made to make texts say things they obviously don't say. But if we think on many levels, many of these problems disappear. When God promised to Abraham that he would make "a great nation" (Gen 12:2), how is that fulfilled—in the people who settled in Canaan? the Kingdom of David? the community who returned from exile in Babylon? the church at the end of time? The answer surely is: yes. All of them. A single promise can have many different fulfillments. We can't understand that with a single straight line. But we can with multistoried waves, for the tension generated by any one "promise" may have many resolutions.

We can take this further. Hope needs to be utterly realistic. It needs to cope with waiting. When I was teaching in Seattle recently, I sent a team of students to a hospital and got them to ask: What kind of worship will best meet the needs of the people there? They came back and answered: worship that helps people to wait. The commonest activity in a hospital is waiting—for results, to see a doctor, for a bed to become free, for a relative to be brought out of the operating room. This kind of waiting also often involves coping with delay when the expected resolution doesn't arrive on schedule. Vast amounts of our time are spent in waiting. And religious literature is full of accounts of people waiting for God, struggling with divine delay ("How Long, O Lord?").

Today, in a culture so enamoured with spiritual "highs" and immediate, pain-free gratification, how can we begin to understand what it means to have hope in the midst of delay, and what might be going on when God seems detained, otherwise held up? Here again music comes to our aid. In most music, the waves are not as neat as in our diagram. They will typically be "stretched." Resolutions are held up. On at least one level, we are made to wait. The most intense form of delay in music is silence—when the music stops. In one of her songs, Alanis Morissette sings about

> The conflicts, the craziness and the sound of pretenses
> Falling all around . . . all around

And then the music ceases, and she sings:

> Why are you so petrified of silence?[2]

Why? In large part because we think silence means nothingness, void, blank space. But music tells us that silence needn't be empty, that waiting can be full of hope. Toward the end of Sibelius's fifth symphony, the vast orchestra simply stops playing, and there follow six crashing chords, separated by silence. But the silence is anything but dead. We are on the edge of our seats. Even in the absence of sound, we sense the waves of meter that have been building up for ten minutes, unfinished waves pulsing through the silence—promise after promise, craving fulfillment. (There's more to music than meets the ear.) To live with God's delay means learning and helping others to learn that the waves of God's activity are "in there," in life's silences. In religious traditions such as Christianity, believers have found that constantly recalling the promises of God for the future means that the present moment—however silent—can become charged with hope. Hope can live in the midst of silence.

Wherever I have spoken about musical waves, I have been astonished at the reactions. I have been told, "That's a picture of my marriage!" An economist once said to me, "That's how economic rhythms operate in the marketplace." A young woman commented, "Isn't spirituality essentially about learning how to believe in an upper wave rising, when all you can hear are waves falling?" What this suggests is that music, in its own unique way, might be tapping into a dynamic that is quite fundamental to what it means to be human, to be creatures who hope.

It may even be that this multilevel dynamism can be found much farther afield, if we are to believe that the God who gives hope to humanity is the same God who gives a future hope to Creation at large. I have argued elsewhere[3] that music has many features that make it especially well-suited to embodying a theological vision of the physical world. It may be that we need to explore these capacities of music much more fully today. In the modern West, we have typically thought of music as chiefly a human creation, the outward expression of inner feelings or ideas. But for a large part of Western history, this would not have been the dominant way of thinking about music. For most of the Medieval era, for example, music was viewed not primarily as the externalizing of the inner human world, but more fundamentally as a way of "tuning in" to the order and beauty of the God-given cosmos, a way of discovering and inhabiting more fully the divinely structured universe.[4] From the Renaissance onward, however, music is pulled out of this theological-cosmological matrix and seen more and more as a human tool (especially of the passions), something we create from our own inner resources and share (or impose on) one another.[5] And this view—which comes in a variety of forms—has come to dominate the way we think about music today.

I am not suggesting a nostalgic return to Medieval music theory in any of its forms. But I am suggesting there were some well-honed intuitions that developed in that epoch that were in many respects far healthier than our own: above all, a concern to ground music in the sonic properties of a physical world, a world that is in turn grounded in the sustaining and redeeming purposes of an intelligent Creator. If music has a unique place in accessing and articulating in sound the dynamic order of the physical world, it means that sciences, both biological and physical, insofar as they seek to disclose and give expression to that order, could well benefit by drawing far more on music. Further, if music has distinctive capacities to access and articulate the *theological* dimensions of this order, then it has unique resources to offer any theologian pursuing such interests.

The Templeton prize–winner Arthur Peacocke is one of a number of scientist-theologians who has drawn extensively on musical models.[6] Long may this continue. The possibility of a rigorous three-way conversation between musicians, scientists, and theologians is surely one of the most exciting and fruitful on the horizon.

✑

JEREMY BEGBIE, PH.D., is Honorary Professor of Theology and Associate Director of the Institute of Theology, Imagination, and the Arts at the University of St. Andrews, United Kingdom. He is also Associate Principal of Ridley Hall, Cambridge, and an Affiliated Lecturer in the Faculty of Divinity there. The Rev. Professor Begbie holds degrees in music and philosophy and gained his Ph.D. in theology from the University of Aberdeen. He also holds music diplomas in performing and teaching from the Royal Academy of Music and the Royal College of Music. A professionally trained musician, Professor Begbie has lectured extensively in the United Kingdom, North America, and South Africa, using multimedia presentations. At St. Andrews, he directs an international research project, "Theology Through the Arts," concerned with the potential impact of the arts on theology. Professor Begbie is author of a number of books and articles on the interface between theology and the arts, including *Music in God's Purposes*; *Voicing Creation's Praise: Towards a Theology of the Arts*; and *Theology, Music and Time*. He also is editor of *Sounding the Depths: Theology Through the Arts*.

NOTES

1 I expand on this at much greater length in Begbie (2000b).

2 From the song "All I Really Want."

3 Begbie (2000a), ch. 8; and (2000b).

4 For a popular presentation, see James (1993).

5 Chua (1999).

6 See e.g., Peacocke (1993), 175ff. Cf. also Begbie (2000b), 67 n. 99.

REFERENCES

Begbie, Jeremy, ed. 2000a, *Beholding the Glory*, London: DLT/Grand Rapids: Baker.

———, 2000b, *Theology, Music and Time*, Cambridge: Cambridge University Press.

Chua, Daniel, 1999, *Absolute Music and the Construction of Meaning*, Cambridge: Cambridge University Press.

James, Jamie, 1993, *The Music of the Spheres: Music, Science and the Natural Order of the Universe*, New York: Copernicus, Springer-Verlag.

Peacocke, Arthur, 1993, *Theology for a Scientific Age*, London: SCM.

NOTIONS OF GOD AND TIME

William Lane Craig

TIME, it has been said, is what keeps everything from happening at once. When you think about it, this definition is probably as good as any other. For it is notoriously difficult to provide any analysis of time that is not, in the end, circular. This is the import of St. Augustine's famous disclaimer, "What, then, is time? If no one asks me, I know; but if I wish to explain it to one who asks, I know not" (*Confessions* 11.14).

Still, it is hardly surprising that time cannot be analyzed in terms of nontemporal concepts, and the usual analyses are not without merit, for they do serve to highlight some of time's essential features. For example, most philosophers of time would agree that the *earlier than/later than* relations are essential to time. Time, then, however mysterious, remains "the familiar stranger."

Now the question theologians face concerns the relationship of God to time. The Bible teaches clearly that God is eternal. In contrast to the pagan deities of Israel's neighbors, the LORD never came into existence, and he will never cease to exist. Minimally, then, it may be said that God's being eternal means that God exists without beginning or end. Such a minimalist account of divine eternity is uncontroversial.

But there the agreement ends. For the question is *the nature* of divine eternity. Specifically, is God temporal or timeless? God is temporal if and only if he exists in time; that is to say, his duration has phases that are related to one another as earlier and later. Given his beginningless and endless existence, God would be omnitemporal; that is to say, he exists at every moment of time there ever is. By contrast, God is timeless if and only if he is not temporal. This definition makes it evident that temporality and timelessness are contradictories: An entity must exist one way or the other and cannot exist both ways without qualification.

Although biblical authors usually speak of God as temporal and everlasting, when God is considered in relation to creation, the biblical writers sometimes portray him as the transcendent Creator of time and the ages and therefore as existing beyond time. As the biblical data are not entirely clear, we seem forced to conclude with James Barr that "if such a thing as a Christian doctrine of time has to be developed, the work of discussing it and developing it must belong not to biblical but to philosophical theology" (1962, 149).

But why, it may be asked, not simply rest with the biblical affirmation of God's beginningless and endless existence, instead of entering the speculative realms of metaphysics in an attempt to articulate a doctrine of God and time? At least two responses may be given to this question.

First, the biblical conception of God has been attacked precisely on the grounds that no coherent doctrine of divine eternity can be formulated. Two examples come immediately to mind. In his *God and the New Physics,* Paul Davies, a distinguished physicist who was awarded the million-dollar Templeton Prize for Progress in Religion in 1995 for his many popular books relating science and religion (and who contributed an essay to this volume), argues that God, as traditionally understood, can be neither timeless nor temporal. On the one hand, God cannot be timeless because such a being "cannot be a personal God who thinks, converses, feels, plans, and so on for these are all temporal activities" (1983, 133–34). Such a God could not act in time, nor could he be considered a self and, hence, a person. On the other hand, God cannot be a temporal being because he would then be subject to the laws of relativity theory governing space and time and so could not be omnipotent; neither could he be the Creator of the universe because in order to create time and space God must transcend time and space. The logical conclusion of Davies's dilemma is that God as the Bible portrays him does not exist. The importance of this dilemma has grown in Davies's thinking over the years; he has more recently written, "No attempt to explain the world, either scientifically or theologically, can be considered successful until it accounts for the paradoxical conjunction of the temporal and the atemporal, of being and becoming" (1992, 38).

A second example is the critique of God as Creator set forth by Stephen Hawking, one of the most celebrated mathematical physicists of the twentieth century, in his runaway bestseller *A Brief History of Time.* Hawking believes that in the context of standard Big Bang cosmology it makes sense to appeal to God as the Creator of the spacetime universe. This is because according to that theory spacetime had a beginning point, called the "initial singularity," at which the universe originated. By introducing imaginary numbers (multiples of $\sqrt{-1}$) for the time variable in the equations describing the very early universe, Hawking eliminates the singularity by "rounding off," as it were, the beginning of spacetime. Instead of having a beginning point akin to the apex of a cone, spacetime in its earliest state in Hawking's theory is like the rounded tip of a badminton birdie. Like the surface of a sphere, it has no edge at which one must stop. Hawking is not at all reluctant to draw theological conclusions from his model: "So long as the universe had a beginning, we could suppose it had a creator. But if the universe is really completely self-contained, having no boundary or edge, it would have neither beginning nor end. What place, then, for a creator?" (1988, 140–41).

The success of Hawking's gambit to eliminate the Creator of the universe hinges crucially on the legitimacy of his concept of "imaginary time." Because on Hawking's view imaginary time is indistinguishable from a spatial dimension, devoid of temporal becoming and *earlier than/later than* relations, the four-dimensional spacetime world just subsists, and there is nothing for a Creator to do.

Both Davies's and Hawking's writings have been enormously influential in popular culture, as well as in scientific thinking. An adequate answer to the challenges they pose requires a coherent theory of divine eternity and God's relation to time.

The second reason that it is incumbent on the philosophical theologian to articulate a doctrine of God and time is that a great deal of careless writing has already been done on this topic. The question is not whether religious believers will address the issue, but whether they will address it responsibly. It is inevitable that when Christians think about God's eternity or divine knowledge of the future or our "going to be with the Lord in eternity," they will form conceptions of how God relates to time. These are usually confused and poorly thought through, a situation often exacerbated by pronouncements made from the pulpit concerning divine eternity. Unfortunately, popular authors frequently compound the problems in their treatments of God and time.

Again, two examples will suffice. Philip Yancey is an enormously popular Christian author. In his award-winning book *Disappointment with God,* Yancey attempts to come to grips with the apparently gratuitous evil permitted by God in the world. The centerpiece of his solution to the problem is his understanding of God's relationship to time (1988, 194–99). Unfortunately, Yancey's view is a self-contradictory combination of two different positions based on a pair of confused analogies. On the one hand, appealing to the special theory of relativity, Yancey wants to affirm that a being co-extensive with the universe would know what is happening from the perspective of any spatially limited observer in the universe. A cosmic observer such as Yancey imagines would experience the lapse of worldwide cosmic time and be able to know what is happening anywhere in the universe. Such a being would be temporal and experience the flow of time. This understanding is, however, inconsistent with Yancey's second analogy of the relation between the time of an author and the time of the characters in his book or film. "We see history like a sequence of still frames, one after the other, as in a motion picture reel; but God sees the entire movie at once, in a flash" (1988, 197). This analogy points in a direction opposite the first, to an understanding of time as static, like a film lying in the can or a novel sitting on the shelf, with a timeless God existing outside the temporal dimension. Yancey's two analogies thus issue in a self-contradictory view of divine eternity—unless, perhaps, he makes the extravagant move of construing eternity as a sort of hyper-time, a higher, second-order time dimension in which our temporal dimension is embedded—and so provides no adequate solution to the problem of disappointment with God.

Our second example is provided by the popular science writer Hugh Ross, who apparently makes so bold as to affirm that God exists and operates in hyper-time. Explicitly rejecting the Augustinian-Thomistic doctrine of divine timelessness, Ross affirms that "The Creator's capacities include at least two, perhaps more, time dimensions" (1996, 24). In attempting to solve the problem of God's creating time (raised by Davies above), Ross asserts that God exists in a sort of hyper-time, in which he created our spacetime universe. Unfortunately, Ross does not accurately represent this notion. A divine hyper-time would be a dimension at each of whose moments our entire time dimension exists or not. On a diagram, it would be represented by a line perpendicular to the line representing our dimension, as illustrated in Figure 1.

But Ross misconstrues the nature of hyper-time, representing God's time on his diagram by a line parallel, rather than perpendicular, to the line representing our temporal dimension (1966, 62). Figure 2 reproduces Ross's Figure 7.1.

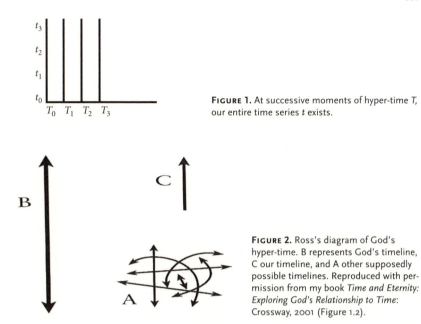

FIGURE 1. At successive moments of hyper-time T, our entire time series t exists.

FIGURE 2. Ross's diagram of God's hyper-time. B represents God's timeline, C our timeline, and A other supposedly possible timelines. Reproduced with permission from my book *Time and Eternity: Exploring God's Relationship to Time*: Crossway, 2001 (Figure 1.2).

What Ross's diagram implies is that God's temporal dimension is actually *the same* as ours, but that he pre-exists for infinite time before the creation of the universe. This is, in fact, a classical, Newtonian view of God and time. Newton believed that God existed from eternity past in absolute time and at some moment created the physical universe. The proper distinction to be drawn on such a view is not between two dimensions of time, but rather, as Newton put it, between absolute time and our relative, physical measures of time. In affirming God's infinite pre-existence, Ross must face the old question that dogged Newtonians: Why would God delay for infinite time the creation of the universe?

In short, Ross's views, while ingenious, are not coherently developed. I suspect that for Ross talk of God's extra-dimensionality is but a *façon de parler* for God's transcending space and time—but then he has expressed himself in a most misleading way, which is bound to create confusion and still leaves us with no clear understanding of God's relationship to time.

The philosopher Max Black once remarked that "a rough measure of the philosophical importance of a concept is the amount of nonsense written about it. Judged by this test the concept of time comes somewhat ahead of the concept of space and behind the concept of deity" (1962, 179). Combine time and deity, and we really have something both important and difficult to write about! If we are to move beyond the nonsense, clear, rigorous thinking, not silence, is called for on this issue.

We therefore have good reason to invite philosophical theology to articulate a coherent account of divine eternity. In carrying out this project, we shall have to keep an eye on science as well as on philosophy. Of course, for the Christian, one's theory of divine eternity will be held tentatively, as our best effort to understand how God relates to time, not dogmatically, as if it were the teaching of Scripture.

Scripture teaches that God exists beginninglessly and endlessly; now it is up to us to figure out what that implies.

L•

WILLIAM LANE CRAIG, PH.D., D.THEOL., is Research Professor of Philosophy at Talbot School of Theology in La Mirada, California. He pursued his graduate studies at the University of Birmingham (England), where he received his Ph.D. in 1977, and the University of Munich, where he received a D.Theol. in 1984. From 1980 to 1986, Dr. Craig taught philosophy of religion at Trinity Evangelical Divinity School. In 1987, he pursued research at the University of Louvain in Brussels, where he remained until 1994. His research interests include the interface of philosophy of religion and philosophy of space and time. The co-author of *Theism, Atheism, and Big Bang Cosmology* (Clarendon, 1993), as well as articles in the *Journal of Philosophy, British Journal for the Philosophy of Science, International Studies in the Philosophy of Science, Philosophia Naturalis, Astrophysics and Space Science,* among others, Dr. Craig has recently completed four volumes on divine eternity and tensed/tenseless theories of time, including *Time and Eternity: Exploring God's Relationship to Time.*

REFERENCES

Barr, James (1962): *Biblical Words for Time.* London: SCM Press.

Black, Max (1962): Critical notice of *The Natural Philosophy of Time,* by G. J. Whitrow, *Scientific American* 206 (April).

Davies, Paul (1983): *God and the New Physics.* New York: Simon and Schuster.

———. (1992): *The Mind of God.* New York: Simon and Schuster.

Divine Temporality and Human Experience of Time 90

Wolfgang Achtner

T IME IS ENIGMATIC. It is seemingly nowhere to be found, the least tangible of anything and still the most basic aspect of experience. What is time? What is eternity? Can eternity enter into time? How does time relate to the structure of human consciousness? How does the experience of time change, if consciousness changes? Can the human consciousness encompass eternity, or is there an insurmountable abyss between time and eternity? How is time conceived in different religious cultures?

What is even more scientifically interesting is this question: Can the *objective* structure of time in theories about physical reality (as in the theory of relativity, quantum mechanics, thermodynamics, and chaos theory) be linked to the *subjective* experience of time in consciousness? Can the gap between objective time in Nature and subjective time in consciousness be closed in order to achieve a comprehensive understanding of time?

These questions have to be tackled in a scientific way in order to make real progress in acquiring "spiritual information" about time, eternity, and consciousness. What is needed is a scientific understanding of (1) the way human beings experience time and eternity, (2) the link between time in physical reality and human perception of time, and (3) a cross-religious understanding of time.

My major thesis is threefold. First, I argue that the neurosciences can help to understand in a scientific way what is recorded as the religious experience of eternity. Second, I argue that this possibility to experience eternity is a basic feature of all human beings encoded in human nature and accessible by different religious techniques. Third, however, I argue that this experience of eternity is closely associated with human creativity. Thus, human creativity points to divine creativity.

To begin, I would like to propose as a working hypothesis a model of time that links it to neurophysiological research, religious experience, and the most recent mathematical concepts. It is in neuroscience, logic, and mathematics where progress in understanding time and consciousness is most likely to emerge. I suggest that the ways relating time to consciousness can be reduced to three basic forms, which I discuss further below:

1. *Cyclical Time*: In mythological religions, as those found in India and early Greece, time is conceived in a cyclical way.
2. *Linear Time*: In commonsense experience, time is perceived as linear. This way of perceiving time is also apparent in classical physics, as in Newton's definition of time as absolute and independent.

3. *Holistic Time*: In the context of the developing psychology of religion, the mystical experience of time was rediscovered in the records of these experiences. The mystics conceive time as timelessness, which might be interpreted as eternity.

From this purely phenomenological approach, we can distinguish three different modes of experiencing time. I refer to them as the (1) mythological-cyclical, (2) rational-linear, (3) mystical-holistic ways of perceiving time. The question is: In what way are these three forms of time-perception present simultaneously in a human being without logical contradiction? I suggest interpreting these three ways of understanding time *as emerging properties of a growing consciousness on a hierarchy of levels.*

Mystical-holistic time perception (highest level)	
Rational-linear time perception (middle level)	growing strength of consciousness
Mythological-cyclical time perception (lowest level)	

In any of these three ways of perceiving time, the consciousness has a certain structure, indicated by the first part of the double-notion. This structure not only determines the way of experiencing time, but also the way to experience the world. We will now explore them from the lowest to the highest strength of consciousness.

✦ In *mythological consciousness*, the world is perceived as a miraculous and frightening entity full of unpredictable interferences by powerful deities. This consciousness is also deeply interwoven into the cycles of Nature, and therefore is itself cyclic.

✦ In *rational consciousness*, this connection of consciousness with Nature is somewhat cut. Consciousness emancipates itself from the cycles in the world, and the world is perceived as a rational intelligible order that is scientifically accessible. From this point of view, the mythological structure of consciousness has to be defeated as a primitive precursor of rational consciousness. In this rational consciousness, time is perceived as linear. The components of memory, perception, and expectation as a feature of the will clearly relate to the linearity of time as past, present (which has a pointlike structure), and future. This linear notion of time in its physical aspect is also well known in Newton's famous definition of absolute time. And it is only in this structure of linear time that the classical rules of logic, discovered by Aristotle, can emerge (the Law of Identity, the Law of Forbidden Contradiction, the Law of Excluded Middle). Also, the concept of causality is associated with this notion of time.

✦ However, there is also a third way of perceiving time that may be called the *mystical consciousness*. What is the structure of this form of time perception like? In it, the linearity of time and the sequence of time units are cut in a unique moment of liberation from time in which eternity enters into time and timelessness is experienced. In this mode of consciousness, the way to experience the world is no longer dominated by its rational intelligibility, but as a unity. The structure of time consciousness and the structure of world perception can be depicted as in the following scheme:

STRUCTURE OF TIME	STRENGTH OF CONSCIOUSNESS	WORLD STRUCTURE	WORLD PERCEPTION
Mystical-Holistic; eternity entering into time	High; peak experience of reativity	Unity *beyond* space and time	Self-transcendence
Rational-Linear; progression in time	Middle; common sense; everyday life	Lawful intelligibility *in* space and time	Self-control
Mythological-Cyclical; recreational time	Low	Disorder counterbalanced by sacred space and time	Dependency

These considerations about the ways humans experience time and its relation to physical reality raise four questions: (1) Is there a link between the subjective experience of time in consciousness and the objective time in physical reality? (2) Is this structure revealed through this purely phenomenological approach based on a neurophysiologic structure, and, if so, what would be the mathematical tools to describe this structure? (3) Does this structure have any relevance for cross-religious similarity or differences in time-experience? (4) What would be the difference to a genuine Christian understanding of time that takes the biblical writings concerning the Trinitarian God actions in history seriously?

All four questions deserve close examination in future research. Here I propose some preliminary considerations about the direction that such future investigation might take:

A. *Subjective time and objective time.* Until now, it has been a mystery how the subjective time of consciousness can be linked to objective time in Nature. In fact, a number of gaps separate subjective and objective time. I offer four examples: (1) *Logic*. Classical Aristotelian logic and causality are associated with linear time. But quantum mechanics has revealed that all features of classical logic are invalidated, including causality. (2) *Arrow of time:* The arrow of time is evident in consciousness, but not in physical reality, except thermodynamics. (3) *Static and dynamic time:* In consciousness, time brings about change, but the physical world of the special theory of relativity is a static four-dimensional space-time without change. (4) *The "now":* Research in neuroscience has shown that the "now" has a duration of three seconds. But in the world of special relativity, the "now" at the intersection of the light-cone has no temporal extension at all. All this means that the relation between consciousness, time, logic, and physical reality is far from being understood.

B. *Neurophysiologic structure of time perception.* It is well known from research that one can distinguish three different parts of the brain. The oldest part, the cerebellum (including the amygdala and the limbic system), is the sea of emotions and basic biological needs. The mesencephalon is a more recent part of the brain and includes the frontal lobe. The youngest part of the brain is the neocortex. Furthermore, the two hemispheres of the brain are interconnected by the corpus callosum. One may consider whether these parts of the brain are associated with the three ways of experiencing time. I would like to suggest testing the following hypothesis: It may be the case that the *mythological-cyclical* way of perceiving time is linked to the oldest part of the brain, the cerebellum. The *rational-linear* way of time perception may belong to the mesencephalon, especially to the frontal lobe. The *mystical-holistic* way to experience time may not be located as exactly as the two preceding ones. However, since this highest form of time experience encompasses the two other ones, one may argue that it is a kind of integration of the three parts of the brain under special predominance of the neocortex. It is also worth considering that a mystical experience of time is associated with a growth of interhemispheric exchange of activity through the corpus callosum. This working hypothesis is well in accord with the recent "connectionist approach" in neuroscience (Atmanspacher et al. 1997, 134). However, time is still not understood as an emergent property of the brain. It is even less understood how the experience of time is genetically determined. Since the brain is a highly complex system, the most recent mathematical concepts, such as chaos theory and complexity theory (which have already been successfully applied in brain research), are needed to describe its functioning. Especially, the three levels of time experience could possibly be understood by the concept of an attractor from chaos theory.

C. *Cross-religious experience of time.* If it is true that these ways of experiencing time have a neurophysiological basis common to all human beings, it makes sense to argue for a similarity in time experience in all major world religions. Especially, the religious peak experience of timelessness in a unique moment deserves further attention and investigation. I pose the question, Can such an experience be identified in different religious traditions pointing to a common anthropological root of religious experience of time?

In fact all world religions have a mystic tradition in which the experience of time and eternity plays a major role:

✦ The Christian mystic Meister Eckhart often describes the unique moment when eternity enters into time. He writes, "Id est *nunc aeternitatis* quod est *verum nunc*" [It is the now of eternity, which is the true now].

✦ In the Islamic tradition, this specific experience of time appeared in Sufism. We find an equivalent word, which is *waqt*, denoting eternity entering into time. Therefore, the Sufi master, who has attained this peak experience, is called, *Ibn al-waqt*, the "son of the present moment." The famous Islamic scholar Annemarie Schimmel describes *waqt* as follows: "The Prophet's expression 'I have a time with God' (*li ma'a Allah waqt*) is often used by the Sufis to point to their experience of *waqt*, 'time,' the moment at which they break through created time and reach the Eternal Now in God. . . ."

✦ In Hinduism, the problem of time has been extensively discussed, and many different ways of interpreting time have been developed. However, in Yoga as well as in Sankhya philosophy, the notion *ksana* denotes the opening of the sequence of time atoms toward timelessness. The same interpretation of *ksana* as a gate to eternity can be substantiated for Yoga philosophy by the exposition about time in the Patanjali, Yoga Sutra III, 52.

✦ Buddhists single out a moment of time in meditation when the sequence of past, present, and future is intersected by eternity. This moment in Zen Buddhism is called *Nikon*.

Although these findings point to a common root of religious experience of time, other religious concepts of time defy such an anthropological basis—yet are no less influential—such as all kinds of apocalyptic and eschatological perceptions of time. A cross-religious investigation would have to take them into account as well.

D. The problem for Christian theology is to take these anthropological structures of experiencing time seriously on the one hand and to relate them to the basic features of Christian belief, such as Christology, historicity, and the Trinitarian God on the other.

A program for "Divine Temporality and Human Experience of Time" would have to investigate in detail:

(i) the relation between objective physical time and the subjective time of consciousness

(ii) the neurophysiological structure for the three modes of time

(iii) the moment of time, mentioned in all world religions, where time and eternity meet

(iv) the relation of these anthropological structures of time to the mentioned basic features of a Christian understanding of time

Such a future-oriented program could yield the following results as spiritual information about the time of humans and divine temporality: (1) A scientific understanding of the religious experience of eternity based on neuroscience, mathematical concepts, and new forms of logic; (2) a better mutual cross-religious understanding and reconciliation based on the scientific insight that all religious human beings share the same possible experience of eternity; and (3) the link between the experience of timelessness and creativity, which may cast new light on the question of divine creativity and thus the way the Trinitarian God operates.

ℒ♥

WOLFGANG ACHTNER, PH.D., a German theologian and mathematician, studied theology at the University of Mainz, Göttingen, Heidelberg, and mathematics by correspondence at the Fern Universität Hagen. A parish minister for fifteen years, he currently is a campus minister and an adjunct professor for science and theology at the Justus Liebig University Giessen; and a scientific consultant for Metanexus Institute, Philadelphia, Pennsylvania. His awards and honors include Kleines Lutherstipendium (1981), translation grant for the book *Dimensions of Time* (Eerdmans, 2000), and LSI-Grant (2002). He served as editor of *Religion und Wirtschaft*, Giessener Hochschulgespräche und Hochschulpredigtender ESG I (2001/2002) and *Ethik in der Medizin*, Giessener Hochschulgespräche und Hochschulpredigten der ESG II (2002).

REFERENCES

Achtner, Wolfgang et al. 2002. *Dimensions of Time*. Grand Rapids: Eerdmans.

Atmanspacher, Harald, and Ruhnau, Eva. 1997. *Time, Temporality, Now*. Berlin, New York: Springer.

PART TEN

Perspectives from World Religions

Progress in Religion? 91

INTERFAITH OPPORTUNITIES

John C. Polkinghorne

I SPENT twenty-five years working as a theoretical elementary particle physicist. In 1952, when I was a novice research student, we believed that matter was made of protons and neutrons. In the course of the subsequent quarter-century, we discovered that the protons and neutrons are themselves composites, made up of quarks and gluons. There was a lot of argument along the way to this conclusion; when the dust finally settled, all agreed that a great advance had been made.

Science makes progress in a way that is deeply impressive. The contrast with religion seems very striking and not a little unnerving. Here the arguments continue for centuries about the simplest and most basic assertions, without attaining any universally agreed resolution (Is there a God?). In view of this, is it at all realistic to hope for progress in religion? One way of addressing the issue is to think about the various ways in which scientific progress is actually made.

One way is by exploring a new realm of experience. Quarks were discovered essentially because experimentalists gained access to higher energies than had ever before been possible. The analogy for religion is not encouraging in this respect. Spiritual experience cannot simply be induced (that is the error of magic), for when it comes it does so as a gracious gift. Moreover, all religious traditions look back to the foundational people and events from which they originated and that are of unique and unrepeatable significance for that tradition. Religion can never rely solely on contemporary resources; it must always have a strong historical dimension. In this respect, the relevant scientific analogy is not with experimental science, but with those historico-observational sciences, such as cosmology or evolutionary biology, that also cannot command their own phenomena, but that have to appeal to a single skein of given experience in forming their understanding. I shall return to this point shortly.

Another means of scientific progress is to make better and more systematic use of material of a kind already available in a fairly straightforward way, but insufficiently analyzed. Medical epidemiology provides a good example of this happening. It was the careful analysis of routine information that revealed the link between smoking and lung cancer. There have recently been some attempts to apply this kind of technique to religious experience, for example by double-blind trials aimed at showing whether intercessory prayer is effective in aiding physical recovery from serious illness. I must confess to feeling some reserve about these investigations. Two problems complicate the evaluation of exercises of this kind, both arising from the multifactorial character of the phenomena. This is an issue that science also faces in its investigations, but it is a difficulty that religion faces in spades because of the deeply personal and individual character of its concerns. The aim of prayer for healing is to seek wholeness for the person prayed for, but this may come not only through physical recovery, but also through the spiritual acceptance of the imminent destiny of death. No one can prescribe beforehand which might prove to be God's will. It is hard to ensure that this latter possibility is properly reflected in the statistics. The second problem is the difficulty of control. Only God knows who is praying for whom at any given time.

However, there are other ways in which science makes progress, particularly in the historico-observational sciences. Charles Darwin did not have a great wealth of entirely new information at his disposal when he wrote *On the Origin of Species* (and it seems that the significance of some of what he did have—such as the differing beaks of the Galapagos finches—did not dawn on him until later). Instead, he was able to organize a vast collection of known facts, and it was then viewing the whole from an entirely new perspective that led him to his great discovery. Here is a much more encouraging analogy for religion to consider.

In fact, I believe that it would be timely for religious thinkers to start to take a similar line. Today we are acquiring a new perspective on how to view the relationships between the world's great faith traditions. Together they represent a vast reservoir of spiritual experience, but in times past it was only too easy to dismiss traditions other than one's own as being simply collections of odd beliefs held by strange people in faraway countries (even if Christians could never properly have thought this way about Jews). Today, however, the adherents of other faiths are no longer exotic oddities, but they are our neighbors, living down the street. We can see for ourselves the spiritual authenticity of their lives. No longer can we simply congratulate ourselves that we are all right and they are all wrong. But neither can we believe the simplistic notion that really we are all saying the same thing, dressed up in culturally different linguistic clothing. There are real differences between us of a most perplexing kind. These matters do not only relate to the obvious points of disagreement between the traditions, such as the status of Jesus or the status of the Qur'an. They also relate to fundamental beliefs about the general nature of reality. Is the human person of unique and persistent significance (as all the three Abrahamic faiths affirm), or is personality recycled through reincarnation according to the law of Karma (as our Hindu friends tell us), or is the self ultimately an illusion from which we have to seek release (as the Buddhist doctrine of *anatta* appears to assert)? Is time a linear pilgrim path to be trodden, or a samsaric wheel from whose revolutions we need to seek to escape?

It cannot be denied that there are grave cognitive clashes between the faith traditions. These contradictions make it scarcely surprising that many people look to science for truth, but believe that religion is no more than culturally molded opinion. Progress in religion must surely require that we make some form of advance in our understanding of these perplexing problems. Yet, if we are to do so, we must also recognize that underneath the puzzling diversities of the world faiths is also a discernible degree of commonality. In their different ways, each is testifying to encounter with a dimension of reality of transcendent importance, one that might properly be called a meeting with the Sacred. I became fully aware of this years ago in the course of watching a television series called *The Long Search*. It consisted of a series of exploratory meetings between Ronald Eyre and a succession of representatives of different faith traditions. The program that sticks in my mind (and the experience which I know had greatly influenced Ronald himself) was an encounter with a Buddhist Zen master. I suppose that Zen Buddhism is a spiritual tradition that is about as far as can be from anything that I find it easy to get my mind or my heart around, but there was an overwhelming spiritual authenticity about that person that was deeply impressive and humbling to behold.

The dialog between the world faiths is only just beginning in earnest. It is a theological task of the highest importance, and I think that many centuries of mutual exploration are likely to lie ahead. (Think about how slow has been the growth of understanding between different Christian sub-traditions, and you will see the magnitude of the interfaith task.) By taking this project seriously, we shall gain a great expansion in the range of religious experience and spiritual testimony available for coherent review in the light of this new perspective of a truly global ecumenism. I simply want to make two comments on the way in which we might seek to proceed.

The first is to affirm that the traditions have to meet one another in the integrity of their understandings and of their differences. I do not believe that we should be seeking a lowest-common-denominator form of "world religion" based on statements so watered down in content that scarcely any adherents of any faith tradition would want to affirm them, or even to take them seriously. I want to meet my brothers and sisters from other faiths and to listen respectfully to them, for I am sure I have things that I need to learn from them; but I can only truly meet them if I do so preserving my identity as a Christian. Only in this way shall I have anything to offer to our mutual encounter. It will be of no use trying to disguise my firm belief in the unique significance of Jesus Christ, the Word made flesh, although I know that this will seem strange, and may even repel some of them. Ultimately, the basis for our meeting can only be the search for truth, and we shall all have to speak for the truth as we have come to understand it. This means that interfaith encounter is inevitably going to be painful and difficult.

This acknowledgment leads me to my second point. The world faiths will have to meet one another initially in ways that are not too threatening. If the status of Christ, or of the Qur'an, is the main item on the opening agenda, defenses will go up at once, and no progress will be made. The grounds for a first encounter have to be serious, but not too intimidating. Considering together how the faiths respond to the insights of science into the nature and history of the universe is a possible initial topic of this kind. In fact, the John Templeton Foundation supports a series of initiatives through the "Science and the Spiritual Quest" (SSQ) project, in which people who have common science backgrounds but are drawn from different religious traditions meet to consider shared concerns. I have had the privilege of participating in some of these activities. The gains are real, even if they are sometimes slow in coming. I believe that here is a fruitful pattern for the future.

I hope that the Third Millennium will be a period of true ecumenical encounter between the world's faith traditions. If that is so, it will be a time of true progress in religion.

❧

JOHN C. POLKINGHORNE holds the degrees of Sc.D. and Ph.D. from the University of Cambridge and honorary doctorates from Durham, Exeter, Kent, Leicester, and Marquette Universities. After twenty-five years working as an elementary particle physicist (Professor of Mathematical Physics, Cambridge University, 1968–79), he trained for the ministry of the Church of England and was ordained priest in 1982. He was President of Queens College, Cambridge, 1989–96, and he is now Canon Theologian of Liverpool and a Fellow of Queens College. Dr. Polkinghorne is a Fellow of the Royal Society (1974), the British National Academy of Science. He was made a Knight of the British Empire in 1997. Dr. Polkinghorne writes extensively on science and religion, including monographs on theoretical physics and popular books on science, such as *The Quantum World* (1984) and *Quantum Theory: A Very Short Introduction* (2002). Other publications include *One World* (1986); his Gifford Lectures, *Science and Christian Belief* (1994; North American title, *The Faith of a Physicist*); his Terry Lectures, *Belief in God in an Age of Science* (1998); *The God of Hope and the End of the World* (2002), and *Science and the Trinity* (2004). In 2002, Dr. Polkinghorne was awarded the Templeton Prize for Progress in Religion.

INTERFAITH DIALOG IN THE GLOBAL WORLD 92

THEOLOGICAL AND INTELLECTUAL CONSTRUCTS FOR THE FUTURE

Bruno Guiderdoni

T HE FRENCH NOVELIST and essayist André Malraux is said to have once sum- marized the uncertain destiny of humankind with a famous assertion: "The twenty-first century will be religious or it will not be." Now, more than forty years after this once futuristic statement was made, it is still not easy to foresee what the future of religions will be in the twenty-first century.

Religions face a great challenge produced by the rapid pace of technological and cultural change with associated dislocation of traditional sources of situation and identity in the world. The sense of place and self are jeopardized by the conflict between the two opposing forces of religion/theology and science/technology, made worse by the tendency toward extreme positions: "relativism," which transforms religions into secularized, ordinary market products; "lifestyle" choices, which can be tried, consumed, and changed at will; and "absolutism," which makes religions into politicized tools used to create a totalitarian, "pseudo-theocratic" organization of societies. Such an unstable tendency toward extremes on the spectrum of thought is more or less the direct result of the incredibly rapid development of science and technology. (This relation is especially strong and much discussed in my own reli- gion, Islam.) So it is prudent to analyze the two opposing forces and to examine the consequences of the interaction between religion/theology and science/technology in the context of the general "modernization" of religious thought.

Two Theological Tasks

Theologians of the twenty-first century find two major tasks on their agenda.

The first is revision of their worldview under the light shed by scientific discov- eries. The effect of science on intellectual culture is ironic: While it has resulted in a devaluing of the importance of traditional cultures and their knowledge or wis- dom based on narrative or story, the turn toward naïve religious fundamentalism often is associated with scientific and engineering training rather than with tradi- tional philosophical education. This is doubly ironic considering that any literalis- tic reading of the Holy Scriptures is not uncommonly contradicted by scientific facts. Such a situation naturally creates tension within religious groups: Those who accept a philosophy of open-minded revision in the way they understand and inter- pret Scripture often find themselves in opposition to those who adhere militantly to a literalistic "doubters-be-damned" approach.

The second task is a collective endeavor for all religions: to understand why there are so many religions. Is this "Babel" of faiths a meaningless accident or the loving wisdom of the Divine? The task of addressing this endeavor is just beginning.

Of course, the existence of many religions is an obvious fact. But there is a gap between recognizing other religions and understanding why other religions exist. If we restrict our focus to the Middle Ages, for instance, Jews, Christians, and Muslims had more or less directly conflicting relationships. Typically, members of one group knew little of the other faiths. Peaceful coexistence was separate coexistence. Few tried to understand their neighbor's religion with any degree of seriousness or sympathy. On the contrary, the necessity of going to war was always justified, on each side, by the belief that one's own group followed the only true faith, whereas the enemy was misguided into following a false or "forged" religion. As a consequence, theologians worked out elaborate systems to explain the reason for the plurality of (false or imperfect) religions and for the uniqueness of the true religion (always their *own*).

The situation is now changing very quickly—a very important matter. The causes of change are several. The development of academic studies and the translation of sacred texts into the most common languages have made the corpus of the main religions available to all. Moreover, modern travel has made encounters between the members of all faiths much easier and more common than they used to be. The model of secular, liberal societies that is spreading on a worldwide scale encourages cosmopolitan discussion and dialog between diverse peoples. Awareness of the diversity of faiths and of the differences in their teachings—as well as of the importance of tolerance and mutualism—is growing. We are the first generation of humankind to experience such a dialog on a global scale, very much as we are the first generation that has ever contemplated the astonishing pictures of planet Earth taken from space. This collective experience brings important opportunities and challenges for gleaning new spiritual information. Theologians are just beginning to investigate and evaluate its consequences. Once a new set of paradigms has been developed, it is probably reasonable to predict that their impact will be dramatic. And toward this end I want to add a note of encouragement.

Two Theological Patterns

It should be clear that traditional theological discourse is typically conducted at the level of *interpretation* of the Holy Scriptures and of oral traditions. The theological work that has been developing for centuries within our faiths is aimed at orchestrating a balance in the interplay of revelation, reason, experience, and tradition. As a consequence, the elaboration of theological thought that has occurred in each religion has mainly been centered on self-consistency. In other words, the existence of multiple faith traditions appeared as a troublesome and unpleasant fact. This "problem" had to be incorporated in some way into the existing theological construct. To this end, an "as-small-as-possible" place was allotted to the disturbing presence of other religions.

The multiplicity of religions has caused two identifiable patterns in thinking about them. The first pattern simply consists of excluding other religions by deny-ing them any status. Thus, only one religion is construed to be "true." Other religions are deemed to be "false," mere imitation systems constructed by human beings to quench their thirst for spirituality or to fight against the only true religion. The fun-damentalist currents in all religions promote this hard, dismissive paradigm. There is simply no room for the other religions in the theological construct of the first kind.

The second pattern consists of finding a peripheral place for the other religions. Other faith traditions, according to this "peripherality" model, are generally under-stood as incomplete, "on-the-road-toward-better-times" systems. They are consid-ered a means of preparing for the final revelation. And when this final revelation occurs, the other, older religions will be incorporated or absorbed into the new Truth. This softer model is, perhaps, the opinion shared by the majority of believ-ers in all religions. In this theological construct of the second kind, the members of other faiths have to be gently persuaded that they will find the plenitude of Truth in the only complete religion.

Let us review two doctrinal examples of the second pattern, drawn respectively from Christianity and Islam. The first doctrine, about the faiths that came before Jesus, was held primarily by Christians. For centuries in mainstream Roman Catholic theology, other faiths were considered to be only preparation for the com-ing of Jesus Christ, the *praeparatio evangelica*, or the "seeds of God's Word" (the *logoi spermatikoi* or *semina verbi*). However, a somewhat similar model has been used by Muslims to interpret Christianity. In mainstream Islamic theology, all reli-gions were considered as actually having been revealed by God through the messages of the prophets. Although all religions were held to have been true at the begin-ning, their disciples were typically understood to have altered and corrupted the original messages so radically that a last revelation (that is, Islam) was made neces-sary. This was called *tahrîf* ("alteration") within Islamic theology and was based on an interpretation of some Qur'an verses.

To summarize, fundamentalists see other religions as simply false, whereas more moderate mainstream theologians view other religions as historically incomplete. At this stage, the main issue is to know how religions can address the new situation brought forth by globalization. Religions are often accused of promoting a world-view that encourages the exclusion of the other faiths, thereby promoting xeno-phobia and prompting people toward inter-ethnic violence. It is obvious that the theological constructs of fundamentalists foment violence. But what is the value of the condemnation of violence that is espoused by less radical, mainstream theolo-gians if they retain a narrow, symmetrically problematic view of other religions? Such theologians may try to promote spectacular interfaith meetings or gatherings of talented theologians. The results of these meetings are often solemn declarations in favor of peace. But can these efforts be more than attempts at diplomatic grand-standing? Religions now suffer a deficit of credibility in public opinion, which crit-icizes their inefficiency in opposing and preventing violence perpetrated in the name of God. But theological problems must have theological solutions.

Cosmological and Theological Constructs: Two Ways of Looking at "Truth"

By analogy, the theological constructs elaborated over centuries may be compared with the cosmological worldview of the Middle Ages. This model was built on Aristotelian physics and Ptolemaic astronomy and was held for roughly two millennia. It interpreted the complexity of astronomical phenomena with an elaborate system of concentric spheres centered on Earth. Theological interpretations of the Holy Scriptures used this Ptolemaic world model. But the theological constructs of the Jews, Christians, and Muslims and the scientific developments in medieval cosmology were contemporaneous. When the Ptolemaic system became increasingly unable to accommodate the accumulation of new astronomical facts, astronomers added new wheels, epicycles, and equants to their complicated machinery to "save the phenomena." But astronomers became more and more skeptical about the ability of astronomy to actually explain the world.

Then along came Nicolas Copernicus. Copernicus demonstrated that a simple and elegant solution could be found that not only reproduced the phenomena, but that also was able to predict them with a greater degree of accuracy. Moreover, this solution proposed a new world model that was much simpler and more geometrically refined in placing the Sun at the center of the known universe. In his book *De Revolutionibus Orbis Cælorum* published in 1543, Copernicus argued that such a position was much more suited to the Sun than to Earth: The Sun was, he argued, the symbol of God's power, providing light and fecundity to the whole of Creation.

Some theological constructs may be viewed as analogous to cosmological models. We now know that our theologies are centered on themselves, somewhat analogous to the medieval cosmos that was centered on the terrestrial observer. These theologies incorporate the existence of other faiths by means of theological constructs that are roughly similar to the wheels, epicycles, and equants of Ptolemaic cosmology. The accumulation of new spiritual facts brought about by a better understanding of what the other religions actually preach requires constructs that are increasingly elaborate. More and more people doubt the intent and authenticity of religions that seem to preach against other truths and claim to own the only Truth. This is perhaps similar to the situation that existed before the Copernican revolution, when many doubted the ability of astronomy to explain a cosmos that was seen as being artificially held together.

Perhaps what is needed is a basic transformation of perspective from "theologicocentric" theologies—that is, theologies centered on the issue of their own self-consistency and robustness with respect to any new fact—to truly "theocentric" theologies—that is, those in which God's light and creativity are at the center of the construct. Thus, we may need a Copernican revolution in theology as much as we needed it in cosmology five centuries ago. In such a new view, the diversity of religions would appear as a "natural" God-given phenomenon, one that was created with purpose.

If such a paradigm shift took place, religious leaders would be driven to view theological constructs as creations by human beings operating in specific, possibly sublimely inspired, contexts. However, the traditions would never be able to encapsulate the whole of Truth, of which only God is the author.

A Third Pattern: Toward a Global View of Religions

Under this paradigm shift, theologians of all religions would want to incorporate new spiritual information associated with their discovery of and new interest in the diversity of religions. They have to not only move away from the narrowness of hateful exclusion, but drop the model of pitiful inclusion. What is needed, in my view, is a third pattern: a "non-exclusive" and "non-inclusive" construct. Here, God's bounty would *require* the existence of other religions to fulfill the spiritual needs of the marvelous diversity of human beings. Similarly, the grandeur of God's mystery, beyond any attempt to describe or summarize the Divine in formulae, would *require* global polyphony of expression and perception of revelation.

As the Qur'an says, "had God pleased, He could have made of you one community: but it is His wish to prove you by that which He has bestowed upon you. Vie with each other in good works, for to God you shall all return and He will resolve for you your differences."[1]

It is perhaps helpful to note that scientific and technological developments have modeled the idea of a plurality of "books" written by God. The natural tendency of theological xenophobia or text-fundamentalism is to state that truth inheres only in a single Book, the book of sacred Scripture specific to the religion or tradition in question. Some theological positions have had to adjust to the idea that God has written two books: the Book of Scripture and the Book of Nature, written in very different languages and frequently seeming to be in contradiction. (The struggle over the "debacle of Galileo" is a classic case of such an evolution of doctrine within Catholicism.) It may be a difficult matter for groups with literalistic tendencies to accept that the Book of Scripture and the Book of Nature speak the same Truth, although this Truth is sometimes difficult to elucidate and enunciate and often requires that religious members and authorities struggle with the hard questions of revision. But this insight is only half the story. The other half is the challenge that has to be embraced. God not only has written the Book of Nature, a single Book for a single cosmos shared by all human beings, but he has written *many* books of Scripture. Is the apparent contradiction that comes out of this plurality caused by the impossibility of capturing the absolute Truth within a single human vision and language? For this reason, the relationships of theological constructs with the scientific worldview and with the existence of other religions are intimately linked. As we progress, perhaps we will realize that God never ceases to speak: He speaks from under the veils of nature's phenomena as well as from under the veils of the revelations that are adapted by and to human cultures.

As the Qur'an also says, "If the sea were ink for the Words of my Lord, the sea would be spent before the Words of my Lord are spent, though We brought replenishment the like of it."[2]

We face an immense challenge. But it may also be surprisingly simple to resolve. Perhaps, in spiritual humility, we need only to incorporate an acknowledgment that our systems are incomplete. In 1931, Kurt Gödel discovered that incompleteness is present within any given formal system powerful enough to include arithmetic. As a consequence, any formal system contains many true statements that cannot be demonstrated. Perhaps something similar occurs with the Divine. Surely, in his infinite reality, God escapes from complete description by any formal system. Why then do we always want to enclose Him within our limited understanding? We need only to remember the teachings of the mystics and holy persons of all our traditions, who repeatedly testified that "God is greater" than the ideas we have about Him. To put it very simply, we need to take *humility* into account. This is the price we pay if we want to save our religions from the double danger of relativism and absolutism. But it is a very attractive price if we consider that by paying it we may contribute to driving humankind from its own arrogant foolishness.[3]

ℒ♥

BRUNO GUIDERDONI, PH.D., has been an astrophysicist at the Institut d'Astrophysique de Paris, Laboratoire du Centre National de la Recherche Scientifique (Paris Institute of Astrophysics of the French National Center for Scientific Research [CNRS]), since 1988. His area of research, observational cosmology, is mainly focused on galaxy formation and evolution. He has published more than one hundred articles and organized several international conferences on these issues. After a two-year stay in Morocco, his spiritual pursuit led him to embrace Islam in 1987. From 1993 to 1999, he has been in charge of the weekly French TV show *Knowing Islam*. In his papers and lectures, he attempts to present the intellectual and spiritual aspects of Islam, reflect on the relationship between science and the Islamic tradition, and promote an interreligious dialog. In 1995, he contributed to founding the Islamic Institute for Advanced Studies (IHEI), aimed at helping European Muslims recover the intellectual dimension of Islam. He has published more than fifty papers on Islamic theology and mysticism, and his book *An Introduction to the Spirituality of Islam* is scheduled for publication in Paris.

NOTES

1 Qur'an 5, 48.

2 Qur'an 18, 109.

3 I acknowledge a fruitful discussion with Charles Harper on these topics in May 2003.

Humility and the Future of Islam 93

Munawar A. Anees

"READ IN THE NAME of thy Lord Who created." This is the first verse of the Qur'an, which in the year 610 announced the advent of Islam as a Revelation continuing the Abrahamic tradition. By the end of the Revelation, which lasted for over two decades, the Qur'an came to contain nearly eight hundred instances of words and nuances associated with "knowledge" (*al-'ilm*).

From this Divine gift of Revelation and out of the Arabian heartland emerged a "Civilization of the Book" that by the year 1100 flourished from the Iberian Peninsula in the West to the Pacific Rim in the East. From the majestic minarets of the Blue Mosque in Istanbul through the winding bazaar of Timbuktu in Mali to the emerald-studded marble façade of Taj Mahal in India, even today a sublime echo of the civilizational grandeur of this world remains.

The early Muslim civilization was heir as well to a diverse intellectual stock. Incorporating aspects of the civilizations of Greece, Rome, India, and Persia as a conglomerate, it accomplished a unique synthesis of ideas in all branches of knowledge. From the eighth to the thirteenth century, there were more religious, philosophical, medical, astronomical, historical, and geographical works written in Arabic than in any other human language of the period.

Today, Muslims do not retain an intellectually rich understanding of their faith as one should expect in view of such a heritage. Even the early discourse on speculative theology (*kalam*) is absent from their circles. Muslims are engulfed in seemingly endless wars of rhetoric and anger among themselves and against the West. Orthodoxy trumps reason. Progress, skepticism, and respect for the value of humane debate are sacrificed at the altar of a totalizing puritanism. We are suffocating because of the loss of pluralism and progressive thought, so distinctive a trait of the Muslim past. The contemporary global Muslim community (*ummah*) continues to suffer after a devastating closure of a great tradition of diverse and polyphonic reasoned argument (*ijtihad*) a millennium ago.

The state of Muslim debate on progress in religion or spiritual information is blurred. It is largely an articulation of a viewpoint that betrays the paucity of knowledge and engagement with the modern scientific ethos. Contemporary discussion tends to perpetuate an ossified style of theological reasoning. Others take it from an extreme apologetic perspective to the point of turning the Qur'an into a book of science containing all necessary insights into astronomy, biology, chemistry, mathematics, and physics. Much of it is promoted as Islamic education. With a ring of authority, critical thinking is demonized.

Similarly, epistemological revisionism in the garb of "Islamization of knowledge" has fallen into the trap of an allegedly value-free science. Advocates have thought it sufficient only to add an adjective to some disciplinary categories (Islamic astronomy, Islamic biology, and so forth).

Then there is the poorly articulated idea of "Islamic science" that randomly makes use of a few common Islamic concepts and values in a rhetoric borrowed from the Western social radicalism.

Against the backdrop of unimpressive intellectual currents lurks a traditionalist discourse that altogether consigns modern science to oblivion and attempts to prop up a fatal mix of mystical and alchemical knowledge. That, too, in the name of Islamic science! Much of the historical discourse on the subject remains panegyric in nature, to the extent of self-delusion. The so-called *jihadi* agenda, although adhered to by only a minority, partially thrives on this nostalgic thread.

Neither scientific apologies for the Qur'an nor the relegation of science to a Quranic literalism are helpful. Both tend to obfuscate the advance of knowledge. Contrarily, we need a dynamic invocation that may play a pivotal role in breaking the impasse that continues to grip Muslim minds and cultures. The concept of humility offers a foundation for the indispensable engagement of religion and science in the Muslim context.

The Qur'an explicitly speaks of humility in relation to one's faith and how it can enhance one's spiritual awareness and commitment to God:

"Has not the time arrived for the believers that their hearts in all humility should engage in the remembrance of God and of the Truth, which has been revealed to them?" (*al-Hadid* 57:16)

Commentary: "Humility and the remembrance of God and His Message are never more necessary than in the hour of victory and prosperity."

"Say whether ye believe in it or not, it is true that those who were given knowledge beforehand, when it is recited to them, fall down on their faces in humble prostration and they say: Glory to our Lord! Truly has the promise of our Lord been fulfilled! They fall down on their faces in tears, and it increases their earnest humility." (*al-Isra* 17:107–9)

Commentary: "A feeling of earnest humility comes to the man who realizes how, in spite of his own unworthiness, he is brought, by God's mercy, into touch with the most sublime truths. Such a man is touched with the deepest emotion which finds its outlet in tears."

"Those who are near to thy Lord disdain not to do Him worship: They celebrate His praises, and bow down before Him." (*al-Airaf* 7:206)

Commentary: "The higher you are in spiritual attainment, the more is your desire and opportunity to serve and worship your Lord and Cherisher and the Lord and Cherisher of all worlds; and the greater is your pride in that service and that worship."

The Quranic term for humility is *khushu'*. The Arabic word *hilm* carries a similar connotation. It is narrated that even the Prophet was exhorted, and he labored to lace his prayers with utmost humility and tears. He, in turn, reminded the believers to follow his example in prayers. The opposite of humility is arrogance (*kibr* in the Quranic terminology). The Qur'an speaks of Satan (*iblis*) as the arrogant one who refused to obey God's command to show humility toward His creature (Adam). In other words, one may consider absence of humility tantamount to arrogance—not an angelic, but a satanic attribute. Arrogance defines its own boundaries, foreclosing new possibilities of knowing. Further, in the Quranic phrase, arrogance leads to tyranny (*zulm*).

Humility was a clearly enunciated theme in the writings of Dr. Muhammad Abdus Salam of Pakistan, the first Muslim Nobel Laureate. He often referred to the role of humility in the understanding of Nature and called for the infusion of this concept into the body of science. The celebrated Pakistani poet and Lenin Prize Laureate, Faiz Ahmad Faiz, was another prominent advocate for the organic necessity for humility. His poetry, often reflective of the bewilderment felt at the cosmic splendor, carries an implicit ode to humility.

The example of a believing physicist and a secular poet tells us that there runs a common thread of humility in the human mind. It may not be uniformly manifested as one attempts to deny it under the guise of secular objectivity. However, as Sir John Templeton articulates, recognition of humility as a universal value reawakens a positive force in human thinking.

The humble approach to progress in religion opens new vistas of knowledge and understanding. While immersing one deeper into spiritual experience, this mindset, contrasted with the positivist heroic approach in science, opens infinitely new avenues for learning. This, we believe, is one of the outstanding characteristics of Sir John Templeton's vision of humility.

Again, in the Muslim context, as well as in other religions, humility could be regarded at once as an agent of both spiritual and cognitive progress. We observe that the Quranic dictum on knowledge is evolutionary at its core. The journey toward spiritual and cognitive excellence commences with human submission to God. This submission symbolizes the pinnacle of humility. The dynamics of knowledge and progress in Islam are thus deeply rooted in a humility originally learned in relation to God and in need of extension to embrace knowledge of the world created and sustained by God.

The Qur'an emphasizes one's obligation to shape one's own future. In that sense, it disapproves of knowledge that creates static minds. Similarly, the Islamic concept of knowledge is intricately woven into action. This integral synchrony of knowledge and action has deeper meanings for both personal and societal progress. First, as an act of obligation, knowing is enjoined. Next, as a corollary of knowing, one is called on to act. Shaping one's future, therefore, becomes an informed, conscious, and knowledge-driven activity.

Fatalism has no place in Islam. If the argument for a nexus between knowledge and action is valid, then the only recourse left is perpetual action toward more knowledge and greater progress. It is this complimentarity of knowledge and action that shapes one's future.

Sir John Templeton has often reminded us of the ambitious desire for a hundredfold increase in spiritual knowledge. Here lies the challenge for the Muslim mind: reconciliation between that ever-increasing knowledge and strategies for action.

Muslims cannot afford to ignore the ongoing evolution of human and spiritual information. Stemming from a single source, the Muslim creed recognizes knowledge as a "unity." It does not distinguish between the secular and the spiritual. Therefore, all knowledge, with its dependent moral contingency, is destined to lead to spiritual evolution.

A humility-centered quest for knowledge is perhaps the key to a better Muslim future. We need not only to recognize humility by its moral or spiritual connotation, but to harness its epistemic potential for the right action. For Muslims, progress in religion or evolution of spiritual information implies a strategy encompassing three tiers: humility, knowledge, action. We earnestly hope, with God's infinite mercy, that Muslim intellectuals will rise to the occasion and contribute to a greater understanding of human quest for spirituality.

ℰ♥

MUNAWAR A. ANEES, PH.D., is Executive Director of Knowledge Management Systems (KnowSys) in Tucson, Arizona and a writer and a social critic. A biologist who earned his doctorate at Indiana University, his contributions in the monthly *Inquiry* (London) have played a pioneering role in the Muslim dialog on religion and science. Author of half a dozen books and more than three hundred articles, book reviews, and bibliographies, he has contributed to the *Encyclopedia of the Modern Islamic World* and *Encyclopedia of the History of Science, Technology, and Medicine in Non-Western Cultures*. His book *Guide to Sira and Hadith Literature in Western Languages* is considered a classic. *Islam and Biological Futures* has brought Muslim bioethical problems to the forefront of contemporary discourse. He founded the journal of current awareness on the Muslim world, *Periodica Islamica*, recognized as "an invaluable guide." He is a founding editor of the *International Journal of Islamic and Arabic Studies*, and an advisory editor of the *Journal of Islamic Science* and *Islamic Studies*. In 2000, he was selected as Religion Editor for the new online encyclopedia, *Nupedia*. Dr. Anees is an elected member of the Royal Academy, Jordan, and a founding member of the International Society for Science and Religion, Cambridge, England. An American citizen, he was nominated for the Nobel Peace Prize in February 2002.

By What Knowledge Is the Spirit Known?

Ravi Ravindra

"Two kinds of knowledge are to be known . . . the higher as well as the lower. . . .
And the higher is that by which the Undecaying is apprehended."
—Mundaka Upanishad *I.i.* 4–5

W ITH ALL the progress in scientific and medical fields, have human beings morally or spiritually advanced? Is it reasonable to assume that future Nobel Prize winners in science will be more spiritually advanced than the past ones because more scientific knowledge will be available to them? What sort of scientific facts or spiritual information will or can lead to this transformation in the nature of human beings? Is a quantitative extension of our information about the universe likely to lead us to a more spiritual life?

All traditions assert that the spirit is higher than and prior to the body-mind, which is sometimes called the "body," for simplicity. One of the ideas that is common to all the great religious traditions of the world is the assertion that, in general, human beings do not live the way they should—and furthermore, the way they could. The Christian perspective claims that we live in sin, but we could live in the grace of God; the Hindu-Buddhist way of saying this is that we live in sleep, but we could wake up. All the traditions suggest ways by which human beings could move toward a life of grace or wakefulness, a shift that is a qualitative transformation of being. Here, I will focus largely on the Indian spiritual traditions, more particularly on the theory and practice of Yoga, the way of transformation.

Yoga begins from a recognition of the human situation. Human beings are bound by the laws of process, and they suffer as a consequence of this bondage. Yoga proceeds by a focus on knowledge of the self. Self-knowledge may be said to be both the essential method and the essential goal of Yoga. However, self-knowledge is a relative matter. It depends not only on the depth and clarity of insight, but also on what is seen as the "self" to be known. The Chandogya Upanishad (VIII.7.2–13.6) instructs spiritual seekers in identifying the self with progressively more and more spiritualized self.

A change from the identification of the self as the body (including the heart and the mind) to the identification of the self as inhabiting the body is the most crucial development in Yoga and is considered a matter of great progress. Yoga identifies the person less with the *body* than with the *embodied*. Ancient and modern Indian languages reflect this perspective in the expressions they use to describe a person's death: in contrast to the usual English expression of *giving up the ghost*, one *gives up the body*. It is not the body that has the spirit, but the spirit that has the body.

The identification of the person in oneself with something other than the body-mind and the attendant freedom from the body-mind is possible only through a proper functioning and restructuring of the body and the mind. The Sanskrit word *sharira* is useful to steer clear of the modern Western philosophic dilemma called the "mind-body" problem. Although *sharira* is usually translated as "body," it means the whole psychosomatic complex of body, mind, and heart. *Sharira* has the same import as *flesh* in the Gospel of Saint John, for example in John 1:14, where it is said, "The Word became flesh." The important point, both in the Indian context and in John, is that the spiritual element, called *Purusha, Atman,* or *Logos* ("Word"), is above the whole of the psychosomatic complex of a human being and is not to be identified with mind, which is a part of *sharira,* or the "flesh."

Sharira is both the instrument of transformation and the mirror reflecting it. The way a person sits, walks, feels, and thinks reveals the connection with the deeper self, and a stronger connection with the deeper self will be reflected in the way a person sits, walks, feels, and thinks. *Sharira,* which is individualized *prakriti* (Nature), is the medium necessary for the completion and manifestation of *purusha* (the inner spiritual being), which itself can be understood as individualized *Brahman* (literally, "the Vastness"), whose body is the whole of the cosmos, subtle as well as gross.

Sharira is the substance through which each one of us relates to the spirit, according to our ability to respond to the inner urge and initiative. The development of this relationship is the spiritual art. To view the *sharira,* or the world, as a hindrance rather than an opportunity is akin to regarding the rough stone as an obstruction to the finished statue.

The most authoritative text of Yoga is the *Yoga Sutras,* which consists of aphorisms of Yoga compiled by Patañjali sometime between the second century BCE and the fourth century CE from material already familiar to the gurus (teachers, masters) of Indian spirituality. Patañjali teaches that clear seeing and knowing are functions of *purusha* (the inner person) and not of the mind.

The mind relies on judgment, comparison, discursive knowledge, association, imagination, dreaming, and memory, through which it clings to the past and future dimensions of time. The mind is limited in scope and cannot know the objective truth about anything. The mind is not the true knower: It can calculate, make predictions in time, infer implications, quote authority, make hypotheses, or speculate about the nature of reality; but it cannot see objects directly, from the inside, as they really are in themselves.

In order to allow direct seeing to take place, the mind, which by its very nature attempts to mediate between the object and the subject, has to be quieted. When the mind is totally silent and totally alert, both the real subject (*purusha*) and the real object (*prakriti*) are simultaneously present to it. When the seer is there and what is to be seen is there, seeing takes place without distortion. Then there is no comparing or judging, no misunderstanding, no fantasizing about things displaced in space and time, no dozing off in heedlessness nor any clinging to old knowledge or experience; in short, there are no distortions introduced by the organs of perception, namely the mind, the feelings, and the senses. There is simply seeing in the present, the living moment in the eternal now. That is the state of perfect and free attention, *kaivalya*, which is the aloneness of seeing and not of the seer separated from the seen, as it is often misunderstood by commentators on Yoga. In this state, the seer sees through the organs of perception rather than with them, or as William Blake says, one sees "not with the mind, but through the mind."[1] Blake speaks about the transformation of perception that this re-ordering allows in "Auguries of Innocence":

> To see a World in a Grain of Sand
> And a Heaven in a Wild Flower,
> Hold Infinity in the palm of your hand
> And Eternity in an hour.

It is of utmost importance from the point of view of Yoga to distinguish clearly between the mind (*chitta*) and the real Seer (*purusha*). *Chitta* pretends to know, but it can itself be known and seen—that is, it is an object, not a subject. However, it can be an instrument of knowledge. This misidentification of the seer and the seen, of the person with the organs of perception, is the fundamental error from which all other problems and sufferings arise (*Yoga Sutras* 2.3–17). It is from this fundamental ignorance that *asmita* ("I-am-this-ness," or egoism) arises, creating a limitation by particularization. *Purusha* says, "I AM"; *asmita* says, "I am this" or "I am that."[2] This is an expression of egoism and self-importance and leads to the strong desire to perpetuate the specialization of oneself and to a separation from all else. The sort of "knowledge" that is based on this misidentification is always colored with pride and a tendency to control or to fear.

The means for freedom from the ignorance that is the cause of all sorrow is an unceasing vision of discernment; such vision alone can permit transcendental insight (*prajña*) to arise. Nothing can force the appearance of this insight; all one can do is to prepare the ground for it. The purpose of *prakriti* is to lead to such insight, as that of a seed is to produce fruit; what an aspirant needs to do in preparing the garden is to remove the weeds that choke the full development of the plant. The ground to be prepared is the entire psychosomatic organism, for it is through that organism that *purusha* sees and *prajña* arises, not through the mind alone, nor the emotions, nor the physical body by itself. A person with dulled senses has as little possibility of coming to *prajña* as the one with a stupid mind or hardened feelings. Agitation in any part of the entire organism causes fluctuations in attention and muddies the seeing. This is the reason that Yoga puts so much emphasis on the preparation of the body, as well as of feelings by right moral preparation and of the mind by immersing oneself in the views from the real world, for coming to true knowledge. It is by reversing the usual tendencies of the organism that its agitations can be quieted and the mind can know its right and proper place with respect to *purusha:* that of the *known* rather than the *knower* (*Yoga Sutras* 2.10, 4.18–20).[3]

If the notion of the spiritual and the corresponding possibilities of enlightenment, freedom, or salvation are taken seriously, then what is spiritual is almost by definition, as well as by universal consensus, higher than what is intellectual. The intellect is contained in being, as a part in the whole, and not the other way around. It is a universal insight and assertion of the mystics and other spiritual masters that spirit is above the mind. Of course, many words other than "Spirit" have been used to indicate Higher Reality, such as God, Brahman, the One, Tao, the Buddha Mind, and the like. Furthermore, it has been universally said that in order to come to know this Higher Reality in truth, a transformation of the whole being of the seeker is needed to yoke and quiet the mind so that, without any distortions, it may reflect what is real.

Paraphrasing St. Paul, it can be said that the things of the mind can be understood by the mind, but those of the spirit can be understood only by the spirit (1 Cor 2:11–14). It is this spiritual part in a person that needs to be cultivated for the sake of spiritual knowledge. In some traditions, this spiritual part, which like a magnetic compass always tries to orient itself to the north pole of the spirit, is called "soul." This part alone, when properly cultivated, can comprehend and correspond to the suprapersonal and universal spirit. Any other kind of knowledge can be about the spirit but cannot be called knowing the spirit.

Of course, to be against knowledge, scientific or otherwise, is hardly any guarantee of transcending the limitations of the mind. Ignorance is not to be commended. For almost all the sages of India, the ultimate cause of all sorrow or bondage is ignorance. As the Buddha is quoted in the Dhammapada (243) to have said, "*avijja paramam malam*" (ignorance is the greatest impurity). To recognize that a certain kind of knowledge is lower, and that the Undecaying is apprehended by the higher knowledge of a radically different sort, does not deny the necessary role of the lower knowledge. But does a quantitative extension of such knowledge and information necessarily lead to wisdom or spiritual life?

In order to understand the sages and the scriptures spiritually we need to undergo a change of being or a rebirth or a cleansing of our perceptions. How can progress in intellectual, scientific knowledge lead to the sort of insight and transformation that takes one beyond the intellect? An intellectual and physical (that is, scientific) understanding neither requires any transformation of our being nor can lead to such a transformation. Neither scientific knowledge about people who have spiritual knowledge nor theoretical knowledge about the spirit makes one a sage.

At the end, I return to the importance of humility and wonder in the presence of the Great Mystery. In my long experience in academic life, I have been struck by the difficulty of freedom from arrogance of knowledge, a major obstacle to spiritual life. I wonder whether this darkness of intellectual conceit worse than ignorance is what a sage in Isha Upanishad (9) has in mind by saying, "Into blinding darkness enter those who worship ignorance and those who delight in knowledge enter into still greater darkness."

It seems to me that it is a matter of spiritual progress when one becomes free not only of the knowledge that is inevitably from the past, but also from the need to know, which is so often permeated by a fear of the unknown and a desire to predict and control—an attempt to squeeze the Vastness into one's mental categories. In this freedom, one can wonder and stand before the Mystery. In a way, one then knows something; but it is not anything that can be expressed in a way that our ordinary mind can categorize and argue about—it is not anything that can be measured as progress in a quantitative sense. It is closer to an insight into the suchness of things, as in the following remark of Albert Einstein:

> There is the cosmic religious feeling of rapturous amazement at the harmony of natural law, which reveals an intelligence of such superiority that, compared with it, all the systematic thinking and acting of human beings is an utterly insignificant reflection.
>
> The most beautiful thing we can experience is the mysterious. It is the source of all true art and science.
>
> To know that what is impenetrable to us really exists, manifesting itself as the highest wisdom and the most radiant beauty which our dull faculties can comprehend only in their most primitive forms—this knowledge, this feeling, is at the center of true religiousness. In this sense, and in this sense only, I belong in the ranks of devoutly religious men.[4]

RAVI RAVINDRA, PH.D., is Professor Emeritus at Dalhousie University in Halifax, Nova Scotia, from where he retired as Professor and Chairman of Comparative Religion, Professor of International Development Studies, and Adjunct Professor of Physics. He received his doctorate in Physics from the University of Toronto and held postdoctoral fellowships in Physics (University of Toronto), History and Philosophy of Science (Princeton University), and Religion (Columbia University). He was a member of the Institute for Advanced Study in Princeton in 1977 and a Fellow of the Indian Institute of Advanced Study, Shimla, in 1978 and 1998. He was the Founding Director of the Threshold Award for Integrative Knowledge and Chairman of its international and interdisciplinary Selection Committee in 1979 and 1980. Professor Ravindra's books include *Theory of Seismic Head Waves*; *Whispers from the Other Shore*; *The Yoga of the Christ* (also published as *Christ the Yogi* and *The Gospel of John in the Light of Indian Mysticism); Science and Spirit*; *Krishnamurti: Two Birds on One Tree*; *Yoga and the Teaching of Krishna*; *Heart without Measure: Gurdjieff Work with Madame de Salzmann*; *Science and the Sacred*; *Centered Self without Being Self-Centered: Remembering Krishnamurti*; and *Pilgrim without Boundaries*. He was a member of the Board of Judges for the Templeton Prize from 1999 to 2001.

NOTES

1 For some further discussion, see the chapter "Healing the Soul: Truth, Love and God," in R. Ravindra, *Science and the Sacred: Eternal Wisdom in a Changing World*, Wheaton, IL: Quest Books, 2002.

2 For a discussion of many utterances of "I Am" by Christ the Logos (Word, *Purusha*), see R. Ravindra, *The Yoga of the Christ*, Shaftesbury, England: Element Books, 1992, 72–81.

(This book has been reprinted with the same pagination under a misleading title of *Christ the Yogi*, Rochester, VT: Inner Traditions International, 1998.)

3　For a more detailed discussion of Yoga, see R. Ravindra, "Yoga: the Royal Path to Freedom," in *Yoga and the Teaching of Krishna: Essays on the Indian Spiritual Traditions*, ed. Priscilla Murray, 52–71. Adyar, Chennai (Madras): Theosophical Publishing House, 1998.

4　Albert Einstein, *Ideas and Opinions*. Based on *Mein Weltbild*. New York: Crown, 1954, 11.

THE SCIENTIFIC FRONTIER OF THE INNER SPIRIT 95

B. Alan Wallace

AS WE ENTER the twenty-first century and look back on the past four hundred years of scientific progress, can we fail to be impressed by the frontiers of knowledge that have been opened to human inquiry? The physical sciences have illuminated the realm of the extremely minute—the inner core of the atomic nucleus; events in the distant past—the first nanoseconds after the Big Bang; and phenomena on the far side of the universe—the constitution of galactic clusters billions of light-years away. At the same time, the biological sciences have made great discoveries concerning the evolution of life, mapped the human genome, and revealed many of the inner workings of the brain. But in the midst of such extraordinary knowledge of the objective world, the subjective realm of consciousness remains largely an enigma. While neuroscience searches for correlates between the functions of the human brain and the depths of the human spirit, the actual nature of the mind/body correlation is still a matter of philosophical conjecture: No hard scientific evidence explains *how* the mind is related to the brain. There is no scientific consensus concerning the definition of "consciousness," and there are no objective, scientific means of detecting the presence or absence of consciousness in anything—mineral, plant, animal, or human. In short, scientists have not yet fathomed the nature of consciousness, its origins, or its role in Nature.

How is it possible that something so central to scientific inquiry—human consciousness—remains so elusive? Is it because it is inherently mysterious or even impenetrable to scientific inquiry? Or have scientists simply failed thus far to devise appropriate methods for exploring the frontiers of the inner spirit? To seek an answer to this question, let us review the ways in which scientists have successfully explored other realms of the natural world.

Looking first to the physical sciences, astronomy began to move beyond its medieval heritage when researchers such as Tycho Brahe devised instruments for making unprecedentedly accurate measurements of the relative movements of the planets. Whereas previous generations of astrologers were content to focus primarily on the alleged *correlations* between the movements of celestial bodies and terrestrial events, Brahe made careful observations of the planets themselves, albeit with the intention to improve the precision of astrological predictions. Similarly, Galileo made precise observations of falling bodies and other terrestrial and celestial phenomena. In short, careful observations of these natural phenomena themselves were the necessary basis for the subsequent explanation of *why* these physical phenomena act as they do.

The life sciences developed in a similar way. In the seventeenth century, the Dutch naturalist Antoni van Leeuwenhoek used the microscope to observe minute organisms, and over the centuries this combination of technology and precise observation of tiny life forms led to the development of cell biology, molecular biology, genetics, and neuroscience. It is important to bear in mind, however, that what the astronomers, physicists, and biologists were observing were mere *appearances* to the human mind, not external, physical objects existing independently of consciousness. The mind has always played a central role in scientific observation and analysis, yet the scientific study of the mind did not even begin until three hundred years after Galileo. The obvious assumption behind this long delay was that consciousness plays no significant role in Nature. But this is a metaphysical conjecture, not a scientific conclusion. Whether that hypothesis is valid or not, it is certainly an oversight to postpone for three centuries scientific examination of one's primary instrument of observation of the natural world: human consciousness.

At the dawn of the modern science of the mind in the late nineteenth century, the pioneering American psychologist William James defined this new discipline as the study of subjective mental phenomena and their relations to their objects, to the brain, and to the rest of the world (1892). He argued that introspective observation must always be the first and foremost method by which to study these matters, for this is our sole access for observing mental phenomena directly (1890/1950: I:185). This approach parallels that of Brahe, Galileo, and van Leeuwenhoek in the development of astronomy, physics, and biology, respectively: Carefully observe the phenomena themselves before trying to explain their origins or the mechanical laws governing their movements. James added that introspective study of subjective mental events should be complemented with objective examination of their behavioral and neural correlates. Since his time, great advances have been made in the behavioral sciences, and even more stunning progress is taking place in the brain sciences. But James's emphasis on the importance of introspectively observing subjective mental phenomena themselves has been largely ignored, so there has been no comparable development of rigorous methods for observing and experimenting with one's own mental phenomena firsthand.

Progress in astronomy before the time of Brahe and his contemporary Johannes Kepler was hampered by both empirical and theoretical limitations. Empirically, medieval astrologers and astronomers failed to devise new, rigorous methods for precise observation of celestial bodies. They were too caught up in their concern with the terrestrial correlates of celestial events. Theoretically, their research was limited by their unquestioning acceptance of the metaphysical assumptions of Aristotelian logic, Christian theology, and medieval astrology. In a similar fashion, contemporary behavioral and neuroscientific research into the mind is empirically limited by the absence of rigorous methods for observing mental phenomena firsthand. And, theoretically, such inquiry is hampered by the metaphysical assumption that all mental events can be reduced to their neural correlates. This materialist premise is not a scientific conclusion, but an assumption that underlies virtually all scientific research into the mind/body problem.

It is with introspection alone that consciousness and a wide range of other mental phenomena can be examined directly. While this subjective mode of perception is still marginalized by the cognitive sciences, the contemplative traditions of the world have for centuries devised a wide range of methods for rigorously exploring the frontier of the inner spirit. Long before the time of Aristotle, the contemplatives of India, for example, devised sophisticated means of refining the attention, stilling compulsive thoughts, and enhancing the clarity of awareness. This discipline is known as the development of *samadhi*, or deep meditative concentration, which was then used to explore firsthand a wide range of mental phenomena (Wallace 2005a, 2005b).

In profoundly stilling the mind, Hindu and Buddhist contemplatives have allegedly probed beyond the realm of ordinary human thought to an underlying substrate consciousness. In their view, experientially corroborated by hundreds of contemplatives throughout Asia (many of them adhering to diverse philosophical and religious beliefs), the human mind emerges not from the brain, but from this underlying substrate that carries on from one life to the next. This substrate consciousness need not be reified into a kind of ethereal substance or immutable soul, but can be viewed more as a continuum of cumulative experience that carries on after death. In each lifetime, this stream of consciousness is conditioned by the body, brain, and environment with which it is conjoined. In the context of such an embodiment, specific mental processes are contingent on specific brain processes. The brain is necessary for the manifestation of those mental functions once the substrate consciousness is embodied, but it and its interaction with the environment are not sufficient for the occurrence of consciousness. Memories and character traits from one life to the next are stored in this substrate, not in the brain, and past-life memories can allegedly be recalled while in *samadhi*. However, if specific brain functions are impaired, one may lose access to their correlated mental functions as long as the substrate consciousness is conjoined with a body.

Pythagoras, Plato, Origen (a highly influential third-century Christian theologian), and much of the Christian community during the first four centuries of the Common Era affirmed the continuity of individual consciousness from one life to the next. While Augustine thought that souls are likely created because of conditions present at the time of conception, he acknowledged that, as far as he knew, the truth of this hypothesis had not been demonstrated (391/1937: III: chs. 20–21). Moreover, he declared that it was consonant with the Christian faith to believe that souls exist prior to conception and incarnate by their own choice (ibid.: 379). This subject, he claimed, had not been studied sufficiently by Christians to decide the issue. Acceptance of the theory of reincarnation in the Western world decreased from the fifth century onward because of its condemnation by ecclesiastical councils and the decline of contemplative practice in general and of deep meditative concentration in particular.

The theory of the substrate consciousness and its relation to the human mind has not been invalidated by contemporary neuroscience. While James did not advocate reincarnation, he believed that the relation of the workings of the brain to the perceptions of the mind is akin to that of a prism refracting light, rather than an organ (the brain) creating mental events (1989: 85–86). He declared that this nonmaterialist view was compatible with the neuroscientific knowledge of his time, and this remains true today. Thus, no purely scientific grounds exist for assuming a materialist view of the mind. While materialists claim that the burden of proof of the non-physical nature of the mind rests on those who can provide evidence to that effect, this is open to question. Introspective observation of mental phenomena does not suggest that they are physical in nature, nor does it provide knowledge of the brain. Likewise, the study of neural events alone provides no knowledge of the mind; one never sees any mental events in the brain, just electrochemical processes. So it takes a leap of faith to believe that mental events are really brain functions viewed from a subjective perspective. Generally speaking, if one believes that two types of phenomena that *appear* to be radically different are in fact identical, the burden of proof lies in demonstrating their equivalence.

Is the belief that the mind is nothing more than a function, or emergent property, of the brain a scientific hypothesis? If so, there should be some way, at least in principle, to falsify that claim; otherwise, it loses its status as a scientific theory. Insofar as scientific research on the mind/body problem is confined to the study of the behavioral and neural correlates of the subjective experience, it is hard to imagine how one could ever test for the existence of nonphysical mental events. One would need to step outside materialist methodologies to detect anything nonphysical. One viable way to put the materialist hypothesis to the test, thereby establishing its status as a scientific theory, is by studying the empirical evidence suggestive of reincarnation. Such research has been done not only by contemplatives exploring their past-life memories, but by modern researchers, such as psychiatrist Ian Stevenson (1997), probing the mysteries of the human mind.

Stevenson's remarkable work, however, has received little attention by the scientific community. The reason for this may be quite simple. As neurologist Antonio Damasio comments, many neuroscientists are guided by one goal and one hope: to thoroughly explain *how* neural patterns become subjectively experienced mental events (1999: 322). So they do not welcome empirical evidence that might suggest that the goal of their research is illusory. This situation is reminiscent of the goal of medieval astronomers to demonstrate how all celestial bodies move in perfect circles. Eventually, Kepler, who was also committed to this belief, was distressed when the empirical evidence accumulated by Brahe forced him to conclude that this long-held assumption was false. (Kepler later deduced that planetary orbits are elliptical; nevertheless, his preliminary calculations agreed with observations to within 5 percent.)

With the union of scientific and contemplative inquiry, humanity may explore the frontier of the inner spirit in unprecedented ways (Wallace 2000). The importance of such collaborative research can hardly be overestimated. The very nature of human identity is at stake, and those who are committed to the pursuit of truth must rely on rigorous, empirical research, even if it invalidates their most cherished assumptions.

ℒ♥

B. ALAN WALLACE, PH. D., earned his doctorate in religious studies at Stanford University in 1995 after obtaining his undergraduate degree in physics and the philosophy of science at Amherst College. He began his studies of Buddhism in 1970 and has been teaching Buddhist meditation and philosophy in Europe and the United States since 1976. Since 1987, Dr. Wallace has helped organize and served as interpreter for a biannual series of Mind and Life conferences on the relation between Buddhism and modern science with the Dalai Lama and distinguished scientists. He is the author, translator, or editor of, or a contributor to, more than thirty books, among them: *Choosing Reality: A Buddhist View of Physics and the Mind* (Snow Lion Publications), *The Bridge of Quiescence: Experiencing Tibetan Buddhist Meditation* (Open Court), *The Taboo of Subjectivity: Toward a New Science of Consciousness* (Oxford University Press), and *Buddhism & Science: Breaking New Ground* (Columbia University Press). Dr. Wallace is the founder and president of the Santa Barbara Institute for Consciousness Studies (http://sbinstitute.com), which promotes the collaboration of scientific and contemplative modes of inquiry into the nature and potentials of consciousness.

REFERENCES

Augustine. (391/1937) *The Free Choice of the Will.* Francis E. Tourscher (trans.), Philadelphia: The Peter Reilly Co.

Damasio, Antonio. (1999) *The Feeling of What Happens: Body and Emotion in the Making of Consciousness,* New York: Harcourt, Inc.

James, William. (1890/1950) *The Principles of Psychology,* New York: Dover Publications.

———. (1892) "A plea for psychology as a science." *Philosophical Review* 1: 146–53.

———. (1989) *Essays in Religion and Morality,* Cambridge, MA: Harvard University Press.

Stevenson, Ian, M. D. (1997) *Where Reincarnation and Biology Intersect,* Westport, CT: Praeger.

Wallace, B. Alan. (1998) *The Bridge of Quiescence: Experiencing Tibetan Buddhist Meditation.* Chicago: Open Court.

———. (2000) *The Taboo of Subjectivity: Toward a New Science of Consciousness,* New York: Oxford University Press.

———. (2005a) *Genuine Happiness: Meditation as a Path to Fulfillment.* Hoboken, NJ: Wiley & Sons.

———. (2005b) *Balancing the Mind: A Tibetan Buddhist Approach to Refining Attention.* Ithaca, NY: Snow Lion Publications.

FROM BIBLICAL STORY TO THE SCIENCE OF SOCIETY 96

HOW JUDAISM READS SCRIPTURE

Jacob Neusner

SIR JOHN TEMPLETON, who celebrated his ninetieth birthday on November 29, 2002, has taken a keen interest in the relationship of science and religion. Some conceive that relationship to be adversarial, but he has viewed science as a medium for advancing human knowledge about God. Those who see conflict between science and religion treat Scripture as a principal battleground, finding contradictions everywhere between its narratives and the laws of science: Creation in six days, the splitting of the Red Sea, the sun's standing still. But cannot Scripture still serve to support the science-religion relationship when contemplated within a different framework?

Why the conflict? Each side—science and biblical religion—finds fault in the other. Science discovers laws of Nature, and Scripture's miracles disrupt those laws. So, science objects to religion. Some of those who affirm Scripture in the name of Creationism take exception to evolution. So, religion finds fault with science. More recently, archaeology has called into question the very historicity of Scripture's narratives, yet another point of conflict between science and the religious knowledge conveyed by the Hebrew Scriptures of ancient Israel (i.e., the "Old Testament").

How can knowledge attained through the scientific method—experimentation, testing, hypotheses—mesh with the Scriptures that Judaic and Christian faithful affirm to be God-given, the medium of God's self-disclosure? Specifically, is there a science to which Scripture may supply valuable data, and is there a program of reading Scripture that science may illuminate? Judaism in its normative sources, the Torah as mediated by the rabbinic sages of the first six centuries CE, answers both questions with a firm "yes." The answer lies in identifying other models for reading Scripture besides the one that today sets Scripture against science. Such a model exists, subject to critical illumination.

The ancient Rabbinic sages read Scripture as God's design for the science of society, for the social order of a sanctified community. They read the facts of Scripture—its narratives, laws, and exhortations—in the manner of social scientists, looking for the "mathematics" of the social order and finding the design of the entire human society that Scripture sustains. When, therefore, we understand how Judaism reads Scripture, we can take a step toward resolving the conflict of science and religion concerning the role of Scripture—its stories and its miracles.

Why social science? Because, just as natural historians seek laws of created order in Nature, and specifically in natural history, so the Judaic sages searched Scripture for patterns indicating laws subject to generalization and testing. The social sciences undertake the effort to uncover patterns out of diverse information, to test generalizations against episodic observations, and to produce "truth" out of "facts." The quest for hypothesis and validation in other contexts marks the Rabbinic sages' writings as a mode of thought congruent with social, and even natural, science.

The comparison may be simply stated. Just as natural history gains knowledge of God in Nature, so the Judaic sages find knowledge of God through Scripture's privileged narratives, the exemplary cases of the Torah. The "facts" of Scripture pertaining to the social order then correspond to the "facts" of Nature pertaining to Creation. So what is to be hoped from systematically finding the patterns and rules yielded by Nature and society? That mode of thought and inquiry bears the promise of improving our understanding of God's plan and intent in forming our concept and knowledge of "ultimate reality."

Let us turn to concrete matters. Precisely how does Judaism address the rules for society contained in Scripture? And what does Judaism learn about God from Scripture, construed within the science of natural history? We turn to a case that shows how the Rabbinic sages looked for generalizations yielded by the episodic narratives of Scripture.

Specifically, in the manner of natural history, they categorized like data with like, all in the quest for the rule governing them all. This they did in relationship to the social rules of Scripture and also to historical events. Here is a simple example of the progress from Scriptural story to the science of society:

> And Abraham rose early in the morning, [saddled his ass, and took two of his young men with him, and his son Isaac, and he cut the wood for the burnt offering and arose and went to the place which God had told him] (Gen. 22:3).
>
> Said R. Simeon b. Yohai [a second-century CE saint, sage, and legal authority], "Love disrupts the natural order of things, and hatred disrupts the natural order of things."
>
> Love disrupts the natural order of things we learn from the case of Abraham: ". . . he saddled his ass." But did he not have any number of servants? [Why then did a slave not saddle the ass for him? Out of his dedication to his son, Abraham performed that menial task.] That proves love disrupts the natural order of things.
>
> "Hatred disrupts the natural order of things we learn from the case of Balaam: 'And Balaam rose up early in the morning and saddled his ass' (Num. 22:21). But did he not have any number of servants? That proves hatred disrupts the natural order of things.
>
> "Love disrupts the natural order of things we learn from the case of Joseph: 'And Joseph made his chariot ready' (Gen. 46:29). But did he not have any number of servants? But that proves love disrupts the natural order of things.
>
> "Hatred disrupts the natural order of things we learn from the case of Pharaoh: 'And he made his chariot ready' (Ex. 14:6). But did he not have any number of servants? But that proves hatred disrupts the natural order of things." (Genesis Rabbah 55:8)

In this perfect case, four facts of Scripture involving Abraham and his opposite, Balaam, and Joseph and his counterpart, Pharaoh, are classified and contrasted. The common classification is "saddling one's own ass," rather than having a servant do the work. This is taken to signal something extraordinary in the transaction. In the one pair, it is the love of Abraham pitted against the hatred of Balaam, the love of Joseph and the malice of Pharaoh. But they have in common the disruption of the natural order of things. Then the social rule follows: *An excess of emotion, whether love or hatred, leads to the violation of social norms.*

What matters in this humble reading is what has happened in Scripture: The question has shifted. Now we no longer ask, did it *really* happen? That question proves monumentally irrelevant, obtuse even. Nor are we engaged by the scientific facts of the matter. We are unconcerned with questions such as what kind of saddles did they have and whether archaeology proves that the saddles in the time of Abraham and Joseph required servile labor to be put into place. Rather, the question is now: How do patterns yielded by Scripture's widely separated facts yield a rule about the social order? Judaism asks Scripture to supply data for analysis and generalization; that is the main point.

The Rabbinic sages found patterns in Scripture because they took for granted that in revealed narrative they would find the lessons they needed for making sense of their own situation. They searched for patterns, or paradigms, because they experienced existence as a pattern. How so? Living in the centuries beyond the destruction of the Jerusalem Temple in 70 CE, they looked back on *two* calamities in sequence—the loss of Jerusalem and its sacrificial service to the Babylonians in 586 BCE and then the repetition of that event in the recent past, 70 CE. The urgent question facing them was, Does the paradigm of exile and return mean that we are trapped in a cycle of destruction and restoration, exile from the Land and return to the Land? And, if not, then what lessons are we to learn?

They thought paradigmatically. What happened once marked an irreversible historical event. Events that occurred twice represented either a cycle or a paradigm, although determining which was a problem. For sages looking for patterns in Scripture, what had taken place the first time, in 586 BCE, and was thought to be unique and unprecedented took place a second time, in 70 CE, in precisely the same pattern. They therefore formed a series from these individual episodes.

Here is where thinking scientifically, in the manner of natural history with its hierarchical classification, intervened: What conclusion is to be drawn from the destruction of the Temple once again? The choice was between a cycle that recurs and a pattern that yields lessons to be learned *and acted upon.* A theory of the cyclical nature of events might have followed. That theory would have held that, just as Nature yielded its spring, summer, fall, and winter, so the events of humanity or of Israel in particular can have been asked to conform to a cyclical pattern, in line, for example, with Ecclesiastes' view that what has been is what will be. But the Rabbinic sages did not take that position at all.

They rejected cyclicality in favor of a different ordering of events altogether. They did not believe the Temple would be rebuilt and destroyed, rebuilt and destroyed, and so on endlessly. They stated the very opposite: The Temple would be rebuilt but never again destroyed. That represented a view of the second destruction that rejected cyclicality altogether. The sages instead opted for patterns of history and against cycles. That is because they retained that notion for the specific and concrete meaning of events that characterized Scripture's history, even while rejecting the historicism of Scripture. They maintained that a pattern governed, and the pattern was not a cyclical one. Here, Scripture itself imposed its structure, its order, its system—its paradigm. And the Official History—Genesis through Kings read as a continuous narrative—left no room for the conception of cyclicality. If matters do not repeat themselves but do conform to a pattern, then the pattern itself must be identified. That is where natural history enters in.

Paradigmatic thinking formed the alternative to cyclical thinking because Scripture defined how matters were to be understood. Viewed as a whole, the Official History indeed defined the paradigm of Israel's existence, formed out of the components of Eden and the Land, Adam and Israel, and then Sinai. This was given movement through Israel's responsibility to the covenant and Israel's adherence to, or violation of, God's will, fully exposed in the Torah, that marked the covenant of Sinai. Scripture laid matters out, and the sages then drew conclusions that conformed to their experience.

So the second destruction in 70 CE precipitated thinking about paradigms of Israel's life, such as came to full exposure in the thinking behind the reading of Scripture. Here is where the thinking of natural history intervenes: the quest for generalizations out of bits of information. In the case of the destructions of 586 BCE and 70 CE, with the episodes made into a series, the sages' paradigmatic thinking asked different questions from the historical ones posed in 586 BCE. The Rabbinic sages brought to Scripture different premises, drew from Scripture different conclusions. Scripture serves as a collection of data, similar to a laboratory where facts are established. These facts concern relationships and one-time events and exemplary transactions. What do they mean, what lessons do they teach?

Asking these questions does not resolve the conflict between evolution and Creationism. Rather, it turns attention to another set of questions Scripture can be asked to answer, questions that I think are more authentic to the purpose of revelation. The faithful who found—and still find—privileged truth ("God's word," in theological terms) have taken an approach to Scripture that treats its statements as exemplary. And science, with its power to frame hypotheses out of bits and pieces of fact and test theories against new facts, cannot object either. Scientific modes of thought, it would seem, transform the study of Scripture into the science of society. And that is what the great theologians of Judaism and Christianity have undertaken for two millennia.

I conclude with a model of paradigmatic thinking that has served Judaism well for two thousand years and that shows the acutely contemporary lessons to be learned from Scripture, read as the Rabbinic sages teach. It concerns the theology of the destruction of the Temple and bears heavy implications for post-Holocaust theology and the response to calamity in contemporary Judaism:

Rabban Gamaliel, R. Joshua, R. Eleazar b. Azariah, and R. Aqiba were going toward Rome. They heard the sound of the city's traffic from as far away as Puteoli, a hundred and twenty *mil* away. They began to cry, while R. Aqiba laughed.

They said to him, "Aqiba, why are we crying while you are laughing?"

He said to them, "Why are you crying?"

They said to him, "Should we not cry, since gentiles, idolators, sacrifice to their idols and bow down to icons, but dwell securely in prosperity, serenely, while the house of the footstool of our God has been put to the torch and left a lair for beasts of the field?"

He said to them, "That is precisely why I was laughing. If this is how He has rewarded those who anger Him, all the more so [will He reward] those who do his will."

Another time they went up to Jerusalem and go to Mount Scopus. They tore their garments.

They came to the mountain of the house [of the temple] and saw a fox go forth from the house of the holy of holies. They began to cry, while R. Aqiba laughed.

They said to him, "You are always giving surprises. We are crying when you laugh!"

He said to them, "But why are you crying?"

They said to him, "Should we not cry over the place concerning which it is written, 'And the common person who draws near shall be put to death' (Num. 1:51)? Now lo, a fox comes out of it.

"In our connection the following verse of Scripture has been carried out: 'For this our heart is faint, for these things our eyes are dim, for the mountain of Zion which is desolate, the foxes walk upon it' (Lam. 5:17–18)."

He said to them, "That is the very reason I have laughed. For lo, it is written, 'And I will take for me faithful witnesses to record, Uriah the priest and Zechariah the son of Jeberechiah' (Is. 8:2).

And what has Uriah got to do with Zechariah? What is it that Uriah said? 'Zion shall be plowed as a field and Jerusalem shall become heaps and the mountain of the Lord's house as the high places of a forest' (Jer. 26:18).

"What is it that Zechariah said? 'Thus says the Lord of hosts, "Old men and women shall yet sit in the broad places of Jerusalem"' (Zech. 8:4).

"Said the Omnipresent, 'Lo, I have these two witnesses. If the words of Uriah have been carried out, then the words of Zechariah will be carried out. If the words of Uriah are nullified, then the words of Zechariah will be nullified.

"'Therefore I was happy that the words of Uriah have been carried out, so that in the end the words of Zechariah will come about.'"

In this language they replied to him: "Aqiba, you have given us comfort."
(Sifre to Deuteronomy 43:3:7–8)

Here is that pattern of the social order that sages find in Scripture. They lay no claim to set forth the laws of natural science, let alone the history of Creation. They find in Scripture answers to a different order of questions altogether. And in light of current events, I can think of no more telling response to the nihilism of post-Holocaust theology and questions such as, "where was God on 9/11?" than Aqiba's discovery in Scripture of the pattern of revealed truth.

JACOB NEUSNER, PH.D., is Research Professor of Religion and Theology and Senior Fellow of the Institute of Advanced Theology at Bard College. He also is a Member of the Institute for Advanced Study in Princeton, New Jersey, and Life Member of Clare Hall, University of Cambridge. He has published more than 850 books and unnumbered articles, both scholarly and academic and popular and journalistic, and is the most published humanities scholar in the world. He has been awarded nine honorary degrees. He was President of the American Academy of Religion (1968–1969), the only scholar of Judaism to hold that position, and a member of the founding committee of the Association for Jewish Studies (1967–1970). He founded the European Association of Jewish Studies (1980–1981). He also served, by appointment of President Carter, as Member of the National Council on the Humanities and, by appointment of President Reagan, as Member of the National Council on the Arts in 1978–1984 and 1984–1990, respectively.

Jonathan Sacks

HISTORY is a journey, and for any journey we need to ask two questions: How do we get there? And, where do we want to go? If we cannot answer the first we get lost. If we fail to ask the second, we may not even know we are lost. That is why we must always have a dialogue between technology and ethics. Technology is the map, ethics the destination; and the more power we have, the more is at stake in how we use it—to heal or harm, mend or destroy. What is fascinating is that the Bible offers a deep perspective on this dialogue, and it does so in its opening chapters. To a surprising degree, its story is ours.

The book of Genesis contains not one account of creation, but two, each supplementing the other. The first is Genesis 1, one of the defining texts of the Western imagination: "And God said, Let there be . . . and there was . . . and God saw that it was good." Contemporary science has added a rich layer of commentary to this spare and multidimensional narrative. We now know about the Big Bang and its astonishing explosion of energy, the formation of atoms coalescing into stars, the emergence of planets, and the birth on earth of ever-more sophisticated forms of life, their ordered complexity swimming against the tide of entropy. The more we discover, the more wondrous and improbable it seems. I, for one, am moved each time I read of a new scientific discovery, to say in the words of Psalm 104, "How many are your works, O Lord. You have made them all in wisdom."

The aspect of God emphasised in Genesis 1 is mirrored in its portrait of mankind. By making Homo sapiens "in his image," the creative God endowed humanity with the power to create. "Be fruitful and increase in number; fill the earth and subdue it." God in the Bible is not like the gods of ancient myth who kept their knowledge to themselves and were angry when Prometheus stole the secret of making fire. Instead, he *wants* us to learn in pursuit of knowledge, fathoming the inner structures of matter and life. Genesis 1 is the biblical mandate for science and technology. It is about how God and human beings *create*.

But the Bible is a subtle book, and its stories rarely end where we expect them to. Genesis 2 contains a second account of creation. This time the vantage point has changed. We no longer see the whirl of galaxies and the echoing vastnesses of space. The focal point of this second account is not man the biological species, but rather the individual, the self, the person. We see God fashioning the first man "from the dust of the ground," breathing into him "the breath of life." There is a tenderness here, a human dimension that we miss in the first chapter. Man is charged not to dominate the earth, but "to serve it and protect it." For the first time the phrase "not good" is heard. "It is not good for man to be alone." God makes the first woman, and waking, man utters the first poem: "This is now bone of my bones and flesh of my flesh." Genesis 2 is about how God and human beings *relate*.

The first chapter is about how order emerges from chaos. The second is about how we redeem our solitude. The first is about power, the second about love. Technology is the ability to control, but true relationship is not. (I love the remark made by one young mother, who said, "Now that I've become a parent, I can relate to God. Now I know what it's like to create something you can't control!") Ethics in the Bible is born in the recognition that the human other has a dignity and independence that must be respected. That is why ethical relationships are based not on dominance or exploitation, but on the coming together of persons in a bond of trust. Without the ability to create, love is lame. But without the ability to relate, technology is blind.

That is why over and above the question, "How?" religion poses the question, "Why?" Science tells us what is. Technology tells us what could be. But the great faiths tell us what should be. In Genesis 1, God invites us to explore, discover, invent, create. Genesis 2, though, is the corollary. It is about where, ultimately, we seek to be. It suggests that the world we make should honour the world God made. It tells us that we were placed on Earth "to serve it and protect it." It asks us to honour other persons as "bone of my bones and flesh of my flesh." Without a sense of destination, we risk the fate of the fabled Russian politician who said, "Comrades, yesterday we stood on the edge of the abyss, but today we have taken a giant step forward!"

By any standards, we live in an age of astonishing technological advance. The twentieth century alone saw the invention of television, the computer, the Internet, the laser beam, the credit card, artificial intelligence, satellite communication, organ transplantation, and microsurgery. We have sent space probes to distant planets, photographed the birth of galaxies, fathomed the origins of the universe, and decoded the genetic structure of life itself.

And yet, today, 1.3 billion people—22 percent of the world's population—live below the poverty line; 841 million are malnourished; 880 million are without access to medical care; 1 billion lack adequate shelter; 1.3 billion have no access to safe drinking water; 2.6 billion go without sanitation. Among the children of the world, 113 million—two-thirds of them girls—go without schooling; 150 million are malnourished; 30,000 die each day from preventable diseases.

Even in the advanced economies of the West, there has been an unprecedented rise in depressive illness, suicide and suicide attempts, drug and alcohol abuse, violence and crime. Since the 1960s, in virtually all the liberal democracies of the West, divorce rates have risen six times, the number of children born outside of marriage five times, and the number of children living with a lone parent three times. Children have become the victims of modernity. In the United States, every three hours gun violence takes a child's life. Every nine minutes a child is arrested for a drug or alcohol offence. Every minute an American teenager has a baby. Every twenty-six seconds a child runs away from home.

Technology transforms the scope of our power, but the great human questions remain. We can communicate instantaneously across the globe—but can we communicate with our marriage partners, our children, our neighbours? We can travel great distances with astonishing speed, but can we traverse the greatest distance of all, between one centre of consciousness and another, my "I" and your "Thou"? In Arecibo, Puerto Rico, a vast reflector telescope scans the heavens for sounds of intelligent life in outer space, yet we can be deaf to the cry of children in our midst. Looking up, we see a heaven of more than a billion galaxies, each with more than a billion stars. Looking down, we see the human body with its hundred trillion cells, each of which contains a double copy of the human genome with its 3.1 billion letters of genetic code. Yet looking forward, there is one thing we do not and will never know: what tomorrow may bring. The future remains the undiscovered country. How then do we face it without fear? By knowing that we are not alone. "I will fear no evil, for you are with me."

The two creation accounts of Genesis complement each other, and we must be mindful of both. From the dawn of civilization, humankind has reflected on its place in the universe. Compared with all there is, we are each infinitesimally small. We are born, we live, we act, we die. At any given moment our deeds are at best a hand waving in the crowd, a ripple in the ocean, dust on the surface of eternity. The world preceded us by billions of years, and it will survive equally long after we die. How is our life related to the totality of things? To this, there have always been two ways of conceptualizing an answer.

One sees the universe in terms of vast impersonal forces. For the ancients, they were earthquakes, floods, famines, droughts. Today, we would probably identify them as the environment, the global economy, the genetic stream, and technological change. What they have in common is that they are indifferent to us, just as a tidal wave is indifferent to what it sweeps away. Global warming does not choose its victims. Economic recession does not stop to ask who suffers. Genetic mutation happens without anyone deciding to whom.

Seen in this perspective, the forces that govern the world are essentially blind. We may stand in their path, or we may step out of the way. But they are unmoved by our existence. They do not relate to us as persons. In such a world, *hubris* (the idea that we can change things) is punished by *nemesis*. Human hope is a prelude to tragedy. The best we can aim for is to seize what pleasure comes our way and make ourselves stoically indifferent to our fate. This is a coherent vision, but a bleak one.

In Genesis 2, a different vision was born, one that saw in the cosmos the face of the personal: God who brought the universe into being as parents conceive a child, not blindly but in love. We are not insignificant, nor are we alone. We are here because someone willed us into being, who wanted us to be, who knows our innermost thoughts, who values us in our uniqueness, whose breath we breathe, and in whose arms we rest—someone in and through whom we are connected to all that is.

That discovery was utterly new and explosive in its implications. It meant that although decoding the natural universe may involve identifying forces or powers, the key to the human universe is the personal—and the personal is anything but blind. All else in the Bible flows from the attempt to make this fact the foundation of a new social order. The question then becomes not, How can we manipulate Nature? but What relationships honour the dignity of the person—of all persons in their dependence and independence? We redeem the world to the degree that we personalize it, taming the great forces so that they serve rather than dominate humanity. That was and remains a marvellous vision. It changed and still challenges the world.

Through God, our ancestors found themselves. Hearing God reaching out, they began to understand the significance of human beings reaching out to one another. Through the words of revelation, they learned that God is not just about power, but also about relationship; that God is found not only in Nature, but also in society, in the structures we make to honour his presence by honouring his image in other human beings.

We must never lose the ethical dimension of technology, the Genesis 2 that weaves its counterpoint to Genesis 1. To the question, Where do we want to go? the answer must surely be: to enhance human dignity; to respect the image of God in the neighbour and the stranger; to make our world a less random, cruel, capricious place; feeding the hungry, tending the sick, healing the brokenhearted, and binding up their wounds.

Every technological advance brings in its wake two opposing dangers. One is portrayed in the Bible in the story of Babel—the hubris that says: we have godlike powers, therefore let us take the place of God. The other is the paralyzing fear that says: in the name of God, let us not use these godlike powers at all. Both, I believe, are wrong. Every technology carries with it the possibility of diminishing or enhancing the human situation. What we need are what I call the three Rs: *reverence* in the face of creation, *restraint* that comes from knowing that not everything we can do we should do, and *responsibility* to those many lives that will be affected tomorrow by what we do today.

✑

JONATHAN SACKS has been Chief Rabbi of Britain and the Commonwealth since September 1, 1991. When appointed, he was Principal of Jews' College, London, the world's oldest rabbinical seminary. He has been rabbi of two major London synagogues. Educated at Cambridge, where he obtained first-class honors in Philosophy, he pursued postgraduate studies at Oxford and King's College, London. In 1990, he delivered the BBC Reith Lectures on The Persistence of Faith. In 2001, the Chief Rabbi was awarded a Lambeth Doctorate in Divinity by the Archbishop of Canterbury. Rabbi Sacks has been Visiting Professor of Philosophy at the University of Essex, Sherman Lecturer at Manchester University, Riddell Lecturer at Newcastle University, and Cook Lecturer at the Universities of Oxford, Edinburgh, and St. Andrews. He holds honorary doctorates from the universities of Cambridge, Glasgow, Middlesex, Haifa, Yeshiva University, New York, the University of Liverpool, and St. Andrews University, and he is an honorary fellow of Gonville and Caius College, Cambridge, and King's College, London. He holds a number of visiting professorships. The Chief Rabbi is a frequent contributor to the national media. He is the author of fourteen books, many of which have been serialized by *The Times*.

A WINDOW FOR RESEARCH

Margaret Poloma

In the coming age we must all become mystics—or be nothing at all.
—*Karl Rahner*

ALTHOUGH modern science has enabled us to abandon the flat-world view of reality and to replace it with the four-dimensional (4-D) perspective of space-time, scientists increasingly are questioning whether the empirical world as we know it is all there is. Religious believers of all ages and persuasions have professed and continue to profess a reality that somehow transcends the four dimensions. In this brief piece, I would like to explore how Pentecostal/Charismatic (P/C) worship can provide a window for research into another dimension of reality commonly referred to in religious writings as "mysticism."

Who Are the Pentecostal/Charismatics?

Pentecostals and their neo-Pentecostal cousins, commonly referred to as "Charismatics," are biblically orthodox Christians who believe that the "gifts of the Holy Spirit" as found in the Acts of the Apostles operate today just as they did in the first-century church. The roots of classical Pentecostalism are found in early-twentieth-century revivals, while many Charismatics trace their origins to the Charismatic Renewal in mainline churches and the countercultural Jesus People Movement in the 1960s and 1970s. The latter gave birth to the so-called Third Wave and the revivals of the 1990s, whose followers may eschew both the Pentecostal and the Charismatic label. Although differing in social context and articulation of specific beliefs, the Pentecostals and neo-Pentecostals (Charismatics) share a common worldview and are generally regarded as a distinct stream of Christianity. "Pentecostalism" has been used generically to refer to the entire movement, but I prefer the compounded term to remind readers that this movement includes both the historic Pentecostalism of the early twentieth century and various forms of neo-Pentecostalism birthed in the second half of the century.

Although assuming diverse structural forms, P/C Christianity nevertheless represents a single cohesive movement reflecting an alternative worldview. The movement that historians date to the beginning years of the twentieth century now accounts for an estimated half-billion believers worldwide and is growing. Its fuzzy denominational boundaries, reticulate and weblike organizational matrices, and syncretistic tendencies (particularly in developing countries) have been catalytic in blurring traditional denominational, ethnic, and geographical divisions. What binds adherents together is a core religious worldview or spirituality that makes them active members of an unseen Kingdom (of God) empowering them to speak in tongues, heal the sick, work miracles, prophesy, and drive out demons. The P/C worldview is a curious blend of premodern miracles, modern technology, and a postmodern mysticism in which the natural merges with the supernatural. Signs and wonders analogous to those described in the premodern biblical accounts are expected as normal occurrences in the lives of believers. Rejecting a Cartesian dualism that separates body from spirit, P/C believers regard "supernatural" phenomena as "natural" experiences.

The P/C worldview is experientially centered, with its followers in a dynamic and personal relationship with a deity who is both immanent and transcendent. God is seen as active in all events. It is a worldview that tends to be "transrational," professing that knowledge is not limited to the realms of reason and sensory experience. Consistent with this transrational characteristic, P/C Christians also tend to be anti-creedal, believing that "knowing" comes from a personal and intimate relationship with God rather than through systematic theology, human reason, or even the five senses. Theirs is a God who is in a loving relationship with each believer, a Divinity who can defy the seeming "laws" of nature. For the most part, however, the P/C worldview incorporates science and technology, believing that God commonly uses modern developments for the betterment of humankind. In summary, a P/C paradigm for truth develops out of an intimate and experiential knowledge of God that alters the believer's approach to experiencing and interpreting reality. Whatever else they may be, P/C Christians tend to be mystics.

P/C Believers as "Main Street" Mystics

I believe that mysticism is a common and possibly universal human experience found in all cultures. Recent research suggests that in its "core" form, it is "natural" to the human species. Psychologist Ralph W. Hood and his collaborators, in accord with other similar studies of cross-cultural mysticism, recently confirmed reports of introversive mysticism (sometimes called a "pure consciousness experience") in both the United States and Iran. Although the unity experience may be universal, the interpretations given to it are contextual and reflect the sociocultural milieu in which they are experienced. Unlike introversive mysticism, interpretations (which have been termed "extroversive mysticism") appear to lack a common core that can be readily found across religious traditions. Not surprisingly, many P/C believers recognize that paranormal experiences are not unique to Christianity, but would eschew any universalistic interpretations. While regarding their experiences as being of divine origin, they commonly teach that paranormal experiences outside their fold are the work of demons.

It is best here not to get sidetracked with the different interpretive schema, as so often happens with a cognitively driven social science of religion. My research on revival experiences of P/C Christians suggests that "pure consciousness experience" (described as entering into God's presence—encounters that leave believers with feelings of love, peace, and joy) is commonplace. The vast majority (nine out of ten) of those involved in the recent revivals reported, for example, that they are more in love with Jesus than they have ever been and that they now know the Father's love in a dramatically new way. Although visions, dramatic physical manifestations, healing in various forms, and prophetic insights are the first things to capture the attention of the uninitiated, at the heart of the revival testimonies are claims of a deeper awareness of the presence and love of God.

In sum, as discussed in detail in my book *Main Street Mystics*,[1] whatever else they are, P/C Christians are modern mystics who walk Main Street. While some of their experiences are as old as shamanism, their interpretations are rooted in Judeo-Christian biblical writings. Their encounter with mysticism is more than a private experience. The medium through which divine empowerment is given and received tends to be communal, particularly in its worship rituals in revitalized P/C churches, in worldwide conferences, and as practiced on Main Street. For many P/C adherents, these mystical experiences occur in a communal setting with spiritual empowerment that has corporate consequences.

P/C Ritual as a Holistic Experience

P/C worship is not designed to talk about God, but to provide opportunities for communion with the divine. Like the expressive religions that preceded it (including that of the Shakers and the Quakers), Pentecostalism encourages worship that engages the individual's spirit, mind, and body within an interpersonal setting. Its worship is holistic in at least two important ways: (1) it involves an entire range of human faculties, including the precognitive and somatic, and (2) its practice is not limited to so-called sacred spaces.

On a personal level, P/C ritual encompasses all three components—spirit, mind, and body—or what Paul MacLean has called the "triune brain," a concept used by the late anthropologist Victor Turner in an attempt to reconcile culturology and neurology. The "instinctual" or "reptilian" brain can find expression in bodily manifestations, especially through glossolalia (speaking in tongues), but also in jerking, shaking, falling, and other seemingly involuntary somatic actions. The "emotional" or "old mammalian" brain finds its expression in a wide range of emotions during P/C rituals where both tears and laughter, sometimes occurring simultaneously, are welcome. The "neo-mammalian" brain with its left and right sectors can be found in both intuitive/prophetic and cognitive/rational expressions. Because their worship services are ideally more than left-brained exercises, early Pentecostals were disparagingly called "holy rollers," and contemporary ones are often critiqued as "mindless." A more neutral and informed description of P/C ritual and its practitioners recognizes the opportunity it provides for catharsis that is rare in contemporary society.

P/C worship, particularly in its revivalist form, seeks to retain a permeable structure where diverse expressions of worship are encouraged. Victor Turner succinctly described religious ritual as being "antistructural, creative, often carnivalesque and playful," a description that fits P/C worship well. Especially during waves of revival that have occurred with regularity throughout P/C history, its worship provides an example of what Turner referred to as "liminality," a phase of culture that is characterized by the subjunctive rather than indicative moods. It is often, to use Turner's description, "a storehouse of possibilities, not a random assemblage but a striving after new forms and structures. . . ." Through the adept use of music, communal prayer, preaching, or teaching, the heavens are opened and God enters to breathe life into the gathering. A palpable presence is often experienced, reflecting what Turner has called "communitas" or what Emile Durkheim referred to as "collective effervescence." Recent revivals have produced services that are partylike, with somatic manifestations of spiritual drunkenness and holy laughter, but they have also spawned somber times with sounds of loud weeping and wailing and cries for divine mercy. For many, these cathartic rituals are both healing and empowering, experiences that have led some to move beyond the sacred space of churches to take to the streets what they have received.

Although P/C Christians have houses of worship, many of their number worship in seemingly secular settings. From the storefront churches and abandoned theaters that characterized much of early Pentecostalism (and still can be found among residents of inner cities), modern and more affluent suburban descendants have set up worship facilities in rented public facilities, especially school auditoriums and civic centers, as well as sports arenas. Although most might aspire to own a typical suburban church and eventually do, the makeshift churches are reflective of the P/C worldview. The natural and the supernatural, the secular and the sacred, the modern and the premodern, and religion and science are more permeable categories for P/C Christians than they are for most modernists. Increasingly they are taking their services to the streets, where young followers can be found singing and praying on the beaches of California or leading worship for the homeless on the streets of downtown Atlanta. Some complement their churches with "healing centers" in rented facilities that are beginning to dot the American landscape or round-the-clock (24/7) "houses of prayer" that are springing up in major cities. Still others take their empowered worldview to their professions where they might pray for healing or incorporate their intuitive abilities into secular counseling techniques. Entrepreneurial followers have set up booths at Renaissance or New Age fairs to pray for healing or to provide dream analysis (prophecy). These ritual exhibitions are not intended for show or for profit, but rather for bringing others into the "Kingdom of God" as followers have experienced it. Through their empowered prayer, many report release from addictions, the lifting of depression, reconciliation in relationships, physical healing, and other modern-day miracles.

P/C Worship and Future Research

As an insider and sociological investigator of the P/C movement for a quarter of a century, I have seen a noticeable improvement in the quality and quantity of scholarly literature on the topic. Few scholars beyond those interested in religious studies, however, have seen the potential significance of moving beyond sociohistorical description toward better explanations of P/C phenomena. Few recognize the window that interdisciplinary study of Pentecostal experience can provide for seeing beyond a modernist 4-D reality.

The P/C movement provides a metaphysical and mystical way of approaching the world for an estimated half-billion people around the globe. Although its growth is much slower and its worldview more domesticated by the forces of modernism in the Western world than in Asia, Africa, and South America, revivals and renewals have continued to revitalize American Pentecostalism throughout its hundred-year history. Waves of renewal ebb and flow, with each wave seeming to leave a clearer articulation of a democratized approach to receiving empowering spiritual gifts.

Scientific research into the P/C "gifts of the Spirit" seems to have begun and ended with the study of glossolalia. Although sometimes made the litmus test for identifying a "true" P/C Christian, more commonly Pentecostal ideology recognizes its limitations. Given its private rather than corporate nature, tongues may be but an entryway to other paranormal gifts that are experienced interpersonally. Prophecy, in its many forms, and divine healing are commonly held in higher accord because of their relevance for the community, but to date scholars have demonstrated little interest in them. The empowerment that the P/C movement claims to experience through its worship rituals suggests a window for scientists to explore another dimension of reality commonly experienced around the globe in Christian and possibly non-Christian contexts.

To study P/C worship rituals scientifically requires teamwork that crosses disciplines. Sociology, history, anthropology, linguistics, and to some extent psychology have already made pioneering efforts to discover the nature of P/C beliefs and practices. Their descriptive findings need to be explored further through the lenses offered by other scientific disciplines. Findings from studies of corporate mystical experience as found in P/C ritual might cast light on a fourth dimension of reality beyond space and time as we know it. These findings have the potential to teach modernists more about what it means to be fully human.

ᴵ℘

MARGARET POLOMA, PH.D., is professor emerita at the University of Akron where she was professor of sociology until her retirement in 1995. During this time, she also accepted visiting professorships at various seminaries and universities. Early retirement has permitted Professor Poloma to focus her research and teaching on her longstanding interest in the integration of spirituality and social science. For much of her career as a sociologist, Professor Poloma has allowed her experiential religious faith and her work as a sociologist to peacefully coexist. Although at times she felt very alone, many others are now engaged in the dialectic, trying to use scientific tools to study the things of the spirit. She feels it is a privilege to stand on the shoulders of Pitirim Sorokin, whose creative sociology on love, which had been eclipsed by the rise of positivism, is now receiving new recognition. Professor Poloma has written five books, including *Main Street Mystics: The Toronto Blessing and Reviving Pentecostalism* (AltaMira Press, 2003), and numerous book chapters and articles.

NOTE

1 *Main Street Mystics: The Toronto Blessing and Reviving Pentecostalism* (AltaMira Press, 2003).

RENEWING THE CONVERSATION

James L. Heft

I T IS TIME for the Catholic Church to resume its conversation with science, a conversation that has never been completely broken off. Over the past fifty years, the Catholic Church has grown into a different understanding of itself and its relationship to science. The Church has taken history more seriously, has understood the Bible better in its historical and cultural contexts, has welcomed dialog with those who think differently, and has come to a clearer understanding of its responsibility for the human rights of the whole human family, especially the poor. It now does not hesitate to recognize the great achievements of modern science, even if it continues to raise questions about their moral applications. It accepts science's independence. The time is ripe for a fruitful conversation.

There are historical and theological precedents for this new conversation. From the time of its origins, and especially in the fourth century, Christianity developed a respectful relationship of intellectual engagement with the Greek and Roman cultures. The Church also affirmed, it might be said, three "revelations": the revelation of God through the creation of the world at the beginning of time, the revelation of God personally in Jesus Christ, and the revelation of the Holy Spirit at Pentecost, which marked the birth of the Church itself. In fact, during the Middle Ages, the Church actually created the conditions for modern science. It then laid the foundations of modern science with its conviction that the world—God's first revelation—is open to rational investigation and that it has within it an order that can be understood.

But as happens in many long-term human relationships, the Church's relationship with science underwent serious strains. That relationship included a spirited and sometimes tense give-and-take between faith and reason, between technological power and the common good, between the desire to know and the desire to dominate. At the beginning of the modern era, science declared its independence and assumed it could go it better alone. Some scientists even thought they could explain everything. The Church opposed these scientists, judging that they were Promethean in their claims. Even though scientists have unleashed some energies that have caused dreadful human catastrophes, they have also made some extraordinary discoveries, sometimes at first opposed by the Church, that have extended and improved the human condition immensely.

But we live in a time when the conversation between the Church and science can begin anew. The Vatican has established the Pontifical Academy of Sciences, through which some of the leading scientists of the world, many of whom are not Catholics, gather to discuss their research and its ramifications for the human family. Perhaps the most striking example of the new possibilities for conversation is a little-known letter, dated September 1987, written by Pope John Paul II to Fr. George V. Coyne, S.J., director of the Vatican Observatory. The letter was occasioned by an international conference held to commemorate the three hundredth anniversary of Newton's *Philosophiae Naturalis Principia Mathematica*. It addresses the relationship of natural science, philosophy, and theology. In it, the pope draws attention to the fragmented state of the world, the growing division between rich and poor nations, and "the antagonism between races and religions that splits countries into warring camps." At the same time, he notes the openness of many in the scientific community to dialog and the search for coherence and collaboration. He says that the time is ripe for a renewed conversation between the Church and modern science, noting that in recent years there has been "a definite, though still fragile and provisional, movement towards a new and more nuanced interchange." The pope does not hesitate to ask some very bold questions about what the Church might learn from modern science:

> If the cosmologies of the ancient Near Eastern world could be purified and assimilated into the first chapters of Genesis, might contemporary cosmology have something to offer to our reflections upon creation? Does an evolutionary perspective bring any light to bear upon theological anthropology, the meaning of the human person as the *imago Dei*, the problem of Christology—and even upon the development of doctrine itself? What, if any, are the eschatological implications of contemporary cosmology, especially in light of the vast future of our universe? Can theological method fruitfully appropriate insights from scientific methodology and the philosophy of science?

The pope's questions exemplify a humility and profound openness to the discoveries of modern science. He sees mutual benefit in the conversation and states that "science can purify religion from error and superstition; religion can purify science from idolatry and false absolutes. Each can draw the other into a wider world, a world in which both can flourish." One is reminded of Albert Einstein's statement of a half-century earlier: "Religion without science is blind, science without religion is lame." Or, in the light of the pope's statement, religion without the benefit of science runs the risk of misinterpreting some of its own sacred texts (e.g., taking literally the two stories of creation in the book of Genesis or thinking that Scripture teaches that the Earth is the center of the universe). Science without the benefit of religion runs the risk of trying to explain everything and, in the process, losing the bigger picture (as it does in the case of various forms of reductionism; for example, of claiming that the mind is only the brain or that consciousness can be fully explained by the ways in which neurons interact).

So much for the pope's openness (which echoes that of many Catholic thinkers) to a conversation with modern science. What about modern scientists? Are they ready to reciprocate and enter that conversation with the Church? A number of recent developments would seem to suggest a positive answer. Developments in modern physics suggest that our ever-expanding universe may well have had a beginning. Physics also tells us that, however precise our instruments, we cannot get a fully objective picture of what we are looking at. Modern biology and environmental studies show us that for us to live at all we require special and hospitable ecological systems. In the striking words of theoretical physicist Freeman Dyson (who contributed an essay in this volume), "I do not feel like an alien in the universe. The more I examine the universe and study the details of its architecture, the more evidence I find that the universe in some sense must have known that we were coming."[1]

Some years ago, the great chemist-turned-philosopher of science Michael Polanyi showed how in order to draw experimental conclusions, all scientists must first affirm a certain worldview, one that they can not account for scientifically. The fact that most scientists do this, unconscious of that fact that they are doing so, makes it no less true that they do it. Several decades earlier in another field, the great mathematician Kurt Goedel showed that it is impossible to demonstrate that any mathematical system is both complete and consistent. In other words, every mathematical system depends on true statements that it cannot demonstrate. These and other discoveries provide grounds for a degree of humility among scientists. These discoveries make clearer the limitations of their scientific disciplines. If scientists have discovered many of the limitations of their disciplines, they should feel them even more when they turn to the great human questions that theologians and philosophers address. As the eminent psychologist William James wrote a century ago, "The science of religions would forever have to confess, as every science confesses, that the subtlety of nature flies beyond it, and that its formulas are but approximations." For that matter, not just the scientists who study religion but also theologians and philosophers should say essentially the same thing about their own capabilities to articulate who God is and what the world is for.

We may conclude, then, from the pope's letter and from recent scientific discoveries that the time is ripe for a renewed conversation between Catholicism and science. Conversations take time; they also benefit from a supportive environment. A new institute dedicated to facilitating such conversations was recently established at the University of Southern California: the Institute for Advanced Catholic Studies (IACS, http://www.ifacs.com/main.asp). Several factors drove the foundation of this Institute. The first is the realization of the profound impact institutes for advanced studies have had on the intellectual developments of the past decades. The institutes at Princeton, North Carolina, Washington DC, Palo Alto, and Berkeley have provided support for multiple breakthroughs in scholarship in the humanities, the physical sciences, and the social sciences. None of these institutes, however, supports much research in religion—still less specifically on Catholicism. Given the recent decline of the great religious orders in the West that have enriched Catholic intellectual traditions over the centuries, IACS—independent and yet fully committed to exploring and developing the intellectual resources of Catholicism—meets an especially urgent need of the Church and the world today.

Catholic intellectual traditions reach far back into history and have assumed many forms and expressions. Like all great traditions, Catholicism represents, in the words of philosopher Alisdair MacIntyre, a historically extended and socially (and artistically) embodied conversation. Not only theologians and philosophers, but also scientists, historians, poets, artists, and musicians give it breadth and depth, texture and shape. Their faith informed their scholarly and cultural traditions, which in turn enriched their faith. The purpose of this Institute is to develop and deepen Catholic intellectual and cultural traditions—and to do so through engaging many of the major issues that face the world today. The goal of IACS is to have eight to ten scholars in place at any given time. When fully operational, it will welcome twenty to twenty-five fellows a year, at least five from other parts of the world than the United States, from all fields and from different faiths or from no religious faith.

Today, scholars most often work in modern universities. These universities are built on the specialization of knowledge. However, specialization "fragments" knowledge because of the unavoidable consequence of "small domain" expertise. In a world of increasing specialization, the good news is that major advances also have come through interdisciplinary research. IACS will encourage this tendency within its specific domain, seeking to enrich and expand the Catholic tradition of scholarship and theological research. Our aim is to bring together specialists and generalists in and across many fields. Our mission will foster cross-disciplinary research and conversation. This approach, we hope, will precisely arrive at a more holistic vision of reality, one that will include a historical perspective as well as philosophical and theological reflections. We affirm a strategic perspective that a holistic vision of reality is desperately needed in our "theologically unchallenged culture."

One of the clearly most important conversations the Institute will facilitate is the dialog between Catholicism and science. The influence of modern science and its application through technology profoundly affects most aspects of modern life. The revolution in information technologies, the genome project, and recent discoveries about the human brain by neuroscientists deeply affect the way we think of ourselves and the way we act. Few theologians and philosophers, however, are deeply engaged within the cultures of modern science. A mirror-image problem is that few scientists know enough philosophy and theology to locate their discoveries in a rich and nuanced way within a larger context of meaning. Having interdisciplinary conversations does not necessarily mean becoming incompetent in two disciplines. Rather, it means that theologians and scientists find the time to learn from one another what they need to know to better appreciate the significance of what they do and how it can contribute to the enhancement of life on this planet.

What scholars most want is time and a stimulating environment. At IACS, scholars will be fully supported for periods of ten months. They will have the benefit and leisure of scholarly support to pursue their research in depth, engage at length in conversations across disciplines, and, in that stimulating environment, create a network of colleagues from many disciplines and different religions interested in learning from one another. If the pope can ask with sincerity whether evolutionary perspectives might shed any new light on how Christians think theologically of Jesus Christ, surely scientists can ask whether theological insights might shed new light on the challenges of understanding how progress in the science of genetics might be engaged in a responsible manner with new concepts affecting our view of the nature and dignity of the human person. Happily, the Catholic Church is open to such a dialog, and IACS is prepared to provide a place and a community of scholars in which new productive conversations between intellectual and scientific leaders can flourish.

ℐ♥

JAMES L. HEFT, S.M., PH.D., is University Professor of Faith and Culture and Chancellor at the University of Dayton. He received his doctorate from the University of Toronto in Historical Theology in 1977. Fr. Heft served as Chair of the Religious Studies Department at the University of Dayton from 1983 to 1989 and as Provost from 1989 to 1996, at which time he was appointed to his current position. He also devotes much of his time to the Institute for Advanced Catholic Studies at the University of Southern California, of which he is the President and Founding Director. Fr. Heft is the author of *John XXII (1316–1334) and Papal Teaching Authority* (Mellen Press, 1986) and has edited *Faith and the Intellectual Life* (Notre Dame Press, 1996), *A Catholic Modernity? An Essay by Charles Taylor* (Oxford University Press, 1999), and *Beyond Violence: Religious Sources for Social Transformation* (Fordham University Press, 2004). Currently, he is working on a book on Catholic higher education. Fr. Heft's article entitled "Mary of Nazareth, Feminism and the Tradition," co-authored with Una Cadegan, won the 1990 Catholic Press Association award for best scholarly article. He has authored more than 150 articles and book chapters and serves on the editorial board of two journals, as well as served on numerous boards and, most recently, chaired the board of directors of the Association of Catholic Colleges and Universities.

NOTE

1 Freeman J. Dyson, *Disturbing the Universe* (New York: Harper & Row, 1979), 250.

THE PILGRIM SOUL FOLLOWS THE "KINDLY LIGHT"

Russi M. Lala

> The breath of God allows each human mind to unfold according
> to its genius . . . the whole man is quickened, his senses are new senses,
> his emotions new emotions, his reason, his affections,
> his imagination, are all new born.
> —*R. W. Trine, "In Tune with the Infinite"*[1]

FOR EIGHTEEN YEARS until April 2003, I was director of one of the largest foundations in India: the Sir Dorabji Tata Trust, Mumbai (Bombay). In this essay, I touch on the faith of a foundation. But primarily I focus on the foundation of my faith. My hope is that my personal reflections help to illuminate the quest for "spiritual information" as I have known it in my work and in my life.

Spiritual Information and Philanthropic Pursuits

There are two ways to start institutions. One is to build the institution and then look for a director to head it. This is what Sir John Templeton did by starting his Foundation to investigate the confluence of science and spirituality and then hiring a planetary scientist, Dr. Charles Harper, as its executive director. The other is to find the director and then build an institution around him. This is what the Trustees of the Sir Dorabji Tata Trust did by taking note of the very good social work that an American missionary, Clifford Manshardt, was doing in Bombay in the 1930s and accepting his proposal to start the Tata Institute of Social Sciences. The Trust gave India not only its first Institute of Social Sciences in 1936, but also its first Hospital for Cancer in 1941 and its first Institute of Fundamental Physics in 1945. It pursued its mission with compassionate outreach and intellectual rigor.

A philanthropic organization such as The Trust has to deal with the emerging needs of a nation on a number of different fronts. Today, one need that is very clear is for ecological preservation alongside essential social and technological development. Dr. M. S. Swaminathan, winner of the first World Food Prize and known as the father of India's Green Revolution, was running a research foundation in Chennai, South India. On a visit, one could see the potential of this work, and a number of Tata Trusts jointly established a practical arm for the research foundation. The J.R.D. Tata Centre for Eco-Technology was inaugurated by the president of India in 1998. A year later, the trustees accepted my proposal to start a Centre for

Research in Tropical Diseases at the prestigious Indian Institute of Science, Bangalore.

The Tata Trust, through its mission, has demonstrated a deep commitment to humanity through the application of remedies in areas of basic, external need. But the journey into the internal world requires a guiding light in addition to a helping hand.

The Pilgrim Soul

There is a pilgrim soul in all of us. Each reaches its destination in a distinctive way. Gathering spiritual information is one step, often followed by embarking on a spiritual quest. The more fortunate have a spiritual experience of their own. Only a few, like St. Paul and Lord Buddha, attain spiritual enlightenment: St. Paul through a flash of lightning that blinded him, Lord Buddha by meditation under a Bodh Tree that gave him insight.

As a child and into my early teens, I had a tenuous faith in God. Then I encountered an atheist Marxist teacher. One day we argued about the existence of God. He won his argument. I lost my faith.

By the age of sixteen, I argued against the existence of God. But in the desert of my atheism, there were no fountains of water for the transcendent thirst in my spirit. I then ceased to argue for atheism and instead searched for the meaning of life. And so from atheism I moved toward agnosticism. I was open to believing in God. However, I wanted to be convinced. I wanted proof of his existence.

In my early twenties, I faced a personal crisis. At that time, I would go to a fire temple (I am a born Zoroastrian) to be quiet and watch the flames. It soothed my spirit, but I had to wait for an answer. The quest had begun.

At age twenty-six, I saw a play produced by "Moral Rearmament" (now "Initiatives of Change") in my hometown, Bombay. At a meeting the next day, I learned about setting out a daily quiet time to listen to one's inner voice and to focus on endeavoring to live by absolute moral standards of honesty, purity, unselfishness, and love. I felt challenged and uncomfortable. Months later, I put right a relationship by being absolutely honest. A fortnight after that, I was walking along at a hill station in Western India, Khandala. In the 1950s, this was a sleepy place, and it had another small hill perched on it. This hill was practically deserted and barren at the time. There was only one hotel at the far end. Walking on the hill at noon, I stood on a small bridge that spanned a gap containing huge black pipes conveying water to a hydroelectric project. Looking down at the pipes from the bridge, I told myself: "If there were a hundred snakes there and I was thrown in their midst and still survived, I would believe there was a God."

No snakes appeared. No bells rang. I walked home. A few days later, at about 11 a.m. on a deserted site not far from the bridge, I sat on the ground absorbed in a book. I heard a rustling in the distance. I said to myself, *I am damned if I am going to be disturbed.* Then a voice within told me powerfully, *Look.* I did. A snake was coming straight at me from less than twenty feet away. There was a depression in front of me, and I jumped back once, twice, thrice. The long snake came exactly to the spot where I had been sitting and slithered down the depression. As I watched the end of his tail, the thought flashed through my mind: *You wanted proof with a hundred snakes. God has given you enough with one.*

Had I not been forewarned and instead been bitten, I would have had to run for almost a mile for help. This is not necessarily proof of the existence of God. But for me it was enough. Since that time, I have never doubted his existence or his interest in my life. W. Stanley Jones put it aptly: "When you find a faith, all your sums add up." For me, they did. My life assumed a new meaning. You first search for a faith that you can hold to and then find that faith upholds you.

Faith flourishes best when you accept that God has a plan and you have a part in it. Quiet times for me became the means to find that plan day by day. In my morning reflections, I sought not only correction but day-to-day direction through the inner voice. I began with a brief prayer or an inspirational reading from the scriptures or elsewhere. As I continued this discipline, life took on a purpose and a shape.

On the hill, he commanded me; but now he whispers and leads me on despite my frailties. It is important to write down these fast-fleeting reflections. The Chinese have a proverb: "The strongest of memories is weaker than the faintest of ink."

The "Kindly Light"

The desire for spiritual information is itself an indication of the soul's search. But spiritual information alone is not adequate to lead to a faith unless one wants that faith. Mark Twain said: "It is not the parts of the Bible I don't understand that worry me. It is the parts I do!" And St. Augustine, although he had potential access to spiritual information through his pious mother, who prayed for her philandering son to no avail for years, himself prayed: "Please, Lord, make me pure; *but not yet.*"

Each person has his or her own time when they are ripe for faith. In his "Confessions," St. Augustine penned the following moving words:

> Too late I loved thee, O Beauty of ancient days, yet ever new! Thou wast within and I went abroad searching for thee. Thou wast with me, but I was not with Thee.

He concluded:

> Our hearts are restless until they find their rest in Thee.

Faith is nourished frequently by streams of silence. "It is in the sphere of the heart that God speaks," says Mother Teresa. "Try speaking directly to God," she adds. "Just speak. Tell Him everything, talk to Him. He is a father. He is father to all, whatever religion we are. We are all created by God, we are all His children . . . but it is not what we say but what He says to us that matters. . . . God is the friend of silence— we need to listen to God."

Over the years, one develops a relationship as expressed in this hymn:

> And He walks with me, and He talks with me,
> And He tells me I am His own;

And the joy we share as we tarry there,
None other has ever known. (Hymn and music by C. Austin Miles, 1912)

God's love became more real and helped me at difficult moments in my life—never more so than when I was told in 1989 that I had cancer. I relate how my experience of faith helped me in *Celebration of the Cells*.[2] I had seven years of remission. Now it has recurred. I am writing this while undergoing radiation; earlier, I had chemotherapy.

Before the first radiation treatment, I read the words: "I uphold you"—not "I will uphold you," but a confident "I uphold you." The first session with a new mask was uncomfortable, and once under the linear accelerator there was little I could do. The words, "I uphold you," sustained me. Even earlier in an MRI tunnel I felt claustrophobic and restless. I recited Psalm 103 as far as I could. My body relaxed. Among the lines in the Psalm are "and forget not all His benefits." This is good to remember when life is rough.

I try to align my life to the moral laws programmed within me. It leads me toward being an integrated person. The flame of the spirit is the "kindly light."

John Henry Newman wrote that beautiful hymn "Lead, Kindly Light" not at a time of triumph, but at a time of deep anguish, when he was torn between his allegiance to the Church of England and his attraction to Rome. He had just recovered after convalescing for a month, victim of an epidemic in Italy. For nearly a week, his ship had been stranded in the Straits of Bonifacio, becalmed and drifting. The passengers were weary of the delay. He read in the Psalms the lines: "Teach me thy way, O Lord, and lead me in a plain path." He prayed to God, for he could not see the path he should traverse. With this experience was born the hymn that was Mahatma Gandhi's favorite:

Lead, Kindly Light, amidst th' encircling gloom;
Lead Thou me on!
The night is dark, and I am far from home—
Lead, Thou me on!
Keep Thou my feet; I do not ask to see
The distant scene—one step enough for me.

Conclusion

The task of philanthropy is to support the quest for human betterment and knowledge. Through my work, I learned that supporting science, technology, medicine, and other human endeavors requires boldly reaching out to help humanity leap forward. But it is within the human heart that the quest for spiritual enlightenment takes place and where spiritual information takes root and flourishes with quiet courage.

There is always the next step for each pilgrim Soul. When we become enlightened as individuals, the path we follow is illuminated and the work we hope to do is accomplished.

✐

Russi M. Lala, publisher, editor, author, and director of the Sir Dorabji Tata Trust from 1985 to 2003, co-founded the Centre for Advancement of Philanthropy. He began his journalism and publishing career in 1948 at the age of nineteen. In 1959, Mr. Lala established and managed the first Indian book publishing house in London. Together with Rajmohan Gandhi (the Mahatma's grandson), Mr. Lala founded the newsweekly *Himmat* in India in 1964 and was its editor for the next decade. His first book, *The Creation of Wealth—The Tata Story*, appeared in 1981 to critical acclaim and was followed by seven other books. Mr. Lala's book *Celebration of the Cells—Letters from a Cancer Survivor* (1999) has helped a number of patients. Inspired by the New York Community Public Trust, he helped to start the Bombay Community Public Trust. Until recently, Mr. Lala was on the Governing Board of the Indian Institute of Science, Bangalore, India's premier scientific and technological institute, and was also on the Governing Board of the first Institute of Social Sciences and the first cancer hospital in India. He has been associated with Initiatives of Change (formerly Moral Re-Armament) for more than fifty years.

NOTES

1 *In Tune with the Infinite* by Ralph Waldo Trine, copyright 1965, The Estate of the late R. W. Trine. Published in the United Kingdom by HarperCollins.

2 *Celebration of the Cells—Letters from a Cancer Survivor.* Viking Penguin, India, 1999.

Contributors

Wolfgang Achtner, Justus Liebig University, Giessen, Germany

Lori Arviso Alvord, Dartmouth Medical School, Hanover, New Hampshire, United States

Munawar A. Anees, Knowledge Management Systems, Tucson, Arizona, United States

Gennaro Auletta, Free University of Urbino, Italy

Hendrik P. Barendregt, Radboud University, Nijmegen, The Netherlands

Robert J. Barro, Harvard University, Cambridge, Massachusetts, United States

John D. Barrow, University of Cambridge, United Kingdom

Gianfranco Basti, Pontifical Lateran University, Rome, Italy

Jeremy Begbie, University of St. Andrews, United Kingdom

Gregory A. Benford, University of California, Irvine, United States

Peter L. Berger, Boston University, Massachusetts, United States

Marco Bersanelli, University of Milan, Italy

John W. Bowker, Gresham College, London, United Kingdom

Steven J. Brams, New York University, New York, United States

Anna Case-Winters, McCormick Theological Seminary, Chicago, Illinois, United States

Michael A. Casey, Staff of the Catholic Archbishop, Sydney, Australia

Hyung S. Choi, Metanexus Institute on Religion and Science, Philadelphia, Pennsylvania, United States

Philip Clayton, Claremont School of Theology, California, United States

Jean Clottes, French Ministry of Culture, Paris, France

Robin A. Collins, Messiah College, Grantham, Pennsylvania, United States

Ramanath Cowsik, Indian Institute of Astrophysics, Bangalore, India

William Lane Craig, Talbot School of Theology, La Mirada, California, United States

Paul C. W. Davies, Macquarie University, Sydney, Australia

Celia Deane-Drummond, University College Chester, United Kingdom

Michael J. Denton, University of Otago, Dunedin, New Zealand

Freeman J. Dyson, Institute for Advanced Study, Princeton, New Jersey, United States

Noah J. Efron, Bar-Ilan University, Ramat-Gan, Israel

George F. R. Ellis, University of Cape Town, South Africa

Robert A. Emmons, University of California, Davis, United States

C. Stephen Evans, Baylor University, Waco, Texas, United States

Kitty Ferguson, Chester, New Jersey, United States

Barbara L. Fredrickson, University of Michigan, Ann Arbor, Michigan, United States

Gregory L. Fricchione, Harvard Medical School, Cambridge, Massachusetts, United States

George H. Gallup Jr., The George H. Gallup International Institute, Princeton, New Jersey, United States

Karl W. Giberson, Eastern Nazarene College, Quincy, Massachusetts, United States

Owen Gingerich, Harvard-Smithsonian Center for Astrophysics, Cambridge, Massachusetts, United States

Marcelo Gleiser, Dartmouth College, Hanover, New Hampshire, United States

Jane Goodall, Jane Goodall Institute, Silver Spring, Maryland, United States

Ursula Goodenough, Washington University, St. Louis, Missouri, United States

William Grassie, Metanexus Institute on Religion and Science, Philadelphia, Pennsylvania, United States

Niels Henrik Gregersen, University of Copenhagen, Denmark

Bruno Guiderdoni, Institut d'Astrophysique de Paris, France

Jonathan D. Haidt, University of Virginia, Charlottesville, Virginia, United States

Charles L. Harper Jr., John Templeton Foundation, Philadelphia, Pennsylvania, United States

Anne Harrington, Harvard University, Cambridge, Massachusetts, United States

John F. Haught, Georgetown University, Washington, D.C., United States

Stevens Heckscher, Natural Lands Trust, Media, Pennsylvania, United States

James L. Heft, The University of Dayton, Ohio, United States

Michael Heller, Pontifical Academy of Theology, Cracow, Poland

William B. Hurlbut, Stanford University, California, United States

Lydia Jaeger, Institut Biblique de Nogent-sur-Marne, France

Max Jammer, Bar-Ilan University, Ramat-Gan, Israel

Philip Jenkins, Pennsylvania State University, University Park, United States

Kevin Kelly, Pacifica, California, United States

Harold G. Koenig, Duke University Medical Center, Durham, North Carolina, United States

Russi M. Lala, Centre for Advancement of Philanthropy, Mumbai, India

Xavier Le Pichon, Collège de France, Aix en Provence, France

Andrei Linde, Stanford University, California, United States

Mario Livio, Space Telescope Science Institute, Baltimore, Maryland, United States

Thierry Magnin, l'École Nationale Supérieure des Mines, St. Étienne, France

David A. Martin, London School of Economics, United Kingdom

Martin E. Marty, University of Chicago, Illinois, United States

Alister E. McGrath, Wycliffe Hall, Oxford, United Kingdom

Nancey C. Murphy, Fuller Theological Seminary, Pasadena, California, United States

David G. Myers, Hope College, Holland, Michigan, United States

Edward Nelson, Princeton University, New Jersey, United States

Jacob Neusner, Bard College, Annandale-on-Hudson, New York, United States

Michael Novak, American Enterprise Institute, Washington, D.C., United States

Martin A. Nowak, Harvard University, Cambridge, Massachusetts, United States & Natalia L. Komarova, Rutgers University, New Brunswick, New Jersey, United States

Kuruvilla Pandikattu, Jnana-Deepa Vidyapeeth, Pune, India

Ted Peters, Pacific Lutheran Theological Seminary, Berkeley, California, United States

Clifford A. Pickover, T. J. Watson Research Center (IBM), Yorktown Heights, New York, United States

John C. Polkinghorne, University of Cambridge, United Kingdom

Margaret Poloma, University of Akron, Ohio, United States

Stephen G. Post, Case Western Reserve University School of Medicine, Cleveland, Ohio, United States

Ravi Ravindra, Dalhousie University, Halifax, Nova Scotia, Canada

Holmes Rolston III, Colorado State University, Fort Collins, Colorado, United States

Nicolaas A. Rupke, University of Göttingen, Germany

Jeffrey Burton Russell, University of California, Santa Barbara, United States

Robert J. Russell, Center for Theology and the Natural Sciences, Berkeley, California, United States

Jonathan Sacks, Office of the Chief Rabbi of Britain and the Commonwealth, London, United Kingdom

Jeffrey P. Schloss, Westmont College, Santa Barbara, California, United States

Arthur J. Schwartz, John Templeton Foundation, Philadelphia, Pennsylvania, United States

Jeffrey M. Schwartz, University of California, Los Angeles, United States

Michael D. Silberstein, Elizabethtown College, Pennsylvania, United States

F. Russell Stannard, Open University, Leighton Buzzard, United Kingdom

Jean Staune, Interdisciplinary University of Paris, France

Antoine Suarez, Center for Quantum Philosophy, Zurich, Switzerland

Alain J.-P. C. Tschudin, University of Cambridge, United Kingdom

Sarah Voss, University of Nebraska at Omaha, Nebraska, United States

B. Alan Wallace, Santa Barbara Institute for Consciousness Studies, California, United States

Paul K. Wason, John Templeton Foundation, Philadelphia, Pennsylvania, United States

Fraser N. Watts, University of Cambridge, United Kingdom

Wesley J. Wildman, Boston University, Massachusetts, United States

Dallas Willard, University of Southern California, Los Angeles, United States

Jennifer J. Wiseman, Johns Hopkins University, Baltimore, Maryland, United States

Robert D. Woodberry, University of Texas, Austin, United States

Everett L. Worthington Jr., Virginia Commonwealth University, Richmond, United States

Robert Wuthnow, Princeton University, New Jersey, United States

Joseph M. Zycinski, Catholic University of Lublin, Poland